CW00694630

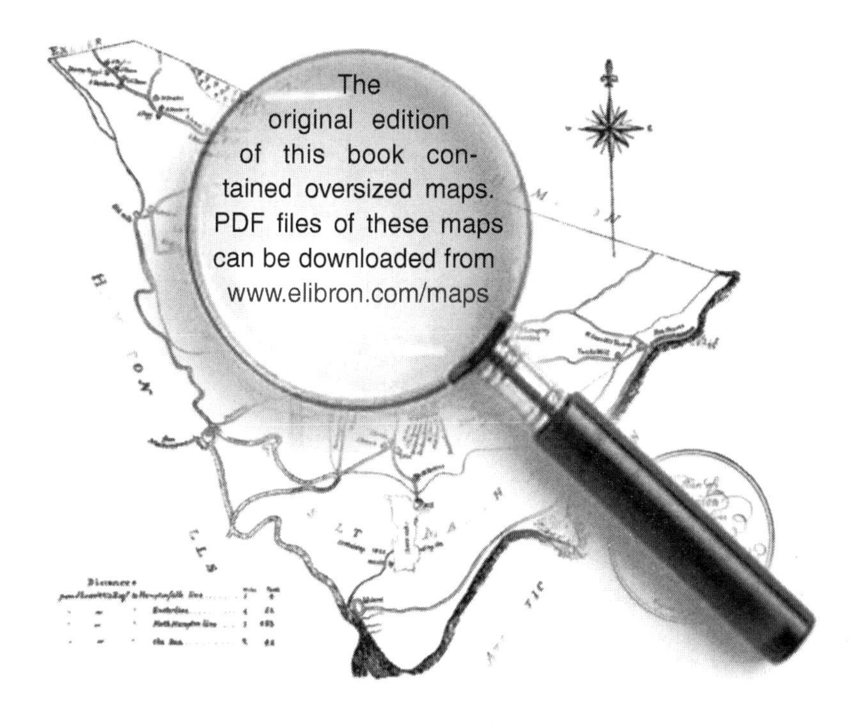
The
original edition
of this book con-
tained oversized maps.
PDF files of these maps
can be downloaded from
www.elibron.com/maps

LEIGH'S
NEW PICTURE OF LONDON

OR, A VIEW OF THE
POLITICAL, RELIGIOUS, MEDICAL, LITERARY, MUNICIPAL
COMMERCIAL, AND MORAL STATE
OF

THE BRITISH METROPOLIS

Elibron Classics
www.elibron.com

Elibron Classics series.

ISBN 1-4021-6237-5 (paperback)
ISBN 1-4212-8022-1 (hardcover)

This Elibron Classics Replica Edition is an unabridged facsimile
of the edition published in 1842 by Leigh and Co.; Orlando Hodgson;
G. Biggs, London.

ROYAL PALACE,

LEIGH'S

NEW PICTURE OF LONDON;

OR, A VIEW OF THE

POLITICAL, RELIGIOUS, MEDICAL, LITERARY, MUNICIPAL, COMMERCIAL, AND MORAL STATE

OF

The British Metropolis:

PRESENTING A

LUMINOUS GUIDE TO THE STRANGER,

ON ALL SUBJECTS CONNECTED WITH

GENERAL INFORMATION, BUSINESS, OR AMUSEMENT.

TO WHICH ARE ANNEXED,

A GENERAL PLAN OF THE METROPOLIS.
AN INDEX TO THE SQUARES, STREETS, &c.
A PANORAMA OF REMARKABLE OBJECTS.
UPWARDS OF ONE HUNDRED VIEWS.
A PLAN FOR VIEWING THE WHOLE IN A WEEK.
A MAP AND DESCRIPTION OF THE ENVIRONS.
TABLES OF FARES FOR COACHES, CABS, BOATS, &c.

ELEVENTH EDITION, CAREFULLY REVISED.

LONDON:
BY ASSIGNMENT FROM LEIGH AND CO.
ORLANDO HODGSON, 111, FLEET STREET,
AND G. BIGGS, 421, STRAND.

With Plan of London, and Map of the Environs, 6s.
Ditto Ditto and 111 Views 9s.
Ditto Ditto and 24 Costumes, 12s.
Ditto Ditto and Rowlandson's Ditto, 15s.

M.DCCC.XLII.

THE READER *is requested to notice that there is affixed to this Volume an* INDEX TO THE PLAN, *by referring to which the situation of any street may be readily found; and also a* GENERAL INDEX, *indicating the page where any edifice or establishment is described.*

DURING the progress of this work through the press, the following alterations have taken place:—

The tolls for passing over Waterloo Bridge have been reduced to one halfpenny for each foot-passenger; for every description of vehicle drawn by one horse, to 2*d.*; each additional horse, to 1*d.*; a horse not drawing, to 1*d.*; empty coaches, cabs, and carts, one half; return chaises, horses, &c., free.

The steam-boats on the Thames now ply as high up the river as Chelsea, for the usual fare, 4*d.* Steamers to Woolwich, Greenwich, Blackwall, the Docks, the Tunnel, and all parts below bridge, several times a day; also to Richmond, Twickenham, Kew, Putney, &c., at different hours daily.

Madame Tussaud's wax-work at present occupies the Baker-street Bazaar. The price of admission is one shilling.

ROYAL EXCHANGE.—A design by Mr. Tite has been adopted; contracts have been entered into for clearing the area and forming the foundation; and several buildings, which obstructed the progress, have been removed. The superstructure will be commenced in the course of the summer, and it is expected the whole will be completed in about three years.

THE NELSON MONUMENT.—The foundation for the column has been laid, and the works are actively proceeding. Several deviations from the plan first proposed have been made, and the column will be thirty feet lower than was originally intended. The site has also been removed from the centre of Trafalgar-square to the south side of it. The ground in front of the National Gallery, which inclined from north to south, will be made level, and the road immediately in front of it, it is expected, will be converted into a terrace fifteen feet higher than the lower area. The enclosure will be about 350 feet from east to west, and 260 from north to south, groups of sculpture being placed at the angles. It is also recommended to erect a splendid fountain between the National Gallery and the column.

Reform Club-House, in Pall Mall.—The loftiness of this building is very striking; it is considered one of the handsomest pieces of architecture in the metropolis. Although the exterior has been exposed for some months, much time will be required to complete the interior. The several club-houses on the south side of this street give it a magnificent appearance.

Several tradesmen's shops in the neighbourhood of Regent-street, Oxford-street, Ludgate-hill, &c., have been fitted up in a style of architectural beauty, which cannot fail to attract observation.

PREFACE.

The unexampled success which has attended the "Picture of London" since the period of its first publication, has prompted the Editor to renewed exertions; and he respectfully submits the present edition to the public, with the hope that it may be regarded as a faithful and entertaining Picture of the existing state of the British Metropolis.

The Editor has been anxious to justify and substantiate the title by which he has introduced this volume to the public. As it is called a "New Picture of London," he has been solicitous to present, in each succeeding edition, such a view of this distinguished Metropolis as may be calculated to convey an adequate notion of its ever-changing mien, as well as to delineate with scrupulous fidelity those severer characteristics which indicate the stamina of an empire's capital. The task he has undertaken is, it must be confessed, one of great magnitude; yet it is from a contemplation of the dignity of the subject that he has derived the necessary stimulus to exertion. If he has occasionally dilated on comparative trifles, it must be recollected that minute parts are of essential importance in a mighty whole: we pass by the isolated block as an abstract object, but gaze with awe at the solemn pyramid. Without pretending to the skill of a painter in arranging his materials with that refinement of composition so necessary to the ends of art, the Editor trusts that their proportionate magnitudes have been observed, their due stations assigned to them, and that no artifices of light or shade have been resorted to, in order to enhance or deteriorate their value. He has endeavoured, in treating of national objects, to evince a national feeling.

Where he has ventured to depart from the ordinary routine of a Guide, he trusts that the few opinions he has felt called upon to advance are in harmony with the conclusions of every cool reasoner and sincere patriot. The materials have been collected from authentic sources, whether by research or personal observation; and it is confidently hoped that such an arrangement has been made as is best calculated to give the visiter to the metropolis a clear conception of the work as a whole, and, by means of two ample indices, to render access to the more intricate branches of the maze a matter of little difficulty. It has been his endeavour to give a compendious and correct view of that justly valued and highly famed political constitution which is the main-spring of all the wonders it has been his duty to enumerate; which pervades our varied institutions, infusing vigour and stability; and which stamps on the British character that integrity of purpose and decision of action which have tended to render Englishmen the arbiters of a world's destiny, and the apostles of rational liberty.

It must, however, be admitted that, notwithstanding the utmost care and diligence, perfect accuracy in a work of this character is unattainable, owing to the changes which are daily taking place: the Editor therefore relies on the indulgence of the public for errors not his own, and will feel obliged by any corrections or suggestions for the further improvement of this Guide, addressed to him at No. 421 Strand.

CONTENTS.

LEIGH'S

NEW PICTURE OF LONDON.

CHAPTER I.

HISTORY OF LONDON, TRACING THE ORIGIN AND FOUNDATION OF THE CITY, WITH THE RISE AND PROGRESS OF ITS PRIVILEGES AND IMMUNITIES; THE GROWTH AND CHARACTER OF SOVEREIGN POWER, FOREIGN AND DOMESTIC; AND THE GRADUAL EXTENSION OF THE BRITISH METROPOLIS.

THE fables of Geoffrey of Monmouth,* with regard to the origin of London, are unworthy of the consideration of the well-informed antiquary; but there is no doubt that it was a city or fortified hold of the Britons before the Roman invasion. Cæsar's Commentaries mention *Civitas Trinobantum*, the district inhabited by the *Trinobantes*, or *Trinovantes*, and called so, it is imagined, from the situation of their country on the broad expanse of water formed by the Thames. Ammianus Marcellinus, who calls London *Augusta Trinobantum*, mentions it as an ancient town, once called *Lundinium*. Pennant adds many corroborating particulars, founded on the etymology of appellations still in use, particularly Dowgate, *Dwr*, or Water-gate, the *trajectus*, a ferry from Surrey to the celebrated Watling-street, which is now believed to have been a British road before it was the Prætorian way of the Romans.

Some writers derive the word LONDON from the British *Llong*, a ship, and *Din*, a town; but as the city was not then celebrated as being the resort of shipping, the prior appellation is with more probability deemed to have been *Llyn-Din*, or the 'town on the lake,' *Llyn* being the old British term for a broad expanse of water, or lake; and such appearance must have been strikingly exhibited when all the low grounds on the Surrey side of the river were overflowed, as well as

* That London was founded by Brute, a descendant of the Trojan Æneas, and called New Troy, or Troy-novant, until the time of Lud, who surrounded it with walls, and gave it the name of Caer Lud, or Lud's Town, &c.; all which may be considered as mere romance.

those extending from Wapping Marsh to the Isle of Dogs. The transition from *Llyn-Din* to LONDON would be easy. The name *Augusta* is evidently Roman. Antiquaries have said it was so called in honour of Constantine the Great's mother, or from the *Legio Secunda Augusta*, which is known to have been stationed in London; but it was doubtless on account of its becoming the capital of the conquered province, as Treves in Germany was for the same reason called *Augusta* Treverorum; Basil, *Augusta* Rauracorum, &c.

The first mention of London by a Roman author occurs in the annals of Tacitus, where he details the spirited revolt of the insulted British queen *Boadicea*. He says, "that about the year 61 *Londinium*, or *Colonia Augusta*, was the chief residence of merchants, and the great mart of trade and commerce, though not dignified with the name of a colony." Dr. Gale, on the authority of Ptolemy, is of opinion that the Roman London was on the south side of the Thames, the site of which is now beginning to lose the name of *St. George's Fields*. It is, however, well known that this spot remained a marsh till the last century. The original London, according to Dr. Stukely, occupied an oblong square; its breadth extending from Maiden-lane, Lad-lane, Cateaton-street, to the Thames; and its length, from Ludgate to Walbrook, which placed it between two natural fosses, the one formed by the small river Fleta, now arched over and used as a common sewer, and the other by a stream called Wall-brook, which has long ceased to exist. This ground-plot at the present moment may be called the heart of the city; but as it scarcely exceeds half a mile in one direction, and a third of a mile in the other, it amounts to a very small part of the space that was subsequently enclosed within the city walls.

As this detail, illustrative of the origin, name, and extent of the city, must be followed up with historical narrative, the next point is, some account of *London under the Romans*. Subjected to the sway of the enterprising and sagacious Romans in the plenitude of their power, a place possessing the many natural advantages of London could not but increase in population and consequence. When the Roman general Suetonius Paulinus marched from the extremity of Wales to avoid the consequences of the merited vengeance of the Iceni under Boadicea, he was obliged to leave London to its fate; and all who could not evacuate the city with him were massacred. This retreat proves that it did not then possess walls or fortifications, and consequently that it had not been founded by the Romans. London appears to have gradually revived from this disaster, for in the reign of the Emperor Severus it was noticed as a great and wealthy city, and regarded as the metropolis of Britain. By the year 359 eight hundred vessels were employed in the port of London for the exportation of corn alone.

The original WALLS OF LONDON were undoubtedly the work of the Romans, though the precise date of their foundation is disputed. Maitland attributes the raising of them to Theodosius, governor of Britain, in A.D. 379; but the majority of authors consider Constantine the Great as their founder, at the instance of his mother Helena—according to Stow, an opinion that is countenanced by the fact of a number of coins of that empress having been found under them. The wall is described as beginning at a fort which occupied a part of the site of the present Tower of London; whence it was carried along the Minories to Aldgate. Thence, after forming a course to the north-west, between Bevis Marks, Chamomile-street, and Houndsditch, it extended in a right line through Bishopsgate churchyard to Cripplegate; there it assumed a southern direction, and approached Aldersgate. Its course was then south-west by the back of Christchurch Hospital and Old Newgate; from which it extended directly south to Ludgate, passing close behind the present site of the prison of Newgate, Stationers'-court, and the London Coffee-house. From Ludgate the direction was western by Cock-court to New Bridge-street, where, turning to the south, it ran by the Fleet-brook to another fort on the Thames, called Baynard's Castle. This circuit, it is related by Stow, measured two miles and a furlong; besides which the whole bank of the Thames, from one fort to the other, was at one time guarded by another wall; but this, according to Fitzstephen, had long been subverted even in his time. This last wall extended one mile and one hundred and twenty yards. Strong towers and bastions of Roman masonry, to the number of fifteen, added to the strength of the defence. The wall when perfect is supposed to have been twenty-two feet high, and the towers forty; one of them stood until within a few years in Shoemaker's-row, Aldgate. The few vestiges at present discoverable are to be found in London-wall, in the courts between Ludgate-hill and the Broadway, Blackfriars, and in Cripplegate churchyard.

There were four principal gates, which opened to the four great military roads from London. The Prætorian way, or

Saxon Watling-street, an original British road, passed under one on the site of Old Newgate; thence it turned down to Dowgate to the ferry, and was resumed from the south bank of the Thames to Dover. Ermine-street passed under Cripplegate; and a vicinal way under Aldgate by Bethnal-green to Oldford, once a pass over the Lea to Layton in Essex. As new roads were formed, more gates were erected, as Bridegate, Ludgate, Aldersgate, Moorgate, Bishopsgate, and the Postern on Tower-hill.

It is scarcely necessary to add, that under the Romans Britain, and of course London, was governed by Roman laws, administered by prefects sent annually from Rome. The importance of the province of Britain was soon exceedingly manifest, as it furnished sufficient strength to nurture several pretenders to the empire. From the many Roman remains, as tesselated pavements, urns, coins, pottery, and foundations of buildings, it is evident that London exhibited much of the grandeur by which the Roman name is so greatly distinguished. Nor is this all; it is supposed by Whitaker, "that the first embankment of the Thames was the natural operation of that magnificent spirit which intersected the earth with so many raised ramparts and roads." There are evident proofs of the existence of this labour on the south side of the Thames; but it is still more obvious in the great sea-wall along the fens of Essex. Britain was conquered by Rome in her maturity; in four centuries she was obliged to abandon it. Her own colossal power had by that time yielded to the usual operation of corruption and misgovernment; and by the rapid decrease of a dominion so stupendous, an ever-memorable lesson has been afforded to mankind.

LONDON next came *under the dominion of the Britons, the Saxons, and the Danes.* When the distracted state of the Roman empire, in the fifth century, compelled that power to withdraw its forces from the distant provinces, London again became a British town. It is mentioned in the Saxon Chronicle for 457, when the Britons fled hither on their defeat by the Saxons under Hengist, who about twenty years afterwards made himself its master; but on his death, in 488, it was retaken by Ambrosius, and retained by the Britons during a considerable part of the next century. It was afterwards subjected to the newly established Saxon kingdom of Essex. On the conversion of the East Saxons to Christianity, London was nominated as the bishop's see, Melitus being appointed the first bishop, in 604; and a cathedral church was erected in 610 on the present site of St. Paul's.

During the *Heptarchy*, few notices of London appear on record. In 664 it was ravaged by the plague; and in 764, 798, and 801, it suffered severely by fires. By that of 798 it was almost wholly consumed, and immense numbers of the inhabitants perished. On the union of the Saxon kingdom under Egbert, London, though not the royal residence or seat of government, was advancing in consequence, as appears from a *wittenagemot*, or parliament, having been held here in 833, to consult on proper means to repel the Danes. In the course of the following twenty years, however, those barbarian invaders plundered the city twice, and massacred a great number of the inhabitants. They also held it in possession, and garrisoned it, in the early part of the reign of ALFRED; but that justly celebrated monarch, with his superior and commanding genius, eventually obtained the mastery, which he principally accomplished by the creation of a fleet. It was in 884 that this excellent ruler gained possession of London, which he immediately repaired and strengthened. Alfred laid down that plan of municipal government of London which gradually moulded into its present form; and, in particular, he instituted the office of sheriff.

In 1013, London, abandoned by the incapable Ethelred II., was obliged to open its gates to Sweyn king of Denmark, who assumed the crown, which he left to his son Canute next year. The Londoners joined in a general rebellion against Canute, which caused him to retire; but he soon returned, and finally obtained the sovereignty on the base assassination of Edmund Ironside. The importance of London, even in those times of vicissitude, was made manifest; for out of an enormous impost of 83,000*l.* Saxon, levied upon the English in this reign, London supplied 11,000*l.*, and in the subsequent reign of Edward the Confessor it had become exceedingly wealthy. On the defeat and death of Harold by William duke of Normandy, 1066, the latter advanced towards London; but the majority of citizens having declared for Edgar Atheling, his admittance was opposed, until the clergy, headed by the archbishops of Canterbury and York, declared in his favour. On the Christmas-day following, anno 1066, he was crowned King of England. From this period London may be considered as the metropolis of the kingdom.

WILLIAM has been erroneously styled "*the Conqueror.*"

He gained the crown, as is evident, indeed, from what is here stated, *by compact*, and not *by conquest*. He killed Harold the usurper, and routed his army; but William claimed a right to the kingdom, was admitted by compact, and took an oath to observe the laws and customs of the realm; and formerly, as is well known, our judges were accustomed to reprehend any gentleman at the bar who casually gave him the title of William *the Conqueror*, instead of William *the First*.

FROM THE ACCESSION OF WILLIAM I. TO THE PRESENT TIME.

WILLIAM, at the commencement of his reign, which began in 1066 and ended in 1087, granted a charter to the citizens, which is beautifully written in the Saxon characters, and is still preserved among the city archives. It consists of only five lines, on a slip of parchment six inches long and one broad; the English of which is simply as follows:—"William the King greeteth William the Bishop, and Godfrey the Portreve, and all the burgesses within London, friendly. And I acquaint you, that I will that ye be all there law-worthy, as ye were in king Edward's days. And I will that every child be his father's heir, after his father's days. And I will not suffer that any man do you any wrong. God preserve you."

In 1077, the greater part of the city was destroyed by fire. In the following year the king founded the fortress now called the White Tower, for the purpose of keeping the citizens in awe, having reason to suspect their fidelity. Henry I., as a reward for the ready submission of the city to his usurped authority, in 1100 granted it an extensive charter of privileges; among which was the perpetual sheriffwick of Middlesex. This is the earliest record that is known to exist which particularly details the city's privileges and customs: it very speedily followed William I.'s charter, and further shews the increased consequence of the citizens by the efforts made to gain their interest and support. On the death of Henry, the citizens took a decided part in favour of Stephen, in his contest with the empress Maude, and greatly contributed to his establishment on the throne. Henry II. does not appear to have held the citizens in any great degree of favour, probably in resentment of their attachment to Stephen; and we find that large sums of money were extorted from them as free gifts. The alleged charter confirmatory of Henry I.'s is not considered authentic. It was in this reign that Fitzstephen, the monk of Canterbury, wrote his curious description of London, which shews it to have been a prosperous and populous city. On the coronation of Richard I., the brutal and misled populace committed a dreadful massacre on the Jews who were settled in London. At the coronation-dinner the chief magistrate of London, who at that time had the title of bailiff, acted as chief butler. Early in this reign the name is said to have been changed to that of *mayor*, in the person of Henry Fitz-Alwyn,* who filled the post for upwards of twenty-four years. Richard granted the city a new charter, confirming all its liberties, with additional privileges. About four years afterwards, 1195-6, on the payment of 1500*l.*, he granted another, providing for the removal of all weirs that had been erected on the Thames. On this charter the corporation of London establish their claim to the conservatorship of the river. In the reign of King John the civic importance of London was greatly increased, and its corporation finally assumed that character which, with few alterations, it has ever since maintained. John granted the city several charters. By one he empowered the "Barons of the city of London" to choose a mayor annually, or to continue the same person from year to year, at their own pleasure.† During the contest between the king and pope Innocent III. London severely felt the consequences of the interdict which was laid upon the kingdom. In the civil feuds which marked the latter years of John, the citizens of London took part with the barons; and when the humbled monarch was compelled to sign *Magna Charta*, it was therein expressly stipulated that "The city of London should have all its ancient privileges and free-customs, as well by land as by water."

The long reign of Henry III., continuing from 1216 to 1272, affords few events worthy of notice respecting London, except the excessive insults and oppressions endured by the magistrates and citizens of London: it is true that *nine* char-

* *Fitz-Alwyn* was descended from the celebrated Ailwyn, "Alderman of all England," and kinsman to king Edgar. He founded Ramsey Abbey.

† Stow incorrectly states this charter to have been given in 1209, but it bears date May *nineteenth*, in the *sixteenth* year of King John's reign. John began his reign in 1199. This charter was acted on at that period in various instances, as many of the mayors were afterwards continued in their offices for several years together; and the same RIGHT was exercised in the case of Mr. Alderman Wood, who filled the office of Lord Mayor during *two* succeeding years, those of 1816 and 1817.

ters, some of them important ones, were granted during this reign.

In 1258 the price of corn was so excessive that a famine ensued; and, according to the Chronicles of Evesham, 20,000 persons died of hunger in London only. In 1264 another massacre of the Jews took place, on a plea that one of that race had taken more than legal interest; and upwards of 500 Jews were put to death by the populace, and their houses and synagogues destroyed.

In the reign of Edward I. the city was divided into twenty-four wards, over each of which presided an alderman. The inhabitants were also allowed to choose common-councilmen as at present. This king likewise granted the citizens a charter in confirmation of their privileges. The suburbs of the city had by this time become enlarged, in consequence of disforesting the great forest of Middlesex, which extended to the river-side, and abounded in beasts of the chase.

King Edward III., at the commencement of his reign, granted to the city two charters. By the first, all the ancient privileges were confirmed and additional ones bestowed. By the other, Southwark was granted to the citizens in perpetuity. In 1348 the terrible pestilence, which, breaking out in India, spread itself westward through every country on the globe, reached England. Its ravages in London were so great, that the common cemeteries were not sufficient for the interment of the dead; and various pieces of ground without the walls were assigned for burial-places. Amongst these was the waste land now forming the precinct of the Charter-house, where upwards of 50,000 bodies were then deposited. This destructive disorder did not entirely subside till 1357. The public entry of Edward the Black Prince into London, May 24, 1356, after the victory he obtained at Poictiers, was celebrated with an unparalleled degree of splendour, and every street through which the cavalcade passed exhibited an extraordinary display of riches and magnificence. This reign was distinguished by the dawnings of the Reformation, under the celebrated Wickliffe, who was much esteemed in London. In 1380 a desperate insurrection, headed by Wat Tyler, took place, which, in its progress, threatened the overthrow of the political and civil establishments of the country; but by the personal intrepidity of the young king Richard, then a stripling, aided by the active courage of Sir William Walworth, mayor of London, the peace of the metropolis and of the kingdom was speedily restored.

At the coronation of Henry IV., in 1399, who, in consequence of the wild and excessive exactions of Richard, was received by the citizens with open arms, the mayor, as usual, officiated as chief butler. The citizens were gratified by the repeal of some obnoxious statutes, and an extension of their privileges. The return of Henry V., after his glorious victory of Agincourt in 1415, was celebrated in London with great magnificence. In this reign the city was first lighted at night by lanterns; and Sir Thomas Eyre, mayor, built Leadenhall for a public granary. The reign of Henry VI. was rendered memorable to London by the insurrection of Jack Cade, who assumed the name of Mortimer, and collected a strong body of malcontents under the pretext of a redress of grievances. They entered the city in triumph, and for some time bore down all opposition, and beheaded the lord-treasurer, Lord Say, and several other persons of consequence. The insurgents at length losing ground, a general pardon was proclaimed; and Cade, finding himself deserted by his followers, fled; but a reward being offered for his apprehension, he was discovered, and refusing to surrender, was killed.

The rents of houses in the city and suburbs during this reign, as appears from a composition for offerings entered into in 1457 between the clergy of London and the laity, increased from six-and-eightpence to three pounds per annum.

In the fatal and bloody contests between the houses of York and Lancaster, London generally shewed a disposition in favour of that of York. On the victorious return of Edward IV., after the decisive battle of Barnet, he bestowed the honour of knighthood on the mayor, recorder, and twelve of the aldermen. In this reign we have the earliest notices of the employment of brick in the building of houses; it was made in Moorfields. New conduits and cisterns for water were also constructed. The reign of Edward IV. will also be ever memorable in the annals of the metropolis for the introduction of printing by William Caxton, citizen and mercer. That of Richard III., beyond the base imposition on the citizens by the Duke of Buckingham in his behalf, had no particular reference to the concerns of the city. Soon after the accession of Henry VII., in 1485, an epidemical disorder of a singular nature, called "the sweating sickness," raged with great violence in London. It appears from Hall's Chronicles, that two mayors and six aldermen died of this complaint in one week. In the thirteenth year of this reign, several gardens were destroyed in Finsbury, out of which a field for archers was formed, which is the origin of the Artillery-ground. The river Fleet was made navigable to Holborn-bridge. Houndsditch was arched over, and the beautiful chapel adjoining Westminster Abbey, still called Henry the Seventh's chapel, erected. The citizens were dreadfully plundered by this king and his iniquitous agents, Empson and Dudley.

Henry VIII. having attempted to raise money without the aid of parliament, the citizens made such determined opposition to the measure, and their example had such an influence throughout the kingdom, that the king, in full council, abandoned his design, and granted a pardon to all who had opposed him. Many improvements were made in this reign in the city and its suburbs, to answer the demands of an increasing population. An immense alteration was made in the aspect of the city by the dissolution of the monasteries. The part of London covered by religious foundations bore so great a proportion to the whole, that it appeared rather a religious than a commercial metropolis. The liberation of so many thousands from the seclusion of the cloister led to increased trade and business. The emperor Charles V., who visited Henry, was treated by the citizens with great magnificence. In 1542 the Bible was first printed in England by royal permission. There were dreadful persecutions during this reign on the score of religion; but the result, in producing the Reformation, was most advantageous to the cause of civil as well as religious liberty.

The events which chiefly characterise the reign of Edward VI., relative to London especially, may be comprised in the foundation of the hospitals of Christ, Bridewell, and St. Thomas; the first for education, and the other two for the reception of the sick, maimed, and helpless poor—charities rendered indispensable by the dissolution of monasteries. By an act of the seventh year of this king's reign, for the general regulation of taverns and public-houses, it was decreed that there should be only *forty* in the city and liberties of London, and *three* in Westminster: there are now upwards of 6,000!

It is unnecessary to allude to the wretched scenes that were acted in London during the unhappy reign of Mary. Under the eventful sway of Elizabeth the metropolis partook largely of the auspicious consequences of her vigorous exertions, in its increase of prosperity, enterprise, and commercial activity. Looking at the present extent of London, it is curious to observe how much anxiety was exhibited in this reign to prevent the increase of buildings and the inconvenience of a too-extensive population. By a decree dated Nonesuch, 7th July, 1580, it was forbidden to erect new buildings where none had before existed in the memory of man. The extension of the metropolis was deemed calculated "to encourage the increase of the plague; created a trouble in governing such multitudes; a dearth of victuals; multiplying of beggars, and inability to relieve them; an increase of artisans more than could live together; impoverishing of other cities for lack of inhabitants. It made lack of air, lack of room to walk, to shoot, &c. And increase of people to rob the queen's customs." Such were the heads of the lord-treasurer's speech. A proclamation was also issued to the same effect by James I. By a map then published, and still extant, it may be seen how much of that which is now the very interior of town was then field and garden. Then, as now, the most crowded part of the city properly so called extended from Newgate-street, Cheapside, and Cornhill, to the banks of the Thames. With the exception of Coleman-street, and a few buildings here and there, from Lothbury to Bishopsgate, and from Bishopsgate to the Tower, all was uncovered or garden ground. Goodman's-fields were only enclosed pasture-grounds; and there were very few buildings east of the Tower. Whitechapel consisted of a few houses only; and Houndsditch, which contained a single row of houses opposite to the city walls, opened behind into the fields. Spitalfields, from the back of the church, lay entirely open. From Bishopsgate Without to Shoreditch church there existed a tolerably regular street, yet still with unoccupied sites intervening. West of Bishopsgate to Moorfields and Finsbury was nearly all unbuilt. From the upper end of Chiswell-street to Whitecross-street there were very few houses; and Goswell-street was called the road to St. Alban's. Clerkenwell was chiefly occupied by the monastery and church; Cow-cross and part of St. John's-street excepted. From the back of Cow-cross to Gray's Inn-lane, which extended a very little way from Gray's Inn, the ground was either unoccupied or pasture and garden ground. From Holborn-bridge to Red Lion-street, the houses continued on both sides, after which the road was open, or bounded on one side by a garden wall, to the *village* of St. Giles, which village was formed by a small cluster of houses on the right; it was therefore called the parish of St. Giles *in the Fields*—a name which it still bears. Beyond, all was country, both northward and westward, Oxford-road having trees and hedges on both sides; indeed, so recently as 1778, a German writer describing the metropolis, speaking of *Tyburn*, the place of execution at that time, mentions it as being "distant from London about two English miles!" From Oxford-road to Piccadilly there was a road called the Way from Reading, proceeding through Hedge-lane and the Haymarket (which avenues were entirely destitute of houses) to St. James's hospital, now the palace; and a few small buildings on the site of Carlton-terrace were all that existed of the present Pall Mall. Leicester-square was all open fields; and St. Martin's-lane had only a few buildings above the church towards the Convent-garden, which extended as a garden to Drury-lane, three buildings alone existing in that extensive site. Long-acre, Seven-dials, and even Drury-lane, to the top of Wych-street, were quite open. The Strand was a street with houses on both sides, but principally formed of the mansions of the nobility and prelates; those on the south side having large gardens open to the Thames. The present names of Norfolk-street, Arundel-street, Surrey-street, Salisbury-street, Cecil-street, Villiers-street, Buckingham-street, &c., point out the relative situations of several of them. At that time it was customary for noblemen resident on the banks of the Thames to proceed to the court at Whitehall in their own barges, and in consequence they retained a number of watermen in livery, who were thereby protected from impressment. Spring-gardens were what the name imports, and the gardens extended to the present Treasury, which occupies the space of the Cockpit and Tilt-yard, opposite to which stood the palace of Whitehall. From King-street to the Abbey the buildings were close and connected, as also from Whitehall to Palace-yard. Several houses also stood near the present Abingdon-street, and on the shore opposite to Lambeth-palace. On the Surrey side of the Thames there were but six or seven houses from Lambeth-palace to the shore opposite White Friars, where a line of houses with gardens commenced, which were continued to Winchester-house in Southwark. On the site of the present Christchurch stood a theatre with gardens; the place was called Paris Garden. Opposite to Queenhithe were the circular buildings appropriated to bull and bear baitings, which Elizabeth often witnessed. Southwark extended but a little way down the High-street. London-bridge was crowded with buildings. Along Tooley-street to Horsleydown was also much built over; after which a few houses and gardens only appeared.

From this sketch, comparing the past with the present, it might appear that the fears of Elizabeth and her ministers were visionary; but such was not exactly the case. The wretched policy of the courts of France and Spain in the religious persecutions of their subjects drove thousands of the most industrious of them to England; and, as they chiefly resorted to London, the houses of the lower ranks of people were crowded to such an excess that disease and pestilence several times occurred. In 1603 upwards of 30,000 persons died of the plague in London. The close manner of building at that period aided the evil; and in the then state of medical science it was not wonderful that an increase of population where plague was so common should alarm a cautious administration. All precautions, however, were fruitless, notwithstanding that some persons were punished for disobeying the proclamation; and in 1583 notice was again taken of this growing evil: the inhabitants of London increased against both restriction and disease, and the natural result followed, in the extension of the suburbs during the whole reign of Elizabeth, and ever since. The commerce of London flourished at this period to an extraordinary degree; indeed, it was almost the only place in the kingdom of very great trading consequence, on which account it could well afford the higher taxation which was laid on it. Against the Spanish armada its exertions were very spirited; the citizens raised and paid no fewer than 10,000 men, and supplied sixteen ships and their equipment. Their aid in the subsequent emergencies was in proportion, their hearts being engaged in the politics of Elizabeth. The Royal Exchange was built in this reign by Sir Thomas Gresham, a public-spirited merchant.

The preparations for the coronation of King James I. were interrupted by a dreadful plague, which ravaged the city with greater violence than any similar visitation since the reign of Edward III. In 1604 the inhabitants of London witnessed the development of that horrible conspiracy, "the Gunpowder Plot;" and, soon after, the punishment of its infamous agents. In 1609 the city acquired a considerable accession of power and property. Almost the whole province of Ulster, in Ireland, having fallen to the crown, the king made an offer of the escheated lands to the city, on condition that they would establish an English colony there. The proposal was accepted; and so rapidly was the colonisation forwarded, that within seven years arose the two capital towns, Londonderry and Coleraine. During the reign of James, the New River was brought to London from Ware, by Sir Hugh Middleton, and London was first paved with flag-stones.

The commencement of Charles the First's reign was marked by the return of the plague, which destroyed in the metropolis 35,000 persons. During the eventful struggle between Charles and his people, London being more directly within the reach of the High Commission and Star-chamber, its inhabitants were more particularly aggrieved by their exactions, and the result was most injurious to trade and commerce. Lord Clarendon speaks of these transactions with becoming sorrow and indignation. It may be added, that London agreed with the parliament, its sufferings having naturally enough driven it to that side of the question. While the civil wars lasted, little new building was undertaken; but under the Commonwealth it again advanced with rapidity, and, strange to say, a similar proclamation to those of Elizabeth, James, and Charles, was, with certain exceptions, made to impede it. Some of these exceptions were the building of the present Covent-garden by the Earl of Bedford, as also the building of Long-acre, Lincoln's-inn-fields, and Clare-market.

On the restoration of Charles II. (1660), in which the city of London materially aided General Monk, it having previously declared for a free parliament, against Richard Cromwell's *Rump* parliament, as it was called, the attention of the legislature was very early directed to the improvement of the capital, by acts for paving and lighting the streets and widening the avenues. The year 1665, in this reign, became memorable in London by the dreadful ravages of the *Great Plague*, as it is styled, in order to distinguish it from all previous ones. It commenced in December 1664, and had not entirely ceased till January 1666. From May to October 1665 it raged with the greatest violence, the deaths progressively increasing from 500 to 8,000 weekly. Whole families, and even whole streets of families, were swept away together. The stoppage of public business was so complete, that grass grew within the area of the Royal Exchange and in the principal streets of the city. All the inns of court were shut up, and all law proceedings suspended. The entire number returned in the bills of mortality as having died of the plague within the year was 68,950. Yet there can be no doubt that this total fell short, by a very large number, of those who actually died by the infection, but whose deaths were not regularly recorded. The aggregate is estimated at 100,000. The whole number of deaths within that year, as given in the bills, was 97,306.

Perhaps the most important event which ever happened in this metropolis, whether it be considered in reference to its immediate effects or its remote consequences, was the *Great Fire,* which broke out in the morning of Sunday, September 2, 1666. Being impelled by strong winds, and the old city being principally built of wood, it raged with irresistible fury nearly four days and nights; nor was it completely got under till the fifth morning. The destructive extent of this conflagration was, perhaps, never exceeded in any part of the world by any fire originating in accident. Within the walls it consumed almost five-sixths of the whole city; and without the walls it cleared a space nearly as extensive as the one-sixth part left unburned within. Scarcely a single building that came within the range of the flames was left standing. Public buildings, churches, and dwelling-houses, were alike involved in one common fate. It may be fairly stated that the fire extended its ravages over a space of ground equal to an oblong measuring upwards of a mile in length and half a mile in breadth. The amount of property destroyed was reckoned at 10,000,000*l.* sterling.

As soon as the general consternation had subsided, an act of parliament was passed for rebuilding the city; and, though all was not done that might have been done, the city was principally rebuilt within little more than four years, and in a style of superior regularity, and infinitely more commodious and healthful than the ancient capital. In this reign and that of James II. many of the large houses of the nobility in the Strand were pulled down; and the year before the Revolution, the suburbs of the metropolis were much increased by the settlement of more than 13,000 French Protestants, who abandoned that kingdom on the revocation of the edict of Nantz. Long-acre, Seven-dials, Soho, and Spitalfields, were in a manner planted by them; and their avocations were chiefly the manufacture of ornamental jewellery and silk-weaving. The city of London most heartily concurred in the invitation to the Prince of Orange; indeed, such a crisis had arrived, that the warmest friends of monarchy could no longer support the weak and ill-advised James II. The fate of all that had been gained for the people—the emancipation of the human mind from priestly thraldom—the protection of religious liberty—the security that cultivated intellect should not be again compelled to retrograde,—all things called for a change in the head of the government. Great facility was afforded to the desired change by the abdication of James; and if all was not accomplished by the "Glorious Revolution" of 1688-9, that the enlightened lover of freedom now might wish should then have been effected, much was gained by the lesson it taught, and the example it set both to the sovereign and to the people.

In the first year of William and Mary an act was passed by which all proceedings of former reigns against the city charters were reversed, and all the rights and privileges of the citizens were fully re-established. In 1692, during the king's absence in Holland, the queen borrowed 200,000*l.* of the city for the exigencies of government; and in 1697 a measure of great utility was carried into execution, namely, *the suppression of the privilege of sanctuary*, which at that time existed in various quarters of the metropolis, as Salisbury and Mitre courts and Ram-alley in Fleet-street; Fulwood's-rents and Baldwin's-gardens, Holborn; Sanctuary, Minories; Savoy, Strand; the Clink, Mint, Montague-close, &c., in Southwark. All these were suppressed, except the Mint, which lasted until the reign of George I. It need not be added that, thus protected, they had become great nuisances, and receptacles of villany and dishonesty. During the reign of William and Mary, the metropolis greatly expanded, particularly to the west; St. Giles's and St. Martin's-in-the-fields becoming then incorporated with the capital, which began to approach the yet distant village of St. Mary-le-bone. The year after the accession of Queen Anne (1703) was remarkable for a dreadful storm of wind which raged through the night of the 26th November. The damage sustained by the city alone was estimated at two millions sterling; and in the suburbs the damage was proportionally great. The ships in the river were driven from their moorings. At sea the destruction was immense; twelve men-of-war, with more than 1,800 men on board, were lost within sight of their own shore.

The increase in the population of London having occasioned a great insufficiency of places for Divine worship, an act of parliament was passed in 1711 for erecting fifty new churches in and about London; the expense of which was defrayed by a small duty on coals brought into the port of London for about eight years. Glass globular lamps were first used in this reign. During this reign several well-known buildings were erected; as Arlington-house, afterwards called Buckingham-house, in St. James's Park; Marlborough-house in Pall Mall, &c. Clerkenwell was much increased, as also Old-street and the lower parts of Shoreditch; Marlborough-street, Soho, was formed; as also Bedford-row, Red Lion-square, and the whole of the neighbourhood immediately north of Holborn. St. Paul's cathedral was completed as to its general structure in 1710. Parish engines were enacted to prevent fires, and party walls directed to be made either of brick or stones. Several municipal regulations also took place for the better watching and guarding of the city.

On the demise of Queen Anne, George I. succeeded to the crown of Great Britain, in pursuance of the Act of Settlement, and made his public entry into London 20th September, 1714. The commencement of the next year, 1715, was marked by a very fatal fire, which destroyed more than 120 houses, and an immense quantity of rich merchandise, in Thames-street; and in the course of it, a rebellion broke out in favour of the Pretender, which caused a great sensation in the metropolis, where many persons were apprehended. At this unfortunate era, the *Septennial* Act passed. The year 1720, in this reign, will be ever celebrated in the annals of London, in consequence of that destructive system of speculation and fraud which history has denominated "The South Sea Bubble." A parliamentary investigation confiscated the estates of the directors for the benefit of those whom their villany had ruined. The sum thus obtained amounted to 2,014,000*l.* The South Sea bubble was the fruitful parent of many similar delusions, although not equally fatal. London was greatly enlarged during the sway of George I. Almost all the streets north of Oxford-road, as far as it at that time extended, viz., to Mary-le-bone-lane, being then in progress; as also Berkeley-square and vicinity, and the fifty new churches.

The metropolis in the early part of the reign of George II. was dreadfully infested with robbers; they paraded in bands during the open day, and had even planned a robbery of the queen on her return from the city in her private carriage, which was prevented only by an accident. In 1733, the city of London and its representatives were much distinguished by their animated opposition to the Excise Scheme of Sir Robert Walpole, which was for the time abandoned. The winter of 1739-40 is noted for the occurrence of one of the most intense frosts ever known in this country; which is recorded in our annals by the appellation of "the Great

Frost." It commenced on Christmas-day, and continued till the 17th of February. Above London-bridge the Thames was completely frozen, and numerous booths were erected on it for selling liquors, &c., to the multitudes who daily flocked thither. In the rebellion of 1745 London again distinguished itself in aid of the reigning family. During the reign of George II. great improvements were made in the metropolis and its neighbourhood. Several new parishes were formed, as St. George's, Bloomsbury; St. Anne's, Limehouse; St. Paul's, Deptford; and St. Matthew's, Bethnal-green. A great part of Fleet-ditch, which had become a vile nuisance, was arched over. A general lighting of London, by parish assessment, was adopted, and one or two acts for regulating the city-watch and police were passed. Grosvenor-square and the various streets in its vicinity were built. Westminster-bridge was erected, and several mean, inconvenient streets were removed to make way for Bridge-street, Great George-street, and Parliament-street. New roads were made across St. George's-fields, now called the Borough and Kent Roads. The houses on London-bridge, which had become dangerous, were removed. A new road was formed from Islington to Paddington: indeed, London expanded itself on all sides, and that unceasing attention to improvements in every thing which concerns health, safety, and convenience, began to manifest itself, by which this great capital has been ever since distinguished.

In speaking of the progress of the metropolis during the long reign of George III., we must confine ourselves to general observations on its buildings, improvements, and population. To these, the amazing extent of warlike operations, all of which have their centre in London, and the consequent growth of a funding system and a proportionate paper currency, have evidently contributed in a great degree. Just before George the Third succeeded to the throne, a power was given to the corporation to make such alterations in regard to the avenues leading to the city as it might think necessary. This act led to much beneficial alteration. The great utility of Westminster-bridge soon became so obvious, that another, at Blackfriars, was undertaken, and attended with similar benefit and improvement. Bridge-street and Chatham-place now occupy the site of the Fleet-ditch, which is arched over, forming the principal sewer of the city. On the Surrey side of the bridge an immense neighbourhood has grown up; and of St. George's-fields, as fields, there are now no remains. After the peace of 1763, the north of the metropolis also extended with surprising rapidity, St. Mary-le-bone and the parish of St. Pancras especially. The new mode of paving commenced about the same time, previous to which few of the streets had level footpaths for passengers, but were formed with small stones, and for the most part with a gutter down the middle. In pursuance of an act of parliament, the enormous signs which hung across the streets, and other protruding incumbrances, were removed. In 1764, a most important act was passed to regulate buildings in reference to fires, being an extension of a former one which was found insufficient. In the early part, also, of the same reign, it became the practice to put the names to the corners of the streets, squares, &c., as also to place the names of residents on brass plates, &c., on house-doors. Sunday tolls were established at the various avenues to London and Westminster, to support a better system of paving, cleansing, and lighting. In 1774, Somerset-house was begun. Manchester-square was commenced in 1776, and various chapels in Mary-le-bone for the increasing neighbourhood. About the same time that village may be said to have become an integral part of the metropolis.

In 1780, from a cause apparently harmless (a petition to parliament from the Protestant Association), arose an insurrection, composed chiefly of the lowest of the people, which during the space of a week bore the most alarming appearance, and gave a great check to improvements. The prisons of Newgate, the King's Bench, and the Fleet, were burnt, and the prisoners set at liberty, most of whom joined the insurgents. The popish chapels and a great number of private houses of Catholics were set on fire; and thirty-six fires were seen blazing at one time in various parts of the metropolis. Military interference became necessary, when many of the rioters were killed; 135 were brought to trial, of whom fifty-nine were convicted, and upwards of twenty of the most active were executed in various parts of the town, immediately contiguous to the scenes of their respective depredations. Lord George Gordon was afterwards tried for having collected the assemblage that occasioned such destructive riots; but as it was clear that he never contemplated such consequences—that he was actuated merely by religious prejudices—he was acquitted. The year 1784 was made memorable by two events of interest, although of minor consequence. One was the "Commemoration of Handel" in

Westminster Abbey and the Pantheon; and the other, the ascent of Vincent Lunardi, an Italian, in a *balloon*, from the Artillery Ground; it was the first aërial voyage in this country. In August 1786 an attempt was made on the life of George III. by an insane woman, named Margaret Nicholson, who, under the pretence of presenting a petition, struck at him with a concealed knife, as he was alighting from his carriage at St. James's. The blow was warded off by a page, and the woman seized. She was afterwards sent to Bethlem Hospital, and died there in 1828.

On the 26th June, 1788, a violent *storm* of rain and thunder visited London. On the 23d April, 1789, that being St. George's day, the metropolis displayed a most splendid festivity and show, in celebration of his majesty's recovery from the calamitous indisposition that had affected his mind from the preceding October. Their majesties on that day went in great state to St. Paul's cathedral, accompanied by the royal family, the foreign ministers, and all the great officers of government, the principal nobility, and members of the House of Commons, the corporation of London, &c.

For some time before 1793, England, as well as France, was alarmingly agitated by the free expression of republican principles; and eventually Louis XVI. became a victim to the disturbed state of things in that country. He was beheaded, and monarchy declared to be abolished. This led to an interruption of intercourse between England and France, after which the Convention declared the French to be at war with the *King* of Great Britain and the *Stadtholder* of the United Provinces. War was thus commenced, and the previous preparations of the English ministry left no doubt that it would be pursued with unusual zeal. The city of London hailed the breaking out of the war with enthusiasm; the common-council thanked his majesty for his "paternal care in the preservation of the public tranquillity, and assured him of the readiness and determination of his faithful citizens to support the honour of his crown and the welfare of his kingdom against the ambitious designs of France:" and, besides this, a bounty of fifty shillings to every able seaman, and twenty shillings to every landsman, who should enter the navy at Guildhall, was voted out of the city-chamber, in addition to the bounties given by the king.

In May 1794, to such a height had political discussion and inquiry risen amongst associations of the people, that many leaders of the societies were arrested and sent to prison on charges of "treasonable practices," and their books and papers seized with a degree of brutal injustice that could not fail to arouse sympathy in behalf of the persecuted, whether they were guilty or not. Hardy, Horne Tooke, and others, were acquitted by juries of their countrymen of the "*treasonable* practices" laid to their charge; and by such verdicts the doctrine of "*constructive treason*" was destroyed, to the joy of every true lover of the constitution, however much he might regret the errors into which the earnest zeal of some persons had led them. A dreadful *fire* broke out in the afternoon of July 23 in this year, at Cock-hill-wharf, Ratcliffe-highway; and in its progress it consumed more houses than any one conflagration since the great fire of 1666. Nearly seven hundred houses were destroyed, and the distress was immense. Government provided tents from the Tower, and the public soon raised nearly 20,000*l.* to afford immediate relief to the sufferers. The year 1797 was distinguished by the extraordinary circumstance of the suspension of payments *in specie* by the Bank of England—a proceeding required by the peculiar situation of public affairs. This suspension continued till 1819, when the Bank returned to cash payments.

THE FOLLOWING ARE THE PRINCIPAL EVENTS WHICH HAVE OCCURRED IN AND NEAR THE METROPOLIS DURING THE PRESENT CENTURY.

1801 Oct. 1. General Lauriston, aid-de-camp to Buonaparte, arrived with the preliminaries of peace.
1802 May 10. Peace with France proclaimed.
1803 Feb. 21. Colonel Despard and six others executed for high treason.
May 16. The declaration of war against France, and a general arming of the people, the volunteers of London and Westminster alone amounting to 27,077.
1806 Jan. 9. Lord Nelson's funeral-procession to St. Paul's.
1807 Feb. 23. Thirty persons crushed to death at the execution of Holloway and Haggarty before Newgate.
1808 Sept. 20. Covent-Garden Theatre burnt down.
1809 Jan. 17. Part of St. James's Palace destroyed by fire.
Feb. 24. Drury-Lane Theatre burnt.
Sept. 18. New Covent-Garden Theatre opened, and the O. P. row commenced.
Oct. 25. Jubilee to commemorate the circumstance of his Majesty George III. having commenced the 50th year of his reign.
1810 April 6. Riots for two days, on account of the committal of Sir F. Burdett to the Tower.
1811 Jan. 8. Thames frozen over.
Feb. 5. Prince Regent took the oaths of office.
1812 May 11. Mr. Perceval shot by Bellingham in the lobby of the House of Commons.

1813 Dec. 27. A fog environed the metropolis for a distance of fifty miles, and continued eight days.

1814 Feb. 4. A fair held on the Thames, which was rendered passable by a severe frost that had lasted six weeks.

Feb. 10. The Custom-house destroyed by fire.

March 31. The Duchess of Oldenburgh, sister of the Emperor Alexander, arrived in London.

April 21. Louis XVIII. entered London on his way to the French metropolis.

June 6. The Emperor of Russia, King of Prussia, Prince Blucher, Prince Platoff, and an immense number of distinguished foreigners, came on a visit to the Prince Regent.

June 18. They were entertained at Guildhall with a splendid banquet, which cost 20,000*l*.

June 20. Grand review in Hyde-park, in presence of the illustrious visitors.

July 7. The Prince Regent went to St. Paul's in state, accompanied by his royal brothers.

August 1. The centenary of the accession of the House of Brunswick, and the return of peace, was celebrated in the Parks by a grand display of fireworks, the erection of a temple of concord, and a pagoda bridge; and by a fair which continued several days.

1815 Feb. 28. March 1, 2. Riots respecting the corn-bill.

1816 May 12. Prince of Saxe-Cobourg married to the Princess Charlotte of Wales.

July 22. Duke of Gloucester married to the Princess Mary.

Dec. 2. An alarming riot, after a public meeting at Spa-fields.

1817 Jan. 28. The Prince Regent shot at, on his return from the opening of parliament.

Feb. 10. Another meeting took place in Spa-fields.

June 9. Watson tried for high treason, and after seven days' trial acquitted. Thistlewood and several others, charged with a similar crime, were not proceeded against.

Nov. 6. The Princess Charlotte expired, after being delivered of a still-born male infant.

1818 July 13. The Duke of Kent married to the Princess of Saxe-Cobourg, and the Duke of Clarence to the Princess of Saxe-Meiningen.

Nov. 17. Queen Charlotte died at Kew.

1820 Jan. 29. His Majesty George III. expired at Windsor.

Jan. 31. His Majesty George IV. proclaimed.

Feb 23. Cato-street conspiracy discovered.

May 1. Thistlewood and four of his associates executed for high-treason.

June 6. Her Majesty Queen Caroline arrived in London.

July 5. A bill of pains and penalties against her Majesty was introduced into the House of Lords.

Aug. 6. The Duchess of York died at Oatlands.

Nov. 10. The House of Peers relinquished the bill of pains and penalties, the majority in its favour on the third reading being only nine.

Nov. 29. The Queen went to St. Paul's to return thanks for the result of the proceedings against her.

1821 July 19. The coronation of his Majesty George IV.

July 31. The King left London on a visit to Ireland.

Aug. 7. The Queen expired at Brandenburgh House.

1821 Aug. 14. Queen Caroline's funeral passed through London.
Dec. 28. An extraordinary high tide of the Thames.
Aug. 12. The Marquess of Londonderry (better known as Lord Castlereagh) put an end to his existence at North Cray, Kent.
1823 Jan. 15. Reduction of the salt-tax took place.
1824 July 8. Died at Osborne's Hotel, Adelphi, the Queen of the Sandwich Islands, who, with her husband, was on a visit to this country. He also expired here on the 14th of the same month.
Nov. 30. Mr. Fauntleroy, the banker, executed at Newgate.
1825 March 2. First stone of the Thames Tunnel laid.
June 15. First stone of the new London bridge laid.
June 28. University College established.
Aug. 4. The Enterprise steam-ship quitted the Thames for India.
1826 Jan. 1. The Imperial Standard for Weights and Measures adopted
1827 Jan 5. The Duke of York died. [killed.
1828 Feb. 28. The roof of the Brunswick Theatre fell in; several persons
June 18. Festival at Freemason's Hall to commemorate the repeal of the Test and Corporation Acts.
Oct. 25. St. Catherine's Docks opened.
1829 March 21. The Duke of Wellington and Earl of Winchelsea fought a duel in Battersea-fields.
April 11. Catholic Relief Bill passed.
Sept. 23. New Post-Office opened.
Sept. 29. Metropolitan Police commenced duty.
1830 June 26. His Majesty George IV. expired at Windsor.
June 28. His Majesty William IV. proclaimed.
Nov. 9. Ridiculous Panic. No Lord Mayor's show.
Nov. 16. Duke of Wellington resigned office.
1831 March 1. Lord John Russell introduced the Reform Bill.
April 20. A majority of eight over Ministers on General Gascoigne's motion.
June 24. Re-introduction of the Reform Bill.
July 6. Second Reading carried by a majority of 116.
Aug. 1. New London Bridge opened.
Sept. 8. Coronation of King William and Queen Adelaide.
Sept. 25. Reform Bill rejected by the Lords.
1832 Feb. 6. The appearance of a virulent disease, or cholera.
March 19. Reform Bill again passed the House of Commons.
May 1. Defeat of the reform Ministry in the House of Lords.
May 9. Resignation of the reform Ministry.
May 18. Recall of Lord Grey.
June 7. Reform Bill received the Royal Assent.
1833 July 2. Hungerford Market opened.
July 29. Wilberforce died.
Aug. 20. Slavery Abolition Bill passed.
1834 April 22. East India Charter expired.
Oct. 16. The Houses of Parliament burnt.
Nov. —. Lord Melbourne resigned. Duke of Wellington held the Seals until the arrival of Sir R. Peel.
1835 April 18. Sir R. Peel resigned; succeeded by Lord Melbourne.
Nov. 17. Grand Aurora Borealis, which caused great alarm.
1836 Sept. 15. Stamp-duty on Newspapers reduced from 4½*d.* to 1*d.*, and on Advertisements from 3*s.* 6*d.* to 1*s.* 6*d.*
Oct. 10. Greenwich Railway opened to Deptford.
Nov. 7. Green's Monster Balloon ascended from Vauxhall, and descended at Weilburg, in Nassau.
1837 April 28. National Gallery opened by William IV.
June 20. His Majesty William IV. expired at Windsor.

1837 June 21. Proclamation of Queen Victoria.
July 13. The Queen took possession of the New Palace.
July 24. Mr. Cocking lost his life in descending with a Parachute.
Nov. 9. The Queen's State Visit to a Grand Dinner at Guildhall.
1838. Jan. 10. Royal Exchange burnt.
March 28. The Sirius steamer left London for New York, followed on the 31st by the Great Western from Bristol.
June 28. Coronation of Queen Victoria. A fair in Hyde-park.
Aug. 10. Drivers, conductors, &c., of carriages plying for hire in the metropolis, or within ten miles thereof, compelled to wear a badge with their number on it, in addition to one for the carriage.
Aug. 17. Birmingham railway opened the whole distance.
Oct. 28. A great hurricane, many houses blown down, and much damage done throughout the metropolis.
1839 April 15. The venerable Thomas Clarkson presented with the freedom of the City of London.
Sept. 7. A banquet in the Thames Tunnel to celebrate its having reached low-water mark.
Dec. 5. The rate of postage reduced to fourpence.
1840 Jan. 10. The rate of postage reduced to one penny.
Feb. 10. Queen Victoria married to Prince Albert of Saxe Gotha.
April 5. Lord William Russell murdered by his valet Courvoisier.
May 10. Her Majesty and Prince Albert shot at while passing up Constitution-hill, by one Oxford, a pot-boy.
Nov. 21. Princess Royal born at Buckingham palace; and a few
1841 Jan. 11. Scott the American diver hung himself while performing his extraordinary evolutions at Waterloo-bridge. (lehem.
Jan. 23. Hatfield, who fired at George III. in 1802, died in Beth-
Feb. 2 Dr. Olinthus Gregory died at Woolwich.
Feb. 8. Camberwell Old Church destroyed by fire.
Feb. 10. Princess Royal christened Victoria Adelaide Mary Louisa.
Feb. 16. Trial of the Earl of Cardigan, for fighting a duel.
June 8. Astley's Amphitheatre destroyed by fire. One life lost.
July 29. Lord John Russel returned for London by a majority of 9.
Foundation for a new Royal Exchange commenced in the early part of the year, after designs of Mr. Tite.
Oct. 30. The Tower of London partly destroyed by fire.
Nov. 9. Prince of Wales born at Buckingham Palace.

CHRONOLOGY OF ENGLISH SOVEREIGNS.

Reign began		
1066	William I., commonly (but erroneously) called "*The Conqueror*."	
1087	William II.	His sons.
1100	Henry I.	
1135	Stephen, William's I.'s grandson, by his fourth daughter, Adela.	
1154	Henry II. (Plantagenet), grandson of Henry I.	
1189	Richard I.	Sons of Henry II.
1191	John	
1216	Henry III., son of John.	
1272	Edward I., son of Henry III.	
1307	Edward II., son of Edward I.	
1327	Edward III., son of Edward II.	
1377	Rich. II., grandson of Edw. III., by his eldest son, the Black Prince.	
1399	Henry IV., son to John of Gaunt, Duke of Lancaster, fourth son of Edward III. .	House of Lancaster.
1413	Henry V., son of Henry IV.	
1422	Henry VI., son of Henry V.	

Reign began		
1461	Edward IV., descended from Edward III., by Lionel, his third son	House of York.
1483	Edward V., son of Edward IV.	
1483	Richard III., brother to Edward IV.	
1485	Henry VII. (Tudor), son of the Countess of Richmond, of the House of Lancaster	House of Tudor, in whom were united the houses of Lancaster and York, by Henry VII.'s marriage to Elizabeth, daughter of Edward IV.
1509	Henry VIII., son of Henry VII.	
1547	Edward VI., son of Henry VIII.	
1553	Mary } daughters of Henry VIII.	
1558	Elizabeth }	

1603 James I., great grandson of James IV., king of Scotland, by Margaret, daughter of Henry VII., and first of the *Stuart* family in England.

1625 Charles I. (son of James I) beheaded Jan. 30, 1649.

1649 Commonwealth and Protectorate, beginning with Oliver Cromwell, who died September 3, 1660.

1660 Charles II. restored May 29.

1685 James II. (both these kings were sons of Charles I.)

1688 { William III., nephew and son-in-law of James II. and Mary.

1702 Anne.

Mary. } Anne. } daughters of James II., in whom the Protestant line of Charles I. was continued: for James II., on abdicating the throne, carried with him his supposed infant son (the Pretender), who was excluded by the act of parliament which settled the succession in the next Protestant heirs of James I. The surviving issue of James at the time of his death were a son and a daughter, viz. Charles, who succeeded him, and the Princess Elizabeth, who married the Elector Palatine, who took the title of King of Bohemia, and left a daughter, the Princess Sophia, who married the Duke of Brunswick Lunenburg, by whom he had George, Elector of Hanover, who ascended the throne by act of parliament expressly made in favour of his mother.

1714	George I.	House of Hanover.
1727	George II., son of George I.	
1760	George III., grandson of George II.	
1820	George IV., son of George III. (after being REGENT upwards of nine years)	
1830	William IV., brother of George IV.	
1837	Victoria I., niece of William IV.; daughter of the Duke of Kent	

CHAPTER II.

GENERAL OUTLINES OF THE METROPOLIS; EXTENT AND LOCALITY; POPULATION; CLIMATE, ETC.

LONDON, in respect to its position on the globe, is ascertained to be 51° 31′ N. lat., and 5′ 37″ W. long., reckoning the first degree of longitude from the Observatory at Greenwich. Its distance from the principal cities of Europe is nearly as follows:

	MILES.	
From Edinburgh	395	S.
—— Dublin	338	S. E.
—— Amsterdam	190	W.
—— Paris	225	N. N. W.
—— Copenhagen	610	S. W.
—— Vienna	820	N. W.
—— Madrid	860	N. E. E.
—— Rome	950	N. N. W.
—— Constantinople	1660	N. N. W.
—— Moscow	1600	E. S. E.
—— Stockholm	750	S. W.
—— Petersburgh	1140	S. W.
—— Berlin	540	W.
—— Lisbon	850	N. N. E.

The immediate site of this vast metropolis is about sixty miles west from the sea, on the banks of the Thames; occupying a gentle slope on the north side of that celebrated river, and an almost uniform flat surface on its southern side. The soil of this district is gravel and clay, with a mixture of loam and sand; and to the abundance of clay, and the facility it affords of making bricks, a part of the rapid increase of building may probably be attributed. London is eminently fortunate in one of the first grand requisites to the health and convenience of a flourishing capital: it is situated on a river of ample extent and excellent water, which carries a tide fifteen miles beyond it, and forms, at the same time, all that is desirable as a medium of commerce. The mean breadth of the Thames at London is about a quarter of a mile: and its usual depth about twelve feet—at Southwark-bridge, from ten to twelve feet low water, and from twenty-five to thirty feet high water, occasioned by spring or other tides. On the Middlesex shore, the buildings of the metropolis, following the natural bend of the river, form a sort of amphitheatre from east to west, in consequence of the gentle rise of the ground from the water-side. The Surrey shore, having been a marsh, is of course flat, but is now covered with a line of buildings, which, from Vauxhall to Deptford, presents an extent of seven miles; the whole forming an assemblage of human habitations second to none but that which distinguished ancient Rome in its prosperity, and at this time certainly the largest in the world.

London, considered as the capital of the British empire, includes not only the city and its liberties, but Westminster,

Southwark, and many villages both in Middlesex and Surrey. Its extent from west to east, or from Knightsbridge to Poplar, is about seven miles and a half. Its breadth from north to south, or from Islington to Newington Butts, is nearly five miles. The circumference of the whole, allowing for various inequalities in the extension of streets, &c., at the extremities, cannot be less than thirty-two miles. Hence it may be fairly estimated that the buildings of this metropolis cover upwards of eighteen square miles. Out of these must be deducted the space occupied by the river Thames, for a length of seven miles, by a breadth of about a quarter of a mile.

Independent of various local and civil divisions, London may be said to consist of five distinguishing parts, or popular divisions;—the West end of the town, the City, the East end of the town, Westminster, and the Borough. "The West end of the town" consists of various handsome squares and streets, occupied by the town-houses of the nobility and gentry, and the most fashionable shops. This quarter has derived additional lustre from the elegant buildings in the neighbourhood of Belgrave-square. The "City" includes the central and most ancient division of the metropolis. This is the emporium of commerce and business of every description, and is occupied by shops, warehouses, public offices, and houses of tradesmen and others connected with business. The "East end of the town," and its inhabitants, are devoted to commerce, to ship-building, and to every collateral branch connected with merchandise. "Southwark," and the whole of the southern bank of the Thames, from Deptford to Lambeth, bear some resemblance to the "East end" of the town, being occupied by persons engaged in commercial and maritime concerns. But this part of London has one feature which distinguishes it from any other: it abounds with numerous and various manufactories, iron-founderies, glass-houses, soap-boiling and dye-houses, shot and hat manufactories, and many other similar establishments. It is therefore chiefly inhabited by workmen, labourers, and the lower classes of society. Many improvements have, however, been made, and many respectable houses erected, in St. George's-fields. "Westminster" contains the palace, the abbey, the parks, the houses of the British legislature, the courts of justice, and many offices connected with government.

Another part of the metropolis, which may be considered as the last enlargement, and the most systematic in its arrangement of squares and streets, is the northern side of the town, comprehending a large mass of new buildings between Holborn and Somers-town, and in the parishes of Mary-le-bone and Paddington. The new quarter of Belgrave-square is one of the most elegant features of the metropolis, and the latest specimen of domestic architecture.

The increase in the size and population of the British metropolis within a few years is truly amazing. It is no unusual event to meet in society persons who recollect those portions of what must now be called the metropolis when they were nothing but fields or swamps; and this remark forcibly applies to Mary-le-bone, St. George's-fields, Russell and Brunswick-squares, Somers-town, Vincent-square, once called Tothill-fields, &c. Such has been the rapid extension of LONDON, that many of those parts of it that are thickly strewed with houses were formerly known as villages. Northumberland-house, at the end of the Strand, which is almost the heart of the metropolis, was formerly described as situated in the "*Village of Charing;*" and when the earl of Burlington was asked "Why he built his house in Piccadilly so far out of town?" he answered, "Because I was determined to have no building *beyond me!*"

At this time, London is computed to contain upwards of 80 squares, and 10,000 streets, lanes, rows, places, courts, &c.: the houses in which are said to amount to no fewer than 197,000. There are two principal ranges of streets, forming a communication from one end of the town to the other. The most southern of these, for the greater part of the way, is within a quarter of a mile of the Thames. It commences at St. James's Palace, in Pall Mall, and is continued through the Strand, Fleet-street, St. Paul's Churchyard, Watling-street, Cannon-street, East-cheap, to the Tower. The northern line of streets commences at Bayswater, and passes through Oxford-street, Holborn, Skinner-street, Newgate-street, Cheapside, Cornhill, Leadenhall-street, and Whitechapel, to Mile-end; a course of at least six miles, with very little undulation. These great avenues, the first of which may be termed the southern, and the other the northern, line of the metropolis, run nearly parallel to each other, and in no part of London can a stranger be far distant from one or other of them; as the streets running north and south which connect them are comparatively short, as are also those from the Strand, &c., to the water-side. Those from the northern line to the New-road, &c., are longer, but still of a moderate length. The lengths of some of the streets and inhabited roads in various parts of the capital are as follow:—

	YARDS.
Aldersgate-street	605
Baker-street	743
Bermondsey-street	836
———— wall	660
Berners-street	330
Bishopsgate-street	1009
Blackman-street	344
Bond-street (New)	733
Bond-street (Old)	209
Borough-road and High-st.	1164
Broad-street, Bloomsbury	341
Broad-street (Old)	339
Cheapside	462
Chiswell-street	385
City-road	1690
Commercial-road	5280
Cornhill	375
Edgeware-road	1397
Fenchurch-street	627
Fleet-street	567
Gracechurch-street	336
Haymarket	352
Holborn (High)	1051
Lamb's-conduit-street	385
Lombard-street	330
Long-acre	457
New Road	3520
Oxford-street	1920
Pall Mall	693
Parliament-street	281
Piccadilly	1650
Portland-street	625
Ratcliffe-highway	625
Regent-street	1728
St. James's-street	385
Shoreditch	710
Snow-hill	127
South Audley-street	539
Strand	1342
Surrey-road	1133
Thames-street (Lower)	484
———— (Upper)	1007
Tooley-street	748
Tottenham-court-road	1155
Waterloo-road, about	1300
Whitechapel	1281
———— road	999

All the streets in London are paved with great regularity, and have a footpath laid with flags, divided from the carriage-way: the latter is formed by small square blocks of Scotch granite. The footpath has a regular curb-stone, raised some inches above the carriage-way; of course the accommodation to the foot-passenger must depend upon the breadth of the avenue: but as every alteration for many years past has tended to widen the streets and lanes of the metropolis, the narrow avenues which admit carriages are gradually increasing in convenience to the pedestrian. In 1823 a new method of forming the carriage-ways of London was commenced in St. James's-square, under the superintendence of Mr. M'Adam. Nearly all the streets are lighted by gas, an improvement which has only been introduced within a few years; and the widening of the footpath in the greater number of streets has added to the comfort of the inhabitants. A new mode of paving streets, with a bituminous mixture, which has proved successful in Paris, has been lately tried in London: a specimen of it may be seen at Whitehall.

The *Climate* of London is temperate, but variable and inclined to moisture. The average temperature is 51° 9′, although it varies from 20° to 81°, the most severe cold usually occurring in January, and the greatest heat in July. Particular instances, however, of extreme cold and heat are occasionally observed. In January 1795 the mercury in

Fahrenheit's thermometer sunk to 38 degrees below the freezing point, and in July 1808 rose to 94 degrees in the shade.

Levels in London above High-Water Mark.

	FT.	IN.
N. end of Northumberland-st., Strand	19	7
N. end of Wellington-street, Strand	35	6
N. end of Essex-st., Strand	27	0
W. end of Coventry-st.	52	0
S. end of St. James's-st.	13	3
N. end of St. James's-st.	46	7
S. end of Air-st., Piccadilly	49	8
W. end of Gerrard-st.	61	4
N. end of Drury-lane	65	0
S. end of Berners-st.	74	3
S. end of Stratford-place, Oxford-st.	59	4
N. end of Regent-st.	76	0
S. end of Orchard-st.	70	4
N. end of Cleveland-st.	80	10
Centre of Regent's Circus	77	2
N. end of Gloucester-place	72	3
N. side of Aqueduct crossing the Regent's Canal	102	6
S. end of King-st., George-st.	5	6

The whole of Westminster, except the Abbey and part of Horseferry-road, is below the level of the highest tide.

Jack Straw's Castle, Hampstead Heath, is the most lofty site in the immediate vicinity of London, being 443 feet above the Thames. The top of the cross of St. Paul's Cathedral is 407 feet, and its base or ground line 52 feet. The lowest building is the Bricklayer's Arms, Kent-road, the south door of which is only six inches above high-water mark.

The most commanding Views of the Metropolis.

Hampstead Heath, Muswell Hill, Hornsey, Greenwich Park, Putney Common, and Primrose Hill.

These points of examination are strongly recommended to the foreign or native visitor of London.

Population.

The following is an Account of the Population of London and its vicinity, according to the Parliamentary returns of 1831 :—

London within the walls	55,778
London without the walls	67,878
Westminster and its Liberties	202,891
Southwark	91,501
Brixton Division, including Barnes, Battersea, Bermondsey, Camberwell, Clapham, Deptford, Lambeth, Mortlake, Putney, Rotherhithe, Tooting, Wandsworth, &c. &c.	245,860
Finsbury Division, including Clerkenwell, Finchley, Hornsey, Islington, Stoke Newington, &c. &c.	151,409
Holborn Division, including St. Giles's in the Fields, St. George's Bloomsbury, Hampstead, Mary-le-bone, Paddington, Pancras, &c. &c.	346,255
Tower Division, including Bethnal Green, Spitalfields, Hackney, Limehouse, Shadwell, Shoreditch, Stepney, Stratford, Wapping, Whitechapel, &c. &c.	359,864
	1,521,436

The London Bills of Mortality, originally instituted in 1533, are founded upon the reports of the sworn searchers, who view all dead bodies after decease, and deliver their report to the parish-clerks. An annual summary of all these accounts is published on the Thursday before Christmas-day, and is called the Bill of Mortality. The original bills comprehend only 109 parishes; but since the year 1660, the number of parishes has been increased to 153. They are divided into 97 parishes within the walls; 17 without the walls; 29 out-parishes in Middlesex and Surrey; and 10 in the city and Liberty of Westminster. A law has recently come into operation for the registration of births and deaths, which, when fully established, will render more correct returns, inasmuch as persons of all religious persuasions will have every opportunity of registering their children, without their religious scruples being affected. Till the passing of this law there was no effective legislative provision for registering births and deaths—the registration of the church being that of *baptisms* and *burials;* and much inconvenience that has been sustained by the decisions in courts of law, that these registers could not be received in evidence of the *time* or *place* of birth, will now be removed.

The number of births during a recent year amounted to 27,028; 13,674 of which were of males, and 13,354 of females. The number of burials in the same year was 23,524; 12,015 were of males, and 11,509 of females.

CHAPTER III.

LONDON VIEWED AS THE SEAT OF GOVERNMENT, LEGISLATIVE AND EXECUTIVE.

The Sovereign and Court.

THE Court may be divided into the *legislative,* the *executive,* and the *fashionable.*

In his LEGISLATIVE capacity, the sovereign's prerogatives are very great; but there are controlling checks on an undue exercise of power provided by the constitution. The monarch alone can convoke, prorogue, or dissolve the parliament; but he cannot originate a bill or raise money without its consent. The House of Lords, which is created by the voice of the sovereign, cannot originate a *money-bill;* all money-bills, all bills imposing taxes or penalties, must commence with the

Commons, and the Lords must agree to or reject them altogether; any alteration, even in the mode of paying a penalty, is fatal to the particular bill. The king may raise an army, but he can procure no money; he may proclaim war, but without parliament he has not the means of carrying it on; and he may resort to the most extravagant expenditure, but it rests with parliament whether one farthing beyond the prescribed income shall be paid.

In the exercise of his EXECUTIVE functions, the sovereign appoints all the ministers of state, the judges, archbishops, bishops, &c.; but the ministers are removable at pleasure, whilst the judges, being appointed for life, can only be affected by impeachment. Through the medium of the judges, the king enforces the execution of all laws; but as the sentences of the law may sometimes be too severe, he has the sole power of mitigating their severity, or of granting a full pardon to the delinquent. Besides being the source of mercy, he is the *fountain of honour*. All degrees of nobility, as well as pensions, &c., flow from him; but here again the king or queen is controlled, for without the assent of parliament there can be no revenue attached to such advancements.

The remaining leading division of the sovereign's power and influence, the FASHIONABLE, now claims our notice.

Next to the solemnization of a coronation, the birth-days, drawing-rooms, and levees, held at one of the royal palaces, constitute the most celebrated court-pageants. Notice is given of drawing-rooms and levees in the *Gazette*; and on those occasions are proffered the compliments of the nobility, persons holding high offices in the state, distinguished members of the law, church, navy, army, &c. On these days, also, it is not unusual to witness the introduction of several of the younger branches of distinguished families, which for females of high rank is deemed a preliminary to their future visits and communication with the fashionable world. The ceremony of presentation is usually performed by the parents, or some near relation or friend. On the first presentation of the daughters of dukes, marquesses, and earls, it is customary for the queen slightly to kiss their cheeks. The king formerly did the same. After this, the queen presents her hand to be kissed. Sometimes ladies send cards to the ladies in waiting, who in that case present them. On these occasions, it is essential that the visitors be full dressed; that is, the gentlemen in the full costume appropriate to their various ranks, professions, and offices; or otherwise to wear the court dress.

The Parliament, its Antiquity, &c.

The Imperial Parliament of Great Britain is the grand assembly of the estates of the realm. Its constituent parts have excited much discussion amongst constitutional writers, some contending that the archbishops and bishops, or *lords spiritual*, constitute *one* estate, the *lords temporal* a *second*, and the *commons* a *third;* but the parliament is usually divided into Lords and Commons. It is summoned, prorogued, and dissolved by the sovereign's voice. Its power is undefinable. Its duty is not only to "*unlock the people's purses,*" but also to *keep the people's accounts;* or, to adopt the legal language of *Coke*, "parliament is the highest and most honourable and absolute court of justice;" "the jurisdiction of this court is so transcendent, that it maketh, enlargeth, diminisheth, abrogateth, repealeth, and reviveth laws, statutes, acts, and ordinances, concerning matters ecclesiastical, capital, criminal, common, civil, martial, maritime, and the rest." Its work is, "to redress grievances, to take notice of monopolies and oppressions, to curb the exorbitancies of pernicious favourites and ill ministers of state, to punish such mighty delinquents as look upon themselves too great for the ordinary reach of justice, and to inspect the conduct of those who are intrusted with the administration of the laws, or disposal of the public treasure of the nation." It can regulate or new model the succession to the crown, as in the reigns of Henry VIII. and William III. It can alter the religion of the land, as was done in the reigns of Henry VIII., Edward VI., Mary, and Elizabeth. It has not only changed, but created afresh the Constitution of the country, and even its own, as in the case of the Reform Bill; but in the former cases the changes have been, or pretended to be, according to the principles laid down in the people's charters; and in the latter instance, alluding to the passing of the *septennial* act, parliament distinctly admitted its violation of constitutional principle and practice, but defended it on the ground of necessity, and as being only a temporary measure. It has never since been repealed, although the occasion of it has long ceased to exist, there being now no pretender to the throne, and monarchy being in no danger.

Parliament derives its name, according to Coke, from every member of that court being enabled sincerely and discreetly *parler la ment* (to speak the mind) for the general good of the commonwealth. Although the derivation of the word may be deemed beyond dispute, there is much doubt about its first application. It was applied to the general assemblies of the state under Louis VII. of France, about the middle of the twelfth century, but it is said not to have appeared in our law till its mention in the statute of Westminster, 1, 3 Edw. I., A. D. 1272; and yet Coke declared in his Institutes, and spoke to the same effect when Speaker (A.D. 1592), that this name was used even in the time of Edward the Confessor, 1041. It is certain that long before the introduction of the Norman language into England all matters of importance were debated and settled in the great *council* of the realm; a practice which seems to have been universal among the northern nations, particularly amongst the Germans, who conveyed it into all the countries of Europe, which they overran at the dissolution of the Roman empire. Instances are upon record of the assembling of this council, to order the affairs of the kingdom, to make new laws, and to amend the old, as early as the reign of Ina king of the West Saxons, Offa king of the Mercians, and Ethelbert king of Kent, in the several reigns of the heptarchy.

Before William I.'s reign, parliaments, or councils of the nation, were to be held *twice* in every year, as appears by *Edgar*, *cap.* 5, the testimony of the Mirrour of Justice, the Institutes, &c.; but the *Commons* of England, represented by knights, citizens, and burgesses, were not specifically named as constituting one of the estates in parliament till the 49th of Henry III., 1265. Hume says, "the commons were no part of the great council till some ages after the conquest." Knights of the shire had previously assembled in a separate house; but the Earl of Leicester, whose attempts on the crown of Henry III. had been defeated, led to the subsequent summoning of two knights from every shire, and also deputies from the boroughs, who were before deemed too inconsiderable to have a voice in legislation. This is the first confirmed outline of a House of Commons. In the earlier reigns, parliament was alternately kept at York, Northampton, Lincoln, New Sarum, Winchester, Gloucester, Leicester, Oxford, Cambridge, and Reading, as well as at Westminster, the latter having been the seat of the legislature since the time of Elizabeth.

The city of London first sent members to parliament in the reign of Henry III.; while Westminster was not represented in that august assembly until the latter end of Henry VIII.th's life, or rather in the first House of Commons of Edward VI. King Edward I., Henry III.'s successor, however, seldom held a parliament more than once in every *two* years: but in the next reign but one it was enacted (4 Edw. III. cap. 14) "that a parliament should be holden *every year once*, and more often if need be." This continued to be the statute-law of the land till 16 Charles II., when an act was passed "for the assembling and holding of parliaments once in *three years* at least;" but parliaments for a longer period than a year were held after Henry VIII. ascended the throne. The *triennial act* was confirmed soon after the Revolution of 1688, by 6 William and Mary, cap. 2. Triennial parliaments thence continued till the first year of George I.'s reign, when, in consequence of the allegation that "a restless and popish faction were designing and endeavouring to renew the rebellion within this kingdom, and the report of an invasion from abroad, it was enacted that the then existing parliament should continue for *seven* years, and no longer." This *septennial* act has ever since been in force.—The PARLIAMENT is England's sheet-anchor:—"England," said Burleigh, "can never be undone but by parliament." The parliament, however, must exist *in fact*, and continue to be the organ of the people's voice—the representative of their feelings and views. Should the time unhappily arrive when the lower house in particular, and the people, shall have separate interests and distinct feelings, then may it be justly feared that the liberties of the nation will be buried amidst the corruptions of a House of Commons.

The LORDS are indefinite in number, excepting the lords spiritual; of these there are two archbishops, and twenty-four bishops, who are supposed to hold certain ancient baronies under the king; in right of which they have seats in the House of Lords, where they intermix their votes with the temporal lords. The lords temporal consist of the peers of Great Britain, in their several orders and degrees of dignity, as dukes, marquesses, earls, viscounts, barons. Some of these sit by *descent*, as do all *ancient peers*: some by *creation*, as in the case of all *new-made peers*; others, since the union of Scotland, by *election*, which is the case of the *sixteen peers* who represent the body of the *Scotch nobility*; and *twenty-eight peers* for *Ireland*, besides *one archbishop* and *three bishops*. The number of lay lords is indefinite, and may be increased at will by the crown. At present the number of peers, temporal and spiritual, is about 410.

The COMMONERS in parliament consist of knights, elected by the counties; and of citizens and burgesses, elected by the cities and borough-towns. There are 658 members, viz.:

ENGLAND—County members		143	
	Isle of Wight	1	
	Universities	4	
	Cities, boroughs, and Cinque Ports	323	
			471
WALES—County members		15	
	Boroughs	14	
			29
SCOTLAND—County members		30	
	Cities and boroughs	23	
			53
IRELAND—County members		64	
	University	2	
	Cities and boroughs	39	105
		Total	658

The two houses having agreed to the measures proposed by either body, the ROYAL ASSENT is necessary to render them laws. The sovereign authority can do this in person, or by appointing three or more peers as commissioners to represent him. When the royal assent is given to a public bill, the clerk says, "*Le roi le veut.*" If the bill be a private bill, he says, "*Soit fait comme il est désiré.*" If the bill have subsidies for its object, he says, "*Le roi remercie ses loyaux sujets, accepte leur bénévolence, et aussi le veut.*" If the king do not think proper to assent to the bill, the clerk says, "*Le roi s'avisera;*" which is a mild way of giving a refusal. It is singular that the King of England should still make use of the French language to declare his intentions to his parliament. This custom was introduced in William I.'s reign.

As to the FORMS observed in the two houses, the Lords, except on state occasions, mingle together promiscuously, only observing the ministerial or opposition side of the house. The archbishops and bishops sit on a bench by themselves. Across the room are woolsacks, continued from ancient custom; and the chancellor, being of course the speaker of the House of Lords, sits on the first woolsack before the throne, with the great seal or mace lying by him; below these are forms. On the other woolsacks are seated the judges, masters in chancery, &c., who give their advice in points of law.

The Commons sit promiscuously: the speaker only has a particular seat; he is elected from amongst their own body, and has an elevated chair at the upper end of the house; the clerk and his two assistants sit at the table below the speaker, towards the middle of the house, dressed in robes. The seat on the floor, to the right hand of the speaker, is called the *treasury-bench;* being the usual position of the members of the government. The side immediately opposite is occupied by the leading members of the *opposition.* When a member of the House of Commons speaks, he addresses the speaker only. If what he says be answered by another, he is not allowed to reply the same day, unless personal reflections have been cast upon him; but when the commons, in order to have a greater freedom of debate, have resolved themselves into a committee of the whole house, every member may speak to a question as often as he thinks necessary.

In the House of Lords they vote beginning at the lowest peer and ascending to the highest, every one answering "Content," or "Not content."

When a bill is objectionable, it is often proposed "that it be read this day six months," so as to be deferred until the next session, or that the period should fall when the house is not sitting. "The order of the day," often called for to put an end to some discussion not previously announced, implies that the matter on the journal should be brought forward in preference; and "that the previous question" be put, is another mode of defeating a measure proposed. "A call of the house" can be insisted on by any member, so as to insure a full attendance; the penalties of disobedience being severe. Cries of "question" and "spoke" imply impatience at a departure from the topic, or the efforts of a tedious orator; while "hear" is a monosyllable of double meaning, implying either derision or attention.

In the House of Commons they vote by "ayes" and "noes;" and if it be doubtful which possess the greater number, the house divides. If the question relate to the introduction of any thing into the house, then the "ayes" go out; but if otherwise, the "noes" go out. In all divisions the speaker appoints four tellers, two of each opinion. In a committee of the whole house they divide by changing sides, the "ayes" taking the right, and the "noes" the left of the chair, and then there are but two tellers. Forty members are sufficient to form a house, and eight a committee. For the reception and discussion of petitions the house meets every day (except Saturday) at noon; but for the regular business of the day it meets at five o'clock.

Accommodations for Members, Reporters, &c.

There are coffee-rooms attached to each house, for the accommodation of the members only; many of whom dine there during a long debate. Strangers from the gallery may get sandwiches, &c. at the bar as a favour; but they are not permitted to enter the rooms. The whole is under the superintendence of the housekeeper. Should the bell ring to announce that a division is about to take place, and to direct the messengers and officers to lock all the doors leading to the house or its lobby, an amusing spectacle is beheld: members are seen running in all directions, with the utmost haste, to get into the house before the fatal key is turned.

For the accommodation of "*strangers*," as all spectators are indiscriminately called, there is a GALLERY at the end of the house, facing the speaker's chair, which, however, will not hold more than about 130 persons, even when the doorways are crowded: it may be cleared at any time at the will of any one member, and all strangers are compelled to withdraw previous to a division. It is understood that visiters are present by courtesy, although a ticket from a member will insure admission; the former mode of paying 2*s.* 6*d.* having been suppressed. Within a few years, in the time of Woodfall and Dr. Johnson, any person seen to take a memorandum was instantly told to put away his paper, or was turned out altogether; and yet a special gallery at the other extremity is now filled with gentlemen openly and undisguisedly taking notes of what is passing, for the known purpose of reporting the debates in the newspapers. Strangers are warned from "being in the eye of the speaker," *id est*, standing upright in the gallery. The salary of the speaker is 6000*l.* per annum, independent of 500*l.* per annum for coals, candles, &c. On every new election he receives 1000*l.* by way of outfit, and 1400*l.* for plate.

COURTS OF JUSTICE.

It is the great glory of this country, that all courts are of right *open to the public*. The prisoner (or defendant) neither makes his appearance nor pleads but in places where every one may have free entrance; and the witnesses when they give their evidence, the judge when he delivers his opinion, the jury when they give their verdict, are all under the public eye; and the judge cannot change either the place or the kind of punishment ordered by the law.

As the remedies of the *unwritten* and *written*, that is, *common* and *statute* law, could not in all cases secure the amplest justice to the subject, COURTS OF EQUITY have been established in this country. The office of the judges in these courts consists in providing remedies for those cases in regard to which the courts of common law, shackled by their original forms and institutions, cannot procure any; or, in other words, the courts of equity have a power to administer justice to the individuals *unrestrained* (not by the law, but) *by the professional law difficulties* which lawyers have from time to time contrived in the courts of common law, and to which the judges of those courts have given their sanction.

Lord Chancellor's Court.

The Court of Chancery is the highest court of judicature in the kingdom, next to the parliament. It has two jurisdictions—one common law, called the ordinary, the other equity, called the extraordinary jurisdiction; the former, however, is seldom resorted to. The lord chancellor, who is called the lord high chancellor of England, sits as sole judge, and he is created by the mere delivery of the king's seal into his custody. The court holds pleas of recognizances acknowledged in the chancery writs, writs of fieri facias, writs for the repeal of letters-patent, writs of partition, &c.; and also of all personal actions by or against any officer of the court; and, by acts of parliament, of several offences and causes. All original writs, writs for the election of members of parliament, patents for sheriffs, commissions of bankruptcy, of charitable uses, and other commissions, as riots, lunacy, &c., issue out of this court. Sometimes a supersedeas, or writ of privilege, has been here granted to discharge a person out of prison; it also considers the intention rather than the words of the law, equity being the correction of that wherein the law, by reason of its universality, is deficient. On this ground, therefore, to maintain a suit in chancery, it is always alleged that the plaintiff is incapable of obtaining relief at common law; and this must be without any fault of his own, *as having lost his bond,* &c., chancery never acting *against, but in assistance of, common law;* supplying its deficiencies, not contradicting its rules—a judgment at law not being reversible by a decree in chancery. This court gives relief for and against infants, notwithstanding their minority; and for and against married women, notwithstanding their coverture. In some cases a woman may sue her husband for maintenance; she may sue him when he is beyond sea, and be compelled to answer without her husband. All frauds and deceits for which there is no remedy at common law may be here redressed, as also unreasonable and deceitful agreements entered into without consideration. Bankrupt business is now settled in a separate court, called Court of Review, but appeals from the decision of this court may be made to the lord chancellor; as also appeals from the decisions of the two inferior chancery courts, viz. Rolls' and Vice-chancellor's.

The lord chancellor has hitherto been removable at pleasure, which is not the case with the common law judges; and hence, from the situation held by him in the lords, his political identity with the ministers, &c., there is a new chancellor with every change of the king's advisers. It has been proposed to bring before the House of Lords a bill to render the office of chancellor permanent; since, by the changes incidental to administrations, fresh difficulties are created in that most important court over which he presides. In term time his lordship sits in Westminster-hall, where an elegant court was constructed in 1823; but during the vacation, in Lincoln's-inn-hall. Both courts are open to the public. The late Sir S. Romilly rose to his great celebrity by his eloquent and courageous pleadings in this court.

Rolls.

The master of the rolls is keeper of the rolls or records of the pleadings, determinations, and acts of these courts, as rules for future decisions. He also decides on cases of equity, and, since the new act, also hears motions; but appeals to the lord chancellor may be made against his honour's decisions. His court joins the Rolls' Chapel in Chancery-lane; and he has a handsome and commodious residence annexed to it. The court is adorned with a statue of George I., and a portrait of Sir W. Grant, formerly master of the rolls. It is open to the public during the transaction of business. A new Record Office is about to be built in the Rolls' Gardens.

Vice-Chancellor's Court.

The office of vice-chancellor was created in 1813. His duty is to assist the chancellor in deciding various petitions, hearing motions, &c. A handsome new court was erected about 1816, contiguous to Lincoln's-inn-hall; but in term time his honour sits at the court erected in 1823 at Westminster-hall.

Exchequer.

The Court of Exchequer is a very ancient institution, having been established by William I., and reduced to its present order by Edward I. It has the power of judging both according to law and equity. In the proceedings according to *law* the lord chief baron of the exchequer and three other barons preside as judges. They are styled barons, because formerly none but barons of the realm were allowed to be judges in this court. Besides these there is a fifth, called *Cursitor Baron*, who has not a judicial capacity, but is only employed in administering the oath to the sheriffs and other officers, and also to several of the officers of the custom-house: the office, however, is little better than a sinecure. When this court proceeds according to *equity*, the lord treasurer and the chancellor of the exchequer are always presumed to be present. All matters touching the royal revenue, treasury, customs, and fines, are here tried and determined. The queen's attorney-general is made privy to all manner of pleas that are not ordinary, and of course those which rise upon the process of the court; and he puts into court, in his own name, informations of seizures, &c. Besides the officers already mentioned, there are the queen's remembrancer, who takes and states all accounts of the revenue, and some others. The court sits at Westminster-hall, and is open to the public.

The exchequer records are of great importance; they are not inferior in interest to Doomsday-book itself. From the very first establishment of the exchequer, it was customary to make a great roll every year, containing an exact account of every branch of the royal revenue as it was collected in each county. The great rolls of most of the years of Henry II., Richard I., and John, are still in existence. The most ancient of the records, THE GREAT ROLL of the fifth year of Stephen, is a famous monument of antiquity, whether the hand-writing or the contents be considered. According to Madox's "History of the Exchequer," it consists of sixteen large rolls, written on both sides.

Queen's Bench.

In the Queen's Bench, which is the supreme court of common law, are determined pleas between the crown and the subject; and those of treasons, felonies, &c., which properly belong to the sovereign. Here likewise are tried breaches of the peace, oppression, and misgovernment; and this court corrects the errors of all the judges and justices of England, not only in pleas of the crown, but in all pleas real, personal, and mixed; except only in pleas of the exchequer. The court is general, and extends to all England; and wherever it is held, the law supposes the sovereign to be present. It has for some centuries past usually sat at Westminster, being an ancient palace of the crown.

The sittings of the queen's bench are held at Westminster-hall and at Guildhall, where new courts have recently been constructed. They are open to the public.

Common Pleas.

This also is one of the royal courts, and is now constantly held in Westminster-hall; one of its judges, however, goes after term to the city of London, to try *nisi prius* causes. In ancient times this court was moveable, as appears by Magna Charta, chap. xi. Its jurisdiction is general, and extends throughout England; it holds pleas of all civil causes at common law between subject and subject, in actions real, personal, and mixed. In personal and mixed actions it has a concurrent jurisdiction with the queen's bench; but no cognizance of pleas of the crown. It does not possess any original jurisdiction; nor has it, like the court of queen's bench, any mode of proceeding in common cases peculiar to itself.

In this court are four judges, created by letters patent; the seal of the court is committed to the custody of the chief justice. The other officers of the court are the custos brevium, three prothonotaries and their secondaries, clerk of the warrants, clerk of the essoines, fourteen filazers, four exigenters, clerk of the juries, cheirographer, clerk of the queen's silver, clerk of the treasury, clerk of the seal, clerk of outlawries, clerk of the enrolment of fines and recoveries, clerk of the errors, &c. To these officers may be added, a proclamator, a keeper of the court, crier, and tipstaffs, besides the warden of the Fleet. The court both at Westminster and Guildhall is open to the public.

Exchequer Chamber.

This court has no original jurisdiction, but is merely a court of appeal, to correct the errors of other jurisdictions. It consists of the lord chancellor, the lord treasurer, and the judges of the queen's bench and common pleas. Into the exchequer chamber are adjourned such causes as the judges find to be of great weight and difficulty, before any judgment is given on them in the court; and here are decided the cases which are reserved for the opinions of *all the judges*.

Bankrupt Court, Basinghall Street,

Is a plain brick and stone edifice, of a quadrangular form (occupying part of the site of Blackwell-hall), erected in 1820 by Mr. Fowler, and opened for public business on the 15th of December in the same year. It contains fourteen public rooms connected by commodious galleries. There is also an office for the registry of all proceedings in bankrupt cases, which is open every day to the public.

Courts of Request.

Of these there are several in different parts of the metropolis, for the settlement of debts under 5*l.*, but extending in the city of London to 10*l.* In the ninth year of Henry VIII. a court of conscience, or court of requests, was erected, which has been confirmed and amended by various succeeding statutes. The practice is by summons; and if the party do not appear, the commissioners have power to apprehend and commit. The commissioners proceed summarily, examining the witnesses of both parties on oath, and, according to their own judgment, pronounce a verdict. The time and expense of obtaining summary redress in this court are very inconsiderable, which renders it of great service to trade. The lord mayor and court of aldermen appoint monthly such aldermen and commoners to sit as commissioners in this court as they think fit; and these, or any three of them, compose a court, held in Basinghall-street every Wednesday and Saturday from eleven till two o'clock, to hear and determine such causes as are brought before them. Besides the court of requests held here for the city, there is one in Vine-street, Piccadilly; one in Kingsgate-street, High Holborn; another in St. Margaret's-hill, Southwark; one in Whitechapel; one in Castle-street, Leicester-square; and one in Swan-street, Southwark. The latter courts are generally managed by tradesmen of respectability.

Court of Admiralty.

This court, held in Doctors' Commons by the lords of the admiralty, takes cognizance of all maritime affairs, whether civil or criminal. All crimes committed on the high seas, or on great rivers below the first bridge next the sea, are cognizable in this court only. The proceedings are the same as those adopted in civil law. The plaintiff gives security to prosecute, and, if cast, to pay what is adjudged. But in criminal cases, as the trial of pirates, and crimes committed at sea, the process, by a special commission, is by a judge, jury, and witnesses, a judge of the common law assisting, on which occasion the court is generally held at the Sessions-house, Old Bailey. The court is open to the public.

Doctors' Commons.

This college of civilians is established for the study and practice of the civil law, in which courts are kept for the trial of civil and ecclesiastical causes, under the archbishop of Canterbury and the bishop of London, as in the court of arches and the prerogative court. There are also offices in which wills are deposited and searched, and a court of faculties and dispensations. The name of commons is given to this college from the circumstance of the civilians commoning together, as in other colleges. This edifice is situated in Great Knight Rider-street, on the south side of St. Paul's cathedral. The old building which stood in this place was purchased for the residence of the civilians and canonists by Henry Harvey, doctor of the civil and common law and dean of the arches; but this edifice being destroyed by the general devastation in 1666, they removed to Exeter-house, in the Strand, where the civilians had their chambers and offices, and the courts were held in the hall. But some years after, the commons being rebuilt in a more convenient and elegant manner than before, the civilians returned thither. The causes of which the civil and ecclesiastical law do or may take cognizance are, blasphemy, apostacy from Christianity, heresy, ordinations, institutions to benefices, celebration of divine service, matrimony, divorces, bastardy, tithes, oblations, obventions, mortuaries, dilapidations and reparations of churches, probates of wills, administrations, simony, incest, fornication, adultery, pensions, procurations, commutation of penance, right of pews, and others of the same kind. Those who practise in these courts are divided into two classes—advocates and proctors. The advocates are such as have taken the degree of doctor of civil law, and are retained as counsellors and pleaders. These must first, upon their petition to the archbishop, obtain his fiat, and then they are admitted by the judge to practise. They wear black robes and hoods, lined with fur. The terms for the pleading and ending of causes in the civil courts are but slightly different from the term times of the common law. The order as to the time of the sitting of the several courts is as follows:—The court of arches, having the pre-eminence, sits first in the morning; the court of admiralty sits in the afternoon on the same day; and the prerogative court also sits in the afternoon. The prerogative office is open from nine to three, except on Sundays and holydays. The expense of searching for a will here is only 1*s.*; and copies or extracts of them may be procured, if required, by paying at a certain rate per folio for the quantity extracted. The original wills of Shakspeare and Milton (among others) are deposited here. Here is a fine marble bust of the late Lord Stowell, by Behnes.

Insolvent Debtors' Court

Was established as an experiment, being chiefly founded on the *cessio bonorum* principle of the law of Scotland; after a short imprisonment, a debtor being entitled to petition for his discharge out of prison, on condition of surrendering all his effects to the use of his creditors. This discharge, if it should not be conditional on the grounds of extravagance or fraud having been committed by the debtor, releases the person; but any property that can be traced to him, although it may have been subsequently acquired, is liable to the payment of his debts. The *person* is for ever released, but *property* never, so long as any debts remain unsatisfied.

The acts constituting the insolvent debtors' court contain the regulations for its guidance, and appoint commissioners to carry them into effect. The construction to be put upon these laws is left to their sole discretion—there is no intervention of a jury, and thus the court partakes of the mingled principles of law and equity, having specific regulations to enforce, at the same time possessing a large discretionary power. The number of persons annually liberated amounts to nearly 5000, more than one-half of whom belong to London. The average dividend resulting from the property given up to the creditors is about a *penny farthing* in the pound! There are four commissioners appointed by the insolvent debtors' act, who sit about four days in every fortnight, and are attended by barristers, and agents who need not be regularly admitted attorneys. The court is a neat building, erected in 1824, from designs by Sir J. Soane, in Portugal-street, Lincoln's-inn-fields. The commissioners go the circuit, and transact the business of the court; indeed, they possess the authority of a locomotive court.

Since the passing of the 1st and 2d Victoriæ, cap. 110, (the act for the abolition of imprisonment for debt,) the law respecting insolvent debtors has been much changed. The insolvent, to obtain his liberation, can now file a petition within twenty-one days after his arrest; but if he should neglect doing so, the detaining creditor may apply by petition in a summary way to the court, for an order vesting the real and personal estate and effects in the provisional assignee of the court. The act, however, only abolishes arrest on mesne process.

The Palace, or Marshalsea Court,

Has jurisdiction over all civil suits within twelve miles of the king's palace, excepting in the city of London. The mode of proceeding is remarkably expeditious, as causes are decided in about three weeks; but neither the plaintiff nor defendant can belong to her majesty's household. The steward, or judge, is a barrister, who sits here every Friday, when the court is open to the public. The building in which the court is held is neat and convenient, and is situated in Scotland-yard.

Old Bailey Sessions.

This court is held for the trial of criminals, and its jurisdiction comprehends the county of Middlesex, as well as the city of London. It is held eight times in the year, by the queen's commission of *oyer* and *terminer*. The judges are, the lord mayor, those aldermen who have passed the chair, the recorder, and the common sergeant, who are attended by both the sheriffs and one or more of the national judges. The offences in the city are tried by a jury of citizens, and those committed in the county by one formed of housekeepers in the county. There are, besides the Middlesex sessions held at Clerkenwell, the Southwark at Horsemonger-lane, and London at Guildhall, for the trial of misdemeanors, &c.

The central criminal court sessions are held once in six weeks; and the new court has jurisdiction of the whole metropolis, and fifteen or twenty miles round.

Connected with the courts previously described are about 800 officers, 450 barristers, 2000 attorneys and solicitors, 130 conveyancers and equity draftsmen, 70 special pleaders, 80 proctors, 40 notaries, 4000 clerks and attendants, besides judges, sergeants-at-law, doctors at law, masters in chancery, king's counsel, and others, amounting altogether to nearly 8000.

INNS OF COURT.

The institutions in which the professors of the law are supposed to be brought up and educated, are now in name only what they were formerly in reality. Instead of any public "moots," exercises, and duties to be observed by students previously to their being called to the bar, they have now only to eat a certain number of dinners during the terms of three or five years, in one of the inns of court, the expense of which, together with a species of fine, amounts to about 130*l*.

Although much pleasantry has been occasioned by the practice of *eating* the way to the bar, it must not be presumed that no preparatory study is pursued. Public courses of study were found inefficacious, and were abandoned; but all those who have risen to celebrity as lawyers laid the foundation of their greatness by hard study. The young men not only apply themselves to courses of law reading, which is necessary to be shewn upon application for admission, but come into the practice of the laws, and the application of their own researches, by placing themselves as pupils with leading special pleaders, counsel, &c. Two or three hundred guineas are frequently paid for permission to study in the office of a special pleader or barrister of high consideration and great practice. The inns of court are governed by masters, principals, benchers, stewards, &c. For light offences, persons are only excluded, or not allowed to eat at the common table with the rest; and for greater, they lose their chambers; and when once expelled from one society they are never received by any of the rest. As the societies are not incorporated, they have no lands nor revenues, nor any thing for defraying the charges of the house but what is paid for admissions, and other dues for the chambers. The members may be divided into benchers, outer barristers, inner barristers, and students. The benchers are the seniors, who have the government of the whole house; and out of these is annually chosen a treasurer, who receives, disburses, and accounts for all the money belonging to the house.

The principal inns of court are four. The *Inner Temple* and *Middle Temple*, *Lincoln's Inn*, and *Gray's Inn*.

The Temple

Is thus called because it was anciently the dwelling-house of the Knights Templars. At the suppression of that order it was purchased by the professors of the common law, and converted into inns. They are called the Inner and Middle Temple, in relation to Essex-house, which was also a part of the house of the Templars, and called the Outer Temple, because it was situated without Temple Bar. The principal entrance to the Temple is the Middle Temple Gate, which was erected from the design of Inigo Jones. It consists of a brick edifice, with four Ionic stone pilasters on a rustic basement, adorned with a figure of a lamb, the badge of the society.

St. Mary's, or the *Temple Church*, situated in the Inner Temple, is an ancient Gothic stone building, erected by the Templars in the reign of Henry II. It is remarkable for its circular vestibule, and for the tombs of the crusaders who were buried here. To the right are four recumbent figures, cross-legged, supposed to be of the Earl of Pembroke and his sons. The five to the left are not cross-legged, and one of them is in a singular attitude, as if preparing to assault. It likewise contains a statue of John Hiscocks, Master in Chancery, the remains of Dr. Mead the physician, and of those eminent lawyers, Plowden, Selden, and Thurlow. The Norman arch forming the entrance is much admired for its workmanship. This church was entirely recased with stone in 1828, under the superintendence of Mr. Smirke.

The Inner Temple

Is situated to the east of Middle Temple Gate, and has a cloister, a large garden, and spacious walks. The hall and chapel are built with Portland stone, and were repaired in 1819; the former is decorated with the story of Pegasus, painted by Sir James Thornhill, and with portraits of King William, Queen Mary, and Lords Coke and Littleton. To the east of the hall is a range of houses, rebuilt of stone in the Gothic style, from designs by Mr. Smirke, in 1829. The paved terrace in front of them forms a good promenade. The *Gardens*, which extend along the banks of the Thames, form a delightful promenade, commanding fine views of Waterloo and Blackfriars' bridges, and of Somerset-house. They are open to the public at six o'clock in the evening, for two or three of the summer months, commencing the first week in June.

The Middle Temple,

Which joins the Inner Temple on the west, is so called from having been the central part of the ancient temple. The hall is adorned with a curious carved screen, a beautiful picture of Charles I. on horseback, by Vandyke, and with portraits of Charles II., Queen Anne, George I., and George II. In the library is preserved a pair of globes made in the time of queen Elizabeth. In the Middle Temple, during the time of the Templars, the king's treasure was kept. The chief officer was the master of the Temple, who was summoned to parliament by Henry III., and from him the chief master of the Temple church is called "Master of the Temple." Part of the north end of King's Bench-walk was lately destroyed by fire, in which many valuable documents perished.

Lincoln's Inn,

Situated between Chancery-lane and Lincoln's-inn-square, derives its name from Henry de Lacey, earl of Lincoln, who erected a mansion on this spot in the reign of Edward I. The buildings form a quadrangle, two sides of which are occupied by the chapel and the hall. On these erections tradition asserts that Ben Jonson was employed as a labouring bricklayer. The former, erected in 1620, from designs by Inigo Jones, contains a tablet in memory of Mr. Perceval, and is richly ornamented with painted glass representing various scriptural subjects. The latter is a handsome room, 62 feet long and 32 broad, in which the lord chancellor sits out of term time; it is adorned with various coats of arms of the members of Lincoln's Inn in stained glass, and with a picture of Paul before Felix, by Hogarth. Here is also a statute of Lord Erskine by Westmacott. Contiguous to the hall is the vice-chancellor's court, erected in 1816. On the west side of the gardens is a fine gravel walk, overlooking Lincoln's-inn-fields; and on the east, a handsome range, termed *Stone Buildings* from the material with which the houses are faced. They were erected by Sir R. Taylor.

Gray's Inn,

Situated in Holborn, is so called from having been the residence of the ancient family of Gray of Wilton, who, in the reign of Edward III., bequeathed it to several students of the law. Like the other inns of court, it is inhabited by barristers and students of the law; and also by many gentlemen of independent fortune, who have chosen it as an agreeable retirement. The hall is adorned with a curiously carved oak-screen, and with portraits of Charles I. and II., James II., and Lord Raymond. The chief ornament of this inn is its spacious *Garden*, which is open every day.

Besides these principal inns of court, there are two *Sergeant's Inns;* the one in Fleet-street, and the other in Chancery-lane.

The Inns of Chancery

Were probably so called because they were anciently inhabited by clerks, who chiefly studied the forming of writs, which regularly belonged to the cursitors, who are officers of chancery.

The first of these is *Thavies Inn*, on Holborn-hill, which derived its name from John Tavye, in the reign of Edward III. It has since been purchased by the Society of Lincoln's Inn, and is now occupied by private persons.

Clement's Inn, Strand, the square of which is adorned with a fine statue of a negro holding a sun-dial, (which rumour states to be that of a negro who murdered his master in one of the opposite chambers, and who was buried here,) and the hall with portraits of several judges, amongst whom is Sir M. Hale.

Clifford's Inn, Fleet-street, formerly the house of Lord Clifford. In the hall is a curious oak-case, containing the ancient laws of the society.

Staple Inn, Holborn, where the wool-merchants were accustomed to assemble, and probably given to law students about the reign of Henry V. The hall contains casts of the Twelve Cæsars, and portraits of Charles II., Queen Anne, Lord Cowper, and Lord Macclesfield.

Lyon's Inn, Newcastle-street, anciently a common inn, with the sign of a lion.

Furnival's Inn, Holborn, which was the residence of lords of that name, whose family became extinct in the reign of Richard II. This edifice was rebuilt by Mr. Peto, in a very handsome style, in 1819.

Barnard's Inn, Holborn, which was so called from a gentleman of that name, who had leased it from the executors of Dean Mackworth, by whom it was given to law students.

Symond's Inn, Chancery-lane, occupied by the masters of chancery previous to their removal to Southampton-buildings.

New Inn, in Wych-street, contiguous to Clement's Inn, belonging to the Middle Temple.

These were considered only as preparatory schools for younger students; and many were entered here before they were admitted into the inns of court. They belong, however, to some of the inns of court, which formerly sent barristers annually to read to them. They are now chiefly occupied by attorneys and solicitors.

The *Law Institute*, Chancery-lane, contains a library, and accommodation for country attorneys to transact the business which may call them to London. Here also the examination of articled clerks takes place, which is of novel introduction, previous to their being admitted as attorneys.

The *Judges' Chambers*, a handsome spacious building, has been erected on a part of the Rolls' Chapel Garden. The approach is through an avenue from Clifford's Inn. The building consists of two floors, with a basement range of rooms below the terrace. In the centre is a door leading to the several chambers appointed for the respective lord chief justices of the queen's bench and common pleas, and the lord chief baron of the exchequer; to the right of the centre is the entrance to the barons of the exchequer, and beyond that those of the puisne judges of the common pleas. The judges of the queen's bench have their chambers assigned at the western angle of the building.

CHAPTER IV.

LOCAL GOVERNMENT OF THE METROPOLIS, POLICE, PRISONS, PAUPERISM, ETC.

THIS division of our labours comprehends the city of London, that of Westminster, the borough of Southwark, &c.; it embraces the municipal regulations of that metropolis which includes Westminster, many parishes in the county of Middlesex, several in Surrey and Southwark; and which, according to Maitland, has "ingulfed one city, one borough, and forty-three villages." And since Maitland wrote, the parishes of St. Mary-le-bone and St. Pancras have been covered with houses.

City of London.

As stated in our general history, William I. granted an important charter to the city of London, confirming Edward the

Confessor's laws; and this is the earliest charter of incorporation existing. It was ever recognised as a charter, and referred to and renewed as such down to Charles II.'s reign. After that charter, London was of so much consequence in the various contests for power and sovereignty, that different monarchs favoured it, granting various privileges and immunities, till the corporation was finally composed of a lord mayor, two sheriffs for London and Middlesex, aldermen, common-council, and livery. At the time of the defeat of Harold by William I., the chief officer of London was called the port-reeve, or port-grave, from Saxon words signifying chief governor of a harbour. He was afterwards called provost; but in Henry II.'s reign, the Norman title of *maire* was brought into use, and soon rendered English by spelling it mayor. In 1354, Edward III. granted to this city the privilege of having gold or silver *maces* carried before the mayor, sheriffs, and aldermen in the city, its suburbs, and liberties, throughout Middlesex; and also when going to meet the king, his heirs, or other royal persons, beyond the county. It was at this period when such a dignity was granted, that the chief magistrate of the city of London was first called *lord* mayor, and gained the style of right honourable. Under him the city is governed by its recorder, aldermen, common-sergeant, &c.

In 1233, King Henry III. granted a charter conferring the liberty of choosing a MAYOR *annually*, and continuing him in that situation from year to year, if the electors so pleased. He was to be presented to the king for approval; but in the 37th of Henry III. a new charter was gained, permitting the presentation to be made to the barons of the exchequer. This was done to avoid the expense of repairing to the king wherever he might be. At first the election was completely popular, resting with the citizens at large, when assembled in general *folk-mote;* but disturbances having resulted from this mode of electing, it was afterwards managed by delegates chosen out of each ward, and this select number was called the commonalty. This method continued till 1475, when an act of the *common-council* vested the election of the mayor and sheriffs in the mayor, aldermen, and common-councilmen, and in the masters, wardens, and liverymen, of the city companies; where the right still continues, it having been confirmed by act of parliament. Although the office of lord mayor is elective, his supremacy does not cease on the death of a sovereign; and when such an event happens, he is considered the principal officer in the kingdom, and takes his place accordingly in the privy-council till the new king is proclaimed.

His *powers* and *privileges* are very extensive. He is not only the king's representative in the civil government of the city, but also first commissioner of the lieutenancy; perpetual coroner and escheator within the city and liberties of London and the *borough of Southwark;* chief justice of oyer and terminer and gaol delivery of Newgate; judge of the court of wardmote at the election of aldermen; conservator of the rivers Thames and Medway; perpetual commissioner in all affairs relating to the river Lea; and chief butler to the king at all coronations, having a fee for that service of a golden cup and cover, and a golden ewer. This privilege was claimed at the coronation of Richard III. and the Lady Anne, and was fully sanctioned. No corporation business is valid without his authority.

The *mode of election*, which takes place September 29, is as follows: the livery in Guildhall, or common assembly, choose two of the senior aldermen below the bar, who are presented to the court of the mayor and aldermen, by whom one of the aldermen so chosen (generally the senior) is declared lord mayor elect. On the 9th of November, that being the day on which the lord mayor elect enters upon his office, the aldermen and sheriffs attend him to Guildhall in their coaches, and about noon proceed to London-bridge, where the lord mayor elect, the aldermen, recorder, and sheriffs, go on board the splendid city barge, and, attended by the several city companies in their barges adorned with flags and pendants, proceed in great state to Westminster, where his lordship, after certain ceremonies, takes the prescribed oaths before the barons of the exchequer. He then proceeds, with the recorder, &c., to the other courts of law, to invite the judges to dinner, and afterwards returns by water to Blackfriars-bridge. Having landed, he is preceded by the artillery company, which is followed by the company of which he himself is free, and in regular order by the other city companies with flags and music; and, among the rest, the armourers have usually persons on horseback, completely dressed in various kinds of armour. To these succeed the domestics and servants of the lord mayor, and then his lordship in his state coach, followed by the aldermen, recorder, sheriffs, chamberlain, common-sergeant, town-clerk, &c., in their several coaches and chariots. This annual cavalcade, generally called the *Lord Mayor's Show*, excites great interest, and exhibits no ordinary display of municipal splendour. It concludes at Guildhall, and is succeeded by an entertainment of appropriate magnificence, at which it is customary to see the princes of the blood, distinguished members of administration, many representatives of the first families in the kingdom, and about a thousand other persons; all of whom are admitted by tickets from the lord mayor, or from one of the sheriffs. The expenses (about 3,000*l.*) are defrayed by the lord mayor and sheriffs, and the festivities of the day are terminated by a splendid ball.

The lord mayor's *dress* is very showy. On public occasions he wears either scarlet or purple robes, richly furred, with a broad hood, and gold chain or collar. When he goes in his state coach, the mace-bearer sits upon a stool in the middle, facing one of the windows, and the sword-bearer upon a stool also, facing the other; and when on foot his train is supported by a page, and the mace and sword are carried before him.

The lord mayor's salary, which is granted annually by the corporation for the expenses of the office, is 8,000*l.*; but the actual expenditure often exceeds this sum by several thousands, and varies according to the wealth or liberality of individuals. The plate used by the lord mayor at his state dinners belongs to the corporation, and is transferred every year, with an inventory of it, to his successor.

The following is a list of the lord mayors of London since 1800:—

1800 Sir R. C. Glynn.
1801 H. Combe, esq.
1802 Sir J. Eamer.
1803 Sir C. Price.
1804 Sir J. Perring.
1805 P. Perchard, esq.
1806 Sir J. Shaw.
1807 Sir W. Leighton.
1808 J. Ansley, esq.
1809 Sir C. Flower.
1810 T. Smith, esq.
1811 J. J. Smith, esq.
1812 Sir C. S. Hunter.
1813 G. Scholey, esq.
1814 Sir W. Domville.
1815 S. Birch, esq.
1816 M. Wood, esq.
1817 M. Wood, esq.
1818 C. Smith, esq.
1819 J. Atkins, esq.
1820 G. Bridges, esq.
1821 J. T. Thorpe, esq.
1822 C. Magnay, esq.
1823 W. Heygate, esq.
1824 R. Waithman, esq.
1825 J. Garret, esq.
1826 W. Venables, esq.
1827 A. Brown, esq.
1828 M. P. Lucas, esq.
1829 W. Thompson, esq.
1830 R. Crowder, esq.
1831 J. Key, esq.
1832 Sir J. Key.
1833 Sir P. Laurie.
1834 C. Farebrother, esq.
1835 H. Winchester, esq.
1836 W. J. Copeland, esq.
1837 T. Kelly, esq.
1838 Sir J. Cowan, bart.
1839 S. Wilson, esq.

The ALDERMEN are of more remote antiquity than the mayors. The office was of Saxon institution. The name is derived from the Saxon *ealdor-man*, a man advanced in years, and accordingly supposed to be of superior wisdom and gravity.

Henry III., after the citizens had suffered many oppressions, restored a form of government, and appointed twenty-four citizens to exercise the power. In his son's reign the city was divided into twenty-four wards. Till 1394, the aldermen were chosen annually; but when Richard II. removed back the courts of judicature from York to London, it was enacted by parliament that they should "continue in office during life or good behaviour." From that time the office of alderman has been for life. There are twenty-six wards, and each ward has its alderman. The mode of election has been several times varied; but it is now regulated by act of parliament, passed in 1725, which act also settles the mode of electing all the other city officers. The right of voting for aldermen is vested in those freemen who are resident householders. The lord mayor presides at the election of an alderman; and if a poll be demanded, it terminates in three days. Those aldermen who have filled the civic chair are justices of the quorum; and all the other aldermen are justices of the peace within the city. They are also the subordinate governors of their respective wards, under the jurisdiction of the lord mayor, and exercise the executive power within their own districts. They hold courts of wardmote for the election of common-councilmen and other ward-officers, the regulation of the business of the ward, the removal of obstructions, &c.; and in the management of these duties each alderman is assisted by one or two deputies, who are annually selected by himself from amongst the common-councilmen of his own ward.

The COMMON COUNCIL is likewise of very early origin; it is a modification of the ancient COMMONALTY. It is beyond dispute (and it is a proud fact for the city of London, as it shews their acknowledged importance at all times,) that the great body of the citizens was very early considered as an integral part of the city constitution. The charter of Henry I. mentions the *folk-mote*, a Saxon appellation, and which may fairly be rendered the *court* or *assembly* of the *people*. The general place of meeting of the *folk-mote* was in the open air at St. Paul's-cross in St. Paul's-churchyard. It was not discontinued till after Henry III.'s reign; until that period it had been considered the *supreme* assembly of the city. It was called together by the tolling of a great bell. From the vast increase of the city's population, the intermixture of the non-freemen with the inhabitants rendered this mode of meeting inconvenient, tumultuous, and sometimes dangerous; and the system of delegation was then had recourse to. A certain number of representatives were chosen out of each ward, who, being added to the lord mayor and aldermen, constituted the *Court of Common Council.* At first only two were returned for each ward; but it being afterwards considered that the collective assembly thus chosen was an insufficient representation, in 1347 the number was enlarged. It was provided that each ward should elect common-councilmen according to its relative extent—not fewer than six, nor more than twelve: since then there has been an alteration in the numbers, and the present aggregate number is 240. The common-councilmen are chosen in the same manner as the aldermen, with this difference—the lord mayor presides at the election of an alderman, and the aldermen at the election of common-councilmen. The court debates with open doors in general, but it has the power, though rarely exercised, of excluding strangers: in the general management of its business, the rules, proceedings, committees, &c., are much like those of the house of commons. They cannot assemble without summons from the lord mayor, and then for one sitting only; but it is his duty to call a meeting whenever it is demanded by requisition, and the law compels him to assemble the court a certain number of times during his mayoralty. The common-councilmen are annually elected on St. Thomas's day; and the elections are usually carried on in the *churches.* Should there be contests, they are conducted in the vestry-rooms or work-houses. The general business of the court is to make laws for the due government of the city, to guide its police, to manage its property; in fact, the court of common-council is the city's legislature. Only twenty-five out of the twenty-six wards return common-councilmen: *Bridgeward without* is unrepresented, except by an alderman.

Names of the wards, with the number of common-councilmen each ward returns:

Ward	No.	Ward	No.	Ward	No.
Aldersgate	8	Castle-Baynard	10	Farringdon-without	16
Aldgate	6	Cheap	12	Langbourn	10
Bassishaw	4	Coleman-street	6	Lime-street	4
Bilingsgate	10	Cordwainers	8	Portsoken	5
Bishopsgate	14	Cornhill	6	Queenhithe	6
Bread-street	12	Cripplegate	16	Tower	12
Bridge	15	Dowgate	8	Vintry	9
Broad-street	10	Farringdon-within	17	Walbrook	8
Candlewick	8				

The SHERIFFS next require our attention. Some writers place them after the lord mayor, but such arrangement would interrupt the narrative respecting the city's legislature. The office of sheriff (from *shire-reeve*, governor of a shire or county) is of great antiquity, trust, and authority. London had its sheriffs prior to William the First's reign. In all general cases, the sheriffs are the king's officers; but the sheriff-wick of Middlesex having been purchased by the city from Henry I., the lord mayor and citizens now hold it in fee, and appoint two sheriffs annually for London and Middlesex. The jurisdictions of these officers are to a considerable extent perfectly separate; but if either die, the other cannot act till a new one be chosen; for there must be two sheriffs for London, which by charter is both a city and a county, though they make but one jointly for the county of Middlesex. Anciently these officers were chosen from amongst the COMMONALTY before spoken of; and any citizen is still eligible, except he swear himself not worth 15,000*l.* Many aldermen who were never sheriffs were advanced to the mayoralty; but greater regularity is now observed, and no alderman can be chosen lord mayor unless he has served the office of sheriff. The mode of choosing the sheriffs has been frequently altered. Formerly, the elder sheriff was nominated by the lord mayor, who drank to him by name as sheriff for the ensuing year; and this nomination was by custom confirmed by the commonalty; but the commons succeeded in abrogating this custom, and for some time both sheriffs were chosen by the livery at large. Sir J. Parsons, lord mayor in 1704, revived the ancient method of nomination, under the authority of a then recent act of common-council. The present mode is for the lord mayor to drink to fourteen respectable citizens, two of whom are elected by the livery on the following Midsummer-day, and they are obliged to serve under a penalty of 400*l.* The opinion of the livery in common-hall is not decisive, and if a poll be demanded it continues open seven days. The lord mayor cannot properly nominate a commoner sheriff, if there be an alderman who has not served, though it is often done; but if the citizen drunk to, pay the fine, he is exempted for three years; nor can he again be drunk to by any future lord mayor, unless he become an alderman. No alderman can be exempted for more than one year, after a previous payment, without the consent of the common-council: whoever serves is obliged to give bond to the corporation for 1000*l.* The sheriffs enter upon their office on Michaelmas-day, having been sworn the day before in Guildhall. On the day after Michaelmas-day, the new sheriffs proceed to Westminster, to be accepted, on behalf of the king, by the barons of the exchequer, and to perform certain ceremonies.* The DUTY of the sheriffs, amongst other things, is to serve writs of process. Where the king is party, the sheriffs may break open doors, or may untile houses, to gain admission, if entrance be denied; but not upon private process, except upon outlawry after judgment; and in every case where the outer door is open, or where admission can be obtained by stratagem, or without force, the sheriffs or their officers may enter and execute their writ. They are also to attend the judges, and execute their orders; to impanel or summon juries "of honest repute and of good ability, to consider of and deliver their verdicts according to justice and the merits of the cause;" to see condemned persons executed; and, in cases of resistance to their legal authority, as in public riots, &c., to raise the *posse comitatûs*. For the county alone, about 25,000 writs are annually directed to the sheriff.

The following is a list of sheriffs since 1800, with the date when their shrievalty terminated:

1801	J. Perring, esq.	1813	J. Blades, esq.
	T. Cadell, esq.		M. Hoy, esq.
1802	W. Rawlins, esq.	1814	C. Magnay, esq.
	R. A. Cox, esq.		T. C. Marsh, esq.
1803	Sir R. Walsh.	1815	J. Leigh, esq.
	Sir J. Alexander.		C. Reay, esq.
1804	J. Shaw, esq.	1816	T. Bell, esq.
	Sir W. Leighton.		J. T. Thorp, esq.
1805	G. Scholey, esq.	1817	G. Bridges, esq.
	W. Domville, esq.		R. Kirby, esq.
1806	J. Ansley, esq.	1818	F. Desanges, esq.
	T. Smith, esq.		G. Alderson, esq.
1807	Sir J. Branscomb.	1819	J. Roberts, esq.
	Sir J. Miles.		L. Gwynne, esq.
1808	C. Smith, esq.	1820	J. Rothwell, esq.
	R. Phillips, esq.		J. W. Parkins, esq.
1809	J. J. Smith, esq.	1821	R. Waithman, esq.
	C. S. Hunter, esq.		W. Williams, esq.
1810	M. Wood, esq.	1822	J. Garret, esq.
	J. Atkins, esq.		W. Venables, esq.
1811	Sir W. Plomer.	1823	M. P. Lucas, esq.
	S. Goodbehere, esq.		W. Thompson, esq.
1812	S. Birch, esq.	1824	G. Whittaker, esq.
	W. Heygate, esq.		Sir P. Laurie.

* The ceremony of counting the hob-nails originated in 1235, when a grant of a piece of ground in St. Clement's, Strand, was made to a farrier, on condition that he annually rendered to the exchequer six horse-shoes, with nails belonging to them. The ground was afterwards given to the corporation of London, by whom the customary payment is still made.

1825 A. Brown, esq.
J. Key, esq.
1826 R. Crowder, esq.
T. Kelly, esq.
1827 C. Farebrother, esq.
H. Winchester, esq.
1828 A. Spottiswoode, esq.
E. A. Wilde, esq.
1829 F. Booth, esq.
W. T. Copeland, esq.
1830 W. H. Richardson, esq.
T. Ward, esq.
1831 C. Marshall, esq.
W. H. Poland. esq.
1832 J. Cowan, esq.
J. Pirie, esq.
1833 J. Humphreys, esq.
R. Peek, esq.
1834 S. Wilson, esq.
J. Harmer, esq.
1835 J. Ilridge, esq.
A. Raphael, esq.
1836 J. Lainson, esq.
D. Salamans, esq.
1837 Sir J. Duke.
J. Johnson, esq.
1838 Sir George Carroll.
Sir Moses Montefiore.
1839 T. Johnson, esq.
T. Wood, esq.

The RECORDER, who is appointed by the lord mayor and aldermen for life, with a salary of 2500*l.*, the chamberlain, common-sergeant, city remembrancer, &c., constitute the other leading city officers.

The term "*livery*" was derived from the custom of the retainers and followers of the lord mayor and sheriffs bearing habiliments of the form and colour displayed by those functionaries. It was usual for the wardens of companies to deliver a purse containing 20*s.* to the lord mayor on the 1st of December, to obtain for individuals, so desiring, sufficient cloth to make a suit, and the privilege of wearing the livery. This circumstance added to the splendour of the lord mayor's train when the civic court went forth to meet the sovereign on his return from a "progress" or a successful expedition.

The JUDICIAL FRANCHISE is amongst the many valuable privileges enjoyed by the city. It is most important; and yet the power of the city courts, for the recovery of debts, or of compensations for injuries, "by action or writ, according to the course of common law," is but little known. There are the Lord Mayor's Court, the Court of Hustings, the Sheriff's Court, &c.

There are ninety-one CITY COMPANIES. The first twelve that stand on the list are called the chief, and are sometimes styled The Honourable. The following is the list, arranged in their order of precedency:

1 Mercers.
2 Grocers.
3 Drapers.
4 Fishmongers.
5 Goldsmiths.
6 Skinners.
7 Merchant Tailors.
8 Haberdashers.
9 Salters.
10 Ironmongers.
11 Vintners.
12 Clothworkers.
13 Dyers.
14 Brewers.
15 Leather Sellers.
16 Pewterers.
17 Barber-Surgeons.
18 Cutlers.
19 Bakers.
20 Wax Chandlers.
21 Tallow Chandlers.

22 Armourers and Braziers.
23 Girdlers.
24 Butchers.
25 Saddlers.
26 Carpenters.
27 Cordwainers.
28 Painter Stainers.
29 Curriers.
30 Masons.
31 Plumbers.
32 Innholders.
33 Founders.
34 Poulterers.
35 Cooks.
36 Coopers.
37 Tilers and Bricklayers.
38 Bowyers.
39 Fletchers.
40 Blacksmiths.
41 Joiners.
42 Weavers.
43 Woolmen.
44 Scriveners.
45 Fruiterers.
46 Plasterers.
47 Stationers.
48 Embroiderers.
49 Upholders.
50 Musicians.
51 Turners.
52 Basket Makers.
53 Glaziers.
54 Horners.
55 Farriers.
56 Paviors.
57 Lorimers.
58 Apothecaries.
59 Shipwrights.
60 Spectacle Makers.
61 Clock Makers.
62 Glovers.
63 Comb Makers.
64 Felt Makers.
65 Framework Knitters.
66 Silk Throwsters.
67 Silkmen.
68 Pin Makers.
69 Needle Makers.
70 Gardeners.
71 Soap Makers.
72 Tin Plate Workers.
73 Wheelwrights.
74 Distillers.
75 Hatband Makers.
76 Patten Makers.
77 Glass Sellers.
78 Tobacco-pipe Makers.
79 Coach and Coach-Harness Makers.
80 Gun Makers.
81 Gold and Silver Wire-drawers.
82 Long Bowstring Makers.
83 Card Makers.
84 Fan Makers.
85 Wood Mongers.
86 Starch Makers.
87 Fishermen.
88 Parish Clerks.
89 Carmen.
90 Porters.
91 Watermen.

Nearly fifty of these companies have halls, some of which are remarkable as buildings, and others for their paintings and curiosities. The following are the principal:—

MERCERS' HALL, Cheapside, is distinguished by a richly sculptured front, adorned with figures of Faith, Hope, and Charity, and contains some interesting reliques of the celebrated Whittington.

GROCERS' HALL, in the court of the same name, in the Poultry, is a handsome building, with stone front, surrounded by an emblem of eastern productions. It contains portraits of Sir John Cutler, Lord Chatham, and his son Mr. Pitt.

DRAPERS' HALL, Throgmorton-street, is a quadrangular edifice, erected on the site of a mansion inhabited by Cromwell earl of Essex. It is enriched with a fine portrait of Nelson by Beechy, a portrait of Fitz-Alwyn the first mayor of London, and another which is said to be of Mary Queen of Scots.

FISHMONGERS' HALL, on the banks of the Thames, close to London-bridge, is a grand pile of building erected in 1833, from designs by Mr. Roberts, in the place of the old hall erected by Sir C. Wren, but pulled down in 1828 to form the approaches to the new London-bridge. It consists of a granite basement devoted to offices, and the superstructure of Portland stone, on a level with the road, which contains the state

MERCERS HALL.

IRONMONGERS HALL.

NEWGATE.

rooms, &c. Over the centre of the road-front, which consists of two fluted Ionic columns with pilasters in antis, the arms of the company are richly carved in stone. The river front, which is equally imposing, presents two ranges, the arched basement supporting columns bearing a pediment. Here is preserved a curious statue of Sir W. Walworth, whose right hand grasps the identical dagger with which he struck Wat Tyler.

SKINNERS' HALL, Dowgate-hill, is a noble building, adorned with pilasters supporting a pediment, in which are the arms of the company.

MERCHANT TAILORS' HALL, Threadneedle-street, is one of the largest in London. It contains portraits of the Duke of Wellington and several other distinguished individuals, and the charter granted to the company by Henry VII.

IRONMONGERS' HALL, Fenchurch-street, is a stately edifice of Portland stone, erected in 1748. It is enriched with some exquisite carving.

BARBERS' HALL, Monkwell-street, contains a fine painting by Holbein, representing Henry VIII. delivering the charter of the barber-surgeons to the company. Amongst the characters introduced is Dr. Butts, mentioned in Shakspeare.

ARMOURERS' HALL, Coleman-street, is adorned with a fine picture by Northcote, representing the entry of Richard II. and Henry Bolingbroke into London.

STATIONERS' HALL, Stationers'-court, Ludgate-hill, contains some good paintings in oil and stained glass.

NEW GOLDSMITHS' HALL, Foster-lane, rebuilt in 1833 from designs by Mr. Hardwicke, is a building of noble proportions, and of massive execution; the centre of which is composed of six Corinthian columns supporting an entablature surmounted by a rich cornice. The five centre windows have balconies, and have over them the sculptured arms, &c., of the company.

SALTERS' HALL, Oxford-court, Cannon-street, rebuilt in 1826, contains portraits of several kings of England, and a remarkably fine one of Sir C. Wren. Here likewise is preserved a bill of fare for fifty people in the year 1506, the whole amount of which did not exceed two pounds.

PAINTER STAINERS' HALL, Little Trinity Lane, is adorned with a view of the Fire of London, and with several portraits, amongst which is one of Camden the antiquarian, who presented this company with a cup and cover still used by them on St. Luke's day.

CLOTHWORKERS' HALL, Mincing-lane, contains carvings, as large as life, of James I. and Charles I.

VINTNERS' HALL, Upper Thames-street, which was partly rebuilt in 1820, contains a picture of St. Martin, who is represented dividing his cloak.

COACH MAKERS' HALL, Noble-street, was long famed for a debating society, in which many eminent men first practised oratory.

SADDLERS' HALL, in Cheapside, was handsomely rebuilt in 1823.

COMMON HALLS, which are assemblies of the livery, are convenable on the requisition of several of the members to the lord mayor, who presides.

The MILITARY GOVERNMENT of the city was another of its peculiar privileges possessed from the earliest times. Its forces consisted of two regiments of militia, raised by ballot, according to an act of parliament passed in 1794, besides a regiment of light horse volunteers. The military force of the city is said to have been highly instrumental in restoring the monarchy to Charles II.

The city of London sends *four* members to parliament, who are chosen by the liverymen; the nomination takes place in Guildhall, and, if a poll be demanded, continues one day. By the Reform Bill, the Tower Hamlets and Finsbury return two members each.

City of Westminster.

That which was once called *Thorney Island* (because, according to Stowe, "it was a place overgrown with thorns and environed with waters,") is now the seat of government, the residence of royalty, and the centre of fashion. For many ages it was a place entirely distinct from London, and the distance between them was considerable. The Strand was the road which formed the communication between the two towns, and Westminster was then open to the Thames and the fields. It appears that in 1385 this road was paved as far as the Savoy; and some years after, Sir Robert Cecil, having built a house at Ivy-bridge, caused the pavement to be extended thither, and many of the houses of the nobility were erected in the Strand. That there was a bridge over the Thames at Westminster in 994 is certain; but it is doubtful whether there was one before that period. Edward the Confessor founded a royal palace here, which was considerably improved by the addition of Westminster-hall. The existence of Westminster is derived from the foundation of the Abbey. In 1257 Henry III. granted to the abbot and convent of Westminster a market and fair, and hence may be traced the origin of "the city and *liberties*" of Westminster. In 1352 Westminster was by act of parliament constituted one of the ten towns in England where the staple or market for wool, &c., should be perpetually held. At the general suppression of religious houses by Henry VIII., Westminster was converted into a bishopric, with a dean and twelve prebendaries; but the only bishop was *Thomas Thirlby*. It was suppressed in 1550, on his translation to Norwich; and Westminster retains the title of city by courtesy. Before it became a city it had many years been the seat of the royal palace, the high court of parliament, and of our law tribunals; many of our sovereigns were crowned and have their sepulchres in the abbey. The ancient palace having been almost destroyed by fire, Henry VIII. purchased his palace of Whitehall of Cardinal Wolsey. From this period, Henry VIII. having built St. James's palace, a tennis-court and cock-pit, and formed the park and places for bowling, the buildings in Westminster began to extend in all directions.

The CITY of Westminster is comprised in the two parishes of St. Margaret and St. John, which are now united; and the LIBERTIES consist of seven parishes,—St. Martin's-in-the-fields, St. James's, St. Anne's, St. Clement Danes, St. Mary-le-Strand, St. George's Hanover-square, and St. Paul's Covent-garden, with the precinct of the Savoy.

ST. MARTIN'S-LE-GRAND, which is situated within the limits of the city of London, is a portion of the liberties of Westminster. Anciently it was the site of a college, consisting of a dean and priests; and Henry VII. conveyed to the abbot of the abbey church of Westminster the advowson of the deanery, &c., of St. Martin's-le-grand. In the thirty-second year of Henry VIII., that monarch granted it to the new see of Westminster, and two years afterwards to the dean and chapter. When Edward VI. dissolved the bishopric of Westminster, he conveyed St. Martin's-le-Grand, with the jurisdiction, to the bishop of London; but an act of parliament restored it (as the abbot and convent had enjoyed it) to the dean and chapter, who are now in full possession of it. The church was taken down soon after the year 1548, and the place covered with buildings. The inhabitant householders, strange as it may seem, have the right of voting for the members for Westminster.

Westminster returns two members to parliament. The election is declared in Covent-garden-market, in front of St. Paul's-church. If more than two members are offered as candidates, and a poll be demanded, the election continues two days, exclusive of the day of nomination. By the Reform Bill, Marylebone and Lambeth return two members each, and separate polling-places are appointed for the various districts.

Its GOVERNMENT, until the Reformation, was arbitrary, under the abbot and monks. It was afterwards under that of the bishop and the dean and chapter; it was next settled by 27 Elizabeth, 1585, fixing the civil government in the hands of the laity, though the dean is empowered to nominate the chief officers. The authority extends to the precincts of St. Martin's-le-Grand, and to some towns in Essex, which are exempted from the jurisdiction of the Bishop of London and the Archbishop of Canterbury. The principal magistrate is the high-steward, who is usually a nobleman, and is chosen by the dean and chapter. His post is similar to that of chancellor of an university, and is generally held for life. On his death or resignation, a chapter is called for the election of another, in which the dean sits as high-steward till the election is concluded. The next great officer is the high-bailiff, who is chosen by the high-steward, notwithstanding which a considerable sum is required to be paid for the place. He also holds his office for life, and has the chief management of the election of members of parliament for Westminster; and all the other bailiffs are subordinate to him. He summons juries, and in the court-leets sits next to the deputy-steward. To him all fines and forfeitures belong, which render the situation very profitable. There are also sixteen burgesses and their assistants, whose functions in all respects resemble those of the aldermen's deputies of the city of London, each having his proper ward under his jurisdiction; and from these are elected two head-burgesses; one for the city, and the other for the liberties, who in the court-leet rank next to the head-bailiff. There is also a high-constable, who is chosen by the court-leet, and has all the other constables under his direction. The government of Westminster has but a slight resemblance to that of a great and opulent city. Its parliamentary representatives, however, are chosen by the householders; and this extensive enjoyment of the elective franchise, together with the circumstance of Westminster being the seat of the court, renders the elections for this city particularly interesting. This city has no power of making freemen, no trading companies, and no courts except those of the leet, the sessions, and a court of requests.

Borough of Southwark.

Southwark, which constitutes another great portion of this widely spreading metropolis, was governed by its own bailiffs till 1327. The city, however, found great inconvenience from the number of malefactors who escaped thither, in order to be out of the reach and cognizance of the city magistrates. A grant was therefore made of that town, and the mayor of London was constituted bailiff of Southwark, and empowered to govern it by his deputy.

In Edward VI.'s reign, the crown granted the "Borough or Town" of Southwark to the city of London for a pecuniary consideration; and within a month after the passing of the patent, in consideration of a further sum paid to the crown by the city, Southwark was made one of the city wards, and named Bridge-Ward-Without. In consequence of the above grant, Southwark became subject to the lord mayor, who has under him a steward and bailiff, the former of whom holds a court of record every Monday at St. Margaret's-hill, for all debts, damages, and trespasses, within his limits. This borough returns two members to parliament. The election takes place in front of the Town-Hall, and if a poll be demanded, continues two days.

Police of the Metropolis.

The police of such a metropolis as that of London cannot fail to excite interest in the minds of inhabitants as well as of visiters; for, next to the blessings which a nation may derive from an excellent constitution and system of general laws, are those advantages which result from a well-regulated and energetic police, conducted and enforced with purity, activity, vigilance, and discretion.

The city of London, as already stated, is under the control of its own magistracy, consisting of the lord mayor and aldermen. There are two police-offices; one in the Mansion-house, where the lord mayor presides; and the other at Guildhall, where the aldermen sit in rotation. All cases which occur east of King-street are taken to the Mansion-house, and those west of King-street to Guildhall. Both offices usually commence business at 12 o'clock.

The principal police-officers under the lord mayor and

aldermen, are two marshals, under whom are eight marshalmen, whose business it is to attend the lord mayor on all state occasions, to attend the courts of aldermen and common-council, the Old Bailey sessions, and to superintend the management of the inferior officers of police. The city has also day and night patrol; and Smithfield patrol, who attend on market-days to keep order.

Besides the general police of the city, similar to that of Westminster, each ward appoints beadles, constables, patrol, watchmen, and street-keepers, according to its size.

The *Metropolitan Police*, established by Sir R. Peel, comprises all parts of the metropolis and its vicinity out of the jurisdiction of the city, and within twelve miles of Charing-cross. It consisted in 1837 of 3421 men, divided into superintendents, inspectors, serjeants, and constables. The expense in 1836 was 216,313*l.* 15*s.* 5*d.* These are placed under the control of a board of police, consisting of three commissioners. This new police was commenced in several of the parishes in Westminster, Sept. 29, 1829, and gradually extended to the other districts. The old watch-rates were abolished, and a general police-tax substituted instead of them. The metropolitan police district is formed into divisions, varying in size, but having the same number of men and officers. In each is a station or watch-house, from which point the duty is carried on. Every division is designated by a local name and a letter of the alphabet. Each division is again divided into eight sections, and each section into eight beats, the limits of which are clearly defined.

The police force consists of as many companies as there are divisions. Each company comprises 1 superintendent, 4 inspectors, 16 serjeants, and 144 police constables. The company is divided into sixteen parties, each consisting of one serjeant and nine men. Four serjeants' parties, or one fourth of the company, form an inspector's party. The whole is under the command of the superintendent. Each man has marked on the collar of his coat the letter of his division, and a number corresponding with his name in the books of the office, so that he may at all times be recognised. The first sixteen numbers in each division denote the serjeants. All the policemen are dressed in blue uniform, and at night wear dark-brown great-coats. Each man is furnished with a rattle, a staff, and a lantern.

The policemen are on duty at all hours, but of course a greater number are employed at night than in the day. One part of the force continues on duty from the evening till midnight, and the other from midnight till morning. The day-police is also relieved in the same manner. The night-police is of great utility in cases of fire, as in the watch-houses of each division is kept an account of the names of the turncocks, and of the places where engines are kept. Besides the parochial engines, many public bodies are provided with them; and the principal insurance-offices have engines stationed in various districts, with active men and horses always in readiness. Water is supplied immediately by means of fire-plugs.

Police-Offices.—For those parts of the metropolis out of the jurisdiction of the city, twenty-seven stipendiary magistrates are appointed. Three at Bow-street, under a jurisdiction long established, and twenty-four by a statute called the "police act," passed in 1792.

These twenty-four have eight different offices assigned to them, at different distances in Westminster, Middlesex, and Surrey; namely, one in each of the following streets; Bow-street; Great Marlborough-street; Hatton-garden; Worship-street, Shoreditch; Lambeth-street, Whitechapel; High-street, Marylebone; Queen-square, Westminster; and Union-street, Southwark. Besides these, there is the Thames Police-office, Wapping.

The duty of the magistrates in these offices extends to several important judicial proceedings, which in a variety of instances they are empowered and required to hear and determine in a summary way; particularly in cases relating to the customs, excise, coaches, carts, pawnbrokers, persons unlawfully pawning the property of others, &c. Their duty also extends to the cases of persons charged with being disorderly, or brought for examination under charges of treason, murder, felony, fraud, and misdemeanours of every description. At each of these offices there are three magistrates, two of whom attend every day except Sunday, and one every evening; two clerks, an office-keeper, &c. Each office has from eight to twelve constables attached to it, who are termed "police-officers." Their pay from government is only a guinea per week; and for the rest of their means of existence they depend on the profits arising out of the services of summonses, warrants, &c., and portions of *penalties*.

The office for regulating disputes relating to hackney-coaches has been removed from Essex-street to Bow-street, a circumstance which appears to have rendered the administration of justice in that particular less easy and certain,

The police-magistrates are now almost invariably selected from amongst barristers, according to regulations established by Lord Sidmouth. They have each an annual salary of 600*l*., and the resident magistrate has the house in which the office is held to live in.

The *Bow-street* police-office is upon a more enlarged scale than the rest. It has three magistrates, with salaries of 800*l*. per annum; the chief-magistrate having 500*l*. a-year in addition, instead of fees. He has also 500*l*. per annum for superintending the horse-patrol. The expense of this office, for a recent year, was 12,270*l*.; while that of the seven other offices, not including the Thames-police, was 24,196*l*. The whole expense, horse-patrols, Thames-police, &c. for the same year, amounted to 51,796*l*. Besides the usual number of constables, horse-patrols ride every evening and night on the principal roads, to the distance of ten or fifteen miles from town. They have small houses to reside in on their various beats, with tablets bearing the title "Horse Patrol Station" affixed to each. This body of men is well armed, and is under the direction of the chief-magistrates of this office. The chief-magistrate of the Bow-street office communicates daily with the secretary of state for the home department, as do the magistrates of the other offices when matters of deep interest affecting the public tranquillity require such communication. Besides this, all the offices make monthly returns of the informations received, and of persons committed and discharged; which return from each office is presented by one of its magistrates, that inquiries may be made if necessary.

The *Thames Police* was established in 1798 for the purpose of repressing the numerous depredations on the Thames, which had then become notorious. Its importance will be admitted, when it is recollected that in this river are engaged upwards of 13,000 vessels, which annually discharge and receive more than three millions of packages. The superintendence of this department of the police extends from Vauxhall to Woolwich, embracing the quays, docks, wharfs, &c., of both banks of the river, with the exception of the space from Tower-stairs to the Temple, belonging to the jurisdiction of the city. There are three principal stations: at Somerset-house, at Wapping, and at Blackwall; and between these, three boats are constantly plying at night. The chief office at Wapping is open during the whole night.

From what has been here said, as well in consequence of

the number of criminals and frequency of crime, which have been voluminously dwelt upon by various writers, the uninvestigating inhabitant, or the inconsiderate visiter of the metropolis, might be tempted to conclude that within its limits there was no safety for property or life. But although there certainly are numerous classes of persons, consisting of plunderers in every shape, from the midnight robber and murderer to the poor perpetrators of petty pillage,—from the cultivated swindler and sharper to the daring street pickpocket; and although thousands of men and women, following the occupations of roguery and prostitution, daily rise scarcely knowing how they are to procure subsistence for the passing hour;—yet, when the extent of the population, merchandise, and commerce, is considered, it is matter of surprise that so little open and daring inroad is made upon our persons and property. There are thousands of persons in this metropolis (which may be said, from the night and day work necessarily pursued in so trading a city, never to sleep,) who have for years passed along the streets at all hours, without ever being robbed, or seriously molested. Robbers lay wait for the timid and unwary, the dissolute and the drunken; they seldom intercept the man who is steadily pursuing his course without intermingling with suspicious company, or passing along by-streets. At night, persons should always prefer the leading public streets; in them there are few lurking holes; and besides, in case of attack, there are almost sure to be passengers who will render assistance when they hear calls for help. Much of course depends on a person's own resolution and discretion.

Mr. Colquhoun very justly traces the origin of much of the crime that exists to the prevalence of public-houses, bad education of apprentices, servants out of place, Jews, receivers of stolen goods, pawnbrokers, gaming-houses, smuggling, *associations in prison*, and prostitution. Not fewer than 30,000 prostitutes are supposed by Mr. C. to live in London; and it is presumed that eight-tenths of these die prematurely of disease and misery, having previously corrupted twice their number of young girls and young men. According to details furnished by the Guardian Society, and noticed in the Commons' Police Report, " out of three parishes, consisting of 9924 houses, and 59,050 inhabitants, there are 360 brothels, and 2000 common prostitutes."

One of the chief encouragements of crime undoubtedly is the receiving of stolen property. In the metropolis Mr. C.

believes there are upwards of 3000 receivers of various kinds of stolen goods, and an equal proportion all over the country; who keep open shops for the purpose of purchasing at an under price, often for a mere trifle, every kind of property brought to them, and this without asking a single question. He further supposes that the property purloined and pilfered in and about the metropolis may amount to 700,000*l.* in one year. There exist in the metropolis a class of dealers extremely numerous, who keep open shops for the purchase of rags, old iron, and other metals. These are divided into wholesale and retail dealers. The retail dealers are the immediate purchasers in the first instance from the pilferers or their agents; and as soon as they collect a sufficient quantity of iron, brass, or other metals, worthy the notice of a large dealer, they dispose of it for ready money. Others are employed in the collection of old rags, and other articles purloined in the country.

Robbery and theft have in many instances been reduced to a regular system. Houses intended to be entered during the night are previously reconnoitred and examined for days preceding. If one or more of the servants are not already associated with the depredators, the most artful means are used to obtain their assistance; and when every previous arrangement is made, the mere operation of robbing a house becomes a matter of little difficulty. Night coaches promote in many instances the perpetration of burglaries and other felonies. Bribed by a high reward, the coachmen enter into the pay of nocturnal depredators, and wait in the neighbourhood until the robbery is completed, and then draw up at the moment the policemen are going their rounds, or off their stands, for the purpose of conveying the plunder to the house of the receiver, who is generally waiting for the issue of the enterprise.

The sharpers, swindlers, and rogues of various descriptions have undergone something like a classification by different writers; and although such an effort must be necessarily imperfect, partially to follow the example in this place may not be without its use. The following is a list of some of the species of cloaked marauders that beset the unwary in this great metropolis—they deceive few but the ignorant and unthinking; these, however, afford too rich a harvest:—

1. Sharpers who obtain licenses as pawnbrokers, and are uniformly receivers of stolen goods.

2. Swindlers who obtain licenses to act as hawkers and

pedlars, and establish fraudulent raffles, substitute plated goods for silver, sell and utter base coin, deal in smuggled goods, and receive stolen goods, with a view to dispose of them in the country.

3. Swindlers who take out licenses as *auctioneers.* These open shops in different parts of the metropolis, with persons at the doors, usually denominated *barkers,* to invite strangers to walk in to attend the *mock auction.* In these places various articles of silver plate and household goods are offered for sale, made up slightly, and of little intrinsic value. Associates, called *puffers,* are in waiting to raise the article beyond its value, when, on the first bidding of a stranger, it is immediately knocked down to him; and when it is too late, he discovers the snare he has fallen into. In addition to the price at which the article may be knocked down, they add certain sums for expenses, duty, &c.

4. Swindlers who raise money by pretending to be discounters of bills and money-brokers. These chiefly prey upon young men of property, who have lost their money by gambling, or spent it in extravagant amusements.

5. Jews who, under the pretence of purchasing old clothes and metals of various sorts, prowl about the houses of men of rank and fortune, holding out temptations to their servants to pilfer and steal small articles, which they purchase at a trifling portion of their value. It is calculated that 1500 of these people have their daily rounds.

6. Swindlers who associate together for the purpose of defrauding tradesmen of their goods. One assumes the character of a merchant, hires a genteel house, with a counting-house, and every appearance of business; one or two of his associates take upon them the appearance of clerks, while others occasionally wear a livery; and sometimes a carriage is set up, in which the ladies of the party visit the shops, in the style of persons of fashion, ordering goods to their apartments.

7. Sharpers who take elegant lodgings, dress fashionably, and assume false names. These men pretend to be related to persons of real credit and fashion, produce letters familiarly written to prove intimacy; and when they have secured the good graces of tradesmen, purchase wearing apparel and other articles, and then disappear with the booty.

Besides these descriptions of rogues who "live by their wits," there are villains who associate systematically together for the purpose of discovering and preying upon persons from the country, or any ignorant person who is supposed to have money, or who has visited London with the view of selling goods, who prowl about the streets where shopmen and boys are carrying parcels, and who attend inns at the time that coaches and waggons are loading and unloading. These have recourse to a variety of stratagems, according to the peculiar circumstances of the case, and in a multitude of instances succeed. Cheats, called *duffers*, go about the streets offering bargains, and attend public-houses, inns, and fairs, pretending to sell smuggled goods, of India and other foreign manufacture. In offering their goods for sale they discover, by long-exercised acuteness, the proper objects to practise upon, and seldom fail to deceive the unwary purchaser, and to pass off forged country or other bank-notes, or base coin, in the course of dealings of any extent.

There are many female sharpers, who dress elegantly, personate women of fashion, attend masquerades; and instances have been known in which, by extraordinary effrontery, they have forced themselves into the circle of St. James's. One is said to have appeared in a style of peculiar elegance on the king's birth-day in 1795, and to have pilfered, in conjunction with her husband, who was dressed as a clergyman, to the amount of 1700*l.*, without discovery or suspicion. Houses are kept where female cheats dress and undress for public places. Thirty or forty of these generally attend masquerades, in different characters, where they realise a considerable booty.

In addition to this detail of swindlers and cheats may be mentioned *gamblers*. The principal gambling-houses are situated in St. James's-street, Pall-mall, Bury-street, the Quadrant, and their vicinity. Some of them are supported by subscriptions, such as Crockford's in St. James's-street, and others are the property of ruined gamblers and pettifogging attorneys. The principal houses, or "hells," as they have been characteristically termed, are only open when the town is full. Play is there carried on every day from one o'clock in the afternoon throughout the night. The games most in vogue are rouge et noir, un-deux-cinq, roulette, and hazard, at which sums of all amounts, from 1*s.* upwards, are staked. Splendid suppers and choice wines are given at these establishments; and luxuries of every description are lavished, in order to attract the inexperienced. The profits of a well-known hell for one season have been calculated at 150,000*l*. In one night a million of money is said to have changed hands at this place.

As to the EXTENT OF CRIME, some few particulars may not be here out of place. Mr. Colquhoun estimates that in the metropolis and its environs there are 6000 licensed alehouses, constantly holding out seductive lures to the labouring classes. To *dram-drinking* he and most writers on the subject who speak from experience attribute the origin of much calamity and crime amongst the poor and indigent; indeed, it appears that the very scenes of idle and unprincipled dissipation often witness the commencement of dishonest practices, as the publicans of London stated to the House of Commons, on applying for relief on the subject, that they were robbed of pewter pots to the amount of 100,000*l*. annually.

When it is recollected that the splendid "gin shops" rise in magnificence on the increasing depravity of the lower orders, we are compelled with sorrow to denounce that improvidence which expends in liquid poison a fund of sufficient magnitude to establish a temple of comfort and enjoyment for the working classes.

According to the returns made to parliament, we look in vain for the proofs of the decrease of crime. The number of committals to the gaols of London and Middlesex from 1811 to 1817 amounted to 13,415; and in an equal period from 1821 to 1827, to 19,883; being an increase of 48 per cent, although the population has not increased more than 19 per cent. The number of persons committed in 1828 amounted to 3560. The entire number committed in 1832 was 3739. The number of executions has greatly diminished since 1829; only one-twentieth of the whole number sentenced having suffered death.

PRISONS.

The PRISONS, HOUSES of CORRECTION, and PENITENTIARIES next claim attention; and an afflicting picture the subject presents to any mind alive to the cries of wretchedness, or affected by the audacious demeanour of hardened vice.

The greatest number of prisoners confined at one time, during the year 1832, in the prisons of the metropolis is as follows:—Newgate, 610; Middlesex House of Correction, 1340; Giltspur-street Compter, 160; Bridewell, 108; Tothill

Fields, 194; Horsemonger Lane (Surrey) Gaol, 210; Penitentiary, 587; Brixton House of Correction, 285: making a total of 3494.

NEWGATE.

Old Bailey.

This prison derives its name from the gate which once formed a part of it, and stood a little beyond the Sessions-house in the Old Bailey. This gate was used as a prison for persons of rank as early as 1218, but was rebuilt about two centuries afterwards by the executors of Sir R. Whittington, whose statue with a cat stood in a niche till the time of its demolition by the great fire of London in 1666. It was then reconstructed in its late form; but the old prison, being an accumulation of misery and inconvenience, was pulled down and rebuilt between 1778 and 1780. During the riots, however, in the latter year, the whole of the interior was destroyed by fire, but shortly afterwards repaired and completed in its present form; the front consisting of a rustic wall broken at intervals by grated windows, and niches partially filled with statues. The centre forms the house of the keeper, whose salary is *500l.* per annum.

Newgate is the common gaol for London and Middlesex, and is under the jurisdiction of the lord mayor, court of aldermen, and sheriffs. It contains not only persons directly committed for trial from the various police-offices, but also those removed from other prisons previous to the commencement of the sessions, and convicts waiting to be sent away. The number of prisoners confined here varies according to circumstances. It has amounted to upwards of 900; though 350 are as many as the governor thinks the prison ought at any time to contain.

The prison is divided into three principal stations: the first is appropriated to convicts; the second contains three yards for persons confined for fines and misdemeanours, and those committed for trial. The passage leading to the cells is for prisoners under sentence of death. The third station is divided into two yards for the tried and untried females. There are fifteen condemned cells, each measuring ten feet by six and a half.

The prison contains a neat chapel, and there is a school for boys under sixteen years of age. The chaplain or ordinary of Newgate receives *265l.* per annum. He reads prayers twice on Sundays, on Wednesdays and Fridays, preaches every Sunday morning, repeats private prayers with those under sentence of death, on Tuesday and Thursday; and, after the report, attends criminals twice a-day, and on the morning of execution.

The prisoners are each allowed a mat and two rugs to sleep on; a pint of gruel for breakfast; and for dinner, alternately, half a pound of beef, and a quart of soup.

Amongst the *females* wonderful improvement has been accomplished by the efforts of the benevolent and persevering Mrs. Fry; who, amidst the severity of prison discipline, has introduced the benefits of religious instruction and stimulating labour, so as to preserve some link of civilisation and utility even in the cell of penitence. The produce of the prisoners' exertions is devoted to their necessaries and comforts; rescuing them from the aggravation of despair, and the callous determination of unredeemed iniquity.

Strangers wishing to see the interior of Newgate must obtain an order from one of the sheriffs.

HOUSE OF CORRECTION,
Cold-Bath-Fields.

This prison is constructed on the late Mr. Howard's plan. It consists of three buildings, separated by kitchen-gardens, and is surrounded with a high wall, and has the best chapel belonging to any prison in the metropolis, excepting, perhaps, that at the Milbank Penitentiary. It was at first designed only as a kind of Bridewell, but having suitable accommodations for various descriptions of prisoners, it is used for criminals generally. A prisoner on entering is put into a bath, and clothed in the prison costume made by those confined in the House of Correction who formerly followed the tailoring trade. The daily occupation of the prisoners is that of picking oakum and coir (the fibre of cocoa-nut), which is sold, the former for 4*l.* 10*s.* per ton, and the latter 6*s.* per cwt. The average daily number of prisoners is 1,100, who are classified as reputed thieves, felons, and those committed for misdemeanours; refractory apprentices are also confined in cells. Each yard has a tread-mill, where the silent system is rigorously enforced.

The prison for females is a separate building with a chapel.

It was originally designed that each prisoner should have a separate cell; but from the number, it has been found necessary to contrive additional dormitories, where several sleep under the superintendence of a monitor. Each cell is 8 feet 3 inches long, 6 feet 3 inches wide, and 8 feet high; they are all arched, airy, and well-constructed.

TOTHILL-FIELDS BRIDEWELL,
Westminster,

Was handsomely rebuilt in 1831, from designs by Mr. Abrahams, the old building having been declared inadequate by the grand jury. The average number of persons daily in this prison may be taken at 97.

GILTSPUR-STREET PRISON

Is situated to the north of Newgate, and forms, with the east end of St. Sepulchre's-church, the entrance of Giltspur-street. It is a vast pile of rustic stone-work, and is intended to supply the place of the old city prisons called Compters. It is appropriated to the reception of vagrants, disorderly persons apprehended during the night, and accused persons waiting for examination. It is also occupied as a house of correction, where those sentenced to hard labour or committed for assaults and misdemeanours are confined. Each prisoner in this department has a bed stuffed with straw, and two or three rugs. The allowance for food is nearly the same as at Newgate. The males are occupied in grinding corn, bruising flax, picking oakum, and in various trades; the females in picking oakum, spinning flax, washing, mending, needle-work, &c. The number of persons committed annually to this prison is upwards of 5000.

NEW DEBTORS' PRISON,
White Cross-street.

This prison was erected in 1813, to confine those unfortunate persons who would otherwise have been incarcerated with felons in Newgate. It is built on the site of the Peacock-brewhouse, and is calculated to hold 400 prisoners.

CLERKENWELL PRISON

Is a common gaol for the county of Middlesex, and receives prisoners of every description. A house of correction was first built here in 1616, Bridewell being found insufficient. It is situate near the old prison, not far from Spa-fields; it was built about 1820, and is calculated to contain 240 persons; but the keeper thinks that 340 may be confined there: the greatest number ever confined in the old building was in September 1817, when 324 prisoners were there at one time,

GILTSPUR STREET COMPTER.

COLD BATH FIELDS PRISON.

PENITENTIARY MILLBANK.

being an excess of nearly 100 above the average amount; from 200 to 230 may be considered as the ordinary number. There are six yards on each side of the prison, making in the whole twelve. Each prisoner is allowed a rug and a blanket, a pound of bread per day, and meat or soup on alternate days.

FLEET PRISON,
Farringdon street.

This prison for debtors was founded as early as the first year of Richard I. It was the place of confinement for those who had incurred the displeasure of that arbitrary court, the Star-chamber. Persons guilty of contempt in the court of Chancery are likewise committed to this place. The prison consists of four stories, nearly 60 yards in length, with a court for exercise. It is divided into two portions, called the masters' side and the common side. The Masters' Side consists of 109 rooms, nearly all of which have fire-places. The Common Side contains four large rooms with fire-places. Each prisoner supplies his own bed and furniture. The average number of persons in this prison is 250 within the walls, and about 60 in the rules. The *rules* extend from the gate of the prison to Chatham-place, including both sides of the way, and from St. Paul's to Salisbury-court and Shoe-lane, including the two churches of St. Bride's and Ludgate, but excepting Ave-Maria-lane and Blackfriars'-gateway.

QUEEN'S BENCH PRISON,
Southwark.

This is a place of confinement for debtors, and those sentenced by the Court of Queen's Bench to suffer imprisonment for libels and other misdemeanours. The building, consisting of about 220 rooms and a chapel, is surrounded by a lofty brick wall, outside of which the marshal, or keeper, has handsome apartments. The rooms in the prison have only one bed in each, but they are remarkably small, few of them being more than nine feet square. Debtors are allowed to purchase the liberties, to enable them to have houses or lodgings without the walls, or to purchase day-rules, to go out of the prison under certain regulations. The rules include the whole of St. George's Fields, one side of Blackman-street, and part of High-street.

BOROUGH COMPTER.

This prison belongs to the city of London, and its jurisdiction extends over five parishes in Southwark. Previous to 1817, when it was visited by a parliamentary committee, it was a mean and confined place, totally inadequate to its purpose; but it has since been very much improved. The different classes of offenders are now kept separate, the convicts are employed, and the whole prison is well arranged.

SURREY COUNTY GAOL,

Horsemonger-lane,

Is a massive brick building, erected in 1781, surrounded by a strong wall. It is appropriated to the confinement of felons and debtors. The keeper has a handsome house on the west side of the building. The place of execution is a temporary erection on the top of the northern lodge. Here Colonel Despard and six of his associates were hanged for high treason in 1803.

NEW BRIDEWELL PRISON,

Near Bethlem Hospital,

Was erected in 1829, as a substitute for the City Bridewell, Blackfriars. It is built of brick, with a slated roof, and comprises two wings, with the governor's house, offices, &c., in the centre. Extending from it, in the rear, is the chapel, dividing the male from the female department. This prison is devoted to the correction and education of the idle and disorderly. The chief employment of the prisoners is turning the tread-mill, which grinds the corn for the supply of Bethlem Hospital. Upwards of 700 persons are annually sent to this prison.

There are also several HOUSES of CORRECTION, besides those particularly mentioned in this division of our work: amongst them are—

New Bridewell, Southwark.

The *Marshalsea Prison*, in Blackman-street, contains about sixty rooms appropriated to the prisoners of the Marshalsea and Palace Court.

The *Savoy Prison*, for the confinement of deserters from the Guards, formerly situated in the Strand, was pulled down in 1819 to make room for Waterloo-bridge. Deserters are now imprisoned on board a vessel moored off Somerset-house.

SHERIFFS' OFFICERS' HOUSES.

Besides the several regular prisons, there are various lock-up houses, commonly called *spunging-houses*, belonging to the sheriffs' officers, who are ready to extend the accommodation of their private rooms for a valuable consideration, till the person under arrest finds the means of satisfying his creditor, or, with a view to less expense, wishes to be removed to a public prison.

PENITENTIARY,

Milbank.

This establishment was formed about 1820 for the purpose of trying a new system of imprisonment, in which the classification and instruction of the prisoners should be particularly attended to. The front faces the Thames, and consists of a gateway, over which is placed the word "Penitentiary" in large letters. The external form of the prison is that of an octagon, enclosing about 18 acres, on which are erected seven distinct though connected buildings, all the rooms in which face the house in the centre, where the principal master resides, and has thus a complete view of the whole. The rooms are about twelve feet by seven, and are each furnished with a bedstead, mattress, rug, bolster, blankets, and sheets; they are likewise well warmed and ventilated, and glazed inside, having iron bars without. The expense of the building is supposed to be about 400,000*l.* or 500,000*l.* It was originally intended for the reception of 400 male and 400 female convicts, but is capable of accommodating 200 or 300 beyond that number. The culprits are kept regularly at work in various manufactures, and their religious and moral habits are strictly attended to. The female prisoners are under the management of officers *of their own sex*, the governor himself being restricted by the rules from going round their part of the prison, except in company with the matron or task-mistress. This circumstance merits particular notice, as the present is the first instance in which it has been attempted in this country to place any number of female prisoners under female officers. The chapel of the prison is a large and commodious building, where the prisoners attend twice on every Sunday. The prisoners are entitled to a per-centage on all their earnings; and the amount is set apart for their use on being discharged out of custody. None of the prisoners are allowed to see their friends, except by an order from the committee; and this privilege is granted to those only whose conduct is approved by the governor, chaplain, or master manufacturer. The interview must take place before an officer, and no provisions of any description are allowed to be brought.

In December 1831 there were 538 prisoners, 144 of whom

were females. In December 1832 there were 519, of whom 136 were females. In 1832, 178 males and 42 females had been admitted. The earnings of the prisoners amounted to 2683*l.* 10*s.*

This prison is governed by a committee named by the privy council, and no person can be admitted to see it without an order from the home secretary of state, or unless he is accompanied by one of the committee.

It has been proposed to make this establishment a receptacle for juvenile offenders, so as to remove them from the contagion of professed thieves and vagabonds.

Pauperism and Mendicity.

As the condition of the poor and the indigent not only constitutes an important feature in the state of society, but also in the character of the government under which we live, some statements regarding the actual extent and progress of Pauperism and Mendicity are necessary to complete this chapter.

Poverty has been well defined to be that condition in society where the individual has no surplus labour in store, and consequently no property but what is derived from the constant exercises of industry in the various occupations of life; that is, the state of every one who must labour for subsistence. Indigence, on the other hand, is that condition which implies *want*, *misery*, and *distress*. Indigence, therefore, and not poverty, is the evil against which good government must guard. Where indigence exists, the burden of what are called paupers must follow; or, which possibly is much worse, mendicity will ensue.

On the subject of pauperism, facts have been developed that excite attention and demand further inquiry. The number of persons relieved permanently in London, on an average of the three years 1817-18-19, was 36,034; occasionally, being parishioners, 81,282: total relieved, 117,316. So that the number of persons relieved from the poor-rates appears to have been 11⅔ nearly in each 100 of the resident population; while the number relieved in 1803 was nearly 7⅓ in each 100; and that while the population has increased about one-sixth, the number of parishioners relieved has advanced from 7⅓ to 11⅔ in each 100. The total of the money raised by the poor-rates was 679,284*l.*, being at the rate of 13*s.* 5½*d.* per head on the population; or 2*s.* 5*d.* in the pound of the total amount of the sum of 5,603,057*l.* as assessed to the property-tax in 1815. The amount raised by the same rates in 1813 was 471,938*l.*, being at the rate of 10*s.* 11¼*d.* per head. This, therefore, exhibits an increase of nearly *one-half* in the amount of money raised to relieve paupers, and 2*s.* 6½*d.* on the rate per head on the population. This increase of pauperism has been marked by a decrease of FRIENDLY SOCIETIES. The number of persons belonging to such societies appeared to be for the three years 1817-18-19, nearly 5 in the 100 of the resident population; a decrease, when compared with the abstract of 1803, of nearly 3½ in each 100.

To cure or alleviate the evil of MENDICITY and VAGRANCY, the House of Commons promoted inquiries by a committee; and the report developed such a body of evidence as to ascertain, beyond all possibility of doubt, the gross and monstrous frauds practised by mendicants in the capital and in its immediate neighbourhood.

The following facts were ascertained:—That considerable sums of money have been found in the pockets and secreted in the clothes of beggars when brought before magistrates; that beggars make great profits by changing their clothes two or three times a-day, and receiving money which was intended for others; and that a blind man with a dog has collected *thirty shillings* a day, and others from *three* shillings to *seven, eight,* and even more per day. There are two houses in St. Giles's which are frequented by considerably more than two hundred beggars. There they have their clubs, and when they meet they drink and feed well, read the papers, and talk politics! Nobody dares to intrude into their clubs except he is a beggar, or introduced by one; the singularity of the spectacle would otherwise draw numbers around them, which would hurt the trade. Their average daily collections amount to from three to five shillings, two shillings and sixpence of which, it is supposed, they each spend at night, besides sixpence for a bed. A negro beggar retired some time ago to the West Indies with *a fortune* of 1500*l.* Beggars have said they go through forty streets in a day, and that it is a poor street that does not yield twopence; and that it is a bad day that does not yield eight shillings and more. Beggars make great use of *children* in practising upon the feelings of the humane. Children are sent out with an order not to return without a certain sum. One man will collect three, four, or five children from different parents, paying sixpence or ninepence for each during the day. Some children have been regularly let out by the day for two shillings and sixpence as the price of their hire; a child that is shockingly deformed is worth four shillings a-day, and even more. Before the Commons' committee an instance was stated of an old woman who keeps a night-school for the purpose of "instructing children in the *street language*."

Mr. Martin, a gentleman residing in Westminster, stated as the result of his inquiries some years ago, the number of beggars about the metropolis to be 15,000. But the committee, from the evidence laid before them, conceived the number to be much larger.

Beggars evade the vagrant act by carrying matches and articles of little intrinsic value for sale. There is no form of distress which they do not assume, in order to practise upon the humanity of strangers.

In Mr. Martin's calculation, formed thirty years ago, there were, out of 15,000 beggars, 5300 Irish; but Mr. Martin's estimate of the whole number is much under the facts of the present moment. Great pains were taken in 1815, by a remarkably humane gentleman, to ascertain the number of mendicants in *London only*, and the result was, that there were 6876 adults, and 7288 children—making the total of 14,164.

Mr. Martin's estimate of their numbers, and of the sums annually extorted from the public by their importunities, follow:—

Parochial individuals	9297
Non-parochial	5991
Total (including 9288 children)	15,288

The amount of sums gained by them was not estimated at a greater rate than what may be deemed absolutely necessary for the maintenance of such a body of people, although in beggary; and the succeeding low sums were accordingly fixed upon:—

	£	s.	d.
For 6000 grown persons, at 6*d*. a-day each, lodging and clothes inclusive	£54,750	0	0
For 9288 children, at 3*d*. per day, clothes inclusive	42,376	10	0
Gross annual expense	£97,126	10	0

As the best security not only against pauperism and mendicity, but also against the extension of crime, will be found to be in exciting and promoting religious and moral habits among the humble, and therefore the frequently neglected classes of the community; and as many have been improvident, and have descended into indigence and criminality from deficient education and idle courses,—in the chapter respecting education, public charities, &c., we shall treat of what efforts have been made to supply securities against the continuance of evils as enormous as they are alarming.

WORKHOUSES.

From what has just been detailed, it will be seen how alarming is the extent of pauperism and mendicity. That there should be such numerous proofs of the benevolent care extended towards the helpless poor is a proud boast for the nation; but, at the same time, it is to be lamented that out of this good should have resulted evil, owing to the inefficacious application of the old system. The claiming as a right, protection from destitution, avoids the degradation attendant upon the solicitation of alms. In a working country like England, so distinguished for the industrious plodding habits of its natives, it never could have been intended that the necessitous poor — necessitous from want of work, loss of parents and friends, or ruinous accidents—should be supported in idleness, because they "threw themselves on the parish." Hence, however, may be traced much of the burden on parishes under the old laws; and no work being provided in these houses, their very name becomes a misnomer. The old system made little or no distinction in the treatment of the youthful and the aged: all partook of the same diet, and were subject to the same rules. A judicious classification was seldom attempted. The new system makes a distinction between the young and able-bodied and the old and infirm, rendering it probably more irksome for the former, but infinitely more comfortable for the latter.

CHAPTER V.

GENERAL HISTORY OF THE COMMERCE AND TRADE OF LONDON; ITS PORT—MANUFACTURES—COMPANIES—POST-OFFICE—MARKETS, ETC.

THIS chapter introduces us to a copious and an interesting subject; one that cannot but arouse the gratitude of Englishmen and the astonishment of foreigners. By its internal activity and external enterprise—its manufactures at home and its commerce abroad—England, in the most trying periods of her history, has been enabled to stand proudly erect amongst afflicted nations.

As to its COMMERCIAL HISTORY, doubtless London was a place of considerable trade at a very early period. Tacitus speaks of it as the *nobile emporium* of his time, the great resort of merchants, and, though not a colony at that period, yet as a city celebrated for its commercial intercourse. After this, little is known of its trade until the close of the second century, when it is again mentioned as having become "a great and wealthy city." In 359, it is said of England, that its commerce was so extended, that 800 vessels were employed in the port of London for the exportation of corn only. Three centuries after, Bede styles it "an emporium for many nations repairing to it by land and sea." Fitz-Stephen, who lived in the reign of Henry II., says, "that no city in the world exports its merchandise to such a distance as London." He does not, however, inform us what goods were exported, or to what countries they were carried. But among the imports, he mentions gold, spices, and frankincense, from Arabia; precious stones from India; and palm-oil from Bagdad.

The close of the 13th century was a remarkable era in the commercial history of London. In 1296 the company of MERCHANT ADVENTURERS was first incorporated by Edward I. The Hanse merchants also received considerable privileges about the same time.

In 1504, all the ancient privileges of the Hanse merchants were confirmed to them by statute; and all the previous acts which had been made in derogation of them were annulled. In 1553, a great geographical and mercantile discovery was made by a company instituted for the purpose of prosecuting discoveries, under the direction of Sebastian Cabot, a merchant of Bristol. One of the ships fitted out by this company accidentally fell into the bay of St. Nicholas, in the White Sea, and landing at Archangel, obtained from the czar of Russia peculiar privileges of trade with the subjects of his dominions. The Russia or Muscovy merchants were incorporated in the reign of Mary, and had their charter subsequently confirmed in the 8th year of Elizabeth. This princess likewise obtained an exclusive grant to the English of the whole foreign commerce of that extensive empire, which they continued to enjoy for a long period.

It was not, in fact, till the reign of Elizabeth that England began to feel her true weight in the scale of commerce. She then planned some settlements in America, particularly in Virginia. About this period the civil dissensions in Flanders caused multitudes of families to flock to London, and to bring with them their trades and their riches. This great addition to the population of the city, and the consequent increase of its commerce, led to the erection of the Royal Exchange by Sir Thomas Gresham. In 1579 the *Levant* or *Turkey* company, and also the *Eastland* company, were established. On the 31st of December, 1600, the queen granted the first patent to the *East India* company. The first adventure proving successful, the company continued its exertions, and hence has arisen the most splendid and powerful mercantile association that probably ever existed in the world. Assurance and insurance companies were now established in London, and the company of Spanish merchants was likewise incorporated.

In the reign of James I. the progress of the foreign trade was rapidly increased. The tonnage and number of ships in the port of London were greatly augmented. Many of the patents granted by Elizabeth were annulled, and the trade thrown open. Among the circumstances which occasioned the vast increase of trade during this reign may be reckoned the colonisation of America and the West India Islands. The new discoveries, likewise, which were every day made in different quarters of the world, had a powerful effect in stimulating numbers of speculating persons to commercial exertion and adventure.

During the peaceful part of Charles I.'s reign, the commerce of the metropolis still continued to make rapid progress. The augmented commerce of its port may in some measure be estimated by the quantum of *ship-money* which this monarch imposed on the city in 1634. About this time *Prices-current* were first printed; and in 1635 an order was issued by the king in council to "the postmaster of England for foreign parts," requiring him to open a regular communication, by running posts, between the metropolis and Edinburgh, Ireland, and a variety of other places.

Previous to 1640, it was usual for the merchants to deposit their money in the Tower-mint. But this deposit lost all its credit by the ill-advised measure of a forced loan, which the king thought proper to make. The merchants in consequence were obliged to trust their money to their apprentices and clerks. The circumstances of the times and opportunity holding forth great inducements to frauds, many masters lost at once both their servants and their money. Some remedy became necessary. Merchants now began to lodge cash in the hands of the goldsmiths, whom they commissioned also to receive and pay for them. Thus originated the practice of *Banking;* for the goldsmiths soon perceived the advantage that might be derived from possessing disposable capital, and began to allow a regular interest for all sums committed to their care: and at the same time they commenced the discounting of merchants' bills, at an interest superior to that which they paid.

In 1651 the celebrated *navigation act* was passed, the provisions of which greatly contributed to promote the naval and commercial greatness of Britain. This year coffee was introduced into London by a Turkey merchant named Edwards. The sugar-trade was now likewise established; and upwards of 20,000 cloths were sent annually to Turkey, in return for the commodities of that country.

The plague in 1665 almost wholly suspended the commerce of London, so that scarcely a single foreign vessel entered the port for the space of three years. The great fire also occasioned incalculable loss to many of the most opulent merchants. Notwithstanding these disastrous events, the spirit of the survivors was roused to uncommon exertions, and in the course of a few years the city rose from its ashes with greater magnificence and splendour. India muslins were first worn in 1670, and soon became prevalent. In this year, also, the Hudson's-bay company was established, with very extensive powers. The Greenland fishing-company was incorporated in 1693, and the institution of the Bank of England rendered the following year justly memorable in the commercial annals of the metropolis.

The commerce to the East Indies having greatly increased, and many disputes arising relative to exclusive trade, a new joint-stock company was incorporated in London in 1698 by the name of the "English Company trading to the East Indies." The existence of two rival companies, however, soon gave rise to innumerable disputes; to remedy which their consolidation took place in the time of Queen Anne, by the title of "The United Company of Merchants trading to the East Indies."

The great progress that commerce made in a few years may be inferred from the following statement:—the number of vessels belonging to the port of London in 1701 amounted to 560, carrying 84,882 tons, and 10,065 men. In 1719, the customs of this city are stated at 1,268,095*l.*, and those of all the outports only at 346,081*l.*

During the reign of George I. the trade of London made little progress, owing to the South-sea scheme, the Scotch rebellion, and the Spanish war. But in 1732 commerce began to revive: its advances, however, were comparatively slow till the peace of Aix-la-Chapelle in 1748, after which it extended with uncommon rapidity. The next check it sustained was occasioned by the American war. But no sooner was peace signed than it proceeded with renewed vigour; for so early as 1784 the value of exports to America only had increased to 3,397,500*l.*, considerably above the greatest amount in any year before the war. The net sum of duties levied in the port of London rose to the vast sum of 4,472,091*l.* From this period to 1790 the commerce of London continued uniformly increasing. In that year, however, in consequence of the commencement of the war, numerous bankruptcies took place.

In the course of the three succeeding years the appearance of things was entirely changed. In 1796 the exports of London amounted in value to 18,410,499*l.*, and the imports to 14,719,466*l.* The number of British ships that entered the port amounted to 2007, carrying 436,843 tons; and 2169 foreign vessels, carrying 287,142 tons. The total entering coastwise was 11,176, including repeated voyages, which made a tonnage of 1,059,915. The following year some alarm was spread among the merchants by the stoppage of bank payments in specie: but, through the intervention of parliament, confidence was soon restored. The net amount of the customs was 3,950,608*l.* In 1798 the revenue of the customs amounted to the sum of 5,321,187*l.*; in 1799 it had increased to 7,226,353*l.*; but next year it fell to 6,468,655*l.* The *official* value of the imports in 1800 was 18,843,172*l.*, and of the exports 25,428,922*l.*, of which 13,272,494*l.* was in British merchandise. Their *real* value exceeded 68,000,000*l.*, nearly two-thirds of the value of the trade of the whole kingdom. The number of vessels belonging to the port in that year was 2666, carrying 568,268 tons, and 41,402 men. Comparing this number with the number returned in the beginning of the last century, the increase is truly astonishing. On the quantity of tonnage it is nearly in the proportion of six to one; and on the amount of men and ships, four to one. The

East India Company's ships alone carry more burden, by 21,166 tons, than all the vessels of London did a century ago. In 1806 the value of the imports and exports of London was 36,527,000*l.*; in 1819, 46,935,000*l.*; in 1825 it had increased to 96,936,000*l.*, and in the year ending January 1829, to 107,772,805*l.* The number of coasters which entered the port in 1814, was 15,139; in 1821, 18,915; and in 1827, 17,677. Of vessels employed in the foreign trade there were 4012 British, and 1534 foreign. In 1837, 17,603 vessels, of 3,132,367 tons, entered the port, and 14,654 vessels, of 2,495,517 tons, cleared outwards, exclusive of vessels in ballast and those in the Irish and English trade, of which there were 9820 inwards, and 14,725 outwards.

Customs duty received in 1839 *at the following ports:—*

London	£11,431,245	Leith	£573,685
Liverpool	4,234,118	Glasgow	468,974
Bristol	1,089,475	Port Glasgow	102,829
Hull	884,443	Greenock	515,084
Dublin	866,056	Newcastle	464,219

The principal enactments and alterations in our commercial intercourse, within a few years, may thus be briefly mentioned: —the general warehousing act (1803); the introduction of the reciprocity system; the intercourse with South America; the alteration in the laws of the customs (1825), and in the navigation laws; the abolition of the slave-trade, and the opening of the trade with the East Indies and China in 1834; the establishment of the new colonies of South Australia and New Zealand; the intercourse with America by steam; the subjugation of Afghanistan and Cabool; and the probability of a proper understanding with China—are amongst the most important features of our new commercial prospects, as is also the overland journey to India. The improvements in the post-office will also have a very important effect on our commercial intercourse.

The Port of London,

As actually occupied by shipping, extends from London-bridge to Deptford, being a distance of nearly four miles, and from four to five hundred yards average in breadth. It may be described as consisting of *four divisions*, called the *upper*, *middle*, and *lower pools*, and the *space between Limehouse* and *Deptford*. The *upper pool* extends from London-bridge to Union Hole, about 1600 yards:—the *middle pool*, from thence to Wapping New-stairs, 700 yards:—the *lower pool*, from the latter place to the Horseferry-tier, near Limehouse, 1800 yards:—and *space below* to *Deptford*, about 2700 yards.—When the House of Commons commenced an investigation respecting the port of London, the land-accommodations were found to consist of only the *legal quays* and the sufferance-wharfs. The former were appointed in 1558. They occupy the north bank of the river, with some interruption, from London-bridge to the western extremity of Tower-ditch, including a frontage of about 1464 feet. This, with the aid of the sufferance-wharfs, was totally inadequate to the purposes of commercial accommodation. It was not, however, till 1793 that a plan was projected for making wet docks for the port of London, in Wapping, the Isle of Dogs, and at Rotherhithe.

THE DOCKS OF LONDON,

Constituting as they do such grand and truly national works, and forming a sort of era in the history of our commerce, merit some particular notice. Owing to the crowded state of the river, and the confined extent of the *legal quays*, a committee was appointed to consider of the best mode of relief; and in consequence Mr. Daniel Alexander was named to make a survey, and prepare plans and estimates for forming docks at Wapping, with the addition of a canal leading to them from that part of Blackwall where the present East-India-docks have been made, and along a line where the West India-docks have been since formed. The plans and estimates were laid before a general meeting of merchants, December 22d, 1795, when they were unanimously approved, and a subscription of 800,000*l.* was filled in a few hours for carrying the same into execution! The application of the merchants experienced opposition from the corporation of London, and from private interests. Ultimately, however, the merchants triumphed, as will be perceived by the succeeding notices of the several docks, the new Commercial-road, &c. Besides fifty privileged warehousing-ports in England, there are twelve warehouses of special security in London.

West India-Docks.

The fund for executing these docks, as already stated, was raised by the subscription of private individuals. The proprietors are repaid an interest, not to exceed 10 per cent, by a rate or charge upon all the shipping and merchandise entering the dock, and the trade of the company has hitherto enabled them to pay that dividend. By the act passed in July 1799, all West-India produce coming to the port of London must be unloaded in these docks. The present capital of the company is 1,100,000*l.* The plan comprehends two docks; the northern one for unloading the ships arrived from the West Indies, covering thirty acres, and capable of accommodating three hundred West-Indiamen; and the southern, for loading outward-bound ships, covering twenty-four acres, and capable of holding upwards of two hundred West-Indiamen. The former was begun February 3d, 1800, and opened August 27th, 1802, being only two years and a half: it is surrounded by extensive ranges of warehouses, capable of accommodating the whole of the West India trade, in which warehouses the goods are lodged till the duty is paid. The dock of twenty-four acres was completed and opened in 1805. These docks are situated across the narrowest part of the Isle of Dogs, which is formed by a circuitous course the river takes, leaving this almost a peninsula; so that the docks communicate with the river at both extremities of the island—at Blackwall and at Limehouse. The canal to the south of the West India-docks was cut in order that ships might avoid the circuitous navigation of the Isle of Dogs; but not being much used, the city sold it to the West India-dock company in 1829. The former East India-warehouses in Fenchurch-street now belong to this company.

The London-Docks

Are situated between Ratcliffe-highway and the Thames. The fund by which these docks were executed was raised in the same way as that of the West India-docks. The first stone of the works was laid June 26th, 1802, and the dock (St. George's) of twenty acres was opened January 31st, 1805. It is capable of receiving 500 vessels, and has a basin attached to it for the reception of small craft. The capital of the company at present is 2,200,000*l.* The great trade of the company consists in the general traffic of the port; the tobacco-warehouse alone covers four acres of ground, and government pay the company 15,600*l.* annually as rent for it. Another dock of fourteen acres is situated to the east of that first constructed, and communicates with it. The first stone of the new basin was laid June 28th, 1830, by Selim Aga, an

Egyptian prince then resident in this country. The business is conducted by twenty-four directors chosen from among the proprietors, together with the lord mayor of the city of London for the time being.

The doors open at seven o'clock and close at six.

East India-Docks.

In 1803 the principal proprietors of East India shipping, seeing the salutary effects derived from the West India-docks, came to a resolution of following the example, by having docks made for the accommodation of East India ships, and for the security of goods brought home by them, which the state of the river and the abuses practised on it had rendered highly necessary. Having succeeded in carrying a bill through parliament, and having opened a subscription to the amount of 300,000*l.*, the directors made purchase of the *Brunswick-dock* at Blackwall, with a view of converting it into a dock for loading the outward-bound shipping. The dock, which received its name in honour of the present race of monarchs, was begun and executed by Mr. Perry from his private fortune, and affords ample proof of his enterprising public spirit. In addition to this, the East India-dock company have formed a large dock of eighteen acres, for the purpose of unloading the homeward-bound ships, with a commodious basin and embrasures to it. This great dock was begun in the end of 1803, and all the works were completed in 1806. All East India produce coming to this port must be unloaded in these docks. The business is conducted by thirteen directors of the East India Company.

The Commercial-Road

Was made for the purpose of opening an easy communication between the city of London and the different docks. It is seventy feet wide, and in the centre of it there is a strong pavement of twenty feet in width. The management is committed to thirteen trustees, who were empowered to raise a sum of 120,000*l.* for its construction. The distance from the Royal Exchange in London to the West India-dock gate is three miles, and to the East India-dock gate three miles and a half.

St. Catherine's-Docks

Are situated between the London-docks and the Tower, on the site of St. Catherine's Hospital, and were opened

October 25th, 1828; little more than seventeen months having elapsed since the first stone was laid. They were constructed from designs by Mr. Telford, and built by Mr. Hardwicke, and cover twenty-four acres; eleven and a half of which are devoted to wet docks, and the remainder to the warehouses and quays. The canal leading to the river is 190 feet long and forty-five broad; and by means of a steam engine of 100-horse power can be filled or emptied, so that ships of 700 tons may be carried into the docks at any time of the tide. It is computed that the docks and basin will accommodate annually about 1400 merchant-vessels. The total cost of these docks, including the purchase of 1250 houses cleared away, is estimated at 2,000,000*l.* The money was raised in shares.

Collier-Dock.

The increasing number of vessels which bring coals to the metropolis, and the obstruction they form to the navigation of the river, have suggested the idea of a dock exclusively appropriated to colliers. It is proposed to be made at the Isle of Dogs, from designs by Mr. G. Rennie.

The Pool

Is that portion of the Thames where colliers are allowed to anchor; it extends from the Custom-house to Botany-bay tier, near the Regency canal: although the bye-laws allow 210 vessels to moor in the pool, the average is about 180. In a late year, 7077 shiploads transported 2,010,409 tons of coals, at the average price of 19*s.* per ton. The vessels are consigned to factors, who sell the produce to the merchants, sharing with them the expense of meterage, 3*d.* per ton.

Manufactures and Trade.

London has been long celebrated for its manufactures, as well as its commerce. In 1327 the skinners were a very numerous and wealthy class of citizens, manufacturing "sables, lucerns, and other rich furs." Clothworkers of different kinds were also noted for the excellence of their goods. In 1556 a manufactory of the finer sort of glasses was established in Crutched-friars; and flint-glass, not excelled by that of Venice, was made at the same time at the Savoy. About five years after, the manufacture of knit-stockings was introduced, in consequence of the ingenuity of an apprentice, who, happening to see a pair from Mantua at the house of an Italian, made another exactly similar to them, which he presented to William earl of Pembroke. A manufacture of knives was shortly after begun by Thomas Matthews in Fleet-street, and has continued to flourish here. Silk stockings were first made in England in the reign of Queen Elizabeth. Coaches were introduced in 1564, and in less than twenty years they became an article of extensive manufacture. In the following year the manufacture of pins was established; and soon after, that of needles. The making of "earthen furnaces, earthen fire-pots, and earthen ovens, transportable," began about the tenth year of Queen Elizabeth; an Englishman of the name of Richard Dyer having brought the art from Spain. In 1577 pocket-watches were brought from Nuremberg in Germany, and the manufacture of them almost immediately commenced. In the reign of Charles I. saltpetre was made in such quantities as not only to supply the whole of England, but the greater part of the continent. The manufacture of silk, as well as of various articles in silver, had also become extremely prevalent. The printing of calicoes commenced in 1676, and about the same time looms for weaving were brought from Holland. The revocation of the edict of Nantz in 1685 having expelled many industrious Frenchmen from their native country, a considerable number came over to England and settled in Spitalfields. By them several of our manufactures were improved, particularly that of silk, which now employs many thousands; and many others were introduced.

The TRADE of London may be divided into the *wholesale* and *retail* business; for they are completely separate, and under different systems of management. The *wholesale* trade is chiefly carried on in the city, and in the vicinity of the river, where large warehouses and counting-houses are established. The *retail* trade is dispersed through all the public streets, in which spacious and handsome shops are opened for the display of all the necessaries as well as the luxuries of life. The shopkeepers of London are an active, industrious, and respectable class of society. The regular and perpetual intercourse which subsists between London and all parts of the kingdom, by means of coaches, waggons, vans, barges, &c., constitutes a marked feature of this wonderful city.

The progress of our work now requires some detailed mention of the principal COMPANIES connected with the trade and commerce of London.

The Bank of England

Is the most important institution of the kind that exists in any part of the world; and the HISTORY OF BANKING furnishes no example that can at all be compared with it, for the range and multiplicity of its transactions, and for the vast influence which it possesses over public and national affairs.

Though banks are of considerable antiquity, it is only in modern times that their power has been so extensively manifested. Between two and three centuries before the Christian era, a banker of Sicyon, a city of Peloponnesus, is mentioned by Plutarch in his life of Aratus. His business appears to have consisted in exchanging one species of money for another. The money-changers of Judea, who were driven out of the temple by Christ, were probably of the description mentioned in the parable of the talents; that is, such as made a trade of receiving money in deposit, and paying interest for it. From Judea the institution of Banks was brought into Europe; and the Lombard Jews are said to have kept benches or banks in the market-places of Italy, for the exchange of money and bills.

In the 14th century the business of banking was carried on by the drapers of Barcelona in Spain, as it was in after-ages by the goldsmiths in London; in both which cases these respective traders were considered the most substantial among the citizens. The bank of Barcelona was established in 1401, by the magistrates, upon the security of the funds of the city.

The bank of Amsterdam, which became proverbial for extensive usefulness and unviolated faith, was founded by the magistrates and merchants of Holland in 1609; and after the credit of the foreign merchants had declined in England, or rather after the spirit and enterprise of our own merchants had obtained for themselves those advantages which had been previously enjoyed by foreigners, the goldsmiths became the principal bankers in London, and more particularly so during the time of the civil wars, and until the revolution of 1688. Several schemes, however, had in the intermediate time been promulgated for a public bank, on a plan similar to that of the bank of Amsterdam. Yet it was not till 1694 that the public mind was sufficiently awakened to the utility of such an establishment, and that legal provision was made to carry it into effect. Great opposition was also excited by the monied men and by others, alleging that it would engross the money, stock, and riches of the kingdom, and eventually render the king absolute.

All difficulties, however, were at length overcome; and an act passed the legislature in 1694, empowering their majesties to incorporate the subscribers under the title of "*The Governor and Company of the Bank of England*," in consideration of the loan of 1,200,000*l.* granted to government, for which the subscribers received almost 8 per cent: the subscription for the whole sum of 1,200,000*l.* was completed in the course of ten days. The charter directs, that the management of the bank shall be vested in a governor, deputy-governor, and twenty-four directors; thirteen, or more, to constitute a court, of which the governor or deputy-governor must be one. They are to have a perpetual succession, a common seal, and the other usual powers of corporations, as making by-laws, &c.; but must not borrow money under their common seal without the authority of parliament. They are not to trade, nor suffer any person in trust for them to trade in any goods or merchandise; but they may deal in bills of exchange, in bullion, and foreign gold and silver coin, &c. They may also lend money on pawns or pledges, and sell those which shall not be redeemed within three months after the time agreed; but this has been little acted upon. No dividend is to be made but by consent of a general court, and that only out of the interest, profit, and produce arising by such dealing as the act of parliament allows. The erection of this celebrated bank, according to the declaration of one of its first directors, not only relieved the ministry from their frequent processions into the city for borrowing money on the best public securities, at an interest of 10 or 12 per cent per annum, but likewise gave life and currency to double or triple the value of its capital in other branches of public credit.

Four general meetings of proprietors are held annually, and a daily committee of three directors presides over the transactions of the institution; the former being qualified by holding 500*l.* bank-stock, and the latter 2000*l.*

Branch banks were established in 1826, in some of the principal cities, for the purpose of counteracting the discredit of country banks, and also to assist them with loans.

The "dealing in bills of exchange" the company has carried on to a very great extent. They *discount* bills for the merchants and bankers at 5 per cent interest; and there is an amount of several millions, constantly floating, devoted to this object. The bills must not have more than three months to run: the bankers or merchants who present them (for persons engaged in the retail trade are not admitted to the direct benefit of these discounts), must be able to swear that they are worth at least 12 or 15,000*l.*; the town bills must be sent in every Wednesday, but the country bills are admitted every day, each party possessing such privilege being limited to a certain weekly amount, which, however, is great; and the next day the bills are punctually discounted or returned; and where any bill is dishonoured, the party on whom the bill is drawn cannot expect his bills to pass there in future. Although the discounting of some bills may be refused on one Wednesday, they may be attended to the succeeding week—the refusal may possibly have been occasioned by the party having previously been accommodated with the prescribed amount. Each merchant has a fair proportion of the amount set apart for the discounting of notes, and no deposits are required. Too much praise cannot be bestowed on the company for the benefits rendered to the commercial world by this laudable practice, which has enabled merchants and bankers to embark in undertakings for their own advantage, the success of the revenue, and the prosperity of our general commerce.

The quarter's liabilities of the bank amounted in 1838 to 30,249,000*l.*, and its assets to 32,964,000*l.*

Nature of the Stocks, &c.

The stocks or public funds comprise the aggregate of all the loans which have been advanced to government for defraying the ordinary and extraordinary expenses of the nation; and, generally speaking, constitute what is appropriately called "The National Debt." The funding system was first practised by the Venetians in 1171, but was not legally established in England till the incorporation of the bank. It consists in the due payment of the interest of every loan, by means of the taxes and duties which are imposed and levied for the service of the state.

The national debt is divided into various portions, under the following denominations:—Bank-stock new 4 per cents; 3 per cents consols; 3 per cents 1726; 3 per cents 1797; 4 per cents consols; 3 per cents reduced long annuities; 3 per cents imperial annuities; imperial annuities for twenty-five years; Irish annuities for fifteen years; deferred stock;

South-sea stock; 3 per cents new South-sea annuities; 3 per cents 1751; 3 per cents old South-sea annuities; omnium; exchequer, navy, victualling, ordnance, and treasury bills.

This variety of denominations has arisen, partly from the exigencies under which the loans were raised, and partly from the terms on which they were negotiated—either on annuities or on the funded property of incorporated companies. In raising loans, a douceur is occasionally given by government of an annuity for a limited time; such are named terminable and redeemable annuities. But the regular stocks, on which the common interest is paid, are called perpetual and also redeemable annuities.

New loans are paid at stated periods by instalments of 10 or 15 per cent; and the terms on which they are made generally occasion an increase on different kinds of stock, to the amount of 3 per cent and upwards (according to the emergency and state of the money-market) more than the sum borrowed. Thus, for every 100*l*. capital, new stock is created to the amount of 103*l*. The difference is called the bonus, and the aggregate of the additional stock of different kinds is termed "omnium." If these be disposed of separately, before all the instalments are paid, the different articles are called scrip, which is an abbreviation of subscription.

The funded debt is that portion of the whole for which taxes have been appropriated by parliament to discharge the interest regularly. But as the necessities of government frequently occasion the borrowing of money, for which no opportunity to make such provision has been afforded, this money is called the "unfunded debt." Of this description are all sums due upon the exchequer, navy, victualling, and ordnance bills, which are issued under legislative authority by those different offices, and which bear an interest of twopence or threepence per day for every 100*l*. till paid off. The value of the stocks is perpetually fluctuating, the variations being occasioned by unfounded as well as real causes. Any occurrence by which the security of the state is either hazarded or strengthened, though one may be as imaginary as the other, has an immediate effect upon the price, which will advance or fall as the news may be considered good or otherwise. The quantity of stock in the market will also either depreciate or raise the value, as purchasers may be more or less numerous.

The manner of buying stock is to give a specific number of pounds for a nominal hundred pounds. Thus, if the purchase be made in 3 per cents, and the current price be 80*l*., that sum is paid for 100*l.* stock, which yields a dividend of 3*l.* per annum. Persons conversant with these things will sometimes obtain a considerable advantage by transferring stock from one branch of the funds to another, the variations in the value of the different stocks not being always adjusted to their proper level.

In the purchase and sale of stocks, it should be remembered that the interest due on them from the time of the last payment of the dividends is always taken into the current price, and the seller never receives any consideration for it, except in the case of India-bonds and exchequer-bills, when the interest due is calculated to the day of sale, and paid for by the purchaser, independently of the price agreed on.

It must likewise be observed, that as the interest on the different stocks is paid at different times, some have always a quarter's interest due on them more than others; and this circumstance occasions a seemingly considerable difference of value, when there is none in reality.

Every possible degree of facility, consistent with prudence, is given to the purchase and sale of stocks; yet the intervention of a stock-broker is generally thought requisite, as the identity of the persons making the transfer must be vouched for, before the witnessing clerk will allow his signature to be made in the bank-books. All transfers of stock are made on the appointed transfer-days, and no stock can be transferred twice on the same day. The space between the shutting and opening the books of any stock is usually about six weeks. At the time of shutting, the dividends due are carried to a separate account, and cannot be transferred with the stock of the proprietor, the warrants being filled up in the name in which the stock stands when the books are shut. The dividends on the bank-stock are payable the day after they become due; but those on the stocks of other companies, and on the government funds, are not payable till about a week after they become due.

The business of a STOCK-BROKER has grown up with the new state of things in the money-market of this country; a condition of credit and paper-circulation. The business of buying and selling different portions of stock, as persons possessed or wanted money, in process of time became of so complex a character, that an ordinary individual could not, with ease and convenience to himself, conduct his own affairs on the "Stock Exchange;" at all events, it was not unpleasant to the general feeling of fund-holders, engaged as many of them were and are in active trades in different parts of the kingdom, to have the opportunity of being able to conduct their money concerns with the Bank of England by means of *agents* or brokers. This gave rise to the profession of "Stock-broker;" and that character is now so completely ingrafted into the system, that private individuals scarcely ever think of conducting their transactions with the bank, except through the medium of a professed broker, who has his *per centage* for his trouble.

STOCK-EXCHANGE.

The persons called STOCK-BROKERS used to assemble and transact business in the Bank-rotunda; but the inconvenience to which they were subjected, and the general interruption of public business occasioned by the *stock-jobbers* who intermingled amongst them, gave rise to the plan of the New Stock Exchange. This building is situated at the upper end of Capel-court, opposite the east door of the Bank; but there are also entrances to it from Shorter's-court and New-court, in Throgmorton-street, and from the Hercules-tavern in Broad-street. It was erected in 1804 by Mr. James Peacock, architect; and is very conveniently arranged and handsomely fitted up. The expense was defrayed by a subscription among the principal stock-brokers of 50*l.* transferable shares. No person is allowed to transact business but regular stock-brokers, and they must be balloted for annually by a committee, and on being chosen subscribe ten guineas each. Under the clock, at the south end of the spacious room in which the subscribers assemble, is a tablet for the purpose of exhibiting the names of such defaulters as have not been able or willing to settle their losses on agreements made for the purchase or transfer of stock, and who are not again suffered to become members. At the north end is a pluviometer, as well as a list of the original proprietors of the building. On the east side is a recess, with an elevated desk, for the use of the "Commissioners for the Redemption of the National Debt," who make their purchases four times a-week—namely, on Monday, Wednesday, Thursday, and Friday, precisely at twelve o'clock. No other business is transacted here than that which relates solely to the purchase and sale of stock in the public funds, exchequer-bills, India-bonds, and similar securities. The hours are from ten to four.—The *jobbers* still assemble in the Bank-rotunda, which exhibits a scene of indescribable confusion.

The practice to which the term *stock-jobbing* is more particularly applicable, is that which is carried on amongst persons who possess little or no property in any of the funds, yet who contract for the sale or transfer of stock at some future period, the latter part of the day, or the next *settling-day*, at a price agreed on at the time. Such bargains are called *time-bargains*, and are contrary to law; and this practice is *gambling* in every sense of the word. The business of *jobbing* is carried on to an amazing extent, and is of this character:—A agrees to sell B 10,000*l.* of bank-stock, to be transferred in twenty days for 12,000*l.* A, in fact, does not possess any such property; yet if the price of bank-stock on the day appointed for the transfer should be only 118*l.* per cent, he may then purchase as much as will enable him to fulfil his bargain for 11,800*l.*, and thus he would gain 200*l.* by the transaction. Should the price of bank-stock advance to 125 per cent, he will then lose 500*l.* by completing his agreement. As neither A nor B, however, may have the means to purchase stock to the extent agreed on, the business is commonly arranged by the payment of the difference—the profit or the loss—between the current price of the stock on the day appointed and the price bargained for.

In the language of the *Alley*, as it is called (all dealings in the stocks having been formerly transacted on 'Change-alley), the buyer in these contracts is denominated a *bull*, and the seller a *bear*. As neither party can be compelled to complete these bargains (they being illegal), their own sense of "honour," the disgrace, and the loss of future credit, that attend a breach of contract, are the sole principles on which this singular business is regulated. When a person refuses, or has not the ability to pay his loss, he is termed a *lame duck*; but this opprobrious epithet is not bestowed on those whose failure is owing to insufficient means, provided they make the same surrender of their property voluntarily as the law would have compelled had the transaction fallen within its cognizance. This illegal practice, which we have already termed *gambling*, is nothing more than a wager as to what will be the price of stocks at a fixed period; but the facility which it affords to extravagant and unprincipled speculation—speculation that is not checked by the ordinary risk of property—and the mischief and ruin which have frequently followed it, very wisely determined the legislature to lay a penalty of

500*l.* on every person making such *time-bargains;* and the like sum on all brokers, agents, and scriveners employed in transacting or writing the said contracts. By the same statute, also, 7 Geo. II. ch. 8, a similar penalty is imposed upon all persons contracting for the sale of stock, of which they are not possessed at the time of such bargain; and 100*l.* on every broker or agent employed in procuring the said bargain.

EAST INDIA COMPANY.

The first idea of this company was formed in Queen Elizabeth's reign; but it has since experienced vast alterations. It was chartered Dec. 31, 1600. Its first shares or subscriptions were originally 50*l.*, and its capital only 369,891*l.* 5*s.*; but the directors having a considerable dividend to make in 1676, it was agreed to join the profits to the capital, by which the shares were doubled, and consequently each became worth 100*l.*, and the capital 739,782*l.* 10*s.*: to which capital, if 963,639*l.*, the profits and stock of the company to the year 1684, be added, the whole will be found to be 1,703,102*l.*—With their capital commerce was established by the Red Sea to Arabia, Persia, India, China, and various islands in the Indian Ocean. About the beginning of the protectorate of Oliver Cromwell, however, it was imagined that opening the trade to the East Indies would benefit the whole nation: commerce was therefore made general, and thus continued till 1657, when experience having proved that the separate trade was detrimental to the undertakers, they were, for the good of the whole, united to the company by the legislature. In 1698 a new East India Company was established, which caused the dissolution of the old company, after the expiration of a certain term, which was allowed for the disposal of their effects. The new company immediately advanced two millions sterling to government at eight per cent. The two companies were, however, ultimately united in 1702, when a new charter was granted to them under the title of "The United Company of Merchants of England trading to the East Indies." In the 6th of Queen Anne, the united company lent the government 200,000*l.*, making their whole loan amount to 3,200,000*l.* In 1730 the company obtained a renewal of their charter from parliament, notwithstanding the powerful opposition which was raised against it by a considerable body of merchants and others in London, Bristol, and Liverpool, who had associated for the purpose of overthrowing the old joint-stock trade, and of establishing a new-regulated company upon its ruins.

In 1744 the East India Company agreed to advance to government one million sterling at three per cent interest, in consideration of having their exclusive privileges prolonged for fourteen years beyond the term prescribed in the act of parliament passed in 1730. By the act which legalised this agreement, the company had authority to borrow any sum not exceeding the million which was wanted, on bonds under their common seal, at similar interest to that which they had covenanted to receive from the state.

The war which broke out between England and France in 1744 produced an extraordinary change in the company's concerns in India, and ultimately led to their present territorial aggrandisement.

The bill which passed the legislature for the government of India for the further term of twenty years took effect on the 10th of April, 1814. This bill limited the operation of the company's exclusive charter to places lying to the north of 11 degrees of south latitude, and between 64 and 150 degrees of east longitude. To other parts within the specified limits, ships of 350 tons burden could trade, and, under certain restrictions, bring all the produce of the East, tea excepted. Persons desirous of going out to India for commercial purposes were bound to apply for a license to the court of directors; and in fourteen days from the time of their application, if it were not complied with, they might apply to the board of control, who could order the court, if they thought proper, to grant a license. This act also acknowledges the duty of this country as a Christian nation "to promote the interest of the native inhabitants of the British dominions in India, and to adopt such measures as may tend to the introduction of useful knowledge, and of religious improvement among them." The effect of the expiration of the charter of the East India Company in 1834 is thus briefly and eloquently expressed by Mr. Pope in his Yearly Journal of Trade:—

"The great and striking distinction between the present and every former charter, lies in the change which it effects in the character and functions of the company. The corporation has hitherto been considered as essentially commercial, and only accidentally political or sovereign, being properly entitled, 'The United Company of Merchants of England trading to the East Indies.' It is now entirely divested of its trading functions, and is only retained as a political instrument for governing the mighty empire which its extraordinary fortunes had thrown in its way, or which extraordinary contingencies had compelled its servants to conquer and to occupy."

The annual exports to India amount to 4,000,000*l*.

SOUTH-SEA COMPANY.—The business of this company consists only in receiving interest of their capital, which is in the hands of government, and in the payment of dividends and transferring stock. It is managed by a governor, sub-governor, deputy-governor, and twenty-one directors.

The *South-Sea House*, in which the affairs of the company are transacted, is a handsome edifice of the Doric order situated in Threadneedle-street. It encloses a quadrangle, surrounded by a piazza with Tuscan pillars. The offices are well laid out, and all the apartments convenient and handsome. The South-Sea establishment has lately been abolished, and the edifice will be devoted to other purposes.

THE LEVANT, OR TURKEY COMPANY, was incorporated by Queen Elizabeth in 1579, and invested with many privileges, but has recently resigned its charter.

THE RUSSIA COMPANY was incorporated in 1555 by Queen Mary, and its privileges were afterwards enlarged by James I. in 1614. This company is under the management of a governor, four consuls, and a numerous court of assistants. Their court is held in Merchant-seaman's office, over the Royal Exchange; and the officers are elected annually on the 1st of March.

THE HUDSON'S BAY COMPANY conduct their affairs in a handsome brick building in Culver-court, Fenchurch-street, where the first Russian ambassador sent to this country resided. The hall contains a vast pair of horns of the moose-deer, and the picture of an elk which weighed 1229 pounds, killed in the presence of Charles XI. of Sweden.

THE EASTLAND COMPANY, which trades with the countries bordering on the Baltic, was incorporated in 1579 by Queen Elizabeth. Its concerns are managed by a governor, deputy-governor, and twenty-four assistants, annually chosen on the first Wednesday after Michaelmas-day. Their meetings are held at the Royal Exchange.

THE LONDON AND WESTMINSTER BANK.

THE LONDON JOINT-STOCK BANK.

Besides these, there are innumerable banking, railway, mining, steam-navigation, dock, canal, bridge, conveyance, agricultural, and other companies, far too numerous and ephemeral to be enumerated in this Guide.

GAS-LIGHT AND COKE COMPANIES.

The chartered *Gas-Light Company* was the first established in London, having been incorporated in 1812; office, Bridge-street, Blackfriars. Its works are situated in the Horseferry-road, Westminster; Brick-lane, Spitalfields; and the Curtain-road; and consume annually upwards of 100,000 chaldrons of coal, which afford light to more than 30,000 lamps. The main pipes extend 200 miles.

The *Imperial Gas Company*.—The works are at St. Pancras, Hackney, and King's-road, Chelsea. This company was established in 1823, and consumes upwards of 80,000 chaldrons.

The *City Gas Company*, incorporated 1817, Dorset-street, Salisbury-square, consumes annually about 35,000 chaldrons of coal, and lights about 11,000 lamps: the main pipes are 50 miles in length.

The *Phœnix*, united with the *South London Company*, at Bankside, consumes annually about 50,000 chaldrons of coal, which light more than 15,000 lamps. The main pipes are about 40 miles long.

The remaining companies are the *British*, the *Ratcliff*, the *Equitable*, the *South Metropolitan*, the *London*, the *Alliance*, the *Brentford*, and the *Westminster*.

WATER-WORKS.

Independently of all the preceding arrangements for the comfort of the metropolis, the inhabitants have a constant supply of water for domestic purposes, which passes beneath the streets by means of cast-iron cylinders or pipes, varying from six to thirty inches in diameter, whence smaller pipes convey the water into each house. The daily supply of all the following companies would cover 32½ acres, at 3 feet depth; equal to 4½ millions of cubic feet, or 117,975 tons weight.

The following is an account of the principal water-works which supply the metropolis, and a table of quantities :—

Company.	Houses.	Barrels per Annum.	Price per Barrel—36 Gallons.	Average height above Water-mark.
New River . . .	66,600	112,500,000	¾ of a farth.	60
Chelsea	12,400	15,000,000	¼*d.* & 1-5th.	60
East London . .	42,000	57,600,000	nearly ¼	60
West Middlesex .	14,500	18,850,000	nearly ½	110
Grand Junction .	8,693	24,266,666	nearly ¼	110

The New River, from the spring at Chadwell, near Ware, has two reservoirs, covering about five acres, averaging 10 feet in depth. These are 85 feet above low-water mark at the Thames. Steam-engines raise the water 60 feet higher than that level, and send it to the upper parts of the houses.

The East London, at Old Ford, on the river Lea, about three miles from its entrance into the Thames. The pipes belonging to this company are 200 miles in length.

The West Middlesex obtains water from the Thames at Hammersmith, whence it is forced into a reservoir at Kensington, 120 feet above low water in the Thames. Another reservoir is on Little Primrose-hill, about 70 feet higher.

The Chelsea, from the Thames near Chelsea Hospital, has two reservoirs; one in the Green-park, 44 feet above the level of the Thames: it has been lately re-constructed and furnished with a very curious filtering apparatus. The other, in Hyde-park, has an elevation of 70 feet.

The Grand Junction, from the Surrey channel of the river Thames, adjoining the grounds of Kew-palace, whence it is forced into three reservoirs at Paddington: these reservoirs are about 89, 104, and 110 feet above low water in the Thames.

The Lambeth, from the Thames between Westminster and Waterloo Bridges, has no reservoir. An engine delivers the water, which is nowhere raised above 40 feet, directly from the river. It supplies 16,000 houses, and daily furnishes 1,244,000 gallons.

The South London or Vauxhall Company derive their supply from the Thames by means of a tunnel, which is carried into the river at Vauxhall-bridge. They serve 10,000 houses, and daily furnish 1,000,000 gallons.

The Southwark, from the Thames, between London and Southwark, supply 7000 houses, and furnish 720,000 gallons daily.

The London and Westminster, from springs in Bushey-Hall meadows, near Watford, called the Colne Waters.

Lloyd's Coffee-House,

On the northern side of the late Royal Exchange, was long celebrated as the resort of eminent merchants, underwriters, marine insurance-brokers, &c. It was afterwards held in a building formerly called the City of London Tavern, which has been recently transformed into the Wesleyan Centenary Hall. The books contain an account of the arrivals and sailing of vessels, and are remarkable for their early intelligence of maritime affairs. In 1803 the subscribers instituted the Patriotic Fund, for the purpose of affording relief to the relatives of those who had died in the service of their country. Now meet at the South Sea House, Broad-street.

INSURANCE COMPANIES.

Insurance, says an eminent writer, is a contract by which the insurer undertakes, in consideration of a premium equivalent to the hazard run, to indemnify the person insured against certain perils or losses, or against some particular event. When insurance in general is spoken of by professional men, it is understood to signify Marine Insurance. Taken in this light, it is a contract of indemnity against those perils to which ships or goods are exposed in the course of their voyage from one place to another. The utility of this species of contract is obvious: insurances give great security to the fortunes of private people, by dividing amongst many that loss which would ruin an individual.

Life-Insurance Offices.

Amicable, Serjeant's-Inn, Fleet-st., 1706.
Argus, Throgmorton-street.
Asylum, Cornhill, 1835.
Britannia, Princes-street.
British Commercial, Cornhill, 1820.
Clergy, Mutual Assurance, Parliament-street.
Clerical and General, Great Russell-street.
Crown, 33, New Bridge-street, 1826.
Eagle, Bridge-st., Blackfriars, 1807.
Eagle, United Empire, Cornhill and Waterloo-place, 1807.
Economic, 34, New Bridge-st., 1823.
Equitable, New Bridge-street, 1762.
European, Chatham-place, 1819.
Hope, 6, New Bridge-street, 1807; 1,000,000*l*.
Law, Fleet-street.
Legal and General, Fleet street.
London Association, King William-street, 1806.
Medical and Clerical, 78, Great Russell-street, 1824; 500,000*l*.
Mutual, 37, Old Jewry, 1834.
National, 38, Old Broad-street; 500,000*l*.
Naval and Military, Waterloo-place.
Norwich Union, Crescent, Blackfriars, and Fenchurch-street; 1,250,000*l*.
Pelican, Lombard-st., and Spring-gardens, 1797.
Promoter, 9, Chatham-pl.; 240,000*l*.
Provident Institution, Regent-st., 1806.
Rock, 14, New Bridge-street, 1806.
Standard, King William-street.
Union, Lancaster-place.
United Kingdom, Marine Insurance, Charlotte-row.
University, Suffolk-street, Cockspur-street, 1825.
Westminster, Strand and Cornhill, 1792.

Fire-Insurance Offices.

Beacon, Chatham-place and Regent-street, 1823
British, Cornhill and Strand, 1799
County, Regent-street, 1807
Hand-in-Hand, New Bridge-st. 1696
Imperial, Cornhill and St. James's-street, 1803
Minerva, King William-street.
Norwich Union, 1797. Crescent, New Bridge-street, & Fenchurch-street; 550,000*l*.
Phœnix, Lombard-street and Charing-cross, 1782
Protector, Old Jewry, Regent-street, and High-st., Southwark, 1825; 5,000,000*l*.
Sun, Cornhill and Craig's-court, Charing-cross, 1710. A new office is building at the corner of Bartholomew-lane, near the Bank.
Westminster, King-street, Covent-garden, 1717.

Fire and Life Insurance Offices.

Albion, New Bridge-street, 1805; 1,000,000*l*.
Alliance, Bartholomew-lane, 1824.
Atlas, Cheapside, 1808; 1,200,000*l*.
Globe, Cornhill and Pall-mall, 1803; 1,000,000*l*.
Guardian, Lombard-street, 1821; 2,000,000*l*.
London Assurance, Birchin-lane, 1720.
Marine Insurance, Cornhill.
Palladium, Waterloo-place and Cornhill, 1824.
Royal Exchange, at the Royal Exchange and Pall-mall, 1720.
Union, Cornhill, 1714.
West of England, 1807, 20, New Bridge-street; 600,000*l*.

Insurance against loss by FIRE is carried on in offices established for that purpose. Their care in providing engines and firemen, the known honour of the directors, and the general respectability of the establishments, have destroyed competition by individuals. Some offices, few in number, are established in the large towns and cities of the kingdom, independent of those in the metropolis, but their operations are merely local; while those in London, by means of agents duly authorised and properly stationed, extend their beneficial operations to all parts of the realm. Several offices insure LIVES, and grant ANNUITIES, &c.; others unite both branches of business.

Taking into consideration the fatal results of some companies who have within a short time imposed on credulous and inexperienced people, and the vast importance of the subject to thousands, no man could, perhaps, serve society more essentially than by affording the public some distinct data for making a prudential choice among so many rival offices; but the attempt would be extremely invidious, and very difficult to perform satisfactorily. The safest general rule is to look well at the list of directors; if they are men of known integrity, moving in some public sphere, and of substantial property, one may feel himself on pretty safe ground: such men are not likely to lend their names to visionary undertakings. This precaution is the more necessary where unusual advantages are offered.

Besides the Insurance Companies may be mentioned the *London Fire-Engine Establishment*, supported by the principal fire-offices: the men wear a grey costume, with strong leathern helmets—they have floating engines on the Thames; and the *Society for the Protection of Life from Fire*, engaged in perfecting the fire-escapes, and keeping watch during the night. Water is laid on in the streets: on drawing the plugs an ample supply is obtained in cases of fire; the engines to the various companies are stationed at convenient distances.

From a report by Mr. Braidwood, the superintendent of the fire-brigade force, the number of fires during the year 1840 amounted to 863, chiefly originated in consequence of intoxication or carelessness of workmen. Out of the entire number, however, 204 commenced in private houses. The number since the establishment of the brigade amount to 3,628. The number of buildings totally destroyed, 195; seriously damaged, 957; slightly damaged, 2,482; lives lost during the past year by fires, 22.

Several of the offices are remarkable as buildings. The *Phœnix and Pelican*, at Charing-cross, erected by Gandy, one of the chastest specimens of architecture in the metropolis. The *Pelican*, Lombard-street, erected by Sir R. Taylor, ornamented with a beautiful group, executed at Coade's manufactory by M. De Verre, from designs by Lady Diana Beauclerc. The *County and Provident*, Regent-street, designed by Mr. Abraham: the front, a rusticated arcade of five arches, over which is a façade of Corinthian columns, supporting an entablature, parapet, and balustrade, the whole surmounted by a statue of Britannia. The *Equitable*, New Bridge-street, rebuilt in 1829, from designs by Sir R. Smirke. The *Union*, Cornhill, adorned with two fine figures of Strength and Justice. The *Amicable*, erected on the site of Serjeant's-inn-hall, formerly used as a chapel. The *Globe*, in Cornhill, rebuilt in 1838 by Mr. Hardwicke. The *Albion*, New Bridge-street, ornamented with a figure of St. George.

POST-OFFICE ESTABLISHMENT.

(*For a description of the edifice, see page* 206.)

The Post-office system may well be deemed the proudest of all the improvements of this commercial city. The progress to its present state was slow. The increase of trade creating a greater necessity for a more speedy and enlarged intercourse with distant parts of the nation, the king, by a proclamation in 1635, ordered his "postmaster of England for foreign parts," to open a regular communication, by running posts between the metropolis and Edinburgh, West Chester, Holyhead, Ireland, Plymouth, Exeter, &c.

The revenues of the post-office in Great Britain and Ireland were, in 1653 and 1654, farmed by John Manley, Esq., for 10,000*l*. Two years afterwards, Cromwell instituted a new general post-office for the commonwealth of the three kingdoms. Charles II., confirming the regulations of the Protector, settled the revenue from it on the Duke of York—the produce in 1665 being 21,500*l*. Ten years afterwards this amount was doubled; and still continued to increase until the reign of William and Mary, when it was considerably influenced by the hostile or tranquil state of the country. The post-office revenue, which during the eight years of war only averaged 67,222*l*. a-year, produced in the succeeding four years of peace, on an average, 82,319*l*. annually. A similar effect was experienced during the reign of Anne, when the war-postage was about 60,000*l*., and in years of peace about 90,000*l*. This disproportion has of late been reversed, and the last years of war were those in which the post-office was the most productive. On the union of England with Scotland, in 1710, a general post-office was established, which included, besides Great Britain and Ireland, our West India and American colonies. This extension increased the revenue to 111,461*l*. What portion of this sum was produced by the respective countries does not appear; but there is reason to believe that it was almost entirely Irish and English, for even so late as between 1730 and 1740 the post was only transmitted three days a-week between Edinburgh and London; and the metropolis on one occasion *only furnished a single letter*, which was for an Edinburgh banker named Ramsay.

A thorough change in the mode of conveying the letters was suggested by Mr. Palmer, in 1784. By the adoption of this plan, the letters are forwarded by strong and well-guarded coaches, each drawn by four excellent horses, which proceed with the utmost regularity between eight and nine miles an hour, stoppages included. In allusion to their employment, they are called *Mail-Coaches*. Formerly the mails were sent by carts or by post-boys on horseback, a mode attended with danger and delay. The first mail-coach was established to Bristol in 1784. From this moment the prosperity of the post-office commenced; and the revenue, which at first was not more than 5000*l*. a-year, and which, after the revolution of two centuries, only produced, in 1783, 146,000*l*. annually yielded, thirty years afterwards, nearly 1,700,000*l*. Yet the expense is now at a less rate per mile than upon the old plan. The total amount of the annual receipts previous to the alteration in 1840, was about 2,400,000*l*. The statistical account given in page 208 applies to the order of things previous to the change caused by the adoption of the uniform rate.

THE PENNY POSTAGE.—As a prelude to the general adoption of the most remarkable event in the history of the post-office, an Act of Parliament (2 and 3 Victoriæ, cap. 52), was passed in the session of 1839-40, for the regulation of the charge of postage by weight instead of by distance. By this act the lords of the treasury were empowered to introduce this wonderful change by degrees, and, on the 12th of Nov., 1839, they issued a warrant for a temporary measure, fixing the rate of a single postage for half an ounce weight at 4*d*. for all places in the united kingdom which had previously paid more than that sum; the inferior rates to remain undisturbed; and all letters to be charged by weight—1 oz.; two postages; 2 oz., four postages, and so on, adding two postages for every ounce up to 16 ounces, the greatest weight allowed, excepting to privileged persons.

In the early part of the year 1840, the uniform penny rate was brought into operation. It was the suggestion of Mr. Rowland Hill, originally a schoolmaster, to whom and to Colonel Maberly, the secretary of the post-office, the public are indebted for the prompt manner in which the intentions of the legislature were carried into effect. As it is generally admitted that postage is not a proper source of revenue, it will be very satisfactory to know that, by the returns made to the 10th of October, 1840, a surplus already accrues to the public revenue, and the number of letters is gradually increasing.

RECEIVING HOUSES.—The principal post-office is in St.

Martin's Le Grand, where business was commenced in 1829; and there are four branch offices; viz., the old office in Lombard-street; Charing-cross; Old Cavendish-street (Oxford-street); and No. 108, Blackman-street, Borough. Besides these, there are branch metropolitan (formerly twopenny) post-offices, at 24, Cornhill; 21, Charing-cross; and 151, Oxford-street; but these latter do not receive general post letters. In addition to these offices, there are numerous houses at convenient distances from each other, appointed for receiving letters in all parts of the metropolis and its environs; and when the boxes are closed in the evening, a considerable number of postmen, ringing bells, are employed for about half an hour in collecting letters, upon payment of a penny each Omnibuses convey the postmen to their districts every morning.

LETTERS.

Prepaid Letters.—The following rates of postage are now charged upon all prepaid letters addressed to any part of the united kingdom, including the Channel Islands and the Isle of Man:—

Not exceeding	Half an ounce	in weight,	One penny.
—	One ounce	—	Twopence.
—	Two ounces	—	Fourpence.
—	Three ounces	—	Sixpence.

and Twopence for every additional ounce up to sixteen ounces.

Unpaid Letters are charged double the above rates, and letters upon which the full and proper rate has not been paid are also charged double.

It is particularly requested by the authorities, that letters may be *fully* and *legibly* addressed, and posted as *early* as convenient.

Manner of Prepayment.—Letters may be prepaid, either by paying the postage in money, or by using a stamped cover, or labels, to the amount of the postage. These covers and labels are sold by all postmasters and receivers of letters, as well as at most stationers' shops. Labels, if used, should be placed at the upper right hand corner, in front of the letter; and if the cover or labels are not of sufficient amount, double postage will be charged on the deficiency.

Foreign, colonial, and ship letters, must be paid, or stamps used covering the full amount of the postage, otherwise they will be returned.

Exceptions.—No letters or packets above the weight of

sixteen ounces can be transmitted by post, except addresses to the Queen, petitions to parliament, parliamentary papers, letters to and from the public departments, deeds, in covers, open at the ends, and letters beyond the sea. Bankers' parcels, specially delivered at the general office, are despatched under particular regulations. Packets above sixteen ounces are sent to the dead-letter office. These regulations also apply to the *local* parts throughout the kingdom.

Members of either house of parliament are not now entitled to receive letters free; but petitions, if open at the ends, may be forwarded without charge. Addresses to the Queen pass free.

Seamen and soldiers, while employed on her Majesty's service, can receive and forward letters to and from most places, under certain regulations, upon payment of one penny in advance.

TWOPENNY POST-OFFICES SUPPRESSED.—The general and twopenny posts are now consolidated; and all letters, may be put in at all the receiving houses. Unpaid letters, and those bearing stamps, must be dropped into the letter-box. Paid letters taken into the office.

HOURS FOR POSTING.—Letters and newspapers for the general post must be put in at the receiving houses before five o'clock in the afternoon, or they will not go the same day, but the branch offices at Charing-cross, Old Cavendish-street, and Blackman-street, Borough, receive letters until three quarters past five, P.M.; and at the general post-office, in St. Martin's-le-grand, and the office, in Lombard-street, letters may be put in until six o'clock. Letters for the morning mails are received only until eight o'clock in the morning.

Newspapers are received at the latter office until half-past seven, upon payment of a half-penny.

By a late regulation, inland letters, the postage on which is paid by stamps affixed to them, also Foreign, Colonial, and Ship letters, on which the postage is to be paid, will be received at the branch offices at Charing-cross, Old Cavendish-street, and the Borough, until a quarter past six P.M.; at Lombard-street until half-past six, and at the General Office, St. Martin's-le-Grand, till seven o'clock P.M. To take advantage of this regulation, an extra penny must be paid with each letter; and at all the offices except that in St. Martin's-le-Grand, that extra penny must be paid by an extra stamp affixed, and not in money; but at the latter office it may be paid either in money or a stamp, as it may be also on Foreign, Colonial, or Ship letters.

COLONIAL LETTERS.—The uniform single rate on all letters conveyed by packet between the united kingdom and the British colonies and possessions, will be one shilling.

SHIP-LETTERS conveyed outwards, in sealed bags, to foreign parts, per ship or private vessel, not exceeding half an ounce, are chargeable with a uniform rate of 8*d.* They must be marked "SHIP-LETTER."

FOREIGN LETTERS.—Letters to most foreign countries must be prepaid; but prepayment is optional to the following places:—British North America, the West Indies, the Bahamas, Demerara, Gibraltar, Malta, Greece, Egypt, St. Domingo, France, &c.

FOREIGN POST DAYS.

Lisbon, Madeira, Spain, Portugal, and Gibraltar, every Saturday.

Malta, Greece, Corfu, Egypt, and India, the last day of every month, and on the Saturday nearest to the 15th of every month, via Falmouth. *Closed mails* are also made up on the 4th of each month, and despatched via Marseilles. Letters may also be sent by the French packets, which leave Marseilles on the 1st, 11th, and 21st of each month.

Madeira, Brazil, and Buenos Ayres, the first Tuesday in each month.

British America, Bermuda, and the United States, on the 18th and 3rd of every month, except November, December, January, and February, then on the 3rd only.

Jamaica, Leeward Islands, Carthagena, Hayti, Porto, La Guayra, and Cuba, the 1st and 15th of every month.

Mexico and Havannah, the 15th of every month.

Spain, France, Italy, Sardinia, and Turkey, daily.

Holland, the Netherlands, Germany, Switzerland, Prussia, Denmark, Russia, Hamburg, Norway, and Sweden, every Tuesday and Friday.

The return of the Packets is calculated thus:—To and from Jamaica, 12 weeks; America, 5 weeks; Leeward Islands, 12 weeks; Brazils, 20 weeks; Mexico, 18 weeks; Gibraltar, 20 days.

From August to January, inclusive, the Packet touches at Pernambuco and Bahia, on her outward passage to Rio de Janeiro; the other six months on her homeward passage.

Letters for places abroad to which there are no post-office packets, are forwarded in sealed ship-letter mails, by vessels sailing from London or the outports. The postage, which must be previously paid, is 8*d*., not exceeding half an ounce.

Foreign letters are received on Tuesdays and Fridays, at the branch offices, Charing-cross, Old Cavendish-street, and 108, Blackman-street, until eight o'clock in the evening; and at St. Martin's-le-Grand and the office in Lombard-street, until ten; and at St. Martin's-le-Grand only until eleven, upon payment of one penny, and until half-past eleven, upon payment of sixpence.

The French post-office allow only a quarter of an ounce for a single rate. Letters to foreign parts should be written on very thin paper, known by the name of "foreign post."

DELIVERIES.—The morning delivery of general post letters received from all parts of the country (inclusive of foreign, ship, and packet letters) commences in the districts within three miles of St. Martin's-le-Grand a little earlier than half-past nine o'clock, and is completed in about two hours, except on Monday, when the number of letters being one-third greater, it is usually delayed from half an hour to an hour. Foreign mails, and morning mails, which are later in the day, are sent out two hours afterwards.

MORNING MAILS are despatched from the general post-office at nine and ten o'clock to Lancaster, Preston, Liverpool, Manchester, Cheltenham, Dovor, Portsmouth, Southampton, Brighton, Dublin, Edinburgh, and Glasgow; and to other places in the route to these towns. Some idea may be formed of the speed of post-office conveyance from the fact that letters for Dublin, Edinburgh, and Glasgow, are delivered in these towns by the middle of the day following that on which they leave London.

The receiving-houses will be open till seven for newspapers, and till eight for letters; the branch offices half an hour later; at the chief office and in Lombard-street another quarter of an hour.

REGISTRATION OF LETTERS.—Frequent frauds having been committed by the non-delivery of money letters, a system of registration has been lately adopted, affording a security to the public which did not previously exist. Upon payment of a fee of one shilling, in addition to the proper rate of postage, letters containing money, bills, or drafts, may be registered at the various receiving-houses, and a printed receipt obtained for them; but these letters must be taken to the office half an hour earlier than usual; and if sent by the twopenny post, an hour before the next delivery.

Foreign, colonial, or ship-letters' registration, will not, however, extend beyond the post of despatch. Letters, whether containing articles of value or not, may be registered.

MONEY-ORDERS.—To prevent the loss of money sent in letters, for which the post-office is not accountable, and for the convenience of persons remitting small sums to any distance, by a recent regulation, the commission formerly chargeable upon money-orders was reduced to *threepence* upon sums not exceeding two pounds, and *sixpence* for sums exceeding two and under five pounds. No order is given for sums above this amount. These orders may now be obtained not only at the chief office, but at the branch offices, and of receivers appointed in the suburbs, and the various villages near London.

These orders are payable to the persons only to whom they are addressed, excepting through the hands of a banker. They are a great public convenience, and have increased threefold since the reduction of the fees.

OVERCHARGES upon the postage of letters are returned upon exhibiting the overcharged letter between the hours of ten and five, at the window in the hall of the general post-office, or by giving it to the letter-carrier of the district.

MISDIRECTED LETTERS are inserted in lists, and publicly exhibited in the hall of the chief office for a certain time, previous to their being placed in the dead-letter office or destroyed.

NEWSPAPERS.

NEWSPAPERS for any part of the United Kingdom (except the metropolitan district) pass free; but must be put up in a cover open at the sides; and if containing anything enclosed or concealed, is liable to treble postage according to its weight: and any person knowingly sending a newspaper with any writing or enclosure, may be prosecuted for a misdemeanour. In case of removal, they may be re-directed and sent free of extra charge.

Newspapers to the British Colonies may be sent, per post-office packets, free of postage, and to any other foreign stations to which there are post-office packets, for twopence, which must be paid when they are posted, provided that they be sent within seven days from the time of publication. The free postage extends to Antigua, the Bahamas, Barbadoes, Berbice, Bermuda, Canada, Halifax, Heligoland, Honduras, Jamaica, Malta, Montserrat, Nevis, New Brunswick, Newfoundland, Nova Scotia, Quebec, St. Kitts, St. Lucia, St. Vincent, Tobago, Tortola, Trinidad, &c. &c.

Newspapers from the British Colonies, brought by government packets, are delivered in any part of the British dominions free of postage. Those brought by private ships are liable to a charge of twopence each.

Newspapers to France, Spain, Denmark, Greece, Hamburgh, Hayti, Peru, Brazil, Buenos Ayres, Honduras, and to some other places abroad, may be sent free; but to most countries a payment of twopence is required in advance.

Newspapers coming from France are liable to the charge of one halfpenny; but from most other countries they are liable to a charge of twopence.

THE METROPOLITAN (OR TWOPENNY) POST.

The metropolitan delivery is divided into two districts—town and country. The London district is comprised within a circle of three miles from the general office in St. Martin's-le-Grand, whilst the country district extends to all places within twelve miles of the same office. Letters for the London delivery are despatched from the receiving-houses to the chief office at eight, ten, and twelve o'clock in the morning, and two, four, six, and eight o'clock in the afternoon. The country delivery takes place at eight and twelve in the morning, and two and six in the afternoon. From 24, Cornhill, 21, Charing-cross, and 151, Oxford-street (or *first-class* receiving-houses), letters are forwarded half an hour later, and from the chief office one hour later than at the other (or *second-class*) receiving-houses.

The same weights, rates, and regulations, are observed as in the general post.

Newspapers are charged the same as letters.

Letters put in on Saturday evening in town, are delivered in the country district on Sunday morning, but letters put into the country district-boxes are not delivered in town till Monday morning.

The date-stamp, or, if there are two, that having the latest hour, shews also the time of the day at which the letters were despatched for delivery from the principal offices.

Any irregularity in the delivery of letters communicated to the comptroller will be duly attended to; and if the covers bearing the date-stamp are produced, they will assist materially in discovering where the fault lies.

Illegal Conveyance of Letters.—By 1st of Victoria, c. 36, sec. 2, former acts are confirmed, with the following penalties:—By 9th of Anne, c. 10, "Any persons illegally conveying letters incur a penalty of 5*l.* for every offence, and 100*l*. for every week the practice is continued." And by 42d of George III. cap. 81, "The sender also incurs a penalty of 5*l*. for every offence, with full costs of suit."

MARKETS, &c.—SUPPLY OF PROVISIONS.

SMITHFIELD-MARKET is famous for the sale of bullocks, sheep, lambs, calves, and hogs, every Monday and Friday: on the latter day there is also a market for horses. The average number of oxen sold at Smithfield annually is 157,739; of sheep and lambs, 1,500,000; of calves, 21,000; of pigs, 60,000: the value of which is estimated at 10,000,000*l*.

NEW SMITHFIELD, Ball's Pond. This market was first established by Mr. Perkins, to obviate the necessity of driving cattle through the crowded streets of the metropolis. It is 800 feet square—upwards of 15 acres of land. It is capable of containing 4000 oxen and 40,000 sheep. It is surrounded by covered stalls, and in the open area has ranges of pens. At the entrance is a handsome building for the offices. This market is not in use.

NEW LEATHER AND SKIN-MARKET, BERMONDSEY. This new market has attracted a great portion of the commerce of Leadenhall.

The HAY-MARKET has been removed from the street of that name to Cumberland-market, Regent's-park.

PORTMAN-MARKET, Edgware-road.

LEADENHALL-MARKET is the greatest in London for the sale of country-killed meat, and was, till lately, the only skin and leather-market within the bills of mortality.

NEWGATE-MARKET is the second great place for country-killed meat; there is also a common market every day for all kinds of provisions. The fruit and vegetables have been removed to Farringdon-market.

At both Leadenhall and Newgate markets are sold pigs and poultry killed in the country, together with fresh butter, eggs, &c., to an astonishing amount. The last three markets supply the butchers of London and its vicinity almost entirely, and pretty generally to the distance of twelve miles and upwards, with meat from the country.

FARRINGDON or FLEET-MARKET, for the sale of butchers'-meat, fruit, and vegetables, was originally formed in 1737, on the site of Fleet-ditch. It was removed to its present situation, between Shoe-lane and Farringdon-street, November 20,

1829. The market is in the form of a quadrangle, 232 feet by 150, and covers an acre and a half. The purchase of the ground and houses taken down amounted to 200,000*l.*, and the building cost about 30,000*l.* An avenue, consisting of a double row of shops, extends round three sides of the quadrangle. It is built of brick, 25 feet in height to the tie beams, and is illuminated by semicircular windows. The chief entrance to the market consists of two gates for waggons, and two for foot-passengers, besides large doors to the avenue.

COVENT-GARDEN-MARKET, for fruit, flowers, and vegetables, was re-constructed in 1829-30, from designs by Mr. Fowler. There are three ranges of shops, running from east to west. On the north side of the middle range is the fruit-market, and on the south side the green-market. The other two ranges form the north and south boundaries: each of these ranges contains 38 fruit-shops. The exterior elevation of the north and south ranges is embellished with a colonnade of granite pillars 12 feet in height, placed eight feet from the front of the shops, so as to form a covered walk. The east front of the market, towards Great Russell-street, presents a colonnade, nearly three times the breadth of the lateral ones, above which is a terrace and conservatory. There are three passages, or alleys, which perforate the area longitudinally, and three which cross it.

At BILLINGSGATE is the fish-market, which is principally supplied by fishing-smacks and boats coming from the sea up the river Thames, and partly with fresh fish by land-carriage from every distance within the limits of England and part of Wales: this market is held daily.

NEW HUNGERFORD-MARKET.—This elegant and convenient structure was begun in 1831, and completed in 1833, from the designs of Mr. Fowler, the architect of Covent-garden-market. It had long been a subject of complaint, that in this vast metropolis there existed but one fish-market whence the minor marts derived their supplies. To remedy this evil, and to provide a general market for the convenience of the west end of the town, a company was formed which, after considerable opposition and delay, obtained an act of parliament incorporating them, with powers to remove the ruinous old buildings which had so long encumbered that neighbourhood, to make a considerable embankment into the river, and to carry the present plan into effect.

It consists of three grand divisions; the upper one forming

HUNGERFORD MARKET.
River Front.

HUNGERFORD MARKET.
Strand Front.

a quadrangle of 140 feet by 70 in the clear, flanked by colonnades, with dwellings over, and shops underneath. The centre, or great hall, is 188 feet by 123, and is formed by four rows of granite columns, with arches springing from them to support the roof, the centre part or nave having an upper tier of open arches for the admission of light and air. On each side of the hall is a line of shops. The east side of the hall and upper quadrangle are appropriated exclusively to the sale of fruit and vegetables, and the west side to butchers'-meat, poultry, eggs, butter, &c. The lower quadrangle contains the fish-market, the descent to which is formed by a spacious flight of open steps, and four staircases under cover. It is 130 feet by 70 in the clear, with double colonnades at the sides, the lower ones containing the fishmongers' shops, and the upper ones forming galleries, corresponding with the colonnades of the upper quadrangle in a straight line, including the hall, of 500 feet in length, and connected at the river end by a terrace, so as to allow an uninterrupted walk round the whole of the building. The river-front is composed of two handsome square buildings, appropriated as taverns, united by a colonnade with a terrace over, whence and from the flat roofs of the taverns, there are very fine views of the most interesting architectural features of the metropolis.

The CORN-MARKET is held in Mark-lane every Monday, Wednesday, and Friday; but the chief business is done on Monday.

At Whitechapel, Smithfield, and the New Haymarket, hay and straw are sold three times a-week, and the metropolis is further supplied with the same articles by a market at Paddington, and by another market for hay and straw held four times weekly in Southwark.

Various other markets are held in different parts of the metropolis, such as NEWPORT-MARKET for butchers'-meat; BOROUGH-MARKET for butchers'-meat and vegetables, Borough Hay-market, Hop-market, Clare-market, Clarence-market, Cumberland-market, Fitzroy-market, Grosvenor-market, Hoxton-market, James-market, Hay-market, Lumber-court for fish, Mortimer-market Tottenham-court-road, Oxford-market, Red Lion-market, St. Luke's, St. George's-market, Shadwell-market, Spitalfields-market, &c.

The WEEKLY MARKETS held in Middlesex amount to nine, independently of those of the metropolis:—namely, at Barnet, on Monday morning; Southall and Finchley, on Wednesday;

Uxbridge, Brentford, Hounslow, and Edgeware, on Thursday; Staines, on Friday; and Enfield on Saturday. At Uxbridge-market a great deal of corn is sold; and there is a large public granary over the market-place, for the purpose of depositing it from one week to another. At Hounslow-market there is a considerable show of fat cattle; and those not disposed of there are sent on to London.

The quantity of LIVE STOCK in and about London is probably less than in any other country, in proportion to the number of acres, with the exception of the cows kept for supplying the metropolis with MILK. The entire number kept by the London cow-keepers is estimated at about 9600; *viz.*, 7900 in Middlesex, 801 in Kent, and 899 in Surrey. The quantity of milk yielded by each cow has been averaged at nine quarts a-day at least; but the total is about 7,900,000 gallons annual produce, from which some deductions must be made for sucklings.

The price at which the milk is sold to the retail-dealer (who agrees with the cow-keeper for the produce of a certain number of cows, and takes the labour of milking them upon himself) varies from 1*s.* 8*d.* to 1*s.* 10*d.* for eight quarts, according to the distance from town: but taking the medium, *i. e.* 1*s.* 9*d.*, the whole amount will be (allowing for sucklings) 328,000*l.* In delivering the milk to the consumer, a vast increase takes place, not only in the price, but also in the quantity, as it is greatly adulterated with water: by this practice, and the additional charge made for cream, the sum paid by the public has been calculated to be as much more, *viz.* 656,000*l.*; nay, one writer has said the advance or profit is 150 per cent!! The milk is conveyed to the consumers in tin vessels called pails, which are principally carried about by women, mostly robust Welsh girls: it is distributed twice daily through all parts of the town.

The annual consumption of BUTTER in London amounts to 11,000 tons, and that of CHEESE to 13,000 tons. The quantity of POULTRY annually consumed is worth from 70,000*l.* to 80,000*l.*, exclusive of game, the supply of which depends on the season. The consumption of wheat annually amounts to 2,000,000 quarters, four-fifths of which are made into bread, forming upwards of 60,000,000 quartern loaves. Vegetables and fruit per annum, 1,000,000*l*; wine, 65,000 pipes: spirits, 11,000,000 gallons.

The Kitchen-Gardens

In the immediate vicinity of the metropolis are estimated at 10,000 acres, about 2000 of which are wholly cultivated by the spade. Shortly after Christmas, when the weather is open, radishes, spinach, onions, and all other seed-crops are sown; and as soon afterwards as the season will permit, which is generally in February, the same ground is planted with cauliflowers from the frames, as thick as if no other crop then had possession of the ground. The radishes, &c., are soon sent to market, and when the cauliflowers are so far advanced as to be earthed up, sugar-loaf cabbages are planted; when these are marketed, the stalks are taken up, and the ground cleared and planted with endive and celery. The average produce of these gardens is supposed to amount to 200*l.* annually per acre, the profit of which is calculated to be very great in successful seasons. The annual produce of all the garden-ground cultivated to supply the London markets is estimated by Mr. Middleton at 645,000*l.*, which, with 400,000*l.* produced by the fruit-gardens, makes a total of 1,045,000*l.* for the consumption of the metropolis and its environs in fruits and vegetables only.

The Fruit-Gardens

Of Middlesex, exclusive of those attached to private houses and gentlemen's villas, are supposed to occupy about 3000 acres, principally situated in the vicinity of Kensington, Hammersmith, Brentford, Isleworth, and Twickenham. They furnish constant employment, on an average, to about ten or twelve persons per acre, men, women, and children; but during the fruit season, this number is increased to about forty, the produce of whose labour, in their various occupations, is thought to amount to 300,000*l.* annually; and to this another 100,000*l.* may be added for the produce of the fruit sent to the metropolis from the surrounding counties; the whole making a total of 400,000*l.* The fruit-gardens have what they call an upper and under crop growing on the same ground at one time. First, the ground is stocked with apples, pears, cherries, plums, walnuts, &c., like a complete orchard, which they call the upper crop; secondly, it is fully planted with raspberries, gooseberries, currants, strawberries, and all such fruit, shrubs, and herbs, as are known to sustain the shade and drip from the trees above them with the least injury; this they term the under crop. Some of these gardens have walls, which are completely clothed with wall fruits, such as nectarines, peaches, apricots, plums, and various others. In order to increase the quantity of shelter and warmth in autumn, they raise earthen banks of about three feet high, laid to a slope of about 45 degrees to the sun; on these slopes they plant endive in September, and near the bottom of them, from October till Christmas, they drill a row of peas: by this means the endive is preserved from rotting, and, as well as the peas, comes to maturity nearly as early as if it had been planted in borders under a wall. Besides the quantity of fruits raised from these gardens, the London markets receive additional supplies from the gardens on the Surrey side of the Thames; and much is also brought from Kent, Essex, Berks, and other counties: these supplies amount to upwards of one-third of the whole consumption of the metropolis.

The Nursery-Grounds

In the vicinity of London are presumed to occupy about 1500 acres, lying principally in the neighbourhoods of Chelsea, Brompton, Kensington, Hackney, Dalston, Bow, and Mile-End. The nurserymen spare no pains in collecting the choicest sort and the greatest variety of fruit-trees, ornamental shrubs, and flowers, from every quarter of the globe, and they bring them to a high degree of perfection. The taste for elegant and rare plants has become so prevalent of late years, that the rearing them for sale now forms a considerable object in commerce; and the English gardeners have attained such celebrity for the cultivation of exotics, that a great exportation of these articles takes place to France, Spain, Portugal, Italy, Russia, and other countries.

ALE AND PORTER.

There are 108 brewers in the metropolis, besides 22 licensed victuallers who brew their own beer. There are also 1017 persons licensed to retail beer, of whom 129 brew. Retailers of spirits and beer, upwards of 10,000.

The quantity of porter brewed annually by the twelve principal houses in London is about 1,400,000 barrels; and the six principal ale-brewers annually make upwards of 80,000 barrels of ale. The annual consumption of beer is about 2,000,000 barrels of 36 gallons each.

SUPPLY OF FISH.

That there should be only one fish-market, that of Billingsgate, to supply the metropolis, is amazing: but that fish should frequently be as scarce and as extravagantly high-priced as if we lived 100 or 150 miles in the interior, will excite no astonishment after this statement.

The following is the quantity of fish brought to London during a recent year. Fresh salmon, 45,446; maids, plaice, and skate, 50,754 bushels; turbot, 87,958; fresh cod fish, 447,130; herrings, 3,366,407; haddocks, 482,493; sprats, 60,789 bushels; mackerel, 3,076,700; lobsters, 1,954,600; soles, 8672 bushels; whitings, 90,604; and eels, 1500 cwt. The number of vessels entered at the office in the same year was 3827. The annual consumption of London is reckoned at 1,000,000*l*. sterling.

COALS.

There is a Coal-Exchange in Thames-street, which is principally occupied by the great dealers, who, having a sort of monopoly of the market, the consumers have no control over it. Above 2,000,000 tons per annum are consumed in Middlesex and Surrey: of this quantity at least two-thirds are for domestic purposes.

SUPPLY OF CATTLE.

The number of HORSES kept in Middlesex amounts to upwards of 30,000, yet very few remarkable for their quality are bred here. The cart-horses, which are compact and bony, are purchased at the different fairs in the neighbouring counties, and at the repositories and stables of the several dealers in the metropolis. Many of the horses employed by the brewers, distillers, and carmen of London, are purchased by the country dealers at two or three years old, and sold by them to the farmers of Wiltshire, &c., who keep them till they are about five years old, when they sell them to the London dealers at high prices, as they are then of a proper age for constant work. The coach and saddle-horses are principally bred in Yorkshire, and brought up from that and other counties by the dealers. The draught-horses belonging to the brewers, distillers, coal-merchants, &c., are scarcely to be equalled as to strength and figure.

Hogs are kept in considerable numbers, but chiefly by the malt-distillers, for whom they are purchased lean, at a large market held on Finchley-common, and to which they are brought from Shropshire and other distant counties; great numbers of fatted hogs are also bought for the hog-butcheries about London; and the bacon cured here is but little inferior to that brought from Wilts and Yorkshire. Much poultry is reared in Middlesex, but chiefly for home consumption; and many pigeons are also bred in this county. Rabbits are bred in and about London, and are sold to the poulterers, who by this means supply the market at those seasons when wild or warren-rabbits cannot be had.

Fairs and Markets.

Great facilities are afforded to internal commerce in England by the establishment of fairs and markets for the sale of commodities of every description. The sovereign is the sole judge where fairs and markets ought to be kept; and therefore, if he grant a market to be established in a place which happens not to be convenient for the country, yet the subjects can go to no other; and if they do, the owner of the place where they meet is liable to an action at the suit of the grantee of the market. The law forbids the holding of markets and fairs on Sundays and the solemn holydays, and declares that they shall not be kept open beyond the time specified in their charters, on pain of forfeiting double the value of the things sold. The grant of a fair or market includes, without express words, the right of establishing a court of *pie poudré*, and of appointing a clerk of the market, who is to receive reasonable fees for marking and allowing weights and measures. These fairs are generally accompanied by the exhibition of plays, drolls, rarities, and a general merriment, which render them the delight of the lower classes of society.

The only fair in London is that of Bartholomew, held in Smithfield on the 3rd of September, which lasts three days. It has been suggested to remedy the flagrant evils of this antique nuisance by establishing a similar recreation during the longest days in summer in Hyde Park.

Railways.

In consequence of the numerous fatal accidents which have recently happened on railways, a meeting of delegates, consisting of directors, engineers, and managers, was held in December, 1840, at Birmingham, for the purpose of a general conference. The parties present were the representatives of upwards of 1200 miles of railway, worth considerably above 50,000,000*l.*; and, probably, a meeting was never held at which a larger amount of property was represented. The directors, fully aware of the grave responsibility which attaches to them, and the obligation under which they lie to adopt all judicious and practicable expedients for insuring the safety, accommodation, and comfort of the public, after many hours' deliberation, agreed to certain regulations, and an uniform system of signals, applicable to all railways, by which means, if carried into operation, an efficient body of men will be disciplined and trained, whose services will be available on any line. It is to be hoped that these rules, aided by such improved arrangement and mechanical adaptations as a more matured experience may suggest, will amply accomplish the desired object.

There are no fixed hours at which the trains uniformly leave the capital. The departures are announced by public advertisement, or by handbill to be had at the principal coach-offices throughout London. Independent of the public conveyances, omnibusses from the principal inns convey passengers to and from the different stations.

In order to avoid confusion, passengers are recommended, especially if they have much luggage, to be at the station a quarter of an hour before the time fixed for starting, as the strictest punctuality is observed.

Parcels are received at all the principal coach-offices.

When carriage-trucks and horse-boxes are required, notice should be given the day previous.

The London and Birmingham.

The terminus is near Euston-square, where a noble Doric entrance has been constructed from designs by Mr. Hardwick. From Euston-square to Chalk-farm the train is drawn by ropes, which are worked by a powerful stationary engine. This railway is 114½ miles in length. From Birmingham, trains proceed to Manchester and Liverpool, and to Chester and Birkenhead.

This railway connects London with Coventry, Leicester, Derby, Sheffield, Leeds, York, Darlington, Selby, Wakefield, Halifax, and Bolton, in a northerly direction; with Preston, Lancaster, and Wyre-harbour, on the north-west coast; with Hull, on the north-east coast; communicates with the Great Western, running south through Worcester, Cheltenham, and Gloucester. Directly or indirectly it unites with the following railways: the Grand Junction, the Chester and Crewe, the Birmingham and Derby, the Midland Counties, the North Midland, the Leeds, the York, the Selby and Hull, the Manchester and Leeds, the Manchester and Liverpool, the Manchester and Bolton, the Bolton and Preston, the Preston and Wyre, the Preston and Lancaster, and the Birmingham, Gloucester, Cheltenham, and Great Western Union railway. The stations near London are—Harrow, Watford, King's Langley, Boxmoor, Berkhampstead, Tring, Aylesbury, &c.

The mail train starts three-quarters past 8 morning, and three-quarters past 8 evening.

London and Bristol (the Great Western).

The terminus is at the Grand Junction-road, Paddington. A branch, midway between Wallingford and Wantage, about ten miles in length, will lead to Oxford. The stations are Ealing, Hanwell, Southall, West Drayton, Slough, Maidenhead, Twyford, Reading, &c.

London and Southampton, or South Western.

The terminus is at Nine-Elms, Vauxhall, to which, besides the usual conveyances, steamboats proceed hourly from all parts on the river. It passes through Kingston, Basingstoke, and Winchester. It is 77 miles in length. The branch to Portsmouth will begin about 5 miles north of Southampton. The steamers to the Isle of Wight, Portsmouth, Jersey, Guernsey, Havre, St. Malo, &c., await the arrival of the trains. The stations near London are, Wandsworth, Wimbledon, Kingston, Esher, Walton, Weybridge, &c.

London and Brighton, by Croydon.

The terminus is in Tooley-street, adjoining the Greenwich railroad, London-bridge. The stations are, New Cross, Forest-hill, Sydenham, Penge, Anerley, Norwood, and Croydon. A branch from this railway will connect London with Tunbridge-Wells, Ashford, Folkstone, and Dover.

S^T PAULS CATHEDRAL.

London and Greenwich.

The terminus is near St. Thomas's Hospital. This line is constructed upon brick arches, and is three miles and three quarters in length. There is a station at Deptford.

London and Blackwall.

The terminii are in the Minories and Fenchurch-street. It is three miles and a half in length. The trains are drawn by means of ropes attached to stationary engines at each extremity of the line. The stations are Shadwell, Stepney, Limehouse, West India Docks, Poplar, and Blackwall, from whence steam-vessels are constantly starting for the fashionable watering-places.

Eastern Counties Railway.

The terminus is in Shoreditch. This railway is open as far as Brentwood, and proceeding with celerity. It will connect London with Romford, Chelmsford, Ipswich, Norwich, and Yarmouth. It is expected that a branch from this railway, near Romford, will connect London with Thames-haven-dock, to be formed a few miles north-west of the Nore, thereby avoiding the circuitous and dangerous navigation of the river. The stations are, Stratford, Ilford, Romford, and Brentwood, &c.

Northern and Eastern Railway.

The terminus is the same as the preceding. The line is open for about twenty miles, as far as Broxbourne, and going rapidly on to completion. The stations are, Leabridge, Tottenham, Edmonton, Ponder's-end, and Waltham-cross.

Iron Steam-boats start every quarter of an hour from London-Bridge to Blackwall, and from London-Bridge to Vauxhall, calling at all the intermediate stairs and bridges. Charge, fourpence each passenger.

CHAPTER VI.

PUBLIC BUILDINGS; INCLUDING CHURCHES, PALACES, PUBLIC OFFICES, NOBLEMEN'S RESIDENCES, SQUARES, BRIDGES, ETC.

ST. PAUL'S CATHEDRAL.

THIS magnificent building has obtained such celebrity, even amongst foreigners, that in an enumeration of the religious edifices of Europe, St. Paul's of London is always mentioned immediately after St. Peter's at Rome.

It stands on an eminence to the north of the river Thames,

on the same spot where in majestic pomp stood the ancient Gothic cathedral so eloquently described by Dugdale and Hollar, and which perished in the memorable conflagration of 1666. The best authority that exists illustrative of the origin of this church, is its great restorer, Sir Christopher Wren. His opinion, that there had been a church on this spot built by the Christians in the time of the Romans, was confirmed; and when he searched for the foundations for his own design, he met with those of the original *presbyterium*, or semicircular chancel of the old church. They consisted only of Kentish rubble stone, artfully worked, and consolidated with exceedingly hard mortar, in the Roman manner, much excelling the superstructure. He explodes the notion of there having been a temple of Diana.

The first church is supposed to have been destroyed during the Dioclesian persecution, and to have been rebuilt in the reign of Constantine. This was demolished by the pagan Saxons, and restored in 1603 by Sebert, a petty prince ruling in these parts under Ethelbert king of Kent, the first Christian monarch of the Saxon race. It was destroyed by the great conflagration in 1086; after which Mauritius, then bishop of London, commenced the magnificent edifice which immediately preceded the present cathedral. Of such magnitude was the building, that neither that bishop nor his successor, De Belmeis, was able to complete the undertaking, though each of them presided twenty years, and expended great sums in the prosecution of it. The latter prelate appropriated the whole revenue of his bishopric to the carrying on of the work. After his death, the further building was for some time interrupted; and the eastern part, or choir, was burnt in 1135. At what period it was restored is uncertain. The grand ceremony of its consecration was performed in 1240. Large additions were afterwards made to the structure; and it was not till 1315 that the church was entirely completed, being 225 years from the time of its foundation by Mauritius.

The noble *subterranean* church of St. Faith was begun in 1257. It was supported by three rows of massy clustered pillars, with ribs diverging from them to support the roof. This was the parish-church. This *undercroft*, as buildings of this sort were called, contained several chantries and monuments. Dugdale relates, that it extended under part of the choir, and the structure eastward, and was supported by three rows of large and massy pillars; a print of it accompanies the description given by that great antiquary. No part is now left of this or of any other ancient crypt, according to Pennant.

The ancient cathedral will ever be regarded as one of the great works of architecture of the middle ages. Pennant says it was a most beautiful Gothic. Its dimensions far exceeded other religious edifices in this country; and it is represented by historians as equally pre-eminent in magnificence and splendour of ornament. In the reign of James I. this cathedral having fallen into decay, a royal commission was issued for its repair; but nothing of consequence was done till the advancement of Laud to the see of London in the succeeding reign. This prelate exerted himself zealously in favour of the neglected building. A subscription was collected to the amount of 101,330*l.* 4*s.* 8*d.*, and Inigo Jones was appointed to superintend the undertaking. He commenced his operations in 1633, and the work went rapidly on till the breaking out of the civil war, which threw all things into confusion; and the parliament confiscated the unexpended money and materials. At the restoration, the repairs were again commenced; but after much labour and expense, the great conflagration of 1666 destroyed the chief part of the building, and irreparably damaged the remainder.

The famous PAUL'S CROSS, which stood before that cathedral, was a pulpit formed of wood, mounted upon steps of stone, and covered with lead, from which the most eminent divines were appointed to preach every Sunday in the forenoon. To this place the court, the mayor, the aldermen, and principal citizens, used to resort. It was in use as early as 1259, and was appropriated not only to instruct mankind by preaching, but to every purpose political or ecclesiastical:—for giving force to oaths, for promulgating laws, &c.; and for the private ends of the ambitious, as well as for the defaming of those who had incurred the displeasure of crowned heads. *Jane Shore*, the charitable and merry concubine of Edward IV., and, after his death, of his favourite the unfortunate Lord Hastings, was brought before this cross in 1483, divested of all her splendour.

After several ineffectual attempts to repair the ancient fabric, every vestige of the original building was demolished. The first stone of the present cathedral was laid on the 21st of June, 1675; and the design was prosecuted with such diligence, that within ten years the walls of the choir and side-aisles were finished, together with the circular porticoes on the north and south sides. The last or highest stone of the building was laid at the top of the lantern in 1710; and shortly after, the queen and both houses of parliament attended Divine service in the new cathedral. The whole structure was thus completed in thirty-five years, by one architect, Sir Christopher Wren, and one master-mason, Mr. Thomas Strong, and while one prelate, Dr. Henry Compton, filled the see of London.

It is built of Portland stone, in the form of a cross, and is divided by two rows of massy pillars into a nave and side-aisles. At the extremities of the principal transept are also semicircular projections for porticoes; and at the angles of the cross are square projections, which, besides containing staircases, vestries, &c., serve as buttresses to the dome.

The west front towards Ludgate-street is extremely noble. The portico forming the grand entrance consists of twelve Corinthian columns, with an upper portico of eight columns of the Composite order, supporting a sculptured pediment. The entablature represents the history of St. Paul's conversion in basso-relievo, by Francis Bird. On the centre of the pediment is a statue of St. Paul, and at the sides are statues of St. James, St. Peter, and the Four Evangelists. The whole rests on an elevated base, the ascent to which is formed by twenty-two steps of black marble.

At the N.W. and S.W. angles of the cathedral, two elegant turrets are erected, each terminating in a dome ornamented with a gilt pine-apple. The south turret contains the clock; the north turret, the belfry.

A semicircular portico, consisting of a dome supported by six Corinthian columns, leads to the great north door, or entrance to the transept, over which is an entablature containing the royal arms supported by angels. The south front of the cathedral corresponds with the north, excepting the entablature, which represents a phœnix rising from the flames—the performance of Gabriel Cibber. Underneath is the expressive word RESURGAM. The east end of the church is semicircular; it is ornamented with a variety of fine sculpture, particularly the cipher W. R. within a compartment of palm branches, surmounted by an imperial crown, in honour of the then reigning sovereign, King William III. The exterior of the walls consists of rustic works ornamented with two rows of pilasters, the lower of the Corinthian, and the upper of the Composite order. The dome, or cupola, rises in beautiful and majestic proportion where the great lines of the cross intersect each other. The dome is terminated by a lantern and globe; and on the summit of the whole is placed the emblem of the Christian faith.

The cathedral is surrounded by a cast-iron balustrade, which weighs about 200 tons, and cost upwards of 11,000*l*: this rests on a dwarf stone wall, and separates the churchyard from the street. Within this enclosure, facing Ludgate-street, is a marble statue of Queen Anne, holding in her hands the emblems of royalty, and accompanied by figures representing Great Britain, Ireland, France, and America. It was executed by Bird.

The interior of the cathedral is not so richly decorated as the exterior. The pavement consists of square slabs of black and white marble, placed alternately; and the floor of the altar is interspersed with porphyry.

A circular staircase within the S.W. pier leads by an easy ascent to the *Whispering-Gallery*, which encircles the lower part of the dome at the extreme edge of the cornice. From this situation, the view of the church, the cupola, and the lantern, is strikingly sublime; and here the paintings by Sir James Thornhill on the compartments of the dome are seen to the greatest advantage. These designs are illustrative of the most remarkable occurrences in St. Paul's life: his miraculous conversion near Damascus; St. Paul preaching before Sergius Paulus, with the Divine judgment upon Elymas the sorcerer; the reverence offered to Paul and Barnabas at Lystra by the priests of Jupiter; the imprisonment of Paul and Silas at Philippi, with the conversion of the gaoler; Paul preaching to the Athenians; the magic books of the Ephesians burnt; St. Paul's defence before Agrippa and Bernice; his shipwreck at Melita.

The *Whispering-Gallery* takes its name from the well-known reverberation of sounds; so that the softest whisper is accurately and loudly conveyed to the ear at the distance of 100 feet, the diameter of the dome in this part. If the door be shut forcibly, it produces a strong reverberation similar to thunder. The same staircase communicates with the galleries over the north and south aisles of the nave, containing the library and model-room.

The *Library* was furnished with a collection of books by Bishop Compton, whose portrait is preserved here; but the flooring, consisting of upwards of 2000 pieces of oak, is pointed out as the object most deserving the attention of a casual visiter. The corresponding room in the north gallery contains a model of the beautiful altar-piece intended by the architect to ornament the east end of the church; and a large model for this building in the style of a Grecian temple. This room contains also some of the funeral decorations used at the interment of lord Nelson.

The *clock-works* are well deserving the attention of the curious. The pendulum is 14 feet long, and the weight at the end is 1 cwt.; the dials on the outside are regulated by a smaller one within; the length of the minute-hands on the exterior dials is 8 feet, and the weight of each 75 pounds; the length of the hour-hands is 5 feet 5 inches, and the weight 44 pounds each; the diameter of the dials is 18 feet 10 inches, and the length of the hour figures 2 feet 2½ inches. The fine-toned *bell* which strikes the hours is clearly distinguishable from every other in the metropolis, and has been distinctly heard at the distance of 20 miles. It is about ten feet in diameter, and is said to weigh 4¼ tons. This bell is tolled on the death of any member of the royal family, of the lord-mayor, bishop of London, or dean of the cathedral.

The Ball and Cross surmounting the lantern, re-erected in 1822, are constructed, as to outline and dimensions, on the same plan as the originals; but the interior has been much improved by the substitution of copper and gun-metal bands for those of iron. The whole height of the copper-work, which weighs above 4 tons, is 27 feet. The iron spindle in the centre, and standards to strengthen the copper-work, weigh about three tons, forming a total weight of above seven tons. The old ball, which has been removed to the Colosseum, measuring 6 feet 2 inches in diameter, was made of fourteen pieces; whilst the new ball, measuring 6 feet, and weighing about half a ton without its ornaments or standards, is constructed of only two, a fair demonstration of the improved state of science. It is capable of containing eight persons. The old ball, including the spindle, standards, &c., weighed two tons and a half, and the cross one and a half. The ascent to the ball is formed by 616 steps, of which the first 280 lead to the whispering gallery, and the next 254 to the upper gallery.

About the year 1790 a scheme was suggested, and has succeeded, to break the monotonous uniformity of the architectural masses in the interior of the cathedral, by the introduction of MONUMENTS and STATUES in honour of the illustrious dead. The first erected was to the memory of John Howard; open to public inspection A.D. 1796. This statue is placed near the iron gate leading to the south aisle. It is the work of the late John Bacon, R.A., and represents the philanthropist in the act of trampling upon chains and fetters, while bearing in his right hand the key of a prison, and in his left a scroll, on which is engraved, *Plan for the Improvement of Prisons and Hospitals.* The eloquent inscription was written by the late Samuel Whitbread, Esq.

The monument in memory of Nelson was executed by Flaxman. The statue of lord Nelson, dressed in the pelisse received from the Grand Seignor, leans on an anchor. Beneath, on the right of the hero, Britannia directs the attention of young seamen to Nelson, their great example. The British lion on the other side guards the monument. On the cornice of the pedestal are the words Copenhagen, Nile, Trafalgar. The figures on the pedestal represent the North Sea, the German Ocean, the Nile, and the Mediterranean.

The following monuments may likewise be seen here: Sir W. Jones, represented leaning on the Institutes of Menù, by Bacon, jun.; earl Howe, by Flaxman: sir Joshua Reynolds, by the same artist; captain Hardinge, by the late C. Manning; lord Rodney, by C. Rossi; captain Westcott, by Banks; sir John Moore, by Bacon, jun.; lord Collingwood, sir Ralph Abercromby, lord Duncan, and Sir Isaac Brock, by Westmacott; captain Duff, by Bacon; captains Moss and Riou, by C. Rossi; general Dundas, by Bacon, jun.; generals Craufurd and Mackinnon, by Bacon, jun,; Dr. Johnson, with an inscription by Dr. Parr; marquess Cornwallis and lord Heathfield, by Rossi; general Picton, by Gahagan; general Ponsonby and Lord Vincent, by Baily; captain Hutt and captain Burges, by Banks; general Bowes, colonel Cadogan, bishop Heber, general Houghton, and general Gillespie, by Chantrey: sir William Hoste, by Campbell; Middleton, first bishop of Calcutta, and Dr. Babbington, by Behnes; together with monuments of captain Faulkner, captain Cooke, captain Millar, by Flaxman, generals Hay, Mackenzie, Pakenham, and Gibbs, Sir William Myers, and Langworth. Over the entrance to the choir is a marble slab with a Latin inscription, which may be translated, "Beneath, lies Christopher Wren, builder of this church and city; who lived upwards of 90 years, not for himself, but for the public benefit. Reader, do you seek for his monument?—look around."

Lord Nelson's remains are interred in a vault under the central part of the building; and near him his friend lord Collingwood.

Among other eminent characters whose bodies have been deposited in these vaults, are—sir Christopher Wren; Dr. Newton, bishop of Bristol; Alexander Wedderburn, earl of Rosslyn; sir John Braithwaite; sir Joshua Reynolds; B. West, esq., and sir Thomas Lawrence, successively presidents of the Royal Academy; James Barry, John Opie, Henry Fuseli, and George Dawes, esquires, painters; and John Rennie, esq., engineer.

The *crypt* beneath the cathedral contains inscriptions to sir Christopher Wren and his daughter, to bishop Newton, the painters Barry and Opie, and other eminent persons. But the chief object of curiosity is the tomb of Nelson. In the middle avenue of the crypt, immediately beneath the centre of the dome, stands a sarcophagus of black and white marble, resting on a pedestal, on which are inscribed the words "HORATIO VISC. NELSON." The sarcophagus and pedestal were brought from cardinal Wolsey's tomb-house at Windsor; they were prepared by the cardinal for his own entombment. Here also may be seen the celebrated figure of Dr. Donne, representing him as a corpse: it was executed in his life-time, and was frequently the object of his contemplation.

The *choir* is divided from the body of the church by an organ-gallery, supported by eight Corinthian columns of black and white marble, and enriched with beautiful carving by Gibbons, whose decorative performances embellish every part of the choir. The episcopal throne near the altar is peculiarly elegant. The bishop's seat for ordinary occasions, on the south side, is distinguished by a mitre and pelican; the lord-mayor's seat, on the opposite side, has the city mace and other appropriate devices. The dean's stall, under the organ gallery, is distinguished by a canopy, and ornamented with sculptures of fruit and flowers.

The *pulpit* was originally placed near the altar, opposite to the bishop's throne, but has been removed to a more centrical situation for the greater convenience of the auditors. The *reading-desk* is supported by an eagle with expanded wings, standing on a pillar, surrounded by rails; the whole of gilt brass.

The *sermons* were anciently delivered in the open air, at a cross in the churchyard, as already stated; from which circumstance they are still termed Paul's-cross sermons. The preachers are nominated by the bishop of London.

The chaplain to the lord-mayor for the time being is the

preacher on all state holydays; and on the first Sunday in Easter and Trinity terms, when the lord-mayor, aldermen, judges, and city officers attend the cathedral church.

The *choral service* is performed daily in great perfection at St. Paul's. The service commences at three-quarters past nine precisely in the morning, and at a quarter-past three in the afternoon; when the solemn harmonies of Tallis, Gibbons, and Purcell, the lighter compositions of Boyce and Kent, and the sublime choruses of Handel, may be heard with the fullest effect: but the greatest treat for the admirers of sacred harmony is the music-meeting in the month of May, for the benefit of the widows and orphans of necessitous clergymen. Handel's grand Dettingen *Te Deum*, several of his most beautiful choruses, and an appropriate anthem by Dr. Boyce, are performed by a powerful orchestra, supported by the principal gentlemen, both clerical and lay, belonging to the three choirs of St. Paul's, Westminster-abbey, and the Chapel-royal, who make a point of attending on this occasion, and who render their assistance gratuitously. One of the royal dukes, the lord-mayor, most of the bishops, and many other distinguished characters, attend as stewards. The doors open at ten, and divine service commences at twelve o'clock. A public rehearsal of this music always takes place a day or two before the meeting. The terms of admission are advertised in the daily papers. The cathedral is likewise open for service every day, except on Sundays, at six in the morning during summer, and at seven in the winter.

Another meeting, equally honourable and gratifying to the benevolence of the age, is held in the month of June, when six or eight thousand children, clothed and educated in the parochial schools, are assembled in the metropolitan church to offer their infant homage to their Creator. A rehearsal of this meeting takes place a day or two before, when persons are admitted at 6*d*. each. Tickets for the meeting itself can only be obtained of persons who patronise the schools.

The Dimensions of the Cathedral are—

	Feet.
Length from east to west, within the walls	500
Breadth of the nave and choir	100
From north to south, through the transept	285
The circuit	2,292
The height, exclusive of the dome	110
Height from the vaults to the top of the cross	404
Height from the centre of the floor to the top of the cross	340
Ground-plot, 2 acres 16 perches 70 feet.	

The whole expense of building the cathedral was about a million and a half.

The public is admitted free of charge daily, from 9 to 11 and 3 to 4, and on Sundays from 10 to 12 and 3 to 5.

Prices of Admission.—Entrance to the body of the church may always be obtained at the north door on payment of 2*d.*; from the body of the church to the upper galleries, including the whispering-gallery, 6*d.*; library, 2*d.*; model and trophy room, 4*d.*; geometrical staircase, 2*d.*; great bell, 2*d.*; ball, 1*s.* 6*d.*; vaults, 1*s.*

WESTMINSTER ABBEY

Bears also the name of the collegiate church of St. Peter. Of the founding of this abbey on "*Thorney Island*," there are so many miraculous stories related by monkish writers, that the recital of them now would hardly be endured: even the relations of ancient historians have been questioned by Sir Christopher Wren, who was employed to survey the present edifice, and who, upon the nicest examination, found nothing to countenance the general belief, that it was erected on the ruins of a *pagan temple*. It may be presumed, that both the ancient church dedicated to St. Paul in London, and this dedicated to St. Peter in Westminster, were among the earliest works of the first converts to Christianity in Britain. With their new religion they introduced a new style of building; and their great aim seems to have been, by affecting loftiness and ornament, to bring the plain simplicity of the pagan architects into contempt. Historians, agreeably to the legend, have fixed the era of the first abbey in the sixth century, and ascribed to Sebert the honour of conducting the work, and of completing that part of it at least that now forms the east angle, which probably was all that was included in the original plan. Till the time of Edward the Confessor, the first abbey remained exposed to the sacrilegious fury of the times; but by the prevailing influence of Christianity in that reign, the ruins of the ancient building were cleared away, and a most magnificent structure for that age erected in their place. In its form it bore the figure of a cross, which afterwards became the pattern for cathedral-building throughout the kingdom. That politic prince, to ingratiate himself with his clergy, not only confirmed all former endowments, but granted a new charter, which concluded with solemn impre-

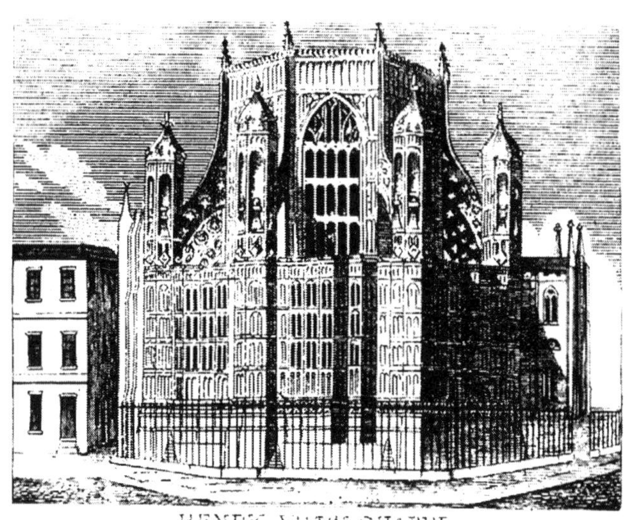

HENRY VIIths CHAPEL

WESTMINSTER ABBEY.

cations against all who should in time to come deface or demolish any part of the building, or infringe the rights of its priesthood. Henry III. not only enlarged the plan of this ancient abbey, but added a chapel, which he dedicated to the Blessed Virgin; but it was not till the reign of Henry VII. that the stately and magnificent chapel now known by his name was planned and executed. Of this chapel, the first stone was laid on the 24th of January, 1502, and when completed was dedicated, like the former chapels, to the Blessed Virgin. Henry designed this as a burying-place for himself and his successors: he expressly enjoined by his will, that none but those of the blood-royal should be inhumed therein.

From the death of Henry VII. till the reign of William and Mary, no care was taken to repair or preserve the ancient church. By the demands which Henry VIII. made upon it, and the ravages it sustained during the unhappy civil commotions, its ancient beauty was in a great measure destroyed; nor did their majesties restore it till it became an object of parliamentary attention, and till a considerable sum was voted for that purpose only. This vote being passed, Sir Christopher Wren was employed to decorate and give it a thorough repair, which that able architect so skilfully and faithfully executed, that the building is thought at this day to want none of its original strength, and to have even acquired additional majesty by two new towers which are situated at the western entrance. It is, however, to be regretted that he should have studied propriety of style so little as to have departed from the pervading Gothic, and to have finished the towers with Roman ornaments. The principal object of attention of the exterior, with the exception of the towers and Henry VII.'s chapel, is the magnificent Gothic portico leading into the north cross, which by some has been styled the Beautiful, or Solomon's Gate, and which is adorned with a window of modern design, admirably executed.

The interior has a commanding appearance; the Gothic arches separating the nave from the side-aisles are supported by forty-eight pillars of grey marble, which are so well disposed that the whole body of the church may be seen on entering the west door.

The *choir*, which is comparatively of recent date, was constructed under the direction of the late Mr. Keene, surveyor to the abbey. It is executed in the ancient Gothic style. The nave is separated from the choir by an elegant stone screen erected from designs by Mr. Blore.

The modern marble altar-piece, which was designed by Sir C. Wren for the chapel at Whitehall, and given to this abbey by queen Anne, was taken down at the coronation of George IV., and the original altar-piece restored as nearly as possible to its ancient design. The *Mosaic pavement* in front of the altar is said to have been executed by Richard de Ware, abbot of Westminster. It is a very curious specimen of workmanship.

On the north side of the choir are the monuments of Aymer de Valence, earl of Pembroke, and his Countess, and Edmund Crouchback, earl of Lancaster: and on the south side are those of Sebert, the original founder of the abbey, and Anne of Cleves; all of which are well worthy the notice of the antiquary.

The roof of the lantern, which was destroyed by fire July 9, 1803, has been rebuilt in a style more suitable to the other parts of the edifice than the old one, and is richly adorned with carving and gilding.

Edward the Confessor's Chapel

Is situated behind the altar at the east end of the choir, and contains the shrine of St. Edward, an exquisite specimen of workmanship, executed by Pietro Cavalini, by order of Henry III. In this chapel are the tombs of Editha, Edward's queen, of Henry III., of his son Edward I., and several other royal monuments. Here also are kept the iron sword of Edward I., a part of his shield, the helmet and shield of Henry V., and the coronation-chairs. The most ancient, under the seat of which is placed the stone said to have been Jacob's pillow, was brought with the regalia from Scone in Scotland, by Edward I., in 1297; the other chair was made for Mary, the consort of William III. The screen of the chapel is adorned with several statues, and with fourteen legendary hieroglyphics respecting the Confessor, executed in basso-relievo. On the floor is a defaced brass figure of John de Waltham, bishop of Salisbury A.D. 1383.

Henry VIIth's Chapel,

Which is so called from its founder, was commenced in 1502, the first stone having been laid by John Islip, abbot of Westminster, in the presence of that monarch, and was completed in about ten years. It is supposed by some to have been constructed under the direction of Sir Reginald Bray, and by others under that of bishop Fox; whilst others imagine that Bolton, the prior of St. Bartholomew's, was the architect employed. The stone was brought from Hudderstone quarry, Yorkshire, and the expense of its erection was estimated at 14,000*l*. It is situated east of the abbey, and is constructed in the florid Gothic style. The exterior is adorned with fourteen octagonal towers jutting from the building in different angles, and ornamented with a profusion of sculpture. The whole was repaired between 1809 and 1823, at an expense of 42,000*l*., which was supplied by parliament.

The ascent to the inside of the chapel is formed by steps of black marble, under a stately portico, which leads to the gates of the body, or nave, on each hand opening into the side-aisles. The gates are of brass, most curiously wrought, the panels being ornamented with a rose and portcullis alternately. The lofty stone ceiling is wrought with an astonishing variety of figures. The stalls are of brown wainscot, with Gothic canopies, beautifully carved, as are the seats, with strange devices. The pavement is of black and white marble, done at the charge of Dr. Killigrew, once prebendary of this abbey.

The view from the entrance presents the brass chapel and tomb of the founder, and round it, where the east end forms a semicircle, are the chapels of the dukes of Buckingham and Richmond; in the former is a monument to the memory of George Villiers, duke of Buckingham. In one of them is the tomb of the Duc de Montpensier, erected by order of his brother Louis Philippe, and executed by Westmacott. The windows, which are fourteen in the upper, and nineteen in the lower range, including the side-aisles and portico, were formerly of painted or diapered glass, having in every pane a white rose, the badge of Lancaster, and portcullises, the badge of the Beauforts, of which a few only are now remaining. The roof is nearly flat, and is supported on arches between the nave and side-aisles, which turn upon twelve stately Gothic pillars, curiously adorned with figures, fruit, and foliage.

This chapel, as already stated, was designed as a SEPULCHRE, in which none but such as were of blood-royal should ever be interred; accordingly the will of the founder has been so far observed, that all who have hitherto been admitted are of the highest quality, and can trace their descent from some of our ancient kings.

In the north aisle are the monuments of queen Elizabeth and her sister Mary; the murdered princes, Edward V. and his brother Richard; Sophia and Maria, infant daughters of James I., who was also interred beneath; Charles Montague, first earl of Halifax; and George Savile, marquess of Halifax. Here likewise is preserved the armour of general Monk.

In the south aisle are the monuments of Mary queen of Scots; Catherine lady Walpole; Margaret Beaufort, countess of Richmond and Derby, the mother of Henry VII.; George Monk, the first Duke of Albemarle, and Christopher his son, the second duke. Here also is a monument on which lies a lady finely robed, the effigy of Margaret Douglas, daughter of Margaret queen of Scots, by the Earl of Angus. This lady, as the English inscription expresses, had to her great-grandfather, Edward IV.; to her grandfather, Henry VII.; to her uncle, Henry VIII.; to her cousin german, Edward VI.; to her brother, James V. of Scotland; to her grandson, James VI.; having to her great-grandmother and grandmother two queens both named Elizabeth; to her mother, Margaret queen of Scots; to her aunt, Mary the French queen; to her cousins-german, Mary and Elizabeth, queens of England; to her niece and daughter-in-law, Mary queen of Scots. There are seven children besides lord Darnley, whose effigy is foremost, round the tomb of Margaret, of whom only three are mentioned in history, the rest having died young. This great lady died March 10th, 1577. At the end is the royal Vault, as it is called, in which the remains of Charles II., William III. and Mary his consort, queen Anne, and prince George, are all deposited.

In the nave of the chapel are installed, with great ceremony, the knights of the most honourable Order of the BATH: which order was revived in the reign of George I., in 1725. In their stalls are placed brass plates of their arms, and over them hang their banners, swords, and helmets. Under the stalls are seats for the esquires; each knight has three, whose arms are engraved on brass plates.

The principal object of admiration here, both for its antiquity and its workmanship, is the tomb of Henry VII. and Elizabeth his queen, the last of the house of York who wore the English crown. It is ornamented with many devices alluding to his family and alliances; such as portcullises, denoting his relation to the Beauforts by his mother's side; roses twisted and crowned, in memory of the union of the two houses of Lancaster and York; and at each end a crown in a bush, referring to the crown of Richard III., found in a hawthorn near Bosworth Field, where that famous battle was fought for a diadem, which turning in favour of Henry, his impatience was so great to be crowned that he caused the ceremony to be performed on the spot with that very crown the competitor had lost.

In a fine vault under Henry VII.'s chapel is the burying-place of the royal family, erected by George II.

The Dimensions of Henry VII.'s Chapel are—

	Feet.
Length from east to west, including the walls . .	115
Breadth, including the walls	80
Height of the Octagonal Towers	71
Height to the top of the roof	86
Height to the top of the West Turrets	102
Length of the Nave	104
Breadth of the Nave	36
Height of the Nave	61
Breadth of each Aisle	17

St. Andrew's Chapel,

Which is next to the north cross, and the others which surround the choir, are crowded with monuments of noble personages, worthy of the attention of the curious.

St. Benedict's Chapel.

Contains the tomb and effigies of Archbishop Langham; and at the corner is an iron gate opening into the south cross-aisle.

The Poets' Corner

Is so called from the number of monuments erected there to celebrate English poets, though we find here a monument to the memory of John duke of Argyle, executed by Roubillac; and others to Camden the antiquary, Doctor Isaac Barrow the divine, and Thomas Parr, who died at the age of 152 years. Amongst the most interesting monuments in Poets' Corner is that to the memory of WILLIAM SHAKSPEARE. On the pedestal are heads of Henry V., Richard III., and queen Elizabeth. This monument was constructed under the direction of the earl of Burlington, Dr. Mead, Mr. Pope, and Mr. Martin. It was designed by Kent, executed by Scheemakers, and the expense defrayed by public contributions.

Near this tomb were interred the remains of Richard Brinsley Sheridan, the poet, the wit, and the orator, whose only monument is a black marble slab, placed there by his friend Mr. P. Moore. Here likewise may be seen the names of "O rare Ben Jonson," Spenser, Chaucer, Butler, Milton, Mason, Gray, Prior, Granville Sharp, Mrs. Pritchard, Thomson, Mrs. Rowe, Gay, Goldsmith; over the entrance of the Chapel of St. Blaize—Handel, by Roubillac; Chambers, Addison, Dr. Hales, by Wilton; Sir J. Pringle, Sir R. Taylor, Wyatt, Grabius, Casaubon, Garrick, Dryden, Cowley, Davenant, Camden, Congreve, Gifford the translator of Juvenal and many years editor of the Quarterly Review, &c. &c.

The monuments in the other parts of the Abbey are too numerous to be minutely detailed. In the south aisle are those of Dr. South, Dr. Vincent, sir Cloudesley Shovel, Dr. Watts, General Paoli, Dr. Burney, Dr. Busby, Dr. Bell, Thomas Thynne, whose murder in his own carriage is here represented, &c. In the west aisle are those of Major André, whose remains were brought from America and interred here in 1821; sir J. Chardin, lord Howe, admiral Tyrell, W. Congreve; W. Pitt, who is represented speaking in his robes as chancellor of the exchequer; sir Thomas Hardy, sir Godfrey Kneller, Banks the sculptor, Dr. Mead, sir Isaac Newton, lord Stanhope by Rysbach, &c.; the last two are in recesses in the new Gothic screen. In the north aisle are those of lord Ligonier, general Wolfe, by Wilton; Pultney earl of Bath, Dr. Arnold, Dr. Croft, Dr. Burney, Mr. Perceval, two Knights Templars, &c., with a superb monument by Bacon, which cost 6,000*l.*

In the north transept were buried near to each other, Pitt earl of Chatham; those celebrated rivals, Pitt and Fox; lord Colchester; Grattan the Irish orator; lord Londonderry; and Mr. Canning. Here likewise are the monuments of lord Mansfield, by Flaxman; earl of Chatham, by Bacon; admiral Warren, by Roubillac; sir Eyre Coote, by Banks; Jonas Hanway, and Mr. Horner, by Chantrey; C. J. Fox, by Westmacott; captain lord R. Manners, Bayne, and Blair, by Nollekens; Holles, Duke of Newcastle, by Gibbs; J. P. Kemble, modelled by Flaxman; George Canning, by Chantrey; general Malcolm, sir S. Raffles, admiral Watson, and Warren Hastings.

St. Erasmus' Chapel

Contains the tombs of lord Hunsdon and lord Exeter in the time of Elizabeth. In a chantry over this chapel are wax figures of queen Elizabeth, William and Mary, lord Chatham, queen Anne, and lord Nelson, ill according, however, with the solemnity of this imposing edifice.

The Chapel of St. John, St. Andrew, and St. Michael,

Is adorned with the monument of lady Nightingale, executed by Roubillac, and remarkable for the beauty of its workmanship; the lady is represented as protected by her husband, whilst a fine figure of Death is seen coming out of a tomb to hurl his dart. Here also are the tombs of sir Francis Vere, sir Edward Holles, admirals Kempenfelt and Pococke, and a bust of Dr. Baillie by Chantrey.

The Dimensions of the Abbey are—

	Feet.
Length from east to west, including walls, but exclusive of Henry VII.'s Chapel	416
Height of the West Towers	225
Length within the walls	383
Breadth at the Transept	203
Length of the Nave	166
Breadth of the Nave	39
Height of the Nave	102
Breadth of each Aisle	17
Length of the Choir	156
Breadth of the Choir	28

Besides the church, many of the ancient appendages of the Abbey remain. The *Cloisters* are entire, and filled with monuments. They are built in a quadrangular form, with piazzas towards the court, in which several of the prebendaries have houses.

The entrance into the *Chapter-house* (built in 1250) is on one side of the cloisters, through a Gothic portal, the mouldings of which are exquisitely carved. By consent of the abbot in 1377, the Commons of Great Britain first held their parliaments in this place, the crown undertaking the repairs. Here they sat till 1547, when Edward VI. granted them the chapel of St. Stephen. It is at present filled with the public records, among which is the original *Doomsday Book*, now above 700 years old: it is in as fine preservation as if it were the work of yesterday. Attendance from 10 till 4.

Beneath the chapter-house is a singular crypt, the roof of which is supported by massy plain ribs, diverging from the top of a short round pillar, quite hollow. The walls are not less than eighteen feet thick, and form a firm base to the superstructure.

The *Jerusalem Chamber*, built by Littlington, formed a part of the abbot's lodgings. It is noted for having been the place where Henry IV. breathed his last: he had been seized with a swoon while praying before the shrine of St. Edward, and being carried into this room, asked, on recovering, where he was? Being informed, he answered, to use the words of Shakspeare, founded on history—

> "Laud be to God!—even here my life must end.
> It hath been prophesied to me many years
> I should not die but in *Jerusalem*,
> Which vainly I supposed the HOLY LAND!"

Not far from the Abbey stood the *Sanctuary*, the place of refuge absurdly granted in former times to criminals of certain denominations. The church belonging to it was in the form of a cross. It is supposed to have been the work of the Confessor. Within its precincts was born Edward V.; and here his unhappy mother took refuge with her younger son Richard, to secure him from his cruel uncle, who had already possession of the elder brother.

To the west of the Sanctuary stood the *Eleemosynary* or *Almonry*, where the alms of the Abbey were distributed. But it is still more remarkable for having been the place where the first printing-press ever known in England was erected. It was in 1474, when *William Caxton*, encouraged by "the great," and probably by the learned Thomas Milling, then abbot, produced "*The Game and Play of the Chesse*," the first book ever printed in these kingdoms. There is a slight difference about the place in which it was printed, but all agree that it was within the precincts of this religious house.

The Abbey is open every day for Divine service, at ten in the morning and at three in the afternoon.

At present the price of admission to this national monument is 1*s*. 3*d*.!!!

ALL SOULS' CHURCH.

Langham-place, Regent-street.

This singular edifice was erected in 1824, from designs by Mr. Nash, and is capable of accommodating 1,760 persons. The steeple consists of a circular tower surmounted by a cone; the tower rests on a flight of steps, and the lower part is surrounded by a peristyle of twelve Ionic columns, the capitals of which are profusely ornamented. The base of the cone is also surrounded by a peristyle consisting of fourteen Corinthian columns, supporting an entablature and balustrade.

CHRIST CHURCH.

HANOVER CHAPEL.

ALL SOULS.

S^T. MARTIN IN THE FIELDS.

S^T. LUKE, CHELSEA.

The cone is fluted, and carried to a point. The church itself is a plain building, cased with stone, lighted by two tiers of windows, and finished with a balustrade.

The interior is very pleasing: three sides are occupied by galleries resting on octangular pillars, and the fourth by the altar, which is adorned with a painting by Mr. Westall, representing Christ crowned with thorns. Above the fronts of the galleries rises a colonnade of Corinthian columns, supporting the ceiling, which is enriched with sunk panels. At the west end of the church is a handsome organ, and at the east end, on either side of the altar, are the pulpit and reading-desk, placed against the pillars sustaining the extremities of the galleries.

St. Martin's-in-the-Fields,

St. Martin's-lane.

This grand stone edifice was rebuilt by Gibbs, between 1721 and 1726, on the site on which there had been a church before 1222. On the west front is a noble portico of eight Corinthian columns: it supports a pediment in which are the royal arms, and underneath a Latin inscription respecting the erection of the church. The ascent to the portico is by a flight of very long steps. The length of this church is about 140 feet, the breadth 60, and the height 45. It has a fine arched roof, sustained by stone columns of the Corinthian order. The steeple, although imposing to the ordinary observer, is considered by architects as the least successful part of the design. In the tower is an excellent peal of twelve bells. *Nell Gwynn* left the ringers of this church, she being buried in its ground, a sum of money to supply them with entertainment weekly. The interior decorations are extremely fine. The ceiling is elliptical, which is said to be much better for the voice than the semicircular. The organ was presented by George III. On the north side of St. Martin's churchyard stand the Vicar's house, the Vestry, and the National School, erected in 1830. The vestry-room contains a fine model of the church, and portraits of the vicars since 1670, and a bust of Dr. Richards. Mr. Scott, the author of "A Visit to Paris," who was killed in a duel in 1821, was buried in the vaults under the church; and here also was interred Mrs. Centlivre, the dramatic writer. Roubillac the sculptor was buried in the adjacent churchyard in 1762. The catacombs surrounding the church were constructed in 1830, and are admirably arranged. In the burial-ground belonging to St. Martin's, on the north-east side of Camden Town, is the tomb of Charles Dibdin, the author and composer.

St. Margaret's Church,
New Palace-yard,

Is situated on the north side of Westminster Abbey, and its existence must be regretted, since it intercepts the view of the cathedral and that exquisite adjunct, Henry VII.'s Chapel, without reconciling the eye to the intrusion by any architectural beauty. It was erected by Edward the Confessor in 1061; rebuilt in the reign of Edward I. by the parishioners; but has been repaired several times since, particularly in 1735, 1758, and 1803, at the expense of parliament, it being considered a national foundation for the use of the House of Commons. In 1758 every part of the structure was ornamented, but especially the east end, which was wrought into a circular sweep, ending at the top in the form of a half-cupola, in squares of beautiful Gothic work. Under the window, and round the sides of the altar, are also various ornaments in a similar style. Over the altar-table is a fine basso-relievo, representing our Saviour and the disciples at Emmaus. One of the disciples is dressed like a Roman Catholic friar, and across his shoulders hangs a cardinal's hat! and behind the other disciple stands a page in Italian costume, with hat and feathers!

The beautiful window was made by order of the magistrates of Dort, in Holland, and designed by them as a present to Henry VII.; but that monarch dying before it was finished, it was set up in Waltham Abbey, where it remained till the dissolution of that monastery, when it was removed to New-Hall, in Essex, then in possession of General Monk, and by him preserved during the civil wars. Some years ago, John Olmius, Esq., the then possessor of New-Hall, sold it to Mr. Conyers, of Copt-hall, who resold it to the inhabitants of St. Margaret's parish in 1758, for 400 guineas. This splendid ornament of the church represents the Crucifixion. The figures at the bottom of the two side-panels, representing Henry VII. and his queen, were taken from the original pictures sent to Dort for that purpose. Over the king is the figure of St. George, and above that a white and red rose.

This church is 130 feet in length, 65 in breadth, and 45 in height. It has ten excellent bells. At the extremity of one of the side-aisles is a tablet with the following inscription:—

"Within the walls of this church was deposited the body of the great Sir Walter Raleigh, Knt., on the day he was beheaded in Old Palace Yard, Westminster, October 18, Ann. Dom. 1618:—

"Reader, should you reflect on his errors,
Remember his many virtues,
And that he was a mortal!"

This church also contains an inscription in honour of Caxton, the printer, placed here by the Roxburghe Club; and a monument to Sir Peter Parker, with an epitaph by Byron.

In the adjacent inclosure is a bronze statue of George Canning, by Westmacott.

ST. LUKE'S, CHELSEA,

Was erected from designs by Mr. Savage. The first stone was laid Oct. 12, 1820, and the church was consecrated Oct. 18, 1824. It is a beautiful edifice in the pointed Gothic style, built of brick, faced with Bath stone, and is divided into a nave and aisles. At the east end is a large window, beneath which is a splendid altar-screen; and at the west end is an organ, built by Nicholls, containing 33 stops and 1,876 pipes. This church is 130 feet long, 61 wide, and 60 high. It will accommodate 2,000 persons. The height of the tower to the top of the pinnacles is 142 feet.

ST. JOHN THE EVANGELIST'S,

Milbank-street.

This singular building is one of the fifty new churches built soon after the time of Sir Christopher Wren. It is the work of Mr. Archer, though Sir John Vanbrugh has the discredit of it. While it was building, the foundations gave way, and it sunk so much as to occasion a material alteration in the original plan. The principal objection to this structure is, that it appears encumbered with ornaments. On the north and south sides are porticoes supported by massive stone pillars. At each of the four angles is a stone tower and a pinnacle. In front is an elegant portico supported by Doric columns, which order is continued in pilasters round the building. This was the first church or public building in London, we believe, that was lighted with *gas*. It is about 140 feet in length, 90 in breadth, and 50 in height. Its interior was very much improved in 1825, from designs by Mr. Inwood. Over the altar is a painted window representing our Saviour's descent from the cross, and the apostles St. Paul and St. John.

St. James's, Westminster,

Piccadilly,

Owes its erection to the great increase in the parish of St. Martin-in-the-Fields. It was founded in the latter part of Charles II.'s reign, and consecrated in the first of James II.'s, and named in honour of both saint and monarch. The font of white marble is finely sculptured by Grinlin Gibbons. Over the altar is a copy of Raffael's Transfiguration in painted glass, by Mr. Backler. It represents the Fall of Man, Salvation of Noah, &c. The building is of brick and stone, about 85 feet long, 60 broad, and 45 feet high, with a steeple 150 feet in height. It was erected by Sir Christopher Wren. Here are deposited the remains of Dr. Akenside the poet: and on the south side of the west porch is a tablet erected to the memory of Tom D'Urfey the poet, who died in 1723. There is also a tablet in honour of Dr. Sydenham.

St. George's,

Hanover-street, Hanover-square,

Is one of the fifty new churches erected in the reign of queen Anne. It was completed in 1724, and measures 100 feet in length, 60 in breadth, and 45 in height.

The ground for the edifice was given by lieutenant-general Steward, who also left 4000*l.* to the parish, towards erecting and endowing a charity school. The portico consists of six Corinthian columns, with an entablature and pediment. The steeple is handsome. The altar-piece, representing the Last Supper, is said to have been executed by Sir James Thornhill.

In the burying-ground, near Tyburn-turnpike, belonging to St. George's parish, was interred Lawrence Sterne, the wit and divine, and Sir Thomas Picton, who was killed at Waterloo.

St. Mary-le-Strand,

Strand.

Is also one of the fifty new churches built in the reign of queen Anne, and is a handsome piece of architecture, erected by Gibbs in 1717. It is 70 feet in length, 30 in breadth, and 46 in height. At the entrance on the west side is an ascent by a flight of steps in a circular form, which leads to a similarly shaped portico of Ionic columns, covered with a dome,

MARYLEBONE NEW CHURCH

BOW CHURCH,
CHEAPSIDE.

S^T BRIDES FLEET STREET.

ST. GEORGE HANOVER SQE.

ST. MARY LE STRAND.

ST. CLEMENT DANES.

ST. GEORGE BLOOMSBURY.

The columns are continued along the body of the church, with pilasters of the same order at the corners; and in the intercolumniations are niches tastefully ornamented. A handsome balustrade is carried round the top of the church, and adorned with vases. The interior contains a modern painted window, two paintings by Brown, and a monument to the memory of J. Bindley, Esq., the collector, who was buried here in 1820.

St. Clement Danes,

Strand.

A church is said to have stood in this place since about the year 700; but the present structure, which was designed by Sir Christopher Wren, was begun in 1680. It is 96 feet in length, 63 in breadth, and 48 in height. It is built of stone, with two rows of windows, the lower plain, but the upper ornamented; and the termination is by an attic. On the north, as well as on the south side of the front, is a portico, with a dome supported by Ionic columns. The steeple, which is lofty and beautiful, was erected by Gibbs in 1719. Otway the poet was buried under this church in 1685, and Dr. Kitchiner in 1827. In the vestry-room, on the north side of the churchyard, is a picture which was formerly the altar-piece to the church, and is said to contain portraits of the Pretender's wife and children.

Joe Miller was interred in the cemetery belonging to this parish, in Portugal-street, Lincoln's-inn-fields, in 1738. His epitaph, written by Stephen Duck, may be seen at the further corner on the left side as you enter the burial-ground.

St. George's,

Bloomsbury,

One of the fifty new churches erected by act of parliament, is distinguished from most others, by standing north and south, and by the statue of King George I. at the top of its pyramidal steeple. It was consecrated in 1731, and is 110 feet in length, 90 in breadth, and about 50 in height. The portico, consisting of eight Corinthian columns, is much admired. Hawksmoor was the architect.

In the western gallery is a monument by Bacon in memory of the late Charles Grant, Esq. It was erected at the expense of the East India Company in 1825. Near it is a tablet in honour of Chief Justice Mansfield. Here also Joseph Planta, Esq., formerly librarian of the British Museum, was buried in 1827.

In the cemetery belonging to this parish, behind the Foundling Hospital, was buried the Rev. S. Ayscough, the compiler of indices, over whom has been placed an epitaph written by his friend Mr. Maurice, author of "Indian Antiquities," &c.

St. Stephen's,

Walbrook.

The old church of St. Stephen being destroyed by the fire of London, Sir Christopher Wren was commissioned to erect the present structure, which has been eulogised by many writers as the master-piece of the architect. The plan is original, yet chaste and beautiful; the dome, supported by eight arches, springing from eight single Corinthian columns, is light and scenic in its effect, scarcely corresponding with the solemnity of religious worship. Over the altar is a fine picture representing the interment of St. Stephen, by West, presented by the Rev. Dr. Wilson in 1776. This church is 82 feet long and 59 broad, and the central roof is 34 feet high.

St. Anne's Soho,

Dean-street,

Was built in 1685, in consequence of the vast increase of inhabitants of St. Martin-in-the-Fields, and dedicated to St. Anne, in honour of the Princess Anne of Denmark. It is a brick edifice, about 110 feet long, 60 broad, and 40 high, and is rendered singular by a circular tower, surmounted by a large ball, containing a clock with four dials. Two paintings of Moses and Aaron adorn the tablets containing the decalogue; and the organ was the gift of William III. At the back of this church is a stone, erected by the Earl of Orford in 1758, with the following inscription:—

Near this place is interred
THEODORE, KING OF CORSICA,
Who died in this Parish
December XI. MDCCLVI.
Immediately after leaving
The *King's-bench Prison*,
By the Benefit of the *Act of Insolvency*,
In consequence of which
He *registered his kingdom of Corsica*
For the use of his Creditors.

The grave, great Teacher! to a level brings
Heroes and beggars, galley-slaves and kings!
But Theodore this moral learn'd, ere dead;
Fate pour'd its lessons on his living head,
Bestow'd a kingdom, and denied him bread!

St. Mary's,

Lambeth.

The tower of this church, which is 87 feet high, was erected about 1375, but the other parts of the edifice appear to have been built towards the end of the fifteenth century. The church is about 110 feet in length, 50 in breadth, and 38 in height. In one of the windows is the figure of a pedlar and his dog, painted on glass: this person is said to have left to the parish the ground called Pedlar's-Acre. This church is remarkable as having afforded a temporary shelter from the rain to the queen of James II., who, after crossing the water from Whitehall, remained here on the night of December 6, 1688, till a coach took her to Gravesend. The south aisle contains a marble slab with a Latin inscription to the memory of Elias Ashmole, the antiquarian. The chancel is ornamented with the monuments of Archbishops Bancroft, Tenison, Hutton, Cornwallis, Moore, and Secker. In the churchyard is the tomb of the Tradescants, father and son, the founders of the Ashmolean Museum; it was formerly ornamented with emblematical devices, but these are defaced, and a new slab has been placed over it, with the original inscription.

In the cemetery belonging to this church, in High-street, are interred Moore, the author of "Fables for the Fair Sex;" T. Cooke, the poet mentioned by Pope in the "Dunciad;" and the celebrated Countess De la Motte.

St. Helen's,

Great St. Helen's, Bishopsgate-street.

This is one of the few churches which escaped the fire of London. It is remarkable for several curious monuments, amongst which may be noticed those of sir Thomas Gresham, the founder of the Exchange; sir Julius Cæsar, master of the rolls to James I.; sir William Pickering, who had served four different sovereigns; sir John Crosby, a great benefactor to the church; and Francis Bancroft, who left a considerable sum of money to the Drapers' company for the erection of almshouses. The remains of the latter are deposited in a chest, the lid of which is without any fastening, and over the face is a square of glass. Here likewise Robert Hooke the astronomer was buried in 1702.

MARY-LE-BONE NEW CHURCH,

New-road,

Was originally designed as an additional chapel-of-ease to the parish; but when the interior had been fitted up and arranged, it was so much admired, that it was thought expedient to make it the parish church. A small stone cupola which had been erected was then taken down, and the present tower, adorned with representations of the Winds, substituted. The front was increased in length, and the portico of six Corinthian columns was tastefully attached to the building. The interior is rendered remarkable by a double gallery. The organ is over the altar, and stands at the south end of the church. The altar-piece, representing the Nativity, is by West, who presented it to the church. The foundation-stone was laid 5th July, 1813; it was consecrated February 4, 1817. Mr. Hardwicke was the architect, and Mr. R. Wade the builder.

Dimensions of the Church.—Length, 125 feet; breadth, 70 feet; height from the ground to the top of the parapet, 53 feet; height of the columns, 34 feet; height of steeple, including the vane, 134 feet; width of the portico, 20 feet. Some idea of the population of Mary-le-bone parish may be formed, when it is known that about 3000 baptisms take place annually in this church.

ST. PANCRAS OLD CHURCH,

And the adjacent churchyard, have been long celebrated as the burial-place of Roman Catholics; and there are many interesting inscriptions to the memory of distinguished foreigners. Here may be seen the tomb of the brave but unfortunate Paoli, and the graves of an archbishop of Narbonne and seven bishops expelled from France, distinguished only by common head-stones. Many of the heads of ancient families of that country, and of her famed marshals, lie near them, in the same undistinguished manner. Here also lie the remains of the Chevalier d'Eon, whose death took place in 1810, at the age of 83, when the controversy respecting his sex was decided in direct opposition to the decision before Lord Mansfield on a policy of insurance. Walker, the compiler of the "Pronouncing Dictionary;" Edwards, who wrote on perspective; Cavallo, the philosophical writer; Woollet, the engraver: Leoni, the architect; Samuel Webbe, the glee composer, and

Mr. Godwin, were likewise buried here. Here also is the monument to Mary Wolstoncroft, afterwards Mrs. Godwin.

St. Mary-le-Bow,

Cheapside,

Was erected in 1673 by Sir Christopher Wren. The original edifice, built in 1087, the crypt of which is remaining, derived its name of Le-Bow from having been erected on arches. The principal ornament of this church is its steeple of Portland stone, which is more than 200 feet in height. It was rebuilt by Mr. G. Gwilt, on the original plan, in 1820, and is surmounted by a vane in the form of a dragon. In the church is a monument to the memory of Dr. Newton, bishop of Bristol. In this church the consecration of the bishops of London takes place; and here are preached the eight lectures instituted by Mr. Boyle, in defence of the Christian religion; they are delivered on the first Monday in each month from January to May, and from September to November.

St. Bride's,

Bride-lane, Fleet-street,

Is distinguished by the beauty of its spire, one of the finest works of Sir C. Wren. It was originally 234 feet high, but having been damaged by lightning, the height has been considerably reduced. Amongst the monuments in the interior is that of Richardson, the author of "Pamela," &c., who was buried in the middle aisle. This church was erected in 1680. It is 111 feet in length, 57 in breadth, and 41 in height. The interior is very imposing; it is divided into aisles by arches, and at the east end is a beautiful stained-glass window by the late Mr. Muss, representing the Descent from the Cross, after Rubens.

In 1826 a clock was put up in the tower of this church, the dial of which is illuminated every evening, so as to render the points of time as distinctly visible as at noon-day. This was the first attempt of the kind made in London. A considerable improvement was effected on the north side after a fire which destroyed some houses standing in the way of the prospect, which has since been obtained by not rebuilding on the spot.

St. Andrew Undershaft,

Leadenhall-street,

Was erected in 1532, and is so called from a may-pole or shaft which stood on this spot. The whole of this building, with the exception of the tower, is concealed behind houses. The interior is decorated with great taste; the ceiling is adorned with angels, and the compartments over the pillars which support it painted in imitation of basso-relievo. The east window is ornamented with five compartments of stained glass, representing Edward VI., queen Elizabeth, James I., and Charles I. and II. The pulpit is a fine specimen of carving, and there are several curious monuments, the most remarkable of which is that of Stow the historian, who is represented sitting at study.

CHRIST CHURCH,
Newgate-street,

Was erected in 1687 by Sir C. Wren, on the site of a church of Franciscans, where, it is said, no fewer than 600 or 700 persons of distinction were interred. The present church is a beautiful structure, with a lofty square tower. The pulpit is carved with representations of the Last Supper and of the four Evangelists. The front is of white marble, and is adorned with alto-relievos. The western window is ornamented with the royal arms and painted glass. Richard Baxter the non-conformist is buried within the walls of this building. The Spital sermons are preached in this church in Easter-week; and here, on St. Matthew's-day, a sermon is annually delivered before the lord mayor, aldermen, and governors of Christ's Hospital.

ST. DUNSTAN'S-IN-THE-WEST,
Fleet-street,

Was rebuilt in 1832, from designs by the late Mr. Shaw, on the site of the old church, which was one of the most ancient buildings in London. It was 90 feet long, 60 broad, and 36 high. At the eastern extremity there was a statue of queen Elizabeth, which was erected in 1766, and formerly stood on Ludgate: on the side facing the Strand behind the clock were two athletic figures with clubs in their hands, with which they struck the quarters. These pets of cockneys and countrymen were, on the demolition of the church, transferred to the guardianship of the marquess of Hertford at his villa in the Regent's-park.

The new building consists of a handsome stone Gothic tower attached to a mass of brickwork, which constitutes the body of the church. Over the entrance is a tablet to the memory of the architect, John Shaw, esq., who died the twelfth day

CHRIST CHURCH SPITALFIELDS.

ST LAWRENCE.

ST LEONARD SHOREDITCH.

ST PAUL COVENT GARDEN

after its external completion. The interior, which is octagonal, is very elegant; the lower part consists of Gothic recesses, in which the monuments are placed, while the upper part is decorated with elegant stained windows. The one over the communion-table represents the four Evangelists.

St. Dunstan's-in-the-East,

St. Dunstan's-hill, Tower-street,

Was rebuilt in the pointed style, under the direction of Mr. Laing, in 1820, with the exception of the tower, which is very much admired for its singular construction; the spire rests on the crowns of four pointed arches—a bold attempt in architecture, and one proof, amongst many, of the geometrical skill of Sir C. Wren, by whom it was constructed in 1678. The windows of the church are decorated with painted glass; that at the east end containing representations of the Ark, with Moses and Aaron, and over them our Saviour and the four Evangelists.

St. Lawrence,

King-street, Cheapside,

Is a handsome stone building erected in 1686 by Sir C. Wren, and ornamented at the east end with four beautiful Corinthian columns, supporting a pediment of the same order. Its spire is surmounted by the gridiron, in allusion to the martyrdom of St. Lawrence. The interior is neat, and the roof is adorned with fret-work. It contains a picture of the martyrdom of the saint, two monuments removed from Guildhall Chapel, and another to the memory of Archbishop Tillotson.

St. Paul,

Covent Garden.

This chaste edifice was erected from designs by Inigo Jones; the interior was burnt in 1795, but has been rebuilt by Mr. Hardwicke on the original plan of that eminent artist. Before this church is erected the hustings for electing members of parliament for Westminster. In the churchyard are deposited the remains of Butler, the author of "Hudibras;" Dr. Wolcot, so well known under the name of Peter Pindar, Michael Kelly the composer, and Johnstone the actor. This church has an illuminated dial.

Christ Church,

Spitalfields,

Is a handsome stone edifice, erected between 1723 and 1729. It has a Doric portico, with a fine flight of steps, and a steeple

234 feet high. The only monument in the interior worthy of notice is that by Flaxman to the memory of Sir Robert Ladbroke, lord-mayor of London. This church is 125 feet in length, 55 in breadth, and about 50 in height.

St. Leonard,
Shoreditch,

Is a plain brick building, with a stone front and spire, erected about 1735, by Dance the elder. It is 75 feet long, and 66 broad. The spire is about 70 feet in height. The portico consists of four Doric columns, surmounted by a triangular pediment. The eastern extremity of the interior is adorned with a painted window representing the Lord's Supper, the reconciliation of Jacob and Esau, Jacob's vision, and Jacob at prayer.

St. Mary's,
Wyndham-place, Bryanstone-square,

Was consecrated January 7, 1824. It is a simple and substantial edifice, erected by Mr. Smirke, and is capable of accommodating 2000 sitters. The principal front consists of a semicircular portico of Ionic pillars in high relief. The interior is almost entirely divested of ornament, and the roof, which is coved, is supported by fluted Doric pillars. Over the altar is a painted window of the Ascension, the figure of Christ being taken from that in the Transfiguration by Raphael; and at the extremity of the church is a fine-toned organ.

St. John-the-Evangelist,
Waterloo-bridge-road.

This church is a recent erection, the first stone having been laid June 30, 1823, by the Archbishop of Canterbury. The architect is Mr. Bedford. It is built with brick and stone, and is surmounted by a handsome steeple. The portico, which consists of six Doric columns, has an imposing appearance. This church will accommodate 2000 persons.

St. Giles,
Fore street, Cripplegate,

Was erected about 1546. Over the south-east door is a beautiful figure of Time, with his scythe, &c.; but the church is particularly remarkable as the burial-place of Fox the martyrologist, Speed the historian, and Milton the poet, whose remains were deposited under the clerk's desk, near those of his father. The monument to the memory of this distinguished man was erected by Bacon, at the expense of the late S. Whitbread, Esq. Oliver Cromwell was married in this church.

ST. SAVIOUR,

Southwark.

On the union of the two parishes of St. Margaret's and St. Mary Magdalen, the church of St. Mary Overy was made the parish church, by the name of St. Saviour. It formerly belonged to a priory founded before the Conquest; but little of its original architecture now remains, as it has been several times repaired, particularly in 1621, in 1703, and in 1825. At the last period its choir was restored by Mr. Gwilt, in the pointed style, of which it presents a fine specimen. The Ladye Chapel, which was formerly let as a *bakehouse* by the *corporation*, is the most beautiful feature of this imposing edifice; and owing to the spirited exertions of a few persons of taste, this exquisite relic has been restored to its pristine beauty. It is proposed to complete the ruinous portion of the edifice in a style in accordance with that already finished, as an additional place of worship for this populous neighbourhood. The church is a noble fabric, with three aisles running east and west, and a cross-aisle. It measures 270 feet in length, 54 in breadth, and 47 in height. The breadth at the cross-aisle is 109 feet. The tower, which is surmounted by four pinnacles, 150 feet high from the ground, is remarkable as the spot from which Hollar took his views of London, both before and after the great fire. The principal monuments are those to the memory of William Wickham, bishop of Lincoln; bishop Andrews; Gower, the contemporary of Chaucer (on the north wall); and A. Newland, Esq., for many years the chief cashier of the Bank of England; all of whom were buried in this church. Here also, in one grave, lie the dramatic writers Fletcher and Massinger.

To the right of the entrance is a stone bearing the city arms and the following inscription: "Christopher Smith, mayor, 1818. The jurisdiction of the city of London, in the town and borough of Southwark, extendeth eastward fronting the river Thames to St. Saviour's-Dock, Dock-Head; and southward to Lambeth, Newington, and St. Thomas-a-Watering, Kent-road, comprehending the parishes of St. Saviour (exclusive of the Clink Liberty), St. George, St. Thomas, St. Olave, and St. John."

ST. GILES'S-IN-THE-FIELDS,

Broad-street, St. Giles's.

This stately edifice, of Portland stone, was erected in 1730 by Henry Flitcroft. At the west end is a tower of the Doric and Ionic orders, terminated by a steeple. The ceiling, which is arched, is supported by Ionic pillars. This church contains a monument to the memory of Sir Roger l'Estrange. Here likewise are interred Andrew Marvel, the inflexible patriot; Richard Pendrell, the conductor of Charles II. after the battle of Worcester; Chapman, the first translator of Homer; and Flaxman, the great sculptor. The clock of this church is illuminated every night. At the north-west corner of the churchyard is a handsome portico, called the Resurrection-Gate, as over it is a fine bronze representation of the Resurrection executed about 1687. On the spot where this church is erected formerly stood an hospital, in front of which Sir John Oldcastle, Lord Cobham, was burnt for his religious opinions in the reign of Henry V. In the burying-ground belonging to this parish at St. Pancras is a handsome mausoleum erected by Sir J. Soane to the memory of his wife, in which he was also interred in 1837.

ST. SEPULCHRE'S,

Skinner-street,

Is a fine stone building, erected by Sir C. Wren in 1670. It is 126 feet in length, exclusive of the ambulatory at the west end, 58 in breadth, and 35 in height. Its venerable tower, 140 feet in height, has four modern spires, surmounted by vanes. The altar-piece is of the Corinthian order, the fronts of the galleries are handsomely carved, and the roof is supported by twelve pillars of the Tuscan order. The exterior was considerably improved in 1833.

ST. ANDREW'S,

Holborn-hill.

This spacious fabric was erected in 1687, under the direction of Sir Christopher Wren. The altar-piece and roof are ornamented with fret-work, and over the former is a painted window, representing the Last Supper and the Ascension. The organ is remarkable for its fine tone, and on each side is a fine painting. The celebrated Dr. Sacheverel used to preach here. This church is 105 feet in length, 63 in breadth, and 43 in height. The height of the tower, which was not finished till 1704, is 110 feet.

STEPNEY OLD CHURCH.

ST SEPULCHRES.

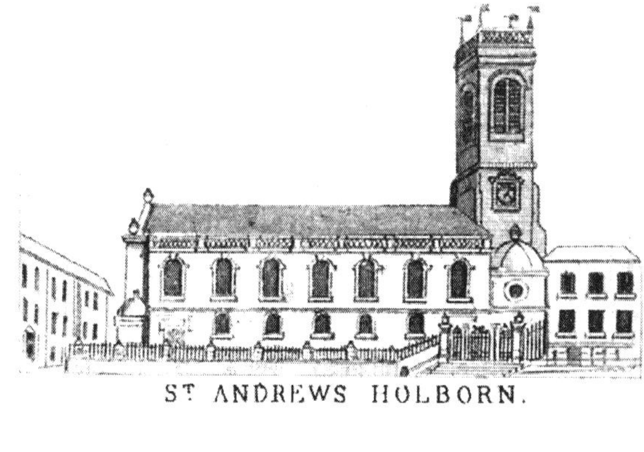

ST ANDREWS HOLBORN.

S.T PANCRAS NEW CHURCH.

S.T PHILIPS CHAPEL REGENT STREET.

Christ Church,

Woburn-square.

This beautiful Gothic edifice was erected in 1833 by Mr. Vulliamy, at an expense of less than 8000*l*. It is in the style of the ecclesiastical architecture of this country which flourished in the 14th and 15th centuries. The materials of which it is constructed are white brick and Bath stone. The principal front has a tower, which is united to a crocketed spire 150 feet high by means of flying buttresses. There are five entrance-doors in the front, and a similar number of windows, with mullions and rich tracery over them. Although insulated (as all Gothic edifices should necessarily be), the adjacent houses sufficiently approximate to impede the view of the side elevations. The interior, which will contain 1500 persons, forms a square of 70 feet by 48 in height, and four massive pillars supporting arches form a transept, the arms of which being equal to the length of the nave, the clerestory becomes a Greek cross. The case of the organ is designed in strict conformity with the style of the church. The great east window, which is enriched with mullions, transom, and elaborate tracery, is 28 feet by 13, and forms an important feature of this elegant church.

St. Dunstan's,

Stepney.

Is a capacious ancient structure, which appears to have been erected about the 14th century. The font is antique and curious, and in the wall of the western porch is a stone with an inscription purporting that it came from Carthage, and once formed part of the walls of that celebrated city. This church is 114 feet in length, 54 in breadth, and 35 in height. The tower is 92 feet high.

St. Pancras New Church,

Tavistock-place.

This splendid church was consecrated May 7th, 1822. The body of the edifice is of brick, but the whole is faced with Portland stone. It was erected by Mr. Inwood, at an expense of 76,000*l*., and is built in imitation of the temple of Erectheus at Athens. The portico is a beautiful erection, consisting of six Ionic pillars, beneath which are three doors, the centre being an exact representation of the entrance to the Greek temple. At the east end of the church are two projecting wings, designed for the registry and vestry-room, and formed upon the model of the Pandroseum which was attached to the Temple of Erectheus. The steeple, which is 168 feet in height, is also from an Athenian model, being built in resemblance of the Temple of the Winds. The interior, which is 117 feet in length, and 60 in breadth, is particularly elegant, the windows being composed of ground-glass with stained borders, the galleries supported by pillars taken from casts of the Elgin marbles, and the end of the church over the communion-table adorned with six verd antique scagliola columns, with bases and capitals of white marble, copied from the Temple of Minerva. The pulpit and reading-desk were formed out of the venerable tree so well known as the Fairlop Oak. Under the church are spacious catacombs.

ST. PETER'S CHURCH,

Wilton-place, Pimlico,

Is a chaste building of the Ionic order, erected in 1826 from designs by Mr. Hakewell. The portico consists of six fluted columns supporting a pediment, behind which rises a quadrangular tower, crowned with a spherical dome and cross. The body of the church is built of brick with stone dressings. The interior is neatly fitted up, and is capable of accommodating 1657 persons. The altar-piece is Mr. Hilton's picture of "Christ crowned with thorns," presented to the church by the British Institution in 1827. This church was burnt 1837, but has since been restored.

TRINITY CHURCH,

Trinity-square, Newington Butts,

Was built from designs by Mr. Bedford, and is capable of accommodating 2048 persons. The first stone was laid June 2d, 1823. The church is in the form of a cross, and the principal front faces the north. It is adorned with a portico consisting of six fluted Corinthian columns, over which rises a square belfry, surmounted by an octagonal tower containing eight bells. In front of the church is a statue of king Alfred.

ST. GEORGE-THE-MARTYR, High-street, Borough, was erected in 1737. Here Cocker the arithmetician and the infamous Bishop Bonner were interred; the former in the old church, erected in 1695, and the latter, who died in the Marshalsea prison, in the adjacent cemetery under the east window. This church is built of brick, with stone quoins. It is

69 feet in length, 60 in breadth, and 35 in height. The tower is 98 feet high.

St. Edmund-the-King-and-Martyr, and St. Nicholas Acon, Lombard-St. So called from the latter parish having been united to the former owing to the demolition of the church, which was never rebuilt. It was thoroughly repaired in 1833, and contains two pictures by Etty, representing Moses and Aaron.

St. Mary's, Newington Butts, erected by Hurlbatt in 1793, was the burial-place of the learned Bishop Horsley. In the churchyard is a monument to the memory of W. Allen, who was shot during the riots in St. George's-fields in 1768.

Allhallows, Bread-street, built in 1684 by Sir C. Wren, contains the remains of John Howe, an eminent nonconformist divine.

St. Luke's, Old-street-road, built in 1732 by Dance, is the only church in London with a steeple in the form of a fluted obelisk.

In the churchyard of St. Mary Rotherhithe, erected in 1739, is the grave of the amiable prince Lee Boo, who fell a victim to the small-pox in 1784.

St. Peter's, Cornhill, which was erected by Sir C. Wren in 1680, contains a monument to the memory of seven children, named Woodmason, who were all burnt in a house in Leadenhall-street, 1782.

St. Botolph, Bishopsgate-street, erected in 1727, from designs by Mr. James Gold, contains the monuments of Sir Paul Pindar, an eminent merchant and zealous adherent of Charles I. In the churchyard is that of a secretary to a Persian ambassador, with an inscription in Persian characters.

St. Catherine Cree, Leadenhall-street (90 feet long and 51 broad), built in 1630, but repaired in 1805, is the burial-place of the famous painter Hans Holbein, as well as of Sir Nicholas Throgmorton, ambassador to Queen Elizabeth.

St. Michael, Cornhill, the tower of which was rebuilt by Sir C. Wren in 1723, is noted for its beautiful tower, surmounted by four fluted turrets. In this church is the monument of Alderman Robert Fabian, the author of the "Chronicle of England and France," published in the early part of the sixteenth century.

St. Mary Aldermanbury, erected in 1676 by Sir C. Wren, was the burial-place of Dr. E. Calamy, a celebrated nonconformist divine, and of the infamous Judge Jefferies. In this church is a beautiful monument representing a female, executed by D. Cardelli of Rome.

St. Mary Woolnoth, Lombard-street, built by Hawksmoor in 1719, contains an epitaph on the Rev. John Newton, written by himself. He was buried here in 1807. It is a square building, the roof of which is supported by fluted Corinthian columns, and it is decorated with richly carved oak wainscoting.

St. Margaret's, Lothbury, built in 1690 by Sir C. Wren, contains a curious font, on the basin of which are carved representations of the Garden of Eden and Fall of Man; the salvation of Noah and his family; the baptism of Jesus; and Philip baptizing the Eunuch. The cover is adorned with a figure of St. Margaret, accompanied by Faith, Hope, and Charity.

St. Olave Jewry, in the Old Jewry, built by Sir C. Wren in 1673, is adorned with three pictures, representing Queen Elizabeth lying on a couch, Charles I., and a figure of Time with emblematical devices.

On the gate of St. Stephen's church, Coleman-street, built in 1670 by Sir C. Wren, is a grotesque representation of the Resurrection.

St. Bartholomew-the-Great, West-Smithfield, one of the most ancient churches in London, having been built in the early part of the 15th century, contains the tomb of Rahere, the founder of the adjacent hospital.

In St. Anne's, Blackfriars, or St. Andrew Wardrobe, built in 1670, by Sir C. Wren, is a beautiful monument by Bacon, erected in memory of the Rev. W. Romaine, who preached many years at this church.

St. Benedict, Bennet's-hill, rebuilt in 1683, was the burial-place of Inigo Jones the architect.

St. Michael, Paternoster Royal, near College-hill, built in 1694 by Sir C. Wren, contains the remains of the famous Sir Richard Whittington.

St. Magnus-the-Martyr, Thames-street, was erected by Sir C. Wren in 1676. The clock is said to be on an exact level with the ground at the end of Cornhill.

St. John Horselydown, built in 1732, has a lofty tower, and contains a picture by the Rev. Dr. Peters, representing St. John in the Isle of Patmos.

St. George, Botolph-lane, built in 1674 by Sir C. Wren, contains an inscription in memory of the patriotic lord-mayor, William Beckford, Esq.

ST. VEDAST, Foster-lane, erected by Sir C. Wren in 1698, is distinguished by a steeple of chaste and elegant architecture. Over the door is an ancient sculpture representing the Christian virtues.

STEPNEY NEW CHURCH, Mile-End-road, is in the pointed style of architecture. It was erected in 1819 from designs by Mr. Walters, who has given the interior, which is of carved oak, a light and elegant appearance.

ST. JOHN-THE-BAPTIST, Savoy-street, Strand, is an ancient Gothic structure, which originally formed the chapel of the Savoy-palace. The roof is remarkably fine, being adorned with carved representations of the holy Lamb, shields of arms, and other ornaments. Several of the monuments are very ancient and magnificent. The whole was repaired and beautified in 1820. It is sometimes called St. Mary-le-Savoy. Its length is about 87 feet, its breadth 26 feet, and its height 33. The tower is 75 feet in height.

ST. JAMES'S, Clerkenwell, rebuilt in 1790 by Mr. Carr, contains a monument with a Latin epitaph on Bishop Burnet, who, as well as Weever the sepulchral historian, was buried in the old church.

ST. PAUL'S, Shadwell, erected in 1820 by Mr. James Walters, is a neat building, with a spire of peculiar beauty.

ST. MARK, near Kennington-common, in Lambeth parish, was erected in 1824. Its form is an irregular octagon, and its steeple is very handsome. It is adorned with a Doric portico, and the interior, which is chaste and elegant, will accommodate 2000 persons. Mr. D. Roper was the architect.

CHRIST CHURCH, Marylebone, was built from designs by Mr. Hardwicke, and consecrated in 1825. The principal front, which is of the Ionic order, is in Stafford-street, Lisson-green. It is surmounted by a tower of bold proportions. The interior is of the Corinthian order, and is very neat. The altar-piece, the Nativity, is by West. It will accommodate 1844 persons.

ST. JOHN'S CHURCH, Hoxton, was erected in 1826, from designs by Mr. Edwards. It will accommodate nearly 2000 persons.

ST. BARNABAS' CHURCH, King-square, between the City-road and Goswell-street-road, was erected from designs by Mr. Hardwicke, and will contain 1608 persons. It has an Ionic portico and a spire. The first stone was laid January 27, 1822, and the building consecrated June 12, 1826.

ST. PETER'S, Beckford-place, Newington, was erected from

designs by Sir J. Soane in 1824. It is a brick edifice with stone dressing and Ionic columns on each side of the principal entrance, and will hold 2000 persons.

TRINITY CHURCH, Mary-le-bone, New-road, near Regent's-park, was erected in 1826, from designs by Sir J. Soane. It is a neat edifice of brick and stone, each side being adorned with six semi-columns of the Ionic order. The portico consists of four columns of the same order, and over it is a tower.

ST. MARY'S CHURCH, Haggerstone, was built in 1826 from a design by Mr. Nash. It is in the Gothic style.

BETHNAL GREEN NEW CHURCH was commenced in July 1825 from Sir J. Soane's designs. It is of Grecian architecture, and has a tower.

ST. MARK'S, Clerkenwell, in Myddleton-square, was consecrated January 2, 1828. It is a building of the Gothic style, and is capable of accommodating 1800 persons. Mr. Mylne was the architect.

TRINITY CHURCH, Rotherhithe, in the pointed Gothic style, erected 1838, will contain 1100 persons.

List of Churches not mentioned in the preceding descriptions, with the years in which they were built.

*St. Alban, Wood-street, 1685.
Allhallows Barking, Tower-st. 1651.
*Allhallows-the-Great, Thames-street, 1683.
*Allhallows, Lombard-street, 1694.
Allhallows, London-wall, built by Dance, 1766.
Allhallows Staining, Star-alley, Mark-lane, 1694.
All Saints, Poplar, 1824.
St. Alphage, Aldermanbury, built by Sir W. Staines, 1777.
*St. Anne's, St. Anne's-lane, Aldersgate, 1685.
St. Anne, Limehouse, built by Hawksmoor, 1729.
*St. Anthony, Budge-row, 1682.
*St. Augustine, or St. Austin, Watling-street, 1695.
*St. Bartholomew, Bartholomew-lane, 1679.
St. Bartholomew the Less, West-smithfield, about 1420.
*St. Benedict Fink, Threadneedle-street, 1673.
*St. Benedict, Gracechurch-street, 1685.
St. Botolph, Aldgate, 1744.
St. Botolph, Aldersgate, 1757.
St. Catherine Coleman, Fenchurch-street, 1734.
St. Catherine's Church, Regent's-park, 1828.
Christ Church, Blackfrs.-road, 1737.
*St. Clement Eastcheap, Clement's-lane, 1686, with a finely-carved pulpit, and a full-toned organ.
*St. Dionis Back Church, Lyme-street, Fenchurch-street, 1674.
*St. Edmund, Lombard-street, 1690.
St. Ethelburga, Bishopsgate-street, about 1420.
St. George-the-Martyr, Queen-square, Bloomsbury, built 1706, but not made parochial till 1723.
St. George-in-the-East, Ratcliffe-highway, built by Hawksmoor, 1729.
St. James, Duke's-place, 1622, but partly rebuilt 1727.
*St. James, Garlick-hill, 1683.
St. James, Bermondsey, 1827.
St. John, Clerkenwell, St. John's-square, 1723.

Those marked thus * were built by Sir C. Wren.

St. John, Wapping, 1789.
St. Margaret, Lothbury, 1690.
*St. Margaret Pattens, Rood-lane, 1687.
*St. Martin, Ludgate-street, 1684.
St. Martin Outwich, Threadneedle-street, 1796.
*St. Mary, Abchurch-lane, 1686.
*St. Mary, Aldermary, Bow-lane, 1681.
*St. Mary-at-Hill, Lower Thames-street, partly rebuilt 1670.
*St. Mary Magdalen, Old Fish-st., 1685.
St. Mary Magdalen, Bermondsey, 1680.
*St. Mary Somerset, Upper Thames-street, 1695.
St. Mary, Whitechapel, 1764.
St. Mary-le-bone Old Church, High-street, 1741.
St. Matthew, Bethnal-green, 1740.
*St. Matthew, Friday-street, 1669.
*St. Michael Bassishaw, Basing-hall-street, 1679,
*St. Michael, Queenhithe, 1677.
*St. Michael, Wood-street, 1669.
*St. Mildred, Bread-street, 1683.
*St. Mildred, Poultry, 1676.
*St. Nicholas, Cole-abbey, Old Fish-street, 1676.
St. Olave, Hart-street, Crutched-friars, date of its erection unknown.
St. Olave, Tooley-street, 1739.
St. Paul's, Ball's-pond, 1826.
St. Peter the Poor, Broad-street, built by Gibbs, 1791.
St. Peter ad Vincula, in the Tower, date of its erection unknown.
*St. Swithin, Cannon-street, 1680.
St. Thomas, Southwark, 1732.
Trinity Church, Minories, 1706.
Trinity Church, Sloane-street.

EPISCOPAL CHAPELS.

Albemarle-st., St. George's Chapel.
Asylum, Westminster-road.—Rebuilt in 1825.
Audley-st., South, GrosvenorChapel.
Baker-street, Portman-square.
Bedford-row, Milman-street. St. John's Chapel is that in which Mr. Cecil formerly preached.
Belgrave Chapel, Brompton.
Bentinck Chapel.
Berkeley-street, Upper, Brunswick Chapel.
Berkeley-street, Soho.
Berwick-street, Chapel-of-Ease to St. James's.
Bethnal-green, Jews' Chapel. This is a handsome modern building, having schools on each side of it for the education of Jewish children.
Bethnal-green, New Church.
Blackfriars-road, Surrey Chapel. This is one of the largest in London, being capable of holding 3,000 persons. It has a very fine-toned organ of extensive powers.
Bridge-street, Bridewell Chapel.
Broad-court, Drury-lane, Tavistock Chapel.
Broadway, Westminster.
Burleigh-street, Strand. St. Michael's chapel of ease to St. Martin's. Built in 1833 from designs by Mr. Savage.
Camden Town. This is one of the new chapels in St. Pancras. It was finished and consecrated in 1824.
Charlotte-street, Bloomsbury, Bedford Chapel.
Charlotte-street, Fitzroy-sq., Percy Chapel.
Charlotte-street, Fitzroy-sq., Charlotte Chapel.
Charlotte-street, Pimlico.
Charter-house-square.
Chelsea, Park Chapel.
Chelsea, Hospital Chapel.
Chelsea, St. George's Chapel.
Church-street, Hackney.
Clarence-street, Park-village, erected by Mr. Pennefeather.
Cloudesly-square.
Conduit-street, Bond-street. Trinity Chapel is built on the site of a wooden chapel on wheels, which was placed here after it had been used by James II.'s army at Hounslow.
Curzon-st., May-fair, Curzon Chapel.
Duke-street, Westminster. This

chapel forms part of a house which was built by the infamous Judge Jefferies.
Eaton-square, Eaton Chapel.
Ely-place, Holborn. Ely Chapel is distinguished by an ancient Gothic window of great beauty.
Foundling Hospital.
Gray's Inn.
Halkin-st., Grosvenor-place, Belgrave Chapel.
Ironmonger-lane, Mercers'-hall.
John-street, Berkeley-square.
Kent-road.
Lincoln's Inn.
Little Queen-street, Lincoln's Inn. Chapel of the Holy Trinity, a chapel of ease to St. Giles's. It is a Gothic edifice, erected in 1829 from designs by Mr. Bedford.
Lisson-grove, St. Paul's, 1838, will contain 1,100 persons.
Lock Hospital.
London-road, Philanthropic Chapel.
London-street, Fitzroy Chapel.
London-wall, Allhallows.
Long-acre.
Magdalen Hospital.
Maida-hill, Christ Chapel.
Margaret-street, Cavendish-square.
Mercers'-hall.
Minories.
Monkwell-street, Lamb's Chapel. This chapel was founded in the reign of Edward I., but derives its present name from Mr. Lamb, a clothworker in the time of Henry VIII., in pursuance of whose will four sermons are annually preached to the company of clothworkers, on the four principal festivals. It was rebuilt, together with the adjacent almshouses, in 1825.
New-road, Paddington Chapel.
New-street-square, Holy Trinity. Built 1837, will contain 1,100.
North Audley-street, St. Mark's Chapel is a chaste edifice, consecrated in 1828. It was built from designs by Mr. Gandy Deering. The front presents a portico of the Ionic order, above which rises a neat tower.
Oxendon-street. This chapel was originally built for a meeting-house, in which the celebrated nonconformist Richard Baxter officiated.
Paddington, Chapel-street, Bentinck Chapel.
Palestine-place, belonging to the Society for Promoting Christianity among the Jews.
Park-street, Grosvenor-square.
Pentonville, St. James's Chapel.
Poplar, E. I. Company's Chapel.
Portland-street, Portland Chapel.
Quebec-street, Portman-square.
Queen-square, Westminster.
Queen-street, Thames-street.
Regent's-park, St. John's Wood, Chapel.
Regent-street, Archbp. Tennison's Chapel. Rebuilt in 1823.
Regent-street. Hanover Chapel was erected in 1824, from designs by Mr. Cockerell, as a chapel of ease to St. George's church. It has an Ionic portico of four columns, and is surmounted by a cupola. In front are two square belfries. The altar is a fine specimen of architectural composition. This chapel will accommodate 1,580 persons.
Regent-street, St. Philip's, or Waterloo Chapel, erected from designs by Mr. Repton in 1820, is a handsome edifice with a noble portico, supported by four fluted pillars of the Doric order. The tower is a copy of the Choragic monument of Lysicrates at Athens. The interior is fitted up in the most elegant style, and is very fashionably attended. It is capable of accommodating 1,500 persons.
Regent-street, chapel of ease to St. James's.
Rolls' Chapel, Chancery-lane, is adorned with some beautiful stained glass, and contains, besides other monuments, one in memory of Dr. Yonge, executed by Pietro Torregiano, a celebrated Florentine sculptor. —Lord Gifford was buried here in 1826.

Saffron-hill, St. Andrew's Chapel, erected in 1831. A brick edifice, with stone Gothic windows, and two turrets over the west entrance; it is 100 feet by 64, and 60 feet high, and will accommodate 2,000 persons.
Seymour-street, Portman-square, Trinity Chapel.
Sidmouth-street, Regent Chapel. This chapel of ease to St. Pancras was built by Mr. Inwood in 1824, and will accommodate 1,832 persons. It is a plain brick building, but has a stone steeple, and a handsome portico of the Ionic order.
Somers-Town Chapel was built in 1824, as a chapel of ease to St. Pancras. It is a neat specimen of the Gothic style, with a tower and pinnacles, and will hold 2,000 persons.
South Lambeth.
Spital-square, Wheeler Chapel.
Spring-gardens.
St. James's Palace, Chapel Royal.
Tavistock-place, Russell-sq., Tavistock Chapel.
Thames-street, St. Mary.
Trinity-street.
Vauxhall, St. Paul's.
Vere-street, Oxford-street, Oxford Chapel.
Vincent-square, Chapel of ease to St. John's. Gothic, from designs by Mr. Blore.
Wapping, Episcopal Floating Chapel.
Welbeck-street, Welbeck Chapel.
West-street, Seven-dials. Service in Irish.
Westmoreland-street, Welbeck Chapel.
Whitehall, Chapel Royal.

ROMAN CATHOLIC CHAPELS.

Chelsea, Chapel-place, Cadogan-street, Sloane-square.
Clarendon-square, Somers-town.
Duke-street, Lincoln's-inn-fields—*Sardinian.*
East-lane, Bermondsey.
Grove-road, St. John's-wood.
Holland-street, Kensington.
Horseferry-road.
Little George-street, Portman-sq.—*French.*
London-road, Prospect-row.
Moorfields.
Parker-row, Dockhead.
Poplar, Wade-street.
Prospect-place, St. George's-fields.
Romney-terrace, Horseferry-road.
South-street, May-fair.
St. Thomas Apostle—*German.*
Spanish-place, Manchester-square—*Spanish.*
Sutton-street, Soho—*Irish.*
Virginia-street, Ratcliffe.
Warwick-street, Golden-square—*Bavarian.*
White-street, Moorfields.

There are Catholic chapels also at Hampstead, Stratford, Greenwich, Woolwich, Isleworth, Richmond, Kensington, and Hammersmith.

At most of the above chapels, but particularly at Moorfields, Spanish-place, and Warwick-street, the instrumental and vocal performances on Sundays and festivals are conducted by eminent professional characters. The door-keepers expect a donation for admitting strangers to the pews. The chapel at Moorfields, built by Mr. Newman, is well worthy of inspection; behind the altar, which is adorned with several fine marble columns, is a fresco of the Crucifixion; and on the ceiling are represented the Virgin Mary, the infant Jesus, and the four Evangelists, surrounded by paintings of the principal events in the life of our Saviour. These pictures were painted by M. Aglio, an Italian artist. Admission may be obtained for 6*d*.

The chapel in Spanish-place, constructed from designs by Bonomi, is much admired for its classical style of architecture.

JEWS' SYNAGOGUES.

The new synagogue in Great St. Helens is an elegant edifice, erected by Mr. Davis, and consecrated Sept. 1838.

Back-alley, Denmark-ct., Strand.
Baker's-gardens, Leadenhall-street.
Bevis Marks, Duke's-place—*Portuguese.*
Bricklayers'-hall, Leadenhall-st.
Carters'-street, Houndsditch.
Church-row, Fenchurch-street.
Dean-street, Soho.
Duke's-place—*German.*
Prospect-place, St. George's-road.
Queen-street, Curzon-street.
St. Alban's-place, St. James's-sq.

MEETING-HOUSES OF THE FRIENDS, OR QUAKERS.

Brook-street, Ratcliffe.
Devonshire-house, Bishopsgate-st.
Houndsditch, No. 86.
Red-Cross-street, Borough.
St. Peter's-court, St. Martin's-lane.
St. John's-street, Smithfield.
School-house-lane, Ratcliffe.
White Hart-court, Gracechurch-st

The meeting-house of the Friends at the latter place, which was burnt down in September 1821, was the oldest in London, and was remarkable as the place where the celebrated George Fox, and the equally celebrated founder of Pennsylvania, inculcated their pacific tenets.

FOREIGN PROTESTANT CHURCHES AND CHAPELS.

ARMENIAN. Princes-row, Spitalfields.

DANISH. Wellclose-square.

DUTCH. 1. Austin-friars. 2. St. James's Palace. The first is a spacious Gothic edifice of great antiquity, having been erected in 1351; and the library attached to it contains several curious MSS., amongst which are letters of Calvin and other foreign reformers.

FRENCH. 1. Austin-friars (same as the Dutch Church). 2. Clements-lane, Lombard street. 3. Little Dean-street. 4. St. John-street, Brick-lane. 5. Threadneedle-street. 6. Trinity-lane, Bread-street.

GERMAN. 1. Austin-friars. 2. Brown's-lane, Spitalfields. 3. Little Alie-street (Lutheran). 4. Little Trinity-lane. 5. Ludgate-hill. 6. St. James's Palace. 7. Savoy-street (Lutheran). 8. Hooper-square, Goodman's-fields.

RUSSIAN. Welbeck-street, Cavendish-square.

SWISS. Moor-street, Seven-dials.

SWEDISH. Princes-square.

DISSENTERS' MEETING-HOUSES.

Explanation:—A. Arian; B. Baptist; C. Calvinist; F. Freethinkers; H. Huntingtonian; L. H. Lady Huntingdon's; M. Moravian; S. Swedenborgian; S. C. Scotch Calvinist; S. Ch. Scotch Church; S. S. Scotch Secession; Sa. Sandemanian; U. Unitarian; W. M. Wesleyan Methodist; Wh. M. Whitfield Methodist.

Adelphi, Strand . . . L.H.
Aldermanbury-postern . . C.
Aldersgate-street, Glass-house-yard . . . . . . C.
Aldersgate-street, Hare-court . C.
Artillery-lane . . . . . U.
Artillery-street . . . . C.
Alie-street . . . . . C.
Back-street, Horselydown . . C.
Barbican . . . . . . C.
Bermondsey, K. John's-court C.
Bermondsey, Neckinger-road . C.
Bermondsey, Paragon Chapel C.
Bethnal-green . . . . . C.
Bethnal-green, Gibraltar Chapel C.
Black's fields . . . . . B.
Blandford-street, Manchester-square . . . . . . B.
Bloomfield-street, Moorfields S.C.
Is an elegant building, erected in 1826 from designs by Mr. Brooks. It is called Finsbury Chapel.
Boar's-head-ct., Petticoat-lane C.
Broad-street, New . . . C.
Broad-street, Wapping . . C.
Brompton, Trevor Chapel . C.
Bull-lane, Stepney . . . C.
Burton-street, Burton-crescent B.
Bury-street, St. Mary Axe . C.
Here Dr. Watts formerly officiated.
Camomile-street . . . . C.
Cannon-street-road, St. George's-in-the-East . . . . . C.
Carnaby-street, near Marlborough-street, (Craven Chapel) . . . . C.
Carter-lane, Doctors' Commons A.
Chapel-street, Soho . . . C.
Chapel-path, Somers-town . B.
Chapman-street, St. George's-in-the-East . . . . B.
Chelsea, Paradise Chapel . . B.
China-terrace, Lambeth . W.M.
Church-lane, Whitechapel . C.
Church-street, Blackfriars . . B.
Church-street, Lambeth . Welsh
Church-street, Mile-end . . C.
City-road . . . . . W.M.
This chapel was erected by the Rev. J. Wesley on the site of the City-foundry, which was used so late as 1715 for casting cannon.
City-road, at the Orphan Sch. C.
———, by Pickford's wharf B.
Clement's-inn . . . . B.
Collier's-rents, Long-lane, Southwark . . . . . . C.
Compton-place, East . . B.
Cook's-grounds, Chelsea . . C.
Crescent, near Jewin-street . F.
Crosby-row, Snow's-fields . . B.
Cross-street, Hatton-garden . S.
This chapel stands on the site of Hatton-house, built by the lord chancellor of that name.
Crown-court, Russell-street S.C.
Crown-street, Soho . . . C.
Cumberland-street, Curtain-road . . . . . Wh.M.
Dean-street, Tooley-street . B.
Denmark-street . . . . B.
Devonshire-square . . . B.
Dudley-street, Soho . . . S.
Eagle-street, Red-lion-square B.
Eagle-street, Spitalfields . W.M.
Eastcheap, Little . . . C.
Edward-street, Soho . . . B.
Essex-street, Strand . . U.
This meeting was formerly a portion of the house occupied by Robert Devereux, earl of Essex.
Ewer's-street, Borough . . B.
Fetter-lane . . . . . . C.
———, Elim-court . . B.
———, Nevil's-court . . M.
Gainsford-street, Borough W.M.
Gate-st., Lincoln's-inn-fields W.M.
Goswell-street-road . . . C.
Gower-street, North . . L.H.
Grafton-street, Soho . . B.
Grange-road . . . . . H.
Gravel-lane, Wapping . . C.

Gray's-inn-lane . . . . . H.
Erected by the notorious William Huntington.
Green-walk, Blackfriars-road . C.
Grub-street . . . . . C.
Guildford-street, Little, Borough . . . . . Welsh
Haberdashers' Hall. See *Staining-lane.*
Hare-street, Spitalfields . . C.
Hinde-street, Manchester-sq. W.M.
Holloway . . . . . . C.
Holywell-mount, Shoreditch . C.
Hope-street, Spitalfields . . C.
Horseferry-road . . . . W.M.
Horselydown, Parish-street . C.
Hoxton . . . . W.M.
Hoxton Missionary College . C.
Ireland-yard, Blackfriars . . S.
Jamaica-row, Rotherhithe . C.
——————— . . B.
Jewin-street . . . . . A.
Called Old Jewry Chapel from its former situation; was built from designs by Mr. E. Aikin in 1808. Here Dr. Rees, the editor of the Cyclopædia, preached till the time of his death in 1825.
Jewin-street . . . . . C.
Jewin-street, Crescent Welsh C.
Jewry-street, Aldgate . . . C.
John-street, Bedford-row . C.
Johnston-street, Old Gravel-lane . . . . . . C.
Kent-road, Alfred-place . . B.
Kent-road . . . . . C.
Kent-street, Southwark . . B.
Keppell-street, Russell-square B.
Lambeth, Walcot-place, Verulam Chapel . . . S.C.
Leading-street, Shadwell . . C.
Leather-lane, Holborn . . A.
——————— . . W.M.
Lewisham-street, Westminster B.
Lisle-street, Leicester-square . B.
Liverpool-st., Battle-bridge W.M.
Lock's-fields . . . . . C.
London-road . . . . . C.
London-wall, Coleman-street S.C.
Long-lane, Southwark . W.M.
Maiden-lane, Covent-garden B.
Mark-lane . . . . . C.
Market-street, May-fair . . C.
Maze-pond, Southwark . . B.
Meeting-house-walk, Snow's-fields . . . . . B.
Middlesex-court, Bartholomew-close . . . . . . C.
Mile-end-road, Brunswick-Chapel . . . . . C.
Mile-end Meeting . . . C.
Mile-end New Town . . C.
Mile's-lane, Cannon-street . S.C.
Mill-lane, Cable-street . . C.
Mitchell-street, Old-street . B.
Moorfields, Albion Chapel . . S.C.
Was erected from designs by Mr. Jay. It has a handsome portico, and is surmounted by a dome, covered with copper, and surrounded by a range of semicircular windows.
Mulberry-gardens, Whitechapel C.
New-court, Carey-street . . C.
This meeting has had several eminent pastors, amongst whom may be mentioned Mr. Daniel Burgess, Mr. Thomas Bradbury, Mr. R. Winter, and Dr. Winter.
Newington Butts . . . . C.
Newman-st., Irving's chapel . S.S.
New Park-street, Southwark . B.
New-road, Paddington . . C.
————, Somers' town . . C.
————, St. George's-in-the-East . . . . . . C.
Nightingale-lane, East-smithfield . . . . . . C.
Orange-st., Leicester-square L.H.
Oxford-court, Cannon-street . B.
Paddington Chapel . . . C.
Palace-street, Pimlico . . C.
Paradise-street, Lambeth . B.
Pavement, Moorfields . . C.
Pell street . . . . . C.
Pentonville, Claremont Chapel C.
Peter-street, Soho . . S.C.
Portland-street (Little) . . U.
A beautiful edifice both in internal and external decoration. Built in 1833.
Poultry . . . . . . C.
This chapel was erected in 1819, on the site of the Poultry Compter or prison.
Prescot-street . . . . . B.
Queen-street, Southwark . . B.
Queen-street, Ratcliffe . . C.
Queen-street, Great, Lincoln's-inn-fields . . . . W.M.
Is a spacious edifice, erected in

1818. The interior is remarkably chaste and elegant, and has a double gallery.
Ratcliffe, Ebenezer . . C.
Red Cross-street, City . . B.
——————— . . Sa.
Regent square . . . S. Ch.
Robert-street, Grosvenor-sq. . C.
Romney-street, Westminster . B.
Rose-lane, Ratcliffe . . C.
Salisbury-street, Bermondsey . C.
Salter's Hall. See *Oxford-court.*
Shakspeare's Walk, Shadwell . C.
Shoe-lane, Fleet-street . . C.
Shouldham-st., Edgeware-rd. . B.
Silver-street, Falcon-square . C.
Sidmouth-street, Gray's-inn-lane. *Scotch Church* . S.C.
Is an edifice in the Gothic style, the first stone of which was laid July 1st, 1824. The interior is 100 feet long and 63 broad, and is capable of accommodating 1,800 persons. It was designed by Mr. Tite.
South-place, Moorfields . . U.
Is a handsome edifice, built in 1823.
——————— . Welsh B.
St. Helen's, Little . . W.M.
St. Thomas-street, Southwark U.
Spa-fields Chapel . . Wh.M.
Was formerly a tavern, but was converted to its present use about 1780, by the celebrated Lady Huntingdon.
Spencer-place, Goswell-street-road . . . . . . B.
Staining-lane, Cheapside . . C.
Stamford-street . . . U.
This chapel is adorned with a noble portico.
Stepney . . . . . . C.
It is reported that the congregation of this ancient edifice has been presided over for the space of two centuries by four ministers alone.
Swallow-street . . . S.C.
Tabernacle-walk, Finsbury Wh.M.
Was erected by the Rev. G. Whitfield.
——————— . B.
Three Crane-lane, Thames-st. C.
Tichfield-street . . . H.
Tottenham-court-road . Wh.M.
In this chapel Bacon the sculptor was buried in 1799.
Unicorn-yard, Tooley-street . B.
Union-street, Borough . . C.
Walworth . . . . . B.
——————— . . . . W.M.
———————, Lock's-fields . . C.
———————, West-lane . . C.
Wardour-street, Soho . . . C.
Waterloo-bridge-road . . S.
——————— . . . C.
Wells-street, Oxford-street S.C.
Wharf-road, Paddington . . C.
White's-row, Spitalfields . . C.
Wild-street, Little . . . B.
Wood-street, London-wall . . B.
Woodd-street, Pancras . . U.
Worship-street, Finsbury U. & B.
York-street, St. James's-square U.

DISSENTERS' BURIAL-GROUND,

Bunhill-fields.

The present Artillery-ground, together with the land on the north side as far as Old-street, was anciently termed Bonhill, or Bunhill-fields. A part of this field, on the north side of the Artillery-ground, now called Tindal's, or the Dissenters' Burial-ground, was consecrated and walled at the expense of the city in the pestilential year 1665, as a common cemetery for the interment of such bodies as could not have room in their parochial burial-ground; but not being used on this occasion, Dr. Tindal took a lease of it, and converted it into a cemetery for the use of the Dissenters.

In this extensive cemetery lie the remains of many distinguished Nonconformists. Amongst them are the following:—

John Bunyan, author of the "Pilgrim's Progress;" Dr. Williams, founder of the Dissenters' Library in Red-cross-street; Mrs. Susannah Wesley, mother of the celebrated John and Charles Wesley; Dr. Isaac Watts; the Rev. D. Neale, author of the History of the Puritans; Dr. Lardner, the learned author of the Credibility of the Gospel History; Dr. John Guise, Dr. Langford, Dr. Gill, Dr. Stennett, Dr. Harris, Dr. S. M. Savage. Dr. Richard Price, author of Reversionary Payments, and other highly distinguished publications; Dr. Henry Hunter, Dr. Fisher, the Rev. Theophilus Lindsey, Rev. Hugh Worthington, Dr. Robert Young, Dr. Lindsey, Dr. A. Rees, the editor of the Cyclopædia; Rev. John Townsend, the founder of the Deaf and Dumb Asylum; George Walker, of Nottingham and Manchester; the Rev. Thomas Belsham; and Dr. W. Harris.

The City Bunhill Burial-Ground.

This cemetery, which is open to all persuasions, contains nearly two acres, lying in the rear of Beech-street, Cripplegate, between Golden-lane and Whitecross-street, from each of which there is a convenient entrance. It is laid down with lawn-grasses, with dry gravel-walks, ornamented with trees and shrubs, and is surrounded by a wall 20 feet high. A clergyman in ordinary is appointed to do funeral duty, but individuals, if they prefer it, may have a clergyman of their own choice.

General Cemetery,

Kensall-green, Harrow-road.

A cemetery for the interment of persons of all religious persuasions has been lately established, under the sanction of an act of parliament, on an elevated and beautiful site on the Harrow-road, within three miles of Oxford-street. It contains nearly fifty acres of ground, surrounded on three sides by a high and massive wall, and on the remaining side, in order to admit a view of the scenery of the adjoining country, by a handsome iron railing of equal height with the wall, the enclosed area being planted and laid out in walks, after the manner of Père la Chaise at Paris.

The greater part has been consecrated, and a small temporary chapel has been erected for the performance of the burial-service according to the forms of the established church, to which office a clergyman of the Church of England has been appointed. In the unconsecrated part, which is appropriated to the use of such persons as object to the burial-service of the Established Church, an elegant Doric chapel has been erected, where the burial rites of every religious sect may be solemnized. In both parts catacombs affording space for the interment of upwards of 2,000 persons have been prepared. Among the many advantages attending this place of sepulture, in addition to the effect on the health of the public by removing interments from the town, may be enumerated the perfect security of the dead, the affording to persons of all religious persuasions the power of having the funeral service performed according to their own ideas of propriety, with the benefit of a burial register authorized and made evidence by an act of parliament; the insuring to the owners of private graves and vaults the perpetual and exclusive right of interment in them, which is unattainable in the ordinary yards, even by purchase, without a faculty; and, lastly, a great reduction in the fees and charges for interments, and the privilege of erecting grave-stones or monuments of every description.

Office of the Establishment, No. 95 Great Russell-street, Bloomsbury, where all applications for interments and information are to be made to Mr. Bowman, the secretary.

Northern Cemetery,

Swain's-lane, Highgate.

The London Cemetery Company, empowered by act of parliament, have commenced their plans of establishing northern, southern, and eastern cemeteries, by erecting a small and elegant structure, from designs by Mr. S. Geary, at the entrance of their northern cemetery, which occupies the southern slope of Highgate-hill, near the new Gothic church. Within the present space of 400 yards by 250 are contained the cemetery-garden, the terrace, catacombs, and Lebanon sepulchres.

Abney-park, at the northern extremity of Stoke Newington, has been purchased by a Cemetery company with a capital of 35,000*l*. in 10*l*. shares.

The South London Cemetery Company have established a cemetery at Norwood, and the City of London and Tower-Hamlets Cemetery Company are located at the Mile-end-road.

PALACES, PARKS, PUBLIC BUILDINGS, &c.

ST. JAMES'S PALACE,

Pall Mall,

Was built by Henry VIII. on the site of an hospital of the same name. It has been the acknowledged town residence of the English kings since Whitehall was consumed in 1695; but though pleasantly situated on the north side of St. James's Park, and possessing many elegant and convenient apartments calculated for state purposes, yet it is an irregular brick building, without a single external beauty to recommend it as a palace. In the front next St. James's-street, little more than an old gatehouse appears, which serves as an entrance to a small square court, with a piazza on the west of it, leading to the grand staircase. The buildings are low, plain, and mean; beyond this are two other courts, which have little appearance of a king's palace. The state apartments look toward the park; and this side, though certainly not imposing, cannot be pronounced mean. It is of one story, and has a regular appearance not to be found in other parts of the building. The south-east wing was destroyed by fire in 1809, and has never been rebuilt, though the whole of the palace was repaired in 1821-2-3.

The state apartments, newly furnished in 1824, are entered by a passage and staircase of great simplicity. The walls are distempered of a dead stone-colour, and are lighted by Grecian bronze lights, with moon-shades placed on plain granite pedestals, which have an air of quakerly neatness quite in unison with this part of the edifice. The exterior walls are sprinkled with black and white in imitation of granite.

On ascending the staircase is seen a sort of gallery or guard-rooom, converted into an armoury, the walls of which are decorated with daggers, swords, and muskets, in various devices. When a drawing-room is held, this apartment is occupied by the yeomen of the guard, in full costume, with their battle-axes in their hands.

The next room is a small chamber, covered with tapestry, in fine preservation, from the ceiling of which hangs an elegant chandelier. When a drawing-room is held, a person attends here to receive the cards containing the names of the parties to be presented, with the circumstances under which such presentation takes place. A duplicate of the card is

ST JAMES'S PALACE.

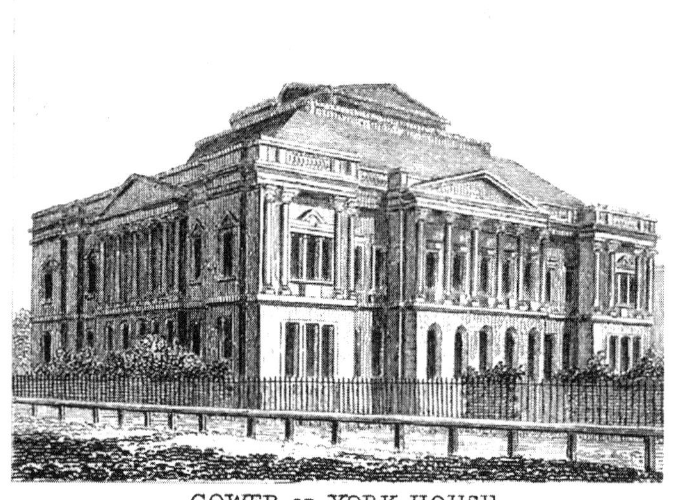

GOWER OR YORK HOUSE

subsequently handed to the lord in waiting, in order to prevent the introduction of improper persons.

The next room is the first of a succession of three rooms, the last of which may be entitled the Presence-Chamber. It is fitted up in a style of matchless splendour. The walls are covered with crimson damask, and the window-curtains are of the same material. The cornices and basements are formed of broad carved and gilt moulding, and extend to every part of the room. On entering, the eye of the spectator is first attracted by a looking-glass of unusual magnitude, which extends completely from the ceiling to the floor. At the east end of the room is a painting of George II. in his parliamentary robes; and on the other walls hang two large pictures of Tournay and Lisle. The furniture consists of sofas, ottomans, and stools covered with crimson velvet, trimmed with gold lace. From the ceiling hangs a superb *or-molu* lustre, containing two rows of lights of three branches each, and at each end of the apartment are two splendid candelabras, elegantly gilt, calculated to receive twelve lights each.

The next room is fitted up in the same style of decoration, and contains an excellent full-length portrait of George III. in the robes of his order. On each side of these are two paintings of the celebrated sea-fights of lord Howe on the 1st of June, and of lord Nelson at Trafalgar. The brilliant effect of the whole is considerably heightened by the addition of three magnificent pier-glasses, reaching from the ceiling to the floor. From the centre of the ceiling also hangs a delicately-chased Grecian lustre.

The third and last room is the Presence-Chamber, in which the queen holds her drawing-rooms. This, in point of gorgeous decoration, far exceeds the preceding rooms, although the style is somewhat similar. The throne is splendid, and, in point of size and magnificence of effect, far exceeds that in the House of Lords. It is composed of rich crimson Genoa velvet, thickly covered with gold lace, and is surmounted by a canopy of the same material, on the inside of which is a star embroidered in gold. There are three steps for her majesty to ascend, which lead to a state-chair of exquisite workmanship, close to which is a footstool to correspond. Over the fire-place is a full-length portrait of George IV. in his coronation-robes, by Sir T. Lawrence. On each side of this picture are paintings of the battles of Vittoria and Waterloo. The piers of the room are entirely filled up with plate-glass, before which are some beautiful marble slabs.

The window-curtains are of crimson satin, trimmed with gold-coloured fringe and lace. The cornices, mouldings, &c. are richly gilt; and the other embellishments and furniture, of corresponding elegance, present a *coup-d'œil* in every way suited to the dignity and splendour of the British court.

Behind the Presence-Chamber is her majesty's closet, in which she gives audience, and receives the members of her own family, foreign ambassadors, cabinet-ministers, and officers of state. It contains a state chair and footstool, elegant writing-table, with buhl inkstand, and other useful furniture. The queen's dressing or private room is beyond this.

There is another room belonging to this spacious suite, which was the old ball-room, but has been entirely new modelled upon the French plan, and forms a supper-room, for which purpose a communication has been made with the old kitchen. The walls are of white ground, richly gilt in compartments of various descriptions. It has five *or-molu* lustres, and it is thought not to be exceeded by any other apartment of the same magnitude in the kingdom.

In one of the rooms, formerly the ante-chamber to the levee-room, James, the son of James II., afterwards styled the Pretender, was born; and at the entrance to this palace an attempt was made on the life of George III. by an insane woman named Margaret Nicholson in 1786.

Buckingham, or St. James's Palace,
St. James's Park.

Was erected in 1703, on the site of what was originally called the Mulberry-gardens, by the learned and accomplished John Sheffield, duke of Buckingham, who died in 1720. In 1761 this palace became the property of the late queen Charlotte, who made it her town residence; and here all her children, with the exception of the eldest, were born. Here likewise several royal marriages have taken place: the late duke of York and princess Frederica of Prussia in 1791; duke of Gloucester and princess Mary, 1816; prince of Homburg and princess Elizabeth, 1818; and the duke of Cambridge and princess of Hesse in the same year.

Between 1825 and 1830, the whole of the building was remodelled under the direction of Mr. Nash; and it is now called

The Queen's Palace in St. James's Park.

The centre is a parallelogram, from each side of which extends a wing, the whole forming three sides of a square. The base-

KING'S PALACE, AS SEEN FROM THE GARDEN.

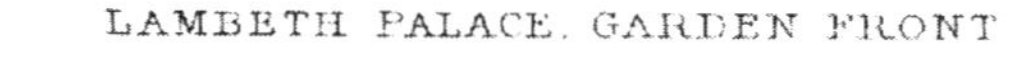

LAMBETH PALACE, GARDEN FRONT

ment is of the Doric and the upper part of the Corinthian order. At the end of each wing is a pediment, with groups of figures illustrative of the arts and sciences. On the left wing are placed statues of History, Geography, and Astronomy; and on the right, Painting, Music, and Architecture. The pediment in the centre of the building contains the royal arms, above which are statues of Neptune, Commerce, and Navigation. Around the entire building, and above the windows, is a frieze, combining in a scroll the rose, shamrock, and thistle.

The completion of this edifice devolved at length upon Mr. Blore, after repeated alterations in form and expense had disappointed all concerned, and had excited public vituperation. After upwards of 600,000*l.* had been drawn from the Treasury, the further sum of 73,777*l.* was voted for its completion.

Mr. Blore found it necessary to extend the wings, to add to the garden front, and to form a more commodious staircase from the kitchens to the dining-room; besides introducing light into various parts of the building, which were before low and gloomy.

The entrance-hall, though low, is very splendid: it is paved with variegated marble, bordered with a scroll of Sienna, centred with puce-coloured rosettes. The walls are of scagliola, and the ceiling is supported by forty-four white marble columns decorated with Corinthian capitals of mosaic gold. Behind the hall is a vestibule of considerable length, forming a sculpture-gallery, against the sides of which are thirty-two columns similar to those in the entrance-hall. In the centre of the vestibule is the door of the libraries, a handsome suite of three rooms looking on to the garden; to the right are private apartments of the queen, and the staircase leading to them; and to the left are the queen's study, and three rooms for secretaries, &c. Returning to the hall, to the left of the entrance is the grand staircase, the stairs of which are of solid blocks of white marble, and the rail is richly formed of mosaic gold and mahogany. A new grand staircase has been recently constructed for the facility of egress at the state parties. The staircase ascends on either side of the lantern-hall (which is adorned with four *bassi-relievi* after Stothard), and leads to the state-rooms, which, though somewhat fantastic, are very splendid. The grand saloon, or principal drawing-room, is adorned with Corinthian columns of imitation *lapis lazuli*, with gilt capitals supporting a rich cornice and frieze. The floor is inlaid with satin and amboyna wood.

The green drawing-room, hung with rich damask drapery and gold bullion fringe, is divided by gilt pilasters. It is ornamented with portraits of the house of Hanover, and two precious cabinets. The yellow or south drawing-room has columns of deep red imitation marble, and mirrors of great size. The whole of these apartments are superbly furnished, and have lustres of great beauty. Besides these are the state and private dining-rooms. The throne-room is richly gilt and hung with crimson silk, the ceiling embossed with great magnificence, and the frieze contains *bassi-relievi* by Bailey, after designs by Stothard, representing the wars of York and Lancaster. The imperial throne is placed in the alcove at the end of the apartment. From this splendid room a door leads into the picture-gallery, a noble saloon running nearly the whole length of the palace, directly in the centre, being 164 feet by 28. It is lighted by three parallel ranges of skylights, decorated with tracery and eastern pendants, assuming a very pleasing appearance. Over the mantel-pieces are carved heads of the great artists of antiquity, and the floor is formed of panelled oak. The octagon chapel has been converted into an armoury. The north wing is appropriated to the queen and her attendants. Two new wings have lately been added, the one to the south forming a guard-house, the other a private entrance. Notwithstanding the enormous sums lavished on this pile, it is to be feared that it will be found deficient in its general design; and that, although it may present isolated beauties, it is far from being considered worthy of pretending to afford a specimen of the architectural skill of the nineteenth century. The garden-front is the most pleasing in effect, presenting a simple elevation with no unpleasant recession of parts to attract yet disappoint the vision.

The grand entrance in front of the palace consists of an arch of white marble, modelled from that of Constantine at Rome, and ornamented with sculpture by Bailey and Westmacott. The central bronze gate is remarkably handsome. On each side of the arch a semicircular railing ornamented with mosaic gold (now corroded) extends to the wings.

Kensington Palace

Was originally the residence of lord-chancellor Finch, from whom it was purchased by king William, who made the road to it through the parks. The gardens were successively improved by queen Mary, queen Anne, and queen Caroline,

KENSINGTON PALACE.

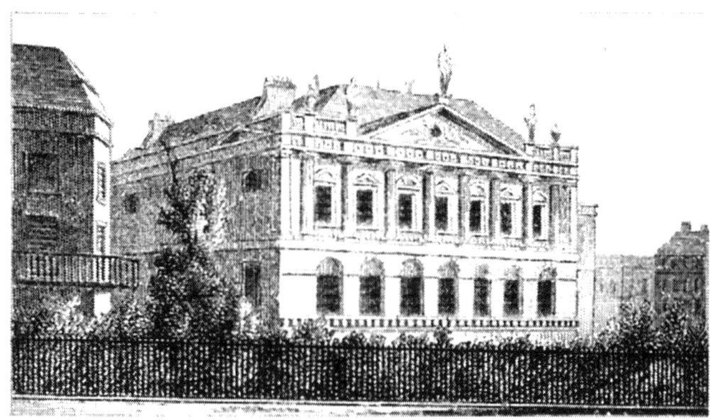

SPENCER HOUSE.

LAMBETH PALACE.

who died within the walls of the palace. George II. and George prince of Denmark likewise expired here. It is the residence of her royal highness the duchess of Kent and his royal highness the duke of Sussex. The building has no pretensions to grandeur, and is very irregular in its architecture; it is composed of brick, and has its principal entrance on the west side. The grand staircase and the ceilings of many of the rooms were painted by Kent. The apartments are adorned with numerous paintings and portraits by distinguished masters. Visiters may see them on application to the housekeeper.

The Gardens are about 3½ miles in circumference, and in summer form a very fashionable promenade. They were laid out, under the direction of queen Caroline, by Bridgman, Kent, and Brown. There are six gates to these gardens, one opening into the Uxbridge-road, four in Hyde-park, and one at the palace. No servants in livery, women in pattens, or dogs, are allowed admission.

Lambeth Palace,

The town residence of the archbishop of Canterbury, is an irregular pile of building on the banks of the Thames. Having been erected at different periods, it displays various kinds of architecture. A considerable portion was built as far back as the thirteenth century. The corners of the edifice are faced with rustic work, and the top surrounded with battlements. The chapel, erected in the twelfth century, contains the remains of archbishop Parker; and in the vestry are portraits of several bishops. In the banqueting-room, which has an old carved ceiling, are the portraits of all the primates from Laud to the present time. Juxon's hall, a noble room forming part of the old palace, has been converted into a library, which was founded by archbishop Bancroft, but has been increased at successive periods by archbishops Abbot, Juxon, Laud, Sheldon, Tennison, and Secker, till the number of volumes now amounts to 25,000. The Lollard's Tower, at the western extremity of the chapel, contains a small room wainscoted with oak, on which are inscribed several names and portions of sentences in ancient characters; and the walls are furnished with large rings, to which the Lollards, and other persons confined for heretical opinions, are supposed to have been affixed. In the grounds, which are laid out with great taste, are two fig-trees of extraordinary size, supposed to have been planted by Cardinal

Pole about 1558. Owing to the munificence and taste of Dr. Howley, the domestic portion of the palace has been greatly enlarged; a new Gothic wing of considerable beauty having been constructed from designs by Mr. Blore, at an expense of 52,000*l*. The whole of the interior is fitted up in a style of simple beauty, oak panelling pervading the edifice, contrasting finely with the fretted ceilings and ornaments. The archbishop's study is a noble apartment, 40 feet by 20; the drawing-room is also of fine proportions, commanding from the ample bay-window a pleasing prospect of the gardens, and a peep at the abbey and bridge through the foliage.

St. James's-Park

Was a complete marsh till the time of Henry VIII., who, having built St. James's-palace, enclosed it, laid it out in walks, and collecting the waters, gave the new enclosed ground and building the name of St. James's. It was afterwards much improved by Charles II., who employed Le Notre to add several fields, to plant rows of lime-trees, and to lay out the mall, which is a vista half a mile in length, at that time formed into a hollow, smooth walk, skirted by a wooden border, with an iron hoop at the further end for the purpose of playing a game with a ball called a mall. He formed a canal 100 feet broad and 2800 long, with a decoy and other ponds for water-fowl. Succeeding kings allowed the people the privilege of walking here, and William III. in 1699 granted the neighbouring inhabitants a passage into it from Spring-gardens. In 1814 the return of peace was celebrated here by fire-works, boat-races, illuminations, and other demonstrations of joy. A pagoda-bridge was erected over the canal, but constructed of such slight materials, that it was obliged to be taken down in 1820. In 1828 the appearance of the park was materially improved. The central portion was laid out in walks and shrubberies, the canal assumed a more picturesque form, being made to flow round an island at each extremity, with a choice collection of aquatic birds belonging to the Ornithological Society; and the whole was surrounded by an iron railing, with gates for the daily admission of the public: besides the public seats, chairs may be had on payment of 1*d.*

Opposite to the Horse-guards, in the fine space between that range of buildings and the canal, are two great guns.

The first is a Turkish piece of ordnance. It is of immense length, and has on it variegated impressions emblematical of the country. It was brought from Alexandria by our troops, and is mounted on a carriage of English structure, which has several Egyptian ornaments.

The second is the grand mortar brought from the siege of Cadiz in 1812, and presented to his majesty by the Spanish regency in 1814, but not placed here till 1816. It is 8 feet in length, 12 inches in diameter at the mouth, and is capable of throwing a shell three miles. The mortar is placed on an allegorical carriage cast at Woolwich, figuratively describing the raising of the siege, and bearing several inscriptions. The weight of the whole is 16 tons.

One of the regiments of the foot-guards daily parades in this park between 10 and 11 o'clock, attended by its band, and afterwards proceeds to relieve the regiment on duty at St. James's-palace, where the bands of both play alternately for about 20 minutes.

The side of the park nearest Pall-mall has been considerably improved by the late alterations. Besides a stately range of elegant houses on the site of Carlton-palace, a handsome square has been formed. The front towards St. James's-park consists of sixteen houses, which are disposed in two ranges, raised on a substructure which contains the kitchens and domestic offices, forming a terrace about 50 feet wide, adorned with Pæstum Doric pillars, surmounted by a balustrade. The superstructure consists of three stories, ornamented with Corinthian columns. In the space between the two ranges is the *Pillar* erected to the memory of the late commander-in-chief—the Duke of York. It is ascended by a spiral staircase, and commands by far the most elegant and imposing view of the metropolis. The column is of pale red granite, 150 feet in height, and is surmounted by a colossal bronze statue, 14 feet high, of "the soldier's friend," by Westmacott. William IV., on his accession to the throne, commanded a way to be broken into the park, and a fine flight of steps to be constructed for the convenience of the public: the level beneath has been paved with variegated asphalte.

Considerable improvements have been effected in Birdcage-walk. The whole line has been straightened, and the railing continued from the barracks to Storey's-gate, where a new keeper's-lodge has been erected. Besides the neat barracks, there is a handsome Doric chapel erected in 1838 for the military. The appearance of this noble chapel is striking from the various points of view, and forms an interesting composition with the towers of the Abbey.

There are carriage-entrances to St. James's-park at St. James's-palace, Constitution-hill, Buckingham-gate, Great George-street, and the Horse-guards; as well as entrances for pedestrians at Spring-gardens, Duke-street, Fludyer-street, Downing-street, through the Treasury, Queen-square, Queen-street, St. James's palace, and Waterloo-place. The entrance at the latter was first opened September 8, 1831, in honour of the coronation, and consists of a noble flight of steps, at the top of which is the York Column.

THE GREEN-PARK

Forms a part of the ground enclosed by Henry VIII. It is situated north of the Queen's Palace, and extends from St. James's-park, from which it is separated by an iron railing, to Hyde-park. *Constitution-hill* is the name given to the fine road which unites the three parks. This park adds greatly to the pleasantness of both palaces, as well as of the surrounding houses. On the north side is one of the reservoirs of the Chelsea Water-works. It was reconstructed in 1829, with a curious filtering apparatus. The promenade round this basin and other parts of this park possesses, for a town scene, considerable attractions. At the N.W. extremity, surrounded by a shrubbery, is the lodge of the deputy-ranger of St. James's and Hyde parks.

HYDE-PARK

Is situated at the western extremity of the metropolis, between the roads leading to Hounslow and Uxbridge. It is bounded on the West by Kensington-gardens, from which it is separated by a sunk-walled fence. This park derived its name from having been the manor of the hyde belonging to the Abbey of Westminster. It contains 395 acres, and abounds with fine trees and pleasing scenery.

At the south-east corner of Hyde-park, near the entrance from Piccadilly, is a colossal statue executed by Mr. Westmacott; and bearing the following inscription:—"To Arthur, duke of Wellington, and his brave companions in arms, this statue of Achilles, cast from cannon taken in the battles of Salamanca, Vittoria, Toulouse, and Waterloo, is inscribed by their country-women." On the base is inscribed, "Placed on this spot on the 18th day of June, 1822, by command of his Majesty George IV." The statue is about 18 feet high, and stands on a basement of granite, making the whole 36 feet above the level of the ground. It was cast from twelve 24-pounders, and weighs upwards of 30 tons.

The sheet of water called the Serpentine River, although in the form of a parallelogram, was made between 1730 and 1733, under the direction of Messrs. Withers and Kimberley, by order of queen Caroline. It is much frequented in summer for bathing, and during frost for skating. At the eastern end of it is an artificial waterfall, constructed in 1817; and at the west end it is crossed by a stone bridge, consisting of five large and two smaller arches, erected in 1826 from designs by Messrs. Rennie. On the north side of the Serpentine are one of the stations of the Humane Society, two powder-magazines, and the keeper's-lodge; and here also are two springs, one a mineral-water fit for beverage, the other used for the cure of diseased eyes. On the south side are the barracks of the Life-guards.

The park is very much frequented as a promenade, particularly on Sundays, between two and five in the afternoon. There are five entrances, which are open from six in the morning till nine at night, but no stages or hackney-coaches are admitted. The gates are adorned with elegant modern lodges, erected from designs by Mr. D. Burton, and that at Hyde-park-corner has a triumphal arch.

Regent's-Park

Is situated on the north side of the metropolis, between the New-road and Hampstead. It originally formed part of the grounds belonging to a palace which stood near the north end of Tottenham-court-road, and was occasionally the residence of queen Elizabeth. This building was pulled down in 1791. From the time of Elizabeth the property was let to various persons, but the leases having expired, it reverted to the Crown; and in 1814 were commenced the improvements, under the direction of Mr. Nash, which have rendered this park the most beautiful part of London.

The park is nearly of a circular form, and consists of about 450 acres, laid out in shrubberies, adorned with a fine piece of water, and intersected by roads which are much frequented as promenades. In the enclosures are several villas, and around the park are noble ranges of building in various styles of architecture.

The following tour of the park will direct the stranger to the various objects which it contains. Commencing at the end of Portland-place, we turn to the right and pass through *Park-crescent*—a handsome semicircular range of private houses adorned with a colonnade of the Ionic order. Crossing the New-road, we enter *Park-square*—a spacious quadrangle, tastefully planted, and bounded on the east and west sides by handsome houses. Proceeding up the east side, we perceive the *Diorama* and the *Colosseum*, both of which are described in another part of this work. The various objects then come to view in the following order:—

Cambridge-terrace is one of the smallest in the park. It consists of a centre and two wings, which have porticoes of the Roman or pseudo-Doric order. The central part is surmounted by an urn and two sphinxes.

Chester-terrace is a grand and commanding range of building, designed by Mr. Nash. It is of the Corinthian order, and is richly decorated. At each end of the terrace is an arch connecting it with pavilion-shaped mansions. This idea is novel, and has a very good effect.

Cumberland-terrace, erected by Mr. Nurse, stands considerably above the road, from which it is separated by a garden. It is approached by a fine carriage-sweep with handsome balustrades. It consists of a centre and wings connected by two arches. The ground-story is rusticated, and in the principal masses of the building serves as a base for Doric columns, surmounted by a balustrade, on which are placed allegorical figures of the seasons, the quarters of the globe, the arts and sciences, &c. The central portion consists of a splendid colonnade of twelve columns, surmounted by a pediment containing sculpture by Mr. Bubb. It represents Britannia crowned by Fame seated on her throne, at the base of which are Valour and Wisdom. On one side are figures of Literature, Genius, Manufacture, Agriculture, and Prudence, bringing forward youth of various countries for instruction: on the other side is represented the Navy, surrounded by Victory, Commerce, and Freedom—the latter extending her blessings to the Africans. Plenty terminates the group on either side. From the sweep in front of this terrace there is a very picturesque view of the park.

St. Catherine's-hospital on the right, and the *Master's House* on the left of the road, are both noticed in another part of this work. Behind St. Catherine's-hospital are barracks capable of accommodating 500 men and horses.

Gloucester-gate leads to the great North road by Camden-town and Highgate. It is a neat structure of the Doric order, consisting of four fluted columns, flanked by stone lodges with pediments.

Zoological Gardens, described in another part of the work.

Macclesfield-bridge is an elegant structure crossing the Regent's-canal on the northern boundary of the park. It was built by Mr. Morgan, and consists of three arches supported by cast-iron pillars of the Doric order. During summer the view of the banks of the canal from the top of the bridge is very picturesque. The road over it leads to Primrose-hill.

The Marquess of Hertford's Villa is situated on the left of the road, surrounded by trees and shrubberies. It was built from designs by Mr. D. Burton. The portico consists of six columns of the same order as that which adorns the entrance to the Temple of the Winds at Athens. Adjoining the villa is a large tent-like canopy covering a spacious room used for *déjeuner* parties.

A new mansion has lately been built in its neighbourhood for Mr. Holdford.

Grove-house, on the opposite side of the road, was likewise erected by Mr. D. Burton, and is a very pleasing specimen of the villa style of architecture. The garden-front, which is the principal, presents a portico of four Ionic columns supporting a pediment and flanked by wings.

Hanover-lodge is situated near Grove-house. It is a very neat building of the Ionic order, surrounded by picturesque grounds.

Hanover-terrace, built from designs by Mr. Nash, consists of a centre and two wings of the Doric order, crowned with pediments surmounted by statues of the muses. In the central pediment is a group of figures in relievo, representing Medicine, Chemistry, Architecture, Sculpture, Poetry, Peace, Justice, Agriculture, Plenty, Music, History, and Navigation.

Opposite Hanover-terrace is a small gate opening into the enclosed part of the park by a footpath, which winds into a serpentine form to a gate opposite Sussex-place, and terminates at another gate fronting York-terrace. To this walk only the inhabitants of the surrounding terraces have admission.

Sussex-place is a whimsical range of buildings erected by Mr. Nash. It consists of a centre with a pediment flanked by octagonal towers, and wings with four similar towers; the whole being disposed in a semicircular form with a garden in front.

All the towers are finished with cupola tops and minarets, which give them a very singular appearance.

Clarence-terrace, built from the designs of Mr. Decimus Burton, consists of a centre and two wings of the Corinthian order, connected by colonnades of the Ilyssus Ionic order. This is the smallest terrace in the park, but it yields to none in picturesque effect.

We then arrive at the entrance-gate from Baker-street.

Cornwall-terrace, one of the earliest erections in the park, was built from designs by Mr. D. Burton, and is very creditable to his taste. It is of the Corinthian order. The basement is rusticated, and the upper part is adorned with fluted columns and pilasters with well-proportioned capitals.

York-terrace is a splendid range of private houses erected from designs by Mr. Nash. The ground-story presents a range of semicircular-headed windows and rusticated piers, above which is a continued pedestal divided between the columns into balustrades in front of the windows of the principal story, to which they form balconies. The centre and the wing of this and the principal chamber-story are adorned with columns of the Ilyssus Ionic order. This terrace rather resembles a single palace than a range of separate houses, all the doors being at the back of the buildings, and the gardens in front having no divisions.

In the centre of York-terrace is *York-gate*, forming, with the two rows of mansions that flank it, a noble entrance to the park. At the end of the avenue is seen the front of Mary-le-bone New Church.

Opposite York-terrace is a building occupied by the *Toxopholite Society*, containing five acres of land for archery sports.

Ulster-terrace forms the west corner of Park-square, and thus completes the tour of the park. It is a plain and simple range, adorned at the basement story with a colonnade of the Ionic order.

Returning to York-gate, we may take the road to the right, and crossing the bridge over the east end of the lake, enter the *Ring*, a fine level drive, planted on each side with trees, and surrounding a shrubbery tastefully laid out.

Around the ring are three villas. The first is *South Villa*, with a portico of Doric columns resting on a rusticated basement. The next is called the *Holme*, from the Saxon word denoting a river-island. It is situated between the ring and the lake, of which it commands a fine view, and is adorned

WESTMINSTER HALL.

HOUSES OF LORDS & COMMONS.

with a portico of the Ionic order. This villa was built from designs by Mr. D. Burton. The third is *St. John's-Wood Lodge*, situated to the north of the ring. It was designed by Mr. Raffield, and is in the Grecian style of architecture.

The visiter may then leave the ring by the same route as he entered, or proceed along the road which extends from its east side in a straight line to the centre of Chester-terrace.

A central portion of the park, between Sussex-terrace and the Zoological-Gardens, has been opened to the public.

The inhabitants of the houses surrounding the park have keys admitting them to the walks within the enclosed area.

ARCHES,

Hyde-Park-corner.

With the exception of that dreary specimen of antiquity, Temple-bar, these beautiful features of architectural decoration have for a long time been wanting in this grand metropolis, where embellishment has hitherto been so little considered, that fountains, statues, vases, terraces, and other comparatively economical beauties, have been neglected as elegant but useless superfluities.

The entrance to Hyde-park was completed in 1828 from designs by Mr. Decimus Burton. It consists of a screen of fluted Ionic columns, with three archways for carriages, two entrances for foot-passengers, and a lodge. The whole frontage extends about 107 feet. The central gateway is adorned with four columns supporting the entablature, above which is a frieze running round the four sides of the structure. This frieze was executed by Mr. Henning, junior, and represents a naval and military triumphal procession. The side-gateways present two insulated Ionic columns flanked by antæ. The gates, which are beautiful specimens of bronzed iron-work, were manufactured by Messrs. Bramah.

The other arch, built about the same time from designs by Mr. Nash, forms the entrance to the gardens of the Queen's Palace. It is of the Corinthian order. Towards Hyde-park are four columns, two at each side of the arch, supporting a portico. The arch itself is adorned with six Corinthian pilasters. The front towards the gardens is exactly similar. The vaulted part in the centre is divided into compartments richly sculptured. A small doorway on each side leads to the porter's apartment, within which are stairs leading to the top. Along the entablature are placed alternately G. R. and the imperial crown. The gates of bronzed iron-work, made by Messrs. Bramah, are adorned with the royal arms.

It is proposed to place the Wellington Testimonial on the summit. This injudicious determination is to be regretted, as it is probable that the talent of the sculptor, Mr. Wyatt, will have too elevated a field for the display of the delicacies of his chisel.

WESTMINSTER-HALL,

New Palace-yard.

The old hall was built by William Rufus in 1097 and 1098; and here, on his return from Normandy in 1099, "he kept his feast of Whitsuntide very royally." It was therefore first used as a banqueting-house to the palace, which stood on the site of Old Palace-yard. It became ruinous before the reign of Richard II., who repaired it in 1397, raised the walls two feet, altered the windows, and added a new roof, as well as a stately porch and other buildings. In 1236 Henry III., on new-year's day, caused 6000 poor men, women, and children to be entertained in this hall and in the other rooms of his palace, as a celebration of queen Eleanor's coronation. The king and queen had been married at Canterbury; and on the day of this great feast made their public entry into London. As a proof of its size, it may be mentioned that Richard II. kept his Christmas festival in the New Hall, accompanied with all that splendour and magnificence for which his court was conspicuous; and that on this occasion 28 oxen, 300 sheep, and fowls without number, were consumed. The number of guests on each day of the feast amounted to 10,000, and 2000 cooks were employed.

The present hall was first called the New Hall-palace, to distinguish it from the Old Palace at the south end of the hall, which, taking in the chapel of St. Stephen, is now used as the two houses of parliament. Westminster-hall is one of the largest rooms in Europe unsupported by pillars;—its length is 270 feet, its height 90, and its breadth 74. The roof consists chiefly of chestnut-wood most curiously constructed, and of a fine species of Gothic. It is every where adorned with angels supporting the arms of Richard II. or those of Edward the Confessor, as is the stone moulding that runs round the hall, with the hart *couchant* under a tree, and other devices of the former monarch. Parliaments often sat in this hall. In 1397, when it was extremely ruinous, Richard II. built a temporary room for his parliament, formed of wood, and covered with tiles. The fine Gothic windows at the extremities were reconstructed in 1820, and the whole hall repaired and beautified during the two following years; and again partially after the burning of the houses of parliament. The front is adorned with two stone towers ornamented with rich sculpture, and on the centre of the roof is a lantern of considerable height, erected in 1821.

The courts of Chancery, Exchequer, Queen's Bench, and Common Pleas, have been held in different apartments of this hall ever since the reign of Henry III. It was within these walls that Charles I. was brought to trial in 1648. It has also been used for the trial of peers and other distinguished persons accused of high-treason, or other crimes and misdemeanors, such as the late Lord Melville, Warren Hastings, &c. In this hall likewise are held the coronation-feasts of the sovereigns of England.

THE COURTS OF LAW

Form a handsome range of building along the north side of Westminster-hall. They were erected from designs by Sir J. Soane, and comprise the Court of Chancery, the Vice-Chancellor's Court, the Courts of Common Pleas, Exchequer, Bail, and Queen's Bench.

The Court of Chancery is a spacious square room, having a handsome circular gallery for the accommodation of students and suitors. It is surmounted by a dome, through each side of which the light is admitted by a large circular window. At the back of the bench is the chancellor's private room.

The Vice-Chancellor's Court is likewise surmounted by a dome, though of smaller size, the light being admitted by windows in the sides of the room.

The Court of Exchequer is a light and spacious hall: on the bench are four seats and desks for the four barons.

HOUSES OF LORDS AND COMMONS,

Old Palace-yard, &c.

Since the last edition of this work, these important fabrics have become a prey to fire, which nearly levelled them with the ground, on the evening of the 16th October, 1834. The Chapel of St. Stephen, containing the House of Commons and the Speaker's dining-room, together with the House of Lords and Painted Chamber, became a mere mass of ruins. After various proposals had been submitted to the ministry, it was resolved to proceed in the temporary restoration of the chambers upon a plan proposed by Sir R. Smirke, at an estimate of 30,000*l.*

The venerable walls of St. Stephen's Chapel being laid bare by the conflagration, the attention of all lovers of ancient architecture was attracted to these picturesque ruins, and a general feeling was expressed in favour of their forming a portion of any new design. From a doubt of their security, the temporary House of Commons was transferred to the former House of Lords—the exterior of which had been exposed to view by the destruction of the Gothic fabric which had screened it. The Chamber of Peers was constructed within the former Painted Chamber, an apartment of lesser dimensions, and which had previously served as a hall of conference for the commissioners of the two houses. It was thus necessary to throw open the royal staircase as an entrance for the peers. The walls of the new house of peers were heightened about one-third, and the edifice presents an admeasurement of 50 feet in length, 20 in width, and 28 in height. The seats for their lordships are of fine oak covered with crimson cloth; and the throne was formerly in Carlton-house.

A committee of the House of Commons having, after due deliberation, decided upon rebuilding the chambers in the *Elizabethan style* (?), architects were invited to send in designs and estimates, without any special sum having been named as the probable extent of the grant to be proposed for that purpose. Before the public voice had decided upon the efforts of competition, the commissioners declared in favour of a splendid design by Mr. Barry, rewarding three others with premiums. At length, in obedience to the loudly-expressed wish of the educated amongst the middle classes, the designs thus selected were allowed to form a portion of a public exhibition, consisting of upwards of 70 designs which had been prepared on this important occasion. The structure, as proposed by Mr. Barry, was estimated at an expense of about 800,000*l.*, of which 100,000*l.* was subsequently retrenched from what was considered superfluous ornament. An embankment 30 feet wide, extending to the second arch of Westminster-bridge, was commenced in 1836; and upon this and the former site it is proposed to erect the superb edifice designed by the talented architect. Exclusive of Westminster-hall and the Law-courts, the new structure will cover six acres.

The river-front will present a superb unbroken range of enriched Gothic, extending at a right angle from Westminster-bridge towards Millbank a distance of nearly 900 feet. Rising to the height of three stories, it will be divided into a centre and wings; the former being carried above the remainder of the structure by a loftier and more enriched battlement, being terminated by rich octagonal embattled towers, in the centre of which are fine oriel windows. These are repeated in the noble wings, whose simple solid square towers terminate so satisfactorily this grand front-elevation. One feature in this design must not be omitted. Terminating the range towards Abingdon-street, there will be a stupendous square tower, 300 feet high, occupying an area 100 feet square. This is to be the royal entrance, being contrived so that the sovereign will be able to drive beneath its massive form, whilst the upper portion will supply that desideratum of a receptacle for the national records in a series of fire-proof apartments. The end towards the bridge, enclosing Westminster-hall (which is to form an entrance to the chambers), will be terminated by a clock-tower of elegant design. The House of Commons will occupy a central situation on the principal floor, between Westminster-hall and the right centre tower of the river-front; whilst the House of Lords will occupy a parallel situation on the opposite side, being separated by a public central hall, lobbies, and anti-chambers.

In our next edition, we hope to give particulars of the progress of this truly magnificent edifice.

The former House of Lords was hung with tapestry representing the victory over the Spanish Armada. A modern porch and staircase (still remaining) was constructed in 1822, by Sir J. Soane, for the access of the sovereign, but is now also used by the peers.

That court of justice, so tremendous in the Tudor and part of the Stuart reign, the *Star Chamber*, took its name, not from the *stars* on its roof (which were obliterated even before the reign of Queen Elizabeth), but from the *Starra*, or Jewish covenants, deposited there by order of Richard I. No *Star* was allowed to be vallid except found in those repositories; and here they remained till the banishment of the Jews by Edward I. It was situated on the south side of New Palace-yard, in the old building on the banks of the Thames.

The *Painted Chamber*, now the House of Lords, was used as the place of conference between the Lords and Commons. It had a mean appearance, being hung with very ancient French or arras tapestry, which, by the names worked over the figures, seems to relate to the Trojan war. It was remarkable, however, as the place in which the death-warrant of Charles I.

was signed, and as the scene of the celebrated conference between the Lords and Commons which was followed by the Revolution.

The vault called *Guy Faux's Cellar*, in which the conspirators of 1605 lodged the barrels of gunpowder, designed at one blow to annihilate the three estates of the realm in parliament assembled, remained till 1825, when it was converted into offices.

Strangers may see the House of Lords on paying 1*s.* to the attendant, and may obtain admission when the house is sitting by an order from a peer, or on application to the doorkeepers.

House of Commons,

Old Palace-yard,

Was connected with the entrance to the House of Lords by a Gothic colonnade cased with stucco, and extending round the north-east corner of Old Palace-yard.

The Commons of Great Britain, previous to the conflagration of 1834, held their assemblies in *St. Stephen's Chapel*, which was built by King Stephen, and dedicated to his namesake the proto-martyr. It was rebuilt by Edward III. in 1347, and by him made a collegiate church, to which a dean and twelve secular priests were appointed. Soon after its surrender to Edward VI., it was applied to parliamentary purposes.

The gallery of the Commons is accessible only to strangers by means of *orders* from the members.

Tower of London.

This ancient edifice is situated on the north bank of the Thames, at the S.E. extremity of the city. The antiquity of the building has been a subject of much discussion ; but the present fortress is generally believed to have been built by William I. at the commencement of his reign, and strongly garrisoned with Normans, to secure the allegiance of his new subjects ; although it appears, from an ingot and three golden coins (one of the emperor Honorius, and the other of Arcadius,) found here in 1777, that the Romans had a fort on this spot.

The Tower is governed by the constable of the Tower, who at coronations and other state ceremonies has the custody of the regalia.

The principal entrance is on the west, and is wide enough to admit a carriage. It consists of two gates on the outside

THE TOWER FROM THAMES STREET.

of the ditch, a stone bridge built over it, and a gate within it. The gates are opened and shut with great ceremony, a yeoman-porter, serjeant, and six men being employed to fetch the keys, which are kept during the day at the warder's-hall, but deposited every night at the governor's house.

The Tower is separated from the Thames by a platform, and by part of the ditch. At each extremity of the platform are passages to Tower-hill, and near that to the east, a place for preving muskets. The ditch, of very considerable width and depth, proceeds northwards on each side of the fortress, nearly in a parallel line, and meets in a semicircle; the slope is faced with brick, and the great wall of the Tower has been repaired with that material so frequently, that it might almost be disputed whether any part of it but the turrets had ever been stone. Cannons are planted at intervals round the line, and command every avenue leading to Tower-hill. The interior of the wall is lined with houses, to the evident injury of the place as a fortress.

The space enclosed by the walls measure 12 acres 5 roods, and the circumference on the outside of the ditch is 3156 feet. On the south side of the Tower is an arch called the *Traitor's Gate*, through which state prisoners were formerly brought from the river. Over this is the infirmary, and the works by which the place is supplied with water. Near the Traitor's Gate is the *Bloody Tower*, in which some have supposed the two young princes, Edward V. and his brother, were smothered by order of Richard III. There is, however, no foundation for this opinion. The Bloody Tower received its present appellation in the reign of Elizabeth, but it is not known on what account. In the south-east angle of the enclosure were the royal apartments; for the Tower was a palace for nearly 500 years, and only ceased to be so on the accession of queen Elizabeth.

The principal buildings within the walls are the Church, the White Tower, the Old Mint, the Record-Office, the Jewel-Office, the Horse-Armoury, the Grand Storehouse—in which is the Small Armoury, the Lion's Tower, which formerly contained the menagerie, and the Beauchamp Tower.

The *Church*, called St. Peter in Vincula, erected in the reign of Edward I., is only remarkable as the depository of the headless bodies of numerous illustrious personages who suffered either in the Tower or on the adjacent hill. Amongst these may be mentioned Fisher bishop of Rochester, executed 1535; Sir Thomas More, 1535; Bullen lord Rochford, 1536; Anna Boleyn, or Bullen, 1536; Thomas Cromwell, the favourite of Henry VIII., 1540; Catherine Howard, 1541; Seymour duke of Somerset, 1552, and his brother the admiral; Dudley duke of Northumberland, 1553; Scott duke of Monmouth, 1685; Lords Lovet, Balmerino, and Kilmarnock.

The *White Tower*, Keep, or Citadel, is a large square irregular building, erected in 1070 by Gandulph bishop of Rochester: it measures 116 feet by 96, and is 92 feet in height. The walls, which are 11 feet thick, have a winding staircase continued along two of the sides, like that in Dover Castle. The building consists of three lofty stories, under which are commodious vaults, and the top is covered with flat leads, whence there is an extensive prospect. On the first story are two fine rooms, one of which contains the *Sea-Armoury*, consisting of muskets for the sea-service, and other warlike implements of every description. Here likewise is the *Volunteer-Armoury*, for 30,000 men. At the top of the building is a reservoir for supplying the garrison with water in case of necessity. The turret at the N.E. angle, which is the highest and largest of the four by which the White Tower is surmounted, was used for astronomical purposes by Flamstead previous to the erection of the Royal Observatory at Greenwich.

Within the White Tower is the ancient *Chapel of St. John*, originally used by the English monarchs. The architecture is Saxon, and it is considered a perfect building of its kind. It is of an oblong form, rounded at the eastern end; on each side are five short round pillars, with large squared capitals curiously sculptured, and having a cross on each. This chapel now forms a part of the Record-Office, and is filled with parchments. A vault beneath it is said to have been the prison of Sir W. Raleigh, in which he wrote his "History of the World."

South of the White Tower is the *Modelling-room*, in which are curious models of Gibraltar and other places; but no strangers are admitted to see them. The *Parade* near the White Tower is much frequented as a promenade on Sundays, when the Tower is open to the public; hours, from 10 till 3.

The *Office of the Keeper of the Records* is adorned with a finely carved stone door-case. It is proposed to collect all the records, and place them in the great tower of the new houses of parliament. All the rolls from the time of King John to the beginning of the reign of Richard III. are deposited in 56 presses at this office. Those since that period are kept at the Rolls Chapel, Chancery-lane. The price of a search is 10*s.* 6*d.*, for which you may pursue one subject a-year. In the *Wakefield Tower*, which forms part of the Record-Office, is a fine octagonal room, where tradition asserts Henry VI. was murdered. This tower derived its name from having been the place of confinement for the prisoners taken at the battle of Wakefield. In this tower the Lollards were also confined.

The *Jewel-Office* is a dark and strong stone room, in which are kept the crown-jewels, or regalia. The imperial crown is enriched with precious stones of every description. Here likewise are preserved the other emblems of royalty used at the coronation of our sovereigns; such as the golden orb, the golden sceptre and its cross, the sceptre with the dove, St. Edward's staff, state salt-cellar, curtana or sword of mercy, golden spurs, armilla or bracelets, ampulla or golden eagle, and the golden spoon. The visiter is likewise shewn the silver font used at the baptism of the royal family, the state crown worn by the sovereign in parliament, and a large collection of ancient plate.

The *Horse-Armoury*, an apartment 150 feet in length and 33 in width, was erected in 1825, when the suits of armour were re-arranged under the direction of Dr. Meyrick. They are now placed in chronological order as follows:—Edward I., 1272; Henry VI., 1450; Edward IV., 1465; Henry VII., 1508; Henry VIII., 1520; Charles Brandon, duke of Suffolk, 1520; Clinton earl of Lincoln, 1535; Edward VI., 1552; Hastings earl of Huntington, 1555; Dudley earl of Leicester, 1560; Lea master of the armoury, 1570; Devereux earl of Essex, 1581; James I., 1605; Sir H. Vere, captain-general, 1606; Howard earl of Arundel, 1608; Henry prince of Wales, 1612; Villiers duke of Buckingham, 1618; Charles prince of Wales, 1620; Wentworth earl of Strafford, 1635; Charles I., 1640; James II., 1685. There is likewise another suit, said to have been presented to Henry VIII. by the emperor Maximilian on his marriage with Catherine of Arragon. The date of the armour is in every instance correct, but only ten suits have been positively identified.

In a recess opposite the centre of the line of horsemen are many curious arms of all sorts and dates; and behind the line of horsemen are specimens of ordnance up to the time of Henry VI.

Between the horses are placed twenty-one small cannon,

presented by George III. to the prince of Wales on his coming of age. This apartment likewise contains several glass cases, in which numerous curious arms are arranged.

The *Grand Storehouse* is a noble edifice north of the White Tower, extending about 345 feet in length and 60 in breadth. It is composed of brick and stone, and on the north side is a stately doorcase, adorned with four columns, and an entablature and pediment of the Doric order. Under the pediment are the king's arms, with carved trophy-work, executed by Gibbons. This noble edifice was begun by James II., and finished by William III. The upper story is occupied by the *Small Armoury*, containing arms for about 200,000 men, all kept bright and clean, and disposed in various tasteful forms, representing the sun, the royal arms, Medusa's head, &c. Here also are preserved eight Maltese flags and a curious cannon taken from Malta by the French, and retaken by the English; the earl of Marr's elegant shield and carbine; two swords carried before the Pretender when proclaimed king in Scotland; the highlander's axe with which colonel Gardiner was killed at Preston-pans; the sword and sash of the late duke of York; the first musket made in the Tower; and numerous curiosities of a similar description. Beneath the Small Armoury, where the Royal Artillery was formerly arranged, are several pieces of cannon curiously carved, and an immense number of musket-barrels piled up in boxes.

Queen Elizabeth's or the *Spanish Armoury* was so called from its having been said to contain the spoils of the Spanish Armada. Dr. Meyrick, however, whose authority on such a point is unquestionable, is convinced that not one atom in the collection belonged to the Armada. The name was recently changed to the *Asiatic Armoury*, as it contains the arms of Tippoo Saib and other Indian princes. Here also are shewn, amongst other curiosities, a representation of queen Elizabeth; the axe which severed the head of Anna Boleyn, as well as that of the earl of Essex—although Hall the chronicler says that "her head was struck off with a sword!"—a wooden cannon used by Henry VIII. at the siege of Boulogne; ten pieces of cannon presented to Charles II. when a child, to assist him in his military studies; a piece of a scythe taken at the battle of Sedgmoor; and a piece erroneously called Henry VIII.'s walking-staff, with which it is said he perambulated the streets of London to see that his constables performed their duty.

At the entrance to the Armoury are two figures called Gin and Beer; they are of the time of Edward VI., and are supposed by Dr. Meyrick to have been originally placed in the great hall of the palace at Greenwich, over the doors which led to the buttery and larder.

The *Council Chamber*, in the *Governor's House*, was so called from having been the place of meeting of the commissioners appointed to inquire into the Gunpowder-Plot.

The *Beauchamp*, or *Cobham Tower*, is noted for the illustrious personages formerly confined within its walls. Amongst them was the good and accomplished lady Jane Grey. The ill-fated Anna Boleyn is said to have written her memorable letter to Henry VIII., in the apartment called the *Mess-house*.

Of the *Bowyer Tower* only the basement-floor remains: here, according to tradition, the Duke of Clarence, brother of Edward IV., was drowned in a butt of malmsey.

The *Lion's Tower*, built by Edward IV., was originally called the *Bulwark*, but received its present name from having been occupied as the *Menagerie;* it is situated on the right of the inner entrance to the Tower. In 1830, the animals were given to the Zoological Society by William IV.

Price of Admission.—The charges have been reduced to 6*d.* each; the jewel-apartment (which has been much improved) to 6*d.* extra; and a trifle to the warder, from each party, is still expected.

THE MINT, TOWER-HILL,

Is a handsome stone building, designed and executed by Mr. Smirke, jun. It consists of three stories, having a centre and wings; the former ornamented with columns, and a pediment displaying the British arms, and the latter with pilasters. The building is well adapted to business, particularly to the purpose intended; but the houses on each side, for the principal officers engaged in the coinage, would have much more correctly assimilated with the fabric if they had been fronted with stucco, and ornamented in the same style. Here are steam-engines, and also those mechanical contrivances which for a time were only to be found at Soho, near Birmingham. The Mint is inaccessible to strangers, unless they can procure a card from the Master of the Mint, or have a special recommendation, or immediate business with the officers. The whole of the interior is lighted with gas.

The Artillery-ground, Finsbury,

Was first converted into a spacious field for the use of the London archers in 1498, but was afterwards employed as a place of exercise for the London Artillery Company, in whose possession it now remains. There are three entrances to this ground by handsome iron gates, namely, in Bunhill-row, Finsbury-place, and Chiswell-street. At the northern extrĕmity is the Armoury-house, surmounted by a lofty flag-staff, and containing several spacious rooms adorned with armour of various descriptions. Admission may be procured by applying to any influential member of the Corporation.

The Monument, Fish-street-hill,

Was erected by order of parliament, to perpetuate the remembrance of the dreadful fire of London in 1666, and the rebuilding of the city in Charles II.'s reign, under the inspection of Sir Christopher Wren. (See p. 15.) It is built in a small square open to the street, and stands on the ground formerly occupied by the church of St. Margaret. A fine view of it is obtained from the street leading to London-bridge.

This noble piece of architecture was designed by Sir Christopher Wren, and is perhaps for proportion the finest modern column in the world. Its erection was commenced in 1671, and finished in 1677, at an expense of 14,500*l*. The column is of the Doric order, fluted, and much exceeds in height* the pillars of Trajan and Antoninus, the stately remains of Roman grandeur, or that of Theodosius at Constantinople. The altitude from the pavement is 202 feet; the greatest diameter of the shaft or body of the column is 15 feet; the ground bounded by the plinth, or lowest part of the pedestal, is 28 feet square, and the pedestal is 40 feet in height. Within is a large staircase of black marble, consisting of 345 steps, 10½ inches broad, and 6 inches risers. Over the capital is an iron balcony encompassing a cippus or meta 32 feet high, supporting a blazing urn of brass gilt. This immense column consists of 28,126 feet of solid Portland stone.

The north and south sides of the pedestal have each a Latin inscription; one describing the desolation of this city laid in

* The greatest of the Roman columns, viz: that of Antoninus, was 172½ feet in height, and 12 feet 3 inches in diameter, English measure. The York Column, in Carlton Gardens, is 150 feet high. The column in the Place Vendôme at Paris, is not more than 140 feet in height.

THE MONUMENT.

THE MINT.

ashes, and the other its glorious restoration. That on the north side (translated) runs thus:—

"In the year of Christ 1666, the second day of September, eastward from hence, at the distance of 202 feet (the height of this column), about midnight, a most terrible fire broke out, which, driven on by a high wind, not only wasted the adjacent parts, but also places very remote, with incredible noise and fury. It consumed 89 churches, the city gates, Guildhall, many public structures, hospitals, schools, libraries, a vast number of stately edifices, 13,200 dwelling-houses, 400 streets; of 26 wards it utterly destroyed 15, and left eight others shattered and half-burnt. The ruins of the city were 436 acres, from the Tower by the Thames to the Temple church, and from the north-east gate along the city-wall to Holborn-bridge. To the estates and fortunes of the citizens it was merciless, but to their lives very favourable, that it might in all things resemble the last conflagration of the world. The destruction was sudden: for in a small space of time the same city was seen most flourishing and reduced to nothing. Three days after, when this fatal fire had baffled all human counsels and endeavours, in the opinion of all, as it were by the will of Heaven, it stopped, and on every side was extinguished." The damage was estimated at 10,714,000*l.* Only eight lives were lost.

The south-side inscription is—"Charles II., son of Charles the martyr, king of Great Britain, France, and Ireland, Defender of the Faith, a most gracious prince, commiserating the deplorable state of things, whilst the ruins were yet smoking, provided for the comfort of his citizens, and the ornament of his city; remitted their taxes, and referred the petitions of the magistrates and inhabitants to the parliament, who immediately passed an act, That public works should be restored to greater beauty with public money, to be raised by an imposition on coal; that churches and the cathedral of St. Paul's should be rebuilt from their foundations, with all magnificence; that the bridges, gates, and prisons should be new made; the sewers cleansed, the streets made straight and regular, such as were steep levelled, and those too narrow made wider; markets and shambles removed to separate places. They also enacted that every house should be built with party-walls, and all in front raised of equal height, and those walls all of square stone or brick, and that no man should delay beyond the space of seven years. Moreover, care was taken by law to prevent all suits about their bounds. Also anniversary prayers were enjoined; and, to perpetuate the memory hereof to posterity, they caused this column to be erected. The work was carried on with diligence, and London is restored; but whether with greater speed or beauty, may be made a question. Three years saw that finished which was supposed to be the business of an age."

The east side has also an inscription, stating the time at which this pillar was begun, continued, and finished.

On the front or west side of the pedestal is finely carved a curious emblem of this tragical scene, by Mr. Cibber, father to the player and poet of that name. The eleven principal figures are done in alto, the rest in basso relievo. The back-ground on the left represents the city in flames, and the inhabitants in consternation. In front appear the insignia of the corporation, partly buried by the ruins, on which is a female figure, denoting London, who is being raised by Time, and encouraged by Providence pointing to the figures of Peace and Plenty. On the right stand Charles II. and his brother Duke of York, preceded by three females, representing Imagination holding the emblem of invention, Ichnographia with rules and compasses, and Liberty, having in her hand a hat inscribed LIBERTAS, in allusion to the freedom granted to those engaged in the restoration of the city. Behind the king are figures of Mars and Fortitude, and beneath, Envy is seen endeavouring to renew the disaster, by blowing flames out of his mouth. The back-ground on the right presents labourers erecting the new buildings.

The inscription on the base of the Monument, which falsely attributed the fire of London to the Roman Catholics, was effaced by order of the Common Council in 1830—an act of tardy justice. It was put there in the reign of Charles II., defaced by James II., and restored by William III.

No fewer than five persons have committed suicide by throwing themselves from the gallery: a weaver, in 1750; John Craddock, a baker, in 1788; Lyon Levy, a diamond merchant, in 1810; Margaret Moyes, daughter of a baker, September 11, 1839; and Robert Hawes, aged 15, an errand-boy, October 18, of the same year.

The price of admission to the gallery of the Monument is 6*d*.

THE MANSION-HOUSE,

Mansion-house-street,

The official residence of the lord-mayor, is situated at the east end of the Poultry, on the site of the ancient Stocks' market,

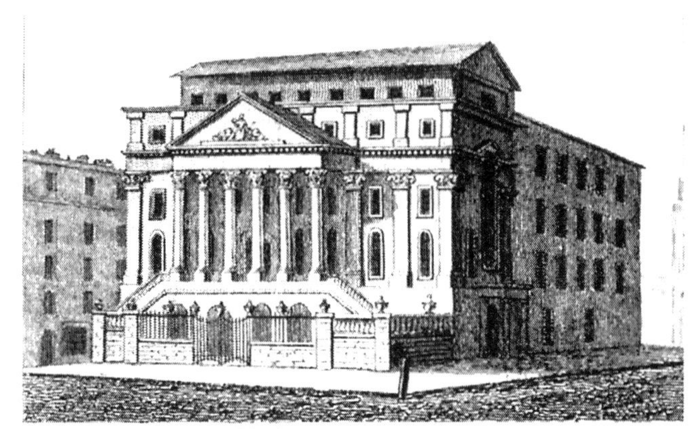
MANSION HOUSE.

EAST INDIA HOUSE.

THE BANK.

It was built by Dance the elder. Its erection was commenced in 1739, but not completed till 1753: it is of an oblong form, and constructed of Portland stone. From its massive style and vast extent, it is calculated to make a magnificent appearance; but the effect is in a great measure destroyed by its still confined situation, and the heavy superstructure over the pediment. A wide and lofty portico, composed of six fluted pillars of the Corinthian order, with two pilasters at each side of the pediment, of the same order, forms the chief ornament of the front. Under this portico is a low basement story, in the centre of which is the gateway leading to the kitchens and offices. A flight of steps ascends to the principal entrance beneath the portico. These stairs are enclosed by a stone balustrade, continued along the whole length of the front. The pediment of the portico is adorned with a piece of sculpture designed by Sir R. Taylor, emblematical of the wealth and grandeur of the city. In the centre is a female figure representing the city, having a wand in her right hand, and the left resting on the city arms. On her head is a mural crown, and under her left foot a figure of Envy. Near her, on the right, is a Cupid, with a cap of liberty affixed to a short staff, leaning on his shoulder; and beyond him reclines a sea-god, to represent the Thames, having at his side an anchor fastened to a cable. To the left of London is Plenty, with a cornucopia; and behind her two naked boys with bales of goods, to denote commerce.

The west side of this edifice presents a range of noble windows, placed between coupled Corinthian pilasters. Its interior exhibits a sufficient degree of splendour; but many of the rooms are dark. Some of the apartments are very large, and fitted up in a sumptuous style, particularly the Egyptian-hall, the ball-room, &c.

The justice-room, where the lord-mayor sits daily to hear complaints, is situated on the left of the principal entrance.

East-India House,

Leadenhall-street.

This edifice comprises the principal offices of the East-India Company. It was originally founded in 1726; but has been so much altered and enlarged since 1798, under the superintendence of Mr. Jupp, as to become an entirely new building. The front, composed of stone, is about 200 feet long, and displays a general air of grandeur and simplicity. In the centre rises a noble portico, supported by six Ionic fluted columns. The frieze is sculptured with a variety of antique ornaments; and the pediment exhibits several figures emblematical of the commerce of the Company, protected by his majesty George III., who is represented in the act of extending a shield over them. Britannia and Liberty are seen embracing each other; while on one side Mercury, accompanied by Navigation, is introducing Asia; and on the other, Order, Religion, and Justice, appear, attended by the city barge, Integrity, and Industry. In the east angle is an emblem of the Ganges; and in the west, that of the Thames. On the apex of the pediment is placed a statue of Britannia; to the east of which is a figure of Asia seated on a camel; and on the west, another of Europe on a horse.

The interior has several noble apartments. The *Grand Court-Room* is light and elegant, and is adorned with a fine basso-relievo of Britannia attended by old Father Thames, and female figures emblematical of India, Asia, and Africa, who are presenting their various productions. Here likewise are several Indian views. The *New Sale-Room* may justly be considered one of the curiosities of the metropolis; it is adorned with pilasters, and with several paintings illustrative of commerce. The *Old Sale-Room* is embellished with statues of Sir Eyre Coote, Lord Clive, Sir G. Pococke, and General Lawrence. The *Room for the Committee of Correspondence* is embellished with numerous views of Indian scenery by Ward, as well as with portraits of Warren Hastings and marquess Cornwallis. The *Library* contains busts of the duke of Wellington, Mr. Orme the historian, and of Warren Hastings, as well as a fine collection of Indian and Chinese manuscripts, together with every book that has been published respecting Asia; and the *Museum*, which adjoins it, abounds with Indian curiosities of every description. The latter may be seen on Mondays, Thursdays, and Saturdays, between 10 and 3, by obtaining a ticket from one of the directors. It has latterly been open to the public without a ticket on Saturdays from 11 till 3, except during September.

In this house the courts of the East India Company are held, and all its official and general business transacted. The East-India Company have extensive warehouses in New-street, Bishopsgate-street, and various parts of London, where imported goods are deposited.

THE BANK OF ENGLAND,

Threadneedle-street.

This immense pile of buildings is more extensive in its range of offices, and more eminent for its architectural ornament and interior arrangement, than any public office in the metropolis. It presented, however, till lately an incongruous medley of styles and forms, having been built at various periods by three different architects.

The centre of the principal or south front, the hall, the bullion-court, and court-yard, were designed and erected by George Sampson in 1733; the lateral wings of this façade and the returns on the east and west sides, with several offices immediately attached, were built by Sir Robert Taylor between 1770 and 1786; and the remaining portion of the building was constructed by Sir J. Soane since 1788. The front and wings, erected by Sampson and Taylor, were rebuilt in 1825 by Sir J. Soane; so that the whole building may now be said to be from the designs of this distinguished architect.

The buildings are included in an area of an irregular form, the exterior wall of which measures 365 feet in front, or on the south side; 440 feet on the west side; 410 feet on the north side; and 245 feet on the east side. This area comprises eight open courts, the rotunda or circular room, several large public offices, committee-rooms, and private apartments for the residence of officers and servants. The principal suite of rooms is on the ground-floor, and there are no apartments over the chief offices; but beneath this floor, and even below the surface of the ground, there is more building and a greater number of rooms than above ground. Part of the edifice is raised on a marshy soft soil; for the stream called Wallbrook ran here, and it has been necessary to pile the foundation, and construct counter-arches beneath the walls.

Of the architectural characteristics of this edifice, its extent, arrangement, and adaptation to the accumulated business of the national Bank, it is impossible to convey satisfactory information in a limited space; but we shall briefly describe a few of the principal features.

The principal entrance is in Threadneedle-street, but there are others in Lothbury and Bartholomew-lane. The *Rotunda* is a spacious circular-room, with a lofty dome, 57 feet in diameter, crowned by a lantern, the divisions in which are formed by caryatides. Here a large and heterogeneous mass of persons, of all nations and classes, assemble on public days to buy and sell stock; but since the building of the New Stock-Exchange, the business transacted in the rotunda has not been of so general and respectable a character. It is still, however, frequented by stockholders, who wait here to learn the result of commissions given to their brokers. The design and construction of the dome are entitled to the particular notice and admiration of strangers.

In the *Three per Cents Warrant-Office* much taste and skill have been displayed. It is an oblong room, with a vaulted ceiling springing from ornamented piers; and in the centre is a handsome dome or lantern-light, supported by caryatides. The soffites of the arches are decorated with panels, roses, and other objects, in strict conformity to the practice of the ancient architects. It is worthy of remark, that the whole is constructed without timber. Branching from this apartment is another, called the *Interior Office*, adapted to clerks whose business it is to guard against forgery. It opens to Lothbury-court, which is a grand display of architectural design, two sides of it being formed by open screens, with handsome fluted columns of the Corinthian order. These are copied from the little temple at Tivoli. On the south side of this court is a noble arch of entrance to the *Bullion-Court*, and to other offices. This arch and façade are designed after the model of the celebrated triumphal arch of Constantine at Rome. On the sides of the great archway are four handsome fluted columns supporting an entablature, and four statues emblematical of the four quarters of the globe. In panels are bassi-relievi executed by Banks, allegorically representing the Thames and the Ganges. The *Drawing-Office*, or Pay-Hall, contains a marble statue of William III. by Cheere. The *Chief Cashier's-Office* is a noble apartment. It is in imitation of the Temple of the Sun and Moon at Rome, and is spacious, simple in decoration, and lighted by large and lofty windows. In the Accountant's-Office, Governor's-Court, Vestibule, and passage from Princes-street, and recessed portico at the north-west angle, are some specimens of architectural design which must excite the admiration of every connoisseur. In all these parts are recognised the forms, style, and detail of the best antique specimens, carefully adapted to their respective situations, and calculated to gratify the eye and satisfy the judgment. Stability is certainly the essential object in such a building, but beauty and grandeur are equally deserving of attention; for the British bank is rich, its proprietors are presumed to be men of education and taste, and under

ROYAL EXCHANGE.

AUCTION MART.

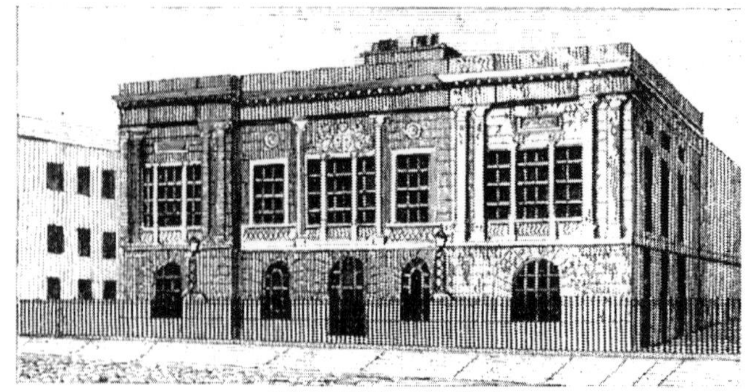
TRINITY HOUSE.

their auspices we are entitled to look for such works as shall be ornamental, and honourable to the character and taste of the kingdom.

The *Clock*, which is in a building over the Drawing-office, is an ingenious piece of mechanism, indicating the time on sixteen dials, which are placed in as many different offices, and striking the hours as well as the quarters. The communication between the clock and the dials is made by about 700 feet of brass rod, which weigh at least 600 pounds. The largest weight is about 350 pounds. The clock is wound up twice a-week.

The Bank is open for business from nine to five, except on Sundays and holydays; and any persons may visit most of the apartments.

The Royal Exchange,

Cornhill,

Founded by Sir Thomas Gresham in 1566, on the site of the ancient Tun Prison, was totally destroyed by the great fire precisely a century after its erection. The late structure was erected by Mr. Nicholas Hawkesmoor, a pupil of Sir Christopher Wren, in 1668, and cost 80,000*l.* It stood upon a plot of ground 203 feet in length and 171 in breadth, containing an area in the middle of 61 square perches, surrounded with a substantial and regular stone building wrought in rustic.

This important structure, once the focus of the world's commerce, no longer exists, having fallen a prey to flames which raged during two days, from the 10th to the 12th of January, 1838. Until the plans for its restoration are ripe, we shall preserve the former description for the curious traveller and the antiquarian. At present, the merchants of London congregate within a temporary structure in the Excise-office, Broad-street.

It had two fronts, north and south, each of which had a piazza; and in the centre were the grand entrances into the area, under a lofty and noble arch. The south front in Cornhill was the principal, on each side of which were Corinthian demi-columns, supporting a compass pediment; and in the intercolumniation on each side, in the front next the street, was a niche with statues of Charles I. and II. in Roman habits. Over the aperture on the cornice between the two pediments were the king's arms in relievo. On each side of this entrance was a range of windows placed between demi-columns and pilasters of the composite order, above which ran a balustrade. This building was 56 feet high; and from the centre of this front rose a tower 72 feet in height, erected in 1821 by Mr. G. Smith. It consisted of a square story, ornamented with colossal griffins supporting the city arms, and with four heads of queen Elizabeth, during whose reign Sir Thomas Gresham lived. Above the square story was an octagon containing the clock, over which was a circular story, surrounded by a colonnade of the Corinthian order, the whole surmounted by a dome, and terminated by a vane of gilt brass in the shape of a grasshopper, the crest of Sir Thomas Gresham's arms. On either side of the square story were façade-walls, containing bassi-relievi by Bubb; one representing queen Elizabeth attended by heralds proclaiming the original building of the Royal Exchange; and the other, Britannia seated amidst the emblems of Commerce, Naval Power, Jurisprudence, and Mercy, accompanied by the polite Arts, Science, Manufacture, and Agriculture. Between the bassi-relievi was a niche containing the statue of Sir Thomas Gresham, and over them statues of the four quarters of the globe. The old tower, which was pulled down in 1820, consisted of three compartments, and was surmounted by a vane similar to the present.

The north front in Threadneedle-street had neither columns nor statues on the outside, but was adorned with pilasters of the composite order, and had triangular instead of compass pediments. The inside of the area was also surrounded with piazzas, the walls of which were hung with advertisements of various descriptions. Above the arches of this piazza was an entablature with curious ornaments; and on the cornice a range of pilasters with an entablature extending round, and a compass pediment in the middle of the cornice of each of the four sides. Under the pediment on the north side were the king's arms; and on the south the city arms: on the east Sir Thomas Gresham's arms; and on the west the Mercers' arms, with their respective enrichments. In these inter-columns were twenty-four niches, twenty-one of which were filled with the statues of the kings and queens of England. Those from Edward I. to Charles I. were sculptured by G. Cibber, those of George I. and II. by Rysbrach, and that of George III. by Wilton; that of George IV. had lately been added. Under these piazzas, within the area, were twenty-eight niches, all vacant excepting that in which Sir Thomas Gresham's statue was placed, in the north-west angle, and that in the south-west, where the statue of Sir John Barnard was placed in his

CUSTOM HOUSE

NEW POST OFFICE.

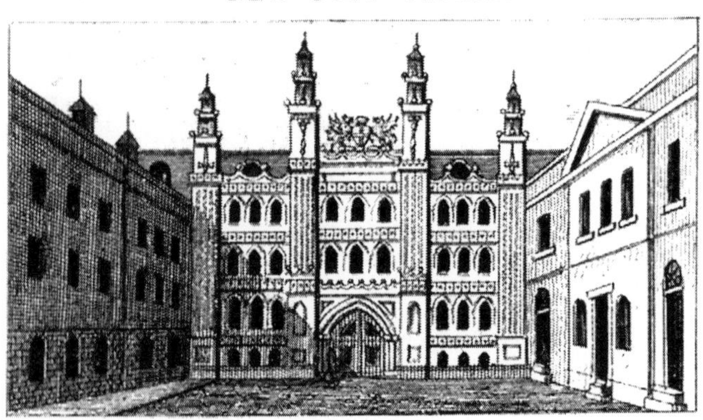
GUILDHALL.

EXCISE OFFICE.

SOMERSET HOUSE STRAND

SOMERSET HOUSE FROM THE THAMES.

ADELPHI TERRACE.

lifetime by his fellow-citizens, to express their sense of his merit. In the centre of this area was a statue of Charles II. by Gibbons, in a Roman habit, upon a pedestal eight feet high, enriched with an imperial crown, a sceptre, sword, palm-branches, and other decorations, and with a flattering inscription.

In this area merchants, and those who had business with them, met every day at 'Change hours; and, for the more regular despatch of business, they disposed of themselves in separate walks, each of which had its appropriate name.

The Exchange was open every day from eight in the morning till half-past four in the afternoon; but was most frequented between one and four o'clock.

The galleries built over the four sides of the Royal Exchange were originally divided into 200 shops; but they were latterly used for the Royal Exchange Assurance Office, Lloyd's Coffee-house, and other purposes, as well as the dry vaults which ran under the whole area.

In the tower was a good clock, with four dials, which was well regulated, and was a standard of time to all the mercantile part of the town; it chimed at three, six, nine, and twelve o'clock. There were likewise dials shewing the direction of the wind. On the right side of the north entrance was a weather-glass which had long been famed for its accuracy. Some idea of the business carried on in the vicinity of the Royal Exchange may be formed from the calculation, that 200,000 persons daily passed the south-west corner.

The Editor regrets that no steps had been taken for the re-erection of this national edifice before this edition went to press.

THE AUCTION-MART,

Bartholomew-lane.

This commercial edifice derives some importance from its immediate contiguity to those active scenes of business, the Bank of England, Royal Exchange, Stock-Exchange, and other public offices. The first stone of this structure was laid in 1808, and it was opened in 1810. Though grand and imposing, the peculiar construction of the building has made it desirable, in some degree, to sacrifice appearance to convenience. It is, however, highly creditable to the architect, Mr. John Walters, who has bestowed on his design the characteristics of a national edifice, combining elegance with simplicity. The interior contains a spacious saloon for the exhibition of particulars of sales of every description, together with various apartments for auctions and auctioneers, coffee-room, &c. Particulars of all sales are preserved here for the purposes of public reference, as are also all charters, acts of parliament, &c., relating to canals, railways, bridges, and other commercial speculations.

Trinity-House,

Tower-hill.

The society of the Trinity was founded by Sir Thomas Spert in 1515, at a period when the British navy began to assume a warlike appearance. It is a corporation, consisting of a master, four wardens, eight assistants, and eighteen elder brethren, selected from commanders in the navy and merchant-service, but as a compliment some of the nobility are occasionally admitted. The revenues are derived from tonnage, &c. They may be considered as the guardians of our ships, warlike and commercial. They examine the children in Christ's Hospital and the masters of king's ships, appoint pilots for the Thames, settle the rates of pilotage, erect light-houses and sea-marks, grant licenses to poor seamen not free of the city to row on the Thames, hear and determine complaints of officers and men in the merchant-service, and all business connected with the Thames.

The present elegant structure was commenced in 1793, under the direction of S. Wyatt, esq., and finished in two years. It is built of Portland stone, and consists of a rustic basement, over which is one story adorned with Ionic pillars and pilasters. It is likewise ornamented with busts of George III. and Queen Charlotte, and allegorical relievi. The interior is embellished with portraits of several eminent men, as well as with numerous naval curiosities, such as the flag taken by Sir Francis Drake in 1588 from the Spaniards, some curious drawings with pen and ink of naval actions, a very large pair of globes, a complete model of a ship, &c. The Trinity-house may be viewed by giving the porter 1*s*.

Custom-House,

Lower Thames-street.

This extensive edifice was erected to obviate the great inconveniences arising from the inadequate size of the former building, and to concentrate various departments of this branch of the revenue, which before were, for want of room, necessarily distributed in remote situations.

After much deliberation on the expediency of altering and enlarging the old Custom-house, the project was abandoned as impracticable to the extent required, and the new Custom-house, as designed by Mr. Laing, the architect, was ordered to be erected on the adjacent ground towards Bilingsgate-dock. It was thus proposed to have removed the business from the old building to the new one, with scarcely any interruption; but before the foundations were quite completed, the dreadful fire took place, February 12, 1814, by which this arrangement was entirely frustrated.

The first stone of the new building was laid on the 25th of October 1813, on which occasion Lord Liverpool officiated, attended by some of his colleagues in the administration and the commissioners of the board of customs. In the stone was deposited a glass urn, containing the several current coins of the realm, various medals illustrative of the great events and personages of the present era, and one engraved with an elevation of the building, inscribed on the reverse with the names of the commissioners, secretary, and architect. On a brass plate inserted in the stone was also an inscription of the date, with the names of the founders, &c.

The new Custom-house was opened for public business on the 12th May 1817, and till 1825 deservedly ranked amongst the most celebrated public buildings of this metropolis. In that year, however, a considerable portion of the long room fell in, and it was ascertained that the foundations of the edifice had been insecurely laid. The whole of the centre was then taken down, and has since been rebuilt under the direction of Mr. Smirke. The principal front, which is towards the river, presents three porticos of the Ionic order, each consisting of six pillars. That in the centre projects more than the others, and is elevated on a sub-basement of five arches. On the top is a balustrade, with a clock in the middle. The long-room is 186 feet 5 inches in length, and 60 in width. It is floored with oak, and the roof is supported by plain square pillars.

The Custom-house is 480 feet in length, and 100 in breadth, and affords accommodation to about 650 clerks and officers, besides 1,000 tide-waiters and servants. In front of it, towards the river, is a broad wharf, with stairs for the public at each end.

The first Custom-house in London was erected in 1559,

and burnt down in 1718. It was rebuilt the same year, and destroyed by fire, as already stated, in 1814.

Excise-Office,

Broad-street.

This edifice was erected in 1763, on the site of the alms-houses and college founded by Sir Thomas Gresham. It consists of two ranges of building, one of stone the other of brick, separated from each other by a large yard. From the centre of each structure, passages and staircases lead to the apartments of the commissioners and clerks. The business is managed by nine commissioners, under whom are numerous clerks, who receive the duty on tea, soap, malt, and other exciseable articles. The Excise-office is open for the transaction of business from nine till three. A temporary structure serves at present as the Exchange.

Guildhall,

King-street, Cheapside.

This extensive but irregular edifice was built in 1411, but so damaged by the great fire as to render its re-erection necessary; an undertaking which was completed in 1669, no part of the ancient building remaining, except the interior of the porch and the walls of the hall. It is occupied by the chief public offices of the city of London, &c. The front, which was not erected till 1789, is in the Gothic style, and consists of three divisions, separated from each other by fluted pilasters: over the centre are the city arms supported by dragons.

The *Hall*, which is built and paved with stone, is 153 feet long, 48 broad, and 55 feet high. It is capable of containing 6,000 or 7,000 persons, and is used for the city feasts, for the election of members of parliament and city officers, and for all the public meetings of the livery and freemen. It has two painted windows, that at the west end representing the city arms, and that at the east the royal arms, and the stars and jewels of the orders of the Garter, Bath, Thistle, and St. Patrick. Beneath the west window are the colossal figures of Gog and Magog, said to represent a Saxon and an ancient Briton. This magnificent room is ornamented with monuments erected at the expense of the city to the memory of Lord Nelson; William Pitt, earl of Chatham; William Pitt, his son; and Beckford, lord-mayor in 1763 and 1770, whose celebrated reply to his majesty George III. is engraved beneath. The monument of the Earl of Chatham was sculptured by Bacon, that of Beckford by Moore, that of Pitt by Bubb, and that of Nelson by Smith. Over the entrance is an orchestra. Beneath the hall is a crypt, which is now used as a lumber-room. In the centre of the north side of the hall is a flight of steps leading to the chamberlain's office, the common-council room, &c.

In three niches at the east end are placed the statues of Edward VI., Elizabeth, and Charles I., which formerly adorned Guildhall-chapel.

This noble hall is the scene of the civic banquets; and here, on the two memorable occasions of the visit of the allied sovereigns, and that of her present majesty, the banquets were on a scale of unparalleled splendour.

The *Chamberlain's Office* is hung with a series of prints by Hogarth; and the drawing-room behind it will gratify the lovers of penmanship, as it is ornamented with about fifty copies of the city's votes of thanks to distinguished personages, which were most of them written by Mr. Tomkins, whose portrait by Sir Joshua Reynolds, said to be his latest production, adds another to the many beauties of this interesting room.

The *Common-council Chamber* is a well-proportioned room, at the upper end of which is a fine statue of his late majesty George III. by Chantrey. It likewise contains a bust of lord Nelson by Mrs. Damer, busts of the duke of Wellington and Granville Sharpe, and a portrait of the late queen Caroline; as well as a fine collection of paintings presented to the corporation by alderman Boydell; amongst them are portraits of marquess Cornwallis, lords Howe, Duncan, Heathfield, and Nelson; the destruction of the Spanish and French flotilla before Gibraltar, by Copley; the death of David Rizzio; the death of Wat Tyler; Domestic Happiness; Miseries of Civil War; Procession of the Lord-Mayor to Westminster by Water; and the Swearing-in of the Lord-Mayor in 1781, containing portraits of the principal members of the corporation at that period. Here also are portraits of Chamberlain Clark, by Lawrence, and — Pinner, Esq., by Opie.

The *Court of Aldermen* has a fine carved ceiling, decorated with paintings.

The hall is always open to strangers, except at the public meetings of the citizens; and the other apartments may be seen for a trifling donation to the officer in attendance.

The *City Library*, in an apartment contiguous to Guildhall, was first opened in 1828. It contains a valuable collection of books, tracts, &c. relating to the city. It is open daily, except during August and on a few holydays. Every member of the corporation has free admission, and may introduce a visiter, either personally or by letter.

Adjoining the library is the *Museum* for the reception of works of art and antiquities belonging to the city.

The *Justice-hall*, where one of the aldermen sits daily, is situated in King-street, to the left of the entrance to Guildhall; and opposite to it are the *Courts of Law for the City*. The *Court of Common Pleas* is decorated with several fine portraits, amongst which are Judge Hale by Wright, and Earl Camden by Sir J. Reynolds. The *Court of Queen's Bench* likewise contains several portraits of its judges.

General Post-Office,

St. Martin's-le-Grand.

The General Post-office was originally established in Cloak-lane, near Dowgate-hill, whence it was removed to the Black Swan in Bishopsgate-street. On occasion of the great fire of 1666, it was removed to the Two Black Pillars in Brydges-street, Covent-garden, and afterwards to Sir Robert Viner's mansion in Lombard-street, where it continued till Sept. 23, 1829, when it was transferred to St. Martin's-le-Grand. It now occupies the site of an ancient college and sanctuary.

This magnificent building was commenced in 1825, from designs by R. Smirke, Esq., and completed in 1829. It is of the Grecian-Ionic order. The basement is of granite, but the superstructure is of brick, entirely faced with Portland stone. The building is 400 feet in length and 80 in depth. In the centre of the front is a portico 70 feet in breadth and 20 in depth. It consists of six columns of Portland stone, resting on pedestals of granite, and supporting a triangular pediment, beneath which is the following inscription:—Georgio Quarto Rege, MDCCCXXIX. At the extremity of each wing is a portico of four columns. In this front are 44 windows. The east or back front is quite plain, and has upwards of 180 windows.

The vestibule, or great hall, occupying the centre of the edifice, forms a public thoroughfare from St. Martin's-le-Grand to Foster-lane. It is 80 feet long, 60 broad, and 53 feet high in the centre. On each side is a line of six columns similar to those of the portico, which have a very noble effect. On the north side of the vestibule are the several receiving-rooms for newspapers, inland and ship-letters; and behind these, farther north, are the rooms for the inland letter-sorters and letter-carriers. These rooms extend the whole length of the front, from the portico to the north wing. That for the letter-carriers is 35 feet in height. Both are conveniently fitted up. The mails are received at the door in the east front, north of the vestibule, leading to the inland-offices, and are taken into the tick-room, where the bags are opened. In this part of the building also are the West Indies, comptroller's, and mail-coach offices. On the south side of the vestibule are the foreign, receiver-general's, and accountant's offices. The foreign-office has an elegant ceiling. At the east end of the vestibule is the twopenny post-office, comprising the receiving, sorters', and carriers' rooms. The sorters'-room is about 46 feet by 24. A novel mode has been adopted for conveying letters which have come into the wrong department from one room to another: they are placed in small wagons beneath the pavement, and made to travel through a tunnel by machinery.

To the right of the principal entrance is a corridor leading to the grand staircase, the dimensions of which are 32 feet by 23. The stairs are of stone, and the balusters of brass bronzed. On the first floor are the board-room, 37 feet by 24, the secretary's-room, and his clerk's office, communicating by passages with the solicitor's offices. All the floors throughout the building are of American oak. At the north-east corner of the vestibule is a staircase leading to the letter-bill, dead, mis-sent, and returned-letter offices. On the upper stories are sleeping-rooms for the foreign clerks, who are liable to be called on duty on the arrival of the mails. The assistant-secretary resides at the south-west extremity of the building.

The basement story is rendered fire-proof by brick vaultings. It comprises rooms for the mail-guards, an armoury, and servants'-offices. There is also some ingenious machinery for conveying coals to each story, and a simple means for forcing water to any part of the edifice in case of fire. The whole building is lighted by gas, of which there are nearly 1,000 burners.

There are two great branches of the General Post-office, the Inland and the Foreign, the details of which are similar, except that attendance at the former is daily, and at the latter only twice a-week; a description of one of them will therefore be sufficient. There are two periods of meeting in the day at the inland-office, one for the distribution of the letters that come up from the country, and another for the despatch of those that are to be sent down. The first commences at six in the morning, and the task is accomplished by half-past eight or nine, except when the mails are delayed by the badness of the roads. The letters to be distributed are counted, and the amount of postage taken, so as to check the accounts of the country postmasters. They are then examined, to ascertain whether the charges on them are accurate, stamped with the date, and arranged for the letter-carriers, to whom they are counted twice over. The postage is paid to the receiver-general three times a-week, when the amount of each letter-carrier's delivery for every day is again checked.

The despatch of the letters in the evening is conducted upon the same admirable system as their distribution in the morning, the whole business being performed in three hours, from five to eight. The letters are first taken out of the receiving-house and arranged in different compartments, named after the mails sent out. This is done by the junior clerks, who thus acquire a perfect knowledge of the situation and distance of all the post-towns. The senior clerks then mark on the letters the proper rate of postage, which they do at an average of one letter per second; and the letters are placed in boxes labelled with the names of the towns. At seven o'clock the receiving-office closes, and the letters for each town are summed up, put in the bag, and a copy of the amount sent along with them. Letters may be sent later than this upon paying a fee, which is allowed as a perquisite to the junior clerks, who also charge 1*d.* for every newspaper sent to the office after the hour at which the bags begin to be closed. The letter-bags, tied and sealed, are all delivered to the respective guards of the mail-coaches by eight o'clock.

The delivery of the letters in the morning is expedited by means of *accelerators*, which were first used on the removal of the office to its present situation. These are lightly-built carriages, which receive the postmen and their letters at the office, and each taking a division of the metropolis, drops the letter-deliverer in his own particular walk in much less time than he would occupy in walking the distance.

The average number of letters which pass through the Post-office in a week exceeds half a million. The Inland-office employs about 200 superintendents, clerks, and sorters, be-

TEMPLE BAR.

CHARING CROSS & COCKSPUR STREET.

THE QUADRANT, REGENT STREET.

sides about 200 persons in delivering the letters; and the Foreign department employs about 20 clerks and sorters, besides 34 persons in delivering. The Two-penny Post employs about 50 sorters and clerks.

The number of letters sent by this post in 1836 was 13,589,925. The amount of receipts seem to be diminishing; in 1826 they were 117,368*l.*; in 1836 they were 112,927*l.*

Herald's College,

Bennet's-hill,

Is an ancient foundation in which are kept records of the blood of every family in the kingdom. It is a brick edifice, erected in 1683, and adorned with four Ionic pilasters; it contains a court of honour, a library, and apartments for the members, consisting of three kings-at-arms, six heralds-at-arms, and four pursuivants-at-arms, whose business it is to attend the king on particular state occasions, to arrange state processions, make proclamations, &c. The north-west angle of the building was erected at the expense of Sir W. Dugdale.

A common search for a coat of arms costs 5*s.*, or a general search 1*l.* 1*s.*; but if a new coat of arms be required, the fees amount to 10*l.* 10*s.* or more, according to the trouble incurred.

Temple-Bar,

Between Fleet-street and the Strand.

This ancient gate is the only one of the city boundaries now remaining. It was built after the great fire, by Sir C. Wren, and has two posterns for the advantage of foot-passengers. It is composed entirely of Portland stone, of rustic work below, and is of the Corinthian order. Over the gateway on the east side, in two niches, are stone statues of queen Elizabeth and James I., with the royal arms over the keystone; and on the west side are statues of Charles I. and II. in Roman habits, executed by Bushnell. Over the east side is an inscription which states that it was erected during 1670-1-2, and the names of the lord-mayors for those years.

The heads of persons executed for high treason were formerly exhibited on this gate. Here also, on particular occasions, the corporation of London receives the royal family, or any distinguished visiters, and the herald's proclamations. When the monarch comes in state, the lord-mayor delivers to him the sword of state, which is returned, and then rides bare-headed immediately before him.

The Adelphi,

Strand,

Is a handsome range of buildings erected about 1770, on the site of Durham-yard, by Messrs. Adams, four brothers whose labours have embellished the metropolis with several edifices of distinguished excellence, and whose many improvements in ornamental architecture will be highly appreciated as long as good taste prevails in the nation. The whole is built on arches, forming subterranean passages from the river to the Strand and George-street. Adelphi is a Greek word denoting the fraternal relationship; and it may not be uninteresting to remark that the family and Christian names of the artists by whom the Adelphi was built are retained in the appellations of the different streets of which it is composed. The Adelphi is one of the principal objects visible from the bridges of Waterloo and Westminster; and the view from the terrace, as it is lofty, and built at a bend of the river, is very commanding. No. 5 on the Terrace was purchased by Garrick, and afterwards became the residence of his widow, who died here in 1822. No. 1 Adam-street was for many years the residence of Dr. Vicesimus Knox.

Somerset-House,

Strand,

Was formerly a palace founded on the site of several churches and other buildings, levelled for the purpose in 1549 by the protector Somerset, whose residence fell to the crown after his execution. In this palace queen Elizabeth resided at certain times; Anne of Denmark kept her court; and Catherine queen of Charles II. dwelt during a portion of the life of her volatile spouse, and continued after his death, until she retired to her native country.

Old Somerset-house, which was a mixture of Grecian and Gothic, was demolished in 1775, and the present magnificent edifice, from a design by Sir William Chambers, erected for the accommodation of all the public offices — those of the treasury, the secretary of state, the admiralty, the war, and the excise excepted. The Royal Society, the Society of Antiquaries, the Geological Society, and the Royal Astronomical Society, hold their meetings here, in apartments which have been allotted to them by royal munificence; and here also are located the University of London, which was incorporated

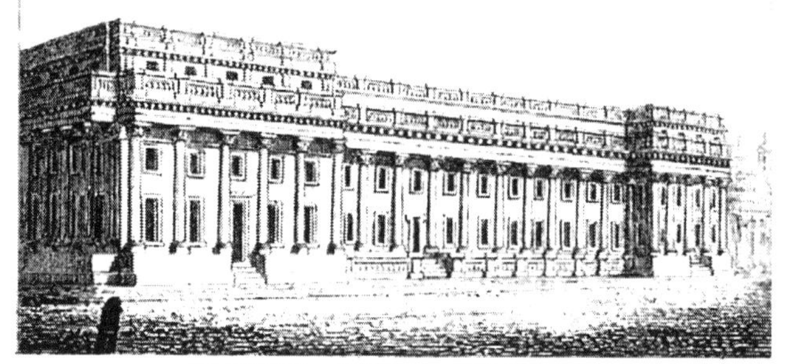

COUNCIL OFFICE WHITEHALL.

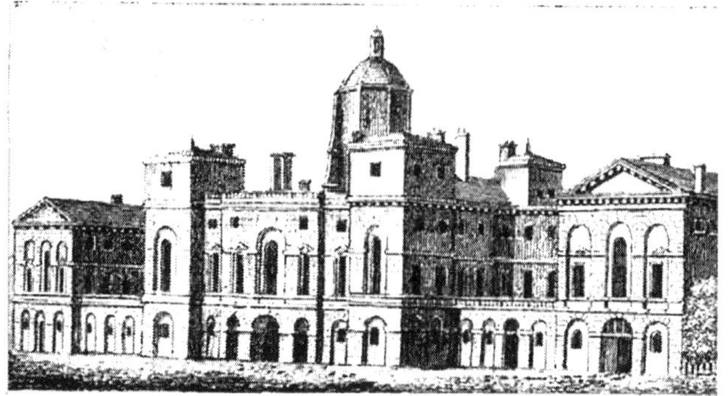

HORSE GUARDS FROM THE PARK.

ADMIRALTY.

by charter of William IV.; and the School of Design, instituted by government in 1837 for the education of industrial artists, and of those engaged in the preparation of patterns for manufacture. Pupils admitted to the morning school pay 4*s.* weekly; to the evening, 1*s.* per week. They are under the superintendence of Mr. Dyson.

Somerset-house, occupying a space about 800 feet in width and 500 in depth, is built in the form of a quadrangle, with a large court in the centre. The Strand front consists of a rustic basement of nine arches, supporting Corinthian columns, surmounted in the centre by an attic, and at the extremities by a balustrade. The key-stones of the arches are adorned with colossal masks in *alto-relievo,* emblematical of Ocean, and the eight central rivers of England, the Thames, Humber, Mersey, Dee, Medway, Tweed, Tyne, and Severn. On the three central windows of the first floor are medallions in *basso-relievo* of George III., his queen, and the prince of Wales. The attic is divided into three parts by four statues of venerable men, representatives of Justice, Truth, Valour, and Moderation, as they bear in one hand the fasces, and in the other the scales, the mirror, the sword, and the bridle. The whole is surmounted by the British arms, supported by Fame and the Genius of England. The three central arches of the basement form the entrance of the vestibule, in which are two busts, by Wilton, of Michael Angelo and Sir Isaac Newton. In the court opposite the entrance is a bronze cast of the Thames, by Bacon, lying at the foot of a pedestal on which is a statue of George III.

Before the front towards the river is a spacious terrace raised on rustic arches, ornamented with a colossal mask of the Thames in alto-relievo. This terrace, however, is not open to the public, which is much to be regretted, as it is a delightful promenade, commanding a fine view of the metropolis, of the river, and of the Surrey hills.

The east wing, forming the King's College, was completed in 1833 in conformity with the charter of that institution.

COMMERCIAL-HALL,

Mincing-lane,

Is an elegant structure, erected by subscription in 1811, for the sale of colonial produce of every kind. It was built from designs by Mr. Woods, and contains five public sale-rooms, a large coffee-room, several show-rooms, and numerous counting-houses let out to various merchants. The front is ornamented with six Ionic columns, between which are introduced five emblematical devices executed by Bubb, representing Husbandry, Science, Britannia, Commerce, and Navigation.

HORSE-GUARDS,
Whitehall.

This edifice is so called in consequence of being the station where that part of her majesty's troops usually do duty. It is a strong building of hewn stone, consisting of a centre and two wings, erected by Ware about 1730. In the former are arched foot and carriage-ways into St. James's-park; and over it in the middle rises a cupola containing an excellent clock. In front are two small archways, where horse-soldiers in full uniform daily mount guard. In a part of the building is the office of the commander-in-chief.

THE TREASURY,
St. James's-Park,

Is a handsome stone building near the Horse-guards, facing the parade. The front, which was erected by Kent, consists of three stories, displaying the Tuscan, the Doric, and the Ionic orders of architecture: the whole surmounted by a pediment. The treasury-board is held in this building. That part of the treasury which fronts Whitehall is a portion of the old Whitehall-palace erected by Cardinal Wolsey; but it has been considerably altered both in the reign of Charles II. and in 1816.

COUNCIL-OFFICE,
Whitehall.

This edifice was rebuilt in 1826, from designs by Sir J. Soane. The Corinthian columns in advance of the front and side of the building are copied from those of the Temple of Jupiter Stator. The council-chamber, which is on the first floor at the west-end, is a magnificent apartment reaching to the top of the edifice; the sides are ornamented with Ionic columns, the shafts of which are executed in scagliola in imitation of Sienna marble, and the capitals in imitation of white marble. The ceiling is slightly curved, and in the centre is an elegant lantern. In this splendid room her majesty's privy council sits to decide on appeals from the subordinate tribunals of the East and West Indies.

The left wing of this building forms one side of the entrance to Downing-street, celebrated as the scene of our foreign di-

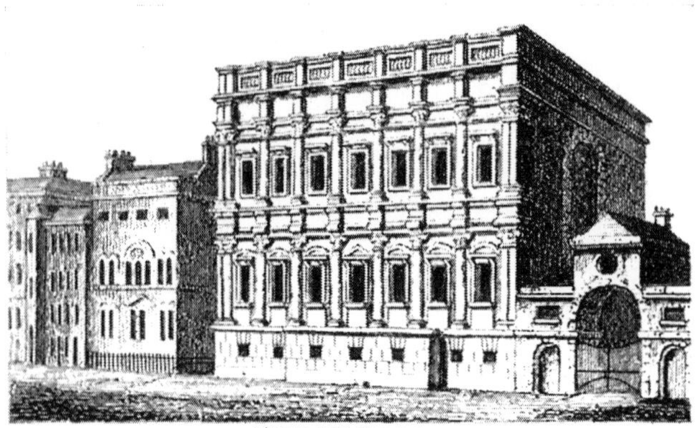

WHITEHALL.

RICHMOND TERRACE.

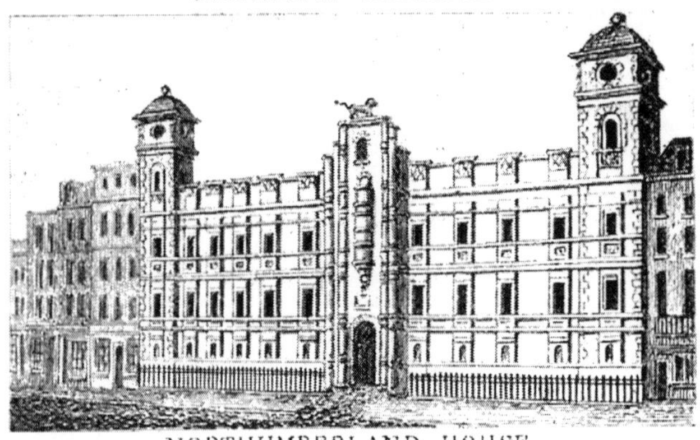

NORTHUMBERLAND HOUSE.

plomacy. New offices for the home-department and foreign affairs, &c. are to be erected on the site of Fludyer-street. It is probable, owing to some defect in the line formed by this edifice, that it will not be completed.

Admiralty-Office,
Whitehall.

This is a large pile built with brick and stone by Ripley, on the site of Wallingford-house, whence archbishop Usher took a last view of his monarch Charles I. The front has two deep wings, and a lofty portico supported by four large stone pillars of the Ionic order. The screen, built in front of the court by Messrs. Adams, is ornamented with naval emblems. Besides a hall and other public apartments, here are spacious houses for the six lords of the admiralty; and on the top of the building is a Semaphore Telegraph, by means of which a correspondence is maintained with various parts of the coast.

Whitehall.

On the banks of the Thames, at the east confine of St. Margaret's parish, was a place called Whitehall, originally built by Hubert de Burgh, earl of Kent, before the middle of the 13th century. It afterwards devolved to the archbishop of York, whence it received the name of York-place, and continued to be the town-residence of the archbishops till purchased by Henry VIII. of cardinal Wolsey in 1530. At this period it became the residence of the court; but in 1697 all was destroyed by accidental fire, except the banqueting-house, which had been added to the palace of Whitehall by James I., according to the extensive and magnificent design of Inigo Jones, in 1619. This is a noble structure of hewn stone, adorned with an upper and lower range of pillars of the Ionic and Composite orders; the capitals and the space between the columns of the windows are enriched with fruit and foliage. The roof is covered with lead, and surrounded with a balustrade. A thorough repair of the whole building was commenced in 1829.

The building chiefly consists of one room of an oblong form, forty feet high. The ceiling, representing the apotheosis of James I., was painted by Rubens, and has since been retouched by Cipriani, the former having received 3000*l.* for his labour, and the latter 2000*l.* George I. converted this noble room into a chapel-royal, in which service is performed every Sunday morning and afternoon. Charles I. was executed on a scaffold in front of this building, January 30, 1649; he was led through an opening made in the north wall, now forming the doorway to a modern erection at that end of the chapel.

Between Whitehall and the Thames stands a bronze statue of James II., which is considered a fine likeness; it was executed by Grinlin Gibbons, a year before he abdicated the throne.

The Queen's Stables,

Pimlico,

Were erected in 1824. They consist of two quadrangles, the entrance to which is formed by a handsome arch of the Doric order. In the first are the coach-houses, and the second is occupied by the horses. The handsome cream-coloured horses belonging to the queen are kept here, and only used on days of public procession.

Admission may be obtained by tickets from the master of the horse.

The royal stables were formerly situated at Charing-cross, and were called the *Mews;* the original building on their site having been devoted to keeping the king's falcons, at least from the time of Richard II. In the reign of Henry VIII. the king's horses were kept there. In 1534 a fire destroyed the building, but it was rebuilt in the reigns of Edward VI. and Queen Mary. In 1732 another edifice was erected, which was occupied by the king's horses till the present stables at Pimlico were built: the edifice was then demolished, and on its site the National Gallery was erected.

Board of Control,

Cannon-row, Westminster,

Was originally built for the New Transport-office, but the peace having almost annihilated that branch of business, it is now appropriated to the Board of Control for India affairs. It is a handsome brick and stone building, with a portico of the Ionic order.

Sessions-House,

Old Bailey,

Is a handsome building of stone and brick. The entrance to the court is formed by two flights of steps, on either side of which staircases ascend to the galleries. On each side of the courts are seats for the sheriffs, who can speak to each other by means of a pipe passing along the front of the bench. The prisoner stands nearly at the extremity of the court, facing the

SESSIONS HOUSE, OLD BAILEY

SESSIONS HOUSE CLERKENWELL.

ST BARTHOLOMEWS HOSPL (Entrance)

CITY OF LONDON LYING IN HOSPITAL

ASYLUM FOR FEMALE ORPHANS.

bench. During the trials admission to the galleries may be obtained on application to the officers, who are constantly in attendance, and demand a sum proportionate to the interest of the case. The fee in ordinary cases is 1*s*., or after five o'clock, 6*d*.

Behind the Sessions-house is a colonnade which was built as a promenade for the witnesses in waiting, over which is a New Court erected in 1824, for the purpose of facilitating the trials during the sessions. The jurisdiction of these courts has already been noticed under the article *Courts of Justice*.

SESSION-HOUSE,
Clerkenwell.

The original Sessions-house for the county of Middlesex, situated in St. John-street, and called Hicks's Hall, having become ruinous, the present building was erected about 1780, from designs by Mr. Rogers. The front is of stone, with a rustic basement, over which are four Ionic pillars and two pilasters, supporting an architrave, frieze, and cornice, with a pediment. Over the centre window is a medallion of George III., and over two others are representations of Justice and Mercy, executed by Nollekens. At each extremity is a medallion of the Roman fasces and sword. The tympanum contains the county arms. The interior is divided into the court, the hall, and rooms for the magistrates, grand jury, &c. In one of the rooms on the side of the entrance is an original portrait of Sir B. Hicks, the builder of the old hall. The court is open to the public.

TOWN-HALL,
Southwark,

Is a modern brick edifice, with a stone front, consisting of a rustic basement, above which are several Ionic pilasters surmounted by a balustrade. The steward of the city of London holds a court of record here every Monday for all debts, damages, and trespasses, within his jurisdiction.

NEW COURT-HOUSE, OR WESTMINSTER GUILDHALL,

Is built on part of the ancient Sanctuary. It is of an octagonal form, and is entered by a few steps under a vestibule, supported by massy columns of the Doric order. It is used as the court of sessions for the city of Westminster, and is open to the public during the transaction of business. The court of review is also held here.

THE CORN-EXCHANGE,

Mark-lane,

Is a quadrangular paved court, surrounded by a colonnade in which are seats for the corn-factors, who have each a desk containing samples of corn. The entrance consists of eight Doric columns supporting a plain building, in which are two coffee-houses. The chief business is transacted here on Mondays, though Wednesdays and Fridays are likewise market-days.

THE NEW CORN-EXCHANGE,

Mark-lane.

This building adjoins the preceding. It was erected in 1828 from designs by Mr. Smith, at an expense of 90,000*l.*, and is a neat specimen of the Greek Doric style of architecture. The façade consists of a peristyle of six fluted columns, with wings of rectangular form, and thin pilasters at the angles. The frieze is adorned with wreaths, and above are represented the royal arms, grouped with implements of husbandry. The interior consists of the sale-room, a spacious and well-lighted hall comprising the corn and seed markets, containing 82 stands for the factors, in the floor of which are inserted circular glasses to light the underground premises, the roof being supported by 12 cast-iron pillars, with wheat-sheaf capitals; the subscription-room where the daily papers are read, containing rolling-maps, &c., an elegant and well-proportioned saloon decorated with four scagliola columns and ten pilasters round the sides, the whole with emblematical capitals—a similar style pervading the edifice even to the balustrade of the staircase. There is an excellent hotel attached to the institution.

EXETER-HALL,

Strand.

This handsome edifice was erected in 1830 from designs by Mr. Gandy Deering, for the meeting of religious, charitable, and scientific institutions, the funds for this purpose being raised in shares. The principal entrance is between two houses in the Strand; but there are doors on each side of the building. It consists of an elegant portico, formed by two pillars and two pilasters, over which is an entablature with the Greek compound *Philadelpheion*, signifying *fraternal love*. Beyond is the vestibule. The ground floor is occupied by offices, committee-rooms, and a room for small meetings, 58 feet by 31, capable of holding 800 persons. On the upper floor is the principal room, 136 feet by 76, capable of accommodating 2500 persons. The building cost about 30,000*l.* Musical festivals, on a grand scale, are occasionally held here.

CROSBY-HOUSE,
Crosby-square,

Is so called from its builder, Sir John Crosby, sheriff of London in 1470. In this house Richard duke of Gloucester lodged when he meditated the murder of his innocent nephews, who had been conveyed to the Tower. The west side is adorned with beautiful Gothic windows, and the roof with exquisite carving. The hall, improperly called Richard III.'s *Chapel*, is 87 feet in length, 28 feet wide, and 36 feet high; but for the convenience of its former occupiers, it has been divided into floors. This house when erected is supposed to have been the highest in London. The mansion of Crosby-house was granted by Henry VIII. to Anthony Bonvica, an Italian merchant. In Elizabeth's time it was appropriated to the reception of ambassadors; and in Charles II.'s reign it belonged to the Non-conformists, who retained it upwards of a century. Crosby-house was lately rented by wharfingers and packers; but, owing to the zealous endeavours of some tasteful individuals, it has been judiciously restored.

THE ALBANY,
Piccadilly,

Which was erected by Sir W. Chambers, derived its name from the second title of the late duke of York, by whom it was formerly inhabited. After his royal highness had left it, the gardens were covered with buildings, which are let out as lodgings to the nobility, members of parliament, and others who have no fixed town residence. This fine range of buildings extends from Piccadilly to Burlington-gardens. There is a porter's lodge at each end, but it is not a regular thoroughfare.

NOBLEMEN'S RESIDENCES.

APSLEY, or WELLINGTON-HOUSE, Hyde-park-corner.—This splendid mansion was originally built by lord Chancellor Apsley, from designs by Messrs. Adams. Having, however, become the residence of the duke of Wellington, it was enlarged and entirely re-modelled in 1828-29, under the direction of Sir J. Wyattville. The basement story is rusticated, and the principal front has a pediment, supported by four Corinthian columns. A bold cornice extends on all sides, which is decorated at the angles with Corinthian pilasters. The front is enclosed by a rich bronzed palisade. The ball-room, extending the whole depth of the mansion, and the picture gallery, are superb. The banqueting-room is splendidly decorated, being of a dead white richly gilt. The celebrated colossal statue of Napoleon, by Canova, is at the foot of the great staircase.

SUTHERLAND-HOUSE, at the corner of the Green-park.—This noble mansion was commenced in 1825, from designs by Mr. B. Wyatt, and was intended to be the residence of his late royal highness the duke of York. On his demise, however, it was purchased by the late marquess of Stafford, and finished in the most splendid style. It is now the residence of his son the duke of Sutherland. Its form is quadrangular, and it has four perfect fronts, all of which are cased with stone. The ground-floor is rusticated, and the upper part is of the Corinthian order. There are in all three stories, but the third is concealed by a balustrade, so as to give a more majestic appearance to the building. Nearly in the centre of the roof is a lantern illuminating the grand staircase.

The north or principal front, which is the entrance, exhibits a portico of eight Corinthian columns. The south and west fronts are alike; they project slightly at each end, and in the centre are six Corinthian columns supporting a pediment. The east side differs a little from the preceding, as it has no projecting columns.

The vestibule, which is of noble dimensions, leads to the grand staircase, 14 feet in breadth. The ground-floor is occupied by the library, bed-rooms, dressing-rooms, baths, &c., all fitted up in a splendid style; and on the first or principal floor are the state apartments, comprising dining-rooms, drawing-rooms, and a picture-gallery 130 feet in length.

NORTHUMBERLAND-HOUSE, Charing-cross.—This magnificent edifice was built in the reign of James I. by Henry Howard, earl of Northampton; during whose life it was called Northampton-house, and consisted originally of three sides only. After his death it came into the possession of his relation the earl of Suffolk, and was then known by the name of Suffolk-house. In 1642 Algernon earl of Northumberland, lord high admiral of England, became its proprietor by marrying Lord Suffolk's daughter, at which time it obtained its present name. The portal was altered in 1750, by Sir H. Smithson, bart., created earl of Northumberland, the ancestor of the present duke.

The front to the street is singular, and is surmounted by a lion, the crest of the Percy family. On entering the first gate, the four sides of the inner court are seen, faced with Portland stone; and two wings, above 100 feet in length, extend from the garden-front towards the river. The principal door of the house opens to a vestibule about 82 feet long, and more than 12 feet wide, ornamented with columns of the Doric order. Each end of it communicates with a splendid marble staircase, leading to the principal apartments, which consist of several spacious rooms fitted up in the most elegant manner. They contain a very large and valuable collection of pictures by the great masters;—among them are the works of Raphael, Titian, Luca Giordano, Paul Veronese, Dominico Fatti, Salvator Rosa, Tempesta, Albert Durer, Old Frank, Rubens, Vandyke, Snyders, Dobson, &c. The whole of the building was completely repaired in 1821, and fitted up in the most sumptuous style.

The garden between the house and the river consists of a fine lawn, surrounded with a great gravel walk.

Burlington-house, Piccadilly, is the residence of Lord Cavendish. The front is remarkable for its beauty, but is hid from public view by a lofty brick wall. The wings of the building are connected with the centre by a colonnade of the Doric order. The Duke of Portland died at this house in 1809, only a few days after he had resigned his seat in the cabinet.

Spencer-house, St. James's-place, the family mansion of earl Spencer, is a noble Palladian edifice, faced with Portland-stone. The pediment of the front towards the Green-park is adorned with statues and vases very judiciously disposed. The principal ornament of the interior is the library, an elegant room, containing one of the finest collections of books in the kingdom.

Marlborough-house, Pall-mall, the town residence of the queen dowager, for whom it was thoroughly repaired and refurnished in 1837, and formerly the residence of the princess Charlotte and the prince of Saxe-Coburg, is a stately brick edifice, erected during the reign of queen Anne, as a testimony of Britain's approbation of the services of the great duke of Marlborough. The wings are adorned with rustic stone-work, and the interior is splendidly furnished. In the vestibule is a painting of the battle of Hochstet, in which the duke of Marlborough, prince Eugene, and marshal Tallard are represented.

Our limits will not allow us to give an ample description of all the noble houses in London. We enumerate those, however, which are of the most distinguished rank.

Shelburne, or Lansdowne-house, Berkeley-square, the residence of the marquess of Lansdowne, is one of the most noble mansions in London, adorned with a fine collection of antique statues, busts, &c. The gallery is a room of imposing proportions, being 100 feet long by 30 wide. In the ante-room is Canova's Venus, and in the dining and drawing rooms are recesses containing statues and busts.

Chesterfield-house, South Audley-street, erected by the celebrated earl of Chesterfield, containing a splendid staircase, brought from Canons in Hertfordshire; the *duke of Devonshire's*, Piccadilly, built from designs by Kent; *Hertford-house*, Manchester-square, formerly inhabited by the duke of Manchester; the *marquess of Anglesea's*, Burlington-gardens, built by Leoni for the duke of Queensbury, and afterwards called Uxbridge-house, from the former title of its present occupant; *marquess of Westminster's*, Upper Grosvenor-street; *lord Harcourt's*, Cavendish-square; *duke of Rutland's*, Arlington-street; *duke of Bedford's*, Belgrave-square; *earl of Harewood's*, Hanover-square; *Melbourne-house*, Whitehall, which has a handsome portico extending over the footpath; *Foley-house*, at the south extremity of Portland-place: *sir W. W. Wynn's*, St. James's-square; *Grosvenor-house*, Upper Grosvenor-street, to which is attached a splendid picture-gallery, erected in 1826 from designs by Mr. T. Cundy; *Gloucester-house*, Piccadilly; *duke of Portland's*, Cavendish-square; the *duke of Norfolk's*, St. James's-square; *duke of Buckingham's*, Pall-mall; *Dorchester-house;* the *marquess of Hertford's*, Park-lane; *Mr. Baring's*, Piccadilly; the *marquess of Hertford's* villa in Regent's-park; *Cambridge*, formerly *Cholmondeley, house*, Piccadilly; *Holderness-house*, marquess of Londonderry's, Park-lane.

STATUES (IN THE OPEN AIR).

The various statues of the metropolis will be found described under the proper heads. The following is a mere enumeration:—

King Alfred, Trinity Church, Trinity-square; sir John Moore and Edward VI., Christ Church; Edward VI. St. Thomas's Hospital; Charles I., Charing-cross; James II., Whitehall-yard; Canning, Palace-yard; George I., Leicester-square; duke of Cumberland, Cavendish-square; William III., St. James's-square; George I., Grosvenor-square; Charles II., Soho-square; C. J. Fox, Bloomsbury-square; duke of Bedford, Russell-square; duke of Kent, Portland-place; queen Anne, St. Paul's Churchyard; Achilles, Hyde-park; Pitt, Hanover-square; duke of York, on the Column; George III., Pall-mall East, and Somerset-house; George I., Bloomsbury Steeple; lord Eldon, School, Wandsworth-road; Elizabeth, James I., Charles I., and Charles II., Temple-bar; Guy, Guy's Hospital; Aske, Aske's Hospital; major Cartwright, Burton-crescent; sir R. Clayton, St. Thomas's Hospital; Henry VIII., St. Bartholomew's Hospital; Whittington, in front of Alms-houses.

The proposed statues of Wellington for the two testimonials, and that of Nelson.

The principal in-door statues are those at St. Paul's, Westminster Abbey, the vestibules of the British Museum, Drury-lane and Covent-garden Theatres, Guildhall, the East India-house, Bethlehem Hospital.

The principal sculptured exteriors are those of the New Palace, the arch of Hyde-park, the base of the Monument, the façades of the British Gallery and the University Club. The frieze of the Athenæum Club, the pediments of St. Paul's, the Mansion-house, the East India-house, the houses in the Regent's-park, the National Gallery, the Gates of St. Giles's, and St. Vedast Churches; the Pelican Insurance, the Provident, the Union, &c. There are also two statues in front of the Asiatic Armoury-tower.

SQUARES.

There are nearly 200 areas bearing the name of square in this metropolis; the greater portion, however, are undeserving of description. The following are remarkable either for historical reminiscences, or for that peculiar beauty which forms one of the chief characteristics of this imposing city.

BEDFORD-SQUARE is neat and spacious: it is 518 yards in circumference. Here, as has been well observed, we have an example of the beauty resulting from an uniform design carried into execution under individual direction; and an instance of the deformities in the architectural appearance of some of the buildings which frequently result from interested speculations.

BELGRAVE-SQUARE was commenced in 1825, on the estate of the marquess of Westminster, and is now one of the most distinguished ornaments of the metropolis. It is 684 feet long and 617 broad: each side is 187 yards long, forming a circumference of 748 yards. The houses are large and uniform, and are adorned with columns of the Corinthian order. At the farther corner of this beautiful square is the *Pantechnicon*—a vast establishment, uniting a bazaar, exhibition-rooms, wine-stores, and carriage-repository. There are also fireproof rooms, in which families may deposit valuable furniture for any length of time.

BERKELEY-SQUARE, on the north side of Piccadilly, is situated on one of the few descents found in London: it is 453 yards in circumference. The south side is occupied by the wall of an extensive garden, in the midst of which is a large stone house of heavy proportions, built by Adams for the late earl of Bute, and sold incomplete to the earl of Shelburne, afterwards marquess of Lansdowne. Lansdowne-house now belongs to the marquess of that name. In the centre of the square, which contains three acres of ground, there was formerly an equestrian statue of George III. by Wilton.

BLOOMSBURY-SQUARE was once called Southampton-square: it is 408 yards in circumference. The house which formerly occupied the north side was built after a design by Inigo Jones, and eventually called Bedford-house; from this place the amiable lady Russell dated her letters, it being her town residence till her death in 1723. To forward those improvements of which Russell, Tavistock, Euston squares, &c. are the result, this house and its gardens were sold, and the whole site is now built over. On the north side, opposite the monument of the duke of Bedford, is a fine colossal statue of the right hon. Charles James Fox, executed in bronze by Westmacott, and elevated on several steps resting on a pedestal of granite; the whole about 16 feet in height. The patriot is represented seated, and habited in a consular robe, with his right arm extended, supporting Magna Charta. The following is the only inscription :—" Charles James Fox. Erected MDCCCXVI."

CAVENDISH-SQUARE contains some very noble mansions: it is 480 yards in circumference. It was planned in 1715, as were some regular streets leading thence to Tyburn or Edgeware-road. In the centre of the square is a gilt equestrian statue of William duke of Cumberland, so celebrated by his successes in Scotland, erected in 1770 by general Strode.

COVENT-GARDEN was so called from having been the garden of St. Peter's convent. It occupies about three acres. The west side of the square is ornamented with the church of St. Paul, and the north with a noble piazza, designed by Inigo Jones, and intended to have been continued on every side. The middle is occupied by the market, rebuilt in 1829-30 from designs by Mr. Fowler. See *Markets*.

EATON-SQUARE, situated to the south-east of Belgrave-square, is a parallelogram 1637 feet by 371. At the north end is St. Peter's Church, designed by Mr. Hakewill.

EUSTON-SQUARE is situated to the north of Tavistock-square, and is bisected by the New-road: it is 143 yards by 248. The north side is a uniform range of building erected about 1812. The south side was built in 1828. On the east side is St. Pancras New Church.

FINSBURY-SQUARE, at the north-east part of the metropolis, is a handsome quadrangular range of building, 495 yards in circumference, surrounding a spacious garden. The houses are lofty and elegant, and are all modern—the west side of the square having been erected in 1777, the north in 1789, the east in 1790, and the south in 1791. In the south-west corner of the square is the house formerly occupied by the eccentric Mr. J. Lackington, and by him denominated the Temple of the Muses.

FITZROY-SQUARE is near the Regent's-park. The houses on the south and east sides are faced with stone, and have a greater proportion of architectural excellence and embellishment than most others in the metropolis. They were designed by the Adams. The north side of the square, which is faced with stucco, was not erected till 1825—the late war having prevented the completion of the original plan: it is 94 yards by 83.

GOLDEN-SQUARE, formerly called Golding-square, from the name of its builder, is near the east end of Piccadilly, but it has no claim to beauty: it is 72 yards square. It was built soon after the revolution of 1688, in what were then called the *Pest-house-fields*. In those fields lord Craven built a lazaretto, which, during the dreadful plague of 1665, was used as a pest-house, and hence arose the name.

GROSVENOR-SQUARE owes its origin to sir R. Grosvenor, bart. It is situated on the south side of Oxford-street, and contains six acres of ground, measuring 165 yards by 215. The houses are magnificent, and the shrubs and walks well arranged. In the centre is a gilt equestrian statue of George I., executed by Van Nost, and erected in 1726 by direction of sir R. Grosvenor.

HANOVER-SQUARE, like the preceding, is a fashionable place, built soon after the accession of the house of Hanover. Both here and in George-street adjoining there are several specimens of the German style of building. The square is 116 yards by 88, and the middle is enclosed with an iron railing. On the east side of the square is a colossal bronze statue of Pitt, by Chantrey, 12 feet in height, placed on a granite pedestal 15 feet high.

ST. JAMES'S-SQUARE is one of uncommon celebrity, chiefly on account of the distinguished characters who have resided in it. It is very large, 138 yards square; and in the centre is an extensive circular sheet of water, from the middle of which rises a pedestal surmounted by a statue of William III. The space within the railing is occupied by walks, ornamented with shrubs, plants, &c. Several houses in this square are remarkable: Norfolk-house as the birth-place of George III.; No. 11, as the residence of lord Ellenborough, who died here in 1818; and No. 14 as the house in which sir P. Francis, the celebrated opponent of Warren Hastings, died in 1819. On the east side of the square is the bishop of London's house—a handsome brick building.

LEICESTER-SQUARE, which is still frequently called "Leicester-fields," contained but few buildings previous to 1658; but Leicester-place, the site of the late house of that name, is found in Faithorne's plan. This house was founded by one of the Sydneys, earl of Leicester, after the removal of that family from Sydney-house in the Old-Bailey. It was for a short time the residence of Elizabeth daughter of James I., the titular queen of Bohemia, who ended her unfortunate life here February 13, 1661. It was afterwards tenanted by prince Eugene. It was, says Pennant, successively the pouting-place of princes; George II., when prince of Wales, lived here for several years after his quarrel with his father. His son Frederick followed his example, succeeded him in this house, and here died. It was at one time used by sir Ashton Lever as a museum of natural history. Savile-house, on the north side, derived its name from the patriotic sir G. Savile, many years member of parliament for the county of York. The Sabloniere Hotel was formerly the residence of

Hogarth, and in the next house to the north lived Mr. John Hunter the eminent surgeon. Sir Joshua Reynolds the painter resided at No. 47; Woollet the engraver was likewise an inhabitant of this square. In the centre is a fine gilt bronze equestrian statue of George I., which originally stood in the park at Canons in Hertfordshire. This square is 396 yards in circumference.

LINCOLN'S-INN-FIELDS is the most extensive square in the metropolis, being 187 yards by 237, or 848 yards in circumference; but owing to a want of uniformity in the buildings, it has not a handsome architectural appearance. Within a few years, however, it has been greatly improved by the decorations of sir J. Soane's house, and the erection of the Royal College of Surgeons. The gardens, which were laid out by Inigo Jones about 1620, occupy the same space as the largest pyramid of Egypt. This distinguished artist likewise formed a plan for the buildings; but the two centre houses (formerly one) on the west side are the only specimens erected. The large house, now likewise divided into two, at the corner of Great Queen-street, was erected by the marquess Powis in 1686, and has been successively inhabited by sir Nathan Wright, lord chancellor Somers, and the duke of Newcastle, from whom it took its present name. This square has likewise been the residence of earl Camden, lord chancellor Loughborough, sir Fletcher Norton speaker of the house of commons, and lord Kenyon the chief justice of the queen's bench. In the centre of this square the virtuous lord Russell was beheaded in 1683.

MANCHESTER-SQUARE (83 yards by 94) was intended to have been called Queen Anne's-square, and to have had a handsome parochial church in the centre of it. This design, however, not having been carried into execution, and the north side lying waste, the late duke of Manchester purchased the site, and erected on it his town residence. Upon the sudden death of the duke, and the minority of his heir, the premises were purchased by the king of Spain as the residence of his ambassador. It afterwards became the property of the marquess of Hertford.

PORTMAN-SQUARE, which is esteemed next to Grosvenor-square, consists of large and elegant mansions. It was begun in 1764, and was not completed for 20 years. It is 606 yards in circumference. The garden of the area is a mere wilderness of foliage, and has a very pleasing effect, not a little improved by the moveable temple erected in it. The north-west angle is closed by the late Mrs. Montague's residence, situated in a little park and lawn, shaded with numerous trees. It was the custom of this amiable lady annually to invite all the little chimney-sweepers, who were regaled in her house and gardens with good and wholesome fare, "so that they might enjoy *one* happy day in the year." These festivities are now discontinued at Montague-house, but the 1st of May is still a day of celebrity with the sooty gentry.

PRINCES-SQUARE is situated a short distance east of Well-close-square. The Swedes' church, which forms its principal ornament, contains the remains of the celebrated Emanuel Swedenborg, who died in 1772. In the vestry-room, amongst several portraits of eminent persons, is one of Dr. Serenius, bishop of Stregnas, the first minister of the Swedish church, and the compiler of an English and Swedish dictionary.

QUEEN-SQUARE is a neat and rural parallelogram, so named in honour of queen Anne, whose statue is placed here in the centre of the gardens. The houses on three of the sides were erected between 1709 and 1720; the fourth is open to Guildford-street. In the south-west corner is the church of St. George the Martyr.

RUSSELL-SQUARE is a well-arranged plot of ground, 803 yards in circumference, surrounded by capital houses. On the south side, facing Bloomsbury-square, is a colossal bronze statue of the late duke of Bedford, by Westmacott. The attitude is graceful and manly; the duke is resting one arm on a plough, whilst the hand of the other is grasping the gift of Ceres. The four seasons are personified by children playing at the feet of the statue, and the pedestal is adorned with rural subjects in basso-relievo. The whole is about 27 feet high, and bears the following inscription:—"Francis duke of Bedford. Erected MDCCCIX." No. 21 in the square is the house in which sir Samuel Romilly terminated his existence, and No. 65 was the residence of sir Thos. Lawrence.

SOHO-SQUARE, 105 yards square, is said to have derived its name from Soho being the word of the day at the battle of Sedgmoor. The duke of Monmouth resided here in a house the site of which is now occupied by Bateman's-buildings. In the centre is a large area within a railing, enclosing trees and shrubs, and a pedestrian statue of Charles II., at whose feet are emblematical figures of the rivers Thames, Trent, Severn, and Humber. No. 32, in the south-west corner of this square, was the residence of sir J. Banks, who left it to the Linnæan Society. At the north-west corner stands the *Bazaar.*

TAVISTOCK-SQUARE is situated a short distance north of Russell-square. It consists of handsome and spacious houses, all of which have been erected within a few years. It is 149 yards by 77.

This square is remarkable for an echo. A person standing against the houses on the north side, when the bell of St. Pancras church is tolling, will hear the sounds reverberated from the houses on the south side in tones more loud and distinct than those immediately from the bell.

TRAFALGAR-SQUARE.—This noble area, 132 yards by 77, which formed the grounds of the Old King's-mews, and was encumbered by the densely-peopled streets and alleys of its purlieus, was cleared during the progress of the improvements which distinguished the reign of George IV. On the northern side is the long elevation of the National Gallery, to the westward the lateral façades of the College of Physicians and the Union Club, and to the east a range of handsome houses of counterbalancing proportions; between these and the Royal Academy of Arts rises the bold form of St. Martin's church. The central space is yet to receive a fitting monument; and in all probability the name of Trafalgar will be united with that of its hero, Nelson, a committee being about to erect what we trust will be a worthy testimonial to that distinguished man.

Constituting the southern part of Trafalgar-square is Charing-cross, one side of which is formed by the curious screen of Northumberland-house.

CHARING-CROSS is so called from one of the crosses which Edward I. erected to the memory of his queen Eleanor, and Charing, the name of the village in which it was built. Some persons, however, deny the existence of any village on this spot, and contend that it derived its name from being the resting-place of the *chère reyne* (dear queen). The cross remained till the civil wars in the reign of Charles I., when it was destroyed on the foolish pretence of being a monument of popish superstition, and replaced by a brass equestrian statue of that monarch, which was cast by Le Sueur in 1633, at the expense of the Howard-Arundel family. This was the first equestrian statue erected in Great Britain. During the civil war, the parliament sold it to John River, a brazier in Holborn, with strict orders to break it to pieces; but he concealed it under ground till the restoration, when it was re-erected in

1678, on a pedestal executed by Grinlin Gibbons, and ornamented with the royal arms, trophies, &c.

On this spot Hugh Peters, "the mad chaplain," was executed in 1660.

Adjoining Charing-cross is a triangular space called PALL MALL EAST, worthy of notice for the beautiful bronze equestrian statue of George III. by Mr. M. C. Wyatt, erected August 1836. Departing from the classical mania which has hitherto *Romanised* the illustrious men of Europe, the sculptor has dared to present to a British public a British monarch in the costume of his age, and borne by a horse of flesh and blood, instead of modelling a Cæsar on a conventional-formed steed. This spirited production is 12 feet in height, but suffers considerably from the paltry proportions of the pedestal, the railing, and the lamps.

TRINITY-SQUARE, Newington-Butts, is situated on the south side of Suffolk-street East. It was built in 1828, and consists of small but neat houses. In the centre is Trinity Church, before which is placed a statue of king Alfred.

WELLCLOSE-SQUARE, which is situated at the east end of the metropolis, is small but neat. The Danish church in the centre was erected, according to an inscription on it, in 1696, at the expense of Christian V., king of Denmark. Caius Gabriel Cibber, the architect of this church, and his wife Jane, the mother of Colley Cibber, are both buried here. The monument of the latter was erected by her husband.

The principal of those which our limits forbid our describing are Addington-square, Blandford-square, Brunswick-square, Bryanstone-square (248 yards by 50), Burton-crescent (with a bronze sitting statue of that venerable reformer major Cartwright), Cadogan-square, Carlton-square, Charterhouse-square, Clarendon-square, Connaught-square, Devonshire-square, Dorset-square, Falcon-square, Gordon-square (154 yards by 110), Haydon-square, Mecklenburgh-square, Montague-square (248 yards by 50), Moorfields, Myddleton-square, Nelson-square, New-square Westminster, Northampton-square (325 yards in circumference), Panton-square, Park-square, Patriot-square, Queen-square Westminster, Ratcliff-square, Red Lion-square, St. John's-square Clerkenwell, St. Thomas's-square Hackney, Salisbury-square, Shepherd's-square, Sloane-square, Southwark-square, Spital-square, Stanhope-square, Suffolk-square Southwark, Surrey-square, Theberton-square, Torrington-square (302 yards by 50), Trafalgar-square, Trinity-square Tower-hill, Vauxhall-

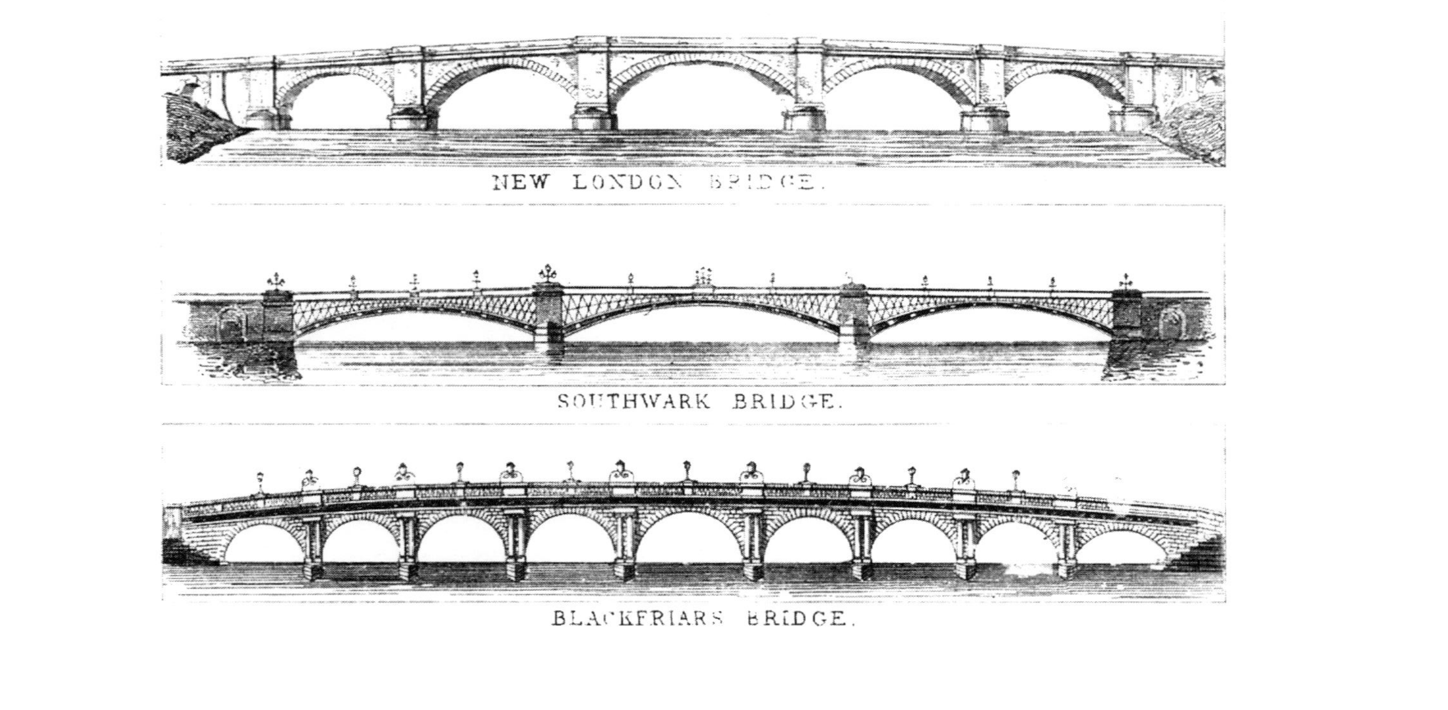

NEW LONDON BRIDGE.

SOUTHWARK BRIDGE.

BLACKFRIARS BRIDGE.

square, Warwick-square, West-square, Wilmington-square, Woburn-square, York-square Regent's-park, &c. &c.

Independent of the squares, there are numerous open spots called by the various names of places, circuses, crescents, polygons, &c., which add to the beauty and salubrity of the metropolis.

BRIDGES.

OLD LONDON-BRIDGE,

Which was demolished to make way for the new structure, was first commenced in 1176, but not finished till 1209. It was then covered with houses connected together by large arches of timber, which crossed the street and gave it a very cumbersome appearance. In 1212 it was the scene of a dreadful accident: a fire having broken out at the Southwark end, an immense multitude came from London to extinguish it, and while engaged in this benevolent purpose the devouring element communicated with the opposite extremity of the bridge, and upwards of 3000 persons perished in the flames or were drowned by overloading the vessels brought for their relief. In 1756 all the houses were pulled down, and the bridge underwent a thorough repair. Amongst the eminent men who resided in the houses which formerly existed on this bridge were Hans Holbein and John Bunyan. The space between the piers of this bridge having been contracted by the size of the starlings, occasioned a fall of water of four or five feet at every flux and reflux of the tides, rendering it unsafe to pass through except at high-water. It consisted of 19 stone-arches, of irregular construction and of various sizes.

NEW LONDON-BRIDGE.

Old London-bridge having been for some years considered destitute of the proper facilities for the transition of passengers and dangerous for vessels, an act of parliament was passed in 1823 for building a new one on a scale and plan commensurate with the other improvements of the metropolis. The first pile of the works was driven 200 feet to the west of the old bridge March 15th, 1824, and the first stone was laid by the lord-mayor (Garratt) on the 15th June, 1825, in the presence of the late duke of York and a numerous company of nobility and gentry. The late Mr. Rennie gave the design for this new bridge, and it devolved on his sons to complete it; a task which was accomplished August 1st, 1831, when the structure was opened by his majesty William IV., and a splendid banquet was given on the occasion. The bridge, which is executed in Scottish, Peterhead, and Derbyshire granite, consists of five elliptical arches, the central one being considered amongst the finest ever constructed. The piers have massive plinths and Gothic pointed cutwaters. The arches are surmounted with a bold projecting block-cornice, which corresponds with the line of road-way, covered with a plain blocking course by way of parapet, which gives the whole a simple grand character.

On either side of each extremity are two straight flights of stairs leading to the water. The pedestals at the top of each flight are formed of single blocks of granite of immense size, each weighing 25 tons. The lamps over each arch were cast by Mr. Parker, from cannon captured on the continent by the British troops.

The foundations of the piers are formed of piles chiefly of beech, pointed with iron, driven from the interior of the coffer dams to a depth of nearly 20 feet into the stiff blue clay forming the bed of the river. On the surface of these piles are laid two rows of horizontal sleepers, about 12 inches square, which are covered with beech-planking six inches thick, on which is erected the lowest course of masonry.

The road to the bridge on the city side commences at the corner of Gracechurch-street and East-cheap. It is supported by eleven brick arches and one stone arch, of beautiful proportions, which crosses Thames-street. On each side of this arch are rustic gate-ways leading to a succession of steps by which foot-passengers may proceed directly from Thames-street to the bridge.

On this side a fine view of the monument may be obtained, also of the new Fishmongers'-hall and the church of St. Michael.

The following are the dimensions of the bridge:—

	Feet.
Length, including the abutments	928
Width of the waterway	692
Width from outside to outside of parapets	56
Height above low-water-mark	55
Width of the stairs	20
Span of the central arch	152
Rise of the central arch	29½
Span of the arches on each side of ditto	140
Rise of ditto	27½
Width of piers on either side of ditto	22
Span of the extreme or land-arches	130
Rise of ditto	24½
Width of abutments at the base	73
Width of the carriage-way	33½

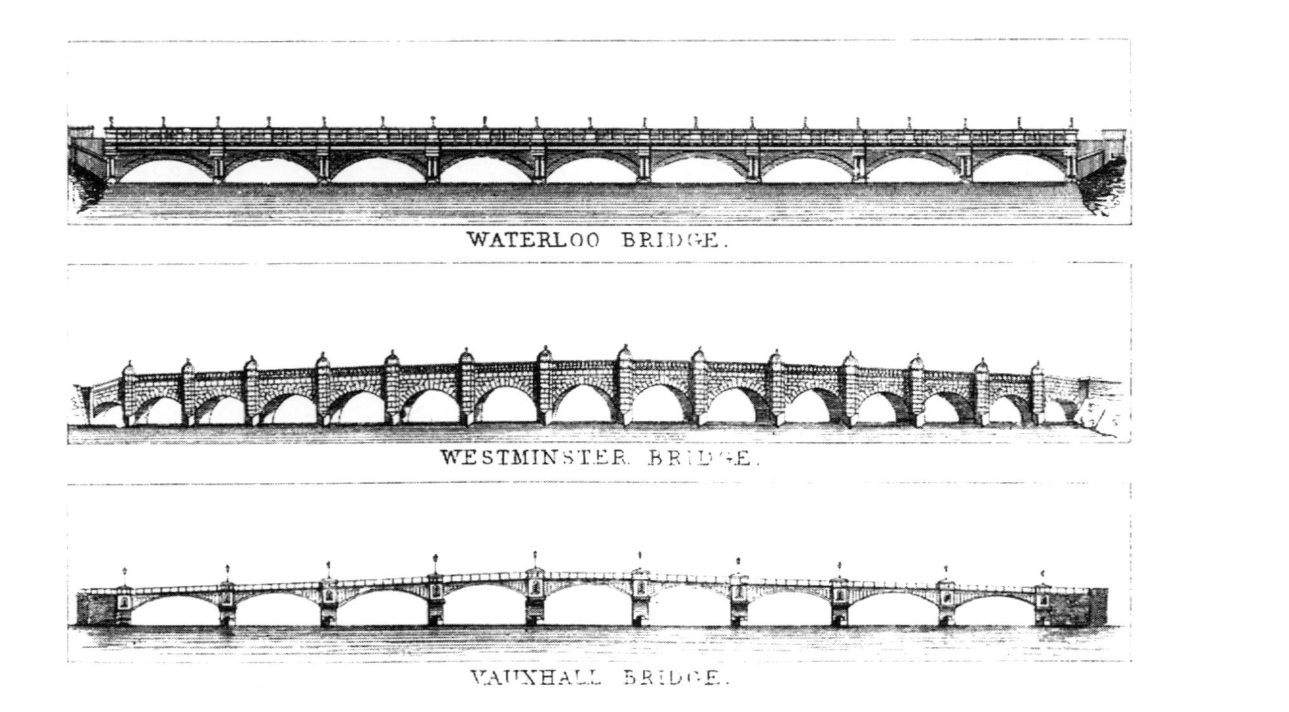

WATERLOO BRIDGE.

WESTMINSTER BRIDGE.

VAUXHALL BRIDGE.

Blackfriars-Bridge

Is an elegant structure, built after a design of Mr. R. Mylne, betwen 1760 and 1768, at an expense of 152,840*l.*, which was defrayed by a toll on the passengers. On a tin-plate placed over the first stone is a Latin inscription, indicating the year in which the erection was commenced, as well as the sovereign and lord-mayor at that period. It also states that the citizens of London had unanimously voted that this bridge should bear the name of William Pitt, earl of Chatham, in honour of that illustrious statesman. The situation of the ground on the two shores obliged the architect to employ elliptical arches, and they have a very fine effect. There are nine arches, the centre one being 100 feet wide. The whole length is 995 feet. The breadth of the carriage-way is 28 feet, and that of the footways 7 feet each. Over each pier is a recess, supported by beautiful Ionic pillars, and at each extremity are stairs leading to the water. This bridge is situated at about an equal distance from those of Southwark and Waterloo. It commands a very fine view of St. Paul's cathedral, as well as of both sides of the river, including the Tower, the Monument, Somerset-house, Westminster-abbey, and about thirty churches. A thorough renovation of the whole fabric was commenced 1837. The old balustrades have been removed, and the steepness of the ascent much diminished.

Westminster-Bridge

Is built entirely of Portland stone, and crosses the river where the breadth is 1223 feet. On each side is a stone balustrade, 6 feet 9 inches in height, with places of shelter from the rain. The width of the bridge is 44 feet, having on each side a footway for passengers 7 feet broad. It consists of 14 piers, and 13 large and 2 small arches, all semicircular, that in the centre being 76 feet wide, and the rest decreasing 4 feet each from the other, so that the last two arches of the thirteen great ones are each 52 feet. The width of the two small arches at the abutments is about 20 feet. It is computed that about 40,000*l.* value in stone and other materials is under water. The proportions of this bridge are so accurate that if a person speak against the wall of any of the recesses on one side the way, he may be distinctly heard on the opposite side; even a whisper is perceptible during the stillness of the night.

This magnificent structure was begun in 1739, and was finished in 1750, at the expense of 389,000*l.* defrayed by parliament. It was built after a design of Monsieur Labelye, a French architect.

The road over Westminster-bridge was macadamized in 1824, in order to give this new method of road-making a fair trial, and in 1837 it underwent considerable repairs.

STRAND, OR WATERLOO-BRIDGE.

The erection of a bridge over this part of the Thames was repeatedly suggested during the last century, but no actual preparations to carry it into effect were made till 1806, when Mr. G. Dodd procured an act of parliament, succeeded in removing objections to former schemes, and gave the present site, plan, and dimensions of the bridge; but in consequence of some disagreement with the committee, he was superseded by Mr. Rennie, who had the honour of completing this noble ornament of the British metropolis. The bridge was commenced in 1811, and finished June 18, 1817, on the anniversary of the battle of Waterloo, when the prince-regent, duke of Wellington, and other distinguished personages, were present. Under the first stone was placed a bottle containing coins of the reign of George III., and over it the following inscription:—

"This foundation-stone of the Strand-bridge was laid on the 11th day of October, A.D. 1811, by the directors for executing the same, Henry Swan, Esq. M.P., chairman, in the fifty-first year of the reign of King George the Third, and during the regency of his R. H. George, prince of Wales; the money for building which was raised by subscription, under the authority of an act of parliament.

"Engineer, JOHN RENNIE, F.R.S."

The style of the architecture is plain but noble, and the materials are of the most durable kind, the outside courses being of Cornish, and the balustrades of Aberdeen granite. All the arches are elliptical and of an equal size, and consequently the road over them is level, in which respect this bridge differs from all others in London. Each pier rests on 320 piles driven into the bed of the river, there being one pile to every yard square; the length of the pile is about 20 feet, and the diameter about 13 inches. At each extremity of the bridge are very handsome stairs to the water.

The following are the dimensions of this noble bridge:—

	Feet.
The length of the stone-work within the abutments	1242
Length of the road supported on brick arches on the Surrey side	1250
Length of the road supported on brick arches on the London side	400
Total length from the Strand, where the building begins, to the spot in Lambeth where it falls to the level of the road	2890
Width of the bridge within the balustrades	42
Width of pavement or footway on each side	7
Width of road for horses and carriages	28
Span of each arch	120
From the springing-line to the crown of the arch	35
From crown of ditto to top of balustrade	14½
From springing-lines to top of piles	11½
Thickness of each pier	20
Clear water-way under the nine arches, which are equal . . .	1080
Number of brick arches on the Surrey side	40

The four toll-lodges are neat appropriate Doric structures, at each of which is a clever contrivance for the purpose of checking. The iron turnstiles, which admit of only one person passing at a time, touch some machinery communicating with a clock locked up in an oak box in each toll-house, the index of which is thereby moved, so that on looking at it the number of those who have passed is directly seen.

The bridge is exactly on a level with the Strand, and fifty feet above the surface of the Thames. During the summer months it is much frequented as a promenade; but there is not at present sufficient traffic to afford the prospect of much profit to the proprietors.

Tolls paid for crossing this bridge.

			s.	d.
Foot-passenger			0	1
Coach, landau, chariot, &c. with four wheels and 6 horses . .			1	6
Ditto,	ditto,	and 4 horses . .	1	0
Ditto,	ditto,	and 2 or 3 horses	0	6
Ditto,	ditto,	and 1 horse . .	0	4
Stage or hackney-coach, ditto, and 2 horses			0	4
Cabriolet, with one horse			0	2
Chaise, chair, tax-cart, &c. with 2 horses			0	6
Ditto,	with 1 horse		0	3
Single horse			0	2
Wagon, cart, or dray, each horse			0	2
Wheelbarrow, truck, &c. not drawn by any beast			0	1½
Oxen per score			0	8
Calves, hogs, sheep, &c. per score			0	4

VAUXHALL-BRIDGE.

This building was originally projected by Mr. R. Dodd, but in consequence of some disagreement he was succeeded, first by Mr. Rennie, and afterwards by Mr. Walker, under whose direction the present elegant fabric was constructed, at an expense of about 150,000*l.*, which is to be defrayed by a toll.

The first stone was laid in 1813 by prince Charles, the eldest son of the late duke of Brunswick, and the bridge was completed in 1816. It consists of nine cast-iron arches, with piers formed by a wooden frame as a foundation, faced with Kentish ragstone and Roman cement. The arches are 78 feet in span and 29 in height, and the length of the bridge is 860 feet. It contributes greatly to the beauty of the metropolis, and affords the inhabitants of Vauxhall, Lambeth, &c. an easy communication with the houses of parliament and courts of law, Pimlico, Chelsea, and their populous neighbourhoods.

Tolls paid for crossing this bridge.

			s.	*d.*
Foot-passenger			0	1
Coach, landau, chariot, &c. with four wheels and 6 horses			2	6
Ditto,	ditto,	4 horses	1	6
Ditto,	ditto,	2 or 3 horses	0	9
Chaise with one horse			0	4
Wagon, cart, or dray, with 6 horses			1	6
Ditto,	ditto,	4 or 5 horses	1	0
Ditto,	ditto,	2 or 3 horses	0	8
Ditto,	ditto,	1 horse	0	4
Single horse or mule			0	2
Oxen, per score			1	0
Calves, sheep, pigs, &c. per score			0	6

SOUTHWARK-BRIDGE

Was originally projected by Mr. John Wyatt, with the view of forming a communication between Bankside, Southwark, and Queen-street, Cheapside. It was begun on the 23d September, 1814, under the direction of Mr. Rennie as engineer, and Mr. Weston as sub-engineer, and completed March 1819, at an expense of 800,000*l.*, including the avenues. Messrs. Joliffe and Banks were the contractors, and the iron-work was furnished from the foundry of Messrs. Walker and Co. of Rotherham.

This stupendous bridge consists of three cast-iron arches, resting on massive stone piers and abutments. The distance between the abutments is 708 feet. The extent of each abutment enclosed, including the land and invert arches, is 71 feet, formed of solid masonry. There are two piers 60 feet high from the bed of the river to the top of the parapet, 24 feet in breadth between high and low water-marks, and 75 feet long, between acme and acme of the salient angles. The foundations of these piers are each about 12 feet below the bed or bottom of the river, and rest on a platform of timber 2½ feet thick; these platforms repose on about 420 piles, most of which are driven 24 feet into the earth, making the depth from the shoe of the piles to the parapet of the piers 98 feet. The two side-arches are 210 feet each in span, and the centre arch 240, with 43 feet clear opening above low-water mark, medium tides. Thus the centre-arch is the largest in the world, as it exceeds the admired bridge of Sunderland by four feet in the span, and the long-famed Rialto at Venice by 167 feet. Many of the iron single or solid castings weigh 10 tons each; and the total weight of iron exceeds 5,308 tons. This bridge was constructed with so much accuracy, that when the centerings of the middle arch were removed, it only sunk at the vertex one inch 7-8ths. The turnstiles are on a similar construction to those of Waterloo-bridge.

Tolls paid for crossing this bridge.

		s.	d.
Foot-passenger		0	1
Coach, landau, &c. with 4 wheels and 6 horses		0	9
Ditto, ditto, 3 and 4 horses		0	6
Ditto, ditto, and 2 horses		0	2
Chaise, &c. with 1 horse		0	2
Wagon, dray, &c. with 4 wheels and 6 horses		0	7
Ditto, ditto, and 4 or 5 horses	5*d*. and	0	6
Ditto, ditto, and 2 or 3 horses	3*d*. and	0	4
Ditto, ditto, and 1 horse		0	2
Cart or two-wheeled vehicle, and 1 horse		0	1½
Single horse or mule		0	1
Oxen per score		0	8
Calves, pigs, sheep, &c. per score		0	4

Some idea of the traffic that takes place across the bridges may be formed from the following statements:—according to an account taken July 1811, it appears that there passed over Blackfriars-bridge, in one day, 61,069 foot-passengers, 533 wagons, 1502 carts and drays, 990 coaches, 500 gigs and taxed carts, and 822 horses. On the same day, July 1811, there passed over London-bridge 89,640 foot-passengers, 1240 coaches, 485 gigs and taxed carts, 769 wagons, 2924 carts and drays, and 764 horses. On October 16th, 1821, there passed over London-bridge 58,180 foot-passengers, 871 coaches, 520 gigs and taxed carts, 587 wagons, 2576 carts and drays, and 472 horses.

According to calculations made daily by Mr. Dodd, during six weeks in summer and six in winter, with a view to ascertain what might be the profits of Waterloo-bridge, the average number of foot-passengers who traversed Blackfriars-bridge during the day of twenty-four hours he estimated to be 48,000, and Westminster-bridge 32,000; but during these calculations, on one fine Sunday in August 1808, 74,427 crossed Blackfriars-bridge.

It has been stated in less accurate calculations, that upwards of 125,000 persons daily cross London-bridge.

THE THAMES TUNNEL.

This novel and stupendous undertaking was projected by Mr. Brunel, under whose direction we trust, notwithstanding the many impediments that have occurred, it will ultimately be executed. It is intended to form a communication between Rotherhithe and Wapping by means of a passage under the Thames, and will certainly, when completed, be one of the most extraordinary constructions of ancient or modern times.

The tunnel consists of two brick archways; and in order that there may be no obstruction to carriages, those going from north to south will pass through one, and those from south to north through the other. These passages are paved or macadamized, and there are distinct paths for foot-passengers. In the centre, and between the two archways, and dividing the two roads, is a line of arches spacious enough to admit of persons passing from one road to the other, and in each of these arches is fixed a gas-light. The approaches to the entrances of the tunnel are formed by circular descents of easy declivity, not exceeding four feet per hundred feet; one of small dimensions for pedestrians, and another of larger for carriages: the descent is so gradual that there is no necessity to lock the wheel of the heaviest-laden wagon. The first stone of the descent for pedestrians on the south side of the river, near Rotherhithe church, was laid by W. Smith, esq., the chairman of the company, March 2, 1825. That portion of the tunnel which is completed is open daily to visiters on payment of 1*s*. each.

Dimensions of the Tunnel.—Length 1,300 feet; width 35 feet; height 20 feet; clear width of each archway, including footpath, about 14 feet; thickness of earth beneath the crown of the tunnel and the bed of the river, about 15 feet.

In the neighbourhood is a curious specimen of Mr. Brunel's ingenuity, being the segment of an arch of 100 feet span built without centering.

CHAPTER VII.

PUBLIC CHARITIES, STATE OF EDUCATION, ENDOWED SCHOOLS, HOSPITALS, DISPENSARIES, ETC.

LONDON contains upwards of 45 free-schools with perpetual endowments for educating and maintaining above 4,000 children; 17 other schools for poor and deserted children; more than 250 parish-schools supported by voluntary contributions, &c., in which about 12,000 or 15,000 boys and girls are constantly clothed and educated; 3 colleges; 22 hospitals for sick, lame, and pregnant women; 107 alms-houses for the maintenance of aged persons of both sexes; upwards of 18 institutions for the support of the indigent of various descriptions; and about 30 dispensaries for the gratuitous supply of medicine and medical aid to the poor.

Besides these various establishments, each parish has a workhouse for the occupation and maintenance of its own distressed or helpless poor; and the several livery companies of the city of London distribute about 75,000*l.* annually in charities. The sums annually expended in public charities have been estimated at 850,000*l.* The hospitals were chiefly founded by private munificence; some of them are endowed with perpetual revenues, and others supported by annual or occasional voluntary subscriptions. The alms-houses were built and endowed either by private persons or corporate bodies of tradesmen; and many of the free-schools owe their origin to the same sources.

The medical assistance in the hospitals is the best which the profession can supply; the attendance is ample, the rooms are generally very clean and wholesome, and the food is suitable to the condition of the patients. The alms-houses and other institutions for the support of the aged and indigent exhibit not merely an appearance, but the real possession of competence and ease. From some of the free-schools pupils have been sent to the universities, as well prepared as those from any of the most expensive seminaries; and all the scholars receive an education adapted to the stations for which they are designed. We shall first notice those charities which more strictly come within the meaning of public endowments: but although they are now chiefly known as public schools, the charters and endowments of most of them contain provisions for the aged and infirm.

CHRIST'S HOSPITAL,

Newgate-street.

This noble establishment is generally known by the name of the *Blue-coat-school*, the title having reference to the costume of the children supported and educated there. The institution is indebted for its establishment to the piety of Edward VI. Dr. Ridley, bishop of London, had the singular and enviable felicity of suggesting before the king, in a sermon preached at Westminster, the imperious demands of poverty upon the attention and commiseration of the powerful and rich. A general report was made to the king on the state and condition of the poor, and the best means of relief and reform; they were divided into three classes—the poor by impotency, by casualty, and by idleness. For the innocent and fatherless was provided *Christ's Hospital*, late the Grey Friars; for the wounded and diseased, the hospitals of St. Thomas and St. Bartholomew; and for the idle and vagabond, Bridewell, where they might be chastised and compelled to labour. Decayed householders, and the poor afflicted with incurable diseases, were to be relieved at their own homes.

The establishment, as first founded, consisted only of a grammar-school for boys, and a separate school for girls, where they were taught to read, sew, and mark. In addition to these Charles II. founded a mathematical school and ward, on the west part of the hospital, for the instruction of 40 boys in the mathematics and navigation, and liberally endowed it with 1,000*l.* paid out of the exchequer for seven years. Another mathematical school, now joined to the preceding, was afterwards founded by Mr. Travers for 37 boys. The lord-mayor and corporation of London are directors and promoters of the institution, and the whole community of Great Britain have the opportunity of carrying on this glorious work. A donation of 400*l.* constitutes a governor. The annual expenditure for the support of the institution is about 30,000*l.*

There are generally in this establishment from 1,000 to 1,200 boys and girls receiving their education, besides being clothed and boarded. The following is a recent annual return:—

Children placed out as apprentices	181
Buried	11
Children under care of the hospital	1,058
To be admitted on presentation	140

The buildings of Christ's Hospital are extensive but irregular; and having been for some time in a state of decay, the governors determined on rebuilding the whole from designs by Mr. Shaw. In 1822 a new infirmary was completed; and on April 28, 1825, the late duke of York laid the first stone of the New Hall, which was opened in 1829. This noble structure is in the Tudor style of architecture. It is 187 feet in length, and 51½ in width, and 46½ high. The south front, in the centre of which is a statue of Edward VI., is of stone, and is flanked by towers, which rise above the other parts. Between these are eight lofty windows separated by buttresses. The interior is adorned with the arms of the governors, and with several portraits, amongst which are Charles II. by sir Peter Lely, and queen Anne. Over one of the galleries is hung Holbein's picture of Edward VI. granting the charter to the hospital. Another picture represents Charles II. and his courtiers giving audience to the governors of the institution, and contains portraits of judge Jefferies, and the painter Verrio himself. At each end of the hall is a gallery, and over one of them an organ.

The *Court-room* is likewise ornamented with numerous fine portraits, particularly one of Edward VI. by Holbein. On the front of the writing-school is a marble statue of sir John Moore, its founder, and over the south entrance to Christ's Hospital is a statue of Edward VI.

An interesting sight is exhibited in the hall every Sunday evening during Lent, at which period the children sup together at seven o'clock. Strangers are admitted by tickets, easily obtained from any person connected with the establishment. In this hall, likewise, the lord-mayor, aldermen, &c. attend on St. Matthew's day, to hear orations from the senior boys. Visiters can only be admitted on this occasion by tickets.

Among the eminent persons buried in the cloisters of Christ's Hospital may be mentioned John of Bourbon, one of the prisoners taken at the battle of Agincourt: Thomas Burdett, the ancestor of sir Francis, who was put to death in the reign of Edward IV. for wishing the horns of a favourite white stag, which the king had killed, in the body of the person who advised him to do it; and Isabella the wife of Edward II.

Charter-House,

Charter-house-square,

Was built upon the site of a monastery founded by sir W. Manny in the reign of Edward III., in a churchyard enclosed by the bishop of London, to which was added a tract of land by the founder, in which upwards of 100,000 bodies were deposited. The name of this establishment is derived by an easy and evident corruption from *Chartreuse*, the place in which it is situated having been a convent of Carthusian monks, who were treated with great cruelty when their possessions were seized by Henry VIII. On May 9, 1611, Thomas Sutton, a man of immense wealth and unbounded liberality, purchased of the heirs of the duke of Norfolk the Charter-house, with its appurtenances, for 13,000*l.*; and on the 22d of June in the same year he obtained letters-patent, with a license in mortmain, to found an hospital and free-school there. This admirable charity was perfected under the directions of his will, making a total expense of 20,000*l.*; and the founder left estates for its endowment valued at 4,500*l.* per annum. The scholars have handsome lodgings, are instructed in classical and other learning, and supplied with all the necessaries of life; the students at the universities have an allowance of 20*l.* per annum each, for the term of eight years. The boys who are incapable of being brought up scholars are put out as apprentices, and the sum of 40*l.* given with each. There are nine ecclesiastical preferments in the patronage of the governors.

The buildings forming the Charter-house have a very ancient appearance. The *Chapel* is a venerable edifice with Gothic windows, in two of which is painted glass representing the arms of Mr. Sutton. The organ-gallery is richly ornamented, and there are numerous monuments; but the principal curiosity is the tomb of the founder, who died in 1614. The *Library* was principally given by Mr. Wray, whose portrait hangs over the chimney-piece. The *Old Court-room* is richly decorated with carving and painting. In the *Governor's-room* is the original portrait of Mr. Sutton, as well as portraits of Charles II., archbishop Sheldon, bishop Bur-

ST PAUL'S SCHOOL.

BRITISH MUSEUM.

SURGEONS HALL.

net, and other eminent men. The *Hall* has a large painted window representing a ship and other emblems. Near the kitchen-garden is a curious pavement representing Mr. Sutton's arms and crest, executed with coloured pebbles by a pensioner.

WESTMINSTER-SCHOOL,

Dean's-yard, Westminster.

This school was founded by queen Elizabeth in 1560, for the education of 40 boys, denominated the Queen's Scholars, who are prepared for the university. It is situated within the walls of the abbey, and is separated into two schools or divisions, comprising seven forms or classes. Besides the scholars on the foundation, many of the nobility and gentry send their sons to Westminster for instruction, so that this establishment vies with Eton in celebrity and respectability. They have an upper and an under master, with numerous assistants. Of these masters many have been eminent in the walks of literature, particularly Dr. Busby, so celebrated for his severity of discipline, and the late Dr. Vincent. In December the friends of the Westminster scholars are invited to witness the representation of one of Terence's plays by the boys of the school.

ST. PAUL'S SCHOOL,

St. Paul's Churchyard,

Was founded in 1509 by Dr. Colet, dean of St. Paul's cathedral, the surviving son of sir Henry Colet, twice lord-mayor. It was instituted for the free education of 153 boys, by a master, an usher, and a chaplain, but now by two upper and two under masters, under the regulation of the Mercers' company, who were appointed trustees of the foundation. The school consists of eight classes or forms. In the first the children learn their rudiments; thence, according to their proficiency, they are advanced to the other forms, till they rise to the eighth, from which, being well instructed in Latin, Greek, and Hebrew, and sometimes in various oriental languages, they are removed to the universities, where many of them enjoy exhibitions, to assist in the expenses of their education. The building in St. Paul's-churchyard was pulled down in 1822, and re-erected in a handsome style during the two following years from designs by Mr. G. Smith.

MERCHANT-TAILORS' SCHOOL,

Suffolk-lane, Cannon-street,

Was founded by the company of Merchant-Tailors in 1561, under the mastership of Emanuel Lucas; Richard Hill, a former master, having previously given *500l.* towards the purchase of a house for that purpose; but that house having been destroyed by the great fire in 1666, the present buildings were erected upon the same spot at the charge of the company. This school is a spacious building, supported on the east by stone pillars forming a cloister, within which are apartments for the three ushers. Adjoining the school are the library and chapel, and contiguous to these is a house appropriated to the head master.

In this school about 300 boys are educated, of which number, by the statutes of the foundation, 100 are taught gratis, 50 at 2*s.* 6*d.* per quarter, and 100 at 5*s.* Certain annual examinations or probations are appointed, at which public exercises are performed by the scholars, of whom several are yearly sent to St. John's College, Oxford, which appears to have been principally founded for their use, as they have no fewer than 46 fellowships there.

CITY OF LONDON SCHOOL,

Milk-street,

Is a handsome building in the Elizabethan style, erected in 1835 from designs by Mr. Bunning. It was established in 1447 for the purpose of affording instruction to boys at a small expense. 500 are educated at about 8*l.* per annum each.

STATE OF EDUCATION.

There are various minor schools maintained by charity, the parish schools, the Lancasterian and national schools, the Sunday-schools, and upwards of 4000 private schools, in and about the metropolis.

The dissemination of the common rudiments of learning amongst all classes, even amongst the most humble, has within the last few years become the laudable and favourite object of all those who had power to estimate the value of education, or had a mite to spare to promote the cause of public charity and public improvement. JOSEPH LANCASTER and his friend Fox began that novel course of instruction which was soon conducted on a grand scale; and schools grew up in all parishes and districts from the labours of private individuals, who triumphed over enormous difficulties, and succeeded in increasing the desire for information amongst the poor and the ignorant. The bishops, the clergy, and the nobility, having witnessed the beneficial effects of the new plan, co-operated in the great design, and commenced the NATIONAL schools. The schools founded on the Lancasterian principles introduce the reading of the Bible without comment, and thus exclude no sect or persuasion. The National schools introduce the creed of the established church.

The number of these institutions, and the extent of their labours, astonish and gratify their most sanguine supporters.

There are more than forty large schools in London alone united to the National Society, each teaching from 200 to 1000 children. The Central School is in Baldwin's Gardens, Gray's-inn-lane, and any respectable person is allowed to visit it. According to the plan pursued in these schools, the expense of books for fifty boys is 1*l.* 3*s.* 11*d.*, amounting to less than sixpence for each child; but as, under good management, each of the tracts comprehended in this calculation will serve six children in succession, the real expense for books, for suitable instruction in reading and the first rudiments of religion, is not calculated at more than one penny for each child. The number of scholars in the National schools of the metropolis is about 20,000.

The LANCASTERIAN schools were not much patronised till about 1808, when Joseph Lancaster's system attracted general attention—a system by which, even if parents were obliged to pay for the school, a child might be completely taught at the expense of 4*s.* 6*d* per annum! But previous to this, our late venerable sovereign George III. had condescended to give Joseph Lancaster a personal interview, and was so much impressed with the value of the simple and economical plan of teaching, and the probable benefits which the country and the world might derive from it, that he became an annual subscriber of 100*l.*, and recommended the queen and other branches of the royal family also to become subscribers to a considerable amount. The prejudices against the founder (who first practised his system in 1798) had so far diminished the subscriptions in 1808, that they amounted to little more than those of the king and the royal family! Mr. Joseph Fox saw that unless a vigorous exertion were immediately made, the whole plan was in danger of being utterly lost. He advanced nearly 2000*l.*, and became responsible for all the debts; and thus saved the system from being abandoned. After that time Mr. Allen and other benevolent individuals co-operated with Mr. Fox, and aided by the powerful patronage already named, as well as that of the dukes of Kent, Sussex, and Bedford, succeeded in bringing the system into extensive, if not full operation. The society afterwards proceeded so successfully, that it has now between 200 and 300 schools for boys, and about 100 for girls. Forty-three of these schools are established in the metropolis, and the remainder in the country. Each school has from 150 to 500 children, who are educated on what is now termed the British system. The school-house for the Spitalfields district cost 1700*l.*, and between 2000 and 3000 children have already been educated in it. It is capable of containing 800 children. The school in the Borough-road contains 500 boys and 300 girls, and has since its establishment afforded education to upwards of 24,000 children. In this building, which was erected in 1817, are kept models of schools for the inspection of visiters. The annual income of the Lancasterian Society is about 1600*l.* The number of scholars in the metropolis is about 12,000.

In aid of all these exertions for the poor, there are the SUNDAY-SCHOOLS. To promote this mode of instructing children, there is a "Sunday-school Union;" an association of gratuitous teachers. According to returns made to this association, upwards of 66,000 children are instructed in the Sunday-schools formed in the metropolis alone. These schools instruct those poor children whose time is fully employed in labour during the week-days, and to them this is the only opportunity of gaining instruction. The children learn their lessons during the week, to repeat to their teachers on Sundays; and the teachers visit the children at their own habitations, and procure the co-operation of their parents, and watch over their conduct as much as possible. There are more than 5000 of these gratuitous teachers in the metropolis; and as they all perform their labour from a sense of duty, they do it much better, generally speaking, than paid teachers; but if they were paid only 2*s.* for each Sunday, which would be very humble pay, considerably above 20,000*l.* per annum would be required for salaries alone!

The British and Foreign School-Society have 86 schools in or near London, in which 14,000 children are educated.

The number of children educated in London by the National, Infant, and Lancasterian Schools, exceeds 200,000.

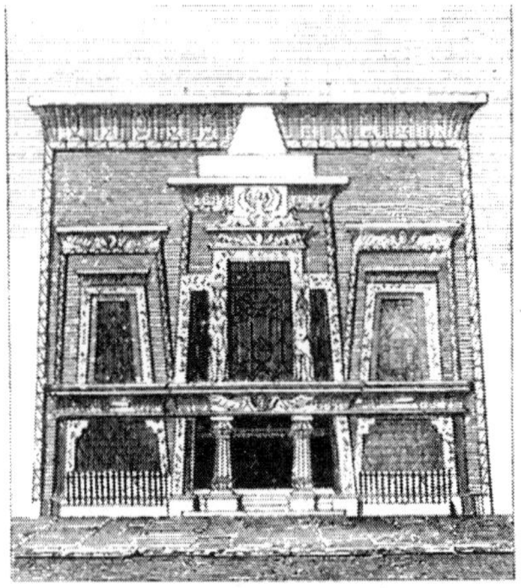

EGYPTIAN HALL.

BRITISH GALLERY.

MILITARY ASYLUM.

FOUNDLING HOSPITAL.

The beneficial effects of these several systems of instruction are demonstrated by the memorable fact, that scarcely one boy who has belonged to any of the institutions has been found in the pursuit of criminal courses. The Rev. Dr. Walmsley, the secretary of the National Society, stated on the authority of the late Recorder, that amongst 497 *juvenile culprits* committed to Newgate, only 14 ever belonged to the National Schools; and of those, six were taken out, after having been in the school only a week, in order to give evidence against a notorious receiver of stolen goods.

PUBLIC CHARITIES, HOSPITALS, &c.

Foundling-Hospital,

Guildford-street.

In queen Anne's reign the scheme of a foundling-hospital was projected; but for want of due exertions it was abandoned: several persons, however, justly expecting that so humane a project would be renewed, bequeathed legacies to promote its establishment. In 1713 the celebrated Addison again called the attention of the public to this subject, in No. 105 of the Guardian; but the desired success did not immediately follow. Some few years afterwards, Mr. Thomas Coram, master of a vessel trading to the American colonies—a man singularly endowed with active and disinterested benevolence—undertook to establish it: and after the labour of seventeen years, succeeded in obtaining the charter from George II., October 1739.

The hospital is built on a spot that was called Lamb's-conduit-fields, and was, in fact, surrounded with pleasant open country; but it is now bounded by Brunswick and Mecklenburg squares, and fronted by Guildford-street and Lamb's-conduit-street. The object of the institution is, to adopt the language of the charter, "the maintenance and education of exposed and deserted young children." The children are not indiscriminately received, in consequence of the mere fact of exposure or abandonment—the introductions are controlled by the committee of management. The age of reception is within twelve months from the birth: but the previous good character and necessity of the mother, and the desertion of the father, must be inquired into; and also whether the reception of the child, together with the secresy observed, will be the means of replacing the mother in a course of virtuous demeanour, and the way of obtaining an honest livelihood. Where these circumstances can be ascertained on the testimony of credible persons, the unfortunate mother is requested to apply personally with her own petition, and assured that patronage will be unnecessary.

There are on the average 120 boys and 130 girls in the hospital, independently of those out at nurse, the whole number being about 460. The receipts of the institution are about 13,250*l.*; resulting from dividends on funded property, *produce of the chapel*, rents, children's work, general benefactions, legacies, improvements of the hospital estates, &c.

The children are not only nursed and educated, but employed under proper regulations, and provided with all necessaries until their dismission from the hospital. On their discharge, the general committee, at their discretion, may give them clothes, money, or necessaries, not exceeding the value of 10*l.* The corporation of the hospital may employ the children in any sort of labour or manufacture, or in the sea-service, and bind them apprentices, or place them out as servants or mariners. The girls are distributed into three classes, under the care of three different mistresses, by whom they are taught needle-work and reading, to assist in the house-work, kitchen, and laundry. The boys are apprenticed at twelve or thirteen years of age, and the girls at fourteen; and they are disposed of with great attention on the part of the committee. The reports as to their subsequent conduct, which is particularly inquired into, have been very favourable.

The building consists of two brick wings, between which is the chapel, and in front are spacious grass-plots and gravel walks. The interior of the house is adorned with paintings, the principal of which are Hogarth's March to Finchley, his fine portrait of captain Coram, Moses discovered by Pharoah's daughter, a sea-piece by Brooking, and representations of various hospitals in London by Gainsborough, Wilson, Wale, &c. Here likewise is a basso-relievo by Rysbrach, representing children employed in navigation and husbandry

The *Chapel*, which so materially contributes to the revenue of the hospital, is much resorted to by the neighbouring families. There is always a popular preacher; and the hymns, anthems, &c., are performed in a very scientific manner. The organ was presented by Handel, who for some time performed his oratorio of the Messiah annually for the benefit of the charity. The altar-piece by West, "Suffer little children to come unto me," is deemed one of his finest performances; and the windows are adorned with the arms of the principal benefactors of the hospital.

The interior of the hospital may be seen on Sundays and Mondays in the middle of the day.

DEAF AND DUMB ASYLUM,

Kent-road.

This institution is indebted for its origin to the humane exertions of the late Rev. John Townsend, who in 1792 attracted the public attention to the afflictions of the deaf and dumb. The present building was erected in 1807, but was enlarged in 1819, and is now capable of receiving 200 children. It contains a fine bust of the Rev. J. Townsend, executed by Behnes, and presented to the institution in 1824 by the patron, vice-presidents, &c. The pupils cannot be admitted before nine years of age nor after fourteen: they are taught to read, write, cipher, and comprehend the meaning and grammatical arrangement of words, and some of them are enabled to *speak*. They are likewise instructed in the arts of mechanism and manufacture. Of those who have left the asylum, but few have been dismissed for mental incapacity, and the greater part of them are now following useful occupations.

MAGDALEN,

Blackfriars-road.

This useful institution was established to reclaim unfortunate females from the paths of prostitution. It was formed in 1758, principally by the exertions of the unfortunate Dr. Dodd; and since that period between 4 and 5000 abandoned women have enjoyed the benefits of the establishment, and have been restored to their families, friends, and society. By far the greater number of those who have been protected here have subsequently continued honourable and correct in their behaviour. No female who has conducted herself with propriety in the house is allowed to leave it unprovided for. The apartments are capable of accommodating 80 females. The chapel is open to the public every Sunday morning at a quarter to eleven, and evening at a quarter to six, when a collection is made on entrance. The females sing in a very affecting manner; but they are screened from general observation. Persons wishing to see through the building may be admitted on application to the treasurer, or to the committee, who meet here every Thursday. The unhappy women who wish to take the benefit of this institution must apply on the first Thursday in the month, between eleven and three, when those whom the committee consider most deserving will be admitted without any recommendation.

THE ASYLUM,

Lambeth,

Is a house of refuge for female orphan children. It was instituted in 1758, principally through the recommendation of sir John Fielding. The asylum was rebuilt in 1825, and forms three sides of a quadrangle. In the centre is a handsome chapel, which is open to the public every Sunday, when collections are made for the benefit of the children, whose cleanly and healthy appearance cannot fail to interest the spectator.

LONDON ORPHAN ASYLUM,

Clapton.

This institution was founded in 1813 for the maintenance and education of destitute orphans, particularly those of respectable parentage, and was formerly situated in the Hackney-road. The present building was erected in 1825, and is capable of accommodating 300 children. It forms three sides of a quadrangle, the centre containing the dining-rooms, and the wings being occupied by the dormitories. In the middle is a chapel connected with the wings by a colonnade. Tickets to see the Asylum may be obtained at the office in St. Mary Axe.

SCHOOL FOR THE INDIGENT BLIND,

Near the Obelisk.

The object of this school is to instruct the indigent blind in trades, by which they may be enabled wholly or in part to provide for their own subsistence. The pupils are also taught to read by means of raised letters. It commenced in 1799, in St. George's-fields; but since that period has been removed to its present situation. It has been lately restored, and a handsome Gothic screen built. The institution has been most successful, for in a little more than eight years it returned thirty persons to their families able to earn from *7s.* to *18s.* per week. There are upwards of sixty persons, males and females, received into the establishment; and from their exertions, between 600*l.* and 1000*l.* a-year are received in aid of general expenses. All under 12 are now deemed inadmis-

GREENWICH HOSPITAL.

CHELSEA HOSPITAL.

sible; but no age between 12 and 30 is considered a disqualification, while the strength remains unimpaired, and the fingers are flexible. The manufactures carried on, particularly in threads, lines, mats, baskets, &c. are extensive; and the ability evinced by many of the pupils is truly astonishing.

Strangers are admitted to view this institution.

GREENWICH HOSPITAL,

Situated on the south bank of the Thames, about five miles from London-bridge, is a retreat for seamen who, by age, wounds, or infirmities, are disabled for service, and for the widows and children of those who are slain in battle. It was originally built as a palace by Charles II.; but in 1694 was appropriated to its present purpose by William and Mary, and its erection completed in the time of George II., though a portion was rebuilt in the succeeding reign. The first stone of the hospital was laid by John Evelyn in 1695.

The principal front faces the Thames, along which there is a beautiful terrace 865 feet in length. The edifice is built with Portland stone, and is divided into four portions, called king Charles's, queen Anne's, king William's, and queen Mary's: between the first two is a space 273 feet wide, forming the grand square, the centre of which is adorned with a statue of George II., carved by Rysbrach from a single block of white marble, which weighed 11 tons, and was taken from the French by sir G. Rooke. On the west side is *King Charles's Building*, the eastern part of which, erected by Webb from a design by Inigo Jones, formed the residence of Charles II.; the western part was rebuilt in 1814. On the east side of the square is *Queen Anne's Building*, which corresponds with that of King Charles'; and behind them are king William's and queen Mary's buildings, surmounted by magnificent domes 120 feet in height.

King William's Building, situated on the west, was erected by sir C. Wren and sir John Vanbrugh. In one of the pediments is an emblematical representation of the death of Nelson, executed from designs by West in 1812. The *Painted Hall* in this part of the building was executed by sir James Thornhill: it was commenced 1708, completed 1727, at the cost of 6,685*l.* for the painting alone. In the cupola of the vestibule is represented a compass surrounded by the four winds, with their various emblems, and beneath is preserved the model of an antique ship found in the 16th century near Rome. From the vestibule a flight of steps lead to the hall, a noble apartment 106 feet long, 56 wide, and 50 high—the painted ceiling of which was repaired in 1808 by Mr. Rigaud. The walls are ornamented with pilasters skilfully painted in imitation of fluting, and with a collection of pictures first placed here in 1824. They consist chiefly of representations of sea-fights and portraits of naval officers. Here also are four statues of lords Nelson, Howe, Duncan, and Vincent. The centre of the ceiling represents king William and queen Mary, surrounded by the cardinal virtues, the four seasons, and the signs of the zodiac; the whole supported by eight gigantic figures. At the west end of the ceiling is seen the Blenheim man-of-war, with a figure of Victory and another of London, accompanied by various rivers and the Arts and Sciences; and at the east end, a galley with Spanish trophies, as well as portraits of Tycho Brahe, Copernicus, and Flamstead. From this splendid apartment another flight of steps leads to the *Upper Hall;* the ceiling represents queen Anne and prince George of Denmark surrounded by several emblematical figures, and in the corners are the arms of England, Ireland, France, and Scotland, between which are introduced figures of the four quarters of the globe: that representing Africa is particularly admired. The sides of the upper hall are adorned with paintings of the landing of William III., the landing of George I., and the family of the latter monarch.

Queen Mary's Building contains the *Chapel,* which is certainly one of the most beautiful specimens in the kingdom; it is 111 feet long, and 52 broad, and is capable of accommodating 1000 pensioners, nurses, and boys, besides the governor and other officers of the establishment. The portico supporting the organ-gallery consists of six fluted marble columns of exquisite workmanship, and the pulpit and reading-desk are richly ornamented with alti-relievi. Over the communion-table is a fine painting by West, 25 feet high and 14 wide, of the preservation of St. Paul from shipwreck, and above it are statues of two Angels by Bacon. The principal events in the life of our Saviour are depicted in chiaro-oscuro round the chapel, and the vestibule is adorned with statues of Faith, Hope, Meekness, and Charity, from designs by West.

A handsome monument, with a bust of sir R. Keats, was erected to the memory of that admiral by William IV.

The council-room and the governor's apartments contain several fine portraits and sea-pieces; but these are not open to the public. In the ante-room is a bust of lord Hawke. The chapel, hall, dining-room, kitchen, and wards, may be seen for a trifling donation to the pensioners appointed to shew them, and all the money they receive is appropriated to the support of the school.

Near the hospital is a brick building containing the Infirmary, and hot and cold baths for the use of the pensioners. The school formerly maintained here was united in 1820 with the Naval Asylum. The hospital generally contains about 3000 pensioners, besides whom there are upwards of 32,000 out-pensioners, who receive, according to their situations, from 4*l.* 11*s.* 3*d.* to 27*l.* 7*s.* 6*d.* annually. The in-pensioners are dressed in blue, and allowed stockings, shoes, linen, and 1*s.* per week for pocket-money. The governors of this hospital are the great officers of state and queen's ministers; but it is under the immediate management of 24 directors, a governor, and lieutenant-governor. It is supported by a revenue derived from various sources, but principally from the payment of 6*d.* a-month from every seaman, from the profits of the Derwentwater-estate, from unclaimed bounty and prize-money, duties arising from the North and South Foreland light-houses, &c.

ROYAL NAVAL ASYLUM,
Greenwich.

This institution was originally commenced at Paddington in 1801, but was removed in 1807 to its present situation, near the entrance to Greenwich-park. It is intended for the reception and education of 800 boys and 200 girls, the children of seamen of the royal navy.

The building consists of a centre connected with two wings by a colonnade of forty stone columns. The interior of the central portion of this building is remarkable, having been commenced in 1613, by Anne of Denmark, and completed in 1635 by queen Henrietta Maria, whose arms still adorn the ceiling of the room in which her son Charles II. was born in 1630. This house, which was afterwards transformed into the ranger's lodge, became the occasional retirement of the prime minister Pelham, from whom it derived the name of Pelham-house.

CHELSEA HOSPITAL, OR COLLEGE,

Is situated on the site of a college founded by James I. for the study of controversial divinity; and is intended to afford an asylum to sick and superannuated soldiers. It was founded by Charles II., carried on by James II., and completed in

1690, in the reign of William III., by sir C. Wren, at an expense of about 150,000*l.* The building is a handsome brick structure, about 790 feet in length, and the grounds occupy a space of 40 acres. The principal edifice forms three sides of a quadrangle, in the centre of which is a bronze statue of the founder. The east and west sides are principally occupied by the pensioners' wards; at the extremity of the former is the governor's house, containing a state-room adorned with portraits of Charles I. and II., William III. and Mary, George II., George III. and his queen. The centre of the building is occupied by a vestibule, having on one side the *Chapel,* with an altar-piece representing the Ascension by Sebastian Ricci; and on the other the *Hall,* adorned with an allegorical picture by Verrio, in which is introduced a portrait of Charles II.; flags are suspended from the roof of the chapel, and the ceiling of the hall is also adorned with flags which were removed from St. Paul's. About 580 men dine in this hall daily.

Besides the main building, there are four wings; one for the infirmary, another for several officers of the house, another for old maimed officers of horse and foot, and the fourth for the baker, laundress, and others.

The number of pensioners is about 400, besides the officers and servants in the house. The out or extraordinary pensioners are also very numerous; and these occasionally do duty in the garrisons whence draughts are made for the army. Their allowance is 7*l.* 12*s.* 6*d.* a-year each. The pensioners are provided with clothes, diet, washing, lodging, and firing. Their dress is red with blue facings.

The candidates for admission must bring a certificate from their superior officer that they have been maimed or disabled in the service of the crown, or have served twenty years, which must be proved by muster-rolls. The expenses of this hospital are defrayed out of the poundage of the army, besides one day's pay of each officer and each common soldier every year, which in time of war amounts to a very considerable sum. In case of deficiency, it is supplied by parliament. The hospital is under the direction of commissioners, a governor, lieutenant-governor, and other officers, with adequate salaries.

THE ROYAL MILITARY ASYLUM,
Chelsea.

Is an institution for the maintenance and instruction of 700 boys and 300 girls, the children of soldiers. The former are educated according to the system of Dr. Bell, in reading, writing, and the useful parts of arithmetic; and the latter in needle-work and household affairs. The boys have a band, which performs every Friday during the summer, from three to five o'clock.

The building was erected in 1801, the first stone being laid by the late duke of York, on the 19th of June. It is of brick, and forms three sides of a quadrangle. The principal front, which is on the west side, has a portico of four noble Doric pillars, supporting a pediment with the imperial arms; and on the frieze is this inscription: "THE ROYAL MILITARY ASYLUM FOR THE CHILDREN OF THE SOLDIERS OF THE REGULAR ARMY." The centre consists of dining and school rooms, one of which is used as a chapel, and the wings are occupied as dormitories; that on the north side for the boys, and that on the south for the girls. On the top of the building is a telegraph communicating with the admiralty.

ST. THOMAS'S HOSPITAL,

High-street, Borough,

Was founded by Richard, prior of Bermondsey in 1213, and surrendered to Henry VIII. in 1538. In 1551 the mayor and citizens of London having purchased of Edward VI. the manor of Southwark, including this hospital, repaired and enlarged it, and admitted into it 260 poor, sick, and helpless objects; upon which the king, in 1553, incorporated it, together with those of Bridewell, Bethlehem, St. Bartholomew, and Christ's hospitals.

The ancient structure having been much damaged by time as well as by fire, it was rebuilt by voluntary subscription in 1693, and greatly enlarged: it then formed three beautiful squares, to which the governors, in 1732, added a magnificent building, consisting of several wards and various offices, at their own expense. It is now composed of four quadrangular courts; but will ultimately be rebuilt in the style of the wing lately completed. In the first court are wards for women; in the second two chapels; the lesser for the private use of the hospital, and the other parochial. In the same court, and adjoining to it, are the houses of the treasurer and other officers. In the third court are several wards for men. The fourth has also wards, hot and cold baths, a surgery, a theatre capable of accommodating 300 persons, for the delivery of lectures, and an apothecary's shop.

In the middle of the second court is a statue in brass of Edward VI., executed by Scheemakers, and beneath him a representation of the halt and the maimed. In the centre of the third court is a stone statue of sir Robert Clayton, lord-mayor of London in 1680, dressed in his costume of chief magistrate. He gave 600*l.* to promote the rebuilding of the hospital, and left 2300*l.* towards endowing it.

The governors of this hospital are the lord-mayor and court of aldermen, and those who, on receiving a governor's staff, give a benefaction of 50*l.* or upwards.

The house contains 18 wards and about 485 beds. It is appropriated to the reception of the sick poor, and of those maimed by accident: the former are admitted by a petition signed by one of the governors; but the latter are received at any hour without recommendation. The annual expenditure at this hospital is about 10,000*l.*: and some idea of the number of objects relieved may be formed from a recent annual return:—Cured and discharged, 10,502; remaining under cure, in-patients, 439; out-patients, 285; buried, 225: making a total of 11,451.

Guy's Hospital,

St. Thomas's-street, Borough.

This benevolent institution is indebted for its origin to Mr. Guy, a wealthy citizen and bookseller of London, who, after having bestowed immense sums on St. Thomas's, determined to be the sole founder of another hospital. At the age of seventy-six, in 1721, he commenced the erection of the present building, and lived to see it nearly completed. It cost him 18,793*l.*, in addition to which he left to endow it the immense sum of 219,499*l.* The entrance to this edifice is formed by an iron gate, opening into a square, in the centre of which is a brass statue of Mr. Guy, by Scheemakers; the front of the pedestal has an inscription, and the other sides are occupied by relievi, representing Mr. Guy's arms, our Saviour healing the impotent man, and the good Samaritan. The building consists of a centre and two wings; behind the former is a separate edifice for the reception of lunatics. One of the wings contains a hall and rooms for public business; and the other a chapel, which contains a beautiful monument to the memory of Mr. Guy. He is represented in his liveryman's robe, raising a half-naked emaciated pauper from the ground, pointing to the hospital in the distance, into which another sufferer is just being carried. The ghastly yet not disgusting appearance of the poor man, and the meekness of the benevolent founder, are admirably contrasted. The leg and foot of the former, in high relief, are finely executed. It is the production of that distinguished sculptor T. Bacon, and cost 1000*l*. Mr. Hunt and Mr. Guy are interred in the vaults.

This hospital was established for the reception of 400 sick and diseased objects, besides 20 incurable lunatics. It contains thirteen wards, and upwards of 400 beds. Its medical establishment consists of three physicians, three surgeons, and an apothecary. The average number of patients admitted annually is about 2,250, besides whom there are 20,000 out-patients. This hospital has a museum, a collection of anatomical preparations, and a theatre for the delivery of chemical, medical, and anatomical lectures. On one evening in the week medical subjects are debated. In the laboratory is a medallion in white marble of the great and pious Boyle.

The governors of the hospital were incorporated by act of parliament: the number to be appointed from those of St. Thomas's hospital by the founder is 60; and it is enacted that if the number do not exceed 40, the vacancies shall be supplied by the lord-chancellor, lord-keeper, or commissioners of the great seal, and lord chief baron of the exchequer, so as to make up 50. It is also enacted that the management be referred to a president, treasurer, and 21 governors, forming a committee, appointed by a general court, seven of whom are annually changed. This committee is empowered to transact the affairs of the hospital, subject to the inspection and control of a general court, which may make any by-laws for the better government of the corporation.

In 1829 a splendid bequest, amounting to 200,000*l*., was made to the governor of this hospital, by the will of Thomas Hunt, esq., on condition that they made adequate accommodation for 100 additional patients.

Patients must apply for admission on Wednesdays at ten o'clock. Petitions may be had gratis at the steward's office. No fee or money is to be paid on admission of patients. Out-patients to attend on Friday mornings at eleven o'clock.—Attendance at the surgery every day, except Sundays, from eleven to two. Accidents admitted at any hour of day or night.

ST. BARTHOLOMEW'S HOSPITAL,

West Smithfield,

Was incorporated in the last year of the reign of Henry VIII. It formerly belonged to the priory of St. Bartholomew in Smithfield, founded by a person named Rahere about

1102. It is supported by the estates of the hospital, which bring in upwards of 30,000*l.* per annum.

This hospital, having escaped the dreadful fire in 1666, was repaired and beautified by the governors in 1691. But becoming ruinous, a subscription was entered into in 1729 for its re-erection. It was constructed by Gibbs, and now consists of four piles of building, surrounding a court, and joined together by stone gateways. One of these piles contains a large hall for the governors at general courts, a counting-house for the committees, and other offices. The other three piles consist of wards for the reception of patients. There are three physicians, three surgeons, three assistant-surgeons, an apothecary, and a chaplain. It contains upwards of 500 beds.

The principal entrance is of Doric architecture, erected in 1702. It consists of a large arch, over which is a statue of Henry VIII. placed between two Corinthian pillars, supporting a circular pediment, adorned with two figures emblematical of Sickness and Lameness. Above is a pediment with the royal arms. The grand staircase, painted by Hogarth at his own expense, is admired for its representations of the good Samaritan; the pool of Bethesda; the pious Rahere, laying the foundation-stone; and a sick man carried on a bier attended by monks. The hall at the head of the staircase is a large room, ornamented with a full-length of Henry VIII., who presented this house to the citizens; as well as with portraits of Charles II., Drs. Radcliffe, Abernethy, and Lawrence; and Percival Pott, esq., a distinguished benefactor to this hospital; the latter was painted by Reynolds. Over the chimney-piece is a portrait of the patron-saint, and in the windows is painted Henry VIII. delivering the charter to the lord-mayor; prince Arthur, and two noblemen with white rods, are standing near him. In the museum is a bust of Henry Earle, esq., by Behnes.

Adjoining the south wing of the hospital is a stone building for the use of the medical establishment.

Persons injured by accidents are received into this hospital at all hours without any delay; but those afflicted with disease can only gain admission by a petition signed by one of the governors. The extensive good done may be inferred from a recent annual return:—Cured and discharged, 4,057 in-patients, and 5,700 out-patients; buried, 314; remaining under cure, 480 in-patients, and 330 out-patients: making a total of 10,881.

BRIDEWELL-HOSPITAL,
Bridge-street, Blackfriars,

Is now a house of correction for dissolute persons, idle apprentices, and vagrants. Its use and character may be inferred from the following return for one year:—

Vagrants committed by the lord-mayor and sitting aldermen	184
Apprentices sent to solitary confinement	38
Persons to be sent to different parishes	633
Apprentices to be brought up to different trades . . .	24

Over the entrance is a bust of Edward VI., during whose reign the hospital was founded. The building consists of a large quadrangle, one side of which is partly occupied by the hall, an extensive room adorned with portraits of Charles II., James II., and Sir Richard Carr Glynn. It is likewise decorated with two pictures, one of which, by Holbein, representing Edward VI. delivering the charter of the hospital to the corporation of London, contains a portrait of the painter; the other, W. Withers, esq., lord-mayor, preceding queen Anne to St. Paul's in 1708. The other sides of the quadrangle are occupied by the prison. A new building connected with this establishment has recently been erected near Bethlehem Hospital, in which are 160 boys and girls, who are instructed in various mechanical employments; it also contains a chapel for the use of its inmates.

ST. GEORGE'S HOSPITAL,
Hyde-park-corner,

Was established in 1733 for the reception of sick and lame. A new building, faced with cement to imitate stone, was commenced in 1828, from designs by Mr. Wilkins. The principal front is 200 feet long. It contains 29 wards and 460 beds; it has a theatre for the delivery of lectures, which will accommodate 160 students; adjoining it is the museum. Patients are admitted every Wednesday by note or recommendation from a governor, and accidents at all times without. There is a fund in connexion with this hospital called "St. George's Charity for Convalescents."

WESTMINSTER-HOSPITAL,
James-street, Westminster,

Was instituted 1719 "for the relief of the sick and needy from all parts." A new edifice, of a handsome Gothic design, has been erected for the purposes of this important hospital, near the great entrance of Westminster-abbey, by Mr. Inwood. It contains 230 beds. Patients are admitted by orders signed by a governor, cases of accident excepted, which are admitted without recommendation at all hours of the day or night, and several beds are reserved for them. A benefaction of 30*l.*, or three guineas per annum, qualifies the donor to become a trustee.

MIDDLESEX-HOSPITAL,

Charles-street, Cavendish-square,

Was instituted in 1745, for the reception of sick and lame patients, the relief of lying-in married women, and the supply of the indigent and laborious poor with advice, medicine, diet, lodging, and other necessaries, when afflicted with disease, or rendered by accident incapable of supporting themselves and families; and further, in 1792, through the munificence of S. Whitbread, esq., a ward was fitted up for patients afflicted with cancer. *Accidents* are admitted at all hours of the day and night without letters of recommendation, and *fevers* at all times with them. Persons who have *cancers* are allowed to remain during their life, unless they wish to be discharged. *Lying-in women* are attended at their own habitations. The hospital is capable of containing 300 patients. The total number of in-patients relieved by this hospital between 1810 and 1819 was 11,359, and the total number of out-patients in the same period, 22,117.

It is under the protection of a patron, a president, fourteen vice-presidents, two treasurers, and a committee of the governors, or those who subscribe three guineas annually, or thirty guineas at one payment. The patients are visited by three physicians, an accoucheur, and three surgeons. The domestic officers are a chaplain, secretary, apothecary, surgeon, and matron.

LONDON-HOSPITAL,

Whitechapel-road,

Was first established in 1740 in Prescot-street, Goodman's-fields, but it was so well patronised that a large and grand hospital was built in Whitechapel-road, and a charter of incorporation granted December 2, 1759. The patients relieved here are sick and wounded seamen, watermen, coal-heavers, shipwrights, ropemakers, labourers in the several docks and on the quays. Attached to this hospital is an *Accumulating Fund*, for the purpose of providing for the future exigencies of the establishment, and securing its permanent support. The fund is under certain orders and regulations, and is subjected to the control of twenty-one guardians, chosen every three years.

Small-Pox-Hospital,
Battle-bridge,

Was instituted by voluntary subscription in 1746, but the present building was not opened till 1767. Soon after the practice of *vaccination* became prevalent, Dr. Woodville, physician to the hospital, first introduced it, January 21, 1799; and since that time upwards of 100,000 patients have been vaccinated here.

A portion of this building is appropriated to cases of *typhus and scarlet fever*. It is supported by voluntary subscriptions. In the court-room of this hospital is a fine bust of George III.

Queen Charlotte's Lying-in-Hospital,
Lisson-green,

Was founded in 1752 for receiving poor pregnant women, as well unmarried as married, who occupy separate wards. Others are attended at their own habitations. It was first established at Bayswater, but afterwards removed to Manor-house, Lisson-green. It is computed that upwards of 50,000 women have received the benefit of this hospital.

British Lying-in-Hospital,
Brownlow-street, Drury-lane,

The first established for this purpose, was instituted in 1749. The qualification of an annual governor is a subscription of five guineas per annum, and of a perpetual governor a single payment of forty guineas, each of whom may present two women in a year. The committee have preserved an account of those who have died, from which it appears that, in the first ten years, one woman died in 42; in the fifth ten years one in 288; and in the sixth ten years one in 216. In the first ten years one child died in 15; in the fifth ten years one in 77: and in the sixth ten years one in 92. The proportion of boys to girls born is 18 to 17; of still-born, about one to 25; of women bearing twins, one to 84.

City of London Lying-in-Hospital,

City-road,

Was instituted in 1750. A subscription of thirty guineas constitutes a governor for life. Those who subscribe five guineas, or three guineas per annum, are governors. Each governor for life has the privilege of relieving eight patients in the year, and of having two of them on the books at a time. Subscribers of five guineas may relieve five patients, and those who subscribe three guineas may relieve two patients. A double subscription acquires a double privilege. This hospital has relieved since its establishment upwards of 30,000 poor married women.

General Lying-in-Hospital,

York-road, Westminster-bridge.

This hospital, formerly called the Westminster New Lying-in-Hospital, was instituted in 1765, for the wives of poor tradesmen and mechanics. It was situated in Westminster-bridge-road, but was rebuilt on its present site in 1828. An annual subscription of three guineas entitles to recommend three in-patients, three out-patients at their own habitations, and any number for advice, and to vote at elections. A subscription of thirty guineas constitutes a governor for life, entitled to recommend yearly three in-patients, three at their own habitations, and any number for advice; also to vote at elections.

Other Lying-in Charities.

Besides lying-in-hospitals may be mentioned two or three institutions for the purpose of delivering poor married women at their own habitations. A useful institution of this kind, the *Royal Maternity Charity*, in Little Knight-Rider-street, dates its rise in 1757. An annual subscription of one guinea or more, or a benefaction of ten guineas or upwards, constitutes a governor. An annual governor for one guinea may recommend eight objects in the year, and in proportion for a larger sum, and the governor for life recommends the same number annually. During the first fifty years of this society the deliveries amounted to 178,983.

Another institution of the same kind, called "*The Benevolent Institution*, for the sole purpose of delivering poor married women at their own habitations," was established in 1780.

DEAF & DUMB ASYLUM.

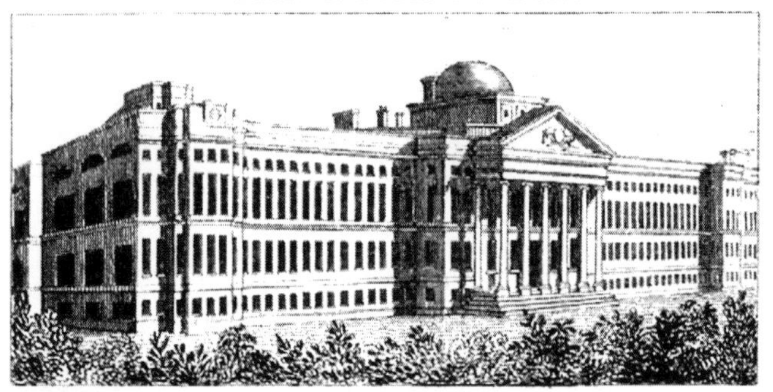

NEW BETHLEHEM.

ST LUKES HOSPITAL.

The Royal West London Infirmary and Lying-in Institution, in 1818, Villiers-street, Strand.

The Westminster Lying-in Institution, 16 Queen-square, for poor married women at their own residences.

The Royal British Ladies' Institution, Beak-street, Regent-street, for poor married women.

Ladies' Benevolent Institution, for the relief of pregnant Jewish married women.

St. Andrew's Ladies' Lying-in Charity.

The Mother and Infant Friend Society, instituted 1812.

Agar-street Benevolent Institution, 1780.

Charlotte-street Lying-in Dispensary, 1778.

Finsbury Institution, 1823.

Long-acre Chapel Dorcas Society, 1813.

Bethlehem Hospital,

Lambeth,

So called from having been originally the hospital of St. Mary of Bethlehem, is a royal foundation for the reception of lunatics, incorporated by Henry VIII. The old Bethlehem Hospital, which was erected in 1675 on the east side of Moorfields, at an expense of 17,000*l*., was 540 feet long, and was pulled down in 1814. It was built in imitation of the Tuileries at Paris, and this copy of his palace gave so much offence to Louis XIV., that he ordered a plan of St. James's palace to be taken for offices of a very inferior nature. The present hospital was commenced in 1812 and completed 1815, on the site of the celebrated Dog and Duck tavern, which was afterwards occupied as the school for the indigent blind. It was designed by Mr. Lewis, and cost about 100,000*l*. The front is truly magnificent, consisting of a centre and two wings, forming a range of building 580 feet in length and three stories high; the centre is surmounted by a dome, and ornamented with an Ionic portico of six columns, supporting the arms of the united kingdom, over which is an additional story. The interior is judiciously fitted up, and is capable of accommodating about 200 patients, 60 of whom are admitted by direction of government. The new buildings, from designs by Mr. S. Smirke, the first stone of which was laid on the 26th June 1838, will accommodate 166 additional patients; the estimated expense of the erection is 20,000*l*. In the hall are placed two fine figures, representing Raving and Melancholy Madness, for which Louis XII. of France once offered 12,000 louis-d'ors; they were executed by the father of Colley Cibber, but repaired in 1820 by Mr. Bacon, and formerly adorned the entrance to the old hospital. The buildings and the grounds for the exercise of the patients occupy above 12 acres. The annual income of the hospital is about 27,000*l.*

The following is an account of the patients in this hospital:—

In the hospital 1st January, 1837	263	
Admitted during the year	311	
		574
Discharged cured	157	
Uncured, improper objects, &c.	104	
Died	27	
On leave of absence	21	
Remaining in hospital	265	
		574

St. Luke's Hospital,

Old-street-road,

Is an institution for the reception of lunatics, which originated in 1732, and was then situated at a place called Windmill-hill, on the north side of Upper Moorfields. The present building, which derives its name from the parish in which it is situated, was commenced in 1751, but not completed till 1786, at an expense of 55,000*l.* It is a solid brick edifice, extending nearly 500 feet in length, and consisting of three stories, besides the basement-floor and attics at the extremities, which are elevated above the other parts of the building. The interior contains apartments for the various officers, and accommodation for 300 patients, 100 of whom are on the incurable list. No persons are admitted except the poor and mad, or those who have been lunatics more than twelve months.

The annual income of the hospital is about 9,000*l.* Persons paying 21*l.* or upwards, or 7*l.* 7*s.* at least, and signing an agreement to pay 3*l.* 18*s.* for the four succeeding years, are admitted governors, nine of whom constitute a general court, held on the third Wednesday in February.

Miscellaneous Hospitals, &c.

North London Hospital, Upper Gower-street. The first stone of this hospital was laid by the Duke of Somerset. It was instituted in consequence of the increase of that portion of the metropolis, and to afford a school of surgery to University College. It is from the designs of Mr. Ainger.

Charing-Cross Hospital, King William-street, from designs by Mr. D. Burton, the first stone of which was laid September 15, 1831, by the Duke of Sussex; supported by voluntary contributions.

Central Lying-in Charity and Dispensary for Females, Great Queen-street, Lincoln's-inn-fields, instituted 1816.

Lock Hospital, near Hyde-park-corner.

Ophthalmic Infirmary, Moorfields.

Ditto, ditto, King William-street, Strand.

Samaritan Society, instituted in 1791, as an appendage to the London Hospital, for the relief and prevention of various kinds of distress, not within the provisions of public hospitals.

Free Hospital for the cure of malignant diseases, Greville-street, Hatton-garden.

Sea-bathing Infirmary for the poor of London, established in 1796, by the late Dr. Lettsom and others, near Margate.

Grey-coat Hospital, Strutton-ground, instituted in 1698, for the education of poor children, 2,000 of whom have been apprenticed since its foundation.

St. John's Hospital, St. John's-square, affords advice and medicine gratis to all sick poor.

St. John's British Hospital, Cross-street, Hatton-garden, admits indiscriminately all sick poor.

Royal Universal Infirmary for children, Waterloo-bridge-road.

London Fever Hospital, Pancras-road, instituted 1803.

Green-coat Hospital, or School, Tothill-fields, founded in 1633, by several of the inhabitants of Westminster, for the instruction and maintenance of poor orphans.

ALMS-HOUSES.

Emmanuel Hospital, or *Lady Dacre's Alms-houses*, James-street, Tothill-fields, founded about 1600. It affords maintenance to a master and mistress, 10 men, 10 women, 10 boys, and 10 girls. The boys and girls have a school-room, and are apprenticed to different trades when their education terminates.

Aske's Hospital, or *Haberdashers' Alms-houses*, Hoxton, founded in 1692, by the company of Haberdashers, in pursuance of the will of R. Aske, esq., who left 30,000*l.* for their erection and endowment. Here 20 poor members of the Haberdashers' company have apartments, and 20 boys are supported and educated. In 1826 these alms-houses were rebuilt in a handsome style. They form three sides of a quadrangle, in the middle of which is a statue of the founder. In the centre of the principal building is a chapel with a portico of the Doric order: on one side of it are the school-room, the court-room, (in which is a portrait of Mr. Aske), apartments for the master, &c.; and on the other the hall, apartments for the chaplain, &c. The houses for the old men form the wings. The chapel is open to the public.

Licensed Victuallers' Asylum, Old Kent-road, erected 1828, consists of 101 houses, forming three sides of a quadrangle, for the reception of decayed victuallers, their wives, and widows. Inmates needing assistance are supplied by an endowment fund connected with this institution.

Bancroft's Alms-houses, Mile-end-road, founded in 1727, in pursuance of the will of Francis Bancroft, and held in trust by the Drapers' Company, for 30 poor men and 200 children.

Trinity Company's Alms-houses, Mile-end-road, founded in 1695, for the reception of 28 poor captains, pilots, &c.

Fishmongers' Alms-houses, Kingsland-road, comprising accommodation for 40 persons, a chapel, and a house for the chaplain.

Whittington's Alms-houses, founded in 1415 at College-hill, but removed to Highgate-hill about 1826; vested in the Mercers' Company.

Drapers' Alms-houses, Greenwich, founded by Lambarde the antiquary in 1576.

Fishmongers' Alms-houses, or *St. Peter's Hospital*, Newington-butts, founded in 1618.

East India Company's Alms-houses, Poplar, for the widows of officers and seamen who have been in the Company's service.

Stafford's Alms-houses, Gray's-inn-road, established in 1613.

Henry VII.'s Alms-houses, Little Almonry, Westminster.

Edward's Alms-houses, Christ-church, Surrey, founded in 1717.

Dame Owen's Alms-houses, Islington, founded in 1610.

Norfolk College, Greenwich, founded in 1613, by Henry earl of Northampton, and held in trust by the Mercers' Company.

Hopton's Alms-houses, Green-walk, Christchurch, for 26 poor housekeepers.

Goldsmiths' Alms-houses, Hackney-road.

Besides these, there are numerous other alms-houses of less magnitude.

Dispensaries.

These very useful institutions, of which there are an immense number, are intended to afford medical assistance in those cases where the poor do not require confinement or absence from employment, or where they have sufficient accommodation at home. They thus form a charitable establishment between the hospital and the workhouse. By this system the necessity of removal is avoided, as well as the expense of maintaining houses, nurses, &c. for the patients, and the sick themselves have the comfort of being surrounded by their families and friends. The General Dispensary in Aldersgate-street was the first established; and this was followed by so many, that upwards of 50,000 patients are now relieved annually at the small expense of 50,000*l.*; a sum not exceeding one-third of the revenue of a single hospital in London. One guinea is the annual subscription of a governor, which enables him to afford relief to at least ten patients.

A list of the dispensaries may be found in the *London Directories.* The following are a few of the principal:—Finsbury Dispensary, 29 St. John-street; Public Dispensary, Bishop's-court, Lincoln's-inn; Westminster General Dispensary, Gerrard-street; St. Mary-le-bone General Dispensary, 77 Welbeck-street; Eastern Dispensary, Great Alie-street, Goodman's-fields; Royal Dispensary for Diseases of the Ear, Dean-street, Soho; Western Dispensary, Charles-street, Parliament-street; City Dispensary, Queen-street, &c. &c.

There are also about a dozen *Vaccine Dispensaries,* where the children of the poor may be vaccinated gratis. About 8,000 are annually vaccinated at these establishments, not more than eighteen of whom, on the average, take the disease afterwards. The average annual number of deaths from small-pox which took place in London previous to the introduction of vaccination was 4,000. The number now scarcely exceeds 600.

Miscellaneous Charities.

Royal Humane Society, Chatham-place.—This institution, for the recovery of persons apparently drowned, was founded in 1774, by Drs. Goldsmith, Heberden, Towers, Lettsom, Hawes, and Cogan; but principally by the exertions of the last three gentlemen. The annual reports of the society, from its institution till 1780, were prepared by Dr. Cogan; from 1780 to 1808, by Dr. Hawes; from 1808 to 1813, by Dr. Lettsom: and after that period by the registrar and secretary for the time being. The society offers rewards to persons who, within a certain time after the accident, rescue drowned persons from the water, and bring them to places where means may be used for their recovery. It likewise confers honorary medals on persons who have exerted themselves in saving the lives of others: these are given at the anniversary of the society, when the individuals who have received benefit from the institution likewise attend and walk in procession. The number of cases in which successful exertions have been made amount to more than 6,000; and the number of claimants rewarded to upwards of 25,000. Forty-three similar institutions have been established in Great Britain, five in the British foreign settlements, and ten in foreign countries.

The society has eighteen receiving-houses in the metropolis, all of which are supplied with perfect and excellent apparatus, and designated by conspicuous boards, announcing their object. The principal receiving-house, however, was erected in 1794, and is situated on a spot of ground given by his majesty George III., on the north side of the Serpentine river in Hyde-park. In this house every thing necessary for the resuscitating process is kept in constant readiness, and during the bathing-season a medical gentleman attends to render assistance in case of accident. The office in Chatham-place, Blackfriars, is open from 11 to 3.

SMALL-DEBT RELIEF SOCIETY, 7 Craven-street, for the discharge and relief of persons imprisoned for small debts throughout England and Wales, was established in February 1772, principally by means of the exertions of the unfortunate Dr. Dodd. It is managed by a committee, who enquire into the character of the applicants. Since its establishment it has procured the discharge of upwards of 40,000 debtors, at an expense of not more than 3*l.* for each individual.

MENDICITY SOCIETY, 13 Red-Lion-square.—This admirable institution was established in 1818 for the purpose of removing from the streets every description of mendicant. Those persons whose characters are found to be good are relieved, whilst those who prefer begging to honest industry are prosecuted and punished. The society is under the direction of a board of management, two of the members of which attend daily at the office to superintend the examination, relief, and disposal of cases. The office hours are from nine to six o'clock. The annual payment of 1*l.* 1*s.* constitutes a governor, and the payment of 10*l.* 10*s.* at one time, or in one year, a life-governor. During two years this society investigated 7966 cases, bestowed 49,858 meals, and committed 965 vagrants.

PHILANTHROPIC SOCIETY, London-road.—This excellent establishment was formed in 1788 and incorporated in 1806. The children taken under its care are such as have been engaged in criminal courses, or are the offspring of convicted felons. It was established by the exertions of Robert Young, esq., (who first suggested the plan,) Dr. Lettsom, the hon. Robert Pusey, Dr. James Sims, and the late duke of Leeds. The first institution was at Cambridge-heath, near Hackney; but the present building was afterwards raised, and soon received within its walls 200 youths of both sexes. For the employment of the children buildings have been erected called the Philanthropic Reform, in which, under the direction of the several master-workmen, are carried on the trades of a printer, copperplate-printer, bookbinder, shoemaker, tailor, &c. The girls are educated as servants, and employed in washing the linen, making their own clothing, shirts for the boys, &c. Industry is excited by rewards that bear a proportion to exertion. Education and religious instruction are also carefully attended to.

The chapel is open to the public every Sunday, when a collection is made in aid of the charity.

PRISON-DISCIPLINE SOCIETY, 18 Aldermanbury.—The society for the improvement of prison-discipline and the reformation of juvenile offenders, held its first public meeting in 1820, although it had been in operation for a considerable time before. Its objects are the amelioration of gaols by the diffusion of information respecting their construction and management, the classification and employment of the prisoners, and the prevention of crime, by inspiring a dread of punishment, and by inducing the criminal, on his discharge from confinement, to abandon his vicious pursuits.

THE MARINE-SOCIETY, Bishopsgate-street, is an institution for qualifying poor and distressed boys for the sea-service. It does not receive boys who have committed theft. It was incorporated in 1772, though it was begun in 1756, and has since clothed and sent to sea nearly 80,000 boys; it has a receiving-ship placed in the Thames, near Deptford, and manned with proper officers to instruct the boys in maritime tactics.

THE AFRICAN INSTITUTION was founded in 1807 for the purpose of instructing and civilising Africa—an immense but laudable undertaking. Many schools have been established, particularly at Sierra Leone, where the number of scholars, male and female, amounts to upwards of 1400. The schools on Dr. Bell's system are usually well attended, and both males and females appear zealous to reap the advantages of instruction.

SION COLLEGE, London-wall.—This institution is situated on the site of a nunnery, which having fallen to decay, was purchased by William Elsynge, citizen and mercer, and converted into a college and hospital, called from his name Elsynge Spital; but in 1340 he changed it into an Austin priory, which was afterwards granted to sir John Williams, master of the jewel-office to Henry VIII., who, with sir Rowland Hayward, inhabited it till its destruction by fire. In 1623, Dr. Thomas White having bequeathed 3000*l.* towards purchasing and building a college and alms-house on the ancient site, his executors erected the present college. It is held by two charters of incorporation, dated July 3d, 6 Car. I. and June 20th, 16 Car. II. By these authorities a president, two deans, and four assistants, with all the rectors and vicars, lecturers and curates, of the city and suburbs, were constituted a corporation, and an alms-house was established for ten men and ten women. Dr. White endowed these by a rent-charge of 120*l.* per annum, besides 40*l.* per annum for the common charges of the college. The bishop of London is visiter. In addition to the founder's benevolence, the college holds a farm in Hertfordshire left by a person of the name of Brewer in 1634.

The library contains several portraits, and a curious piece of antique plate, having on one side an image of the Deity, and on the other a representation of the decollation of John the Baptist.

ST. CATHERINE'S HOSPITAL, on the east side of the Regent's-park, was originally founded by Matilda queen of Stephen about 1145. Queen Eleanor afterwards appointed a master, three brethren chaplains, and three sisters, ten poor women, and six poor clerks. Several other queens of England have been benefactors to this hospital. Its present name is derived from Catherine the wife of Henry VIII., who founded a guild, of which many distinguished persons were members.

This establishment was formerly situated near the Tower, but in 1826 was removed in consequence of the construction of St. Catherine's Docks. The building, erected from designs by A. Poynter esq., is of white brick, in the pointed style of architecture, and consists of two ranges, each forming three houses. In the centre, but detached, is the collegiate church, consisting of a nave and aisles. This is also built of white brick, but the front is cased with stone, and surmounted by two pinnacles. Over the central window are the royal arms and those of the college. The organ, which was brought from the old church, has a larger swell than any other in England. The curious wooden pulpit and stalls have likewise been reinstated here. On the opposite side of the road is the master's house, surrounded by about two acres of pleasure-ground.

WESTMINSTER BENEVOLENT SOCIETY.

This useful institution, which was established in 1810, is for the relief of the afflicted poor, particularly the families of soldiers and distressed married women at the time of child-birth. The society grants the loan of a box of child-bed linen to each poor married woman during her confinement; and pecuniary aid to the amount of 10*s*. or 20*s*. during the month. The business is conducted by two committees, male and female, who personally investigate every case.

MISCELLANEOUS CHARITABLE SOCIETIES.

Masonic Society, founded in 1798, for clothing and educating the sons of deceased or indigent freemasons.

Freemasons' Charity for Female Children, Melina-place, instituted in 1788 to clothe, maintain, and educate the female children and orphans of indigent brethren. The building is adorned with three elegant and appropriate statues of Faith, Hope, and Charity.

Society of Charitable Sisters for the relief of poor aged widows and single women of good character.

Ladies' Charitable School, King-street, Cornhill.

Infant Orphan Asylum. Office, 52 Threadneedle-street.

Royal Highland School Society, supporting upwards of 300 schools, and educating 20,000 children.

Law Association, for the benefit of the widows and families of professional men in distress in the metropolis and the vicinity. Established in 1817.

Royal Naval Charitable Society, instituted 1791

Guardian Society for Penitent Females. Asylum. New-road, St. George's East.

Philological School, Gloucester-place, near Lisson-grove, New-road, established in 1792 for the general instruction and clothing of the sons of poor clergymen, naval and military officers, reduced tradesmen, and mechanics.

National Benevolent Institution, 45 Great Russell-street, founded by Peter Hervé, esq., in 1812, for the relief of distressed persons in the *middle ranks* of life, of whatever country or persuasion.

Raine's Charity, in St. George's in the East, founded by Henry Raine, esq., who, about 1719, built two schools in Fawdon-fields, near where he had lived and realised property. He made provision for the maintenance and instruction of *fifty* boys and *fifty* girls, and for the support of a master and mistress. By his will he made a singular provision for bestowing annually on one girl of six who should in the course of the year leave the school, with proper certificate of regularity and exact observance of religious duties, the sum of 100*l.* as a *marriage-portion*, to be paid on her wedding-day. The female to whom the donation is given becomes entitled to it by *drawing a lot;* and on the day of her marriage, which is always on the 1st of May, 5*l.* in addition to the portion is to be expended in a dinner.

Philanthropic Society, Mile-end, instituted in 1803 for procuring the discharge of persons confined for small debts, and for the temporary relief of the necessitous manufacturers and labourers in London and its vicinity.

General Philanthropic Society, Clerkenwell.

Commercial Travellers' Society.

German and Dutch Jews' Hospital, Mile-end Old Town, arose in 1795 from the benevolent exertions of the celebrated Benjamin and Abraham Goldsmid, esqrs.

London Female Penitentiary, established in Pentonville in 1807, to afford prompt reception to all females who have fallen into vice, and are desirous of reforming.

Refuge for the Destitute, in Hackney-road, instituted in 1806, for the purpose of providing for persons discharged from prison or the hulks, unfortunate and deserted females, and others, who, from loss of character and extreme indigence, could not, though willing to work, obtain an honest maintenance. The house appropriated to the males is situated at Hoxton.

Quakers' Workhouse, 51 Goswell-street-road, founded about 1692, but then situated in Bridewell-walk, Clerkenwell, where there is still a piece of ground appropriated to the sepulture of the Society of Friends.

Benevolent Society of St. Patrick, Stamford-street, Blackfriars, a flourishing institution, established in 1784, for the purpose of affording education and clothing, and ultimately, in cases of good behaviour, of placing out the children (not under seven nor above ten years of age) of one or two Irish parents born in London, whether of the Catholic or the Protestant faith. There are 300 boys and 200 girls.

Welsh School, Gray's-inn-lane-road, established about 1714, for the education and maintenance of poor children of Welsh parents, born in or near London. It contains some curious MSS. relating to the history of the ancient Britons, amongst which is a copy of the laws of Howel Dha.

French Hospital, in Bath-street, Old-street, instituted for the relief of poor French Protestants and their descendants.

Society of Schoolmasters, formed in 1798, for the purpose of affording assistance to the wives and orphans of schoolmasters, and to schoolmasters and ushers in necessitous circumstances.

Scottish Hospital, Crane-court, Fleet-street, for relieving distressed natives of Scotland, originally founded by Charles II. and re-incorporated by George III. In the hall is a bust of Charles II., and an exquisite whole-length of Mary queen of Scots. It likewise contains a portrait of William IV. by Wilkie.

The Polish Society, a literary society for the relief of distressed Polish refugees.

Society for the relief of Foreigners, formed in 1807 for the purpose of giving money, legal and medical advice, &c., to those indigent persons who are not natives of this kingdom.

Caledonian Asylum, Copenhagen-fields, Islington, established in 1815 for the support and education of the children of indigent natives of Scotland.

Highland Society, for relieving distressed Highlanders, and establishing Gaelic schools in the Highlands of Scotland.

Literary Fund, Lincoln's-inn-fields, intended to relieve authors and literary men who by age or infirmities are reduced to poverty. Founded 1790, incorporated in 1818.

National Benefit Institution, 51 Threadneedle-street; formed for the relief of the sick and infirm poor.

Covent-Garden Theatrical Fund, instituted in 1765, for the support of aged and infirm actors, actresses, and their children.

Drury-Lane Theatrical Fund, for a similar purpose, formed by Garrick in 1777.

Queen Adelaide's Fund, for the relief of lunatics discharged from the county hospitals.

Orphan Working School, City-road, established in 1760, and principally supported by Dissenters.

Clergy Orphan School, St. John's-wood-road, for clothing and educating the orphan children of clergymen.

Licensed Victuallers' School, Kennington-lane: the school was established in 1803, but this new and handsome edifice was erected 1836; it will accommodate 250 children.

Seamen's Hospital, established on board the Grampus lying off Deptford. It was instituted in 1821, since which time about 2000 sailors have been received into it.

Royal National Institution for the Preservation of Life from Shipwreck, established in 1824.

Society for the Conversion and Education of Negro Slaves.

Besides these, there are the *Royal Society of Musicians*, the *Choral Fund*, and the *New Musical Fund*, established for the support of sick and infirm musicians; *Society for the suppression of Juvenile Vagrancy*, 32 Sackville-street; the *Artists' Benevolent*, for decayed members, their widows, and children, instituted 1810; the *Society for the Encouragement of Servants*, founded in 1792; the *Hibernian Society*, for forming schools and circulating the Bible in Ireland; the *Society for the Relief of the Widows and Orphans of Medical Men*, founded 1788; the *Artists' General Benevolent Institution*, instituted 1814; the *Phœnix Annuitant Society*, for relieving its members in old age; the *Irish Charitable Society*, for the assistance of distressed natives of the sister kingdom, held in Crane-court, Fleet-street; *Distressed Sailors' Asylum*, Cannon-street-road, St. George's East; the *Society for the Relief of poor pious Clergymen*, instituted in 1788; *Society for improving the Condition of Chimney-sweepers*, instituted in 1803; *Guardian Society for the Preservation of Public Morals*; *Benevolent Annuity Society of Blues*; *Printers' Pension Society*; *Newspaper Press Benevolent Society*; *Bookbinders' Pension Society*, 1830; *County Societies* without number; *General Endowment Association*, established 1829 under the Friendly Society Act, &c. &c. A College for decayed Artists is about to be founded.

Banks for Savings.

Owing to the perseverance of the late Mr. George Rose, the ideas of various writers, particularly of Mr. Colquhoun, in his treatise on "*Indigence*," to establish banks in which the poor might deposit their *savings*, received the sanction of parliament. The system has been very successful. There are at present about 37 banks for savings in and near the metropolis, and others in every part of England.

Small deposits of not less than one shilling are received, but are not entitled to interest till they amount to one pound sterling, and no interest is allowed on the fractional parts of a pound. Deposits withdrawn before they have been left one month are not entitled to interest. Deposits received from minors as well as other persons. Notice of withdrawing money must be given a week beforehand.

CHAPTER VIII.

MEDICINE AND SURGERY, COLLEGES, LECTURES, ETC.

Schools of Anatomy were first opened in London early in the eighteenth century, when pupils began to attend the practice of the hospitals, and thus to acquire a *scientific* knowledge of their profession. The advantages of this, the *only* true method of obtaining the requisite information, became apparent; and in the course of a few years almost every hospital in London became a school, at which not only anatomy, but every other branch of medical and chirurgical science was taught. This gave rise to private theatres in various parts of the metropolis, where anatomical instruction was given by men of great worth and talents; and this effective system of imparting a knowledge of the healing art has ever since continued in operation, with great benefit to the student and credit to the country. At the head of the several hospitals are men of first-rate eminence, who visit the various patients accompanied by pupils, &c., and prescribe, or ascertain the accuracy of what has been prescribed. Lectures are delivered to the pupils during the winter season, generally in the theatres of the hospitals; and on these occasions *practice* is combined with theory. Pupils must "walk" the hospitals for a limited period, many of them attending as "dressers,"

&c.; and if at the end of one or two years they are deemed qualified, certificates to that effect are delivered, which enable them afterwards to apply for diplomas.

College of Physicians,

Pall-mall East.

The College of Physicians owes its foundation to Dr. Thomas Linacre, of All Souls, Oxford, one of the physicians to Henry VIII., who, through his interest with cardinal Wolsey, obtained in 1518 letters patent constituting a corporate body of regular physicians in London, with peculiar privileges. Linacre was elected the first president of the college, which held its meetings at his house in Knight-rider-street, and was succeeded by Dr. Caius, the founder of Caius College, Cambridge. Dr. Harvey, to whom we are indebted for the discovery of the circulation of the blood, was also another ornament and benefactor to this institution: the college having removed to a house at Amen-corner, Dr. Harvey built them a library and public hall, which he granted for ever to the college, with his books and instruments. The college was afterwards held in a building in Warwick-lane, erected by sir C. Wren, where it continued till 1823, when the present elegant stone edifice was erected from designs by sir R. Smirke.

The portico is formed by six columns of the Ionic order, and leads to the spacious hall, the roof of which is supported by fluted Doric pillars, each consisting of a single block of stone. On the left is the dining-room, extending the whole depth of the building; it contains numerous portraits, amongst which are those of Henry VIII., cardinal Wolsey, sir Hans Sloane, &c. The floor and walls are of polished wood, and the chimney-slabs of black marble. From the hall a stone staircase with a chaste bronze railing, capped with mahogany, leads to the library. This noble room is surrounded by a gallery, and contains a good collection of books and anatomical preparations. Here also are portraits of Drs. Harvey and Ratcliffe, and an exquisite bust of George IV. by Chantrey. The Examiners' room is also adorned with several portraits, as well as with busts of sir H. Halford and Dr. Baillie by Chantrey, Dr. Mead by Roubiliac, and Dr. Sydenham by Wilton. The wainscoting, which is curiously carved, was brought from the old building. Beyond this apartment is a reading-room. The theatre is small, but neat; it contains some portraits, and a picture representing Mr. Hunter delivering a lecture to the members of the college. The collection of *materia medica* belonging to the college is very extensive.

The rapid improvement which the science of physic has undergone by the institution of this college, is the best proof of its utility. England, which in the beginning of the sixteenth century had been behind all the then civilised world in medical knowledge, finds herself in the commencement of the nineteenth inferior to none in any branch, superior to most in some, and taking a decided lead in all the ramifications into which the science of physic and the sister arts have divided themselves. The college consists of a president, elects, and fellows; and no persons except those included in the following classes are legally entitled to practise as physicians:—1. Those who being graduates of the universities of Oxford and Cambridge, are licensed to practise by the college in London and within seven miles, during their respective periods of probation, previous to their becoming fellows. 2. The medical graduates of the two universities. 3. The licentiates, who are admitted to practise in London and within seven miles; and the extra-licentiates, who are admitted to practise in the country, but not within the privileged district of the college.

Besides the quarterly meetings for the granting of diplomas, &c., the Guestonian Lecture and the Harveian Oration in Latin, are delivered in the course of the year. The celebrated Dr. Akenside once delivered the Harveian oration.

Royal College of Surgeons,

Lincoln's-inn-fields.

Till 1800, the surgeons remained united in the charter granted by Henry VIII., which incorporated them with the barbers; but at that time they obtained a new charter, making them a separate college. Since that period, various legislative and other important regulations have been adopted to promote their utility and respectability; and no person is legally entitled to practise as a surgeon in the cities of London and Westminster, or within seven miles of the former, who has not been examined at this college.

Surgeons' Hall, or Royal College and Theatre, was erected by Mr. Dance; but reconstructed in 1836 by Mr. Barry. It is a noble building of the Ionic order, with a handsome portico, on the frieze of which is inscribed, "*Collegium regale chirurgorum*;" and on the summit are placed the arms of the college, supported by Machaon and Podalirius, two sons of Esculapius. The back entrance is in Portugal-street.

The interior is grand, spacious, and appropriate. The *museum* is an extensive building, of an oblong form, with galleries; and among its valuable possessions is the collection of the great JOHN HUNTER, purchased by order of government. To adopt the language of sir Everard Home—"In this collection we find an attempt to expose to view the gradations of nature from the most simple state in which life is found to exist, up to the most perfect and most complex of the animal creation—man himself." It contains preparations of every part of the human body in a sound and natural state; as well as a great number of deviations from the natural form and usual structure of the several parts. A portion of it is allotted to morbid preparations; and there are few of the diseases to which man is liable of which examples are not to be found. There is also a rare and extensive collection of objects of natural history, which, through the medium of comparative anatomy, greatly contribute to physiological illustration; likewise a very considerable number of fossil and vegetable productions. The whole amount to TWENTY THOUSAND specimens and preparations. They are displayed in the gallery, except such parts as consist of specimens too large for preservation in spirits, or are better preserved or seen in a dried state, and those are on the floor of the museum. There is no printed catalogue of the Hunterian collection.

The museum also contains many valuable contributions made by sir Joseph Banks; 500 specimens of natural and diseased structure presented by sir William Blizard; specimens in natural history, and contributions to the library, by sir E. Home, &c. Amongst the many curiosities is the *preserved wife* of the celebrated Van Butchell, in a long square mahogany box, with a square of glass over the face, which may be removed at pleasure; an Inca of Peru in a remarkable attitude; some heads of savages; the skeleton of a remarkable female dwarf; the skeleton of Chuny the elephant shot at Exeter-change; and several other curiosities.

The other buildings connected with the institution, the theatre, &c., possess equal merit; utility and architectural excellence having been successfully combined.

There are at least twenty-four LECTURES delivered annually at this college, called the "Museum Lectures," the subjects of which are illustrated by the preparations, according to an agreement made with government when the Hunterian collection was presented to it. There are also anatomical lectures, called "Arris' and Gale's Lectures," according to the intention of alderman Arris and Mr. Gale, the donors of funds for that purpose. Besides these, an annual oration has been instituted, called the "Hunterian Oration," delivered every 14th of February.

The library is only accessible to the members, except by special tickets. Permission to view the museum may be obtained by an order from any member of the college, or on Tuesdays and Thursdays during the months of May and June, by previously leaving the name and address of the applicant. It is open on Mondays, Wednesdays, and Fridays, from twelve till four, except the gallery, which is not open after two o'clock.

VETERINARY COLLEGE,

Camden-town.

The objects of this institution are the reformation and improvement of farriery. It was established in 1791, under the auspices of persons of distinguished rank, and is managed by a president, 10 vice-presidents, 24 directors, a professor, treasurer, &c. The school, in which there are on an average 30 pupils, is under the direction of the professor. The buildings are extensive, and admirably adapted for their various purposes. The stables are scientifically arranged, and the institution has connected with it a theatre for dissections and the delivery of lectures, an apartment containing anatomical preparations, and an infirmary for 60 horses.

THE APOTHECARIES' COMPANY

Was originally incorporated with the grocers by James I. in 1606: but eleven years afterwards he granted the apothecaries a distinct charter, forbidding grocers and others to retail any medicines or drugs, and ordaining the sale of such articles to be entirely under the direction of this company. There were then only 104 apothecaries' shops in London and the suburbs. They have since gained various privileges by act of parliament, and no person is now allowed to practise as an apothecary in any part of England and Wales without having first obtained a certificate of his qualification from the Court of Examiners belonging to this company. The freehold of the physic-garden at Chelsea was given to them by sir Hans Sloane, on condition that they should present annually to the Royal Society 50 new plants, till the number should amount to 2000. This condition was punctually fulfilled, and the specimens are yet preserved in the society's collection. The company's hall is a spacious building in Water-lane, Blackfriars, which was finished in 1670. The hall contains a portrait of James I., as well as a bust of Gideon Delaune, his apothecary. Here prescriptions are prepared, and unadulterated drugs are sold to the public as well as to the profession. The whole of the medicines used in the army and navy are received from this hall. A general *herbarizing* takes place annually amongst the members of this company, for the improvement of students, apprentices, &c., and several others of less extent are made in the course of the summer.

Medical Society,

Bolt-court, Fleet-street,

Was instituted to give the practitioners of the healing art frequent opportunities of meeting together; to receive medical papers and useful facts respecting difficult and extraordinary cases; to excite practitioners to increased exertion, by the bestowment of honorary rewards; and to found a medical library for the use of the members. The library now consists of 30,000 volumes, 10,000 of which were given by Dr. Sims. The society is composed of physicians, surgeons, apothecaries, and other persons versed in sciences connected with medicine. Its first meeting was held January 7th, 1773, when an address on the state of medical knowledge was delivered by Dr. Lettsom. The meetings were held in Crane-court, Fleet-street, till 1788, when Dr. Lettsom presented the society with the house they now occupy.—This was not the residence of Dr. Johnson, as has been erroneously stated. Dr. J. resided in the building afterwards occupied by Mr. Bensley the printer.

Medical and Chirurgical Society,

Lincoln's-inn-fields,

Was founded in 1805, and is similar in its objects to the Medical Society. It has an extensive library, and ranks amongst its members some of the most eminent of the faculty in the metropolis.

Besides the above, there is a *Physical Society* at Guy's Hospital, the *Anatomico-Chirurgical Society*, the *Westminster Medical Society*, the *Philo-Medico-Chirurgical Society*.

MEDICAL LECTURES

On Anatomy, Physiology, Surgery, Medicine, Obstetrics, Chemistry, &c., are delivered at stated times at the various hospitals, at University College, and at King's College, by the most celebrated men in the profession. Many eminent surgeons and physicians likewise lecture at the Theatre of Anatomy, Great Windmill-street; at Mr. Taunton's Theatre, 87 Hatton-garden; at the Theatre of Anatomy and Medicine, Webb-street, Maze-pond, Borough; or at their own houses. The lectures are generally advertised in the newspapers; but information respecting them may be obtained of the medical booksellers. The terms vary from two to five guineas for the first course: but a reduction is made by each lecturer for the second and third courses; also for an annual or perpetual ticket of admission. The first course usually commences in October, and the second in January.

CHAPTER IX.

RELIGION OF THE METROPOLIS; CHURCHES AND CHAPELS; SOCIETIES TO PROMOTE CHRISTIANITY, ETC.

LONDON is distinguished by the number and variety of its places of worship. It contains 1 cathedral, 1 abbey-church, about 130 parish-churches, about 70 episcopal chapels, about 180 meeting-houses, 18 meeting-houses for foreigners, 15 Roman Catholic chapels, and 6 synagogues: making a total of more than 400.

THE BRITISH AND FOREIGN BIBLE SOCIETY was instituted in 1804, for the circulation of the Scriptures without note or comment. It is supported by churchmen and dissenters, and has succeeded beyond the most sanguine expectations of its projectors: it has expended more than two millions. The Bible has been printed in almost every language; and upwards of nine millions of Bibles and Testaments have been distributed. More than a thousand auxiliary societies have been established in Britain alone, and a considerable number on the continent, in the East Indies, &c. The society's house is situated in Earl-street, Blackfriars, where it has a collection of curious editions of the sacred Scriptures.

THE PRAYER-BOOK AND HOMILY SOCIETY was formed about 1814, with a view to distribute *gratis*, and to circulate at reduced prices, the authorised formularies of the Established Church. Its office is in Salisbury-court, Fleet-street.

THE CHURCH-MISSIONARY SOCIETY was established in 1800 for the diffusion of divine truth throughout the world. It is conducted by members of the Established Church, and publishes monthly a Missionary Register, which contains an account of the principal transactions of the various institutions for propagating the Gospel, and of the proceedings of this society at large. Its office is No. 14 Salisbury-court.

THE HOME-MISSIONARY SOCIETY was established in 1819. Its design is the improvement of the unenlightened inhabitants of the towns and villages of Great Britain, by the preaching of the Gospel, the distribution of religious tracts, and the establishment of Sunday-schools. The directors send missionaries into those places *only* where the extent and moral condition of the population may appear to require assistance. The society has at the present time 105 agents in the several counties of England, who have above 60,000 hearers, and give instruction to more than 8000 children, by 500 gratuitous teachers. More than *two millions*, even in Britain, are still unprovided with the means of religious instruction. The society publishes a Home Missionary Magazine monthly, containing intelligence from the stations, &c. Its office is No. 11 Chatham-place, Blackfriars.

THE WESLEYAN METHODIST MISSIONARY SOCIETY was originally commenced by the Rev. John Wesley, Rev. Dr. Coke, and others; and is now conducted by the Methodist Conference. It extends its operations to every part of the globe, and has upwards of 100 missionaries.

There are likewise several other missionary-societies, having nearly similar objects to the preceding, such as the *London*, the *Baptist*, the *Moravian*, &c.

THE RELIGIOUS TRACT SOCIETY was instituted in 1799, in order to circulate the truths of the sacred Scriptures in a plain and unobtrusive form, by way of narrative, precept, or doctrine. Since its establishment it has circulated upwards of forty millions of tracts, many of which have been sent to the remotest parts of the globe. A donation of ten guineas constitutes a member for life, and an annual subscriber of 10*s*. 6*d*. is considered a member The repository of the Tract Society is situated in Paternoster-row.

Besides those institutions, the objects of which we have briefly detailed, to afford some idea of the immense efforts made by religious classes of this metropolis, there are various other societies connected with the advancement of religion and the improvement of morals. Amongst them are :—

SOCIETIES.

1. For the Suppression of Vice, Essex-street, Strand, instituted in 1803.

2. For promoting Christian Knowledge, Lincoln's-inn-fields, founded 1699.

3. For the Propagation of the Gospel in Foreign Parts, incorporated in 1701, No. 77 Great Queen-street.

4. For the Conversion of Negro Slaves.

5. For the Support of Sunday Schools throughout the British Dominions, instituted in 1785.

6. For the Instruction of Adults.

7. For Protecting Trade against Sharpers and Swindlers, instituted 1776..

8. For giving Effect to the King's Proclamation against Vice and Immorality, established in 1787.

9. For distributing Religious Books to the Poor, instituted in 1750.

10. For giving Bibles to Soldiers and Sailors, instituted in 1780.

11. For giving Bibles, and otherwise furthering the purposes of Sunday-schools, 1785.

12. For providing Parochial Libraries, founded by Doctor Bray.

13. Queen Anne's Bounty for the Augmentation of Small Livings of Clergymen.

14. For promoting the Enlargement and Building of Churches and Chapels, formed in 1818.

15. For the Conversion of the Jews, having a chapel and two schools at Bethnal-green.

16. For prosecuting Felons, Swindlers, &c., instituted in 1767.

17. For discovering the best means of diminishing the number of prostitutes, termed the "Guardian Society," instituted in 1812.

18. For abolishing slavery, called the Anti-Slavery Society.

19. For propagating Christian Knowledge in the Highlands and Islands of Scotland.

20. For distributing the Canonical Books of Scripture, instituted 1831.

21 For distributing small cheap Tracts, inculcating moral conduct upon Christian principles.

22. For promoting the due Observance of the Lord's Day.

23. For the encouragement of Sunday-schools, the Sunday-school Union.

24. For promoting the Religious Principles of the Reformation.

25. For the Relief of Small Debtors.

26. For the Protection of Life from Fire.

27. For the Prevention of Cruelty to Animals.

28. For the Protection of Aborigines.

The following statement of the receipts of the principal religious charities in London for a recent year, will give some idea of the immense sums of money bestowed in charity in the metropolis of the British empire :—

African Institution	£1,134
Anti-Slavery Society	748
Baptist Missionary Society	14,759
Baptist (General) Missionary Society	1,256
British and Foreign Bible Society	97,062
British and Foreign School Society	2,053
Christian Knowledge Society	54,891
Church Missionary Society	35,462
Church of England Tract Society	636
Hibernian Society	8,984
Home Missionary Society	9,000
Jews' Society	11,400
London Missionary Society	31,266
Merchant Seaman's Bible Society	648
National Education Society	1,996
Naval and Military Bible Society	1,929
Prayer-Book and Homily Society	2,082
Religious Tract Society	8,809
Society for the Propagation of the Gospel	15,560
United Brethren or Moravian Society	7,332
Wesleyan Missionary Society	31,748

CHAPTER X.

GENERAL STATE OF LITERATURE, SCIENCE, AND THE ARTS IN LONDON; INSTITUTIONS ESTABLISHED TO PROMOTE THEM; EXHIBITIONS; PERIODICAL WORKS; NEWSPAPERS, ETC.

The encouragement given to learning, the patronage extended to the arts, and the result which has attended the efforts made to advance human knowledge, would warrant a far more extended detail than can be indulged in here. The formation of libraries and the establishment of literary institutions have tended greatly to promote the diffusion of knowledge amongst all ranks of society; and hence this country is enabled to boast of an immense number of men distinguished by cultivated intellect, superior genius, and extraordinary learning.

The number and variety of works which annually issue from the metropolitan press are truly astonishing; while in point of ability and usefulness they were probably never exceeded. There is not a single department either in science or general literature, which has not made considerable progress within a few years. The publishing and bookselling business is conducted upon a very extended scale; and a succession of new and interesting volumes is constantly appearing.

The character and extent of periodical literature form a prominent feature of the present age; for the reviews, magazines, newspapers, and other periodical journals, far exceed in number those of any former period. Hence much political and general knowledge has been disseminated through the country; a spirit of inquiry has been excited, and a literary taste imbibed by almost every class of society.

In the scientific departments England stands very high, and in various branches of mathematical knowledge her professors have never been surpassed. The arts, however, have not been for many years in progression; and their present state is unworthy of so opulent a country, the lower branches alone being duly encouraged.

BRITISH MUSEUM,

Great Russell-street, Bloomsbury.

The old building of the British Museum forms a square, enclosed by a high brick wall, which excludes the house from view: at each corner is a turret; and over the Ionic arch of the entrance is a large cupola. On entering the gate of the Museum, a spacious quadrangle presents itself, with an Ionic colonnade on the south side, and the main building on the north. The building measures 216 feet in length, and 57 in height to the top of the cornice. The two wings are occupied by the officers. The architect, Peter Paget, a native of Marseilles, and an artist of great eminence in his time, was sent over by Ralph first duke of Montagu, for the purpose of constructing this splendid mansion.

Sir Hans Sloane may with truth be pronounced the founder of this great receptacle of valuable curiosities; but it would be injustice, in thus mentioning sir Hans, not to advert to a predecessor of still greater liberality, who *gave* his invaluable collection to the public; this was sir Robert Cotton. The books and other articles which were offered to the public by sir Hans Sloane for 20,000*l.*, and which had cost him 50,000*l.*, being purchased by the government, it was found necessary to provide a place for their reception. Fortunately Montagu-house, one of the largest mansions in the metropolis, was obtained in 1753, and hence the origin of this celebrated museum, which has been gradually increased by gifts, bequests, and purchases of every species of curiosity in animals, vegetables, fossils, minerals, sculpture, books, MSS. &c. &c.

It is impossible to give an account of all the objects of literature and art in this repository; but a slight enumeration of some of the principal collections, and the means by which they were accumulated, may be attempted. The *Harleian Library* contains 7000 manuscripts, bought by the right honourable secretary Harley, and the noble collection of sir Simon D'Ewes, amongst which are numerous ancient manuscripts, books, charters, &c., some in Saxon, others of high antiquity, which throw great light on history: this valuable collection of MSS. was purchased for 10,000*l.* Here likewise is deposited John Stowe's collection, as well as several original ledger-books, coucher-books, and cartularies of monasteries in this kingdom, as Bury St. Edmund's, St. Alban's, and other religious houses, besides 40,000 original rolls, letters-patent, signs-manual, &c.; and it is also rich in heraldic collections, including the genealogies and histories of most of the British sovereigns. In 1767 an act was passed to enable the trustees to sell or exchange any duplicates of books, medals, coins, &c., and to purchase others in their places. In 1772 the house of commons voted 8410*l.* for purchasing antiquities brought from Italy, and 840*l.* to provide a proper receptacle for them; and in 1804, 16,000*l.* for building additional galleries and apartments for Egyptian and other articles. One of the first gifts to the public after the establishment of the institution was the legacy of colonel Lethieullier, consisting of a curious collection of Egyptian antiquities; to which Pitt Lethieullier, esq., nephew to the colonel, added several others, collected by himself during his residence at Grand Cairo. As an addition to the Cotton library, Mrs. Maddox, relict of the late Mr. Maddox, historiographer royal, left by her will her husband's large and valuable collection of manuscripts, which had engaged his attention many years. Major Edwards bequeathed many books, together with 7000*l.* after the decease of Elizabeth Mills; and the trustees obtained the collections of Dr. Birch. In 1760 Mr. Da Costa presented several Hebrew manuscripts; and since that period numberless gifts have been made; one of the principal of which was that of the Rev. Dr. Cracherode, of the *Principes Editiones* of the Greek and Roman classics. It now contains 218,957 printed books, and 21,604 MSS.

The recent additions are the Greek coins of R. P. Knight, esq.; a collection of architectural and other casts presented by the Royal Academy; Egyptian antiquities, purchased for 855*l.* 5*s.* 10*d.*; antique vases, for 3473*l.* 18*s.* 7*d.*; etchings by Dutch masters, for 5000*l.*; Charlemagne's Bible, for 750*l.*; in addition to which is the valuable collection of the late Dr. Mantell of Brighton.

The *Cottonian Library* was collected by the indefatigable exertions and excellent judgment of sir Robert Bruce Cotton, who was born in 1570 and died in 1662. This inestimable treasury of knowledge, after being with difficulty rescued from the fury of the republicans during the interregnum, was secured to the public in 1700, by a statute entitled "An act for the better settling and preserving the library kept in the house at Westminster, called Cotton-house, in the name and family of the Cottons, for the benefit of the public." The library was removed in 1712 to Essex-house, Essex-street, Strand, but for what precise reason is not known, where it continued until 1730. From this place it was subsequently conveyed to a house in Little Dean's-yard, Westminster, purchased by the crown of lord Ashburnham. On the 23d of October 1731 a conflagration destroyed a portion of the library; but the remaining books were deposited in the dormitory of the Westminster school, whence they were removed to their present situation. The collection of *sir Hans Sloane* was made by that excellent physician during the course of an active life, protracted to the term of ninety-one years, spent in the pursuit of knowledge and the practice of benevolence; and it was augmented by a collection bequeathed to him by W. Courteen, esq. The *King's Libraries* consist of printed books and manuscripts collected during several centuries, and munificently bestowed upon the public by George III., whose name is inscribed on many of them.

The British Museum also received a considerable accession in 1823, by the liberality of his majesty George IV., who presented the library collected by George III. at Buckingham-house, for the use of the public.

To these collections have been added the *Elgin Marbles* obtained by lord Elgin during his mission to the Ottoman Porte, and purchased by government for 35,000*l*. The marbles are in the very first class of ancient art. They formed part of the frieze and pediment of the Parthenon and the temple of Erectheus, and were executed from designs by Phidias.

Dr. Burney's rare and classical library was purchased by government for 13,500*l*. Amongst the printed books, the whole number of which is from 13,000 to 14,000 volumes, the most distinguished portion consists of the collection of Greek dramatic authors, which are arranged so as to present every diversity of text and commentary at one view; each play being bound up singly, and in so complete but expensive a manner, that it occasioned the sacrifice of two copies of every edition, and in some instances of rare editions. Amongst the manuscripts of classical and other ancient authors are Homer's Iliad, formerly belonging to Mr. Townley, considered superior to any other that exists, at least in England: two copies of the series of Greek orators, deemed the most important ever introduced into this country, because they supply more *lacunæ* than any other manuscripts; two beautiful copies of the Greek Gospels of the 10th and 12th centuries; the Geography of Ptolemy, &c. Another part of this collection comprises a numerous and rare series of newspapers from 1603 to the present time, amounting in the whole to 7000 volumes, which is more ample than any other extant. There is also a collection of between 300 and 400 volumes in quarto, containing materials for a *History of the Stage*, from 1600 to the present time, and particulars relating to the biography of actors and persons connected with the stage.

1.—*Regulations for general Admission.*

The Museum is open for public and general inspection from *ten* to *seven* o'clock from May to September, and from *ten* till *four* o'clock during the other part of the year, on the *Monday, Wednesday,* and *Friday, in every week,* except the first week in January, May, and September, on Christmas-day, Good-Friday, and Ash-Wednesday, and all special fast and thanksgiving days.

Persons who wish to see the Museum must inscribe their names and places of abode in a book kept for that purpose.

No children apparently under ten years of age will be admitted.—No money to be given to the attendants or servants.

2.—*Directions respecting the Reading-room.*

The reading-room of the Museum is open every day, excepting Sundays, Ash-Wednesday, Good Friday, Christmas-day, and the first week in January, May, and September. The hours are from *nine* till *seven,* from 1st May to August 31, and *nine* till *four* during the rest of the year.

Persons desirous of admission are to send in their applications in writing (specifying their Christian and surnames, rank or profession, and places of abode) to the principal librarian, who will lay the same before the next general meeting or committee of the trustees. But as it might be dangerous, in so populous a metropolis as London, to admit perfect strangers, it is expected that every person who applies should produce a recommendation from a trustee, or an officer of the house. Applications defective in this respect will not be attended to.

In all cases which require such despatch as that time cannot be allowed for making an application to the trustees, the principal librarian, or in his absence the senior under-librarian in residence, is empowered to grant a temporary leave till the next general meeting or committee.

Permission will in general be granted for six months, and at the expiration of this term fresh application is to be made for a renewal.

No reader (except in particular cases, at the discretion of the principal librarian,) will be entitled to more than two volumes at a time; but they may be changed as often as he may require.

Readers will be allowed to take one or more extracts from any printed book or manuscript; but no whole, or greater part of a manuscript is to be transcribed, without a particular leave from the trustees. The transcribers are not to lay the paper on which they write on any part of the book or manuscript they are using, nor are any tracings allowed without particular permission of the trustees.

No person is, on any pretence whatever, to write on any part of a printed book or manuscript belonging to the Museum; but if any one should observe a defect in such book or manuscript, he is requested to signify the same to the officer in waiting, who will make proper use of the information.

It may be sufficient merely to suggest that silence is absolutely requisite in a place dedicated to the purpose of study.

Persons under eighteen are not admissible.

3.—*Regulations respecting the Admission of Students into the Gallery of Antiquities.*

Students desirous to be admitted are to send their applications in writing to the principal librarian, or, in his absence, to the senior under-librarian in residence. These officers will lay the same before the next general meeting or committee of trustees, who will, if they see no objection, grant admission for a term not exceeding half a year; but in case of applications being made when an early meeting of the trustees is not at hand, the principal librarian, or in his absence the under-librarian, is empowered to grant a temporary leave till the next general meeting or committee.

Students who apply for admission to the gallery are to specify their descriptions and places of abode: and it is expected that every one who applies do produce a recommendation from a trustee or officer of the Museum, or from one of the professors in the Royal Academy.

The SYNOPSIS of the contents of the British Museum, with which we shall conclude this portion of our work, will be a useful guide to the visiter.

The *ground or first floor*, as it is called, consisting of sixteen rooms, contains the old library of printed books. Strangers are not introduced into these apartments, because the mere sight of the outside of books cannot convey either instruction or amusement.*

The *hall* contains the statue of Shakspeare by Roubiliac, which formerly adorned Garrick's villa at Hampton; Guadma, a Burman idol, presented by Captain Marryatt; an Indian

* An alphabetical catalogue of this library was printed in 1787, in two volumes folio; a new edition, in seven volumes 8vo, was published in 1820. A catalogue of the Royal Library was printed in five volumes folio, and privately distributed by order of George IV. soon after it was presented.

fountain; a statue of Mrs. Damer by Cerrachi; and one of Sir Joseph Banks by Chantrey.

The decorations of the great staircase are worthy of notice. The paintings on the ceiling, representing Phaëton petitioning Apollo for leave to drive his chariot, are by Charles de la Fosse, who in his time was deemed one of the best colourists of the French school; and who executed the paintings on the cupola of the dome of the Invalides, which are ranked among the *admiranda* of Paris. The landscapes and architectural decorations are by James Rousseau, whose particular skill in perspective has at all times been held in high estimation. On the stairs are placed the musk-ox and white bear brought from the North Pole, a male and a female camelopardalis, a young Indian elephant, and a large seal.

Upper Floor.

The first room contains artificial curiosities from the less-civilised parts of the world. In a glazed case in the centre of the room is the original Magna Charta, with a fac-simile engraving by Pine. The cases contain articles from the west coast of North America and the South Sea Islands, presented chiefly by captain Cook and Sir Joseph Banks, consisting of fishing implements from Nootka Sound and Oonalashka; water-proof fishing-jackets made of the intestines of the whale; several caps of wood representing heads of beasts; a wooden coat of armour; warlike implements and various tools, clubs, adzes, &c. Otaheite winter and summer clothes, made of the bark of the paper-mulberry; a mourning-dress; a canoe composed of many pieces of wood sewed together, from Queen Charlotte's Island; Esquimaux dresses and implements, brought to England by captain Parry; Peruvian and Mexican idols, statues, &c.

The second, third, and fourth rooms contain the herbariums of Sir Hans Sloane and Sir Joseph Banks; the fifth, sixth, and seventh rooms are at present occupied by Sir J. Banks' library; in the sixth room is also preserved the general collection of insects: these rooms are not open to casual visiters. They formerly contained the MSS., which are now deposited in the New Building.

The grand and splendid SALOON, painted by La Fosse, represents the birth of Minerva. The landscapes and architectural decorations are by J. Rousseau, and the garlands of flowers by John Baptist Monoyer. The general collection of quadrupeds is contained in this apartment. Over the chimney is a fine hunting-piece by Weenix.

The eighth room contains a fine collection of casts from ancient regal, monastic, and other seals; the collection of Greek, Hindoo, and Celtic bronzes, &c.

In the ninth room are deposited the mammalia supplementary to the saloon; they are placed here at present for want of room. It likewise contains the specimens of crustacea, the reptiles in spirits, &c.; and round the room are the horns of various species of the rhinoceros.

The tenth room contains a collection of reptiles in spirit, dried reptiles, sea-eggs, star-fish, &c.: over the cases are placed the horns of different species of deer. In the centre of the room are skeletons of an Indian elephant, presented by sir Jasper Nicholl and general Hardwicke; also skeletons of a Virginian deer, great kangaroo, and Arctic wolf.

In the eleventh room are deposited the general collection of fish, corals, and sponges. In the table-cases are the radiated animals; and round the room is placed a series of horns of the family Bovidæ.

New Building.

A new and more commodious building, from designs by Mr. Smirke, is now erecting in the gardens of the British Museum, and is intended to receive the collections deposited in the present edifice. When completed, it will form a quadrangle, and be one of the noblest buildings in the metropolis. The east wing, which is already finished, is an edifice of noble proportions, 500 feet long. It is built of brick and faced with stone. In the centre is a portico of four Ionic columns, fronting the inner side of the quadrangle.

The ground-floor comprises the reading-room, the room for MSS., and the king's library.

The *Reading-room* is surrounded with shelves of books secured by wire. Tables are placed on each side for the use of the readers, and are furnished with pens, ink, and rests for the books. Catalogues are placed in the room, which the visiter consults at his pleasure, writes his notes from them, pulls the bell-rope, a messenger immediately obeys the summons, and in as short a time as possible returns with the wished-for book.

The *MSS.-room* is in the form of a cross. Amongst the valuable literary stores deposited in this apartment are the following:—The Lansdowne manuscripts, consisting of 1,352 volumes, of which 114 contain an ample collection of lord Burleigh's state papers, many of them originals; 46 volumes of sir Julius Cæsar's papers, all relative to the time of queen Elizabeth and James I. The Hargrave manuscripts, in 499 volumes, purchased in 1813 for 800*l.*, are mostly devoted to the laws; 107 volumes of historical collections of Dr. White Kennett, bishop of Peterborough; Dr. Birch's MSS., consisting of 337 volumes, chiefly on history, biography, divinity, and literature, who also bequeathed 522*l.* 18*s.* annually; sir Hans Sloane's MSS., consisting of 4,100 volumes, principally on physic, natural history, and natural philosophy; Kempfer's MSS.; Mr. Halhed's, and some other collections of oriental MSS.; a collection of MSS. and rolls, consisting of 62 articles, relating to Kent, purchased of Mr. Hasted; the Harleian MSS.; 57 volumes containing a series of public acts relating to the history and government of England from 1115 to 1608, collected by Thomas Rymer, but not printed in his *Fœdera;* 47 volumes relating to the history of Ireland, presented by the Rev. Jeremiah Milles, dean of Exeter; 43 volumes of Icelandic MSS., presented by sir Joseph Banks; 41 volumes containing the decisions of the commissioners for settling the city estates after the fire of London; 24 volumes relating to the history of music (bequeathed by sir John Hawkins); 27 volumes of music, chiefly motets and other church music, by Prenestini, Palestrina, Pergolese, Steffani, Handel, &c. &c., bequeathed by J. Mathias, esq.; the Cottonian library of manuscripts; and 94 volumes of extracts, transcripts, and notes, chiefly relating to the exchequer, collected by Thomas Maddox, esq., historiographer to queen Anne and George I.

The *King's Library* is a splendid apartment 300 feet in length, 40 in width, and 30 in height. The flooring is of oak inlaid with mahogany, and the roof is divided into compartments richly decorated with stucco-work. The walls and doorways are adorned with white marble and scagliola, and the doors are of oak with bronze ornaments. The whole room is surrounded by bookcases of uniform pattern, ornamented with brass moulding. At intervals along each side of the apartment are placed cabinets, which contain the atlases and larger works, and also serve as tables. On either side of the middle of the room is a recess, adorned with pilasters and two pillars of Scotch granite. Each of these pillars is a single block, with a Corinthian capital formed of Derbyshire spar. In the corners of the recesses are four staircases leading to the gallery, which runs round the upper part of the room, and is bordered by an elegant brass railing. This library consists of 65,000 volumes in every class of literature, arranged in 304 presses. In 124 cases is a splendid collection of general atlases.

The upper floor contains an apartment (*The Long Gallery*) the same length and breadth as the king's library, but not so lofty, and illuminated by flat windows in the roof. This room is appropriated to the general collection of mineralogy and geology, including secondary fossils, arranged according to the system of Baron Bazelius. It consists chiefly of the collections of sir Hans Sloane, C. Hatchet, esq., Dr. Cracherode, the collection of George IV. added 1816, and the collection of fossils of Mr. Brander; there is also a human skeleton embedded in lime-stone, from Guadaloupe, presented by sir A. Cochrane; and some bones of the mammoth and megatherium. The walls of the gallery are decorated with upwards of 100 portraits; a great part of them have belonged to the Sloaneian, Cottonian, and other collections. Among the principal are Henry VIII. by Holbein, Cromwell by Barnard, Edward III. (an early portrait), George I., Henry VII. (a curious portrait), Richard II., the duke of Monmouth, queen Elizabeth by Zuchero, Joseph Planta, sir Hans Sloane by Kneller, Louis XIV., sir Isaac Newton, &c. Adjoining it is a room (the thirteenth) appropriated to the general collection of birds, and in the table-cases the shells. Beyond this is a room (the twelfth) in which British birds and shells are arranged, together with a small collection of birds' eggs. Next to this is the print-room. The prints are well arranged in portfolios. Over the glass-cases in which they are kept are placed busts of eminent men; the walls are adorned with numerous portraits of sovereigns and eminent men; on the landing-place is an immense meteoric iron. The west wing of the building, which is not yet completed, contains the collection of sculpture. *The Grand Central Saloon* is the first, which contains some Roman sculptures and the Persepolitan casts. *The Phigalian Saloon* consists chiefly of bas-reliefs. *The Elgin Saloon* contains the Elgin marbles; the fragments of the frieze and metopes are in the wall; in the centre are the celebrated remains of the Theseus and Illysus, as well as the sculptures from the pediments of the Parthenon. In the *Egyptian Saloon*, which, as well as the Elgin Saloon, is a room of noble proportion, are many articles which were captured by the British army in Egypt, and presented to the Museum by George III.; there are also several from the collections of Messrs. Salt and Sams, and two fine sphinxes presented by lord Prudhoe. Up the stairs at the end of this are the Egyptian and Etruscan rooms; in the Egyptian are mummies in every stage of development, as well as many antiquities from Thebes, &c. In the Etruscan room are the vases lately purchased.

Ground-Floor—Gallery of Antiquities.

This department of antiquities, which is very extensive, occupying several apartments, is, for the most part, in the old building, and contains in fifteen rooms nearly 1,000 articles of sculpture.

Over the door fronting the entrance to the *first* room is a marble bust by Nollekens of Charles Townley, esq., to whom the Museum is indebted for the fine collection of terra-cottas this apartment contains, as well as for many of the other valuable antiquities in this gallery. The *second, third, fourth, sixth, eleventh,* and *twelfth* rooms contain Greek and Roman sculptures; the *fifth,* Roman sepulchral antiquities; in a temporary building opposite the fifth room is the large and valuable collection of casts which belonged to the late sir Thomas Lawrence; they were presented by the Royal Academy. The *seventh,* British antiquities; the *eighth,* Egyptian antiquities; these latter, however, will in all probability be removed to the new gallery. In the *ninth,* in the centre of the room, at the head of the stairs, is placed the celebrated Barberini Vase, which was for more than two centuries the principal ornament of the Borberini palace. This vase was purchased of sir William Hamilton nearly thirty years ago by the duchess of Portland, since which period it has been more generally known by the name of the Portland Vase. It was found, about the middle of the sixteenth century, two miles and a half from Rome, in the road leading to Frascati. At the time of its discovery the vase was enclosed in a marble sarcophagus, within a sepulchral chamber under the mount called *Monte del Grano.* The material of which the vase is formed is glass; the figures, which are executed in relief, are of a beautiful opaque white. The *tenth* contains sir William Hamilton's collection of miscellaneous antiquities. The medal-room, leading out of the tenth, contains the collection of coins and medals, the basis of which was formed by the cabinets of sir Hans Sloane and sir Robert Cotton, and has been from time to time enlarged by many valuable purchases and donations; but principally by the munificent donation of George IV. and the valuable bequests of the rev. C. M. Cracherode and R. P. Knight, esq. It is comprehended under three heads:—1. Ancient Coins; 2. Modern Coins; 3. Medals. The first of these heads consists of Greek and Roman coins; the second, Anglo-Saxon and other coins; and the third, the more modern.—This room can only be seen by a special order.

The number of persons admitted to view this national repository during 1836 was 383,157.

A synopsis or catalogue of the contents of the Museum may be purchased on entering, price 1s.

National Gallery of Arts,

Trafalgar-square.

This edifice occupies a commanding situation, forming the northern side of Trafalgar-square. It presents a frontage of 460 feet, while its depth is only fifty-six feet. It consists of a central portico of eight fluted Corinthian columns (which formerly belonged to Carlton-house), and two wings of four columns, each connected with the centre by a long low two-storied structure, surmounted by a balustrade. The lower portion is lighted by windows, and the upper presents a range of statueless niches, the rooms having skylights visible in every direction.

Beneath the side-porticos are passages, one leading to Castle-street, the other to the barracks. The central portico, remarkable for the richness of its columns and the poverty of its pediment, is surmounted by a dome with an ornamented roof. The niches beneath the columns are filled with statues. —*See* National Gallery and Royal Academy.

Royal Society,

Somerset-house.

The origin of this learned, scientific, and useful body is ascribed to the honourable Robert Boyle and sir William Petty, who, together with several doctors of divinity and physic, Matthew Wren, and Mr. Rook, frequently met in the apartments of Dr. Wilkins, in Wadham College, Oxford, where the society continued till 1658, when the members were called to various parts of the kingdom on account of their respective functions; and the majority coming to London, constantly attended the lectures at Gresham-college, where, being joined by several persons of the greatest learning and distinction, they continued to meet once or twice a-week, till the death of Oliver Cromwell, when the college was converted into a barrack for the reception of soldiers. Charles II., by his letters-patent, April 22, 1663, constituted them a body politic and corporate by the appellation of the *President, Council, and Fellows of the Royal Society of London for improving Natural Knowledge.*

For the good government of the society, the charter ordains that the council shall consist of twenty-one persons (the president always to be one); and that all persons who shall be chosen by the said president and council, and noted in a register to be kept for that purpose, shall be fellows of the said society. The statutes which were afterwards framed and approved by the king established the affairs of the society on a more respectable and prudent footing. Their principal provisions were, that each fellow should sign an obligation promising to promote the good of the society, attend its meetings, and observe its statutes; with a proviso that any one may withdraw on giving notice in writing to the president. Each member pays an admission-fee of eight guineas, and is subject to an annual payment of four guineas, unless he redeem it by paying at once fifty guineas. The society publishes an annual volume in two parts under the name of *Philosophical Transactions of the Royal Society of London.* The society being thus established, men of all ranks and professions vied in promoting its designs by communicating every thing within their power relating to natural and artificial discoveries. Charles II. presented them with a stately gilt silver mace,* to be carried before the president, and in 1667 gave them Chelsea College, and twenty-six or twenty-seven acres of land surrounding; but the society not having converted part of it into a physic-garden, as was intended, and the king having resolved to erect an hospital for old and maimed soldiers, purchased it back February 8, 1681, for the sum of 1,300*l.* On their removal from Gresham-college, the Royal Society purchased a house in Crane-court, Fleet-street; but when Somerset-house was converted into a public building, his majesty George III. was pleased to assign to them the spacious apartments which they now occupy.

* It had previously been used in the House of Commons, and was the same to which Cromwell referred when, dissolving the Long Parliament, he said, "Take away that bauble."

The meetings of the society are held at half-past eight every Thursday evening, from the beginning of November to the end of Trinity Term. Strangers may attend them by permission of the president and fellows present.

The museum of this society is a collection worthy its character, and the library is furnished with a large and valuable stock of the best authors. Sir Christopher Wren and sir Isaac Newton were presidents of this society. Sir Humphry Davy was elected president of the Royal Society on the death of sir J. Banks, in 1820; but retired in 1828, and was succeeded by Davies Gilbert, esq., who in 1830 was succeeded by the duke of Sussex, who resigned 1838. The Marquess of Northampton is the present president. The annual meeting for the election of officers is held on St. Andrew's day.

Society of Antiquaries,

Somerset-house.

Research into the history, beauties, defects, and properties of those objects which have survived the ravages of time, has always been a favourite pursuit of the liberal and enlightened. These dumb witnesses speak with irrefutable certainty of the manners, customs, and habits of the ages in which they were formed, and enable us to pronounce a correct judgment on matters connected with the history of those times. Societies for the prosecution of this study have been often attempted in England. Sir H. Spelman speaks of a society of antiquaries in his time, to whom his treatise on the terms, written in 1614, was communicated, he himself being one of the number. The society was founded in 1572 by archbishop Parker, Camden, sir R. Cotton, Stowe, and others. Application was made in 1589 to queen Elizabeth for a charter; but by her death the application proved abortive, and her successor, James I., was far from favouring the design. In 1717 this society was revived, and in 1751 it received its charter of incorporation from George II. The statutes provide for the due management of the revenues, and for the publication of drawings and papers; the latter are, as often as the council think fit, collected in volumes, under the title *Archæologia*, of which 18 volumes are published. The society of antiquaries possess a good library, the books in which may, on proper application, be lent to the fellows. Their apartments are contiguous to those of the Royal Society, and contain several curious antiques, and two valuable pictures, representing the Champ d'Or and the meeting of Henry VIII. with Francis I., and the battle of the spurs.

The meetings are held every Thursday evening from the beginning of November to the end of Trinity Term. Strangers are allowed to attend them by permission of the president and fellows present. Each member of the society pays four guineas annually, besides eight guineas on admission; or fifty guineas at once, which exempts him from all further contribution.

SOCIETY OF ARTS,
John-street, Adelphi.

The Society for the Encouragement of Arts, Manufactures, and Commerce, was formed in 1754. It originated in the patriotic zeal of Mr. William Shipley, brother of the bishop of St. Asaph; and the active and liberal patronage of the late lord Folkstone, its first president, and the late lord Romney, his successor, perfected its establishment. The chief object of the society is the promotion of the arts, manufactures, and commerce of the United Kingdom, by the donation of premiums and bounties for useful inventions, discoveries, and improvements. In pursuance of this plan, they have already expended upwards of 50,000*l.* derived from voluntary subscriptions and legacies. The institution consists of a president, sixteen vice-presidents, two chairmen of each of the committees, a principal and assistant secretary, a housekeeper, a collector, and a messenger, and about 1700 members. The general meetings are held every Wednesday at seven o'clock in the evening, from the first Wednesday in November to the second Wednesday in June. There are *nine* committees; their meetings are appointed by the society to be held on other evenings, according to convenience.

No invention or improvement for which a patent has been obtained can receive either premium or bounty, as every object on which the society bestows its rewards is laid open for public use and inspection. By this system the society has become possessed of a most valuable repository of models and machines in every department of the economical and useful arts. The society publishes an annual volume of its transactions.

The society's house, erected by the Adams, is a handsome brick building, ornamented with four Ionic stone columns, supporting a pediment, on the entablature of which is inscribed "ARTS AND COMMERCE PROMOTED." The grand series of paintings by Barry, which occupies the whole circumference of the great room, an extent of 114 feet by 11 feet 10 inches in height, forms a great ornament of the institution. Its design is to illustrate this maxim :—"That the attainment of happiness, individual and public, depends on the cultivation of the human faculties." The first of the six pictures of which this series is composed represents man in his uncultivated state, with its attendant misery, invited by Orpheus to the enjoyment of social order; the second, a Grecian thanksgiving to Ceres and Bacchus; the third, the victors of the Olympic Games; the fourth, the triumph of the Thames, or Navigation; the fifth, the Society of Arts, &c. distributing its rewards; and the sixth, Elysium, or the State of Retribution.

These noble productions and the models may be seen any day except Wednesday.

The list of premiums is published early in June in each year, and may be had gratis on application to the porter, between ten and two.

Since 1787 the society has adopted the practice of distributing the premiums and bounties at the close of each session, instead of bestowing them monthly in the several committees by the hands of their respective chairmen. The anniversary by this change becomes a most interesting and gratifying proceeding. Members of the society are entitled to no reward, except an honorary medal. The anniversary was for several years held in the King's Theatre, on the last Tuesday in May; but it now takes place at Exeter Hall. Admission to it may be obtained by tickets from the members.

The first public exhibition by the artists of the British metropolis took place in 1760 at the rooms of this society, and was repeated there for several years, till in process of time the Royal Academy was founded.

Royal Academy,

Trafalgar-square.

The establishment of the "Incorporated Society of Artists, and Royal Academy," has been alluded to in the preceding article. The *fine arts* in England, previous to the accession of George III., had experienced total neglect; but at the commencement of his auspicious sway more than common attention to them began to manifest itself among the professors, as well as among the higher ranks of society. This bias in favour of the liberal arts was not unnoticed by his majesty; and when the artists formed their plan of uniting to perpetuate their public exhibitions, and assumed a permanent character, the royal assent was graciously conceded, and their charter granted Jan. 26, 1765. From this "Incorporated Society of Artists of Great Britain" arose the Royal Academy, in consequence of a dispute between the directors and the fellows, which occasioned a separation of interests. On the 10th December, 1768, the institution of the present Royal Academy was completed, under the immediate patronage of his majesty; and sir Joshua Reynolds, who received the honour of knighthood on the occasion, was appointed its first president. It is instituted for the encouragement of design, painting, sculpture, &c., and is under the direction of forty artists of the first rank in their several professions. It furnishes, in addition to busts, statues, and pictures, living models of different characters for study in drawing and painting. Nine of the academicians are annually elected out of the forty, whose business it is to attend by rotation, to set the figures, to examine the performances of the students, and to give them necessary instructions. There are likewise five professors—of painting, of architecture, of anatomy, of perspective, and of sculpture, who annually read public lectures on the subjects of their several departments; besides a president, a council, and other officers. Mr. Howard lectures on painting; Mr. Wilkins on architecture; Mr. Green on anatomy; Mr. Turner on perspective; and sir R. Westmacott on sculpture. Sir Joshua Reynolds, Mr. West, and sir Thomas Lawrence, were successively presidents. On the death of the latter in 1830, sir M. A. Shee was elected. The number of associates is twenty.

Royal Society of Literature,

St. Martin's-place.

The first public meeting of the fellows of this society was held on Tuesday June 17th, 1823, under the patronage of George IV., and the immediate superintendence of the learned Dr. Burgess the bishop of Salisbury. The object of the society is to promote the advancement of literature,—by the publication of inedited remains of ancient literature, and of such works as may be of great intrinsic value, but not of that popular character which usually claims the attention of publishers;—by the promotion of discoveries in literature;—by endeavours to fix the standard as far as is practicable, and to preserve the purity, of our language, by the critical improvement of lexicography;—by the reading, at public meetings, of interesting papers on history, philosophy, poetry, philology, and the arts, and the publication of such of those papers as shall be approved of in the Society's transactions;—by the assigning of honorary rewards to works of great literary merit, and to important discoveries in literature; — and by establishing a correspondence with learned men in foreign countries, for the purpose of literary inquiry and information. The society consists of fellows and associates, the latter being divided into ten royal associates, who each receive 100 guineas per annum from the privy purse; and ten society associates, who are appointed on the funds of the society. Besides these there are honorary associates, from amongst whom the preceding are selected. The management of the society is vested in a council, consisting of the president, vice-president, and a certain number of the fellows. The meetings are held every other Wednesday at three o'clock, except during a short vacation in the summer.

UNIVERSITY COLLEGE,
Gower-street, Bedford-square.

The first public meeting with a view to establish this important institution was held at the City of London Tavern, July 1st, 1825, and was attended by a great number of distinguished senators, merchants, and literary gentlemen.

The plan of the institution comprehends public lectures, with examinations by the professors; mutual instruction among the pupils; and the aid of tutors in those parts of knowledge which most require to be minutely and repeatedly impressed on the memory. The professors derive their income principally from the fees paid by their pupils. The course of instruction consists of languages, mathematics, physics, the mental and the moral sciences, together with the law of England, history, and political economy; and the various branches of knowledge which are the objects of medical education.

The University is governed by the council, which is elected by the body of shareholders every two years; and the superintendence of the establishment is confided to a warden. The capital proposed to be raised is 300,000*l.*, which is divided into shares of 100*l.* Donors of 50*l.* are entitled to the same privileges for life as the subscribers of 100*l.* Each subscriber or

HANOVER TERRACE, REGENT'S PARK.

NEW ENGLISH OPERA HOUSE.

LONDON UNIVERSITY.

donor is entitled to the presentation of one student, the annual expense of whose education is about 30*l*.

The building for the University was designed by Mr. Wilkins, and when completed will consist of a centre and two wings, advancing at right angles from its extremities. The central part only has been erected. The first stone was laid April 30, 1827, by the duke of Sussex, and the building was opened for the delivery of lectures Oct. 1st, 1828. The front, which faces the west, is a chaste elevation of stone, adorned with a noble portico consisting of twelve Corinthian columns, supporting a pediment, in which is a basso-relievo emblematical of science and literature. Behind the portico, and over the octagonal vestibule in the centre of the edifice, rises a handsome cupola surmounted by a lantern. The building extends about 400 feet in length and nearly 200 feet in depth, including the hall and lecture-rooms in the rear. On the basement are rooms for the anatomical school, kitchens, rooms for the steward and housekeeper, refreshment-rooms, &c.

The ground-floor comprises four lecture-rooms 46 feet by 24; two lecture-rooms 44 feet by 38; several rooms for the professors; two cloisters, 107 feet by 23, for the exercise of the pupils during the intervals of lecture; two semicircular theatres 65 feet by 50; chemical laboratory; museum of materia medica, containing a very complete collection; university-office, council-room, &c.

In the centre of the upper floor is the vestibule forming the chief entrance, the great door of the portico leading into it. From this spot the whole extent of the building is seen. To the east is the hall, 90 feet by 45, intended for public examinations and other meetings of ceremony. To the north is the museum of natural history, 120 feet by 50, with a gallery round it; and at its extremity is the museum of anatomy, containing an excellent collection of preparations, several mummies, a valuable series of coloured delineations of morbid structure, &c. Adjoining this apartment are two professors' rooms, and a semicircular theatre 65 feet by 50.

To the south of the vestibule is the Great Library, 120 feet by 50; and beyond it the small library, 41 feet by 22, with a gallery round it capable of containing 12,000 volumes. Adjoining it is the librarian's room. At this end of the building is another semicircular theatre 65 feet by 50; and here also are rooms for the apparatus of natural philosophy, which is very extensive, and admirably suited for public instruction.

Persons respectably dressed are allowed to see the interior of the University every day.

KING'S COLLEGE,

East wing of Somerset-house.

This establishment was founded shortly after University College, and was opened October 8th, 1831, when an address was delivered by the bishop of London. Its object is to secure to the rising generation in the metropolis and its vicinity the benefits of an economical, scientific, and religious course of instruction, according to the doctrines of the Church of England. This college is patronised by the dignitaries of the church, and by a great number of the nobility: its government is vested in a council of forty-one, of which the bishop of London is president. It received the sanction of a royal charter; and the ground on which the building is erected was given by the government (at an annual rent of 20*s.*) to the trustees, the archbishop of Canterbury, the bishop of London, and the duke of Rutland, with the stipulation that the eastern wing of the river-front of Somerset-house should be completed within five years.

The building, designed by sir R. Smirke, forms the entire wing of Somerset-house, which has so long remained in an unfinished state. It comprises a chapel and public hall, a library and museum, ten lecture-rooms, a house for the principal, apartments for the professors, &c. The college consists of two departments; a college, in which is a school of medicine and surgery for senior, and a grammar-school for junior students; and provides for the residence of some of them in the houses of the tutors. It is under the superintendence of a principal and 30 masters.

ROYAL ACADEMY OF MUSIC,

Tenterden-street, Hanover-square.

The professed object of this establishment is to promote the cultivation of music among the natives of this country, and to afford the first facilities for attaining perfection in this branch of the arts to a certain number of pupils. The school is supported by contributions and annual subscriptions, and its government is vested in a committee consisting of twenty-five directors. The terms of admission are, for in-students, fifty guineas per annum, entrance ten guineas; out-students, thirty guineas per annum, entrance five guineas. There are four king's scholarships; the scholars receive their education gratuitously for two years, after which the scholarships are again open to competition, the late scholar not being excluded from competing a second time. The students are directed in the study of any particular branch of music by the principal professor, according to the disposition he may observe in them; and they are also instructed in harmony, composition, and the pianoforte, as well as in the English and Italian languages, and in writing and arithmetic.

Zoological Society and Gardens,

28 Leicester-square, and Regent's-park.

This society was instituted in 1826, under the auspices of sir Stamford Raffles, lord Auckland, sir H. Davy, and other lovers of science. Its object, as its name imports, is to promote the study of zoology.

The *Museum* in Leicester-square contains several thousand stuffed animals, or parts of animals, the greater portion of which have been given to the society. Amongst them are an ostrich presented by his majesty, the collection made by sir Stamford Raffles in Sumatra, and a curious collection of horns presented by general Hardwicke.

The *Gardens* and *Menagerie* on the north-east side of the Regent's-park were opened in 1828, and have since become a place of great resort. To this a considerable plot on the other side of the road has since been added, and the communication is by means of a tunnel. The gardens, independent of their zoological attractions, form a delightful promenade, being laid out with great taste, and adorned with parterres of flowers. The buildings are from designs by Mr. D. Burton. The animals are exhibited in paddocks, dens, and aviaries, suited to their various habits. In 1830 William IV. presented the society with the animals from the Tower.

To obtain admission to the museum or the gardens, strangers must procure an order from one of the members of the society, and pay 1*s.* at the entrance.

The gardens are open from 10 o'clock till sunset, and the museum from 10 o'clock to 6. Descriptive catalogues may be obtained at the doors. During a recent year 112,000 persons were admitted.

SURREY ZOOLOGICAL GARDENS,

Walworth.

Entrances—Penton-place and New-street, Kennington, and Manor-place, Walworth.

On the demolition of Exeter Change, the menagerie of Mr. Cross was temporarily lodged in the King's-mews, whence it was ultimately removed to the present spot, where no pains or expense have been spared to render it worthy of public patronage. A large piece of water, with two islands, containing a boat-house and summer-house, present a very pleasing appearance from various parts of the garden, whilst the light and elegant circular glass-house surrounding the cages of the larger and fiercer animals conveys a peculiar impression, from the contrast afforded by the powers of the forest-lords and the apparently feeble barrier opposed to their violence.

There is a den and pole for bears, a cottage for the wapiti and camel, a ruin for eagles, folds for deer, and a variety of sheds, &c. for various beasts and birds.

Seats are disposed in such a manner that the circuit of this agreeable garden may be performed with ease. During the season there are frequently fêtes, balloon-ascents, fireworks, &c.

Tickets of admission may be easily obtained, and 1*s.* is paid at the door by each person.

NAVAL AND MILITARY LIBRARY AND MUSEUM,

Whitehall-yard.

Patroness—The Queen. *Vice-Patron*—The duke of Wellington.

This admirable institution is of recent origin, and is well calculated to afford to the members of the two warlike professions that species of information which must tend to enhance the dignity of their characters, as individuals on whom the most important duties necessarily devolve. It is calculated to shed lustre on the British arms by prompting them to plant the standards of freedom and civilisation on the farthermost corners of the globe, and to twine the garlands of peace round the ruder emblems of war. It is instituted as a central repository for objects of professional art, science, and natural history, and for books and documents relative to those studies, or of general information. The delivery of lectures is included in the design of the institution. The museum and library are

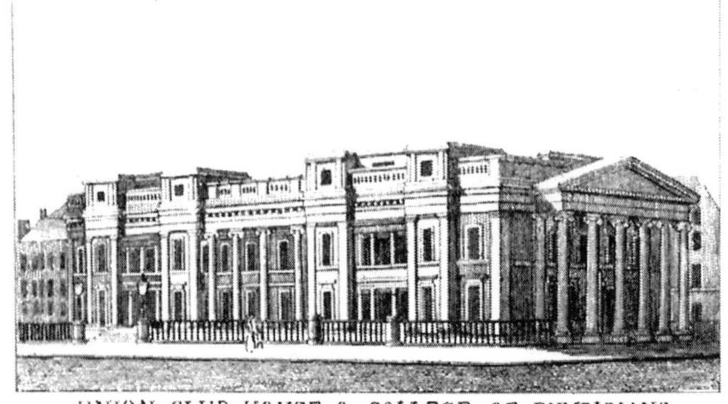

UNION CLUB HOUSE & COLLEGE OF PHYSICIANS.

UNIVERSITY CLUB HOUSE &c. PALL MALL EAST.

LONDON INSTITUTION.

comprised in four rooms, and 1200 volumes have already been presented, besides various curious objects of professional interest, amongst which is the sword the duke of Wellington wore at Waterloo. The annual subscription is ten shillings, and the sum of six pounds constitutes a member for life. The institution already reckons 3,700 members.

The Royal Institution,

Albemarle-street.

This institution was formed in 1800, under the patronage of his majesty George III., and incorporated by royal charter, as "The Royal Institution of Great Britain," for diffusing the knowledge and facilitating the general introduction of useful mechanical inventions and improvements, and for teaching, by courses of philosophical lectures and experiments, the application of science to the common purposes of life. The investigations and the important discoveries of sir H. Davy, who lectured on chemistry here, conferred no small degree of celebrity on this establishment. A new professorship was created in 1833, by J. Fuller, esq., with an endowment of 100*l*. per annum. The present professor is Dr. Faraday.

The house is very large, and well adapted to the purposes for which it is intended. It has double windows, to keep out the heat in summer and the cold in winter, and contains a chemical laboratory on an extensive scale, a handsome library, a commodious theatre in which the lectures are delivered, rooms for the perusal of periodical publications, apartments for the professors, &c.

A new stone front was constructed in 1837 by Mr. Vulliamy: it presents a range of 14 Corinthian columns, between which are three tiers of windows.

The London Institution,

Finsbury Circus,

Was opened in January 1806. The principal objects of this institution are the acquisition of an extensive library, consisting of books in all languages, both ancient and modern; the establishment of rooms for newspapers and other periodical works; and the general diffusion of science, literature, and the arts, by means of lectures and experiments. To accomplish these purposes, nearly 1000 gentlemen and merchants subscribed 75 guineas each for the supply of the requisite funds, and selected a committee to prepare laws for the government of the institution. In January 1807 the London Institution was made a corporate body by royal charter. Its affairs are directed by a committee of 26, chosen from amongst the proprietors, who meet annually for this purpose. The newspaper and magazine rooms are open to the proprietors from 8 o'clock in the morning till 11 at night, and the library from 10 in the morning till 10 at night, every day except Sundays, Christmas-day, Good-Friday, and fast and thanksgiving days. On Saturday the library is closed at 3 o'clock. The proprietors have each a transferable ticket admitting the bearer to all parts of the house. Annual subscribers pay 3*l.* 3*s.* each.

The institution originally occupied the house in the Old Jewry built by sir Robert Clayton, but afterwards another in King's-arms-yard, Coleman-street, whence it was removed to the present elegant stone building, which was erected for the purpose. The first stone was laid November 4, 1815, by the lord-mayor (S. Birch, esq.), attended by a numerous body of the proprietors. The architect was Mr. W. Brooks. The building is 108 feet in length, exclusive of the wings, which are each 16 feet. The centre of the front is adorned with a handsome portico, consisting of four Tuscan pillars, supporting an equal number of the Corinthian order, the whole surmounted by a pediment. The ground-floor is occupied by the entrance-hall, decorated with pilasters and columns, the newspaper, magazine, and committee-rooms, &c. The great staircase is at the end of the hall, and leads to the library, which is 97 feet in length and 42 in width, having a gallery on every side. On the first landing of the great staircase is the entrance to a hexagon vestibule communicating with the lecture-room, which is 63 feet by 44, and is capable of accommodating about 750 visiters. The celebrated professor Porson was elected to the office of librarian to this institution, and continued to fill it to the period of his sudden dissolution.

The Institute of British Architects.

Lower Grosvenor-street.

President—Earl de Grey.

This institute was founded for the general advancement of civil architecture; for promoting and facilitating the acquirement of the knowledge of the various arts and sciences connected therewith; for the formation of a library and museum; for establishing a correspondence with learned men in foreign countries; for the purpose of inquiry and information upon the subject of the said art; and for establishing an uniformity and respectability of practice in the profession.

The institute consists of three classes of members—fellows, associates, and honorary fellows: in the former alone are vested the control and management of the society; the honorary fellows consist of noblemen who have contributed at one time a sum of not less than 25 guineas; the fellows pay 5 guineas admission, and 3 guineas annually, or 30 guineas at first; the associates 3 guineas first year, and 2 guineas after-years.

Russell Institution,

Coram-street, Russell-square.

The objects of this institution are the formation of an extensive library, consisting of the most valuable books in ancient and modern literature, to be circulated among the proprietors; the delivery of lectures on literary and scientific subjects; and the establishment of a reading-room. The building was erected about 1800, as an assembly-room, and was converted to its present purpose in 1808. It is adorned with a Doric portico of four columns, and comprises a library, newspaper-room, and theatre. The number of proprietors is limited to 700.

London Literary Institution,

165 Aldersgate-street,

Was established in 1825 for the diffusion of literature and science amongst commercial and professional young men, by the formation of reading-rooms, the delivery of lectures, instruction in languages, &c. It is supported by annual subscriptions and donations.

Western Literary Institution,

Leicester-square,

Is similar to the preceding both as to its objects and the mode in which it is supported. Subscriptions, two guineas per annum.

Marylebone Literary Institution,

17 Edward-street, Portman-square.

This institution was established April 23d, 1832, and contains a valuable library of circulation and reference, and a reading-room. Terms, 1*l.* 10*s.* per annum, or 7*s.* 6*d.* per quarter.

Eastern Literary Institution,

Trafalgar-place, Hackney.

Subscription, two guineas per annum: entrance, one guinea.

Besides these there are—
The *Eastern Athenæum*, Stepney-square, founded in 1833.
The *Southwark Literary Institution*, Bridge-house-place.
The *Belgrave Institution*, 30 Sloane-street.
The *Islington Institution*, Upper-street.
The *Pimlico Institution*, Ebury-street.
The *Westminster Institution*, Little Smith-street.
The *Metropolitan Institution*, Bishopsgate-street.

The Mechanics' Institute,

Southampton-buildings, Chancery-lane,

Held its first public meeting at the Crown and Anchor Tavern, Nov. 11, 1823. It is chiefly indebted for its existence to the exertions of Dr. Birkbeck, and is intended, as its name imports, to diffuse information respecting the arts and sciences amongst the mechanics of the metropolis. It possesses a theatre for the delivery of lectures, and a library.

Similar institutions have also been formed in Spitalfields, Rotherhithe, St. George's-in-the-East, &c.

Gresham College

Was founded and endowed by sir T. Gresham, but the building no longer exists. He devised a portion of his property in trust to the city and the Mercers' Company for the purpose, amongst others, of paying four lecturers in divinity, astronomy, music, and geometry, and three readers in civil law, physic, and rhetoric; and in order to promote general instruction, the lectures were to be read *daily* both in Latin and English. The intention of the founder was deviated from to a considerable degree, as the lectures were for a long time delivered only in term-time, in a room at the corner of the Royal Exchange, were purposely made very short, and the professors' places rendered little better than sinecures. In 1830, however, an arrangement was made for the delivery of the lectures in the theatre of the London Institution; and it is hoped that the public will now derive considerable advantage from the liberal endowment of sir Thomas Gresham. The yearly salary of each professor is 100*l*. The lectures are advertised in the daily journals, and the public are admitted gratuitously.

Red Cross-street Library

Was founded for the use of Protestant Dissenting Ministers by Dr. Williams, who was born about 1643. He died after an active, memorable, and useful life, in 1716, leaving his library, now increased by the purchase of Dr. Bates's to near 17,000 volumes, for public use; and he directed that his trustees should purchase or build a proper house for its reception. This building was opened in 1729 in Red Cross-street, where the doctor's collection is preserved with peculiar care and neatness, and where the dissenting ministers frequently meet to transact business. The great room contains several glazed cases, in which are the works of Grævius and Gronovius, Rymer's "Fœdera," the early editions of Milton's works, with the first edition of his "Paradise Lost," and many other curiosities.

At this library is kept a register of the births of children, which is equally valid in point of law with the parochial registers under the new regulations.

Any person procuring a written order from one of the trustees may have access to the library between 10 and 3 every Tuesday, Wednesday, Thursday, and Friday, except during the Christmas and Whitsuntide weeks, and the month of August.

Law Institution,

Chancery-lane.

This institution was formed in 1825, but the building was commenced in 1829, from designs by Mr. Vulliamy. A grand portico of Portland stone, extending nearly 60 feet in width, presents a beautiful elevation of four Grecian Ionic columns and two antæ (side-pilasters), supporting an entablature and pediment: the former, to attain the requisite altitude, are placed on pedestals, which, as well as the basement story and podium of the inner wall of the portico, are of Aberdeen granite. The entrance and two ranges of windows in the front wall complete the superstructure. The interior, which is admirably adapted to the requisites of the profession, consists of a hall above 30 feet high and 57½ feet long by 50 wide, which is lighted by a lantern 40 feet by 20; a library 55 feet by 31½, and 23½ high, divided by a screen of columns and pilasters of scagliola into two unequal parts, both surrounded by bookcases of oak, and a gallery which supports a second range of cases; a club-room (which occupies all the ground-floor, 50 feet by 27, and 18 high) ornamented with scagliola columns, a paneled ceiling, and appropriate ornaments. The remainder of this commodious edifice consists of rooms for dinner-parties and for the various transactions connected with the law, apartments for the officers of the institution, the office for the deposit of deeds, with 52 strong-rooms of various dimensions, and the portion devoted to the domestic wants of the establishment.

Miscellaneous Literary and Scientific Societies.

The *Linnæan Society*, 32 Soho-square, was instituted in 1788, by sir J. E. Smith, and incorporated in 1802. Its object is to promote the study of natural history, particularly of that branch for which Linnæus, from whom it takes its name, was celebrated. The house in which the society holds its meetings was formerly the residence of sir Joseph Banks, who bequeathed it to the members for this purpose.

The *British Mineralogical Society*, 17 Old Bond-street, was established in 1799, for the express purpose of examining gratuitously the composition of all specimens of minerals and soils, sent for that purpose by the owners of mines, agriculturists, or others interested in the inquiry.

The *Royal Asiatic Society*, 14 Grafton-street, Bond-street, is instituted for the investigation and encouragement of arts, sciences, and literature, with respect to Asia. It is under the management of a council, and its members consist of persons eminent for their literary talents, but particularly as oriental travellers and scholars. It has a library and a museum.

The *Entomological Society*, instituted in 1806, is particularly directed to the study of insects found in Great Britain. It likewise attends to the best methods of destroying noxious insects, making known those which are useful, &c.

The *Mathematical Society*, Crispin-street, Spitalfields, was originally formed by the association of some journeymen mechanics. The lectures delivered here generally commence in November and terminate in April; they are previously advertised, and tickets may be procured of most opticians.

The *Medico-Botanical Society*, 32 Sackville-street, was established in 1821, for the purpose of promoting, by means of experiments and lectures, the sciences of medical botany, pharmaceutic chemistry, and materia medica. It is supported by the subscription of the members.

The *Architectural Society*, Lincoln's-inn.

The *Literary Association of the Friends of Poland*, 10 Duke-street, St. James's.

Society for the study of Architectural Topography, for the advancement of that delightful portion of history and art which age has traced in venerable characters.

The *Architectural Society*, also for the advancement of architecture and the introduction of scientific and artistic meetings, held at Exeter-hall.

The *Artists' Drawing-Society*, 3 Savoy-street.

The *Philosophical Society* of London was established in 1810, under the auspices of Mr. Pettigrew and Dr. Lettsom.

The *Geological Society*, Somerset-house, established in 1813, has published several volumes of its transactions.

The *Horticultural Society*, 23 Regent-street, was founded in 1804. It has a garden at Turnham-green.

The *Board of Agriculture*, in Sackville-street, was formed in 1793 under the direction of A. Young, esq. and sir J. Sinclair.

The *Society of Civil Engineers*, incorporated in 1828, Great George-street, Westminster.

Society for the Promotion of Practical Design, as applicable to trade, have schools, Saville-house, Leicester-square.

The *Phrenological Society*, Panton-square.

Besides these, there are the *London Architectural Society*, which has published some useful essays; the *Astronomical Society*, formed in 1820; the *Hunterian Society;* the *Societa Armonica;* the *City Philosophical Society*, in Dorset-street, Salisbury-square; the *Meteorological Society;* the *Philomathic Society*, Burton-crescent; the *Philological Society;* the *Royal Geographical Society;* the *London Statistical Society;* the *Dilettanti;* &c. &c.

The number and variety of lectures which have been read in these societies have proved highly beneficial to science, by exciting inquiry and investigating facts by experiment. Few public lectures were delivered till the establishment of these institutions. The following are the names of some of the persons who have delivered lectures:—sir H. Davy, sir E. Smith, Dr. Roget, Dr. Crotch, Dr. Shaw, Dr. Birkbeck, Dr. Spurzheim, Dr. Allen, Messrs. Good, Singer, Accum, Westley, Hardie, Bakewell, Brande, Faraday, W. Hazlitt, Millington, C. F. Partington, Phillips, Macculloch, Wallis, Black, Wood, S. Knowles, &c. &c.

MUSICAL SOCIETIES.

The *Philharmonic Society* was founded in 1813, for the revival and encouragement of the highest class of instrumental music. It consists of some of the most distinguished members of the musical profession, and has been attended with the most decided success. Eight concerts are given each season, generally commencing in February and ending in June; and whatever profit accrues from them is devoted to the objects for which the society was formed. The band engaged for these concerts is the very best that can be procured.

The *Ancient Concerts*, held at the Hanover-square rooms, every Wednesday from February to June, were founded during the last century, for the performance of ancient music. They are under the direction of six noblemen, who alternately select the pieces for the night. The performers, both vocal and instrumental, are of the highest class.

The *City of London Classical Harmonists*, held at the London Tavern.

The *Cecilian Society*, for the performance of sacred music, is held at the Albion Hall, Moorfields, every Thursday evening at eight o'clock. Tickets may be obtained of any member of the committee at a trifling expense. There are generally three grand nights in the year, Christmas-eve, St. Cecilia's-day, and one during the first quarter.

Besides these are the *Royal Society of Musicians*, 12 Lisle-street, Leicester-square; and there are frequently concerts at Exeter-hall, which are always advertised; and where also the *Sacred Harmonic Society* meet.

EXHIBITIONS OF WORKS OF ART, &c.

These are numerous, and a careful examination of them will furnish the visiter with ample means to appreciate the individual and aggregate merits of English artists. Besides the public exhibitions, some artists have galleries of their own; and in these will be found some of the most meritorious works of the age. The best productions of the modern sculptors will be found in the cathedral of St. Paul, and in Westminster-abbey; while the true talents of the architects can only be appreciated by a personal examination of the buildings which they have erected.

The names and residences of the principal painters and sculptors may be found in the catalogues of the Royal Academy, British Gallery, Society of British Artists, and Water-colour exhibitions.

Royal Academy,
Trafalgar-square.

In the rooms granted to this society there is an annual exhibition of new paintings, drawings, sketches, models, and proof-prints. No works are admitted which have been publicly exhibited before, and no copies of any kind, excepting paintings in enamel and impressions from unpublished medals: so that a visiter to this exhibition may form a just estimate of the present state of the arts in Great Britain. The exhibition, as it is generally denominated, is opened on the first Monday in May, and continues so every day from eight to seven, for six weeks or more, at the discretion of the council. The price of admission is 1*s.*; the catalogue 1*s.*; the produce of which (generally about 6000*l.*) has of late years proved fully sufficient to support the expenses of the establishment; but at its commencement it was assisted by royal bounty to the amount of 5000*l.* The Royal Academy had at first its rooms in Pall-mall, afterwards apartments were allotted to it in Somerset-house, but in 1837 it was removed to the new National Gallery, of which it occupies the east wing.

The permanent beauties of the academy's rooms are well worthy of notice. The statue of Hercules in the great hall is a noble work of art. The *Library* is adorned with a painted ceiling by Angelica Kauffmann, representing Invention, Composition, Design, and Colouring. Over the fireplace is a most beautiful unfinished sculpture of the Holy Family, by Michael Angelo, presented by sir G. Beaumont.

This neat apartment contains an excellent collection of books of prints, which are accessible to students on Monday and Thursday evenings.

Behind it is the Council-room, containing amongst the diploma pictures of the various academicians, two fine whole-lengths by Reynolds of George III. and queen Charlotte.

In this portion of the ground-floor are the keeper's apartments. Crossing the passage leading from Trafalgar-square to Castle-street, you enter the hall of casts, which contains a choice collection of casts sent by pope Pius VII. as a present to George IV. when prince regent; beyond which you ascend by a double flight of steps to the great hall, behind which is a semicircular apartment built out from the main edifice, devoted to the purposes of the Antique Academy and Sculpture Gallery. A side staircase leads from the Hall of Casts to the Life Academy, a small apartment in the central dome.

From the great hall a central flight conducts to the Painting-school and Lecture-room, the former containing the palettes of Reynolds and Hogarth; the latter, a fine copy of the Last Supper, by Leonardo da Vinci. Sir J. Thornhill's copies of the Cartoons are preserved in these apartments.

The British Institution,

Pall-mall,

Was established in 1805, on a plan formed by sir Thomas Bernard, for the purpose of encouraging British artists, and affording them opportunities of exhibiting historical subjects to a greater advantage than in the rooms of the Royal Academy, where the multitude of paintings, particularly of portraits, prevented them from being viewed with the attention they deserved. It is patronised by the first characters in the country, and supported by voluntary subscriptions, and by the produce of the exhibitions which are formed under its sanction. There are generally two exhibitions in the course of the year, one of old pictures, and the other of new.

The gallery purchased for the use of this institution was erected by alderman Boydell, for the exhibition of paintings for his edition of Shakspeare, and it is well adapted for its present purpose. The sculpture in front, representing Shakspeare accompanied by Painting and Poetry, is light and elegant. It was designed by Banks, who likewise executed the unfinished colossal statue of Achilles bewailing the loss of Briseis, which ornaments the hall.—Admission 1*s.*; catalogue 1*s.*

Society of British Artists,

Suffolk-street, Pall-mall-east.

In consequence of the limited size of the rooms at Somerset-house (the former Royal Academy), this society was instituted May 21, 1823, for the annual exhibition and sale of the works of living artists in the various branches of painting, sculpture, architecture, and engraving. The exhibition is opened during the months of April, May, June, and July.

The gallery, which was completed in 1824, is entered by a Doric portico, and consists of a suite of six rooms, one of which is used by the committee. They are the most extensive rooms in London for the exhibition of works of art, having 700 feet of wall illuminated by skylight.

The first exhibition of this society opened April 19, 1824. Admission 1*s.*; catalogue 1*s.*

The National Gallery of Ancient Pictures,
Trafalgar-square.

Since the days of the elegant-minded Charles I. England has ever been rich in works of ancient art. It would appear, however, that the intense political interest excited by the stirring events of the last half century had totally incapacitated successive ministers for a fosterage of the fine arts. To this day the government of England has done nothing for the patronage of modern art; and had it not been for the munificence of private individuals, we might have disgracefully justified the contumelious assertions of Winkelmann and Du Bos. The name of Boydell must ever be endeared to English artists for an encouragement unparalleled in the annals of patronage, since he rendered painting at once useful and ornamental. Until the year 1824 we had no national collection of ancient pictures; and the editor records with pain, that in 1839 we had still no collection of modern pictures and statues.

In 1824 a nucleus of a national collection was formed by the purchase of the greater portion of the pictures belonging to the late Mr. Angerstein. The sum of 40,000*l.* was granted for these forty works of art. For some years these treasures were immured within the residence of the late proprietor, No. 100 Pall-mall (now demolished), but were at length removed, together with numerous additions, to the new structure in Trafalgar-square, which was opened to the public in April 1838.

The English, who had been deemed insensible to artistic beauty, speedily vindicated their character for taste; and 8000 individuals visited this gallery on Whit-Monday 1838. The zeal and respectful conduct of those who contemplate the treasures of this gratuitous exhibition contrast forcibly with the different demeanour of the visiters of paid exhibitions. Of the apartments devoted to the purpose it is advisable to say little, since the architect was greatly shackled by superior orders.

The collection, augmented by the bequests of sir G. Beaumont, the rev. Holwell Carr, Lord Farnborough, &c., now contains about 150 pictures, the principal of which are :—

No. 1. A noble picture by Michael Angelo and Sebastiano del Piombo of "the Resurrection of Lazarus."

No. 33. A grand picture by Parmegiano of "the Vision of St. Jerome."

No. 35. A gorgeous specimen of colour by Titian, "Bacchus and Ariadne."

No. 26. A fine bold effort of Paul Veronese, "the Consecration of St. Nicholas."

No. 13. A graceful sketchy picture by Murillo of "the Holy Family."

No. 15. A fine broadly painted work of Correggio, "the Ecce Homo."

No. 10. Mercury instructing Cupid in presence of Venus, by Correggio.

No. 23. A sweet miniature of the Holy Family, by Correggio, replete with his charming qualities.

No. 12. A superb composition by Claude, but considered by many to be a copy.

Nos. 2, 5, 6, 14, 19, 30. Beautiful landscapes by Claude.

No. 34. Venus and Adonis, by Titian. The tone is low, probably from age.

No. 32. A grand study, the Rape of Ganymede, by Titian.

No. 8. An extraordinary picture, more for the artist than for the ordinary observer ; it is called Michael Angelo's Dream.

No. 9. A fine production by A. Carracci, representing Christ appearing to Simon Peter after his resurrection.

No. 4. An harmonious and richly coloured picture by Titian of the Holy Family.

No. 18. A highly laboured production of Christ disputing with the Doctors, attributed to L. da Vinci, but doubted by many.

No. 27. A remarkably grand and characteristic portrait by Raffael of Pope Julius II.

No. 20. A glowing picture of Cardinal Hippolyte de Medici and the painter S. del Piombo.

No. 52. A splendid head of Gevartius by Vandyk.

No. 46. A noble gallery picture of Peace and War by Rubens.

No. 45. An exquisite gem by Rembrandt, "the Woman taken in Adultery."

No. 38. A rich dashing performance by Rubens of the Rape of the Sabines.

Nos. 43 & 47. Small pictures by Rembrandt.

No. 51. A noble portrait by the same.

No. 50. A bold sketch by Vandyke.

No. 53. A glowing picture by Cuyp.

No. 57. A study for the grand picture of St. Bavon by Rubens.

No. 55, 58, & 61. Sweet bits by Claude.

No. 59. A solemn picture of the Brazen Serpent by Rubens.

No. 71. A beautiful landscape by Both.

No. 76. Christ praying in the Garden by Correggio.

No. 81. A richly coloured picture of the Vision of St. Augustin by Garofolo.

No. 83. A grand composition of Phineus and his Followers turned to stone by Perseus, with the Gorgon's Head. This, as well as a picture of the Plague, by Poussin, are noble specimens of this classical painter. They have both suffered from the dark grounds on which they were painted. Nos. 40, 42, 62, 65, 91, are by the same pencil.

Besides these are 84, Mercury and the Woodman, by S. Rosa; 67, Holy Family by Rubens; 66, a landscape by Rubens; 88, Erminia discovering the Shepherds, by Carracci; 87 and 96, Two large pictures by Guido.

In the side-rooms are fine landscapes by Canaletti, Hogarth's admirable series of the Marriage à la mode, Wilkie's Village-Festival and Blind Fiddler, Lawrence's Hamlet, Reynolds' Lord Heathfield, &c. &c.

On the walls of the passage are two grand Cartoons by A. Carracci.

The gallery is open on the first four days of the week from ten to five, and all persons are admitted gratis. Artists are allowed to have admission on the other two days of the week, by tickets, which may be obtained from the keeper of the gallery. Catalogue, price 1*s*.

Exhibition of Water-colour Drawings,

Pall-mall-east.

The rooms at the Royal Academy appropriated to water-colour pictures not being sufficiently capacious, the painters in this style determined in 1804 to exhibit their works separately from those of other artists. Two distinct societies were formed, one of which opened an exhibition in Lower Brook-street, and the other in Old Bond-street. The latter has long ceased to exist; but the former, being transferred to Spring-gardens, annually exhibited a collection of drawings, in oil as well as in water-colours, till 1821, when the original intention of confining the exhibition to water-colours only was reverted to, and the exhibition removed to the Egyptian-hall. The exhibition now takes place in Pall-mall-east, in a house built expressly for the purpose. It generally opens in May.—Admission 1*s.*; catalogue 6*d.*

New Society of Painters in Water-colours,

Bond-street.

Similar in plan to the preceding.—Admission 1*s.*

Miss Linwood's Gallery,

Leicester-square,

Is an interesting display of ingenuity and taste, consisting of copies in needlework of some of the best English and foreign pictures. They are exhibited in elegant apartments, comprising a gallery 100 feet long, a grotto of the same length, and a room appropriated to sacred subjects. Amongst the works which Miss Linwood has copied with unparalleled taste and skill are, the Girl and the Kitten, the Laughing Girl, the head of Lear, and the Sleeping Girl, by sir J. Reynolds; the Woodman, by Barker; Moonlight, by Rubens; Madonna, by Raphael; the Gleaner, by Westall; Virgil's Tomb, and Cottage in Flames, by Wright; David with his Sling, by Carlo Dolci; St. Peter, by Guido; Eloisa, and Jephtha's Rash Vow, by Opie; Hubert and Arthur, by Northcote; Children in a Cottage, by Gainsborough; two Landscapes, by Francisco Mola; Dead Birds and Shell-fish, by Haughton; the judgment of Cain, from a French picture; a head of Christ, by Carlo Dolce; a portrait of Napoleon Buonaparte; a portrait of herself, &c. Open all day.—Admission 1*s.*; catalogue 6*d.*

MADAME TUSSAUD'S EXHIBITION OF WAX-WORK is very amusing and well got up, and consists of groups and full-length figures of the most noted persons of the age, dressed as in life, and excellent likenesses. Two groups may be particularly noticed—the coronation, and the Napoleon group.—Admittance to the whole 1*s.* 6*d.*

EXHIBITION OF GLASS-PAINTING.—Mr. Backler, Newman-street, has a good collection of this description of art.

MR. SASS'S ACADEMY FOR DRAWING AND PAINTING, 6 Charlotte-street, Bloomsbury.—Although this academy cannot be ranked amongst the exhibitions of the metropolis, the excellence of its design entitles it to a particular notice amongst the institutions connected with the arts. It is an establishment for the education of artists, possessing a good collection of casts from the antique, drawings, paintings, and other requisites for advancing the progress of the student in the knowledge of the human figure and of the various branches of the fine arts.

THE LIFE ACADEMY.—This society was first established in consequence of the time required to obtain permission to study at the Royal Academy. It is held at the premises belonging to Mr. Shade, Soho-square.

RUSTIC, HISTORIC, AND LIFE ACADEMY, Clipstone-street. —This is another highly useful institution, presenting to the student all those varieties of models which are so conducive to the development of his talent.

PRIVATE COLLECTIONS AND GALLERIES.

The *Bridgewater Gallery*, Cleveland-row, (late the Stafford Gallery,) is an unrivalled collection of pictures, bequeathed to the late duke of Sutherland, which he allowed the public to view once a-week, from 12 to 5, during the months of May and June. Persons wishing to have tickets of admission must be known to the duke, or to Lord Francis Egerton, or have a recommendation from some one who is. Artists may obtain admission by a recommendation from any member of the Royal Academy.

The *Marquess of Westminster's* new and splendid gallery, Upper Grosvenor-street, contains a grand collection of pictures, both ancient and modern. It was originally commenced by the purchase of Mr. Agar's pictures for 30,000 guineas, and has since received very considerable additions. The noble marquess permits strangers to visit it, under certain regulations, during the months of May and June.

Mr. Hope, Duchess-street, Portland-place, possesses a valuable collection of pictures, vases, and statues. The furniture and decorations of the apartments, principally designed by Mr. Hope himself, are very elegant. They may be viewed by tickets during the season.

Soanean Museum, Lincoln's-inn-fields, is a splendid suite of four rooms, ornamented with paintings by Canaletti and Hogarth, and with designs by sir J. Soane himself. They are likewise enriched with a choice collection of Roman and Grecian specimens of architecture, Etruscan vases, Egyptian antiquities, &c., particularly the alabaster sarcophagus brought by the late enterprising traveller Belzoni from the ruins of Thebes. This unique collection, endowed with 30,000*l.*, was presented to the nation by the late liberal proprietor in 1833, an act of parliament having sanctioned the disposal of this valuable museum in its present form. Visiters may obtain admittance by leaving their names and address beforehand.

Besides those already mentioned, the most celebrated are the collections at Northumberland-house; duke of Devonshire's, Piccadilly; lord Ashburton's, Piccadilly; earl of Ashburnham's, Dover-street; Mr. J. Harman's, Finsbury-square; G. Hibbert, esq., Portland-place; Mr. W. Fawke's, Grosvenor-place; sir R. Peel's; Mr. Vernon's, &c.

The Egyptian Hall,

Piccadilly.

Derives its name from the style of its architecture. It was erected in 1812 by Mr. Bullock, from a design by Mr. G. F. Robinson, and was originally occupied by that fine collection of artificial and natural curiosities, the London Museum; but was subsequently divided into several compartments, which are used as exhibition-rooms. There is at present (1839) exhibiting here a model of the Battle of Waterloo, shewing the position of the troops and the undulations of the ground; 190,000 figures are introduced.

COLOSSEUM.

BURLINGTON ARCADE.

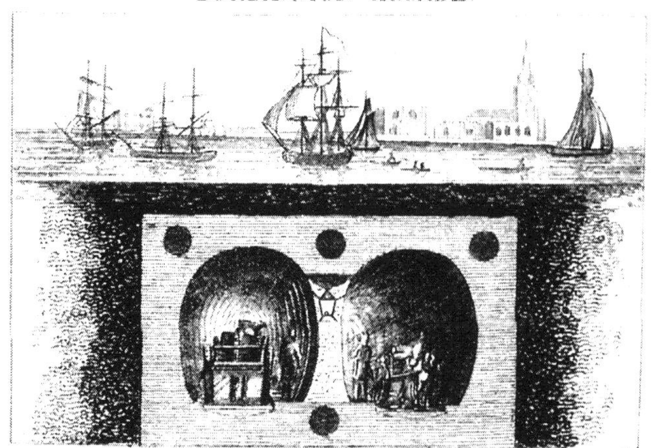

THAMES TUNNEL.

COADE AND CO.'S MANUFACTORY OF ORNAMENTAL STONE AND SCAGLIOLA MARBLE,

New-road,

Is an extensive repository for the exhibition and sale of every species of architectural ornament, executed in artificial stone, which, having undergone the operation of a particular process, is capable of resisting frost and retaining its original sharpness. It possesses all the advantages of natural stone, and is much cheaper. Many of the specimens shewn here are from models by Bacon and other eminent sculptors. This manufactory was originally established in 1769, and situated in Narrow-wall, Lambeth.

PHRENOLOGICAL CASTS.

Persons interested in the study of Phrenology will find at the establishment of Mr. De Ville, modeller, Strand, a very extensive collection of casts, comprising subjects of every nation and of every character.

DIORAMA,

Regent's-park.

The diorama, which had long been an object of wonder and delight at Paris, was first opened in London Sept. 29, 1823. It differs from the panorama in this respect, that, instead of a circular view of the objects represented, it exhibits the whole picture at once in perspective; and it is decidedly superior both to the panorama and the cosmorama in the fidelity with which the objects are depicted, and in the completeness of the illusion. The interior of the building resembles a small theatre, the part allotted to spectators consisting of a tier of boxes elevated three or four feet above the amphitheatre or pit. Above is a circular ceiling ornamented with transparent devices, and surrounded with medallions of eminent painters and sculptors. The whole is movable, and is made to revolve with the spectators at intervals of a quarter of an hour, so that as one picture recedes the other comes gradually into view. Such is the effect produced by the disposition of the building, and by the various modifications of light and shade, that the optical deception is complete, and it is difficult for the spectator to persuade himself that he is only contemplating a work of art. Messrs. Bouton and Daguerre are the artists employed. Admission 2*s.*; description gratis.

PANORAMAS.

The principal panorama in the metropolis, besides the Colosseum, is that belonging to Mr. Burford, at the eastern corner of Leicester-square, where a series of unrivalled productions, from the pencil of that distinguished painter, afford a truly gratifying treat to the curious in topographical delineations. There are generally views of two celebrated places. Admission to each view 1*s.*; and description, containing an outline sketch of the panorama, 6*d.*

THE COLOSSEUM,
Regent's-park,

Derives its name from its colossal size. It was erected in 1827-8, for the purpose of exhibiting Mr. Horner's Panorama of London. The building was designed by Mr. D. Burton, and is certainly one of the noblest edifices in the metropolis. It presents a Greek Doric portico of six columns, and is surmounted by a dome 126 feet in diameter, 75 feet of which are entirely of glass. Its form is that of a polygon with 16 faces, each 25 feet, so that the circumference of the whole building is 400 feet. The height of the walls on the outside is 64 feet, and on the inside 79 feet, while the skylight of the dome is 112 feet from the ground The whole of the exterior is covered with cement, tinted to imitate stone.

Beyond the entrance are vestibules, one of which leads to a saloon for the exhibition of works of art, and the other to the various galleries from which the panorama is to be viewed. There is also in the centre of the building a curious contrivance, by means of which visiters are raised at once to a level with the panorama, and saved the trouble of ascending the staircase.

The Panorama of London far surpasses in extent and accuracy every thing of the kind hitherto attempted. Some idea of its size may be formed from its occupying 40,000 square feet, or nearly an acre of canvas. The various objects are depicted as seen from the top of St. Paul's, where Mr. Horner made the original sketches in 1821, when the ball and cross of the cathedral were being replaced. The original ball and a model of the cross are shewn in the Colosseum. Mr. Parris was the artist under whose superintendence the painting of the panorama was executed.

The gardens surrounding the Colosseum are laid out so as to appear much more extensive than they really are. They comprise conservatories, waterfalls, fountains, a Swiss cottage, &c., constructed under the direction of Mr. Robinson.

During the winter, concerts and balls are held here.

Admission; panorama, ball, and saloon for works of art, 1*s.*; conservatories, fountains, Swiss cottage, and marine grotto, 1*s.*

Cosmorama,

209 Regent-street,

Is intended to present correct delineations of the celebrated remains of antiquity, and of the most remarkable cities and edifices in every part of the globe. The subjects are changed every two or three months.

Open from eleven till dusk. Admission 1*s.*; descriptive catalogue 6*d.*

Missionary Museum,

26 Austin-friars,

Is a collection of curiosities obtained by the London Missionary Society from their various foreign stations, but principally from Africa and the South Sea Islands. Admission on Wednesdays from 10 to 3 from Michaelmas to Lady-day, and from 10 to 4 from Lady-day to Michaelmas. A catalogue is printed, the price of which is left to the liberality of the visiters.

Weeks' Exhibition,

202 Piccadilly,

Is a singular collection of mechanical curiosities.

Exhibition of Ancient Arms and Armour,

3 Lower Grosvenor-street.

This is a valuable and curious collection of Arms and Armour, belonging to Mr. Pratt of Bond-street, and various noblemen and gentlemen who lend curious specimens for the use of artists, and for the purpose of exhibition: most of the specimens are for sale. Among the most remarkable objects may be mentioned a group of cavaliers in plate-armour, intended to portray a council of the time of James the First; a suit of armour said to have belonged to the Maid of Orleans; a suit of polished tilting-armour, which, with many of the other specimens, was taken from the collection of the Duc de Ferrara. Various suits of plate and chain-armour, of the time of the Crusades; a jazarine, or suit of concealed armour, said to have belonged to Henry VIII.; Moorish chain-armour worn by one of the kings of Granada; a variety of ancient swords, banners, maces, helmets, &c.; and a curious collection of guns, from the ancient matlock to the modern rifle. Open all day; admission 1*s.*; catalogue 1*s.* 6*d.*

THE POLYTECHNIC INSTITUTION,

309 Regent-street.

The objects of this truly valuable institution are "the advancement of practical science in connexion with agriculture, the arts, and manufactures; and the demonstration, by the most simple and interesting methods of illustration, of those principles upon which every science is based, and the processes employed in the most useful arts and manufactures affected."

The entrance hall, 45 feet by 40, contains the following objects of interest:—a printing establishment, an optician's, a glass-worker's, a revolving steam-engine, power-looms, and a turner's shop. Beyond this is the great hall, 120 feet by 40. Occupying the centre of the floor is the canal or reservoir, displaying the appurtenances of a dock-yard, &c. At one end is a pool of considerable depth, above which is suspended a diving-bell, weighing three tons, capable of containing four persons, a charge of 1*s.* extra being made for a personal experiment. The pool can be emptied in less than one minute. Before the diving-bell practice, at about 11 o'clock, a diver proceeds to shew the mode of raising sunken vessels, and remains under water for 20 minutes.

Above the entrance-hall is the theatre, capable of containing 500 persons. The wonders of the hydro-oxygen microscope are exhibited on the largest disc yet formed.

National Gallery of Practical Science,
Lowther Arcade,

Is a noble gallery, lighted by circular skylights, devoted to models and designs of inventions and improvements in the various branches of science. In the centre is a canal, on which are models of steam-boats; a steam-gun on a small scale is exhibited, which discharges 75 shots a-second. The saloon is surrounded by galleries, where are exhibited various objects of fine art or of science. Lectures are delivered at two o'clock every day by celebrated professors. Admission 1*s.*

The Apollonicon,
101 St. Martin's-lane,

Is a grand mechanical musical instrument, invented and constructed by Messrs. Robson and Son, under the patronage of King George IV. By its mechanical or self-acting powers, it is capable of performing any piece of music which may be arranged on it, with a grandeur and precision unequalled by any orchestra of the most scientific performers. Any piece of music may likewise be played on it by one or six performers at the same time.

This exhibition is open daily from 1 to 4; and an eminent professor is engaged to play on Saturdays during the winter-season. There are sometimes evening performances, which are advertised in the daily journals. Admission in the day 1*s.*

BAZAARS, &c.

Soho Bazaar, Soho-square, an establishment for the sale of light goods, formed by the late Mr. Trotter in 1815. It consists of several rooms hung with red cloth, and fitted up with mahogany counters, divided into stands, which are occupied by upwards of 200 females. The nature of the mart, and the variety of goods exhibited, daily attract numerous visiters, and render it quite a fashionable lounge.

The Pantheon, Oxford-street.—This bazaar unites the usual advantages of a mart for fancy goods, and exhibition-rooms for the display of works of art. There is a good collection of pictures, ancient and modern, which are placed here for sale.

QUEEN'S BAZAAR, now theatre, Oxford-street, similar in intention to the preceding, though not of the same extent. There are rooms on the upper floor for various exhibitions, one of which is devoted to dioramic effects. The first building was destroyed by fire in 1829.

ST. JAMES'S BAZAAR, St. James's-street.—This bazaar was erected in 1832, by Mr. Crockford. It consists of two spacious halls on the ground and first floors. The exterior presents in its lateral elevation an imposing line.

WESTERN EXCHANGE, Bond-street, similar to the preceding.

Many individual speculations on a smaller scale have been dignified by the name of bazaars.

ARCADES, &c.

BURLINGTON ARCADE,
Piccadilly,

Is a covered avenue, 210 yards long, containing 72 shops, erected in 1819, on the west side of Burlington-house. It extends from Piccadilly to Burlington-gardens, and has a triplicated entrance at each end. This novel building is much frequented, and is rendered particularly attractive by its seclusion from the heat and inclemency of the weather, as well as by the care of its inhabitants, who have appointed two porters to keep out improper visiters.

LOWTHER ARCADE.

This beautiful arcade, built by Mr. Herbert, is 245 feet long, 20 feet broad, and 35 feet high, and consists of 25 small but elegant shops. At the end towards St. Martin's Church is the National Gallery of Practical Science.

MAGAZINES, &c.

In our former editions we ventured to enumerate the various periodicals which issued from the London press; a task of no great difficulty when the candidates were few, and their claims on stability confirmed. The case is now altered; each week gives birth to a fresh "impartial organ" of some sect or other, political, literary, or religious, and beholds also the extinction of some work which in its latest agonies proclaimed its "increasing circulation." To avoid the discrepancy which must necessarily exist in such a shifting scene between our list and the actual state of the literary market, we subjoin but a few, refraining from offering any remarks on the variety of principle to be traced in the various magazines, since the tenets of each occasionally vary to suit the circumstances of the times.

The following are the principal:—

Blackwood's Magazine, Edinburgh Review, Quarterly Review, Church of England Quarterly, Westminster Review, Fraser's Magazine, Monthly Review, British Critic or Quarterly Theological Review, Eclectic Review, Foreign Quarterly Review, Monthly Magazine, New Monthly Magazine, Gentleman's Magazine, Metropolitan Magazine, Church of England Magazine, Monthly Chronicle, Bentley's Miscellany, British Magazine, United Service Journal, Court Magazine, Asiatic Journal, Botanical Magazine, Medical Quarterly Review, Edinburgh Philosophical Journal, &c. &c.

The Athenæum and the Literary Gazette are the two principal weekly literary and artistic journals. The Penny and Saturday Magazines, and a variety of works of a similar price, have inundated the minor channels of literature: an honourable place must, however, be assigned to the Mirror, which has manfully and successfully stood its ground amidst the most determined competition.

It is to be regretted that this increased vitality in the minute organs of information should have degenerated, in too many instances, into a liveliness which assails the innocent, and a vigour which destroys the weak; the conscientious partizan has been greatly superseded by the hireling slanderer; principles are sacrificed, and interests are betrayed; the once-respected bulwarks of public honour and private worth are shamelessly overthrown; and the taint of malignant scurrility (the sure herald of the decay of manly virtue) is rapidly invading our national taste.

ANNUALS.

This elegant class of publications was introduced from Germany only a few years ago; the first, entitled the "Forget

Me Not," having been published by Ackermann in 1823. It has since become so popular that each year ushers new candidates into the arena of taste. They make their appearance about November, so as to be available as Christmas presents. They consist of tales, essays, and minor poems, of eminent writers, are illustrated with plates engraved in the very first style of the art, and done up in an elegant form. They vary in price from *7s. 6d.* to *2l. 12s. 6d.*

THE NEWSPAPER PRESS.

> "The folio of four pages, happy work!
> Which not even critics criticise; that holds
> Inquisitive attention . . . .
> Fast bound in chains of silence, which the Fair,
> Though eloquent themselves, yet fear to break;
> What is it but a map of busy life,
> Its fluctuations, and its vast concerns?"

THE DIURNAL PRESS is a mighty political engine, and is no where exercised with so much liberty as in this country. *Junius*, with his peculiar force, observes that "they who conceive that our newspapers are no restraint upon bad men, or impediment to the execution of bad measures, know nothing of this country." In the list of those national privileges which distinguish Britain from all other countries, that which is derived from an extended and free press, and particularly from daily and other papers, is the most prominent. On this theatre of exhibition, the aggregate population of the country, as well as the lesser masses in their corporate and other capacities, and even insulated individuals, possess the power of stating their sentiments—of displaying important information—of giving wise counsel—of expressing their patriotic anxiety concerning any pending measure affecting the common weal—and of unmasking the designs of foreign or domestic foes, whether the latter be found in the higher or lower orders of society. The enlightened Englishman, the man who loves the constitution of his country, and rightly estimates its genuine principles, will ever lend his aid to preserve this invaluable privilege from the violations of power on the one hand, and the equally injurious outrages of popular licentiousness on the other.

In the present day the English newspapers have extended their circulation and influence through every rank and order of the state; they have generated a new era in the public mind;—have placed political, moral, scientific, and commercial information within the reach of understandings hitherto uncultivated;—and have rendered the great mass of Englishmen respectable for the possession of knowledge unparalleled in any former state of this island.

The first *Newspaper* that ever appeared was printed in England in 1588. It was called "*The English Mercurie,*" and was published about twice a-week, in Elizabeth's reign, when the famed Spanish Armada threatened our shores. No. 50 of the paper, which is now in existence, constituting No. 4106 of Sloane's collection, gives a formal account of the introduction of a *Scotch ambassador* to queen Elizabeth! Thus it appears that newspapers arose soon after the introduction of printing; and scarcely a century elapsed before the diurnal press assumed a settled and decisive character.

The FREEDOM OF THE PRESS, however, was not gained without long and fearful struggles; for Henry VIII., Elizabeth, and Charles II., were particularly inimical to it; and it was not till four years after that "glorious Revolution" which seated William III. on our throne, that the basis of the liberty of the press was firmly laid, by the parliament *refusing* any longer to continue those *restrictions* which had previously been imposed on it.

NEWSPAPER ESTABLISHMENTS are now of great importance. The number of Newspapers published in London is 71; and the number of stamps used in one year (1837) was 29,172,797, the duty upon which was 121,553*l.* The number of copies of the morning journals daily put in circulation is about 32,000; and of evening journals about 13,000.

Of the Sunday papers not fewer than 150,000 copies are circulated. Besides these are papers published once, twice, and three times a-week. The total number of copies of newspapers printed in Great Britain during the year is about 53,496,207.

In 1833 the stamp-duties upon advertisements were lowered from 3*s.* 6*d.* to 1*s.* 6*d.*; and in 1837 the paper-stamp was lowered from 4*d.* to 1*d.*

The morning papers have their editors and sub-editors, the salaries of the former varying from 600*l.* to 1000*l.*, and those of the latter from 400*l.* to 600*l.* The editor's duty is to write what are called the leading articles of the paper, and to sustain its political tone. The sub-editor's office is to look over and control all the other departments; to investigate the reports and other articles of intelligence, to bring them within proper limits, and to protect the journal from improper or ill-written articles. Each morning paper employs collectors of foreign news in the city and on the Royal Exchange; translators of foreign journals and books; and from six to twelve parliamentary and law reporters. They receive 200*l.* and 300*l.* a-year each. In addition to these, are persons who collect paragraphs of police and other news for all the papers, and receive an allowance for as much as happens to be inserted.—The evening papers generally copy their reports, &c. from the morning papers, and therefore are only at the expense of an editor and a translator, besides collectors of city and foreign news, journals, &c.

The morning papers engage about twenty compositors, besides boys and pressmen, though most of them are now worked by machine; and the evening papers and weekly journals employ a proportionate number. Thus the expense of the composition of a newspaper, in procuring intelligence, in employing writers, compositors, pressmen, &c., is immense—in some instances as much as 400*l.* and 500*l.* a-week; besides the expenditure for house-room, type, clerks, &c., and the *stamp duty.* The machinery of the Times-office is the most extensive in London.

The *News-Exchange*, or *Newsmen's Hall*, where, every morning and evening, the London journals are divided amongst hundreds of venders, is situated in Black-horse-court, Fleet-street.

The impossibility of giving an accurate list of the newspapers is still more apparent than in the instance of the magazines: were we to attempt a classification of the ephemera which rise above the literary horizon to sink as quickly beneath it, we should be found guilty, at the end of a few months, of recording facts unimportant and forgotten. We therefore subjoin but a few of the principal:—

The Times, The Morning Chronicle, The Morning Herald, The Morning Post, The Standard, The Courier, The Globe, The Sun, The Examiner, Bell's Messenger, The Atlas, The Spectator, John Bull, The Age, The Weekly Dispatch, The Observer, The London Gazette, The Court Journal, Metropolitan, Conservative Journal, The Sunday Times, The News, Bent's List, Publishers' Circular, &c. &c.

The prices vary; but 5*d.* is the usual price for the daily, and from 4*d*. to 10*d*. for the Sunday papers. The charge for reading is, from a newsvender, 1½*d*. an hour.

All the newspapers may be seen at Deacon's Coffee-house, Walbrook; Peel's Coffee-house, Fleet-street; or the Chapter Coffee-house, Paternoster-row.

CHAPTER XI.

AMUSEMENTS OF THE METROPOLIS: ITALIAN OPERA; ROYAL THEATRES; ORATORIOS; MINOR THEATRES; VAUXHALL; CONCERTS; PROMENADES; &c. &c.

CONSIDERING the vast extent and wealth of the British capital, it might be expected that it should possess an ample fund of amusement for its enormous population. This, in truth, it does—the theatre of course holding the first rank. The English stage is conspicuous as having produced some of the most able writers and the best actors ever seen in the world.

THE QUEEN'S THEATRE, OR ITALIAN OPERA-HOUSE, Haymarket,

Is the most fashionable place of amusement in the British metropolis, having been erected to gratify the increasing taste of the public for exquisite music and elegant dancing. The performances consist of Italian and German operas and ballets, and the performers are the most celebrated from the Italian, German, and French stages. The original building is generally supposed to have been constructed by sir John Vanbrugh, though Mr. Pennant attributes it to sir C. Wren. It was burnt down in 1790, and shortly after rebuilt on an improved plan, though the exterior was not erected in its present style till 1818, from designs by Mr. Nash. It is now a handsome edifice, cased with stucco, and adorned with an elegant colonnade supported by cast-iron pillars of the Doric order. The front is decorated with a relievo, executed by Mr. Bubb in 1821, representing the Origin and Progress of Music. The interior is magnificent, and is nearly as large as the theatre of La Scala, at Milan. The stage, within the walls, is 60 feet long and 80 broad; and the space across from the boxes on each side 46 feet. Each box is enclosed by curtains, according to the fashion of the Neapolitan theatres, and is furnished with six chairs. There are five tiers of boxes, all of which are private property, or are let out for the season to persons of rank and fashion. The boxes will accommodate about 900 persons, the pit 800, and the gallery 800.

The grand concert-room, which is fitted up in the most elegant manner, is 95 feet long, 46 broad, and 35 high. The Opera usually opens for the season in January, and continues its performances on Tuesdays and Saturdays till August.

Price of Admission.—Pit, 10*s.* 6*d.*; Stalls, 14*s.* 6*d.*; Gallery, 5*s.*; Upper Gallery, 3*s.*—Performance commences at half-past seven o'clock.

DRURY-LANE THEATRE,

Brydges-street,

Derives its origin from a cock-pit near this spot, which was converted into a theatre in the time of James I., in whose reign it was pulled down and rebuilt under the appellation of the Phœnix. After the restoration, the king granted a patent for stage-performances to Thomas Killigrew, who in 1662 erected a new theatre on the site of the present edifice. The actors were the king's servants; and ten of them, who were called gentlemen of the great chamber, had an annual allowance of ten yards of scarlet cloth, with a suitable quantity of lace: hence the performers at this house are styled "her majesty's servants." Killigrew's theatre was burnt down in 1671, but rebuilt by sir C. Wren, and continued standing till 1793, when it was replaced by a very large house, erected from designs by Holland. This, however, fell a prey to the flames, February 24th, 1809; and the present heavy though substantial edifice was construced in 1811 by B. Wyatt, esq. The front is of the Doric order; and the portico, surmounted by a statue of Shakspeare, was added in 1820. An *Ionic* colonnade was injudiciously added a few years since. The grand entrance leads through a spacious hall supported by five Doric columns, to an elegant rotunda, whence staircases ascend to the boxes. The interior of the house, which was entirely rebuilt in 1822 by Mr. Peto, under the direction of Mr. Samuel Beazley, presents about three-quarters of a circle from the stage, and has a splendid, though not gaudy appearance. It is principally illumined by an elegant gas chandelier, which hangs over the centre of the pit. The stage at the

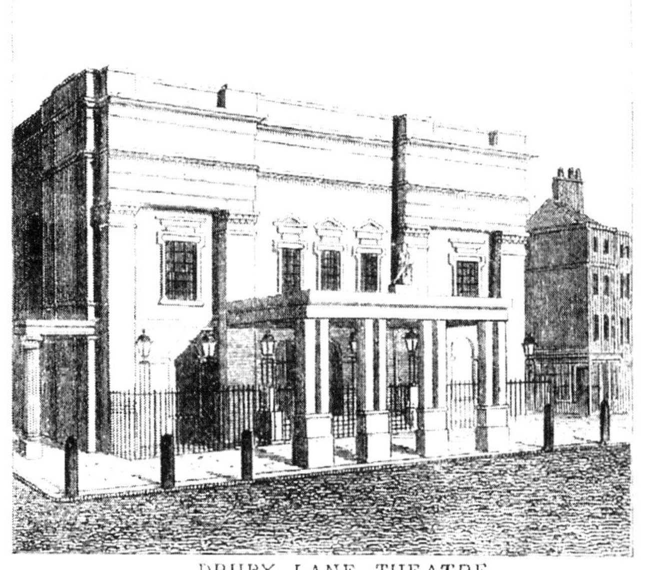

DRURY LANE THEATRE.

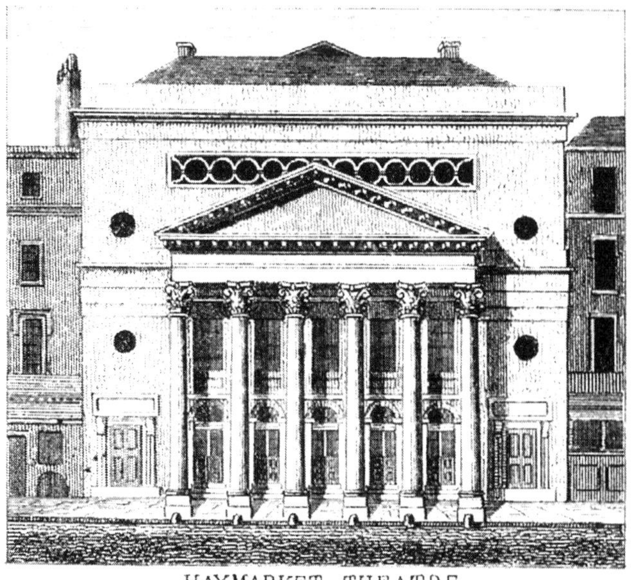

HAYMARKET THEATRE.

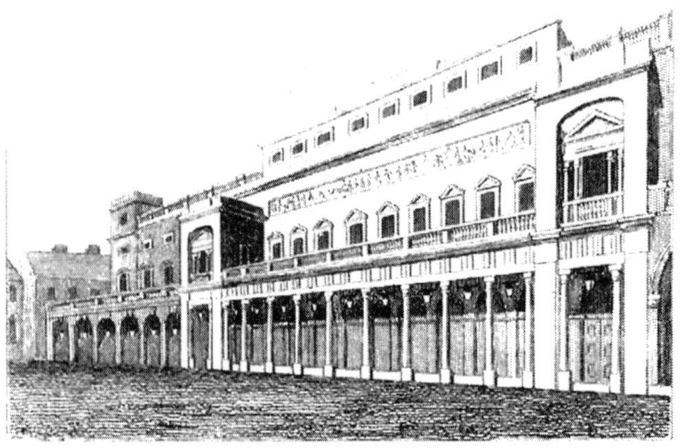

OPERA HOUSE.

COVENT GARDEN THEATRE.

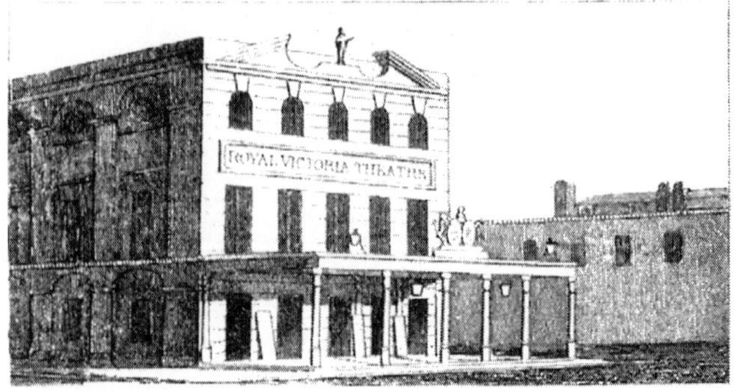

VICTORIA THEATRE.

opening of the curtain is 43 feet in width, and 38 in height; the diameter of the pit is 53 feet, and the height of the house from the pit-floor to the ceiling is 50 feet 6 inches. There are three tiers of boxes, the first and second each containing 29, and eleven back boxes. In the space on each side of the lower gallery, above the third tier, are nine boxes on each side; and on a level with the pit are eight private boxes. It is estimated that the house will accommodate 3611 persons with seats; the boxes containing 1828, the pit 800, the lower gallery 675, and the upper gallery 308. The grand saloon is an elegant room about 86 feet in length.

The national drama is not strictly adhered to at this house; the splendour of spectacle, the fascinations of opera, and the wonders of ballet, have been displayed with a lavish expenditure.

Oratorios and selections of miscellaneous music are performed at this theatre and at that of Covent-garden, on the Wednesday and Friday evenings during Lent. There is generally an oratorio also on the 30th of January, and on Whitsun-eve.

Price of Admission.—Boxes, 5*s.*; Pit, 3*s.*; Lower Gallery, 2*s.*; Upper Gallery, 1*s.*—The performance commences at seven o'clock.

Covent-Garden Theatre,

Bow-street,

Is indebted for its origin to a patent granted in 1662 to Sir W. Davenant, whose company was denominated the Duke's Servants, as a compliment to the Duke of York, afterwards James II. The theatre which preceded the present was first opened by the celebrated Rich, about 1732; but after undergoing several alterations, was destroyed by fire September 20, 1808. The new theatre was erected during the ensuing year, and opened September 18, 1809, with *Macbeth.* It is on an extensive scale; and the management was formerly vested in John Kemble, who made many improvements and reforms in the internal economy, science, and costume of dramas.

This great ornament of the metropolis is nearly of a square form, and is insulated. The architect, Mr. Smirke, jun., took for his model the finest specimen of the Doric from the ruins of Athens—the grand temple of Minerva, situated in the Acropolis. The principal front exhibits a portico, which, though magnificent, is greatly inferior to the Athenian original; it is embellished with statues of Tragedy and Comedy by Flaxman, and with two bassi-relievi representing the ancient and modern drama. The following description will enable the spectator to distinguish the various figures :—

The *Ancient Drama* (that towards Hart-street).—In the centre, three Greek poets are sitting: the two looking towards the portico represent Aristophanes, as Old Comedy, and Menander, as New Comedy; before whom appear Thalia with her crook and comic mask; Polyhymnia playing on the great lyre, Euterpe on the less, Clio with the pipes, and Terpsichore as the muse of action; followed by the Hours or Seasons attendant on Pegasus. The third figure, sitting in the centre, represents Æschylus, the father of tragedy, holding a scroll on his knee, and looking at Minerva, who is seated opposite. Between Æschylus and Minerva, Bacchus stands leaning on a faun, and behind Minerva appears Melpomene, or Tragedy, holding a sword and mask; then follow two Furies pursuing Orestes, who supplicates protection from Apollo, who is represented in the four-horse chariot of the Sun. The *Modern Drama*.—The centre figure, looking from the portico, represents Shakspeare seated, and calling before him the following characters in the Tempest: Caliban, laden with wood, Ferdinand sheathing his sword, Miranda entreating Prospero, and Ariel playing on a lyre. This part is terminated by Hecate in her car, attended by lady Macbeth, and Macbeth, who is turning with horror from the body of Duncan lying behind him. In the centre, looking towards the portico, is seated Milton contemplating Urania. At his feet appears Samson Agonistes chained. The other figures represent the mask of Comus: the two Brothers appear driving out three Bacchanals, with their leader Comus, and the Enchanted Lady is seen seated in the chair. The group is terminated by two tigers, in reference to the transformation of Comus's devotees.

The interior of the theatre is elegant, and larger than the old house. The staircase is adorned with Ionic columns, between which are suspended Grecian lamps; and at the head of it is an ante-room, containing a statue of Shakspeare by Rossi. The fronts of the boxes are appropriately ornamented with the national emblems, the rose, the thistle, and the shamrock. The stage is very spacious, and there are three circles of boxes, one gallery, and an extensive pit. The house is illuminated by a superb chandelier hanging from the centre of the roof. This theatre is calculated to hold upwards of 3000 persons. It is now under the admirable management of the talented Mr. Charles Mathews (son of the celebrated comedian) and his gifted wife, the accomplished and indefatigable Madame Vestris, whose united and zealous endeavours to rescue the legitimate drama from neglect, have hitherto been attended with great success; and it has now become, for the selection of the performances, the ability of the corps dramatique, the beauty of the scenery, the propriety of costume, and the minutiæ of stage arrangements, the most perfect establishment in the British dominions. Foreigners and strangers visiting the metropolis, desirous of knowing the present state of the national drama, should not fail to visit this theatre.

The company it would be useless to detail, as the perpetual removals and accessions, at this as well as at the other theatres, would soon render such accounts imperfect.

Price of Admission.—Boxes, 5*s.*; Pit, 3*s.*; Gallery, 1*s.*—The performance commences at seven o'clock.

THE HAYMARKET THEATRE

Was opened for the first time in 1821. It is situated, as its name imports, in the Haymarket, almost on the site of the original building, which was erected in 1702. The designs for this elegant and commodious building were made by Mr. Nash. The front is ornamented with a lofty portico, supported by six columns of the Corinthian order, over which are nine circular windows, connected together by rich sculpture. The interior is smaller than any of the regular theatres. It contains two tiers of boxes, besides two rows of side boxes. This theatre is licensed to exhibit regular dramas during the summer. It has been for several seasons under the spirited management of Mr. Webster, supported by Mr. Macready.

Price of Admission.—Boxes, 5*s.*; Pit, 3*s.*; Lower Gallery, 2*s.*; Upper Gallery, 1*s.*—Performance commences at seven. There is no half-price at this theatre.

ENGLISH OPERA-HOUSE, OR LYCEUM,

North Wellington-street.

The old theatre was entirely destroyed by fire, February 16, 1830. The new building, erected from designs by Mr. Beazley, was opened in 1834; it has two tiers of boxes, and a gallery, and is lighted by a magnificent chandelier, which cost 650*l.* The front of the theatre towards Wellington-street is formed by an elegant portico of six Corinthian columns. The pit-entrance only is in the Strand.

Price of Admission.—Boxes, 4*s.*; Pit, 2*s.*; Gallery, 1*s.*—The performance commences at seven o'clock.

Promenade Concerts, *à la Musard*, with a full and select orchestra, have been successfully given during several seasons, to which the price of admission is only 1*s.*

St. James's Theatre,

King-street, St. James's.

This elegant theatre was erected for Mr. Braham, from designs by Beazley, and somewhat resembles the theatre in the palace at Versailles. The interior is elegantly fitted up, from designs by Messrs. Crace, with white and gold decorations. It has two tiers of boxes, besides galleries and slips.

This theatre is occasionally occupied by the French and German companies.

Price of Admission.—Boxes, 5*s.*; Pit, 3*s.*; Gallery, 2*s.*

The Royal Circus, or Surrey Theatre,

Blackfriars-road,

Was originally devoted to the exhibition of equestrian performances, under the direction of Mr. Hughes; but being burnt down in 1805, it was rebuilt in its present tasteful form, and the equestrian circle occupied by a spacious and convenient pit; horses being only occasionally introduced on the stage. The theatre afterwards fell into the hands of Mr. Elliston, who introduced ballets, melo-dramas, &c., a style of performance which is still continued here, and which seldom fails to attract good audiences. It is now under the control of Mr. Davidge and his partner.

Price of Admission.—Boxes, 2*s.*; Pit, 1*s.*; Gallery, 6*d.*—The performance commences at half-past six o'clock.

The Royal Victoria Theatre,

Waterloo Bridge-road,

Was commenced in 1816, the first stone having been laid by Alderman Goodbehere, as proxy for the Prince and Princess of Saxe-Coburg, according to an inscription at the corner of the building. It was opened in 1818. It is of an oblong form, and is admirably adapted for dramatic representations, the stage being very extensive, and every part of the house so constructed as to afford a good view of it. There are two tiers of boxes, and the lower is connected with a small saloon containing some fine marine paintings, as well as excellent likenesses of the Prince and Princess of Saxe-Coburg.

After the panic in the two national theatres, during the disastrous season of 1833, some of the principal actors enlisted under the banners of Messrs. Abbot and Egerton, and performed for some time at this house. It is now conducted by Mr. Osbaldiston.

Price of Admission.—Boxes, 2*s.*; Pit, 1*s.*; Gallery, 6*d.*—The performance commences at half-past six.

Sadler's Wells,

St. John-street-road,

Is so called from the wells formerly situated here, and from the name of the person by whom a summer theatre was first opened on this spot in 1683. It is appropriated to the performance of pantomimes, burlettas, spectacles, dancing, &c. A few years ago it was famous for its aquatic exhibitions, the whole space beneath the stage being filled with water, and allowing a display very different from that of other theatres.

Price of Admission.—Boxes, 2*s.*; Pit, 1*s.*; Gallery, 6*d.*

The Royal Amphitheatre, late Astley's,

Westminster-Bridge-road,

Is a summer theatre, where pantomimes, burlettas, and unrivalled feats of horsemanship, rope-dancing, &c., are exhibited. It was first established about 1767, as an open riding-school, but in 1780 was covered in, and formed into a regular theatre. It has been since thrice destroyed by fire—in 1794 and 1803; was rebuilt, and one of the best frequented theatres in London, managed by the far-famed Ducrow; it was again burnt down 8th June, 1841, and is now rebuilding; it generally commenced its season on Easter-Monday, and closed in October.

Price of Admission.—Boxes, 4*s.*; Pit, 2*s.*; Gallery, 1*s.*—The performance commences at half-past six o'clock.

The Royal Adelphi Theatre,

Strand,

Is open during the winter, for the performance of burlettas, pantomimes, and dancing. It was formerly called the "Sans Pareil," and was at that time the property of Mr. and Miss Scott; but in 1820 it changed its proprietors, and the performances were very much improved. In 1828 it became the property of Messrs. Mathews and Yates, and subsequently of Messrs. Yates and Gladstanes. The whole management devolves upon that versatile actor Yates, who has contrived with a small stage to produce scenic illusions superior to any other theatre. The transformation in 1840 of the unmeaning front to the present elegant façade, was unprecedented for celerity. Being only a narrow upright slip of building, its architectural appearance is remarkably striking; and though it may not be perfectly correct in principle, the design possesses great character. When illuminated, the corridor has a splendid effect, which must be seen to be appreciated.

Price of Admission.—Boxes, 4*s.*; Pit, 2*s.*; Gallery, 1*s.*

The Olympic Theatre,

Wych-street,

Was erected in 1806 by the late Mr. Astley, for the exhibition of equestrian performances and rope-dancing; but it was afterwards sold to Mr. Elliston, by whom the interior was much improved. It subsequently passed into the hands of Madame Vestris, and is now used for the performance of vaudevilles.

Price of Admission.—Boxes, 4*s.*; Pit, 2*s.*; Gallery, 1*s.*

The Princess's Theatre,

Formerly the Queen's Bazaar, in Oxford-street.

After being shut up for some time, it was re-opened in the autumn of 1840 for promenade concerts. It somewhat resembles the St. James's, but is of loftier proportions, and the general effect is much richer.

Strand Theatre,

Near Somerset-House.

Farces, burlettas, travesties, &c.

Price of Admission.—Boxes, 4*s.*; Pit, 2*s.*; Gallery, 1*s.*

City of London Theatre,

Norton-falgate.

Burlettas, farces, &c.—Boxes, 2*s.*; Pit, 1*s.*; Gallery, 6*d.*

Royal Fitzroy Theatre, late The Queen's,

Tottenham-street, Tottenham-court-road.

Burlettas, farces, &c. Formerly the Regency Theatre.

Price of Admission.—Boxes, 4*s.*; Pit, 2*s.*; Gallery, 1*s.*

The Royal Clarence Theatre, or Panarmonion,

Liverpool street, Battle-bridge.

Price of Admission.—Boxes, 2*s.*; Pit, 1*s.*; Gallery, 6*d.*

London-Bridge Theatre.

Price of Admission.—Boxes, 2*s.*; Pit, 1*s.*; Gallery, 6*d.*

City Theatre,

Milton-street.

Price of Admission.—Boxes, 2*s.*; Pit, 1*s.*; Gallery, 6*d.*

GARRICK THEATRE,

Leman-street, Goodman's-fields.

Price of Admission.—Boxes. 2*s.*; Pit, 1*s.*; Gallery, 6*d.*

DUCROW'S OLYMPIC CIRCLE,

Whitechapel.

There are also small theatres at Whitechapel and in Catherine-street. Entertainments are also given at Saville-house.

VAUXHALL GARDENS.

This celebrated place of summer resort is situated near the Thames, in the parish of Lambeth, about 1½ miles from Westminster-bridge. It is denominated from the manor of Vauxhall, or Faukeshall; but the tradition that this house, or any other adjacent, was the property of Guy Fawkes, is erroneous. The premises were in 1615 the property of Jane Vaux, and the mansion-house was then called Stockdens. From her it passed through various hands, till, in 1752, it became the property of Jonathan Tyers, esq. There is no certain account of the time when these premises were first opened for the entertainment of the public; but the Spring Gardens at Vauxhall are mentioned in the "Spectator" as a place of great resort.

These gardens are now beautiful and extensive, and contain a variety of walks; when open for public amusement, they are illuminated with variegated lamps, and embellished with transparent devices. Nearly facing the west door is an orchestra, and opposite to it is a pavilion of the Composite order.

The different boxes and apartments of these gardens are adorned with paintings, many of which were executed by Hogarth and Hayman. The latter has chosen his subjects from Shakspeare. The musical performance is in a great room, or rotunda, 70 feet in diameter. Beyond is a piazza of five arches, which open in a semicircle, with a temple and dome at each end; in the centre is a grand portico of the Doric order.

The entertainments keep the company engaged every night but Saturday till after eleven o'clock; and the parties who sup are well supplied and accommodated in the boxes, whilst others dance to the light music played by small bands in various parts of the gardens.

Vauxhall Gardens generally open in May and close at the end of August. The doors are opened at seven, the concert begins at eight, and the fire-works at ten or eleven o'clock. During the entertainments about 400 persons are engaged, nearly 100 of whom are vocal and instrumental performers.

Fêtes, flower-shows, &c. often take place here in the day-time: they are always advertised.

Admission, 1*s*.

ALMACK'S BALLS,

Which are held every Wednesday during the season at Willis's-rooms, King-street, St. James's-square, are very numerously and fashionably attended. Several ladies of distinction are styled lady-patronesses, and in order to render the balls more select (the price of the tickets being only 7*s*.), it is necessary that a visiter's name should be inserted in one of these ladies' books, which of course makes the admission difficult. Other balls are occasionally given at Willis's-rooms, but they have no connexion with Almack's.

ARGYLE ROOMS,

Regent-street.

This rendezvous of fashion was, a few years since, a private residence, which was purchased by colonel Greville, and converted into a place of entertainment, frequented only by the upper classes of society. In 1818 it was rebuilt from designs by Mr. Nash, and contained a splendid suite of rooms for concerts, exhibitions, &c. The whole was burnt down in February 1830, and there is at present but a small concert-room.

NEW ROOMS, HANOVER-SQUARE,

Are a handsome suite of apartments, fitted up in a most splendid style, and let out for the performance of concerts, &c. The usual price of tickets for the concerts is 10*s*. 6*d*.

BALLS, CONCERTS, AND MASQUERADES.

No metropolis boasts of more amusements than London, when the veil which ordinarily hides them from the casual observer is drawn aside. During the season scarcely a day passes without two or three morning or evening concerts, and balls are to be found in as great profusion. To prevent the introduction of improper company, a little form is observed in the management of the latter. He who possesses means and inclination to launch into gaiety, will find in this vast metropolis ample opportunity for ruining his constitution and his purse.

Balls and concerts are also frequently held at Willis's-rooms, King-street, St. James's-square; Freemasons'-hall, Great Queen-street; Crown and Anchor, Strand; City of London-tavern, Bishopsgate-street; Albion, Aldersgate-street; Horns, Kennington.

Masquerades take place at the Opera House; at the Lyceum; at the Lowther-rooms, King William-street, Strand; and at the Eagle-tavern, City-road. An imitation of Musard's Promenade Concerts was attempted at the Lyceum in 1838, admission 1s.; and will, it is to be hoped, be crowned with success.

CONVERSAZIONI.

These agreeable meetings have of late years become very general, and the professors of the liberal arts especially have now an opportunity of becoming more acquainted with their brethren and their works. Among the principal artistic meetings are:—

The Graphic Society, Thatched-house.

Artists' Conversazione, Freemasons' Tavern.

Ditto, London Coffee-house.

Scientific Conversazione, National Gallery of Science.

The Soirées at the British Institution, Royal Institution, Society of Arts, &c.

PROMENADES.

The promenades of the metropolis are numerous as well as pleasant. For a description of the principal, the reader is referred to the following articles:—Hyde Park, Kensington Palace, the Green Park, Inner Temple, Gray's Inn, Waterloo Bridge, St. James's Park, Tower of London. Bond-street, St. James's-street, Pall-mall, Regent-street, and the Regent's Park, are likewise very much frequented as promenades.

FASHIONABLE PARTIES.

The social meetings of the fashionable world consist of balls, musical parties, and routs. The latter appear to be formed on the model of the Italian conversazioni, except that they are in general so crowded as entirely to preclude conversation. Cards upon these occasions are usually provided for the senior part of the company.

The expense of these entertainments depends entirely on the species of amusement which is provided. If balls are given the expense is considerable, as it is usual to give a supper to the company; and at some seasons fruit is necessarily very scarce and of high price. These repasts are generally provided by some confectioner of repute at a stipulated sum, who also provides chairs, plates, and glasses.

The time for assembling is generally from ten to twelve o'clock, or even later, as many persons visit several of these places in one evening. The hours of departure are various and uncertain; but from balls it is sometimes six or seven o'clock in the morning before the whole have separated.

The Sporting World.

The sports of the metropolis have not only found a conspicuous place in the researches of our early writers, but in the present day supply many of our modern periodicals with "columnar variety," in all the peculiar phraseology of the lower arts and sciences. The mock battles in Lent, when "young men, being greedy of honour and desirous of victory, did thus exercise themselves in counterfeit battles, that they might bear the brunt more strongly when they came to it in good earnest"—the Easter sea-jousting—and the fierce hunts, when "foaming boars fought for their heads, or else lusty bulls and huge bears were baited with dogs,"—have all subsided into less exciting games; and the far-famed religious representations have dwindled into decorous oratorios.

The Hippodrome,

Notting-hill.

This extensive undertaking was, after much opposition, sanctioned by parliament in 1838, for the purpose of horse-racing and other sports. It consists of an enclosure about two miles in circumference, and is well laid out.

Amongst the most prominent sports peculiar to England are *Horse-racing*, *Prize-fighting*, *Cock-fighting*, &c. On our race-courses may be seen some of the finest animals that art can rear or money purchase; and the noble and the "black-leg" may be found there interesting themselves in the result of the day's sports. Cups, plate, &c. are allotted to be run for at the several races, but the betting forms the prominent feature; and the settling of the bets takes place at Tattersall's Repository, Hyde-park-corner, which then presents as curious a scene as can well be imagined.

Boxing is peculiar to England, and is defended by many as calculated to maintain the British character and spirit. In Alfred's time wrestling and boxing constituted part of the sports; but pugilism has not been practised as an art more than a hundred years. In 1791 it was in such high repute, that *Dan Mendoza* opened the Lyceum in the Strand for public exhibitions of sparring. Since that period boxing has become a complete system, as there are regular prize-fighters who contend for a purse made up by the lovers of the sport. On these occasions a large ring is formed on some common, round which a motley group of lords, gentry, and plebeians, assemble to witness the contest.

Sparring, which is boxing in gloves, takes place at the Tennis-court, Windmill-street, Haymarket. The exhibitions are previously advertised, and the price of admission is generally 3*s*.

Cock-fighting, though a barbarous sport, is much encouraged. Till within a few years there was a *Cock-pit Royal* in St. James's-park; but as the ground belonged to Christ's Hospital, that body would not renew the lease for a building devoted to cruelty. A more commodious cock-pit has since been built in Tufton-street, Westminster; where also dog-fights take place, and badgers and bears are baited. Visiters are made to pay for entrance, and it is advertised in the newspapers when these fights are to take place.

Pigeon-shooting has also its votaries; and near the Red-house at Battersea is an establishment expressly intended for the lovers of this sport.

Archery. The principal societies for the pursuit of this delightful amusement are the *Toxophylite Society*, Regent's-park; *Fraternity of St. George*, Lord's Cricket-ground; *Robin Hood Society*, Archery-ground, Bayswater.

Rifle-galleries. These are in every part of London, and are much frequented.

The river Thames affords an admirable opportunity of fostering on a small scale that naval spirit which is our bulwark. *Sailing* and *Rowing Matches* are constantly taking place during the season.

BILLIARDS.

The game of Billiards has of late years become a general favourite, and numerous saloons have been opened for public accommodation. The general price is 1*s*. per hour, or 3*d*. per game.

Cigar Divans.

That habit which was noticed by Mrs. Barbauld in her early works as a fresh importation, has now become an established custom and a favourite recreation. The state of the metropolitan atmosphere may be said to have experienced a total change owing to the introduction of gas and cigars; the latter article, which was formerly the characteristic appendage of foreigners, has now become the badge of all classes.

The cigar divans are generally fitted up with great elegance, and afford an agreeable lounge for young men in public offices and the various professions. The admission is generally 1*s*., for which a cup of coffee and a cigar are obtained, and a sight of the periodicals. The principal of them are:—

The Royal Cigar Divan, Strand.
Gliddon's Cigar Divan, King-street, Covent-garden.
Royal City, St. Paul's Churchyard, &c. &c.

CHAPTER XII.

CLUB-HOUSES: GENERAL ACCOMMODATIONS: HOTELS, TAVERNS, &c.: TEA-GARDENS: HACKNEY-CARRIAGES: WHERRIES: STEAM-BOATS: BATHS, &c.

Subscription, or Club-Houses.

These establishments, which have of late years assumed a splendour unknown to the sober taste of their originators, are the resorts of political, fashionable, and literary characters, for the purposes of conversation, reading, or refreshment. Persons desirous of admission must be proposed by members and balloted for. The subscription varies according to the character of the Club, from 20 guineas to 25 guineas entrance, and from 5 to 6 guineas per annum.

The principal are:—

The Union Club-house, at Charing-cross, a noble building, erected in 1824 from designs by Smirke, containing some of the finest rooms in the metropolis.

THE UNIVERSITY CLUB-HOUSE, Suffolk-street, was built in 1824. It was designed by Messrs. J. P. Gandy and W. Wilkins, and exhibits a very tasteful combination of the Grecian, Doric, and Ionic orders; as regards the latter it is a copy of the triple Temple of Minerva Polias and Pandroseus at Athens. The staircase is particularly handsome; the walls are adorned with casts from the frieze of the Parthenon, and the light is introduced in a novel and admirable manner. The apartments, which are fitted up with elegance, comprise breakfast, coffee, and dining-rooms, a saloon, and library.

THE SENIOR UNITED SERVICE CLUB, in Pall-mall, was erected in 1828, from designs by Mr. Nash, on the site of Carlton-palace. It contains two rooms, 150 feet by 50, and is splendidly furnished.

THE JUNIOR UNITED SERVICE CLUB-HOUSE, corner of Charles-street, Regent-street, is adorned with a basso-relievo representing Britannia distributing rewards to naval and military heroes. It was built by Smirke.

CROCKFORD'S CLUB-HOUSE, St. James's-street, is devoted to play. It was built in 1827, from designs by Messrs. B. and P. Wyatt, and is a very chaste specimen of architecture. Four Corinthian pilasters, with an entablature surmounted by a balustrade and pedestals, form the front. The building consists of two principal stories; the doors and windows of the ground-floor are in the Venetian style, and the windows of the upper story in the French. The entrance-hall is divided right and left by a screen of Roman Ionic columns of verd antique scagliola marble, with capital and bases of white marble. On the right is the coffee-room, and opposite to it the library, adorned with Sienna columns and antæ of the Ionic order, taken from the Temple of Minerva Polias. Behind the library is the dining-room. A splendid staircase, paneled with scagliola of various colours, and adorned with Corinthian columns, leads to the upper rooms. These consist of an ante-room, a saloon or drawing-room, a cabinet or boudoir, and a supper-room, all adorned with curious paneling, gilding, looking-glasses, &c., in a style far surpassing description.

THE ATHENÆUM CLUB was instituted in 1824, for the association of individuals known for their scientific or literary attainments, artists of eminence in any class of the fine arts, and noblemen and gentlemen distinguished as liberal patrons of science, literature, and the arts. The club-house is situated in Pall-mall, on the site of Carlton-palace. It was erected in 1829, from designs by Mr. Decimus Burton, and cost with the furniture about 40,000*l*. It is an elegant edifice, of Grecian architecture. The frieze is an exact copy of the Panathenaic procession which formed the frieze of the Parthenon. It was executed by Mr. Henning. Over the portico is a copy of the statue of Minerva by Bailey. The house is open to the members every day, from nine o'clock in the forenoon till two in the morning.

TRAVELLERS' CLUB, 106 Pall-mall, rebuilt in 1832 by Mr. Barry, is a beautiful elevation, at once simple and imposing, the back-front presenting a Palladian design of great elegance.

THE CITY CLUB, established in 1833, occupies a handsome building erected on the site of the Old South-Sea House in Broad-street, from designs by Mr. Hardwicke, at an expense of 8000*l*.

THE LITERARY UNION, 12 Waterloo place, has lately been dissolved, and is re-modelled under the title of the CLARENCE CLUB.

ARTHUR'S CLUB-HOUSE, 69 St. James's-street, was rebuilt in 1827. The front is of stone. It presents a rusticated basement of five arches, above which are six columns of the Corinthian order, supporting an entablature, cornice, and balustrade.

ROYAL NAVAL CLUB, 160 Bond-street.

VERULAM CLUB, 35 Lincoln's-inn-fields.

ORIENTAL CLUB, Hanover-square.

ALFRED CLUB, 23 Albemarle-street.

WYNDHAM'S CLUB, 8 St. James's-square.

BROOKE'S SUBSCRIPTION-HOUSE, corner of Park-place, St. James's-street, a handsome building, ornamented with Corinthian pilasters.

BOODLE'S SUBSCRIPTION-HOUSE, 31 St. James's-street.

WHITE'S SUBSCRIPTION-HOUSE, 43 St. James's-street, is a handsome stone building.

GRAHAM'S CLUB, 87 St. James's-street.

COCOA-TREE CLUB, 65 St. James's-street.

PORTLAND CLUB, 1 Stratford-place.

CITY CONSERVATIVE, Threadneedle-street.

GUARDS' CLUB, St. James's-street.

ALBION CLUB, 85 St. James's-street.

COLONIAL CLUB, 60 St. James's-street.

ST. JAMES'S CLUB, 50 St. James's-street.

OXFORD AND CAMBRIDGE NEW UNIVERSITY CLUB, Pall-mall, is a splendid building, from designs by Mr. S. Smirke: it is adorned with some fine bassi-relievi by Nicholls.

THE REFORM CLUB, now in course of erection by Mr. Barry, will present a similar elevation to that of the adjoining club (the Travellers').

CARLTON CLUB, Pall-mall, from designs by Smirke.

WESTMINSTER CHESS-CLUB, 101 Strand.

THE WESTERN CLUB, OR CHAMBER OF COMMERCE.

CLUB-CHAMBERS are being erected in Regent-street, opposite the Carlton Hotel. This building will contain 81 rooms, exclusive of rooms for gentlemen's servants; and the house will have warm baths.

CERCLE DES ETRANGERS, Regent-street.

HOTELS, &c.

The accommodation for strangers and occasional residents in London have the same comparative excellence as those enjoyed by the inhabitants themselves. The hotels, inns, taverns, and lodging-houses, possess both convenience and cleanliness; and in all the principal ones an inmate may either reside in privacy or mix with company, as inclination dictates. Commodious private lodging may be found in many eligible situations throughout the metropolis; and in many of the first situations at the west end of the town are hotels where the most elevated in rank and distinction meet with adequate and comfortable residences and entertainments. The accommodations of the principal taverns and coffee-houses in all the other quarters of London, and more particularly in the city, are equally respectable, though perhaps not so splendid. It is calculated that in London there are 200 inns, 400 taverns, and 500 coffee-houses. The charges, of course, vary according to the style of the accommodation.

At coffee-houses and inns, breakfast of coffee or tea is generally charged from 1*s.* 6*d.* to 3*s.*; dinner from 3*s.* to 14*s.*: tea from 1*s.* 6*d.* to 2*s.* 6*d.*; beds from 1*s.* 6*d.* to 5*s.*; and servants' beds from 1*s.* 6*d.* to 2*s.* Port or sherry is charged about 5*s.* or 6*s.* a bottle; Madeira, 8*s.* or 10*s.*; Claret or Burgundy, from 8*s.* to 12*s.*; Hock or Champagne, from 10*s.* to 12*s.* If the visiter has a separate sitting-room, the expense is increased from 3*s.* to 10*s.* 6*d.* per day. The waiter expects about 1*s.* or 1*s.* 6*d.* per day, and the chamber-maid 1*s.* At the first-rate hotels, a sitting and bed-room are charged from

10*s.* to 1*l.* 1*s.* per day; and extra bed-rooms about 4*s.* or 5*s.* The charges likewise for meals are proportionably high.

At livery stables, horses may be kept from 1*l.* 1*s.* to 1*l.* 10*s.* per week, and hostlers expect about 6*d.* a-night for each horse.

Good furnished lodgings may be obtained by the week or month in private houses, in most of the respectable streets at a moderate price: apartments on the first floor from 1*l.* 11*s.* 6*d.* to 6*l.* 6*s.* per week; and on the upper floors from 1*l.* 1*s.* to 4*l.* 4*s.* per week; a single bed-room may be procured from 7*s.* to 12*s.* per week.

At boarding-houses, visiters may be accommodated with board and lodging, from 1*l.* 11*s.* 6*d.* to 3*l.* 3*s.* per week.

A list of the hotels, taverns, and coffee-houses may be found in the London Directories, Court Guide, and Blue Book.

Supper-Rooms.

At most of these houses some good singing is to be heard, they being attended by professional men: the principal are in the neighbourhood of the theatres; viz.—

Evans's, Covent-garden.
Offley's, Henrietta-street.
Garrick, Bow-street.
Coal-Hole, Strand.
Albion Tavern, Great Russell-street, where there is no singing.

Tea-Gardens.

These places of summer amusement are frequented, particularly on Sundays, by the middle classes of society. The charge for tea or coffee is generally from 1*s.* to 2*s.* a-head. The following are the principal in the vicinity of the metropolis:—

Bagnigge-wells, Spafields.
New Bagnigge-wells, Bayswater.
New Bayswater Tea-gardens.
Bull-and-Bush, Hampstead-heath.
Camberwell Grove-house.
Canonbury-house, Islington.
Chalk-farm, Primrose-hill.
Copenhagen-house, Holloway-fields.
Eel-pie-house, or Sluice house, on the New River, near Hornsey.
St. Helena Gardens, near the Lower Road, Deptford.
Highbury-barn.
Hornsey Wood-house, the grounds of which include a fine wood and an extensive piece of water.
Hoxton-gardens.
Jack Straw's Castle, Hampstead-heath.
Kilburn-wells, Edgeware-road.
Mermaid, Hackney.
Montpelier, Walworth.
Mount-pleasant, Clapton.
Red-house, Battersea.
The Eagle, City-road.
Southampton Arms, Camden-town.
Union Gardens, Chelsea.
White Conduit-house, Islington.
Yorkshire Stingo, Lisson-green.

STAGE-COACHES, POST-HORSES, &c.

Besides the mail-coaches for the conveyance of letters and passengers, stage-coaches are established which travel to and from all parts of the kingdom, carrying persons and goods at fixed rates. These vehicles perform their journeys with great regularity: they are supplied in stated places with relays of horses, and meals are furnished for passengers at prices varying from 2*s.* to 3*s.* 6*d.* at the various inns on the road. The names of the inns whence the stages set out, as well as the days and hours of their starting, are to be found in the London Directories.

Post-chaises do not perform stated journeys, but are hired according to the occasion of the traveller, and travel with greater or less despatch in proportion to the number of horses engaged. The charge for a pair of horses varies from 1*s.* 3*d.* to 1*s.* 9*d.* per mile. It is usual to give the post-boy 2*d.* or 3*d.* per mile.

HACKNEY COACHES, CABRIOLETS, AND OMNIBUSES.

Hackney-coaches abound in the metropolis, and are always to be found at the legal stands. They are divided into two classes, the day and the night coaches. The fares will be found at the end of this volume.

The CABRIOLETS are of Parisian origin, but the aristocratic taste of Englishmen suggested the propriety of obliging the driver to be seated on the outside of the vehicle. They are now of an infinite variety of shapes.

The OMNIBUSES are likewise of foreign birth, and are found to be of the greatest convenience to persons whose occupations lead them to various parts of the town in the course of the day. The fares vary from 6*d.* to 1*s.*

STEAM-CARRIAGES occasionally ply in different parts, but cannot yet be said to deserve the appellation of a metropolitan vehicle.

New regulations have been adopted for the better management of hackney-coaches, &c., the drivers of which are now obliged to wear badges with their respective numbers. A person wishing to complain, should be careful to note down the number of the coach as well as that of the driver. The registry-office is in Adam-street, Adelphi.

WHERRIES, PLEASURE-BOATS, &c.

The Thames is supplied with about 2000 small boats, which

are stationed at the various stairs on its banks, to convey passengers from one part of the river to another. The watermen's rates, as fixed by law in 1828, will be found detailed at the end of the work.

Pleasure-boats and sailing-vessels may also be hired at several places between Westminster and Vauxhall bridges. At Messrs. Serle's, Roberts', Lyon's, Judge and Needham's, Paul's Wharf, Blackfriars, &c., boats may be hired at the following prices:—A wherry, 1*s*. first hour, 6*d*. each hour afterwards; a four-oared boat, 1*s*. 6*d*. the first hour, and 1*s*. each hour afterwards; a shallop, 25*s*. per diem.

Steam-Packets.

The first vessel propelled by steam on the Thames was brought by Mr. G. Dodd from Glasgow in 1815. It was called the Thames, and was used as a Margate packet, often conveying between 200 and 300 passengers. Since then, other vessels on similar principles have been built; and London now possesses steam-vessels to Aberdeen, Antwerp, Arbroath, Belfast, Boulogne, Calais, Cologne, Cork, Dublin, Dundee, Falmouth, Gravesend, Hamburgh, Hull, Leith, Margate, New York, Newcastle, Ostend, Plymouth, Ramsgate, Richmond, Rotterdam, Scarborough, Southend, and Yarmouth. The time at which these vessels start, and the fares, are advertised in the daily papers.

The fourpenny boats which ply from London-bridge to the Southampton Railway every quarter of an hour, call at Dyer's-hall Wharf, Bankside, Hungerford-market, and Westminster-bridge.

Horse-Repositories.

These establishments are used for the sale of horses, carriages, &c. by public auction or by private contract. The principal are the following, with the days on which the auctions take place:—

Dixon's, Barbican, Tuesdays and Fridays.

Horse-Bazaar, King-street, Portman-square.

Morris's, late Aldridge's, Little St. Martin's-lane, Wednesdays and Saturdays.

Robinson's, 29 Little Britain.

Tattersall's, Grosvenor-place, Hyde-park-corner, Mondays.

Baths.

The baths of London are numerous and commodious, and

are fitted up with every attention to the convenience of visiters. The usual price for a cold bath is 1*s*., or a warm bath 2*s*. to 3*s*. 6*d*.; but if the visiter subscribe for a quarter of a year or a longer time, the expense is proportionably diminished. The sea-water baths are 3*s*. 6*d*. each time, or if warm, about 7*s*. 6*d*. The following are the principal baths in the metropolis:—

St. Agnes le Clerc, Old-street-road, is a spring of considerable antiquity, having been known in the time of Henry VIII. It is said to be efficacious in rheumatic and nervous cases. The house for the accommodation of visiters contains two baths, the larger for the use of gentlemen, and the smaller for ladies.

Addington-square, Camberwell, warm, cold, and vapour.
Albany-place, York-road, tepid swimming-baths.
Alpha-road, fumigating, plunging.
Argyll-street, No. 30, medicated vapour.
Bagnio-court, Newgate-street, No. 3.
Bath-street, No. 11, cold, shower, and warm.
Beaufort buildings, Strand, warm and cold.
Chapel-place, Cavendish-square, warm, shower, aud salt-water.
Cold-bath-square, Clerkenwell, warm, cold, shower, and chalybeate.
Coulson's hotel, Lower Brook-street, warm.
Duke-street, Adelphi, warm, cold, and vapour.
Fenton's hotel, St. James's-street.
Floating-bath, Blackfriars-bridge.
———— Waterloo-bridge.
———— Westminster bridge.
George-street, Adelphi, sea-water.
Gracechurch-street, warm and vapour.
Great Marlborough-street, No. 40, sulphur, chlorine, vapour, and warm or hot air.
Harley-street, No. 75, warm and shower.
Old Hummums-hotel, Covent-garden, warm and cold.
Jermyn-street, No. 7, medicated and warm.
Leicester-square, No. 27, warm, vapour, salt, cold, and shower.
Lothbury, Founder's-court, shampooing, vapour, hot-air, sea-water, &c.
Mivart's hotel, Brook-street, warm.
National Baths, Westminster-bridge-road, cold and tepid. A very extensive and well-arranged establishment.
New Bridge-street, Blackfriars, warm and cold.
New-road, near Fitzroy-square, cold, warm, and shower.
Oxford-street, No. 72, portable baths.
Park-place, Harrow-road, cold.

Peerless Pool, City-road, having been formerly a dangerous pond, was called *Perilous* Pool till 1748, when it was fitted up in a commodious style by Mr. Kemp, who denominated it Peerless, a name to which it is justly entitled, being the completest public bath in the metropolis. It measures 170 feet in length, and 100 in breadth, and is surrounded by boxes for the convenience of the bathers. Here likewise is a commodious cold bath, 40 feet long and 20 broad.

St. James's-place, vapour and shampooing.
St. Mary Axe, No. 34, warm and cold.
Strand-lane, near Somerset-house, cold.
Suffolk-place, No. 9, Pall-mall-east, shampooing, Turkish medicated-

vapour, humid sulphur-vapour, Barège, and other artificial baths, plain, warm, cold, and shower-baths. This establishment is conducted by Mr. W. Seaman, and is the most complete in London. The baths are of marble, and every possible attention is shewn to those who frequent them. The humid sulphur-vapour baths, in imitation of those at Baia, Tritole, St. Germano, &c. were invented by Mr. S.

Warwick-street, Golden-square.

Waterloo-road, cold and swimming.

York-terrace, Regent's-park, warm, cold, and vapour.

St. Chad's Wells, Gray's-inn-lane-road, were formerly celebrated for their medicinal properties, but are now little frequented. They are said to have derived their name from St. Chad, the first bishop of Lichfield.

LONDON BANKERS.

Ashley, James, and Son, 185 Regent-street.
Barclay, Bevan, and Co. 54 Lombard-street.
Barnard, Dimsdale, and Co., 50 Cornhill.
Barnetts, Hoare, and Co., 62 Lombard-street.
Bosanquet, Pitt, Anderdon, and Co., 73 Lombard-street.
Bouverie, Norman, and Murdock, 11 Haymarket.
Brown, Janson, and Co., 32 Abchurch-lane.
Call, Sir W., Marten, and Co., 25 Old Bond-street.
Child and Co., 1 Fleet-street.
Cockburns and Co., 4 Whitehall.
Cockerell, Trail, and Co., 8 Austin Friars.
Cocks, Biddulph, and Co., 43 Charing-cross.
Coutts and Co., 59 Strand.
Cunliffe, Brooks, and Co., 29 Lombard-street.
Curries and Co., 29 Cornhill.
De Lisle, Janvin, and Co., 16 Devonshire-square, Bishopsgate.
Dennison, J., and Co., 4 Lombard-street.
Dixon, Son, and Brooks, 25 Chancery-lane.
Dorrien, Magens, and Co., 22 Finch-lane.
Drewett and Fowler, 4 Princes-street, Bank.
Drummonds and Co., 49 Charing-cross.
Feltham and Co., 42 Lombard-street,
Fuller (Richard and George) and Co., 84 Cornhill.
Glyn, Sir R. Carr, Halifax, Mills, and Co., 66 & 67 Lombard-street.
Goslings and Sharpe, 19 Fleet-street.
Hammersleys and Co., 69 Pall-mall.
Hanburys and Co., 60 Lombard-street.
Hankey and Co., 5, 6, 7 Fenchurch-street.
Herries, Farquhar, and Co., 16 St. James's-street.
Hill and Sons, 17 West Smithfield.
Hoare (Henry) and Co., 37 Fleet-street.
Hopkinsons and Co., 3 Regent-street.
Jones, Lloyd, and Co., 43 Lothbury.
Jones and Son, 41 West Smithfield.
Kinloch and Sons, 1 New Broad-street.
Ladbrokes, Kingscote, and Co., 2 Bank-buildings.
London Joint-Stock Bank, Princes-street, Bank.
London and Westminster Bank, 9 Waterloo-place, Pall-mall; 38 Throgmorton-street; Lothbury; 213 High Holborn; 155 Oxford-street; 47 Skinner-street.

Lubbock, Sir J. W., and Co., 11 Mansion-house-street.
Masterman, Peters, and Co., 35 Nicholas-lane, Lombard-street.
Pocklington and Lacey, 60 West Smithfield.
Praeds, Mackworth, Fane, and Co., 189 Fleet-street.
Prescott, Grote, Prescott, and Grote, 62 Threadneedle-street.
Price, Sir C., Marryat, and Co., King William-street.
Puget, Bainbridge, and Co., 12 St. Paul's Churchyard.
Ransom and Co., 1 Pall-mall-east.
Robarts, Curtis, and Co., 15 Lombard-street.
Rogers, Olding, and Co., 29 Clement's-lane, Lombard-street.
Scott, Sir C., and Co., 1, Cavendish-square.
Smith, Payne, and Smiths, 1 Lombard-street.
Snow, Strachan, and Paul, 217 Strand.
Spooner, Attwoods, and Co., 27 Gracechurch-street.
Stevenson and Salt, 20 Lombard-street.
Stone, Martins, and Stone, 68 Lombard-street.
Twinings, 215 Strand.
Veres and Co., 77 Lombard-street.
Wakefield, F., and Co., 70 Old Broad-street.
Weston and Young, 6 Wellington-street, Borough.
Whitmore, Wells, and Whitmore, 24 Lombard-street.
Williams, Deacon, Labouchere, and Co., 20 Birchin-lane.
Willis, Percival, and Co., 76 Lombard-street.
Wright, Selby, and Robinson, 5 Henrietta-street, Covent-garden.
Young and Son, 11 West Smithfield.

CHAPTER XIII.

RECENT AND PROJECTED IMPROVEMENTS IN LONDON.

LONDON, ever fertile in improvements, has experienced innumerable changes since the accession of George IV., during whose reign a mania for building was developed, which, though involving the ruin of individual speculators, tended to the beauty and convenience of the metropolis. From that period to the present the power of the office of Woods and Forests has rapidly changed the face of large portions of the modern Babylon. It were fruitless, amidst the comparatively anomalous alterations which have been effected, to expect to trace that homogeneous beauty or propriety which might reasonably be expected to result from original and unshackled plans on unembarrassed sites; yet, let any impartial observer endeavour to recollect what London was on the demise of Geo. III., and then consider what it is at the present moment, and the result will be a feeling of wonder and admiration at the power and wealth displayed in the successive improvements.

Although the Regent's-park may not exactly demand a place in this chapter, we cannot resist adverting to it as the most beneficial and beautiful alteration which has been effected; and it were unjust to refuse the architect the high praise to which he is entitled for the able manner in which, by his plans, linear and literary, he enabled the Commissioners of Woods to achieve that vast undertaking.

The re-modelling of St. James's-park is another change calculated to embellish the court end of the metropolis, and to add to the pleasures of the public, as well as conciliate its good will. There remains, however, much to be effected before our parks are other than tasteless areas—the Green-park, to wit, which is a disgrace to the metropolis.

The additions to the Zoological-gardens will be viewed with satisfaction by all classes; by the scientific as an extension of opportunities for the acquirement of knowledge, and by the curious unlearned as a most agreeable lounge during hours of recreation.

One of the most important architectural works belonging to this portion of our Guide is the New Palace, in St. James's-park, a description of which will be found in another chapter.

The National Gallery of Painting, Sculpture, and Architecture, erected from the designs of Mr. Wilkins, is another important addition to the public edifices. In the area of Trafalgar-square it is proposed to erect the Nelson monument. May it be worthy of him!

The grand design, by Mr Barry, for the New Houses of Parliament will be found described in another portion of this work. This stupendous and noble edifice will, when completed, be the finest edifice of modern times.

The British Museum slowly advances towards completion under the auspices of sir R. Smirke. The grandeur of the finished portion makes us regret that it should be deemed prudent to restrict the issue of sums necessary to complete it. Our country has hitherto been justly reproached with a want of taste in architectural decoration; but we shall shortly be able to produce, with exulting patriotism, a building destined to rival continental grandeur, and to efface the stain on our national fame.

The improvements in the neighbourhood of Charing-cross next demand our attention. The entrance to the Strand, which was formerly confined and gloomy, has been widened, and two ranges of handsome houses have been erected, bearing the name of West Strand. The lateral elevations form one side of Trafalgar-square, Duncannon-street, Adelaide-street, and William-street; the main pile being intersected by the Lowther-arcade. The demolition of 550 houses and the erection of 200 new edifices on their site, together with the purchase of leases and grants of compensation, was effected by the Commissioners of Woods at an expense of upwards of 1,108,000*l.* The average value of frontage is 5 guineas per foot.

THE NEW HUNGERFORD-MARKET is described in another chapter.

THE NEW STREET from Waterloo-bridge to the British Museum is intended to join Great Russell-street after crossing the Strand, the site of the old Lyceum Theatre, Exeter-street, Tavistock and York streets, up Charles-street, and up Holborn.

One of the most important improvements is the line forming a portion of the LONDON-BRIDGE APPROACHES, leading from King William-street to Moorgate. The road diverges to the left at Eastcheap, and merging into the Poultry by the Mansion-house, runs down Princes-street, one side of which has been rebuilt with a range of handsome edifices, and proceeds, to the right of Coleman-street, to the Pavement, Moorfields. Various other improvements are to take place in the neighbourhood of the Bank and Lothbury. The Wellington statue and the new Exchange will add to the beauty of this much-frequented spot; but of the latter nothing can be said until the four parties concerned—the city, the government, the Mercers' Company, and the Gresham committee, shall have agreed on the plans.

The views from the avenues leading to the bridge are very imposing. On the Southwark side the eye is attracted by the massive warehouses and other buildings at the foot of the bridge, the new entrances to St. Thomas's Hospital, and the Church of St. Saviour, with the beautiful Ladye Chapel. On the opposite side, the double front of the New Fishmongers' Hall, the opening to the monument, and the buildings newly erected, combine to render it a very imposing prospect.

Improvements are to be made in the approaches to Southwark-bridge.

St. George's, the New Westminster, the North London, and the Charing-cross Hospitals have sprung up within a short period: they will be found described in another portion of this work.

The *New Cemeteries* are likewise important features in the

last improvements; the repugnant idea of the heart of an overgrown metropolis being devoted to the purposes of sepulture having stimulated a spirit of enterprise likely to rescue the habitations of the living from the taint of corruption.

Fleet-Market has been rebuilt in a more convenient situation, and the spot whereon it formerly stood has assumed a noble appearance, forming a portion of an intended improvement by which a road will be opened to Islington. It is in contemplation, in order to obviate the dangerous descent of Snow-hill, to construct a viaduct by which the communication between Newgate-street and Holborn will be facilitated.

It has long been in contemplation to remove the Fleet Prison from its present situation, in order to profit by the increased value of ground since the widening of Farringdon-street. A spot in St. George's-fields, opposite New Bethlehem, has been decided on, and the intention may probably be carried into execution.

The improvements which have taken place in St. George's-fields are very great: part of the waste ground has been granted to Bethlehem-hospital, and laid out with a shrubbery, &c.: further improvements are in contemplation. The new *Blind School*, from designs by Mr. Newman, is a pleasing composition in the Tudor and Gothic style.

The interior of Westminster-hall has been coated with Portland stone, which much improves its appearance.

Alterations are likewise being made in the *East India Docks*. A dock is to be made at Blackwall for the reception of steam-boats, and the East India import dock is also devoted to a similar purpose. A new market is about to be established in the neighbourhood of Westminster-abbey, to be called the *Westminster-Market*. The proposed capital of the company is 150,000*l*., in shares of 25*l*. each.

A variety of new companies have sprung up for the improvement of the paving of the metropolis by means of asphalte, a composition of bitumen with various sorts of concrete.

Amongst the many changes which have lately taken place may be enumerated the following:—The rebuilding of London-bridge, the Goldsmiths' and Fishmongers' Halls, the erection of the New Palace, the British Museum, the Post office, the University College, the King's College, the new portion of Lambeth Palace, the Council Chamber, Whitehall, the Triumphal Arches Hyde-park-corner, the new terraces on the

Uxbridge-road, the Surgeons' Hall, the Atlas Assurance Office, the marquess of Westminster's Gallery, the formation of the two Zoological Gardens, the improvements in the neighbourhood of Charing-cross, Carlton-square, the York Column and Statue, Marlborough-house, St. James's-park; the Green-park also is to be laid out in a similar manner; Hyde-park is also being replanted; Wellington chapel, and many new churches; and the London-bridge approaches. Most of these will be found fully described in a former chapter, others can only be hinted at as intentions. Alterations have been made in Sutherland-house; great additions and improvements also have been made to Christ's Hospital; the City of London School has been rebuilt; the Railway Termini will be found described in another part of this work.

The spirit of improvement is rapidly extending, and in all probability an ample chapter of proposed alterations awaits our editorial scrutiny. The giant nucleus of the commercial world already extends over an astounding space, yet each day beholds some portion of verdant fields grasped within the arms of the rapacious metropolis.

Gymnastics, Fencing, &c.

These exercises have been introduced within a few years by Professor Voelker.

At Mr. Angelo's Rooms, Old Bond-street, the science of fencing, and the use of weapons in general, is taught in great perfection.

The Calisthenic exercises for ladies have been recommended by the highest surgical authorities, as conducive to the full development of the female form, and to the preservation of health in the fair sex.

At Cremorne-house, the establishment of Baron de Beranger, archery, riding, gymnastics, and various athletic and chivalric exercises, are taught under the superintendence of the proprietor and his sons.

STRANGER'S GUIDE

TO THE

REMARKABLE BUILDINGS, ANTIQUITIES, AND OTHER CURIOSITIES

OF

LONDON.

*** The Streets are arranged alphabetically, and the remarkable objects in each are mentioned according to their relative distance from St. Paul's.

CHAPTER XIV.

ABCHURCH-LANE. St. Mary's Church.

ADDLE-STREET. See ALDERMANBURY.

ADELPHI. In John-street, House of the Society of Arts. —Fine view from the Terrace.—Subterranean passages leading from the Strand, and from George-street, to the river.

ALBEMARLE-STREET. Louis XVIII. had apartments at Grillon's hotel in 1814, previous to his departure for the French metropolis.—No. 21, the Royal Institution, newly faced.

ALDERMANBURY. Corner of Love-lane, St. Mary's church. —No. 18 was formerly the residence of judge Jeffereys.—In Addle-street, Brewer's-hall.—Near London-wall, church of St. Alphage.

ALDERSGATE-STREET. New Post-office, from the north end of which there is a fine view of St. Paul's dome.—In St. Anne's-lane, church of St. Anne.—At the corner of Little-Britain, St. Botolph's church.—Nos. 35 and 38 formed part of Shaftesbury-house, formerly the residence of Anthony Ashley Cooper, earl of Shaftesbury; it was originally called Thanet-house, and was ornamented under the direction of Inigo Jones.—On No. 116 is a tablet stating that on the 20th November, 1790, two incendiaries were executed here for having set fire to several houses on the 16th of May of the same year.—The Half-Moon tavern, which stood in this

PANORAMA OF REMARKABLE OBJECTS IN LONDON

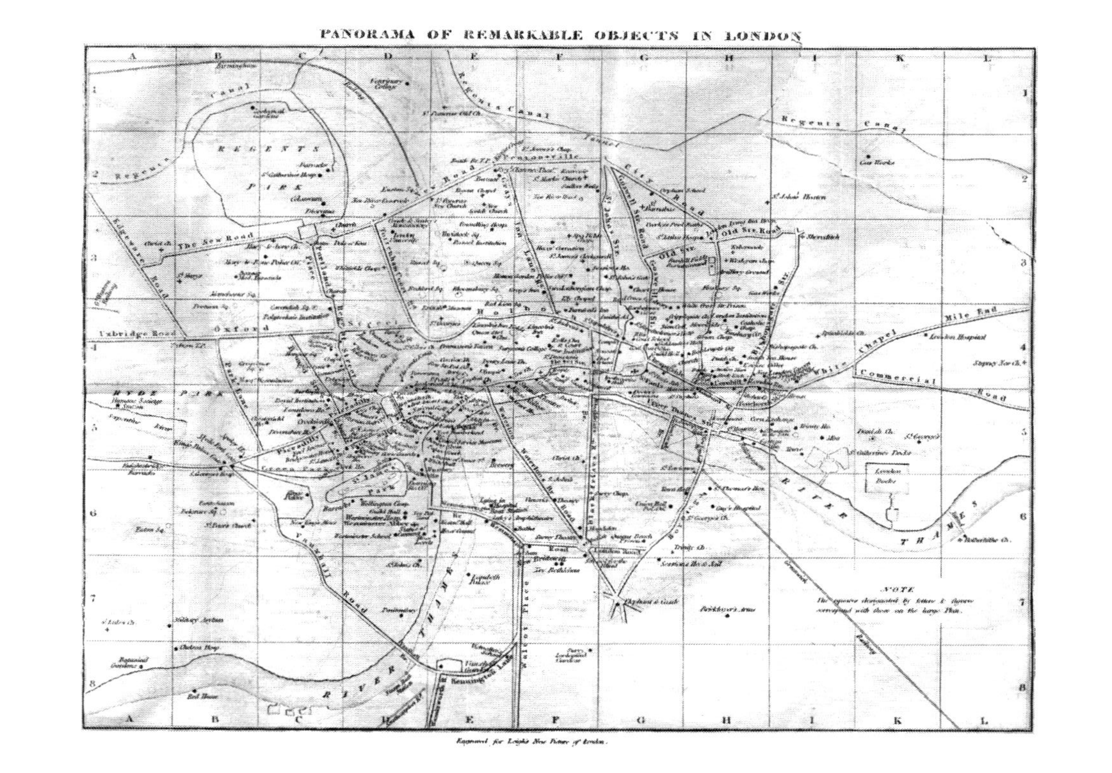

Engraved for Leigh's New Picture of London.

street, was very much frequented by the wits of the reign of Charles II.

ALDGATE. At the corner of Houndsditch, St. Botolph's church.

ARLINGTON-STREET, PICCADILLY. At Rutland-house, No. 16, the duke of York expired, January 5th, 1827.

AUDLEY-STREET. See SOUTH AUDLEY-STREET.

AUSTIN-FRIARS is so called from having been the residence of the Augustines, whose noble church still remains, and is now used by the Dutch.—No. 26, Missionary Museum.

AYLESBURY-STREET, CLERKENWELL. At the corner of Jerusalem-passage stood the residence of Thomas Britton, the musical coalman.

BAKER-STREET, PORTMAN-SQUARE. No. 58, Bazaar for the sale of horses, carriages, furniture, and miscellaneous articles; and the exhibition of Panoramas, Dioramas, &c.—At No. 68, Mr. Grattan, the Irish orator, died, June 1820.

BARBICAN. No. 21 was the residence of alderman Staines, by whose liberality the adjoining chapel was erected.

BARTHOLOMEW-CLOSE is the site of the ancient monastery of St. Bartholomew, some vestiges of which may be seen in the livery-stables at No. 69; part of the walls of the refectory are likewise visible in Middlesex-passage, at the north corner of the close.

BARTHOLOMEW-LANE. At the corner of Threadneedle-street, St. Bartholomew's church.—In Capel-court, the Stock Exchange.—Opposite, east entrance to the Bank.—Auction Mart.

BASINGHALL-STREET. Public office for Commissioners of Bankrupts.—In Mason's-court, Mason's-hall, now occupied as a warehouse.—Between Nos. 75 and 76, back-entrance to Guildhall.—Opposite, Weavers'-hall.—No. 71, Coopers'-hall. —Opposite, in Sambrooke-court, the house where Dr. Lettsom resided.—Church of St. Michael Bassishaw.—No. 39, Girdlers'-hall.

BASING-LANE. Gerrard's, or Gisor's-hall, is a part of a large ancient house; it is remarkable for its vaults, which are said to be 600 years old, and are supported by 16 pillars brought from Caen.

BEECH-LANE, BARBICAN. In the court between Nos. 11 and 12 stood the residence of Prince Rupert, which was pulled down in 1820, and the site built upon.—The almshouses here are ancient, having been erected by the Drapers' company about 1540.

BENNET'S-HILL. Herald's College.—At the corner of Thames-street, the church of St. Benedict.

BERKELEY-SQUARE. On the south side Lansdowne-house.

BERMONDSEY-STREET. Church of St. Mary Magdalen.

BISHOPSGATE-STREET. At the corner of Threadneedle-street, church of St. Martin-Outwich.—In Crosby-square, Crosby-house.—In St. Helen's, St. Helen's church, and Leather-dressers'-hall.—Between Nos. 52 and 53, St. Ethelburga's church.—On Nos. 1 and 64, mitres, designating the place where Bishops-gate formerly stood.—Opposite Houndsditch, St. Botolph's church.—No. 199 is the White Hart, a tavern established in the 15th century, but rebuilt in 1829.—No. 169 is a very old house, which was the residence of sir Paul Pindar, an eminent merchant, who died in 1650.

BLACKFRIARS-ROAD. Contiguous to the bridge is the British plate-glass manufactory.—No. 3 was formerly occupied by the Leverian Museum, and afterwards by the Surrey Institution, both of which are now dissolved.—Between Nos. 26 and 30, Christ church.—At the corner of Charlotte-street, Surrey chapel.—Magdalen hospital.—Surrey theatre.—The Obelisk at the south extremity is situated at the junction of the roads from the bridges of Westminster, Waterloo, London, and Blackfriars.—Opposite is the School for the Indigent Blind.

BLOOMSBURY-SQUARE. Statue of C. J. Fox.

BOROUGH, BLACKMAN-STREET. In Suffolk-street-east, Trinity church.—Corner of Borough-road, King's-Bench Prison.—In Horsemonger-lane, Sessions-house and Jail for the county of Surrey.—In the Borough-road, British and Foreign School Society.

BOROUGH, HIGH-STREET. Between Nos. 36 and 37, St. Thomas's Hospital, and a little to the south, Guy's Hospital.—Beautiful view of St. Saviour's and the Ladye Chapel.—No. 75 is the Talbot inn, over the entrance to which is the following inscription: "This is the inn where Geoffrey Chaucer, knight, and nine-and-twenty pilgrims, lodged in their journey to Canterbury in 1383." In the yard is a picture representing their entrance into Canterbury; the original house, called the Tabard (Talbot being a corruption), was burnt down in 1676, and the present building raised on the site.—At the corner of County-street, Town-hall, Southwark.—At the corner of Great Dover-street, St. George's church.

BOTOLPH-LANE is noted as the residence of orange-merchants.—Between Nos. 8 and 9, St. George's church.

BOW-LANE, CHEAPSIDE. Near the corner of Watling-street, church of St. Mary-Aldermary.

BOW-STREET, COVENT-GARDEN. No. 3 is the Police-office. —Covent-garden Theatre.

BREAD-STREET, CHEAPSIDE. At the corner of Watling-street, Allhallows church.—Between Nos. 36 and 39, St. Mildred's church.

BRIDE-LANE. See BRIDGE-STREET.

BRIDGE-STREET, NEW, BLACKFRIARS. No. 42, Albion Insurance-office.—No. 38, National Union-office.—In Little Bridge-street are vestiges of the old London wall. No. 1, Hand-in-Hand Insurance-office.—No. 6, Hope Insurance-office.—In Bride-lane, church of St. Bride.—No. 13, Bridewell.—No. 14, Rock Insurance-office.—In Crescent-place, Norwich Union-office.—In Water-lane, Apothecaries'-hall.—In Chatham-place, Equitable and European Insurance-offices, Humane Society's office.—At the south extremity, Blackfriars'-bridge.

BROAD-STREET, BLOOMSBURY. St. Giles's church.

BROAD-STREET, CITY. Between Nos. 62 and 63, church of St. Peter-le-poor.—Nearly opposite, the Excise-office.

BRYDGES-STREET. Drury-lane theatre.

BUCKINGHAM-STREET, STRAND. The last house towards the river on the east side was occupied by Peter the Great, during his residence in London.—This and the adjoining streets are erected on the site of a palace of the archbishops of York, which was rebuilt by Villiers, duke of Buckingham; but the only vestige remaining is the water-gate, called York-stairs. This beautiful specimen of architecture was erected by Inigo Jones. On the south side it bears the arms of the Villiers family, and on the north their motto, "FIDEI COTICULA CRUX," (the Cross the touchstone of faith).

BULL-AND-MOUTH-STREET, ST. MARTIN'S-LE-GRAND. The name of the Bull-and-Mouth Inn, in this street, has been strangely perverted from its original, the "Mouth of Boulogne harbour," which became a popular sign after the capture of that place by Henry VIII.

BURLINGTON-GARDENS. Albany.—Uxbridge or Anglesea-house.—Burlington Arcade.

CANNON-ROW, WESTMINSTER, more properly spelt Canon, derived its name from having been the residence of the canons of St. Stephen's chapel.—Office where the London Gazette is published.—Board of Control.—Phrenological Society.

CANNON-STREET, CITY. Between Nos. 81 and 82, St. Swithin's church, in the south wall of which is London-stone, one of the oldest antiquities of the metropolis, having been known before the time of William I. It was formerly much larger, and stood on the opposite side of the way, but the time and purpose of its erection are alike unknown. Some have supposed it to be the spot whence the Romans measured the distance of their several stations. It was against this stone that Jack Cade struck his sword, exclaiming, "Now is Mortimer lord of London."—No. 19 bears a representation of London Stone, with the date 1669, and some assert that this was the first house erected after the fire of London.—In Swithin's-lane, Salter's-hall.

CASTLE-STREET, LEICESTER-SQUARE. Next to St. Martin's Workhouse is a library, founded by Dr. Tennison for the use of the parish of St. Martin, of which he was vicar.—Barracks.

CATO-STREET, EDGEWARE-ROAD. No. 6 is the place where Thistlewood and his associates assembled, February 1820, with the intention of assassinating his majesty's ministers.

CAVENDISH-SQUARE. Statue of William, duke of Cumberland.

CHANCERY-LANE. Between Nos. 105 and 109, Law Institution.—New Judges' Chambers and Serjeants' Inn.—Rolls chapel and court.—Between 22 and 23, Symond's-inn.—Opposite, Lincoln's-inn.—No. 3 Took's-court is the house where lord Byron passed three vacations, of six weeks each, in order to receive instruction in the French language from the Abbé de Rouffigny.—In Southampton-buildings, Office of the commissioners of Bankrupts, a handsome building of the Doric order; and London Mechanics' Institute.—Beyond Lincoln's-inn, Six Clerks'-office, Inrolment-office, and part of Stone-buildings ornamented with Corinthian pillars.

CHARING-CROSS. Statue of Charles I.—Phœnix Insurance-office.

CHARTER-HOUSE-SQUARE was formerly the churchyard of the Chartreusian monastery.—Charter-house.

CHEAPSIDE. Between Nos. 142 and 144, Saddlers'-hall.—Between 55 and 56, Bow church.—No. 92, the Atlas Fire-office.—No. 90 was formerly the residence of that distinguished patron of the fine arts, alderman Boydell.—Between Nos. 86 and 87, Mercers'-hall.—No. 73 was erected by sir C. Wren.

CITY-ROAD. At the end of Finsbury-place, the Artillery-ground.—Bunhill-fields Burial-ground.—Opposite, the Wesleyan chapel; the first house on the right in the court in front was the residence of the Rev. John Wesley, and here he died in 1791.—At the corner of Old-street-road, the London Lying-in hospital; and opposite, an extensive vinegar manufactory.—Peerless-pool baths.—Bridge over a basin of the Regent's-canal.—Orphan working-school.—Bridge across the New-river.

CLEMENTS-LANE. Church of St. Clement, Eastcheap.

CLERKENWELL. See AYLESBURY-STREET, RAY-STREET, and ST. JOHN'S-SQUARE.

CLERKENWELL-CLOSE. Here formerly stood the house of Oliver Cromwell, where some suppose the death-warrant of Charles I. was signed.

CLERKENWELL-GREEN. Sessions-house, St. James's church.

CLINK-STREET, SOUTHWARK, was so called from a prison of that name which formerly stood here.—St. Saviour's church. —Ladye chapel. Near St. Saviour's dock are vestiges of the palace inhabited by the bishops of Winchester as far back as the time of Edward I.—Globe-alley, in the vicinity, derived its name from the theatre here, which had a license granted to Shakspeare, Fletcher, and others, to perform plays. In this neighbourhood, likewise, was the Paris or Bear-garden, so celebrated in the time of Elizabeth for the exhibition of bear-baiting, which was then a fashionable amusement.

CLOAK-LANE. See DOWGATE-HILL.

COCK-LANE, WEST-SMITHFIELD, is celebrated for the deceptions of a female ventriloquist, who in 1762 contrived to make many persons believe that she was a ghost. The house in which this occurred is No. 33.

COCKSPUR-STREET. Union Club-house.—Messrs. Hancock and Co.'s glass manufactory, one of the most splendid establishments in the metropolis.—Statue of George III.—In Pall-mall East, College of Physicians, Society of Painters in Water-colours, University Club-house.

COLEMAN-STREET. Between Nos. 35 and 36, St. Stephen's church.—In Pitcher's-court, Bell-alley, was the house where Bloomfield, the author of the Farmer's Boy, followed the occupation of a shoemaker.—No. 81 is the Armourers' and Braziers' hall.

COLLEGE-HILL derived its name from a college founded here by the celebrated Whittington.—Church of St. Michael Royal.—Mercers' school.

CORAM-STREET. Russell Institution.

CORNHILL. Guy, the bookseller and founder of the hospital, first commenced business in this street, at the corner of Lombard-street.—In Bank-buildings, the Sun Fire-office.—Between Nos. 5 and 7, Globe Insurance-office.—No. 21, British Fire-office.—Site of Royal Exchange. An inscription on the pump in front of the Exchange states that the well beneath was first sunk in 1282.—No. 35, the British Commercial Assurance-office, adorned with sculpture, representing Britannia protecting the widow and orphan.—No. 83, Eagle Insurance-office. —No. 81, the Union Insurance-office.—Behind No. 44, in St. Michael's alley, St. Michael's church.—Between Nos. 55 and 56, St. Peter's church.—In Sun-court, opposite, the Imperial Fire-office.

COVENT-GARDEN. St. Paul's church.—Market.

CRAVEN-STREET. No. 7 was inhabited by Dr. Franklin.

CROSS-STREET, HATTON-GARDEN. Here are the remains of Hatton-house, built by the lord-chancellor of that name in the time of queen Elizabeth. On the site of part of it is the Caledonian chapel.

CURTAIN-ROAD is said to have derived its name from an obscure theatre called the Green Curtain, in which Ben Jonson was an occasional performer.—Gas-works at the corner of Worship-street.

DEAN-STREET, SOHO. St. Anne's church.

DISTAFF-LANE. Cordwainers'-hall.

DORSET-STREET, FLEET-STREET. The ground occupied by the Gas-works is that on which, it is said, Shakspeare's theatre formerly stood.

DOWGATE-HILL. In Cloak-lane, No. 6, Cutlers'-hall.—No. 5, Tallow-chandlers'-hall.—No. 8, Skinners'-hall.—In Checquer-yard, Plumbers'-hall.

DOWNING-STREET, WESTMINSTER. Secretary of State's office, Foreign Department.—Secretary of State's office, Colonial Department.—Between this street and Fludyer-street new offices are to be built.

DUKE'S-PLACE has been the residence of Jews since the time of the Commonwealth.—St. James's church.—Dutch synagogue.

EASTCHEAP. See GREAT and LITTLE EASTCHEAP.

ELBOW-LANE. See THAMES-STREET, UPPER.

EUSTON-SQUARE. Birmingham Railway Terminus.

FARRINGDON-STREET. On the east side, Fleet Prison; on the west side, New Fleet-market.

FENCHURCH-STREET. Between Nos. 3 and 4, Hudson's bay Company's house.—No. 53 is the King's Head Tavern, which was visited by the princess (afterwards queen) Elizabeth, on her liberation from the Tower. She dined here on pork and pease, and the dish in which they were served up is still preserved in the coffee-room, together with her portrait. —Opposite, Ironmongers'-hall.—Between Nos. 70 and 78, East India warehouses.

FINSBURY-CIRCUS occupies the site of Moorfields. On the north side is the London Institution.

FINSBURY-PLACE NORTH is a handsome row of buildings on the site of Moorfields.—Riding-school.—Albion chapel, on the south side of which is a sun-dial, with this appropriate motto, "Dum spectans fugio," placed over a figure of Time.

FISH-STREET-HILL. Monument.—At the south end, St. Magnus' church and remains of Old London-bridge, and near the latter, New London-bridge and Fishmongers'-hall.

FLEET-STREET. The obelisk at the east end denotes the extent of the Fleet-ditch in 1775, when it was filled up, and Bridge-street erected on its site.—The Waithman testimonial, a granite obelisk erected by subscription in 1833, opposite the preceding.—St. Bride's church.—Between Nos. 151 and 152, Bolt-court, where Dr. Johnson resided.—Between Nos. 64 and 65, the Bolt-in-Tun Inn, one of the oldest in London.—In Serjeant's-inn, the Amicable Assurance-office. —Between 186 and 187, St. Dunstan's-in-the-West.—Between Nos. 16 and 17, entrance to the Inner Temple.—No. 17 was once the residence of Prince Charles Stuart, son of James I.—No. 7 was Tothill's printing-house, where Shakspeare's earliest plays were printed.—Between Nos. 5 and 6, entrance to the Middle Temple.—At the corner of Chancery-lane was Izaac Walton's house.—No. 1, Child's banking-house, was the Old Devil's Tavern, of celebrated notoriety.— At the west end, Temple-bar.

FOSTER-LANE. St. Vedast's church.—New Goldsmiths'-hall.—General Post-office.

FRIDAY-STREET. St. Matthew's church.

GEORGE-STREET, HANOVER-SQUARE. St. George's church.

GILTSPUR-STREET. The Compter Prison.—St. Sepulchre's church.—The Fortune-of-War public-house, in this street, is situated on the spot where the fire of London terminated. In front of it was formerly placed the figure of a very fat boy, with this inscription, "This boy is put up in memory of the great fire of London, occasioned by the sin of gluttony, 1666;" an assertion, the origin of which is unknown.

GOSWELL-ROAD. In King-square, St. Barnabas's church.

GOWER-STREET, BEDFORD-SQUARE. University College. —Hospital.

GRACECHURCH-STREET. At the corner of Fenchurch-street, St. Benedict's church.

GRAY'S-INN-LANE and ROAD. Verulam-buildings, named from the title of the celebrated Francis Bacon.—Baldwin's-gardens were so called from one of queen Elizabeth's gardeners, who erected the buildings; and the Hole-in-the-Wall here was much frequented by the facetious Tom Brown.—Welsh school.—St. Andrew's burying-ground.—(formerly) City Light-Horse barracks.—In Sidmouth-street, Regent chapel, and New Scotch church.—London Horse Repository. —In Liverpool-street, Theatre, late Panarmonion.—St. Chad's Wells.

GREAT EASTCHEAP. On No. 2 is a stone figure of a boar's head, bearing the date 1668. The house on which it is placed occupies part of the site of the Boar's Head Tavern alluded to by Shakspeare in Henry IV., as the residence of Mrs. Quickly, and the scene of Sir John Falstaff's merriment. At the public-house, No. 12 Miles-lane, is still preserved a tobacco-box, on the lid of which is a representation of this celebrated tavern.

GREAT MARLBOROUGH-STREET. No. 21, Police-office.

GREAT QUEEN-STREET, LINCOLN'S-INN-FIELDS. At the printing-office of Messrs. Cox and Son is the identical press at which Dr. Franklin once worked as a journeyman.—No. 62, the Freemasons' Tavern; the hall is one of the largest rooms in London, and is adorned with portraits of the royal family; it was erected in 1780, from designs by T. Sandby.

GREAT RUSSELL-STREET, BLOOMSBURY. Between Nos. 92 and 93, the British Museum.

GREAT ST. HELENS. Handsome New Synagogue.

GREEN-PARK commands a fine view of the W. end of Piccadilly.—On the E. side, Sutherland-house and earl Spencer's.—On the N. side, the Ranger's lodge.

GROSVENOR-SQUARE. Statue of George I.

GRUB-STREET was formerly inhabited by the lowest class of literary characters, from which circumstance the epithet "Grub-street" is applied to bad compositions.—In Hanover-court formerly stood a large house, said to have been the residence of General Monk.

GUILDFORD-STREET. Foundling-hospital.

GUTTER-LANE, CHEAPSIDE. No. 36, Embroiderer's-hall.

HANOVER-SQUARE. Pitt's statue.

HART-STREET, BLOOMSBURY. St. George's church.

HART-STREET, CRUTCHED-FRIARS, was the residence of the celebrated Whittington, whose house was standing so late as 1806.—St. Olave's church.

HATTON-GARDEN was named after the lord chancellor Hatton. No. 54, Police-office.

HAYMARKET is so called from the purpose to which it was appropriated.—Italian Opera-house, or King's theatre.—Haymarket theatre.

HIGH-STREET, MARYLEBONE. No. 86, Police-office.—Old church, Marylebone.

HOLBORN derived its name from a stream which formerly ran here, called the Oldbourne. On Holborn-hill, St. Andrew's church.—In Ely-place, an ancient chapel.—Opposite, Thavies' Inn.—Between Nos. 22 and 23, Barnard's Inn.—Opposite, Furnival's Inn.—Behind Nos. 1, 2, 3, and 4, which are some of the oldest houses in London, Staples Inn. Between Nos. 20 and 21, Gray's Inn.

HORSEMONGER-LANE. See BOROUGH.

HORSELYDOWN. St. John's church.

HYDE-PARK. Arch. —On the E. side, New Lodges, Statue of Achilles, Reservoir and Riding-house. On the S. side, Life-guard or Knightsbridge barracks.—On the W., Magazine.—Serpentine river, with new stone bridge.—Humane Society's house.—Kensington-gardens and palace.

IVY-LANE derived its name from the ivy with which the canons' houses, formerly situated here, were covered.—Dolly's chop-house, which once stood here, was famed at the time the Tatler was published for its literary club, of which Dr. Johnson and many other eminent men were members.

KING-STREET, CHEAPSIDE. St. Lawrence's church.—Guildhall.—Courts of Law.

KNIGHTSBRIDGE. Barracks for foot and horse-guards.

LEADENHALL-STREET. Corner of Lime-street, the East India-house and museum.—At the corner of St. Mary-Axe, church of St. Andrew Undershaft. No. 46 was long celebrated as the japan and cutlery warehouse of Mr. Bentley, commonly called Dirty Dick.—No. 52, Bricklayer's-hall, now a Jews' synagogue, rebuilt in 1820.—Between Nos. 84 and 86, church of St. Catherine Cree.—Under No. 71, which is built near the site of the house inhabited by Stow the historian, are vestiges of the chapel of St. Michael, a beautiful specimen in the Gothic style, erected in 1189, and discovered here in 1789.

LEICESTER-SQUARE. Zoological Museum.—Burford's Panorama.—Saville Palace.—Linwood's Exhibition.—Western Literary and Scientific Institution.—Statue of George I. See SQUARES.

LINCOLN'S-INN-FIELDS. On the S. side, College of Surgeons.—On the N. side, sir J. Soane's Museum.—On the E. side, Lincoln's-inn Gardens, and Stone-buildings.

LINCOLN'S-INN NEW-SQUARE. At the N.E. corner, Lincoln's-inn hall and chapel.—Vice-chancellor's Court.

LITTLE EASTCHEAP. The Weigh-house was so called because in former times all goods from abroad were weighed here by the king's beam, to prevent fraud.

LOMBARD-STREET is so called from having been the residence of the Lombards, the money-lenders of former times, whose usurious transactions caused their expulsion from the kingdom in the reign of Elizabeth. It is now chiefly occupied by bankers.—Next to No. 11, St. Mary Woolnoth.—No. 11, the Old Post-office.—No. 70, the Pelican Insurance-office.—No. 68 occupies the site of sir Thomas Gresham's house, which bore the sign of a grasshopper.—No. 19, the Phœnix Insurance-office.—Between Nos. 58 and 59, church of St. Edmund the king.—Between Nos. 47 and 48, Allhallows church.—No. 43 was the residence of Jane Shore, whose husband kept a silversmith's shop here, which continued in the same line of business till the present century.

LONDON-WALL. No. 5, Curriers'-hall—At the corner of Philip-lane, Sion-college.—In the burying-ground opposite St. Alphage's church, remains of the old city-wall. Albion-rooms for the delivery of lectures and the meetings of the Cecilian Society.—Near Winchester-street, Carpenter's-hall.—Near the corner of Broad-street, Allhallows church.

LOTHBURY. St. Margaret's church.—N. entrance to Bank.—London and Westminster Bank.

LUDGATE-HILL. No. 24 is the London coffee-house, in which is preserved a stone of hexagonal form, with a Latin inscription to the memory of Claudia, the wife of one of the Roman generals who came to this country. It was discovered here in digging a foundation in 1806.—No. 38, the Belle Savage Inn, is said by Stow to have derived its name from Arabella Savage, who gave this inn to the Cutler's company, whose arms still adorn the front; but the Spectator asserts that it is indebted for its designation to La Belle Sauvage, a beautiful woman described in an old French romance as having been found wild.

LUDGATE-STREET.—In Stationers'-court, Stationers'-hall. —Next to No. 41, St. Martin's church.

LYME-STREET. At the corner of Fenchurch-street, St. Dionis back-church.—No. 17, Pewterers'-hall.

MAIDEN-LANE, CHEAPSIDE. No. 13, Waxchandlers'-hall. —No. 8, Haberdashers'-hall.

MARK-LANE. In Star-alley, church of Allhallows Staining. —No. 23, back of Commercial-hall.—Between Nos. 52 and 59, the Old and New Corn-exchanges.

MARLBOROUGH-STREET. See GREAT MARLBOROUGH-STREET.

MILE-END-ROAD. London Hospital.—A short distance to the south, Stepney new church.

MILBANK, WESTMINSTER. St. John's church.—Penitentiary, in front of which is a fine gravel walk along the river. —Vauxhall-bridge.

MINCING-LANE. Between Nos. 40 and 41, Clothworkers'-hall.—Between Nos. 30 and 36, Commercial-hall.

MINORIES. Trinity church.—At the south end, the Tower.

MONKWELL-STREET. No. 33, Barbers'-hall.

MOORFIELDS. The north and east sides are principally inhabited by upholsterers.—In Eldon-street, Unitarian chapel, and Welsh chapel. — In Bloomfield-street, Mr. Fletcher's chapel, Roman Catholic chapel, and Ophthalmic Infirmary.

MOORFIELDS, LITTLE. No. 24 is an old house in the foliated style of building, erected probably about 1600.

MOORGATE-STREET. A fine new street.

MOTCOMB-STREET. Pantechnicon.

NEWCASTLE-STREET, STRAND. Entrance to Lyon's Inn.—Olympic Theatre.—In Wych-street, New Inn.

NEWGATE-STREET. On No. 52 is an ancient sculpture, representing Adam and Eve standing by the forbidden tree; it bears the date 1669, and was formerly, no doubt, one of these signs by which each shop in London was designated.—Pannier-alley, see PATERNOSTER-ROW.—Bagnio-court is said to have contained the first bath established in England for hot bathing.—No. 80 is decorated with another sculpture, dated 1669; it represents Jeffery Hudson, the dwarf, and William Evans, the gigantic porter of Charles I.—Between

Nos. 91 and 92, entrance to Christ's church and hospital.—On No. 9, at the corner of Warwick-lane, is a stone figure of Guy, earl of Warwick, whose house stood near this spot; he was renowned in the days of king Athelstan for killing the Danish chief Coldbrand. It bears date 1668, but was renovated in 1817.

NEWMAN-STREET, OXFORD-STREET, is principally inhabited by painters and sculptors.—No. 14 was for many years the residence of B. West, Esq., the venerable president of the Royal Academy, who died here in 1820. It was afterwards occupied by a gallery of his pictures, which were sold by auction in 1829, and the gallery converted into the late Mr. Irving's chapel.

NEW PALACE-YARD is the spot where the meetings of the electors of Westminster are generally held, except during the sitting of parliament.—On the south side, Westminster-hall, and the Courts of Law.—Canning's statue.—On No. 9, exactly opposite the entrance to Westminster-hall, is a dial with these words, "Discite justitiam moniti," (Learn to administer justice,) an inscription which relates to the fine imposed on chief-justice Radulphus de Hengham, in the reign of Henry III., for erasing the court-roll. The fine was employed in building a bell-tower, containing a clock, which, striking hourly, was to remind the judges in the hall of the fate of their predecessor. This clock-tower remained here till 1715.—A short distance west, stands the Guildhall, Westminster; and behind it, the Mews intended for the use of the members of the houses of Lords and Commons, a quadrangular building of the Doric order; also the New Westminster Hospital, a handsome Gothic building.

NEW ROAD, from Islington to Paddington. Near Islington, Claremont chapel and New River reservoir. On Pentonville-hill, St. James's chapel.—At Battle-bridge, Small-pox hospital.—A short distance west, St. Pancras old church.—Near Euston-square, St. Pancras new church.—Coade and Sealey's manufactory.—Trinity church.—Circus at Regent's-park.—Mary-le-bone new church.—Mary-le-bone workhouse.

NOBLE-STREET, CHEAPSIDE. No. 14, Coachmakers'-hall, formerly noted for a debating society.

NORFOLK-STREET, STRAND. The last house on the west side nearest the river has been successively inhabited by three eminent men: Penn, the founder of Pensylvania; Dr. Birch, the antiquary; and the Rev. Theophilus Lindsey.

NORTH AUDLEY-STREET. Chapel.

OLD BAILEY. Sessions-house.—Newgate prison.—On the west side resided the notorious Jonathan Wild.—In a house over Break-neck-stairs, in Greenarbour-court, Oliver Goldsmith wrote his *Vicar of Wakefield.*—Break-neck-stairs are remarkable as one of the places where watermen plied for fare on the Fleet-ditch.

OLD FISH-STREET. Opposite Lambeth-hill, church of St. Mary Magdalen.—Between Nos. 5 and 6, St. Nicholas Cole abbey.

OLD JEWRY. No. 8 was the residence of Sir Robert Clayton, lord-mayor in 1680; it was afterwards occupied by the London Institution; and here Porson died. Nearly opposite, St. Olave's church.

OLD PALACE-YARD. On the west side, St. Margaret's church.—Statue of Canning.—Westminster abbey.—Henry VII.'s chapel.—On the east side, Houses of Parliament.

OLD-STREET ROAD is a part of the Roman military way, which led, by the north side of London, from the west to the east part of the kingdom.—St. Luke's church.—St. Luke's hospital.

OXFORD-STREET. Between Nos. 73 and 74, the Royal Bazaar, fitted up as a theatre.—Between Nos. 359 and 360 is the front and portico of the Pantheon.

PALACE-YARD. See NEW and OLD PALACE-YARD.

PALL-MALL. South side of the Opera-house.—United Service Club.—Travellers' Club, Reform Club, Carlton Club.—No. 29, Royal Exchange Insurance-office.—No. 91, the duke of Buckingham's. — No. 86, Ordnance-office.—No. 73, Globe Insurance-office.—No. 52, British Gallery.—No. 65, Marlborough-house.—At the west end, St. James's Palace.

PALL-MALL EAST. See COCKSPUR-STREET.

PARLIAMENT-STREET. On the east side is Richmond-terrace, a noble range of houses adorned with Ionic columns, erected in 1823 on the site of Richmond-house. No. 52 was for many years the residence of C. J. Fox.

PATERNOSTER-ROW was so called from the manufacturers of beads, and other emblems of devotion, who formerly inhabited this street; it is now noted as the residence of booksellers.—The Chapter Coffee-house has long been famed as the resort of literary characters, and here are kept files of most of the London and country newspapers.—In Lovell's-court, Richardson the novelist wrote many of his works, at the house of his friend, alderman Bridgen.—In Pannier-alley is an ancient piece of sculpture, representing a boy on a pannier, and underneath is this inscription:—

When ye have sovght
The citty round,
Yet still this is
The highest ground.
Avgvst the 27
1688.

PETER-STREET, WESTMINSTER. Gas-works.—At the corner of Tufton and Peter streets resided the notorious colonel Blood, but the house is no longer standing.

PICCADILLY. Circus formed by Regent-street:—Between Nos. 196 and 197, St. James's church.—Between Nos. 46 and 47, Albany.—Between Nos. 48 and 52, Burlington-house and Arcade.—Opposite, the Egyptian-hall.—At the corner of Berkeley-street, Devonshire-house.—No. 80, formerly 78, is the house where sir Francis Burdett resisted the speaker's warrant, and from which he was conveyed to the Tower, April 9, 1810.—No. 82, lord Ashburton's, whence there is a fine view of lord Spencer's, the Palace, and the Green-park. —No. 94, Cambridge-house.—No. 105, formerly the Pulteney-hotel, a handsome stone building of the Corinthian order, where the emperor of Russia and the duchess of Oldenburgh resided in 1814.—Opposite, the Green-park and the Ranger's-lodge.—At the corner of Park-lane, Gloucester-house.—Corner of Hamilton-place, lord Eldon's.—At the west extremity, Apsley or Wellington-house, and Arch into Hyde-park.—On the opposite side of the road, an Arch forming the entrance to the Palace.—St. George's-hospital.—From this spot there is a picturesque view of Westminster-abbey, Green-park, &c.

PORTLAND-PLACE is the handsomest brick street in the metropolis, the houses being regular, elegant, and lofty. It is about 200 yards in length, and about 42 in breadth.—The south end is terminated by the garden of Foley-house, and the north is open to the Regent's-park.—In Park-crescent, at the north end of Portland-place, is a bronze statue of the late duke of Kent, by Mr. Gahagan, erected by public subscription. The statue is seven feet two inches high, and weighs two tons.

PORTLAND-STREET (Little). Unitarian chapel.

PORTMAN-STREET. No. 22 was for a short time the residence of queen Caroline.

PORTUGAL-STREET, LINCOLN'S-INN-FIELDS. Insolvent

Debtors' Court.—The Theatre where pantomimes were first performed, under the direction of Rich, is now occupied as a china warehouse.—Next to it is the back of Surgeons'-college. —Opposite, St. Clement's burial-ground, containing the tomb of Joe Miller.

POULTRY. Grocers'-hall, in the court of the same name. —On No. 9 is one of the ancient signs by which the shops in London were designated.—Between Nos. 30 and 31, Chapel built on the site of the Compter-prison.—St. Mildred's church. —In Mansion-house-street, which connects the Poultry with Cornhill, the Mansion-house.

PRINCES-SQUARE. The Swedes' church.

PUDDING-LANE, LITTLE EASTCHEAP. On the east side of this street, 202 feet from the monument, the great fire of London commenced.—No. 34 Butchers'-hall.

QUEEN-SQUARE. Statue of queen Anne.—Church of St. George the Martyr.

QUEEN-STREET. See GREAT QUEEN-STREET.

RATCLIFFE-HIGHWAY. The church of St. George-in-the-East.—No. 29 was the house of Mr. Marr, who, with his family, was inhumanly murdered December 8, 1811.

RAY-STREET, CLERKENWELL. At No. 3 is a pump, with an inscription stating that it is furnished with water from a well about four feet eastward, round which the parish clerks of London assembled annually in former times, to perform sacred plays. From this circumstance it was called Clerks' Well, and thence arose the name of the parish in which it was situated.

RED-CROSS-STREET. At the west end, church of St. Giles, Cripplegate.—Back of New Debtors' Prison.—Immediately adjoining, Dr. Williams's Library.

RED LION-STREET, SPITALFIELDS. Nicholas Culpepper, the herbalist and astrologer, died in 1654 at the corner of Red-lion-court; the house has been often repaired since his time, and is now occupied by a publican.

REGENT'S-PARK. On east side, Diorama; Colosseum with Panorama of London; Gloster, Cambridge, Chester, and Cumberland terraces; St. Catherine's Hospital, and Horse-guards barracks.—On the north side, the Zoological-gardens and Primrose-hill.—On the south side, Ulster, York, and Cornwall terraces, and the Lodge of the Toxophilite society.—On the west side, Clarence-terrace, Sussex-place, and Hanover-terrace.—In the centre is a circular road surrounding a nursery-ground, where the London Botanical Society hold their meetings.

REGENT-STREET. At the corner of Charles-street, Junior United Service Club-house.—Nearly opposite, St. Philip's, or Waterloo chapel, Club-chambers.—No. 24, Microcosm Exhibition.—County Fire-office, terminating the view from Pall-mall.—Quadrant, extending from Piccadilly to Glass-house-street, ornamented by colonnades, supported by 140 cast-iron columns.—No. 174, Archbishop Tennison's chapel. —No. 209, Cosmorama.—Near Oxford-street, the Argyle-rooms.—Opposite, Hanover chapel.—In the upper part, facing Margaret-street, the Polytechnic Institution.—At the corner of Langham-place, All Souls' church.

ROOD-LANE. Church of St. Margaret Patens.

RUSSELL-SQUARE. Statue of the duke of Bedford.

RUSSELL-STREET. See GREAT RUSSELL-STREET.

SACKVILLE-STREET is the longest in London without a turning or any street leading into it.

ST. ANDREW'S-HILL. See THAMES-STREET, UPPER.

ST. ANNE'S-LANE. See ALDERSGATE-STREET.

ST. DUNSTAN'S-HILL. See THAMES-STREET, LOWER.

ST. JAMES'S-PARK. On the east side, back of Admiralty and Horse-guards, and front of Treasury.—Two pieces of Ordnance on the Parade.—Ornamental water and shrubbery in the centre.—The Mall.—To the right of the Mall, Carlton-terrace, on the site of Carlton-palace-gardens.—York Column. —Marlborough-house. — St. James's-palace. — Sutherland-house.—Green-park.—On the west, the New Palace on the site of Buckingham-house.—On the south side, Bird-cage-walk and noble new barracks for foot-soldiers, and the handsome Wellington chapel.

ST. JAMES'S-SQUARE. Statue of William III. See article SQUARES.

ST. JAMES'S-STREET. No. 85, Albion Subscription-house. —No. 5, the Imperial Insurance-office.—No. 69, Arthur's Club-house.—At the corner of Park-place, Brooke's Subscription-house.—No. 31, Boodle's Subscription-house.—No. 43, White's Subscription-house.—Between 50 and 54, Crockford's Club-house.

ST. JOHN'S-SQUARE, CLERKENWELL. Nos. 36 and 37 formed the residence of bishop Burnet.—St. John's-gate, forming the south entrance to this square, is the finest vestige of monastic building in the metropolis; it was originally the gate to the priory of St. John of Jerusalem, but is also remarkable as the place where the early numbers of the "Gentleman's Magazine" were published. It was often visited by Dr. Johnson, Garrick, and other eminent characters. It is now occupied partly as a tavern, and partly as a watch-house.

ST. JOHN'S-STREET ROAD. At the Old Red-lion public-house, Paine wrote his "Rights of Man."—Sadler's-wells theatre.—A short distance to the west, the New-river Head, and St. Mark's church, Myddleton-square.

ST. MARTIN'S-LE-GRAND. The east side of this street was pulled down in 1818 to make room for the new Post-office, and vestiges were discovered of a building erected in the 13th century.

ST. MARTIN'S-LANE. Church of St. Martin.—Messrs. Woodburn's Gallery.—No. 101, Exhibition of the Apollonicon.

ST. MARTIN'S-STREET, LEICESTER-SQUARE. The house between the chapel and Long's-court was the residence of sir Isaac Newton.

ST. PAUL'S CHURCHYARD. In the centre, St. Paul's cathedral.—On the north side, Chapter-house.—On the south, Doctors' Commons.—On the east, St. Paul's school.

SAVOY-STREET, STRAND, leads to the site of the ancient Savoy-palace, which was built by Peter, earl of Savoy, in 1245. Here the amiable king John of France was confined, and died in 1364. It was afterwards used as a prison for deserters, but was pulled down in 1816 to make room for Waterloo-bridge.—St. Mary-le-Savoy.—Lutheran church.

SCOTLAND-YARD was so named from being the site of a magnificent palace, for the reception of the kings of Scotland when they visited London.—The Palace-court.—Naval and Military Museum and Library.—Metropolitan Police-office.

SHOE-LANE. New Fleet-market.

SHOREDITCH derived its name from sir John Sordig, lord of the manor in the time of Edward III., and not, as vulgar tradition reports, from Jane Shore having died here in extreme poverty.—At the north end, church of St. Leonard.

SKINNER-STREET. St. Sepulchre's church.

SMITHFIELD. See WEST SMITHFIELD.

SOHO-SQUARE. Statue of Charles II.—The Bazaar.

SOUTH AUDLEY-STREET. At the corner of Curzon-street, Chesterfield-house.—No. 77 is the house to which her late majesty queen Caroline repaired, on her arrival in London, June 6, 1820.

SPA-FIELDS. The house next to the east end of the chapel in Exmouth-street was the residence of the countess of Huntingdon.—To the west, the House of Correction.

SPITAL-FIELDS is chiefly inhabited by silk-weavers, whose predecessors came over to England and settled here after the revocation of the edict of Nantes.—See UNION-STREET and RED LION-STREET.

STAINING-LANE. Front of Haberdashers'-hall.

STAMFORD-STREET. Unitarian chapel.—Benevolent Society of St. Patrick.

STRAND. St. Clement's church.—Between Nos. 15 and 16, Picket-street, Clement's-inn.—In Holywell-street, Lyons-inn.—Between Nos. 168 and 169, Strand Theatre, formerly Burford's Panorama.—St. Mary-le-Strand, or New church.—Between Nos. 151 and 152, Somerset-house and King's College.—No. 345 was occupied by Jacob Tonson the bookseller.—Between Nos. 130 and 135, Wellington-street, leading to Waterloo-bridge, at the corner of which is the Duchy of Cornwall-office, a handsome brick-building with stone front, erected in 1821.—Exeter-hall.—At the corner of Beaufort-buildings resided Lilly the perfumer, mentioned in the Spectator.—No. 411, the Adelphi Theatre.—No. 427, decorated with busts of George I., II., and III.—No. 429, British Fire-office.—Lowther-arcade.—National Gallery of Practical Science.—Hungerford-market.—No. 1, Branch Post-office.—Northumberland-house.

STRATFORD-PLACE. No. 11 was inhabited by the archdukes John and Louis of Austria, during their visit to London in 1815.

SUFFOLK-STREET. Society of British Artists.

SUFFOLK-STREET, EAST. See BOROUGH.

THAMES-STREET, LOWER. On St. Mary's-hill, No. 18, Waterman's-hall.—No. 17, Fellowship Porters'-hall, and church of St. Mary-at-Hill.—Billingsgate Fish-market.—Opposite, the Coal-Exchange.—Custom-house.—On St. Dunstan's-hill, church of St. Dunstan-in-the-East.—No. 16 Harp-lane, Bakers'-hall.—At east end, the Tower.

THAMES-STREET, UPPER. On St. Andrew's-hill, church of St. Anne, Blackfriars.—At the corner of Bennet's-hill, church of St. Bennet.—At the corner of Old Fish-street-hill, church of St. Mary Somerset.—At the corner of Trinity-lane, St. Michael Queenhithe.—No. 9 in Trinity-lane, Painter Stainer's-hall.—On Garlick-hill, church of St. James.—Next to No. 70, Vintners'-hall, handsomely rebuilt in 1823.—Entrance to

Southwark-bridge.—In Elbow-lane, at the corner of Little Elbow-lane, Innholders'-hall; and No. 3, Dyers'-hall.—At the corner of Allhallows-lane, church of Allhallows. — In Suffolk-lane, Merchant Tailors'-school.—Between Nos. 112 and 113, Fishmongers'-hall.

THEOBALD'S-ROAD, and the adjacent street, called KING'S-ROAD, derived their names from being frequented by James I., in coming from his palace at Theobald's.

THREADNEEDLE-STREET. Principal front of the Bank.—North front of Royal-exchange.—Opposite, St. Bartholomew's church.—Between Nos. 12 and 15, St. Benedict's church.—Between Nos. 51 and 53, a French church.—Between Nos. 30 and 31, Merchant Tailors'-hall.—At the east end, South Sea-house. See BISHOPSGATE-STREET.

THROGMORTON-STREET. Drapers'-hall.

TOOLEY-STREET. St. Olave's church.

TOTTENHAM-COURT-ROAD. The chapel where Whitfield preached.

TOWER-HILL was, till 1746, the usual place of execution for state criminals.—On the south side, the Tower; and to the east of it, St. Catherine's Docks.—On the east, the Mint.—On the west, the Trinity-house.

TOWER-STREET. Allhallows Barking church.

TRAFALGAR-SQUARE. National Gallery. — St. Martin's church.—College of Physicians.—Union Club.

TRINITY-LANE. See THAMES-STREET, UPPER.

UNION-STREET, BISHOPSGATE. At the east end, Christ church, Spitalfields.

UNION-STREET, BOROUGH. No. 190, Police-office.

WALBROOK. St. Stephen's church.

WATER-LANE, BLACKFRIARS. See BRIDGE-STREET.

WATERLOO-BRIDGE-ROAD. To the west of Waterloo-bridge, Shot-manufactory, having a tower nearly 100 feet high.—Infirmary for children.—St. John's church.—Sion chapel.—New Jerusalem chapel.—Victoria theatre.

WATERLOO-PLACE. York column.—Athenæum club.

WATLING-STREET was one of the Roman military roads.—At the corner of Budge-row, St. Antholin's church.—No. 33, entrance to St. Mary Aldermary.—Corner of Bread-street, Allhallows church.—Corner of Old 'Change, church of St. Faith and St. Augustine.

WELBECK-STREET. No. 1 is a specimen of Egyptian architecture, built in 1810, as a picture-gallery, but afterwards converted into an auction-room.

WELLCLOSE-SQUARE. Danish church.

WEST SMITHFIELD is remarkable as the largest cattle-market in England, and is the place where Bartholomew fair is held, the charter for which was granted by Henry II. It has likewise been the scene of tournaments, theatrical performances, and martyrdoms. The spot where the latter took place is situated in the centre of the pens, where the gas-lamp now stands.—Here Wat Tyler was killed by the lord-mayor Walworth, in consequence of which the dagger was added to the city arms.—On the south side, St. Bartholomew's hospital, and church of St. Bartholomew the Less.—In the south-east corner, St. Bartholomew the Great.

WESTMINSTER-BRIDGE-ROAD. At the north end, Westminster-bridge.—To the right, Lambeth-palace.—Astley's Amphitheatre.—In the York-road, General Lying-in-hospital.—New chapel.—Asylum.—Bethlem-hospital.—Blind school.

WHITECHAPEL is principally inhabited by butchers.—St. Mary's church.

WHITECROSS-STREET. New Debtors' prison.

WHITEHALL. Asphalte experimental pavement.—Admiralty.—Army Pay-office, from which, through Whitehall-place, there is a fine view of St. Paul's cathedral.—Horse-guards.—Whitehall chapel or Banqueting-house.—Behind Whitehall, statue of James II.—Dover-house.—Treasury.—New Council-office, and Board of Trade.

WINCHESTER-STREET. In the south-west corner are vestiges of Winchester-house, which was erected by a marquess of that name in the reign of Edward VI.

WOOD-STREET. Between Nos. 114 and 115, St. Michael's church.—At the corner of Love-lane, St. Alban's church.—No. 83, Parish Clerks'-hall.

WYCH-STREET. See NEWCASTLE-STREET.

LITERARY RECOLLECTIONS.

Blackstone was BORN in Cheapside; lord Byron in Holles-street, Cavendish-square; Camden the antiquary in the Old Bailey; Colley Cibber in Southampton-street, Strand; Cowley in Fleet-street, at the corner of Chancery-lane; Gray in Cornhill; Hogarth in Ship-court, Old Bailey; Holcroft the dramatic writer in Orange-court, Leicester-square; Ben Jonson in Hartshorn-lane, which was near Charing-cross; Milton in Bread-street, where his father was a scrivener;

lord chancellor More in Milk-street; Pope in Lombard-street; Spenser in East Smithfield; Stow the historian in Cornhill.

Lord Bacon RESIDED in Gray's-inn; Barry the painter in Castle-street, Oxford-street; Beaumont and Fletcher at Bank-side; Butler, the author of "Hudibras," in Rose-street, Covent-garden; Cibber the elder in Holborn, near St. Andrew's-church; sir Edward Coke in Hatton-Garden; Defoe in Cornhill, where he kept a hosier's shop; John Fox in Grub-street, where he compiled the greater part of his "Martyrology;" Garrick in Southampton-street, as well as in the Adelphi; Gibbon in Bentinck-street; Handel in Brook-street, Grosvenor-square; Hans Holbein in Duke's-place, as well as on old London-bridge; Hume in Lisle-street, Leicester-square; Dr. Johnson in Temple-lane, and in Bolt-court, Fleet-street; Ben Jonson, in Bartholomew-close; sir Godfrey Kneller in Great Queen-street; Milton in St. Bride's churchyard, Aldersgate-street, Jewin-street, Barbican, Bartholomew-close, and Scotland-yard; Prior in Duke-street, Westminster; sir J. Reynolds in Newport-street, St. Martin's-lane, and Leicester-square; sir R. Steele in Bury-street; Dr. Stillingfleet in Hatton-garden; sir J. Thornhill in Covent-garden; and Voltaire, while at London, in Maiden-lane.

Boswell, the biographer of Johnson, DIED in Great Portland-street; sir Francis Bourgeois in Portland-place; Chatterton in Brook-street, Hatton-garden; Congreve in Surrey-street; Dryden in Gerrard-street; Garrick in the Adelphi; Glover in Albemarle-street; Gibbon in St. James's-street; Holcroft in Clipstone-street; Hoyle the whist-player in Welbeck-street; archbishop Leighton at the Bell-inn, Warwick-lane; Milton in Artillery-walk, Bunhill-fields; Nollekens the sculptor in Mortimer-street, Cavendish-square; sir J. Reynolds in Leicester-square; Richardson the novelist in a passage leading from Water-lane to Salisbury-court; Sheridan in Saville-row; Spencer at an inn in King-street, Westminster; Sterne in Old Bond-street; H. Walpole in Berkeley-square.

PLAN FOR VIEWING LONDON

IN

EIGHT DAYS.

By pursuing the following method, the stranger will be enabled to take a cursory view of every remarkable object in a short space of time. To inspect them all minutely would, of course, occupy many weeks.

Each day's excursion commences at Charing-cross, as a great majority of the visiters of the British metropolis fix their residence in that vicinity. The various objects are described in other parts of the work.

FIRST DAY. Statue of Charles I. at Charing-cross—Scotland-yard police-office—Admiralty—Horse-guards—Whitehall-chapel—Statue of James II. at the back—Council-office—Treasury—Richmond-terrace—Board of Control—Palace-yard—Westminster-hall Courts of Law—House of Commons—House of Lords—Statue of Canning—St. Margaret's-church—Westminster-abbey, Poets' Corner, Henry VII.'s chapel—Westminster-school—St. John the Evangelist—Penitentiary—Fine gravel road and view of Lambeth-palace—Vauxhall-bridge—Vauxhall-gardens—Lambeth-church—Lambeth-palace—Westminster-bridge—Charing-cross.

SECOND DAY. St. James's-park—Back of Treasury and other offices—Parade, with two pieces of ordnance—Terraces on the site of Carlton-palace—York Column—Specimen of Asphalte pavement—Mall-walk—Marlborough-house—Gower-house—Palace—Wellington-chapel and Barracks—Royal Mews at Pimlico—Chelsea-Hospital and Ground—Royal Military Asylum—Botanical Garden.—Return by Eaton square—St. Peter's-church—Belgrave-square—Pantechnicon—St. George's Hospital—Hyde Park-corner—Entrance to the Palace—Entrance to Hyde-park—Green-park—Spencer house—St. James's-palace—British Institution—St. James's Theatre—St. James's-square—New University Club—Carlton Club—Site of New Reform Club—

Travellers' Club—Athenæum Club—Opera-house Colonnade—United Service Club—Statue of George III.—National Gallery, Trafalgar-square—Charing-cross.

THIRD DAY. Union Club-house—College of Physicians—Water-colour Exhibition—United University Club-house—Society of British Artists, Suffolk-street—Italian Opera-house—Haymarket Theatre—Junior United Service Club-house—St. Philip's Chapel—Club Chambers—County Fire-office—St. James's Church—Burlington-house—Burlington-arcade — Devonshire-house — Cambridge-house — Duke of Wellington's, Apsley-house—Hyde-park—Statue of Achilles—Serpentine River—Cascade, Conduit, and New Bridge—Kensington Palace and Gardens. — Return by Bayswater, Archery-ground, and Park-lane—Marquess of Westminster's Gallery—Dorchester-house — Chesterfield-house—Piccadilly—Charing-cross.

FOURTH DAY. Leicester-square—Miss Linwood's Exhibition—Burford's Panorama — Zoological Museum—Western Literary and Scientific Institution—Piccadilly—Bond-street—Western Exchange—Berkeley-square— Lansdowne-house—Grosvenor-square—Statue of George I. — Portman-square—Bryanston-square—Montague-square —Baker-street Bazaar, Madame Tussaud's Exhibition — Mary-le-bone Church—Through the Regent's-park, by the New Walk—Marquess of Hertford's and other villas—Zoological Gardens—St. Catherine's-Hospital —Colosseum — Diorama — Park-square and Crescent—Statue of the Duke of Kent—Portland-place—All Souls' Church—Polytechnic Institution—Cavendish-square—Hanover-square—Statue of Pitt—St. George's Church—Regent-street—Hanover Chapel—Archbishop Tenison's Chapel—Regent's Quadrant—Charing-cross.

FIFTH DAY. St. Martin's Church—Apollonicon — St. Giles's Church—Soho-square—Bazaar — New Theatre (late Queen's Bazaar) — Pantheon —Bedford-square—University College—Euston-square—Terminus of Birmingham railway—St. Pancras Church — Tavistock-square — Russell-square — Bloomsbury-square—British Museum—Freemasons' Tavern—Covent-garden Theatre—Drury-lane Theatre—St. Paul's Church, Covent-garden—Market—Charing-cross.

SIXTH DAY. Branch Post-office — Northumberland-house—Hungerford Market—Lowther Arcade and Gallery of Practical Science—Charing-cross Hospital—Adelphi-terrace—Water-gate—Cellars beneath—Garrick's House—Society of Arts — Exeter-hall — Burleigh-street Chapel — Somerset-house—King's College—St. Mary's Church—St. Clement's Church—Temple Bar—Law Life Assurance-office—St. Dunstan's New Church—Temple Church, Hall, and Gardens—St. Bride's Church—Waithman's and Wilkes's Monuments—New Farringdon Market—Fleet Prison—Bridewell—Blackfriars-bridge—Shops in Ludgate-hill—St. Paul's Cathedral—St. Paul's school—New Post-office—Goldsmith's-hall at the back—Bow Church — Guildhall — Mansion-house — St. Stephen's, Walbrook — City of London School — Bank — New street leading to Finsbury—Site of Royal Exchange—Stock-exchange — Auction-Mart— Excise-office—Roman Catholic Chapel, Moorfields—London Institution—Finsbury-square—St. Luke's Hospital—Charter-house—West Smithfield—St. Sepulchre's — Newgate — St. Andrew's, Holborn-hill—Furnival's Inn — Chancery-lane—Law Institution — Lincoln's-Inn — Lincoln's-inn-fields—Soane's Museum — Surgeon's-Hall and Museum—thence to Charing-cross.

SEVENTH DAY. London-bridge by 4*d.* steamer from Westminster-bridge or Hungerford—King William-street—Cannon-street, in which is the London-stone—New Fishmonger's-hall—Monument—Billingsgate Fish-market—Custom-house and Quay—Tower—Mint—St. Catherine's Docks—London Docks—Cross the River and visit the Thames Tunnel at Rotherhithe, and Brunel's arch—St. Mary's Church.—Recross the River to West-India Docks—East-India Docks—East-India Tram-road.—Return by omnibus along the Commercial-road to Leadenhall-street—Commercial-Hall—Corn Exchanges—East-India-house and Museum—St. Michael's, Cornhill—Return by Cheapside, Ludgate-hill, and Strand.

EIGHTH DAY. Steam-boat from Hungerford to Westminster-bridge—Astley's Theatre—Orphan Asylum—Bethlehem Hospital—School for the Blind—Philanthropic Institution—Obelisk—Elephant and Castle—Surrey Zoological Gardens—Surrey Theatre—Magdalen Asylum—Deaf and Dumb Asylum—Queen's Bench Prison—British and Foreign School—Guy's-Hospital —St. Thomas's Hospital—St. Saviour's Church — Greenwich Railroad — Return by Union-street, across Blackfriars-road—Victoria Theatre—St. John's Church, Waterloo-road — Waterloo-bridge — Wellington-street, and the Lyceum Theatre—Return along the Strand to Charing-cross.

ENVIRONS.

The most remarkable places in the vicinity of London may be visited in five days.

FIRST DAY. Fulham—Putney—Richmond—Twickenham—Hampton Court.

SECOND DAY. Deptford—Greenwich, by railroad—Woolwich—Shooter's-hill—Blackheath.

THIRD DAY. Slough—Eton—Windsor, by railroad.

FOURTH DAY. Camberwell—Dulwich—Norwood—Beulah Spa—Sydenham—Lewisham.

FIFTH DAY. Primrose-hill—Highgate—Hampstead—Harrow, by railroad.

DIARY OF AMUSEMENTS IN LONDON,

POINTING OUT THE PRINCIPAL OCCURRENCES WORTHY OF NOTICE DURING THE YEAR.

JANUARY.

6th. Twelfth Day. Epiphany is celebrated at the Chapel Royal, St. James's. Gold, frankincense, and myrrh are presented at the altar, in imitation of the offering made by the Wise Men of the East; and the music and singing, on this occasion, is generally performed by the first professional talent in the metropolis.

In the evening the confectioners' and pastry-cooks' shops present a brilliant display of ornaments.

On Plough Sunday, or first Sunday after Epiphany, the Lord Mayor, Sheriffs, and Aldermen, go in state from the Mansion-house to St. Lawrence's Church, and afterwards return to dinner.

On Plough Monday, the Common-councilmen and other Ward officers are sworn into office at Guildhall.

11th. Hilary Term commences. On this, as well as on the first day of the other terms, the Judges breakfast at the Lord Chancellor's house, and afterwards proceed, about 12 o'clock, to Westminster-hall, to open the courts of law. The judges, as well as the counsel, are, on this occasion, full-dressed, and the whole spectacle is well worthy a stranger's attention.

During each term, the Gresham lectures are delivered. The time and place of delivery, and the subjects, are advertised in the daily papers, and the public are admitted gratis.

FEBRUARY.

The British Gallery generally opens in this month, for the exhibition and sale of works by British artists.—Admission 1*s.*; Catalogue 1*s.*

On the Wednesday and Friday evenings in Lent, Oratorios, or Selections of Music, are performed at Covent-garden and Drury-lane theatres; and the minor theatres are generally opened with sleight of hand and mechanical exhibitions.

MARCH.

1st. St. David's Day. The anniversary of the Welsh Charity School is held.

17th. St. Patrick's Day, when the anniversary of the Benevolent Society of St. Patrick is held.

During March, and the two succeeding months, most of the charitable institutions hold their anniversaries. They are generally celebrated by a public dinner, preceded by a sermon on the same day or on the previous Sunday. They are always advertised in the daily papers, and tickets for the dinner, generally 15*s.* or 1*l.* 1*s.*, may be procured of the stewards, or at the tavern.

From March to May inclusive, the Blue-coat boys sup in public. See page 239.

APRIL.

23d. St. George's Day.

On Maunday Thursday a confirmation of the juvenile branches of the nobility takes place at the Chapel Royal, St. James's; and at Whitehall-chapel, the annual royal donations are distributed by her majesty's almoner, to as many poor men and women as the king or queen is years of age. The service at Whitehall commences at three o'clock; and strangers who cannot obtain tickets may procure admission to the gallery by giving 1*s.* to the doorkeeper.

Easter Sunday. The queen, if in town, attends the Chapel Royal, St. James's, and receives the sacrament.

Easter Monday. The lord-mayor, sheriffs, aldermen, &c., proceed from the Mansion-house in state, accompanied by about 600 Blue-coat boys, to Christ-church, Newgate-street, where they hear the Spital sermon, and afterwards return in procession to the Mansion-house to dinner.

On the same day, according to annual custom, a stag is turned out near the Bald-faced Stag, in Epping-forest. The queen's hounds also generally meet in the vicinity of Windsor.

On Easter Monday, Tuesday, and Wednesday, is held Greenwich fair, which presents an extensive field of amusement for the lower orders of society.

On Easter Monday also, the Royal Amphitheatre, Sadler's Wells, and the Surrey theatre, open for the summer season.

15th. Easter Term begins.

During April, May, June, and July, the Society of British Artists exhibit a collection of modern paintings at their gallery in Suffolk-street, Haymarket.—Admission 1*s.*

The Society of Painters in Water-Colours also open their exhibition towards the end of April.—Admission 1*s*.

MAY.

1st. On this and the two following days the chimney-sweepers parade the streets in various whimsical dresses.

17th. Her majesty's birth-day is kept on this day. A drawing-room is held at St. James's, and the Park and Tower guns fire a royal salute at one o'clock. In the evening the houses of her majesty's tradesmen, and many public buildings, are illuminated.

23d. Trinity Term begins. On the first Sunday in this term, the lord-mayor, sheriffs, aldermen, &c., go in state to St. Paul's cathedral, to meet the judges and attend divine service.

The exhibition of the Royal Academy opens on the first Monday in May. On the preceding Friday, a numerous company enjoy what is termed a private view of the exhibition; and on the Saturday, the Royal Academicians and a select party dine together at Somerset-house.

On Holy Thursday, the churchwardens, overseers, &c., of each parish of the metropolis, accompanied by the charity-children, attend church, and walk the bounds of the parish.

In May, the anniversary of the Sons of the Clergy is held at St. Paul's, when a fine concert of sacred music is performed. A rehearsal of this music takes place a day or two before. All persons contributing to the charity, at the doors, are admitted.

In May, also, the medals and rewards offered by the Society of Arts are distributed to the successful candidates. Tickets may be obtained of any member of the Society.

Vauxhall opens towards the end of this month.

JUNE.

On the first Thursday in this month, the charity children of London, to the number of 7000 or 8000, attend divine service at St. Paul's cathedral. Tickets of admission can only be obtained of persons connected with the schools. A rehearsal of this meeting takes place on the preceding Tuesday, to which persons are admitted at 6*d*. each.

Whit-Monday, Tuesday, and Wednesday. Greenwich fair is repeated, as at Easter; and Woodford races are held.

In the second week after Whitsuntide, Ascot races take place.

24th. The sheriffs are elected at Guildhall.

During this and the two succeeding months, numerous cricket-matches take place in the vicinity of London; and there are frequent rowing and sailing-matches on the Thames.

The theatres of Covent-garden and Drury-lane close about the end of this month or beginning of the next; and the Hay-market and English-opera open.

On Trinity Monday a grand procession leaves the Trinity-house, Tower-hill, and proceeds by water to Deptford.

Woolwich races take place in June.

In the last week in June, the glass-cutters of the metropolis go in procession through the streets, exhibiting various curious specimens of their labour. The brass-founders also make a similar display about this time.

JULY.

The parliament is generally prorogued during this or the preceding month, and if the queen goes in person, a grand procession, similar to that when the parliament is opened, takes place from the Palace to the House of Lords. The state-carriage, drawn by eight beautiful cream-coloured horses, magnificently caparisoned, the splendid equipages of the royal family and the nobility, the number of soldiers in state dresses, and the multitude assembled to witness the spectacle, combine to present a scene of unrivalled interest. Her majesty leaves the palace at about one or two o'clock.

31st. The British Museum is closed for two months.

AUGUST.

1st. A rowing-match takes place for a coat and badge, which was bequeathed by Doggett, an actor, to be annually rowed for by six watermen, in the first year after they were out of their apprenticeship.

On the first Wednesday in this month, Edgeware fair; and on the two following days, Edgeware races.

SEPTEMBER.

3d. Bartholomew fair begins. It is held in Smithfield, and continues three days.

Egham races are held in this month.

21st. St. Matthew's Day. The lord-mayor, sheriffs, &c., repair to Christ-church, Newgate-street, to hear a sermon, and afterwards proceed to the hall of Christ's-hospital, where two of the senior Blue-coat boys deliver orations.

28th. The sheriffs are sworn into office at Guildhall, before the lord-mayor, aldermen, &c. The hall is open to the public.

29th. Michaelmas-day. The lord-mayor, sheriffs, and other city officers, go in state from the Mansion-house to Guildhall, whence they walk to St. Lawrence's church, and hear service. They then return to Guildhall, to hold a common hall, for the purpose of electing a new lord-mayor; after which the old mayor gives the new one a grand dinner at the Mansion-house.

30th. The sheriffs proceed in the barges of their respective companies to Westminster-hall, in order to be accepted, on the part of the queen, by the barons of the Exchequer. On their return the senior sheriff gives a dinner at the hall of the company to which he belongs.

OCTOBER.

1st. The British Museum opens. See p. 287.

NOVEMBER.

2d. Michaelmas Term begins.

8th. The lord-mayor is sworn into office at Guildhall.

9th. The lord-mayor's show takes place. See p. 53.

DECEMBER.

About the middle of this month an annual show of cattle is held at Dixon's Repository, Goswell-street.—Admission, 1s. It was instituted by the late Francis duke of Bedford, who offered prizes for rearing cattle, sheep, pigs, &c.

The number of cattle brought to Smithfield on Monday in the week preceding Christmas is generally larger than on any other day of the year.

21st. St. Thomas's-day. The common-council-men are elected.

25th. Christmas-day. Good music and singing may be heard at the Roman Catholic chapels.

Besides these various sources of amusement, there are many others, which have already been described in Chapters X. and XI.

CHAPTER XV.

CONCLUDING OBSERVATIONS.

A CONTEMPLATION of the material structure of London, even a review of its varied curiosities, however instructive and amusing, affords but a feeble index of its intellectual characteristics. The secret of the astounding development of wealth and power is to be discovered only by the patient investigator of statistics, who unites with this a philosophical observation of man. Still, without an abstruse attempt at reaching the depths of the metropolitan resources, we may be pardoned for offering a few general remarks on the social, moral, and intellectual condition of London.

To attempt any delineation of the character of Londoners would be a vain task; for the metropolis of the world has as little decided character as could be supposed to belong to a vast emporium of every species of enterprise, opinion, and habit. The extent of the wants of citizens being in proportion to their means of purchase, and the amount of objects created or imported, all capitals therefore have features in common; and the fewer objects to generalise the character of a metropolis, the more striking its identity. The individuality of Bern or of Madrid is little exposed to the variations of cosmopolitism; while London, like a sea that receives the influx of tributary streams, mingles the varied attributes of its condition till it assumes an universal rather than an identical mien. The English character, however, in its most extended sense, is undoubtedly stamped upon the metropolis. A commanding sum of public and private virtue—a startling degree of corruption (the badge of all overgrown cities)—vastness of enterprise, vigorous competition of talent, unbounded extent of resources, and indefatigable industry, are amongst the most obvious features of the British metropolis.

As a mass of astonishing extent, upheld by the intellect and toil of hundreds of thousands, London is a stupendous spectacle; as the scene of human happiness and misery, it cannot fail to be one of intense interest. The conflict between the discordant prescripts of antiquity and the expanding perceptions of the present; the struggles between riches and penury, virtue and vice, wisdom and folly, benevolence and cupidity,

—present a picture of such varied interest, that even ancient Rome, with more aggregate splendour and power, but less individual independence, scarcely affords a parallel. In the British metropolis the shrines of religion, of grandeur, and of commerce, the temples of mirth and dissipation, the asylums for the distressed, and the receptacles of guilt, suggest the ideas of progressive civilisation and rational co-operation, rather than that virulence of design and inflated appeal to the imagination which were so obvious in the mistress of the early world. Rome was a discordant vortex, supplied for a period, through violence and fraud, by the tributary streams of vassal wealth; London is composed of heterogeneous materials tending to a homogeneous result; the latter is the abode of freemen, the former was the tomb of heroes.

The vast extent of London, and its immense population, cannot fail to strike every visiter with astonishment. The influx of foreigners, attracted chiefly by the advantages of commerce, swells an already exuberant population to an astounding computation; while the dense line of vehicles and pedestrians through the principal thoroughfares seems to proclaim the capital of Great Britain the rendezvous of the commercial world. London within the walls (or the heart of the city) is the great repository of the mercantile wealth, not merely of the metropolis, but of the whole country. Its aspect is that of commercial activity; its denizens bespeak the importance of their negociations and their ardent pursuit of wealth; while the ground is crowded at every step with the offices of bankers, merchants, and traders, and the various agents in the mighty commercial scheme.

London will not excite much admiration in the minds of those whose ideas of beauty and grandeur are derived from the isolated remains of Grecian and Roman architecture. Neither will its dusky fabrics bear a comparison with the chasteness and cleanliness of the edifices of Berlin or Paris. The dull uniformity presented by rows of brick buildings of the same general form and appearance, possesses but little attraction for the eye: notwithstanding this disadvantage, the interiors of the metropolitan dwellings are unrivalled for grandeur, elegance, and convenience, according to the respective ranks of those to whom they belong; in short, nothing is wanting to convey an adequate conception of the opulence, ingenuity, and industry of a great capital: even beneath its soil is a region teeming with mechanical wonders. The shops are also remarkable both for external appearance and for the riches and variety of the articles on sale. However inferior it may be to many other cities in point of general architectural splendour, the want of external advantages is more than counterbalanced by the comfort and convenience which it has derived from increasing information and practical science.

Society in large cities necessarily assumes a tone more suited to its extension of privileges than can be expected in a smaller sphere. Yet even in the metropolis, where communion would be supposed to spread a liberality coequal with its pervading knowledge, the spirit of sociality is blighted by a prejudicial affectation of refinement, which distinguishes all ranks in different degrees. The perception of individual wealth is less striking in London than it is in the country, where the wealthy rule over the habits and feelings of their neighbours. In the capital, the appreciation of wealth is applied more to masses than to single examples, yet strikes with such unerring power, that *sets* rule in London while individuals sway in the country. The high-bred and restrictive mandates of the respectable portion of the noble families, the flippant assumption and unrestrained levity of the *half-castes*, the ignorant dogmatism of the aristocracy of wealth, and the timid respectability and craving imitation of the middle classes,—are traits which characterise and laws which bind. The supreme power with all ranks is wealth; and although it may fail to make profligacy or ignorance respectable, it seldom fails to render them sufferable. Yet it would be unjust to deny that in this land there exists a scrutinising spirit of decency that could never tolerate the species of laxity which in many countries conveys no reproach and calls down no retribution. The besetting sin of English society is the overwhelming sway of fashion; yet it would not, perhaps, require much argument to maintain that, in a corrupt state of civilisation, where the varied channels of commerce demand a continued flow, some advantages may be derived even from the mutations of fashion.

The Clubs of London have had a very decided influence on the state of society, and on the interests of hotels and taverns. These once-flourishing resorts of men in the upper grades of society have been abandoned for the club-houses, where the advantages of co-operation have been so conspicuously displayed, that the humbler purveyors of comfort have sunk in the unequal contest, and their establishments are now frequented by scarcely any others than temporary sojourners. The effect of this change on the domestic character of these grades is conspicuous; those who have discovered sources of gratification where a moderate expenditure ensures a splendid entertainment, cannot help contrasting the sober hue of domesticity with the cheerful and inspiriting tone of extended communion. To such as possess homes without the usual endearing associations, club-houses present advantages not to be resisted; but to the family-man, who has a higher duty than to pander to selfish gratification, they are too often replete with fatal effects. A contrast which serves only to undermine the stability of private virtues and enjoyments, is dearly purchased indeed. Still, there is probably no innovation without some redeeming advantages, and it may be thought a somewhat Quixotic spirit to assail the fame of established favourites.

The march of intellect has discountenanced in a great degree that profuse extravagance which was formerly the characteristic of all classes. The ostentation which but lately pervaded every rank has been attributed to pride and vanity; it were more just to attribute it to a desire to keep up the hypocrisy of appearances, and to that contagious timidity and irresolution which stimulate men to *become* beggars rather than *appear* poor. Fraternity of profusion poisoned the sources of hospitality: display bespoke a hearty welcome, and inebriety was the climax of good-will; the host imagined that to do *much* was to do *well;* and the guest parasitically applauded the efforts of a man whose mind was racked with the pangs of incipient ruin.

While treating of the state of society, it may be proper to notice a feature in the national character which has been greatly misunderstood and misrepresented. The thoughtless, who delight in any appearances which, by offering a palpable conclusion, may save the trouble of investigation, have seized with avidity that habitual reserve which characterises the inhabitants of London in particular, upon which to build an hypothesis of disdainful taciturnity and supercilious egotism. Nothing, certainly, can be more apparent than the characteristic; nothing more unjust than the deduction. Surrounded as the metropolitan is with hosts of disreputable persons who feed on the produce of others, it becomes a matter of essential security to weigh with some caution the probable chances of an association which irretrievably taints by contact. He who can lightly afford, by bandying fellowship with every fresh face, to sacrifice the prudent dignity of the citizen for the doubtful fascinations of the cosmopolite, can have little property and still less reputation at stake. The value of character is no where so fully appreciated as in England, being the basis of man's success and the apex of his undertakings. It appears, then, that this apparent defect results from a protecting principle founded both on justice and morality.

The most striking feature of the metropolis is the splendour it derives from being the residence of royalty and the seat of parliament. England is a republic on a magnificent scale; and the monarch is a perpetual president, supported in a manner worthy of a powerful nation, and wisely shielded from personal insult by the spirit of the British constitution.

The emanation of power *from* the people, without the immediate operation of democratic machinery, forms one of the bulwarks of our civil existence. Popular influence purified by the ordeal of collective intelligence, popular wants remedied by enlarged views and efficacious measures, and popular demands acceded to or rejected with fearless equanimity,—are the signs of a national parliament, the only faithful guardian of a nation's liberties. All classes of interests are represented by the elect of the nation, whilst individual claims of an extraordinary nature can be brought within the walls of parliament. The Reform Bill has, in a great measure, equalised the power of classes; and the check which each branch of the legislature opposes to the other is replete with advantageous effects. Yet every innovation, whether beneficial or otherwise, excites a quickened circulation in the arteries of the social state. The restless dispositions of the factious find stimulus in every change; and with the elements of improvement it is to be expected that particles of evils should be mingled, so as to render its progress unsteady even if it retard not its full operation. The very essence of the British constitution is equality of rights; yet examples of the undue influence of rank and wealth, and the power of the quibbles and subtleties of sophistry, are to be found in the annals of the law: frequently, the purity of intention proclaimed by the constitutional code suffers for the errors of a corrupt interpretation. All are equal before the law; but as the law is a mere letter or breath, it is necessary, in order to ensure its integrity, that the agents of that law should entertain the same purity of principle.

We now come to that portion of intellectual London which appeals so forcibly to our amusement-loving natures during moments of relaxation and recreation. London possesses its due share of objects that come under the denomination of sights; yet, owing to a system of exaction at once anti-national and degrading, it presented till lately little to the humble admirer of greatness and grandeur, except what he could glean from the exterior of those institutions whose treasures he is debarred from appreciating. Whilst the metropolis of the British empire boasts of being upheld by the freemen of the world, these very citizens, by whose funds the wonders of London are supported, pusillanimously submit (with the exception of ill-timed murmurs alone) to the galling demands which await them at the doors of almost all our public buildings, not even excepting cathedrals. This system, which is so foul a blot on the legislature and the independence of freemen, has justly rendered us the object of wonder and contempt to foreigners. It has an immediate and fatal effect upon our hospitality, for, instead of experiencing a patriotic delight in displaying the attractions of London to country friends and to foreigners, we dread their announced visit as a double tax upon our time and our purses. A society has been established for the laudable purpose of gaining for the people those civil rights which are connected with the acquirement of knowledge and the improvement of taste. Through its influence, the admission to the Tower has been lowered, and St. Paul's partially thrown open. In England most of the important undertakings are the result of private speculations, and are managed by societies and companies, in whose hands competition becomes the stimulator to excellence. In other countries, on the contrary, the governments are the sources of improvement, and it has been clearly demonstrated that in private undertakings there is generally a spirit and variety wanting in government works; yet, for want of expansive views, and a truly national enthusiasm, a want of taste is too apparent.

London, being the focus of intelligence, affords a fair specimen of the intellectual claims of the empire; although at the same time a spirit of improvement has been developed in the country also, which has tended to lessen our exclusive admiration of the power and intelligence of the metropolis. Many county towns have, independent of literary and scientific institutions, societies for the advancement of the fine arts, which have annual exhibitions of works of art.

The fountains of scientific, literary, and artistic knowledge, are numerous and influential, and although many may fail to present that *primâ facie* imposing appearance which distinguishes some few continental associations emanating directly from the governments, they are nevertheless well calculated to disseminate information and to create taste. The Royal and London Institutions, the Royal Society, the Society of Arts and Sciences, the Society of Antiquarians, the Linnean, the Geological, the Zoological, and numerous other societies, tend to the diffusion of knowledge in their various departments. Indeed, such is the desire for intellectual improvement in this great city, that the societies established for the promotion of useful attainments would outnumber the whole of the institutions in any capital of the world. The interests of the arts are dependent upon the British Museum, the Royal Academy, the British Gallery, the National Gallery, the Society of British Artists, and the two societies of water-colour painters; and whatever may be advanced against the partial evils resulting from undigested plans, it cannot be denied that the Arts derive a permanent character from established institutions.

While the pride of intellect is thus fostered and invigorated, its decline is not unmarked in the metropolitan calendar. The labourers in the too often sterile vineyard of intellectuality are welcomed, in their "sear and yellow leaf," to asylums where their latter days may be passed in tranquillity, or they become entitled to pensions which protect them from penury and despair. In this view London presents much to animate the philanthropic mind. Whilst the arm of commerce directs the destinies of a wondering sphere, the hand of benevolence closes the wounds of affliction; while the merchants of the world command the flow of Nature's blessings, the philanthropists of the universe plead the cause of Christianity. The capital of the British empire is literally studded with the labours of charity; and although the propriety of the varied modes in the application of charity may often with justice be questioned, the origin of the benefits demands heartfelt gratitude and admiration. An attempt to remedy the ills resulting from a corrupt state of circumstances is worthy of a being endowed with reason. It may not be in his power to insure happiness, but it is generally possible to alleviate misfortune. There is no profession or trade which does not boast of some society for the relief of its decayed members; and although the idea is necessarily suggested that there must be a mass of misery to demand such an immense number of charitable institutions, there is still a source of gratification in the reflection that these evils are not irremediable. It is in accordance with the designs of Providence that disease shall assail man, and it is in the nature of man to be improvident; we are therefore permitted to employ antidotes to disease, and to suggest schemes to counteract improvidence.

Let us now turn our attention to the progress that has been made and the station we hold in the highest intellectual pursuits. Architecture first claims notice, as holding the chief rank in civic embellishment. Although the present age may boast a greater number of scientific architects than any former period, we have not one of the commanding abilities of sir Christopher Wren, considering all the disadvantages under which he laboured. In many respects, a purer taste prevails; yet it is to be regretted that, whilst architecture is viewed by one class merely as an art, by the other it is regarded merely as a science; neither endeavouring to unite the two grand requisites, without which it becomes either a puerile affectation of taste or a contracted and graceless imitation. The intention of architecture is primarily to supply the wants of man, and, secondly, to afford as much refinement as may be consistent with a skilful adaptation of means to the ends of security and comfort. It is either palatial, ecclesiastical, mercantile, or domestic; and in each style the feeling of the architect should adorn the science by which he is guided. Utility and ornament being its essential features, if deficient in either respect it ceases to be worthy of being considered an art or science: and as the effect produced on the minds of the unlearned is one of the chief tests of architectural beauty, a building that pleases the educated few alone fails to answer its grand intention.

Of palatial architecture we have but few examples, and these will convey to posterity no very flattering opinion of the merits of precursive ages. The only one which can at all be viewed as a fitting abode for the powerful monarch of a mighty empire is the castellated specimen of "regal Windsor;" yet even that must be regarded as a peculiar combination of the splendour of succeeding periods, rather than as an architectural whole, to be criticised by rules of science or dogmas of taste.

The mansions of our nobility may be cited with pride: they display every variety of architecture and every luxury of decoration.

Warwick-castle, Chatsworth, Castle Howard, Blenheim, Alton Towers, Stowe, Trentham Hall, Arundel Castle, Hatfield House. Wrest. Highcliffe. Cobham Hall. Goodwood, Wardour

Castle, Wentworth House, Clumber Park, Longleat, Luton Hoo, Eaton Hall, &c. &c., are all objects of exceeding interest to the foreigner and of gratulation to the native.

Ecclesiastical architecture is perhaps one of the most striking features of the metropolis, and one of the least faulty branches of the art. It is true that the proportions of Grecian and Roman buildings have been copied with slavish accuracy; and too often defects in the originals, engendered by necessity, have in modern hands been erected into standards of excellence. Still, however much originality may be valued, a pleasing imitation is to be preferred to a faulty invention. The genius of the country and of its architects, be it said, is greatly in favour of the Gothic, which seems the genial architecture of the English mind and climate: consequently, we shall find our Gothic specimens more uniformly successful than the other branches; though the modifications of the Grecian and Roman in many of our churches present a pleasing aspect to all who are liberal enough to perceive that although the necessities of Greece did not suggest the introduction of steeples and spires, such a fact does not preclude any endeavour on the part of modern artists to superadd a requisite in temples of Christian worship. What has been done is only a partial guide as to what may be done; and to shackle succeeding ages by the trammels of the past is at once unjust and humiliating.

Our mercantile architecture has lately degenerated into an affectation of pomp, ill suited to the stability and modesty of trade. Flaunting pillars have obscured that light which is but too much diminished by a cloudy atmosphere, while glaring and irrelevant ornaments have presented projections more calculated to collect floating smoke than to please the startled vision. Thus, while the greater portion of the metropolis shocks the refined taste by rows of dusky houses, the remainder often displeases by eccentric elegance and misplaced splendour.

To render London an uniform and pleasing city would be an impossible task; yet it is to be regretted that more regard is not paid to propriety and uniformity. Much that formerly devolved on architects is in the present day the work of builders; the former had in general too little practical knowledge, the latter have too little taste. We have, however, a few noble examples of domestic architecture; the dull brick walls, with unarchitraved windows, have yielded to the more elegant style conspicuous in the beautiful quarter of Belgrave-square, where may be seen some of the most chaste and dignified specimens of modern building.

It appears, then, that great works were executed when, with the exception of a meteor here or there, architectural taste was at a low ebb, and that in the present day, with a more widely diffused knowledge, we do not achieve works of such commanding beauty. The Post-office, the portico of University College, the British Museum, and a few other structures, may be advanced as claims on admiration; but St. Paul's, Westminster-abbey, Greenwich-hospital, and Somerset-house, preceded these memorials of the architectural beauties of the nineteenth century.*

In painting and sculpture we hold a comparatively creditable situation; yet we are lamentably deficient in productions of an Epic character, without being able by a sufficient number of examples in other styles to lay claim to a decided English school. Government does actually nothing for the arts; and without desiring the baneful *fa presto* patronage which has rendered Versailles a forest of mediocrity in its pictures, and the Louvre a wilderness of canvass, we may yet sigh for a discerning fosterage which would bring forth the latent talent of the country. If the amount expended on objects of art be the indication of patronage, there has been no lack of it; but of judicious, enlightened patronage, there has been but little. Patrons have required objects of a minor class, and artists have not been behind the demands of the market. While the capital of Scotland boasts a series of large works by the gifted Etty, the metropolis of England possesses not, in a single public edifice, a production of this ornament of the English school.

Reynolds is termed the father of English art, and justly so; yet his disciples, with a superstitious veneration for even the errors of their parent, while they have exaggerated his defects, have but slightly imitated his beauties. He carried portrait-painting to a high pitch of intellectual refinement, yet sowed the seeds of carelessness and affectation of manner. His laxity as a draughtsman has been considered as a generous contempt for shackling lines, while his vigorous and mellow pencil has in the hands of his followers dwindled into a gross

* Be it recollected, however, that the ancient architects were not stinted in their means, as seems to be generally the case with the moderns. We find, on referring to the annals of St. Paul's, that, independent of government assistance, the sum of 51,217*l.* was subscribed towards a fund for rebuilding that important edifice.

and glaring tool. West introduced a totally different style, and failed in the other extreme, the generality of his pictures being but tinted outlines. He erred, however, rather from the fearlessness of overweening confidence than from the mystery of ignorance. He was a fine artist, but was weak enough to imagine that, by painting great pictures, he deserved to be ranked amongst great painters. Lawrence followed, and carried portrait-painting to the highest pitch of refinement—a refinement too often detrimental to the dignity of art. His pencil was the courtly delineator of rank and beauty, both assuming in his hands an air of luxury, suavity, and languishing ease, which was unknown before. He became the founder of a new style; but as imitators are generally exaggerators, their affectation and frippery have inflicted an injury on the succeeding school by a futile attempt at reproducing excellence. The last few years have witnessed a sad prevalence of the technical over the spiritual language of art.

It must not be forgotten, however, that West was an American, and that his talent was formed in Rome before he came to this country. Fuseli, Rigaud, and De Loutherbourg, were also foreigners, yet their names are to be found in our academic annals. We can, however, boast of Barry and Opie, two of the greatest names of British art; and although the paucity of excellence in our school in the higher departments be somewhat depressing, we have some few noble proofs of the fallacy of the puerile conclusions of Winklemann and Du Bos. In the present day we have hosts of meritorious artists in the various departments; but few, however, in that style which alone can raise a nation to the pinnacle of intellectual greatness. There is a want of stimulus to great exertions: genius languishes unless fostered by public enthusiasm, and that is devoted to more generally interesting and less-ennobling pursuits. We have Hilton, Etty, Haydon, Wilkie, Landseer, M'Clise, Briggs, Eastlake, Patten, Foggo, and others of distinguished talent, to uphold our character with the world; yet even they are forced to succumb to the false taste and to the falser plea, that there is no room in the huge mansions of our nobility and gentry for works of history. Historical pictures, however, need not necessarily be of great dimensions. The fact is, that all see clearly the value of opera-dancers and racers, while few feel the beauties of dignified works of art; but as men are not to be argued into a perception of beauty, nor taunted into a patronage of intellect, the evil must depend for its cure on the unerring corrector of abuses—time.

Sculpture appears to have met with more patronage than painting in the higher branches, the glorious achievements of heroes, legislators, and sages, having been perpetuated in "monumental marble." Owing to this patronage, sculptors have assumed a higher station than painters; and without pretending to examine the comparative difficulties of the two arts, we may safely affirm, that more power is displayed by the chisel than by the pencil. Banks and Flaxman are the two greatest names in British sculpture: while in the present day the claims of that art are upheld by Westmacott, Baily, Chantrey, Gibson, and other sculptors of considerable merit.

Engraving has met with great encouragement, but has experienced a fate similar to that of the sister arts. The graver has been employed as a producer of saleable merchandise, rather than as a perpetuator of artistic excellence: and although, in a mere commercial point of view, this circumstance may be fraught with advantage, yet in the higher sense, this extinction of emulation in a more noble career is painful and humiliating. Nothing can surpass the exquisite beauty of the plates in many of the annuals and other periodicals: the result of these works has been to teach merit the fatal lesson, that minor efforts command the greater patronage. Much of the reward of genius is nominal, but it is ennobling from its nature; and when those rewards are discarded for more worldly stimulants, the producer of excellence degenerates into the manufacturer of attractions.

In music the taste of the public has experienced a decided improvement, while the science and feeling of professors appear to have retrograded. The enormous patronage bestowed on music, as a science appealing to the whole world, independent of all considerations of nationality, is a sufficient proof that neither melody nor harmony is lost on the English ear. It is true that we have by no means the same taste or feeling for the art as the Italians or Germans; yet, to say that we are utterly destitute of either, is an insult to common sense and to nature.

The quality of music, however, is but little considered: and it is viewed more as an innocent pastime than as a scientific attainment and an intellectual gratification. We seldom hear of a truly English original opera, although the last few seasons have been more prolific, but are harassed with cramped imitations of foreign works, produced with infinite labour, little skill, and less effect. Our composers are arrangers of pretty melodies rather than authors of elaborate and scientific works: they seek for melody more than for harmony; and although the former is the soul of music, it derives its chief beauty from the enriching harmony. The early English composers obtained a more sterling reputation than is enjoyed by their successors, and appeared more likely to form a decided English school. Foreign talent, so decidedly superior to our own in this respect, appears to have checked the English muse, and to have diverted her efforts into a fresh channel without an immediate prospect of successful competition. Much is attributed to the bad taste of the public: true it is that that taste is bad; but it is for the learned to lead the unlearned: true greatness never yet urged the plea of a mastery beyond it, nor ever required an apology for pusillanimous subserviency.

The drama, as one of the principal features of the metropolis, next demands our attention; and it is with regret we are forced to echo the tocsin of the drama's decline. The zealous endeavours of our first living tragedian have, however, rescued for a time the legitimate drama from neglect; and under the auspices of Mr. Macready, Shakspeare has been fittingly produced before a British audience. The most brilliant repertory must, however, in time operate unfavourably upon satiated audiences; and each age, however delighted with the noble productions of the past, requires the energies of contemporaneous writers to sustain the drama's wonted fire. Attention to the interests of authors is one of the great means of insuring dramatic success; for it can hardly be supposed that men of talent will devote their lives to that pursuit which exposes them to the caprice of managers and actors, without offering any adequate reward. Still, there are other causes which have operated unfavourably towards the stage; an undue subserviency to a depraved taste has in the end disgusted the very class of people for whom the legitimate drama was sacrificed. But the sin of appealing to "the groundlings" has not been confined exclusively to managers; actors have willingly availed themselves of a laxity which has rendered their task the easier: vehemence of gesture and peculiarity of intonation have supplanted propriety of action and purity of elocution; rage has foamed, pathos has whined: the stately march of the hero and the unequal tread of passion have dwindled into a monotonous stage tramp. The mind is sacrificed to the eye, and the soul-stirring drama is a relict of the past, not a badge of the present.

Sheridan Knowles, Sergeant Talfourd, Sir E. L. Bulwer,

Douglas Jerrold, the authors of the "Provost of Bruges," the "Cavalier" and "Francis I.," Miss Bailie, &c. are the most successful dramatists of the day. The numerous adapters and translators of foreign pieces, Buckstone, Serle, H. Bayley, C. Mathews, Poole, Peake, Planché, Dance, Lemon, &c. &c., are indefatigable in their vocation, while the midnight horrors of melo-dramatic scribes daily inundate the channels of romance. Still, the drama has lost its wonted fire, and ages of misrule have forfeited the confidence and support of the public.

When we add to this desultory examination of our pretensions to fame, as advanced by the remaining branches of science, we shall find that our station in European reputation is enviable, and that the intellectual attainments of Great Britain are objects of reference and respect to emulous neighbours. In medicine we hold a very high rank; and although the French are distinguished by an admirable perception of the theory of medicine, we are unrivalled in purely practical physic. Our surgical practitioners are also in many respects unequalled in the world. One great advantage possessed by our continental rivals is the ease with which their dissecting-rooms are supplied, and the moderate expense of a professional education. It must also be remarked, that if the fees of the London physician be double and treble those of the Parisian *médicin*, the former is opposed by the domestic apothecary, while the moderate expense of an educated adviser on the Continent obviates the necessity of a minor practitioner. In mechanics we are allowed to be pre-eminent, and in civil engineering we are not only able to minister to our own wants with unequalled rapidity and perfection, but to direct the energies of other countries in the march of social improvement. The power of the press, the operations of the legal courts, and the various minor topics of intellectual London, will have been duly examined in the various chapters devoted to them.

We have thus endeavoured, within the narrow limits assigned to us, to take an impartial survey of the moral greatness of London, and of its highest characteristics—a survey which, notwithstanding the various discrepancies it has been our duty to point out, can leave no doubt as to the overwhelming moral and physical power concentrated in the metropolis of the British empire. In despite of the inequalities to be traced in our condition, whether as regards refinement or happiness, and of the shades which occasionally darken the metropolitan horizon, it is still a mighty shrine of greatness

LEIGH'S NEW MAP OF THE ENVIRONS OF LONDON.

London. Published by Leigh & Son, 421 Strand

and goodness, where intellect towers in proud pre-eminence, justice fearlessly awards her verdict, and domestic virtues grace the private sphere. In whatever respect we view it, an imposing magnitude and a swell of power are distinguished mingling with the milder and more endearing peculiarities of an enlightened community. The destinies of the world seem to revolve on it as on an axis; and from the heart of this mighty body the voice of liberty, humanity, and morality, is wafted to the distant shores of the globe. It is from this spot of earth, a geographical atom, that the world's laws receive their sanction or doom; and although the crusade of liberty would, without a prudent regard for political necessities, engender irremediable evils, yet are the eyes of nations emulous in the career of civilisation,—of those awakening with dawning energies, and finally, of those at present crushed beneath an appalling despotism,—fixed upon this sacred asylum of freedom, all their hopes and fears of regeneration or eternal thraldom being registered in the universal annals of mighty, imperial LONDON.

CHAPTER XVI.

THE ENVIRONS OF LONDON.

*** In the following description, we profess to notice only the most remarkable places in the vicinity of London, as an account of *every* spot would far exceed the limits of this work.

ACTON is a village about five miles from London, on the road to Uxbridge. It is noted as having been the residence of sir Matthew Hale, the upright judge; of Richard Baxter, the nonconformist divine; and of Skippon, the parliamentary general. None of the houses, however, in which these persons resided are now standing.

Coach.—Crown, Aldersgate-street.

ASCOT-HEATH is about six miles from Windsor, on the road to Bagshot. It is celebrated for the races held here in the second week after Whitsuntide, which afford four or five days' amusement to the numerous spectators, amongst whom some of the royal family may generally be distinguished.

BARNES is a village on the Surrey side of the Thames, about

six miles west of London. About a quarter of a mile from it is *Barn Elms*, which derives its name from the majestic trees in the vicinity, and is remarkable for an old house called queen Elizabeth's dairy, where Jacob Tonson died. Here this celebrated bookseller erected a gallery for the reception of the Kit-Cat Club, and ornamented it with portraits of the members. Barn Elms was likewise the residence of Cowley the poet, and of Heidegger, the master of the revels to George II.

Inn.—White Hart. *Coach.*—Goose and Gridiron, St. Paul's.

BATTERSEA is a village in Surrey, on the banks of the Thames, about four miles from London. Here the celebrated Bolingbroke was born and died; and here, in a room forming part of the family mansion, he often enjoyed the conversation of his friend Pope. This room still remains, but the greater portion of the house has been pulled down. In the church is a monument to the memory of Bolingbroke, executed by Roubiliac. Here likewise are buried Curtis the botanist; Astle the antiquary; and Collins the author of the Peerage. This village has long been noted for its asparagus. The wooden bridge over the Thames here was erected about 1772.

Coaches.—Black Horse, Coventry-street; Gracechurch-street, Leadenhall-street, and Strand.

BLACKHEATH, Kent, 5¼ miles from London, is a fine elevated heath, in the parishes of Greenwich, Lewisham, and Lee. It commands some delightful prospects, particularly from the lawn called the *Point*, behind a grove at the west end of Chocolate-row. Amongst the many pleasant villas which adorn this heath, may be noticed Westcomb-park and the Woodlands. The house formerly occupied by the princess of Wales has been pulled down. In 1780 a cavern was discovered on the side of the ascent to Blackheath. It consists of several rooms, from 12 to 36 feet wide each way, which have a communication with each other by arched avenues. Some of the apartments have large conical domes, 36 feet high, supported by a column of chalk. The bottom of the cavern is 50 feet from the entrance; at the extremities, 160 feet; and it is descended by a flight of steps. The sides and roof are rocks of chalk, the bottom is a fine dry sand, and 100 feet underground is a well of very fine water, 27 feet deep. This cavern is said to have been the retreat of Jack Cade in the reign of Henry VI., and was occupied by banditti in the time of Oliver Cromwell. The entrance to it may be seen from the great road leading to Dartford. Admittance, 6*d.*

Near the cavern is the new Trinity Church, the first stone of which was laid by the Princess Sophia, July 18, 1838.

Morden College, on the east side of Blackheath, was erected by sir John Morden, a Turkey merchant, who in 1702 devised all his estates to the Turkey company, for the support of the college and the maintenance of poor aged and decayed merchants of England. The pensioners, who are allowed 40*l.* a-year, must be single men, members of the Church of England, and not less than 50 years of age. Over the gate of the building are statues of sir John and lady Morden.

Coaches.—Gracechurch-street, Charing-cross, Leadenhall-street, and Fleet-street.

BLACKWALL is situated on the Thames, about 2½ miles from the metropolis. It is particularly noted for its dock-yards, which belong to the East India Company. On the side of the river are several taverns, which are much frequented, particularly by parties who come here to eat white bait. The windows command fine views of Woolwich, Greenwich, Shooter's-hill, and the adjacent country.

Coaches.—Whitechapel and Leadenhall-street.

BOX-HILL is a delightful eminence, on the road to Worthing, about 22 miles from London, and three beyond Leatherhead. It is supposed to have received its name from the box-trees planted on the south side of it by the earl of Arundel in the time of Charles I. Its situation is quite romantic, and it commands views of London, the greater part of Middlesex, a considerable portion of Kent and Surrey, and Sussex as far as the South-Downs.

Coaches.—Gracechurch-street.

BRENTFORD is a market-town on the Thames, 7½ miles from Hyde-park-corner. It has a church, and a chapel in which is a picture of the Lord's Supper by Zoffany. In a field adjacent to this town, called the Half-acre, the freeholders of Middlesex assemble to elect representatives. Adjoining Brentford is Sion-house, the seat of the duke of Northumberland. The market-day is Tuesday.

Inn.—Royal Hotel. *Coaches.*—St. Paul's Churchyard; Crown, Aldersgate-street; and Gloucester Coffee-house, Piccadilly.

BROMLEY is a market-town in Kent, 10 miles from London. It possesses a college founded by John Warner, bishop of Rochester, for 20 widows of loyal and orthodox clergymen. The church, a part of an ancient Benedictine monastery, contains the monument of Dr. Hawkesworth, author of the "Adventurer," who died at this place in 1773. In the vicinity is a palace belonging to the bishop of Rochester, adjacent to which is St. Blaizewell, a mineral spring similar to that of Tunbridge.

Coaches.—Gracechurch-street, Fleet-street, Charing-cross, Water-lane, Bridge-street Westminster, and Borough.

BUSHY-PARK is a royal demesne near Hampton-court, about 12 miles from London.

Coaches.—Bell or Bull, Holborn; and White Horse-cellar, Piccadilly.

CAMBERWELL is a pleasant village in Surrey, three miles from London-bridge. It has two churches, one of which (St. George's) is a handsome modern building. The Grove, which is an embowered walk about half a mile in length, forms a delightful promenade.

Coaches. — St. Paul's Churchyard, Gracechurch-street, Leadenhall-street, Charing-cross, and Fleet-street.

CARSHALTON, Surrey, about 11 miles from London, is a picturesque village upon the banks of the Wandle: it has an ancient church.

CHELSEA is a village on the Thames, two miles from London, and is particularly noted for two charitable institutions, the Military Hospital and the Military Asylum, which have been already described. In the old church is a monument to sir Thomas More, erected by himself; and in the churchyard is the tomb of sir Hans Sloane, whose collections formed the foundation of the British Museum; and a monument erected by the Linnæan and Horticultural Societies to the memory of Miller the author of the "Gardener's Dictionary." The duchess of Mazarine, Eleanor Gwyn, sir Robert Walpole, sir Hans Sloane, and sir Thomas More, were residents in this parish. At Chelsea likewise is a Botanical Garden, which was bequeathed by sir Hans Sloane to the Company of Apothecaries, who have erected a marble statue of their benefactor, by Rysbrach, in the centre of the garden. On the south side are two very large cedars of Libanus, which were planted in 1685, and on the north is a green-house and a botanical library. Don Saltero's is a famous coffee-house in Cheyne-walk, which was so called from the name of its first proprietor, Salter, who by his eccentric conduct and collection of curiosities attracted much company to his house. These curiosities were sold by auction in 1799, since which period the house has gradually declined in celebrity. Chelsea has been famous for its buns for upwards of a century. The new church, or St. Luke's, Chelsea, has already been described.

Coaches.—Strand, Charing-cross, Leadenhall-street, Ludgate-hill, Coventry-street, and Fleet-street.

CHERTSEY, in Surrey, 21 miles from London, is a place of considerable antiquity, with a handsome bridge of seven arches over the Thames. The church (St. Anne's) is handsome and spacious. The Porch-house was once the residence of Cowley the poet.

Coaches.—Bolt-in-tun, Fleet-street.

CHISWICK is a village on the Thames, about six miles from London. In the earl of Burlington's vault in the church are deposited the remains of Kent the famous gardener; and in the churchyard are interred the following remarkable characters:—Earl Macartney, who conducted the embassy to China; sir John Chardin, the oriental traveller; Ralph the historian; Griffiths the original editor of the Monthly Review; Loutherbourg the landscape-painter; Hogarth, on whose tomb is an epitaph by Garrick; Mary countess of Faulconberg, the daughter of Oliver Cromwell; Dr. Morell; Tomkins the penman, to whose memory a tablet has been erected in the church, by Chantrey; and Ugo Foscolo, an Italian of considerable literary attainments.

A small tunnel belonging to the Middlesex Water-works, leads under the Thames at this place.

Chiswick-house, the seat of the duke of Devonshire, is a very fine specimen of architecture, and is richly adorned with sculptures, paintings, &c. The gardens are tastefully laid out, and ornamented with statues and other decorations. At this mansion Mr. Fox expired in 1806, and Mr. Canning in 1827.

Admission may be obtained on application to the housekeeper.

Coaches.—Piccadilly, St. Paul's Churchyard.

CLAPHAM is a village in Surrey, 3½ miles south from London, consisting chiefly of many handsome houses surrounding a delightful common, which was formerly little better than a morass, and the roads were almost impassable. The latter are now in an excellent state, and the common itself so beautifully planted with trees, both English and exotic, that it has much the appearance of a park. Near the road to Wandsworth is a reservoir of fine water, from which the village is supplied. At the north-east corner of the common is a church erected in 1776; and on the spot formerly occupied by the old church is an elegant chapel. The manor-house, now a boarding-school for young ladies, is situated near this spot, and is rendered conspicuous by a curious octagonal tower. In St. Paul's chapel are some curious monuments.

Coaches.—Bank, Gracechurch-street, Fleet-street, Charing-cross, Strand.

CLAREMONT-HOUSE, near Esher, about 17 miles from London, is situated on a charming spot of country. It was the residence of the late lamented and beloved princess Charlotte, and the scene of her death. The house was originally built by sir John Vanbrugh, and was successively occupied and improved by the earl of Clare, afterwards the duke of Newcastle, lord Clive, viscount Galway, earl of Tyrconnel, and C. R. Ellis, esq., of whom it was purchased by parliament for the prince and princess of Saxe-Cobourg, for 65,000*l.* It still belongs to the King of the Belgians, by whom it is sometimes visited. The duke of Newcastle adorned the park by many plantations under the direction of Kent, and on a mount erected a building in the shape of a castle, and called it Claremont, from his own name, by which the place has been since known. While the estate was in the possession of lord Clive, the mansion was rebuilt, and the grounds laid out by Mr. Brown, at the cost of 100,000*l.* The house is an oblong, 44 yards by 34. On the ground-floor are eight rooms, besides the hall and the great staircase. In the principal front, a flight of steps leads to the grand entrance under a pediment, supported by Corinthian columns.

CROYDON is a market-town in Surrey, ten miles from London. It is divided into the old and new town; in the former are the church (St. John's) and the remains of the archbishop of Canterbury's palace; and in the latter, which is situated on the high-road to Brighton, stand the butter-market, the court-house, and Whitgift's Hospital. The latter is a brick building, endowed in 1596 and 1599, for the maintenance of a warden, schoolmaster, and about 30 poor brethren and sisters, who are nominated by the archbishop of Canterbury. A chapel in this hospital contains a fine portrait of the founder. The church is a capacious building, with a lofty embattled tower: it contains the remains and monuments to the memory of archbishops Sheldon, Wake, Grindall, Whitgift, Potter, and Herring. Croydon has three churches, several charity-schools, and other charitable institutions; a theatre, and numerous meeting-houses. The iron railway from Wandsworth passes by this town to Merstham, and a railroad leads from Croydon to London.

Coaches.—Gracechurch-street, Bishopsgate-street-within, Holborn, Borough, and Bridge-street Westminster.

DEPTFORD, a large town in Kent, divided into Upper and Lower, was anciently called West Greenwich and Deptford. It is seated on the Thames, four miles S.S.E. from London, and is remarkable for its capacious victualling-yard and docks, which may be viewed by an admiralty-order, or by personal application to the principal officer. It has a wet-dock of two acres, and another of an acre and a half, with great quantities of timber, extensive storehouses, &c. Here the royal yachts are generally kept. The manor-house of Say's-court was the seat of John Evelyn, esq., a celebrated natural philosopher of the last century, and the residence also of Peter the Great during the time that he worked as a shipwright in the yard. But this house has been demolished many years, and on its site now stands the workhouse of St. Nicholas. In Deptford are the two parishes of St. Nicholas and St. Paul; and two hospitals, one of which was incorporated by Henry VIII., and is called Trinity-house of Deptford Strond; it contains 21 houses, and is situated near the church. The other, called Trinity-hospital, has 38 houses. Both are for decayed pilots or masters of ships, or their widows. On Trinity Monday a grand procession comes here by water from Trinity-house, and is received with firing of cannon and other marks of joy and festivity. Besides the churches, there are chapels belonging to the methodists, to the baptists, and other classes of dissenters; and a small theatre.

About half a mile south of Deptford, on the banks of the Ravensbourne, is a large building in which gun-barrels, bayonets, halberts, &c., are manufactured by machinery set in motion by a steam-engine of vast power. Over Deptford Creek, which was formerly passed in boats, and frequently attended with danger, a commodious wooden-bridge has been erected for foot-passengers.

Coaches.—Charing-cross and Gracechurch-street.

Or by Greenwich railroad from London-bridge.

DORKING, in Surrey, 23 miles from London, is surrounded by very beautiful scenery. The rock-caves are remarkable. *Inn.*—Fox and Hounds. Leith-hill, Box-hill, Norbury-park, and Mickleham, in its vicinity, are well worthy of a visit.

About half a mile from Dorking is *Deepdene*, the elegant mansion of viscount Beresford.

Coaches.—Cross-keys, Gracechurch-street; Golden-cross, Charing-cross.

DULWICH is a hamlet of Camberwell, about five miles from London, remarkable for the beauty of its scenery. It was formerly noted for its medicinal waters, and was the birthplace of Nan Catley, the actress, afterwards Mrs. Lascelles. God's Gift College, at this place, was founded by Edward Alleyne, esq., a player of great celebrity, and a contemporary of Shakspeare, who having realised a considerable fortune, retired to Dulwich, and superintended the erection of his college, which he devoted to the maintenance, education, and relief of poor and needy people, of St. Botolph Bishopsgate Without, St. Saviour's in Southwark, part of St. Giles's Cripplegate, and Camberwell. The manor of Dulwich belongs to the corporation of this college, and the estate being much increased by enclosures, donations, and the advanced value of land, while the original number of persons relieved has not been enlarged, a situation in God's Gift College is extremely desirable, and approaches to opulence.

The chapel of the college contains a copy of Raphael's Transfiguration, by Julio Romano: but the principal object of curiosity is the *Picture-Gallery*, which was erected in 1813, under the direction of the late sir J. Soane. It contains a fine collection of pictures, which were left by sir Francis Bourgeois, an eminent historical painter, and intended to form the foundation of a National Gallery. The public are allowed to view this gallery every day, except Fridays and Sundays. The hours of admission, from April to November, are from ten to five; and from November to April, from eleven to three. Tickets of admission may be obtained gratis of Mr. Lloyd, Harley-street; Mr. Colnaghi, Pall-mall-east; Mr. Ackermann, Strand; and some other places.

Coaches.—Gracechurch-street, Charing-cross, and Fleet-street.

EGHAM is a village in Surrey, 18 miles west of London, remarkable for its races, which are held at Runnymead in September. This mead is likewise celebrated as the place where king John was compelled to sign Magna Charta. The church, which is ancient, contains some curious monuments, amongst which is one to sir John Denham, the poet's father. In this parish also is Cooper's-hill, the subject of Denham's celebrated poem.

Coaches.—White-horse Cellar, and Holborn.

ELTHAM, about eight miles from London, has the remains of a palace, well worthy of notice, in which Edward II. resided. They may be viewed on application to the keeper.

Coaches.—Charing-cross, and Fleet-street.

EPPING, a town in Essex, 17 miles from London, famous for its butter and sausages. On Epping-forest a stag is turned out annually on Easter Monday, for the amusement of the public.

Coaches.—Aldgate.

EPSOM is a town in Surrey, about fifteen miles from London. It was formerly famous for mineral springs, but is now more noted for its horse-races, which are held in May and October, and attract an immense number of spectators. The race-ground is an elevated spot, about half a mile from the town. A handsome race-stand, which will accommodate nearly 5000 persons, was erected here in 1829. *Pitt-place*, near Epsom church, is an elegant mansion, where lord Lyttleton expired, three days after a singular dream, in which he was warned of his approaching dissolution.

Coaches.—Charing-cross; Bridge-street, Westminster; Holborn; Gracechurch-street; Fetter-lane.

ESHER, a pleasant village on the Portsmouth road, about 16 miles from London; it has a neat church built by the duke of Newcastle. Near Esher, Esher-place, a handsome mansion, the seat of J. Spicer, esq.

Coaches.—Golden-cross.

ETON, 21 miles from London, a village on the Thames, in Bucks, opposite Windsor, from which it is only separated by a bridge, was in ancient times, and is at present, famed for its royal college and school, founded by Henry VI. in 1440, for the support of a provost and seven fellows, and the education of seventy youths in classical learning. It consists of two quadrangles; one appropriated to the school and the lodgings of the masters and scholars, in the midst of which is a copper statue of the founder; the other to the apartments of the provost and fellows. The library is one of the finest in England. The chapel is a stately structure, resembling that of King's College, Cambridge; and at the west end is a marble statue, by Bacon, of the ill-fated Henry. The seventy king's scholars, as those are called who are on the foundation, when properly qualified, are elected, on the first Tuesday in August, to King's College in Cambridge, but are not removed till there are vacancies, and then according to seniority. After they have been three years at Cambridge, they claim a fellowship. Besides those on the foundation, there are seldom fewer than 300 noblemen and gentlemen's sons, called oppidans, who board at the masters' houses, or within the bounds of the college. The revenue of the college amounts to about 5000*l.* a-year. The lover of poetry will always recollect Gray's "Ode to Eton College" with pleasure and satisfaction. The celebrated Porson was educated here.

Eton College and Chapel may be seen on application to the attendant.

The Eton Montem is a singular custom, which takes place triennially on Whit-Tuesday. The young gentlemen of Eton College march in procession to Salt-hill, a small mound on the side of the Bath road, where their captain, who is the best scholar among those belonging to the foundation, recites a passage from some ancient author. The young gentlemen called salt-bearers, who are arrayed in fancy dresses, then disperse in various directions, to collect money from all passengers, none being permitted to pass without bestowing something; a ticket is then given, which is generally worn in the hat, that they may not be again solicited. The money thus collected, which has amounted to 800*l.*, is given to the captain, to enable him to take up his residence at one of the universities. This ceremony is generally honoured by the attendance of the royal family and a fashionable company.

Splendid regattas take place, June 4, and the last Saturday in July. On these occasions the young gentlemen of Eton go in procession, in several boats, to a meadow opposite Surly-hall, where a cold collation is provided, and, on their return, fireworks are exhibited on an island a little above Windsor-bridge.

The Great Western railway runs near Eton.

Coaches.—Fleet-street, and White-horse Cellar.

FAIRLOP-OAK, a celebrated tree in Hainault forest, Essex, was blown down February 1820; part of it has been converted into a handsome carved pulpit at St. Pancras church. It was remarkable for its extended branches, which covered a space more than 300 feet in circumference, and under which a fair was annually held on the first Friday in July. This fair originated with the eccentric Mr. Day, a pump and block-maker of Wapping, who having a small estate in the vicinity, annually repaired here on the day above mentioned, with a party of friends, to dine on beans and bacon. Every year added to the number, and in the course of a short time it assumed the appearance of a regular fair, which is still continued, though the eccentric institutor and the venerable oak are no longer in existence. The pump and block-makers of Wapping always attend in a boat drawn by six horses, and accompanied by music.

FROGMORE is a charming estate, about half a mile from Windsor, originally the property of the hon. Mrs. Egerton, but in 1792 purchased by the consort of George III., by whom it was greatly improved. The grounds are tastefully laid out, and adorned with several ornamental buildings, some of which were designed by Wyatt, and others by the princess Elizabeth. Her majesty had a private printing-press here, under the superintendence of her librarian. It is now the residence of the princess Augusta.

FULHAM is a village four miles from London, on the north bank of the Thames, over which is a wooden bridge, where a toll must be paid. The church, a large irregular stone building, contains numerous monuments, one of which was erected in memory of Dr. Butts, mentioned by Shakspeare in Henry VIII.; and in the churchyard are deposited most of the bishops of London since the Restoration. In Fulham-house, near the bridge, Granville Sharp, esq., the zealous friend to the abolition of the slave-trade, died in July 1813. On the banks of the Thames, a short distance west of Fulham, stands the palace of the bishop of London, the gardens of which contain numerous botanical curiosities. Here the amiable bishop Porteus expired in 1809. The nursery-grounds and market-gardens of Fulham supply Covent-garden with large quantities of vegetables and fruits.

Inns.—Golden Lion, Swan. *Coaches.*—St. Paul's churchyard, Strand, Coventry-street, and White-horse Cellar.

GRAVESEND is situated on the Thames in Kent, 22 miles from London. Here vessels entering the river are visited by the custom-house officers. Gravesend has a church (St. George's), built 1730, a chapel of ease in the modern Gothic style, and several Dissenters' chapels. Among the public buildings may be mentioned the town-hall, the custom and excise-offices, gas and water works, the new baths, &c. It has also a theatre, and zoological gardens are about to be established at Rosterville. Steam-boats leave London for this place several times a-day; the fare is usually 2*s*. The river here is a mile in width. Adjoining Gravesend is Milton, an agreeable place of resort. About four miles from Gravesend is *Cobham Hall*, the seat of earl Darnley. The country near Gravesend is very picturesque.

New piers have lately been erected, by which the inconvenience of landing in boats is avoided.

Coaches.—Bull, Leadenhall-street; Golden-cross, Charing-cross ; Cross-keys, Wood-street.

GREENWICH, a town in Kent, five miles E.S.E. from London, is situated on the south bank of the Thames. The old church is a handsome stone fabric : it contains three portraits of sovereigns, and a curious painting, on board, representing a monumental effigy of queen Elizabeth. The church, dedicated to St. Mary, was commenced in 1823, from designs by Basevi, and consecrated July 25, 1825. It is situated between the hospital and the park, and is capable of accommodating 1713 persons. This edifice is of Grecian architecture. It is built of white brick, with stone dressings. The front, which presents a portico of four Ionic columns, is of stone, and is surmounted by a stone tower of two stories. The interior is chastely ornamented, and over the altar is a picture by Richter, representing Christ healing the blind.

Among the charitable foundations are two colleges for poor people; one founded by the celebrated antiquary, William Lambard, being the first erected by an English Protestant subject; and the other by Henry Howard, earl of Northampton. This town has been the residence of many noble and literary characters. William Courtenay, earl of Devonshire, resided here after his release from prison by Henry VIII., till his death in 1512 ; bishop Gastrell lived here before his promotion to the see of Chester, in 1714; the brave sir John Lawson, the scourge of the Dutch, died here of the wounds received in the great engagement with the Dutch fleet in May 1665; the latter days of sir John Leake were passed here, in a villa built for his own residence ; and Dr. Johnson had lodgings in Church-street in 1737, when he composed a great part of his Irene as he walked in the park.

Greenwich was the birth-place of queen Mary and queen Elizabeth ; and here Edward VI. died. A palace erected here by Humphry duke of Gloucester, who named it Placentia, was enlarged by Henry VII., and completed by Henry VIII. ; but becoming ruinous, was pulled down by Charles II., who began a magnificent edifice, and lived to see the first wing finished. He also enlarged the park, walled it round, planted it, and erected a royal observatory on the top of the hill, for the use of the celebrated Flamstead, whose name the house retains. The present astronomer-royal is Mr. Pond, and the instruments made use of are considered the best in Europe; but the observatory is not open to the public. From the meridian of Greenwich all English astronomers make their calculations. An instrument has lately been erected, consisting of a ball suspended on a perpendicular frame, by the dropping of which the hour of one is proclaimed to the vessels in the river, so as to enable them to obtain correct chronometers.

The park and hill are distinguished for their beautiful scenery, and extensive prospects of London and the adjacent country. They are much frequented during summer by picnic parties, who either bring their own provisions, or obtain refreshments from the numerous tea and coffee rooms in the street leading to the entrance of the park. They are likewise much resorted to at the fairs which are held here on the Monday, Tuesday, and Wednesday of Easter and Whitsuntide weeks.

The Hospital and Naval Asylum, which form the principal ornaments of this place, have been already described in another part of the work.

It returns two members to parliament.

The Greenwich railroad was the first completed in the neighbourhood of the metropolis; it is built on brick arches, and extends nearly in a straight line: its length is about 3¾ miles; the time of transit is about 10 or 12 minutes.—Fare 6*d.*

Coaches and Omnibuses.—Charing-cross, Gracechurch-street, Fleet-street; Midnight coach, Catherine-street. *Boats* go during summer, every half-hour, from the Tower-stairs, and the fare is only 6*d.*

HACKNEY is an extensive and populous village, about two miles from Shoreditch church, having for its hamlets Upper and Lower Clapton, Shacklewell, Dalston, and Homerton. It is noted as the birth-place of the witty Dr. South and the benevolent Howard; and is said to have given name to hackney-coaches, though the term *hackney*, as applied to any thing hired, was made use of before this village was in much repute. The principal objects worthy of notice are the mansion at the extremity of Church-street, formerly the residence of Ward, whose infamy has been immortalised by Pope; the nursery-grounds of Messrs. Loddiges, containing one of the finest collections of exotics in the kingdom; Brooke-house, at Clapton, erected on the site of a mansion inhabited by lord Brooke; and the London Orphan Asylum at Clapton. The church, erected in 1797, is a heavy brick building, to which a stone steeple and porticoes were added in 1813: the vestibules are ornamented with several monuments, brought from the old church, only the steeple of which remains. The churchyard is planted with trees, which give it a very rural appearance, and render it a pleasant promenade. Hackney has several chapels of ease, and numerous meeting-houses, in one of which Dr. Priestley formerly officiated. A new church also, called West Hackney church, was erected at Shacklewell in 1823. The meetings of the freeholders of Middlesex are held at the Mermaid tavern here.

Coaches.—Royal Exchange; the Flower-pot, Bishopsgate-street; Strand; Snow-hill; Oxford-street.

HAMMERSMITH is a populous village about four miles west of London, with a church, two chapels of ease, several meeting-houses, and a charity-school established by bishop Latimer; in one of the former is a monument to the memory of the earl of Mulgrave, who resided nearly opposite the chapel, and died in 1646; in the chancel is a bronze bust of Charles I., placed here by sir Nicholas Crispe, whose heart is deposited in an urn beneath. Hammersmith has a nunnery, the inmates of which are denominated English Benedictine Dames. It is situated in King-street, and has a chapel attached to it. Thomson wrote a considerable portion of his "Winter" at the Dane coffee-house in this village; and the terrace was for many years the residence of Loutherbourg the painter, and of Murphy the dramatic writer. Hammersmith is interspersed with numerous villas. Brandenburgh-house, formerly the residence of the margravine of Anspach, and afterwards of her majesty queen Caroline, who expired there August 7, 1821, was pulled down in 1823.

Hammersmith-bridge was erected in 1827, and is designed to form a shorter route to Barnes, East Sheen, and other places on the opposite side of the river. It consists of a horizontal roadway suspended to iron chains, which are carried over two stone piers and archways, and made secure to abutments at each end of the bridge. The extreme length of the road is 822 feet, and the clear water-way 688 feet. The road is 16 feet above the high-water mark, and 20 feet in width; besides a foot-path of five feet. The whole cost of this elegant structure was about 80,000*l.* Mr. Tierney Clark was the architect.

HAMPTON COURT.

ETON COLLEGE.

CLAREMONT.

Inn.—Bridge Hotel. *Coaches and Omnibuses.* — St. Paul's Churchyard, Strand, and White-horse Cellar.

HAMPSTEAD is situated in Middlesex, four miles N.W. from London. It lies on the declivity of a hill, which is surmounted by an extensive heath. The fine views of the metropolis from the heath, and from most parts of the village, particularly from Shepherd's-fields, are not the only beauties of the scene; the home-landscape, consisting of broken ground, divided into enclosures, and well planted with trees, is extremely picturesque. This village is noted for its medicinal waters: besides the old spa, which is of a chalybeate quality, there are two other kinds of mineral waters; the one a purgative saline, similar to that of Cheltenham, the other of a sulphureous nature. On the left of the entrance to Hampstead is a house supposed to be that in which sir Henry Vane resided at the time of the Restoration. It afterwards belonged to Dr. Butler, author of the Analogy between Natural and Revealed Religion, who ornamented the windows with stained glass (principally subjects from Scripture), which still remains. On the side of the hill is an ancient building, called the Chicken-house, which, tradition says, was a hunting-seat of James II.: one of the windows was formerly ornamented with small portraits, in stained glass, of James I. and the duke of Buckingham. The church was rebuilt in 1747; and its spire, rising through the trees, forms a picturesque object from whatever part of the adjacent country it is seen.

Hampstead has been the residence of many literary characters as well as noblemen. Sir Richard Steele lived in a house on Haverstock-hill, which is still called Steele's cottage; it is situated on the left of the road from London: in the same tenement died sir Charles Sedley. Gay, Akenside, Dr. Sewell, and numerous other literary characters, were likewise residents at Hampstead. At *Hollybush-hill*, in the house formerly frequented by the Kit-Cat Club, Steevens the editor of Shakspeare lived and died. Near it is an elegant assembly-room, formed out of a house built by Romney the painter. *Child's-hill*, west of Hampstead-heath, commands an extensive prospect, including Windsor-castle, the obelisk on Bagshot-heath, the Surrey hills, and, on a clear day, the Hog's-back in Hampshire.

Coaches.—James-street, Covent-garden; Exchange; Tottenham-court-road; Bank; Blue Posts, Holborn.

HAMPTON COURT is a royal palace, on the northern borders of the Thames, about 13 miles from London. It was erected by cardinal Wolsey, on the site of a manor-house belonging to the Knights-hospitallers, and was so capacious, that it was said to have been provided with 280 beds for visiters of superior rank.

Wolsey presented it to Henry VIII. in 1526. Edward VI. was born at Hampton-court, October 12, 1537, and his mother, queen Jane Seymour, died there on the 14th of the same month. On the 8th of August, 1540, Catherine Howard was openly shewn here as queen. Catherine Parr was married to the king at this palace, and proclaimed queen July 12, 1542. Philip and Mary kept their Christmas at Hampton-court with great solemnity in 1558; when the *great hall* of the palace was illuminated with 1000 lamps curiously disposed. Queen Elizabeth after she came to the throne frequently resided at Hampton-court. In this palace was held, in 1603, the celebrated conference between the presbyterians and the members of the established church, which led to a new translation of the Bible, and some alterations in the liturgy. Charles I. retired to Hampton-court on account of the plague in 1625. This palace was occasionally inhabited by Charles II., James II., and William III. The duke of Gloucester, son of queen Anne, was born in this palace, July 24, 1689. George I. occasionally visited Hampton-court, as did his successor to the throne; but the palace has not since been inhabited by the royal family.

The usual approach to the palace is from the *west*. Here, on the right and left, are seen ranges of subordinate chambers and domestic offices, portions of the building constructed by Wolsey, and on the latter side are the royal stables. The *west front* of the palace comprises three stories. Beyond the archway of the portal is the first, the *western* or *entrance court*, a quadrangle, 167 feet from N. to S., and 141 from E. to W. This leads through a groined archway to the second, the *clock-court*, or *middle quadrangle*, which measures 133 feet from N. to S., and 92 feet from E. to W. On the turrets are introduced busts of the Cæsars. On the left is the large Gothic hall, with a fine oriel window, where Henry VIII. held his revels, and in which queen Caroline, the consort of George II., ordered several plays to be performed, particularly one for the late emperor of Germany, when he visited England in 1730. On the front of the third story is a large and curious astronomical clock, made by Tompion: on the S. side is a stone colonnade of fourteen columns, leading to the great staircase. The *third great quadrangle*, usually termed the *eastern or fountain court*, from the fountain in the centre, consists chiefly of buildings constructed by sir C. Wren in the time of king William. This quadrangle is 110 feet by 117. On the N. side is the queen's staircase, the side of which, painted by Vick, represents Charles II. and his queen, with the duke of Buckingham as Science in the character of Mercury, while Envy is struck down by naked boys.

The *chapel* on the N. side of the fountain-court forms the S. side of a small quadrangle. On the outer wall, at each side of the door, are the arms of Henry VIII. impaled with Seymour; and the initials H. I., united by a true-lover's knot. The interior was fitted up in the reign of queen Anne. The original roof remains, and is ornamented with ranges of large pendants, each being formed into the representation of a balcony, on which are placed winged angels with musical instruments; the altar-piece is Grecian, and adorned with Corinthian columns.

The *great eastern façade*, or grand front, comprehends the whole of the state apartments. It was begun in 1690, and completed in 1694, after the designs of sir C. Wren. The grand elevation towards the east is about 330 feet in extent. The material chiefly used is brick, of a bright-red hue; but the numerous decorations are of stone. The *southern front*, which is 328 feet in length, has a central compartment of stone, but is less embellished than that towards the E. On the entablature, which is sustained by four columns, is inscribed GULIELMUS ET MARIA, R.R.E., and on the parapet are placed four statues—Flora, Ceres, Diana, and Pomona.

Painted Gallery.—The *State Apartments* are approached by the *King's Staircase*, which was painted by Antonio Verrio. On the left side are represented Apollo and the nine Muses, at whose feet sits the god Pan, with his unequal reeds; and a little below is the goddess Ceres, holding in the one hand a wheatsheaf, and pointing with the other to loaves of bread. At the feet of Ceres is Flora, surrounded by her attendants, and holding a chaplet of flowers. Near her are the two river gods, Thame and Isis, with their urns; and in the centre a large table decorated with flowers.

On the ceiling are Jupiter and Juno, with Ganymede riding on Jupiter's eagle, and offering the cup; and in the front is Juno's peacock. One of the Parcæ, with her scissors in her hand, seems to wait for Jove's orders to cut the thread of life. These figures are covered with a canopy, and surrounded with several Zephyrs with flowers in their hands; and on one side of them is Fame with her two trumpets. Beneath is a figure of Venus riding on a swan, Mars addressing her as a lover, and Cupid riding on another swan.

On the right hand are Pluto and Proserpine, Cœlus and Terra, Cybele crowned with a tower, and other figures.

In the front are Neptune and Amphitrite, with two attendants, who are serving them with fruit. Bacchus, leaning on a rich ewer, and accompanied by his attendants, places his left hand on the head of Silenus, who sits on an ass that is fallen down. Diana, above, is pointing with her finger to a table supported by eagles: on one side of which sits Romulus, founder of Rome, with a wolf; and on the other, Hercules leaning on his club; between these is Peace, holding in her right hand a laurel, and in her left a palm-branch over the head of Æneas, who seems inviting the twelve Cæsars, together with Spurinna the soothsayer, to a celestial banquet. Over them hovers the genius of Rome with a flaming sword and a bridle; the latter the emblem of government, and the former that of destruction. The next is the emperor Julian, writing at a table while Mercury dictates to him. Over the door at the head of the stairs is a funeral pile. These pictures have suffered much from age.

State Apartments.—The first room is the *Guard-Chamber*, containing arms for a thousand men, placed in various forms. It also contains portraits of many distinguished admirals, all painted by Kneller; over the fire-place is Vespasian's amphitheatre at Rome, by Canaletti; and opposite, George prince of Denmark; with some battle-pieces by Rugendas.

The *King's First Presence-Chamber* is hung with a rich tapestry. Opposite the entrance is the chair of state. In this room is a fine picture, by Kneller, of William III. on a grey horse. Here also may be seen the portraits of queen Mary, consort of William III., and the following eight distinguished ladies of her court:—the duchess of St. Alban's; Isabella, duchess of Grafton; Cary, countess of Peterborough; the countess of Ranelagh; Mary, countess of Essex; Mary, countess of Dorset; lady Middleton; and Miss Pitt.

The *Second Presence-Chamber* is hung with tapestry, representing Abraham offering up Isaac; the lights of this tapestry are in gold, and the shades in silk. The paintings are Christian IV. of Denmark, by Van Somer; Bandinelli the sculptor, by Correggio; queen Elizabeth, when a child, by Holbein; Charles I., when young; prince Rupert; Isaac and Rebecca; Charles I., on horseback, by Vandyke; the present royal family, by Knapton; and three pieces of ruins and landscapes, by Rousseau.

The *Audience-Chamber.*—In this room is a silver chandelier of sixteen branches, also a chair of state. The tapestry represents parts of the history of Abraham. The paintings are, Elizabeth queen of Bohemia, by Honthorst; two Madonnas; Jesus, John, Mary, and Elizabeth, by Bassano; Virgin and Child; five pictures by S. Ricci, representing part of the history of our Saviour. Lewis Cornaro and family, copied from Titian, by Stone; George III., in his 42d year, and Queen Charlotte, by West.

The *Drawing-Room.*—The tapestry represents a continuation of the history of Abraham; a portrait of Charles I., by Vandyke; David with Goliath's head, by Fetti; the Deluge, by Bassano; the Muses, by Tintoretto; the Cornaro Family, by Old Stone; the Holy Family, by Correggio; and George III. reviewing dragoons at Bagshot, by Sir William Beechey.

The *State Bed-chamber* contains a bed of crimson velvet, decorated with plumes of feathers. The tapestry is descriptive of the history of Joshua. The ceiling, by Verrio, represents Night and Morning. The paintings are Joseph's Chastity, by Gentileschi; Danaë, by Genaro; Anne Duchess of York, by Sir Peter Lely; and flower-pieces, by Baptiste. Also a clock that goes one year and a day without winding.

The *King's Dressing-room.*—The ceiling, by Verrio, represents Mars reposing in the lap of Venus, while Cupids steal his armour, sword, and spear. The pictures are Christ and St. John, by da Vinci; St. Peter in prison, by H. Steenwick, &c.

Queen Mary's Closet is hung with needle-work, said to be wrought by herself and her maids of honour. The paintings are, a Holy Family, by Dasso; Moses striking the Rock, &c.

The *Queen's Gallery* is hung with seven pieces of Gobelin tapestry, representing the history of Alexander the Great.

The *Queen's Bed-chamber* contains the state-bed of Queen Anne. The ceiling represents Aurora rising out of the ocean. The Shepherd's Offering was painted by old Palma.

The *Queen's State Audience-room* is provided with a canopy of state, and the walls are hung with tapestry representing Abraham receiving bread and wine.

The *Dining-room* contains the model of a palace intended to have been built at Richmond. Round the room are the Triumphs of Julius Cesar, in water-colours, by Montagna.

The *Prince of Wales's Presence-chamber* is hung with tapestry, expressive of the story of Tobit and Tobias; and contains portraits of Louis XIII., two Spanish Ambassadors, &c.

The *Cartoon Gallery*, built by Sir C. Wren, is so called from containing the Cartoons of Raphael. These esteemed works were executed by desire of Leo X., about 1510. They represent, 1. The Miraculous Draught of Fishes; 2. The Charge to Peter; 3. Peter and John healing the Lame at the gate of the Temple; 4. The Death of Ananias; 5. Elymas the Sorcerer struck with Blindness; 6. The Sacrifice to Paul and Barnabas by the people of Lystra; 7. Paul preaching at Athens. They have been finely lithographed by Mr. Foggo.

Renovations are still proceeding; and the decorations being completed of *Cardinal Wolsey's Hall* and his *Presence-chamber*, they were, in the early part of 1841, thrown open to the public. The collection has been considerably increased, and visitors are no longer hurried through the rooms by a parrot-guide, neither is any gratuity exacted. The visitor may proceed direct by coach, as indicated at p. 424, or go by railroad either to Kingston or Esher, or by steamer to Richmond, where conveyances are always to be met with.

The *Pleasure-Gardens* are very extensive. Opposite the southern front are two large marble vases; that on the right represents the triumphs of Bacchus, and that on the left Amphitrite and the Nereids. There are also two large vases at the bottom of the walk, one of which represents the judgment of Paris, and the other Meleager hunting the wild boar. In the parterres are four fine brass statues, which formerly stood at the parade in St. James's-park, and were placed here by Queen Anne; one is an original, and was brought from Rome, being the workmanship of Desitheus, of Ephesus; the second is a young Apollo; the third a Diana; and the fourth a Saturn about to devour one of his own children. In the Privy Gardens are five figures: Ceres; Bacchus, holding a cup over his head; Vulcan; Apollo, gazing at the sun; and Pan, with a young Apollo.

In a greenhouse is a celebrated vine, allowed to surpass any in Europe; it is 72 feet by 20, and has in one season produced 2272 bunches, weighing 18 cwt. It was planted in 1769; the stem is about 13 inches in girth. In the gardens is a walk called Queen Mary's Bower, and a quantity of orange-trees. They are open daily from an early hour till dusk.

On the north of the palace is the Wilderness, in which is the

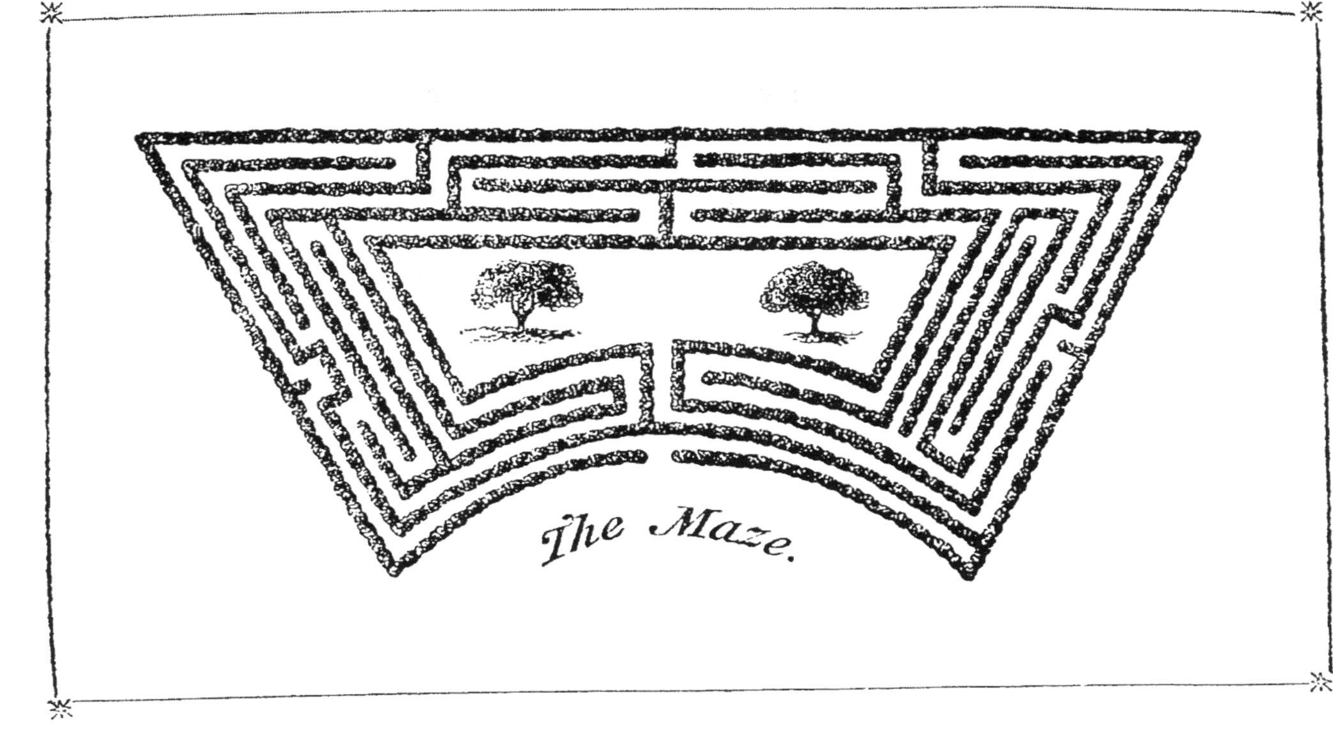
The Maze.

curious *Maze* that affords great amusement to the juvenile visiters. The mode of obtaining direct access to the centre is, by turning to the left of the entrance, and following the hedge on the right hand.

The palace is supplied with water by a conduit from Combe, near Kingston, and by a canal from Isleworth river, near Longford. Both these works are said to have been executed by Wolsey. The conduit from Combe passes under the Hogsmill river near Kingston, and under the Thames, east of the palace. No charge is made for viewing the palace, but 6*d*. each is expected from a party: the gardener and maze-keeper likewise expect a fee. The village of Hampton, at the extremity of Bushy-park, has good inns, The Toy, King's Arms, and Bell; and a handsome church consecrated in 1831. There is a carriage and post-road through Bushy-park to Hampton-court.

Hampton-house was the villa of the celebrated Garrick. In the garden on the banks of the Thames he erected a temple in honour of Shakspeare, and placed in it the statue of the great bard by Roubiliac, which is now in the British Museum.

Coaches.—Bolt-in-Tun, Fleet-street; Strand; Royal Exchange; Holborn-bars; Tottenham-court-road.

HARROW-ON-THE-HILL is a village 9½ miles from London. The hill on which it is situated is the loftiest in Middlesex, and commands delightful and varied prospects of the surrounding country. Part of the parish church was erected in the time of William the Conqueror; it is adorned with a monument in memory of Dr. Garth, the poet and physician. Harrow is principally noted for its free-school, founded in the reign of Elizabeth by John Lyon, and considered one of the first public seminaries in the kingdom. Amongst the eminent persons who have been educated here may be mentioned, Dr. Parr, sir W. Jones, Sheridan, lord Byron, sir R. Peel, Mr. Perceval, earl Spencer, and the marquess of Hastings. During the summer, passage-boats go two or three times a-week to this village from Paddington, and return the same day.

Coaches.—Bull, Holborn; Railway station.

HIGHGATE is a hamlet of the parishes of Hornsey and Pancras, and is situated on a lofty hill 4½ miles from London. It is interspersed with many handsome houses belonging to persons of rank and opulence. The new church of St. Michael, erected in 1832 by Mr. Vulliamy, is an elegant and simple Gothic pile, with a graceful tower and spire 145 feet high; from the elevation of the spot, it forms a landmark to the surrounding country. In 1813 a new road was cut from Upper Holloway to between the 5th and 6th mile-stone on the Barnet-road, in order to avoid the steep acclivity of Highgate-hill. This road is crossed by Hornsey-lane, which is supported at this part by a stone archway, surmounted by balustrades, whence there is a delightful view of the metropolis and surrounding country.

In Holloway, at the bottom of Highgate-hill, are *Whittington's Alms-houses*, with a statue of Whittington, erected in 1827 from a design by Mr. G. Smith.

On an eminence between Highgate and Hampstead, is *Caen* or *Kenwood*, the seat of earl Mansfield, who has a fine collection of pictures. The pleasure-grounds, which are laid out with great taste, consist of about fifty acres.

Coaches.—Blue-posts, Holborn; Tottenham-court-road; James-street, Covent-garden; Newgate-street; Bank.

HOLLAND-HOUSE, the seat of the noble lord of that name, is situated in Kensington, two miles from the metropolis. It was built in 1607 by sir Walter Cope, from whose son-in-law, Rich earl of Holland, it derived its name. In 1716 it became the property of the celebrated Addison, and was the scene of his affecting interview with his son-in-law, the earl of Warwick, to whom he had been tutor, and whose licentious conduct he had vainly attempted to repress. As a last effort, he sent for him when at the point of death, hoping that the solemnity of the scene might make some impression on him. When that young nobleman arrived, and requested to know his commands, he received the memorable answer, "See in what peace a Christian can die!" Tickell has alluded to this in his address to the earl of Warwick:—

> "He taught us how to live; and, oh! too high
> A price for knowledge, taught us how to die."

On the death of this nobleman in 1721, the estate devolved on lord Kensington, who sold it in 1762 to the right hon. Henry Fox, afterwards lord Holland. Here the right hon. C. J. Fox, the patriotic statesman, was born in 1748. The apartments are ornamented with portraits of the Lennox, Fox, and Digby families.

HOMERTON is a hamlet of Hackney, and is well known for the education of dissenting ministers. Amongst the leading men who have conducted the college there, were Dr. Conder and Dr. Fisher. This edifice was rebuilt in 1824. There are also alms'-houses for twelve widows of dissenting ministers.

HORNSEY is a neat village situated at the foot of Muswell-hill, and is remarkable for the number of villas and the beautiful views which it commands. The church is new, but the tower is ancient.

HOUNSLOW, a market-town ten miles W. of London, has extensive cavalry-barracks and powder-mills. Its heath used to be famous for robberies.

HOXTON is a hamlet of Shoreditch, and has a college for the education of missionaries, removed from Gosport in 1826. Aske's Hospital, erected by the Haberdashers' Company, is situated in Pitfield-street.

ISLINGTON is an extensive village about two miles from London, with a church and three chapels of ease, one of which was erected at an expense of upwards of 20,000*l.*, and several chapels and meeting-houses. The Pied-bull-inn is said to have been inhabited by sir Walter Raleigh, and to have been the first house in England where tobacco was smoked. Islington is remarkable for the salubrity of its air and the number of its chalybeate springs, and is likewise noted for supplying a great portion of the metropolis with milk. Amongst the eminent men who have made it their residence, were Collins the poet and Morland the painter. On the south-west side of the village is the New River-head, and on the north side stands *Highbury-place*, where Mr. Newland, the chief cashier of the bank, died in 1807. Near Highbury-place is *Highbury-barn*, a tavern and tea-gardens, which are very much frequented, particularly during the summer. At Highbury also is the Dissenting-college, removed from Hoxton in 1826. It was built from designs by Mr. Davis. At *Canonbury*, immediately adjoining Islington, is a tower, which formed part of a mansion built by the priors of St. Bartholomew. This tower has been the residence of Goldsmith the poet, and Chambers the compiler of the "Cyclopædia." Colley Cibber died at Canonbury-house in the immediate vicinity. The Church Missionary Society has a college at Islington.

Coaches.—Holborn-bars, Royal Exchange, Fleet-street, Cheapside.

KENSINGTON is a village 1½ mile from Hyde-park-corner. The royal palace at this place has already been described. Several of the earls of Warwick are entombed in the church. Dr. Jortin the divine, and Mrs. Inchbald the actress, were buried in the adjacent cemetery. Pratt earl of Camden was a native of this place; and Hunter the celebrated surgeon resided for many years at *Earl's-court*, which is a hamlet of this parish. A new theatre has lately been erected, called the New Kent Theatre.

Coaches.—Leadenhall-street, Bank, Strand, and Piccadilly.

KEW is situated on the Thames, about seven miles from London, and 1½ mile from Richmond. The church contains an epitaph by Hayley, on Mr. Meyer the painter; but Kew is particularly famed for the royal residence called KEW PALACE, which has been successively occupied by the Capel family, by S. Molineux, esq., by Frederick prince of Wales, occasionally by Thomson the admired author of the "Seasons," and by his late Majesty George III.; here also queen Charlotte expired. The house was improved by Kent, and contains some pictures; but the gardens are the principal object of attraction. They are not very large, nor is their situation advantageous, as it is low and commands no prospect; but they contain the finest collection of plants in the world, and are decorated with various ornamental buildings, most of which were erected by sir W. Chambers about 1760. On entering from the palace, and turning towards the left, the first building which appears is *the Orangery*, or *Green-house*, 145 feet long. Near it in a grove is *the Temple of the Sun*, of the Corinthian order, embellished with a representation of that luminary, surrounded by the signs of the zodiac in basso-relievo. There is also a *Physic-garden*, and contiguous to it *the Flower-garden*, of which the principal entrance forms one end; the two sides are enclosed with high trees; and the other end is occupied by an aviary of vast depth. From the Flower-garden, a short winding walk leads to *the Menagerie*, the centre of which is occupied by a large basin of water, stocked with curious water-fowl, and enclosed by a range of cages for exotic birds. Near the menagerie stands *the Temple of Bellona;* and towards the lake, in a solitary walk on the left, *the Temple of the god Pan*, the profile of which is imitated from that of the theatre of Marcellus at Rome. On an eminence stands *the Temple of Æolus;* and near the south front of the palace, *the Temple of Solitude*. At the head of the lake stands *the House of Confucius*, a Chinese octagon, built from the designs of Goupy, and painted with historical subjects relating to Confucius and the Christian missions to China. Near the house of Confucius is the engine which supplies the lake and basins in the gardens with water, contrived by Mr. Smeaton. It raises, by two horses, upwards of 3600 hogsheads of water in 12 hours. *The Temple of Victory* was built in commemoration of the victory obtained in 1759, near Minden, by prince Ferdinand of Brunswick, over marshal De Contades. On an open space near the centre of the wilderness is *the Great Pagoda*, designed as an imitation of the Chinese Taa. The base is a regular octagon, 49 feet in diameter, and the superstructure is likewise a regular octagon, of ten stories, measuring, from the base to the top of the fleuron, 163 feet. The walls are composed of very hard bricks, the outside with grey stocks, laid with such care that there is not the least crack or fracture in the whole structure, notwithstanding its great height. The staircase is in the centre of the building, and from the top is a very extensive view, in some directions upwards of 40 miles, over a rich and variegated country. Near the Grand Pagoda stands *the Mosque*, over the entrance to which is an Arabic inscription, extracted from the Koran. In the way from the Mosque, towards the palace, is a Gothic building representing a cathedral, and *the Gallery of Antiques*. Near the lake stands *the Temple of Arethusa*, and over a portion of it is a bridge from one of Palladio's designs. *The Ruin*, which forms a passage for carriages over one of the principal walks, is built in imitation of a Roman antiquity.

These gardens are opened every Sunday from midsummer to the end of autumn.

The old house opposite the palace was taken by queen Caroline, consort of George II., of the descendants of sir R. Levett, and has been inhabited by different branches of the royal family. His majesty George IV. was educated there, under the superintendence of the late Dr. Markham, archbishop of York. Near this spot a *New Palace*, in the Gothic style of architecture, was erected by George III., under the direction of Wyatt; but this edifice was pulled down in 1827.

Inn.—Rose and Crown. *Coaches.*—Strand, Piccadilly, St. Paul's Churchyard, Gracechurch-street.

LALEHAM, 18½ miles from London, is a small village near Staines. In the church is a picture by Harlowe, representing Peter walking on the sea.

Laleham-house is an elegant villa surrounded by 40 acres of ground, which were laid out by the earl of Lucan. This mansion was appropriated to the queen of Portugal when she came to England in 1828.

LEITH-HILL, five miles from Dorking, commands a prospect of amazing extent and beauty.

MILL-HILL is a village of Middlesex, 9½ miles from London. Here is the Protestant Dissenters' Grammar-school, erected in 1826 from designs by Mr. Tite.

Coaches.—Blue-posts, Tottenham-court-road.

MORTLAKE is a village in Surrey, seven miles from London, and is remarkable as the burial-place of Dee and Partridge the astrologers, sir John Barnard, alderman Barber, and sir B. Watson; here likewise sir P. Francis was buried in 1819. An ancient house in this place is supposed to have been the residence of Oliver Cromwell, and was afterwards inhabited by E. Colston, esq., the benefactor of Bristol.

Inns.—Queen's-head, King's-arms. *Coaches.*—St. Paul's Churchyard, Strand, and Piccadilly.

NEWINGTON, or STOKE-NEWINGTON, is a village in Middlesex, about 2½ miles from London. The manor-house was for many years the residence of Dr. Watts, and here he died in 1748. In this village also Dr. Aikin and Mrs. Barbauld expired. Behind the church is a grove called Queen Elizabeth's Walk. The churchyard contains a monument to the memory of alderman Picket, his son, and daughter: the latter was burnt to death.

Coaches.—Exchange, Bishopsgate-street.

THE NEW RIVER, an artificial stream for the supply of the metropolis with water, was originally projected by Mr. (afterwards sir Hugh) Myddleton, a citizen and goldsmith, who was aided in the undertaking by King James I., the city having refused him any assistance. It has its principal source at Amwell, in Hertfordshire, where several springs are collected into a basin, on the side of which is placed an inscription on stone, indicating that the stream was opened in 1608, and that the length of its course is 40 miles. Thence it flows by Hoddesdon, Broxbourne, Cheshunt, Waltham-cross, Enfield, Hornsey, and Stoke-Newington, to the basin at Islington, termed the New River-head, which is a large circular reservoir, enclosed by a brick wall, whence the water is conveyed by means of pipes to various parts of the metropolis. This immense undertaking was completed in 1613, and in 1619 the proprietors (the property having been divided into shares) were incorporated under the title of the New River Company.

NORWOOD is a village in Surrey, six miles from London, of which it commands a fine view. It is much frequented by pic-nic parties. A mineral spring called the *Beulah Spa* was opened to the public at this place in 1830. It is surrounded by about 40 acres of ground tastefully laid out. The water resembles that of Cheltenham, containing a large portion of magnesian salts. The following is the analysis according to Mr. Hume:—

	Grs.
Sulphate of Magnesia	123
Sulphate of Soda and Magnesia . . .	32
Muriate of Soda	19
Muriate of Magnesia	18½
Carbonate of Lime	15
Carbonate of Soda	3
	210½

At Norwood is the South Metropolitan Cemetery, with catacombs and two chapels.

Inns.—The Park Hotel, the Beulah Spa Hotel. *Coaches.*—Half-moon, Gracechurch-street; King and Keys, Fleet-street.

OATLANDS (Lord Francis Egerton's), formerly the seat of the late duke of York, is situated near Weybridge, in Surrey, about 18 miles from London. The estate consists of about 3000 acres; the house, which stands on a terrace near the centre of the park, is a magnificent building commanding extensive prospects. Beneath the terrace is an artificial serpentine piece of water, so judiciously disposed that the stranger would probably mistake it for the Thames, particularly as the bridge at Walton is made to appear as if it crossed this water. The grotto, consisting of two rooms covered with shells and minerals, is uncommonly beautiful and romantic. It was executed by a father and his two sons, and is said to have cost the duke of Newcastle, to whom the estate formerly belonged, upwards of 10,000*l.* On the side of the park towards Walton is a gateway, erected from a design by Inigo Jones. Here the duchess of York died in 1820.

Coaches.—Bolt-in-tun, Fleet-street.

OSTERLEY-PARK, the seat of the earl of Jersey, is situated a short distance beyond Brentford, and about nine miles from London. It is a noble mansion rebuilt by sir F. Childs in 1750, and measures 140 feet by 117. The apartments are fitted up with great taste, and the grounds are beautiful.

PADDINGTON is a village in Middlesex, about a mile from London. The church is a beautiful modern edifice, on an eminence, and in the churchyard are interred the following eminent artists:—Vivares and L. Schiavonetti, engravers; Barrett and Nollekens (father of the sculptor), painters; and

Arminger, Banks, and Nollekens, sculptors. The late marquess of Lansdowne, who died in 1809, is buried under the chancel of the church, and in the vaults are deposited the remains of the right hon. J. P. Curran. The canal which leads from this village to the Grand Junction Canal at Bull-bridge, has contributed greatly to its prosperity, and renders it a very populous place. The terminus of the Great Western Railway is also here.

Coaches and *Omnibuses.*—Bank, Charing-cross.

PRIMROSE-HILL is a delightful eminence between the Regent's-park and Hampstead, commanding a very fine view of the metropolis. It has been called " Green-berry-hill," from the names of the three persons who were executed for the supposed assassination of sir Edmunbury Godfrey, and who were said to have brought him hither after he had been murdered near Somerset-house. This hill, even in modern times, has been contaminated with blood, as several duels have been fought here. That of most note was between colonel Montgomery and captain Macnamara in 1803; the former fell, and expired at Chalk-farm, a house of public entertainment on the spot. The same fate befel Mr. Scott, the editor of the London Magazine, in 1821.

REGENT'S-CANAL was opened on the 1st of August, 1820. It commences at Paddington, where it joins a cut to the Grand Junction, and passing by a tunnel under Maida-hill, continues its course by the Regent's-park and Pancras to Islington, where another subterranean excavation, about three-quarters of a mile in length, has been formed for its passage. It then proceeds by Hoxton, Hackney, and Mile-end, to Limehouse, where it joins the Thames. The whole length of its course is nine miles, and within that space are comprised 12 locks and 37 bridges; the former are so admirably constructed, that a barge can pass through each in 3½ minutes. They are capable of admitting barges 83 feet long and 14 wide. The tunnel at Islington commences near White Conduit-house, and terminates at the New River, near the City-road, where a large basin has been formed. This canal cost upwards of half a million of money, and was seven years in hand. It was executed under the superintendence of Mr. Nash.

RICHMOND is a village in Surrey, nine miles from London, and is certainly the finest, most luxuriant, and most picturesque spot in the British dominions, whence it has been termed the *Frascati* and the *Montpelier* of England. It was anciently called *Sheen*, which in the Saxon tongue signifies *resplendent*. Here stood a palace in which Edward I. and II. resided, and Edward III. died of grief for the loss of his heroic son, the Black Prince. Here also died Anne, queen of Richard II., who first taught the English ladies the use of the side-saddle. The palace was repaired by Henry V., who founded three religious houses near it, and in 1497 it was destroyed by fire; but Henry VII. rebuilt it, and commanded that the village should be called Richmond,—he having borne the title of earl of Richmond before be obtained the crown; and here he died. Queen Elizabeth was a prisoner in this palace for a short time during the reign of her sister. When she became queen, it was one of her favourite places of residence; and here she closed her illustrious career. It was afterwards the residence of Henry prince of Wales; and bishop Duppa is said to have educated Charles II. here. The Pretender, son of James II., is also supposed to have been nursed here. The houses adjoining the gateway are parts of the old palace, and are described in the survey taken in 1649; the old yew-tree, likewise mentioned in that survey, still exists. On the site of this palace also is Cholmondeley-house, built by George third earl of Cholmondeley, afterwards the property of the late duke of Queensbury.

Near Richmond-green are the gardens formerly called the Old or Little Park, which contains the Observatory, built by sir W. Chambers in 1769, and furnished with a fine set of instruments. The grounds were laid out by Bridgman, but afterwards improved by Browne. The banks along the Thames are judiciously varied, forming a noble terrace, which extends the whole length of the gardens. The gardens are open to the public every Sunday, from midsummer till the end of autumn.

At the foot of Richmond-hill, on the Thames, is the villa of the late duke of Buccleuch. From the lawn there is a subterraneous communication with the pleasure-grounds on the opposite side of the road, which extends almost to the summit of the hill. Near this is the charming residence formerly inhabited by lady Diana Beauclerc, who herself decorated one of the rooms with lilacs and other flowers. Here likewise are several other villas of the nobility. On Richmond-green is a house formerly belonging to sir Matthew Decker, bart., an eminent Dutch merchant, who built a room here for the reception of George I. In this house is an ancient painting of Richmond-palace by Vinkeboom; and another said to be the work of one of Rubens' scholars, supposed to represent the lodge which formerly stood in the Old Park. The green is surrounded by lofty elms; and at one corner of it is a theatre.

Richmond has four almshouses, one of them built by bishop Duppa, in the reign of Charles II., for ten poor widows. An elegant stone bridge of five semicircular arches, from a design by Paine, was erected here in 1777. The summit of Richmond-hill commands a luxuriant prospect, which Thomson, who resided in this beautiful place, has celebrated in his Seasons.

Thomson's residence, Rossdale-house, is in Kew-foot-lane. In the poet's favourite seat in the garden is placed the table on which he wrote his verses. Over the entrance is inscribed—

"Here Thomson sung the Seasons and their change."

The inside is adorned with suitable quotations from authors who have paid due compliments to his talents; and in the centre is an elegant inscription. Thomson was buried at the west end of the north aisle of Richmond church, where a brass tablet with the following inscription has been put up by the earl of Buchan:—"In the earth below this tablet are the remains of James Thomson, author of the beautiful poems entitled 'The Seasons,' 'The Castle of Indolence,' &c., who died at Richmond on the 22d of August, and was buried there on the 29th, O. S., 1748. The earl of Buchan, unwilling that so good a man and sweet a poet should be without a memorial, has denoted the place of his interment for the satisfaction of his admirers, in the year of our Lord 1792." Underneath is this quotation from his "Winter:"—

"Father of Light and Life! Thou Good Supreme!
O, teach me what is good! teach me Thyself!
Save me from folly, vanity, and vice,
From every low pursuit! and feed my soul
With knowledge, conscious peace, and virtue pure;
Sacred, substantial, never-fading bliss!"

In the churchyard were buried the Rev. Gilbert Wakefield, who died in 1801; and Dr. Moore, the author of Zeluco. In the church lies Mrs. Yates, the celebrated actress.

Richmond-park, formerly called the Great or the New Park, to distinguish it from that which was near the Green, was made by Charles I. The great lodge, erected by Robert lord Walpole, who was ranger, is a stone edifice standing on a rising ground, and commanding a fine prospect of the park. Here also is another house, called the Stone-lodge, which was built by George I. This park is eight miles in circumference, and contains 2253 acres, of which about 100 are in Richmond parish, 650 in Mortlake, 265 in Petersham, 230 in Putney, and about 1000 in Kingston.

Inns.—Star and Garter, Castle, and Talbot. *Coaches.*—Gracechurch-street, Old Bailey, St. Paul's Churchyard, White Horse Cellar, Piccadilly.

During summer *Steam-boats* go every day from Queenhithe to Richmond.

SHOOTER'S-HILL is situated eight miles from London, on the Dover road. The summit commands a fine view of the metropolis, but the most delightful prospect is from the tower of Severndroog castle, which was erected to commemorate the reduction of a fort of that name near Bombay. This tower is generally called the Folly, and is much frequented by pic-nic parties, who are accommodated at the adjacent lodge. At the summit of the hill, which is more than 400 feet above low-water mark, is a spring of excellent mineral water.

Coaches.—Charing-cross, Gracechurch-street.

SION-HOUSE, the seat of the duke of Northumberland, is situated in Isleworth, on the Thames. The mansion is a noble edifice of white stone, which was repaired by Inigo Jones, but has been recently modernised. It commands a fine view of the river. The first mulberry-trees planted in England are now standing in the gardens attached to this house. The conservatory, recently erected at an expense of 40,000*l.*, is one of the finest in the world.

SLOUGH is a little village about 20 miles from London, and about one mile and a half from Windsor. It is worthy of notice as having been the residence of Dr. Herschel the astronomer, who expired here in 1822. His extraordinary telescope is minutely described in the "Philosophical Transactions" for 1795. It may be viewed on application at the house, where his son still resides.

Slough is one of the Great Western Railway stations.

Coaches.—Bolt-in-tun, Fleet-street; White Horse Cellar, Piccadilly.

STAINES is a very ancient market town, 16 miles W.S.W. from London. It is supposed to have derived its name from the stone (*stana*) which marks the extent of the jurisdiction possessed by the city of London over the western part of the Thames. This boundary-stone is situated on the margin of the river near the church, and bears the following inscription on a moulding round the upper part:—"God preserve the city of London. A. D. 1280." The town consists of one wide street, terminating at the Thames, across which is an iron bridge of one arch. The church was rebuilt in 1829, from designs by Mr. J. B. Watson. It is in the Gothic style, and is capable of accommodating 1100 persons.

Coaches.—Bell, Holborn.

St. Albans is about 21 miles from London on the northern road. The abbey is a curious remain of antiquity; and in St. Michael's church is a monumental effigy of Francis Bacon, lord Verulam. This place was once the capital of Britain, and previous to the invasion of Julius Cæsar was the residence of British princes.

Coaches.—Smithfield.

Strawberry-hill, near Twickenham, Middlesex, the villa of the late earl of Orford (better known as Mr. Horace Walpole), is situated on an eminence near the Thames. It was originally a small tenement, built in 1698 by the earl of Bradford's coachman, and let as a lodging-house. Colley Cibber was one of its first tenants, and there he wrote his comedy called "The Refusal." It was afterwards taken by persons of consequence, as an occasional summer residence, and in 1747 was purchased by Mr. Walpole, who erected the present beautiful Gothic structure. Great taste is displayed in the embellishments of the edifice, and in the choice collection of pictures, sculptures, antiquities, and curiosities that adorn it. The approach to the house through a grove of lofty trees, the embattled wall overgrown with ivy, the spiral pinnacles and gloomy cast of the building, give it the air of an ancient abbey. In the grounds is a pretty Gothic chapel, containing a curious mosaic shrine.

By lord Orford's will this mansion was bequeathed to the hon. Mrs. Damer, who resigned her claim to it in favour of the countess of Waldegrave. It is at present the seat of earl Waldegrave.

Streatham is a village in Surrey, about five miles from London, on the road to Croydon. The church contains two Latin inscriptions, to the memory of Mr. Thrale and his mother-in-law, Mrs. Salisbury, written by Dr. Johnson, who was a frequent visiter at Streatham-park when it belonged to Mr. Thrale.

Inn.—The White Lion.

Teddington, a pretty rural village in Middlesex, about 12 miles W.S.W. from London. The manor-house is a fine mansion; the church contains some monuments.

The Thames, to which the metropolis is so much indebted,

rises in Trewsbury Mead, two miles from Cirencester, in Gloucestershire, and becomes navigable for barges of 80 or 90 tons at Lechdale, 138 miles above London. Ships of the largest size may ascend the river as far as Deptford, and vessels of 700 or 800 tons can come up to London-bridge. The entire course of the river from its source to the Nore is about 200 miles. From Oxford to Maidenhead it falls 12½ feet every five miles, and from Maidenhead to Brentford, 10 feet every five miles, although the fall from Brentford to the Nore, a distance of 60 miles, is only seven feet. The breadth of the Thames at London is about a quarter of a mile, and at Gravesend about a mile. The tide flows up to Richmond, which, following the winding of the river, is 70 miles from the sea—a greater distance than the tide is carried by any other river in Europe. The water, however, is not salt much higher than Gravesend, which by the river is 30 miles from London. The Nore is 40 miles from London; and it is high-water at London-bridge two hours after it is high-water at the Nore.

TILBURY-FORT, in West Tilbury, opposite Gravesend, may be termed the key to London. It was designed by sir Mr. Beckman, chief engineer to Charles II. It has a double moat, the innermost of which is 180 feet broad, with a good counterscarp, covered way, ravelins, and tenailles. Its chief strength on the land side consists in its being able to lay the whole level under water. On the side next the river is a strong curtain, with a noble gate, called the Watergate, and before it is a platform, on which are planted 106 guns, from 24 to 46-pounders each, besides smaller ones between them; the bastions and curtains are also planted with guns. Here is likewise a high tower, called the Block-house, said to have been built in the reign of Elizabeth.

TWICKENHAM is an extensive and populous village on the Thames, about 10½ miles from London. Between Richmond-bridge and this village is a public but rural walk, on the border of the river, and probably no promenade of a similar extent, in any part of this island, presents a display of scenery so soft and so highly cultivated. At a short distance from the river is Marble-hill, built by George II. for the countess of Suffolk. The margin of the Thames, through its whole progress along the village, is lined with stately dwellings, whose ornamental grounds descend to the water's edge; among these is one endeared to memory as the residence of Pope. The house was not large, but Pope took great delight in embellishing the grounds. Towards the front of the house stood a far-famed weeping-willow, supposed to have been planted by him; but it perished in 1801, and another has been planted on the spot. Here he translated a part of the "Illiad," and wrote the "Dunciad," the "Essay on Man," the "Epistles," and numerous minor poems; and hence are dated the greater number of those letters so universally admired for elegance and wit; here also Pope died. This villa was taken down by baroness Howe in 1807, and a new dwelling erected about 100 yards from the site. The grotto which Pope constructed has been stripped of its most curious spars and minerals by the zeal of those who have been desirous of procuring a memorial of the poet. In a retired part of the grounds is an obelisk raised by Pope to the memory of his mother. In the church of Twickenham Pope and his parents are interred. To their memory he himself erected a monument; to his own, the gratitude of Warburton erected another. On the outside of the church, on a marble tablet, are some lines by Miss Pope to the memory of Mrs. Clive the actress.

UXBRIDGE is a market-town in Middlesex, 15 miles from London, on the road to Oxford. At the Crown inn is the room in which the commissioners of Charles I. and the parliament met in 1646, whence the house is called the Treaty-house.

WIMBLEDON is a village in Surrey, on a fine heath, seven miles from London. In the church, Mr. Perry, for many years editor of the Morning Chronicle, was buried in December 1821. The eminences in the park attached to lord Spencer's seat at this place, command delightful prospects, including Norwood, Epsom-downs, Highgate, Harrow-on-the-hill, and the metropolis, in which may be distinguished his lordship's house in the Green-park. Adjoining earl Spencer's grounds is a house which formerly belonged to M. Calonne, the comptroller-general of France before the revolution, and was afterwards inhabited by the prince de Condé. There are numerous other good houses on Wimbledon-common, in one of which John Horne Tooke died in 1812. At the south-west corner is an encampment, surrounded by a ditch, and enclosing about seven acres. It is supposed to have been the scene of battle, in 568, between Ethelbert king of Kent, and Ceaulin king of the West Saxons.

Coaches.—Gracechurch-street.

WINDSOR, 21 miles from London, is situated on the east border of Berkshire. It was declared a free borough as far back as 1276. The church, in High-street, dedicated to St

John the Baptist, is in the plain Gothic style, and is capable of accommodating 1800 persons. It was built in 1822, and contains several ancient monuments, as well as two Gothic chairs presented by the princess Augusta. The rail surrounding the altar was carved by Gibbons.

The guildhall was erected in 1686. It contains numerous portraits, amongst which is that of his majesty George IV. by sir T. Lawrence. Windsor also contains a free-school, several meeting-houses and charitable institutions, a theatre, and barracks. At the bottom of Thames-street is the bridge which connects Windsor with Eton. It was erected in 1824, and consists of three cast-iron arches, resting on granite piers. It is 200 feet long and 26 wide.

WINDSOR-CASTLE has long been the favourite residence of the British monarchs. This magnificent palace occupies more than 12 acres of ground; it was originally built by William the Conqueror, but enlarged by Henry I. The monarchs who succeeded him likewise resided in it, till Edward III., who was born here, caused the old building, with the exception of three towers at the west end, to be taken down, and re-erected the whole castle, under the direction of William of Wykeham. He likewise built St. George's chapel, and instituted the Order of the Garter. Charles II. entirely changed the form of the upper court, enlarged the windows, and made them regular, richly furnished the royal apartments, decorated them with paintings, and erected a magazine of arms. He likewise enlarged the terrace-walk made by queen Elizabeth, on the north side of the castle, and carried another terrace round the east and south sides of the upper courts. With the exception of trifling repairs, the building remained as it was left by Charles II. till the reign of George III., who made it his principal residence. Under his direction various improvements were effected, and many others suggested, the execution of which was deferred by his lamented illness. In 1824 a parliamentary grant of 300,000*l*., subsequently increased to 771,000*l*., was voted for the repairs and alterations of the castle, which were immediately proceeded with, from designs by sir Jeffrey Wyatville.

The castle is divided into two courts, or wards, with a large round tower between them, called the middle ward, the whole containing about twelve acres of land, with many towers and batteries. It is situated upon a high hill, which rises by a gentle ascent, and on the declivity is the *Terrace*, which is 1870 feet in length; it is faced with a rampart of freestone,

WINDSOR CASTLE.

NEW CEMETERY HARROW ROAD.

HOLLAND HOUSE.

and allowed to be the noblest walk in Europe, with respect to strength, grandeur, and prospect.

The *Lower-ward* is much more extensive than the other, and includes the following towers: Winchester, originally built by William of Wykeham; Store, or the Lieutenant's tower; Salisbury, Garter, and Julius Cæsar's, or the Belfry. The ward is divided by St. George's chapel, which stands in the centre. On the north or inner side are the houses and apartments of the dean and canons of St. George's chapel, with those of the minor canons, clerks, and other officers; and on the south and west sides of the outer part are houses of the poor knights of Windsor.

St. George's Chapel, or the *Collegiate Church* of Windsor, is the largest in dimensions, the most chaste and elegant in architectural style and character, and the most diversified in external and internal arrangement, of the three royal chapels in England. It was founded by Edward III., but much improved by Edward IV., and afterwards by Henry VII., whose prime minister, sir Reginald Brag, assisted in the construction of the roof, which is decorated with an infinite number of devices. The roof is built in the form of an ellipsis, and is supported by lofty pillars. On each side of the choir are the stalls of the sovereigns and knights of the order of the garter, with their arms, banners, &c.; and in the vaults beneath are interred Henry VI., Edward IV., Henry VIII., his queen Jane Seymour, Charles I., and a daughter of queen Anne. The monument of Edward IV. is adorned with a curious specimen of wrought steel, said to have been executed by Quintin Matsys of Antwerp. The carving which ornaments the organ and the stalls is particularly fine. About 1790, various alterations were made in the chapel, under the direction of Mr. Emlyn, by order of George III., who contributed 15,000*l.* from his own private purse towards defraying the expenses. The altar is an elegant screen, elaborately carved, and adorned with the arms of Edward III., Edward the Black Prince, and the first knights of the garter, as well as with a picture of the Last Supper by West, over which, from designs by the same artist, is a painted window, representing the Resurrection, executed by Mr. Jarvis and his pupil Mr. Forest. The other windows contain paintings of the arms of the knights by Mr. Eginton. The organ, made by Mr. Green, is considered one of the finest in the kingdom.

In a small chapel, at the north-west angle of the nave, is

the cenotaph of the princess Charlotte, erected by public subscription in 1825. It was executed by Mr. B. Wyatt.

At the east end of St. George's chapel is a freestone edifice, built by Henry VII. as a burial-place for himself and his successors; but afterwards altering his purpose, he began the more noble structure at Westminster; and this remained neglected till Cardinal Wolsey began a sumptuous monument for himself, whence the building obtained the name of *Wolsey's tomb-house*. The cardinal, dying soon after his disgrace, was buried in the abbey at Leicester, and the monument remained unfinished. James II. converted the building into a popish chapel, but it afterwards fell to decay, and remained so till the reign of George III., when it was formed into a royal mausoleum under the direction of Mr. Wyatt. The entrance is in the choir of St. George's chapel. Here are deposited the remains of George III., his consort queen Charlotte, his daughter the princess Amelia, his sons George IV., William IV., the dukes of York and Kent, and his grand-daughter the princess Charlotte, with her infant son. This mausoleum also contains the bodies of the infant princes Alfred and Octavius, which were removed from Westminster-abbey.

Between the two wards of the castle stands the *Round-tower*, which contains the governor's apartments. It is built on the highest part of the mount, and is ascended by a flight of stone steps. This mount is laid out in sloping walks round the hill, covered with verdure, and planted with shrubs. The apartments command an extensive view to London, and into the counties of Middlesex, Essex, Herts, Bucks, Berks, Oxfordshire, Wilts, Hants, Surrey, Sussex, Kent, and Bedfordshire. In the guard-chamber are shewn the coats of mail of king John of France, and David king of Scotland, both prisoners here at the same time; and here is the room in which marshal de Belleisle resided when a prisoner in 1744.

The *Upper-ward* is a noble quadrangle, having the state apartments on the north side, the Round-tower on the west, and the king's private apartments, with those of the royal household, on the east and south. On the west side of the square is an equestrian bronze statue of Charles II., executed in 1679. The pedestal is adorned with bassi-relievi by Gibbons. The state-apartments, which are shewn to the public, are adorned with carving by Gibbons, and painted ceilings by Verrio, and contain a rich collection of pictures by the ancient masters, as well as an historical series by the late Mr. West.

The principal improvements made by sir J. Wyatville are in the Upper-ward. Connected with the Round-tower is the Devil-tower, near which was the old principal gateway. The new gateway is a noble and imposing arch, 24 feet in height, above which are apartments for the attendants, the whole surmounted by machicolated battlements. It immediately faces the Long-walk. On the east side of the gateway stands York-tower, and on the west Lancaster-tower, the first stone of which was laid by his majesty Aug. 12, 1824. Opposite this gateway is the principal entrance to the state apartments, in front of which is a magnificent tower, the lower part being arched, and allowing carriages to pass under. Above is an apartment forming a communication with the state-rooms on the north front. In the upper division of the tower is a clock with musical chimes, bearing the date 1827.

At the north-east corner of the court-yard is the gateway to the domestic offices, and near it is a small tower, forming an entrance for her majesty's visiters. An elegant vestibule, at the top of the staircase, communicates with the corridor, which extends round the south and east sides of the building, and from which folding-doors open at intervals into the apartments. At the south-east corner of the court is the queen's private entrance, adorned with the royal arms. It is nearly of a triangular form, and communicates with the corridor by a small landing, above which rises an embellished lantern.

The principal apartments are in the east front, and comprise two dining-rooms, drawing-room, library, &c. They are lighted by large oriel windows; the ceilings are enriched with various devices, and several of the doors are ornamented with carved work originally intended for a saloon for Napoleon.

The east front has a splendid appearance. A pentagon terrace, with bastions at the angles, extends a considerable distance into the park, and communicates with the old terrace on the north and south sides. The space which it encloses is laid out as a flower-garden, with a fountain in the centre. Upon this front are four towers, the principal of which, at the south-east angle, is called the King's-tower, and is of such massive construction, that upwards of 1000 tons have been added to the original weight on the foundation.

The Waterloo-gallery contains portraits of the sovereigns of Europe, and various distinguished characters, by Lawrence.

Brunswick-tower, near the east end of the north terrace, is

of octagon form, and rises 120 feet above the level of the terrace. The principal apartment in it is a private dining-room for her majesty. In a central position between the principal suite of apartments and St. George's hall, is the music-saloon. Brunswick-tower and the state-apartments are connected by a corridor, terminating at the Royal Guard-chamber, where George III.'s tower has been erected. The alterations in the south front have been confined to the new gateway, and raising the building to a level with the other portions of the edifice.

The round-tower and state-apartments are open every day for the inspection of the public; and St. George's chapel may be viewed during the intervals of service, which is performed daily at half-past ten and half-past four.

The royal foundations in this castle are, the most noble order of the garter, which consists of the sovereign and twenty-five knights companions; the royal college of St. George, consisting of a dean, twelve canons, seven minor canons, eleven clerks, an organist, a verger, two sacristans, and eighteen alms knights. The order of the garter is also called the order of St. George, the patron of England, under whose banner the English always went to war; and St. George's cross was made the ensign of the order.

Coaches. — Bolt-in-tun, Fleet-street; White-horse-cellar, Piccadilly.

The Great Western Railway runs to Slough, about two miles from Windsor, whence coaches go on the arrival of every train.

WINDSOR LITTLE PARK, immediately adjoining the Castle, is about four miles in circumference, and contains about 500 acres. It was enclosed by a brick-wall in the reign of William III. The ground forming the declivity of the hill on the north terrace of the castle is laid out with shrubs and flowers, and is called, from its situation, the Slopes. Divided by the London road from the Little Park is *Frogmore*, already noticed.

WINDSOR GREAT PARK lies on the south side of the town of Windsor. It is fourteen miles in circumference, and contains about 1800 acres. This park was much improved by his majesty George III. It is intersected by several roads, the principal of which is the Long Walk, a noble avenue nearly three miles in length, adorned on each side with a double row of trees, and leading from the Castle to a hill whence there is a delightful prospect. In this walk, about two miles from the town, is a saline spring, of considerable efficacy in chronic disorders. An equestrian statue of George III. has also been erected here.

Near the end of the Long Walk is *Cumberland Lodge*, so called from William duke of Cumberland, who lived here. In the vicinity of the Lodge is the lake called *Virginia Water*, surrounded by pleasing grounds. Over various parts of the lake are bridges, one of which is a single arch, 165 feet in span; and on the south-west margin is a temple and fishing-gallery.

The lodges to the park present nothing remarkable, with the exception of the Sandpit-gate, built from a design by Mr. J. Wyatt in 1800. It consists of an embattled archway, with two octagonal towers. Near it are the enclosures for her majesty's menagerie.

Adelaide Lodge, erected in 1831, is a pretty summer retreat for her majesty, situated in the park, towards Datchet.

Between the park and the forest stands *Cranbourn Lodge*, built by the earl of Ranelagh in the reign of Charles II. It was once occupied by William duke of Cumberland, afterwards by the princess Charlotte of Saxe Cobourg.

WOODFORD is a pleasant village on the road to Epping, about eight miles from London, formerly noted for its mineral waters. In the churchyard is a yew-tree of extraordinary size, and an elegant monument of the Corinthian order, designed by sir R. Taylor, and erected in memory of the descendants of sir E. Godfrey, who formerly lived in this village. Here also Oliver Cromwell and Milton are said to have resided. Pony races are held at Woodford at Whitsuntide.

WOOLWICH is a market-town in Kent, about nine miles from London, situated on the Thames. It is famed for its dock-yards, in which men-of-war are built, and for its royal arsenal, called the *Warren*, where immense military stores are deposited. The *Royal Arsenal* was formed about 1720, on the site of a rabbit-warren; it contains numerous buildings, consisting of store-houses, manufactory of Congreve rockets, barracks, model-house, cannon-foundry, boring-houses, smiths' and carpenters' shops, establishment for filling cartridges, grenades, and bombs, and shot-manufactory. Here likewise are machines, set in motion by steam, for sawing and planing wood, &c. &c.

On the common is a noble range of building, forming the *Artillery Barracks*, which contain a library, mess-room, guard-room, and capacious chapel. This beautiful edifice is 400 yards in length and 300 in depth. Behind it is a riding-school, and on the descent leading from the common to the arsenal are the military hospitals.

The *Marine Barracks* occupy an eminence on the west side of the barrack-field. In front of the artillery barracks is a fine parade, where the soldiers are frequently exercised in throwing shells at a mark, and other military evolutions.

The *New Military Academy* is a handsome castellated edifice, situated on the common, about a mile from the barracks; it was built from designs by Wyatt, and is upwards of 200 yards in length. The governor is always the master-general of the ordnance, who has the appointment of the principal officers and of the cadets.

The *Royal Military Repository*, on the south-west side of the barrack-field, contains canals, and a piece of water on which experiments are occasionally made with gun-boats, &c. During war upwards of 3000 labourers and artificers are employed at Woolwich, exclusive of the convicts belonging to the hulks, which are anchored opposite the dock-yard and arsenal.

Coaches.—Gracechurch-street and Charing-cross.

HACKNEY COACHES.

Number.

THE registrar may license 800 coaches, by 9 Anne, c. 23; 200 more by 11 Geo. III., c. 24; and 100 more by 42 Geo. III., c. 78. Total, 1100.

By 54 Geo. III. c. 147, he may license 200 chariots; and by 55 Geo. III., he is empowered to license, if he thinks fit, 200 more; making 400 chariots.

Drivers, Conductors, and Watermen.

Drivers, conductors, and watermen attending carriage-stands must not be under 16 years of age, must be licensed by the registrar, and must wear a metal ticket conspicuously on their breasts, containing their respective numbers. Drivers, conductors, or watermen acting without license liable to a penalty not exceeding 5*l*.

Size of Horses.

No horse shall be used with a hackney-coach or chariot which shall be under 14 hands high.

Number of Passengers.

Coaches are not compellable to take more than four adults in the inside, and a servant out; but if the coachman agree to take more, the fare will be 1*s*. for each extra person, of whatever age he or she may be, not being a child in arms or lap; and if taken in the country, 1*s*. for going, and 1*s*. for returning.

By 55 Geo. III., chariots are compellable to take three adults, or grown-up persons, not being children in arms or lap, and a servant on the outside; but if the coachman should agree to carry, or should actually carry, above that number, he shall be paid at the same rate as in the preceding article respecting coaches.

One-horse Chaise.

It will likewise be lawful in the registrar, with the approbation and direction, in writing, of the lords of his majesty's treasury, or any three or more of them, to license such number of carriages with two wheels, and drawn by one horse, as shall be specified by them, subject to the same laws and regulations as hackney-coaches and chariots; and they shall be entitled to demand and take two-thirds of the amount of fares, rates, and benefits as established by law for hackney-coaches and chariots, and not compellable to carry more than two persons.

Abusive Language.

By 9 Anne, c. 23, the drivers of coaches and carriers of chairs, on demanding more than their fare, or giving abusive language, are to forfeit not more than 5*l*.; and in default of the payment, they are to be sent to the house of correction for seven days.

Extortion.

By 1 Geo. I., c. 57, coachmen refusing to go on, or extorting more than their fare, are to forfeit not more than 3*l*., nor less than 10*s*.

Not only the registrar, but also justices, may determine offences and inflict punishments.

Returning from the Country.

Coaches hired to go into the country in the day-time are to have for their return empty—for ten miles, 5*s.*; eight miles, 4*s.*; six miles 3*s.*; and for four miles, 2*s.*; but there is no allowance for less than four miles.

Obligation to go.

And they shall be compellable on every day, and at any hour of the night, although they may have been out twelve hours, to go with any person or persons desirous of hiring them, and no more than the regular fare allowed on such occasions.

Deposit for Waiting.

Persons taking coaches to places of public resort, to be kept in waiting, are to pay the coachman a reasonable deposit, to be accounted for when the coach is discharged.

Check-String.

The registrar is to order check-strings to every hackney coach; and every hackney coachman plying without such shall forfeit 5*s.*

Coach-Stand.

By 11 Geo. III., c. 20, coaches are to stand eight feet asunder, and room to be left for waggons, on penalty of 20*s.*

Inspection.

By 39 and 40 Geo. III., c. 47, the registrar may appoint inspectors of hackney coaches and horses, and suspend the license of any person whose coach shall be defective or horses unfit; and may annul licenses if the inspectors are refused to examine coaches.

Off the Stand.

Hackney coachmen, whose coaches are standing in the streets, although off the stand, are compellable to go with any person desirous of hiring them; and, in case of refusal, are liable to be fined, unless they prove they were hired at the time. And in case of leaving their coaches unattended, whether hired or not, are liable to a penalty not exceeding 5*l.*

Not Stage-coaches.

By 48. Geo. III., c. 87, hackney-coaches are not to ply for promiscuous passengers when returning from the country, on pain of a penalty not exceeding 3*l.*, nor less than 20*s.*; but this is not to prevent their taking up regular fares.

Tickets or Certificates.

By the last act, the clause relative to tickets is repealed.

Option of Fares or Distance.

Fare to be calculated for time or distance, at the option of the coachman, and not by the day, as heretofore.

Agreement for more than the regular Fare not binding.

No agreement to pay more than the regular fare is binding. Any person may, notwithstanding such agreement, refuse to pay more than the established fare; and if he pay more he may recover the overplus, the driver being subject to a penalty of 5*l.* for non-payment.

Time of Sunset.

As the period of sunset has been found constantly liable to dispute, it is therefore now regulated that the sunset hours shall be after eight in the evening between Lady-day and Michaelmas, and after five in the evening between Michaelmas and Lady-day; and the back-carriage, after such hours, shall be taken to the carriage-way pavement, or next standing beyond which the coach was hired from (if hired at any stand off the said pavement), at the full fare back to either, at the option of the party discharging.

How Property left in Coaches or Chariots is to be disposed of.

The drivers of hackney coaches wherein any property is left shall carry such property, in the state in which it was found, within four days, to the Hackney Coach Office, and deposit the same with one of the clerks, under a penalty not exceeding 20*l.*

General Rules of Distances.

	s.	d.		s.	d.
Not exceeding one mile	1	0	Seven miles	8	6
One mile and a half	1	6	Seven miles and a half	9	0
Two miles	2	0	Eight miles	9	6
Two miles and a half	3	0	Eight miles and a half	10	6
Three miles	3	6	Nine miles	11	0
Three miles and a half	4	0	Nine miles and a half	11	6
Four miles	4	6	Ten miles	12	0
Four miles and a half	5	6	Ten miles and a half	13	0
Five miles	6	0	Eleven miles	13	6
Five miles and a half	6	6	Eleven miles and a half	14	0
Six miles	7	0	Twelve miles	15	0
Six miles and a half	8	0			

And so on at the rate of 6*d.* for every half mile, and an additional 6*d.* for every two miles completed.

Time.

Not exceeding thirty minutes	1	0	Not exceeding two hours and twenty minutes	6	0
Forty-five minutes	1	6	Two hours and forty minutes	7	0
One hour	2	0	Three hours	8	0
One hour & twenty minutes	3	0	Three hours and twenty min.	9	0
One hour and forty minutes	4	0	Three hours and forty min.	10	0
Two hours	5	0	Four hours	11	0

And so on at the rate of 6*d.* for every fifteen minutes further time.*

* For further information see the "Arbitrator, or Metropolitan Distance Map," for regulating Hackney Coach Fares, &c. by Distance or Time, according to the last act; shewing at one view the whole of the metropolis, in half-mile measurements; accompanied by an alphabetical list of about five hundred of the principal streets, and their admeasurements; with other useful information. Price in sheet, coloured, 2*s.*; mounted, coloured, in case, or in the form of a book, 3*s.* 6*d.*; ditto, roller and varnished, 4*s.* 6*d.* Published at 421 Strand, and sold by all booksellers.

SUNDRY FARES.

Admiralty to

	s.	d.		s.	d.
Islington church	4	0	Shoreditch church	4	0
India-house	3	0	Tower	3	0
Mile-end turnpike	4	6	Union-street, Borough	3	6
Ratcliff-cross	5	6			

Bank to

	s.	d.		s.	d.
Berkeley-square	3	6	Piccadilly	3	0
Haymarket	3	0	Pantheon, Oxford-street	3	0
Hyde-park corner	4	0	Ratcliff-cross	3	0
Islington church	3	0	Tyburn turnpike	4	0

Berkeley-square to

	s.	d.		s.	d.
Clerkenwell-green	3	6	Newgate	3	0
Foundling hospital	3	0	Obelisk, Fleet-street	3	0
Guildhall	3	6	Ratcliff-cross	6	0
Islington church	4	0	St. Paul's, west end	3	0
India-house	4	0	Shoreditch church	4	6
Lincoln's-inn, near side	3	0	Tower	4	0
Mile-end turnpike	5	6	Union-street, Borough	4	0

Clerkenwell to

	s.	d.		s.	d.
Hyde-park corner	4	0	Shoreditch church	3	0
Mile-end turnpike	3	6	Tyburn turnpike	3	6
Ratcliff-cross	4	0	Union-street, Borough	3	0

Foundling Hospital to

	s.	d.		s.	d.
Hyde-park corner	3	0	Shoreditch church	4	0
India-house	3	0	Tower	3	6
Mile-end turnpike	4	0	Tyburn turnpike	3	0
Ratcliff-cross	5	6	Union-street, Borough	3	6

Guildhall to

	s.	d.		s.	d.
Haymarket	3	6	Piccadilly	3	0
Hyde-park corner	4	0	Pantheon, Oxford-street	3	0
Islington church	3	0	Tyburn turnpike	3	6

Hyde-park Corner to

	s.	d.		s.	d.
Islington church	5	6	Ratcliff-cross	6	6
India-house	4	0	St. Paul's, west end	3	6
Lincoln's-inn, near side	3	0	Shoreditch church	5	6
Mile-end turnpike	6	0	Temple-bar	3	0
Newgate	3	6	Tower	4	6
Obelisk, Fleet-street	3	0	Union-street, Borough	4	6

Islington Church to

	s.	d.		s.	d.
India-house	3	6	Ratcliff-cross	5	6
Lincoln's-inn, near side	3	0	Temple-bar	3	6
Mile-end turnpike	4	6	Tower	4	0
Piccadilly	4	0	Tyburn turnpike	4	6
Haymarket	4	0	Union-street, Borough	4	0
Pantheon, Oxford-street	3	6			

Leicester-square to

	s.	d.		s.	d.
Aldgate	3	6	Hyde-park corner . . .	1	0
Aldersgate-street . . .	2	0	India-house	3	0
Battersea	5	6	London-bridge . . .	3	0
Battle-bridge	3	0	Minories	3	6
Blackfriars-bridge . .	2	0	Paddington church . .	3	0
Blackwall	7	0	Ratcliff-cross . . .	5	6
Chelsea hospital . . .	3	0	Rotherhithe church . .	5	6
Custom-house	3	6	Royal exchange . . .	3	0
Charter-house	2	0	Shadwell church . . .	4	6
Grosvenor-square . . .	1	0	Shoreditch church . .	4	0
Houndsditch	3	0	Tower-gate	3	6

Minories to

	s.	d.		s.	d.
Adelphi	3	0	Foundling hospital . .	3	0
Admiralty	3	6	Gray's-inn	2	0
Aldersgate-street . . .	4	0	Hanover-square . . .	4	0
Barbican	1	6	Haymarket	3	6
Battle-bridge	3	6	Hoxton-square . . .	1	6
Bedford-row	3	0	Hyde-park corner . .	4	6
Berkeley-square . . .	4	6	Lambeth-palace . . .	3	6
Blackfriars-bridge . .	2	0	Limehouse church . .	3	0
Bloomsbury-square . .	3	0	Lincoln's-inn-square . .	3	0
Bond-street, Piccadilly .	4	0	Ludgate-hill	1	6
Bow-street	3	0	Newgate	1	6
British museum . . .	3	6	Norfolk-street, Strand . .	2	0
Buckingham-gate . . .	4	6	Palace-yard	3	6
Cavendish-square . . .	4	0	Pall-mall east . . .	3	6
Charing-cross	3	6	Piccadilly, Bond-street .	4	0
Chelsea church . . .	7	0	Pickett-street, Strand . .	2	0
Clerkenwell-green . . .	2	0	Portland-place . . .	4	0
Coventry-street . . .	4	0	Rotherhithe church . .	4	0
Downing-street . . .	3	6	Soho-square	3	6
Exeter-change . . .	3	0	Wimpole-street . . .	4	6

Moorfields to

	s.	d.		s.	d.
Admiralty	3	0	Mary-le-bone church . .	4	6
British museum . . .	3	0	Parliament-street . .	3	0
Cavendish-square . . .	3	6	Portman-square . . .	4	0
Downing-street . . .	3	0	Rathbone-place . . .	3	0
Greenwich	8	0	Spring-gardens . . .	3	0
Hanover square . . .	3	6	St. Martin's-lane . . .	3	0
Haymarket	3	0	Temple-bar	1	6
Lambeth-palace . . .	3	6			

Oxford-street (Bond-street) to

	s.	d.		s.	d.
Adelphi	1	6	Buckingham-gate . . .	2	0
Aldgate	4	0	Charing-cross	1	6
Bank	3	6	Clerkenwell-green . . .	3	0
Billingsgate	4	0	Custom-house	4	0
Blackwall	8	6	Downing-street . . .	1	6

	s.	d.		s.	d.
Gracechurch-street	3	6	Newgate	3	0
Hyde-park-corner	1	6	Parliament-street	1	6
Lambeth-palace	3	6	Shoreditch church	4	0
London-bridge	4	0	Temple-bar	2	0
Mansion-house	3	6	Walbrook	3	6

Palace-yard to

	s.	d.		s.	d.
Aldersgate-street	3	0	Holborn-bridge	2	0
Aldgate	3	6	Lamb's-conduit-street	2	0
Blackwall	8	0	Leadenhall-street	3	0
Bank	3	6	Limehouse church	6	0
Bedford-row	2	0	Middlesex hospital	2	0
Bloomsbury-square	1	6	Moorfields	3	6
Cavendish-square	2	0	Old Jewry	3	0
Coventry-street	1	0	Paternoster-row	2	0
Custom-house	3	0	Poultry	3	0
Fenchurch-street	3	0	Rotherhithe church	4	6
Fetter-lane	2	0	St. Paul's churchyard	2	0
Foundling hospital	2	0	Temple-bar	1	6
Grosvenor-square	2	0	Walbrook	3	0
Hanover-square	1	6	Walworth	8	0

St. Paul's Churchyard to

	s.	d.		s.	d.
Adelphi	1	6	Greek-street, Soho	1	6
Albemarle-street	3	0	Haymarket	2	0
Aldgate	1	6	Hoxton-square	2	0
Bedford-square	2	0	Leicester-square	1	6
Blackwall	6	0	Manchester-square	3	6
Bond-street, Piccadilly	3	0	Newman-street, Oxford-street	2	0
British museum	1	6	Parliament-street	2	0
Broadway, Westminster	3	0	Pimlico	3	6
Cavendish-square	3	0	Portman-square	3	6
Charing-cross	1	6	Red-lion-square	1	6
Cockspur-street	1	6	Rotherhithe church	4	0
Custom-house	1	6	Shoreditch church	2	0
Downing-street	2	0	Westminster-hall	2	0
Foundling hospital	1	6			

Strand (Catherine-street) to

	s.	d.		s.	d.
Argyle-street	1	6	Manchester-square	2	0
Bank	2	0	Mary-le-bone church	3	0
Cavendish-square	1	6	Pimlico	2	0
Conduit-street	1	6	Ratcliff-cross	4	6
Custom-house	2	0	Rotherhithe church	5	6
Dover-street	1	6	Royal exchange	2	0
Grosvenor-square	2	0	Shoreditch church	3	0
Hoxton-square	3	0	Tooley-street	2	0
Lambeth-palace	3	0	Wimpole-street	2	0

Temple-bar to

	s.	d.		s.	d.
Aldgate	2	0	America-square	2	0
Albemarle-street	1	6	Bank	1	6

	s.	d.		s.	d.
Bayswater	3	6	Mary-le-bone church	3	0
Billingsgate	1	6	Minories	2	0
Blackwall	5	6	Newman-street	1	6
Bridge-street, Westminster	1	6	Old Palace-yard	1	6
Bruton-street	2	0	Oxford-street, Bond-street	2	0
Burlington-street	1	6	Parliament-street	1	6
Chelsea-college	4	0	Pimlico	2	0
Clerkenwell-green	1	6	Portman-square	3	0
Coventry-street	1	6	Rathbone-place	1	6
Golden-square	1	6	Rotherhithe church	4	6
Grosvenor-square	2	0	St. Luke's hospital	2	0
Hanover-square	2	0	Shoreditch church	3	0
Hoxton-square	3	0	Soho-square	1	6
Knightsbridge	3	0	Spitalfields church	2	0
Lambeth-palace	3	0	Threadneedle-street	1	6
Manchester-square	2	0	Tower-gate	2	0
Mansion-house	1	6			

Tower-gate to

	s.	d.		s.	d.
Adelphi	3	0	Lambeth-palace	3	0
Albemarle-street	4	0	Leather-lane	2	0
Barbican	1	6	Leicester-square	3	6
Battle-bridge	3	6	Limehouse church	3	0
Berkeley-square	4	0	Lincoln's-inn-fields	2	0
Blackfriars-bridge	1	6	Long acre	3	6
Bloomsbury-square	3	0	Middlesex hospital	4	0
Bruton-street, Bond-street	4	0	Newgate	1	6
Catherine-street, Strand	2	0	Oxford-street, Bond-street	4	0
Charing-cross	3	0	Parliament-street	3	6
Conduit-street	4	0	Piccadilly, Bond-street	4	0
Downing-street	3	6	Portland-place	4	0
Exeter-change	2	0	Portman-square	4	6
Foundling hospital	3	0	Red-lion-square	3	0
Greek street, Soho	3	6	Rotherhithe church	3	6
Grosvenor-square	4	6	St. Luke's hospital	2	0
Hanover-square	4	0	Soho-square	3	6
Haymarket	3	6	Temple-bar	2	0
Holborn-bridge	1	6	Tyburn turnpike	4	6
Hyde-park corner	4	6	Westminster-hall	3	0
Jermyn-street	3	6	York-street, Covent-garden	3	0
Knightsbridge	5	6			

Charing-cross to

	s.	d.		s.	d.
Aldersgate-street	2	0	Mansion-house	2	0
Aldgate	3	0	Mary-le-bone church	2	0
Bank	3	0	Mile-end turnpike	4	0
Blackwall	7	0	Minories	3	0
Chelsea church	4	0	Newgate	1	6
Guildhall	2	0	Royal exchange	3	0
Goodman's-fields	3	6	Shoreditch church	4	0
Houndsditch	3	0	St. Paul's	1	6
Hyde-park corner	1	6	Tower	3	0
Leadenhall-street	3	0	Wellclose-square	4	0
Limehouse church	6	0			

Gracechurch-street to

	s.	d.		s.	d.
Adelphi	2	0	Limehouse church	3	6
Albemarle-street	3	6	Lincoln's-inn-fields	2	0
Barbican	1	6	Mary-le-bone church	4	6
Bedford-row	2	0	Oxford-market	3	6
Berkeley-square	4	0	Palace-yard	3	0
Blackwall	4	0	Piccadilly (Haymarket)	3	6
British museum	3	0	Portland-place	4	0
Catherine-street	2	0	Ratcliff-cross	2	0
Cavendish-square	3	6	Rotherhithe church	3	6
Cockspur-street	3	0	Soho-square	3	0
Downing-street	3	0	Southampton-row	2	0
Foundling hospital	2	0	Strand, New Church	2	0
Golden-square	3	0	Temple-bar	1	6
Hanover-square	3	6	Welbeck-street	4	0
Hyde-park corner	4	6	Westminster-hall	3	0
Lambeth palace	3	0	York-street, Covent-garden	3	0
Lamb's-conduit-street	2	0			

Bloomsbury-square to

	s.	d.		s.	d.
Aldermanbury	1	6	Hyde-park-corner	2	0
Aldgate	3	0	Knightsbridge	3	0
Bank	2	0	London-bridge	2	0
Barbican	1	6	Mansion-house	2	0
Berkeley-square	1	6	Mary-le-bone church	2	0
Blackwall	6	0	Parliament-street	1	6
Cavendish-square	1	6	Portman-square	2	0
Custom-house	3	6	Poultry	1	6
Greenwich Hospital	9	0	Rotherhithe church	4	6
Guildhall	2	0	Royal exchange	1	6
Grosvenor-square	2	0	Shoreditch	3	0
Houndsditch	3	0	Tower	3	0
Hoxton-square	3	0	Westminster abbey	2	0

Newgate to

	s.	d.		s.	d.
Adelphi	1	6	Greenwich	8	6
Aldgate	1	6	Haymarket	2	0
Bedford-square	1	6	Lambeth Palace	3	0
Bond-street, Piccadilly	3	0	Leicester-square	2	6
British museum	1	6	Mary-le-bone church	3	6
Charing-cross	1	6	Palace-yard	2	0
Custom-house	1	6	Rotherhithe church	4	6
Foundling hospital	1	6	Tower-gate	1	6

India House to

	s.	d.		s.	d.
Piccadilly	3	6	Pantheon, Oxford street	3	6
Haymarket	3	6	Tyburn-turnpike	4	0

Mile-End Turnpike to

	s.	d.		s.	d.
Newgate	3	0	Pantheon, Oxford-street	4	6
Obelisk, Fleet-street	3	0	Temple-bar	3	0
Piccadilly	4	6	Tyburn-turnpike	6	0
Haymarket	4	6	Union-street, Borough	3	0

Ratcliff-cross to

	s.	d.		s.	d.
St. Paul's, west end	3	6	Tyburn-turnpike	6	6
Shoreditch church	3	6	Union-street, Borough	3	0
Temple-bar	4	0			

LIST OF THE PRINCIPAL COACH-STANDS.

Adam-street West, Portman-sq.
Adelaide-street, Strand.
Agar-street, Strand.
Aldersgate-street, Barbican.
Ditto, New Post-office.
St. Ann's church, Soho.
Battle-bridge.
Bedford-street, Covent-garden.
Bishopsgate-street Within.
Ditto, Four Swans.
Ditto, Artillery-lane.
Blackfriars, Bridge-street.
Blackman-st., over London-bridge.
Ditto, over Blackfriars-bridge.
Borough, High-street.
Bricklayers' Arms.
Buckingham-gate.
Camberwell-green.
Charing-cross.
Charles-street, Covent-garden.
Cheapside, King-street.
Ditto, Foster-lane.
Ditto, St. Paul's-churchyard.
Chelsea College.
Cold Bath-square.
Compton-street, Tavistock-square.
Conduit-street, Bond-street.
Cornhill, Leadenhall-street.
Ditto, Gracechurch-street.
Elephant & Castle, Prospect-place.
Farringdon-street, Obelisk.
Fenchurch-street, Mark-lane.
Foundling Hospital.
St. Giles's, High-street.
Grosvenor-street West.
King-street, Cheapside.
Hackney, Church-street.
Haymarket, Opera.
High-street, Borough, over Westminster-bridge.
Ditto, over Blackfriars-bridge.
Holborn, King-street.
Ditto, Red Lion-street.
Ditto, Hatton-garden.
Ditto, Southampton-buildings.
Horse Guards.
Hyde-park-corner.
Islington-green.
St. James's-street.
Kennington-cross.
Ditto, Horns.
Kensington, High-street.
King's-bench, Westminster-bridge
Knightsbridge.
Lambeth-turnpike, Marsh-gate.
Leicester-square.
St. Luke's Hospital.
Marlborough-street.
Mary-le-bone, High-street.
Mile-end-turnpike.
Minories, near Tower-hill.
Moorfields, Finsbury-pavement.
Newgate-street, Old Bailey.
New-road, Welstead-street.
Oxford-street, Charles-street.
Ditto, Pantheon.
Ditto, Bond-street.
Ditto, Orchard-street.
Paddington-street.
New Palace-yard, Westminster.
New River Head, Goswell-st.-road
St. Paul's-churchyard, Ludgate-st
Park-road, Boston-street.
Piccadilly, Haymarket.
Ditto, Bond-street.
Praed-street, Edgeware-road.
Ratcliffe-highway.
Shoreditch Church.
Smithfield, near St. John-street.
Southampton-row.
Strand, Somerset House.
Temple-bar.
Tottenham-court-road, Goodge-st.
Ditto, New-road.
Tower-gate.
Trafalgar-square West.
Ditto, East.
Vauxhall-road, Pimlico.
Wellington-street, London-bridge.
Whitechapel-bars.
Ditto Church.

FARES TO THE OPERA-HOUSE, DRURY-LANE, AND COVENT-GARDEN THEATRES.

From	Opera House.		Drury-lane Theatre.		Covent-garden Theatre.	
	s.	*d.*	*s.*	*d.*	*s.*	*d.*
Aldersgate-street	3	0	2	0	2	0
Bishopsgate-street Within	3	0	2	0	2	0
Bishopsgate-street Without	3	0	3	0	3	0
Blackman-street, over London-bridge	3	6	3	0	3	0
Ditto, over Blackfriars	3	6	3	0	3	0
Ditto, over Westminster	3	0	3	0	3	0
Bloomsbury-square	1	6	1	0	1	0
Buckingham-gate	1	0	2	0	2	0
Charing-cross	1	0	1	0	1	0
Cheapside, Foster-lane end	2	0	1	6	1	6
Ditto, end of King-street	2	0	1	6	2	0
Chelsea College	3	0	3	6	3	0
Cornhill	3	0	2	0	2	0
Fenchurch-street	3	0	3	0	3	0
Fleet-street, Obelisk	1	6	1	0	1	0
Gracechurch-street	3	0	3	0	3	0
Hackney Church	5	6	5	0	5	0
Holborn, end of Leather-lane	1	6	1	0	1	0
Hyde-park-corner	1	6	2	0	2	0
Islington	3	0	3	0	3	0
Knightsbridge	2	0	3	0	3	0
Mile-end-turnpike	3	6	3	0	3	6
Minories	3	0	3	0	3	0
Moorfields	3	0	2	0	2	0
Oxford-street, Pantheon	1	0	1	6	1	6
Ditto, end of Orchard-street	1	6	2	0	2	0
Palace-yard and St. Margaret Church	1	0	1	6	1	6
Ratcliffe-cross	5	0	3	6	4	0
St. Anne's Church, Soho	1	0	1	0	1	0
St. James's Palace-gate	1	0	1	0	1	0
St. Paul's Churchyard	2	0	1	0	1	0
Shoreditch Church	3	6	3	0	3	0
Smithfield	2	0	1	6	1	6
Temple-bar	1	0	1	0	1	0
Tottenham-court-road, Goodge-street	1	6	1	0	1	0
Tower-gate	3	0	3	0	3	0
Union-street, end of Borough	3	0	3	0	3	0
Whitechapel-bars	3	0	3	0	3	6

FARES TO VAUXHALL, SADLER'S-WELLS, ASTLEY'S, AND THE CIRCUS.

From	Vauxhall.		Sadler's Wells.		Astley's.		Circus.	
	s.	*d.*	*s.*	*d.*	*s.*	*d.*	*s.*	*d.*
Aldersgate-street	3	6	1	6	2	0	2	0
Arundel-street, Strand	3	0	2	0	1	6	2	0
Bedford-street, Covent-garden	3	0	3	0	1	6	2	0
Bishopsgate-street Within	3	0	3	0	3	0	2	0
Blackman-street	2	0	3	0	1	6	1	0
Bloomsbury-square	3	6	2	0	2	0	3	0
Bond-street, Piccadilly	3	0	3	0	1	6	2	0
Buckingham-gate	3	0	3	6	1	6	2	0
Charles-street, Covent-garden	3	0	2	0	1	6	2	0
Cheapside, end of Foster-lane	3	0	1	6	2	0	1	6
Chelsea-college	4	6	5	0	3	0	3	0
Cornhill, Freeman's-court	3	0	2	0	2	0	2	0
Fleet-street, Obelisk	3	0	1	6	2	0	1	6
Gracechurch-street	3	6	2	0	2	0	2	0
Haymarket, Piccadilly end	4	6	3	0	1	6	2	0
Holborn, end of King-street	3	6	2	0	2	0	3	0
Hyde-park-corner	5	0	3	6	2	0	3	0
Islington	5	0	3	0	3	6	3	0
Leicester-square	3	0	2	0	1	6	2	0
Mile-end-turnpike	4	6	3	0	3	6	3	6
Minories	3	6	3	0	3	0	3	0
Moorfields	4	6	1	0	3	0	2	0
Newgate	3	6	1	0	2	0	1	6
Oxford-street, end of Charles-street	3	6	3	0	2	0	3	0
Ditto, Pantheon	3	6	3	0	2	0	3	0
Ditto, Bond-street	3	6	3	0	3	0	3	0
Ditto, Orchard-street	4	0	3	6	3	0	3	6
Palace-yard and St. Margaret's church	3	0	3	6	1	0	1	6
Ratcliffe-cross	5	6	3	6	4	6	3	6
St. Ann's Church, Soho	3	0	5	0	1	6	3	0
St. James's Palace	3	0	3	0	1	6	3	0
St. Paul's-churchyard	3	6	2	0	2	0	1	6
Shoreditch Church	4	6	2	0	3	6	3	0
Smithfield	3	6	1	0	3	0	2	0
Strand, Catherine-street	3	0	3	0	1	6	2	0
Temple-bar	3	6	2	0	2	0	2	0
Tottenham-court-road, Goodge-street	4	6	3	0	2	0	3	0
Tower-gate	4	6	3	0	3	0	2	0
Union-street, Borough	2	0	3	0	1	6	1	0
Whitechapel-bars	4	6	3	0	3	0	2	0

REGULATED FARES OF WATERMEN.

ESTABLISHED AUG. 1, 1828.

Watermen are obliged to carry four persons with sculls, and six persons with oars, at the following fares:

WESTWARD OF LONDON-BRIDGE.

	Sculls.	Oars.
London-bridge to Southwark-bridge, or any intermediate stairs	3*d.*	6*d.*
Southwark-bridge to Blackfriars bridge	3	6
Blackfriars-bridge to Waterloo-bridge	3	6
Waterloo-bridge to Westminster-bridge*	3	6
Westminster-bridge to Lambeth-stairs, or Horseferry-stairs .	3	6
Lambeth-stairs, or Horseferry-stairs, to Vauxhall-bridge . .	3	6
Vauxhall-bridge to Nine-elms, or opposite side of the river .	3	6
Nine-elms to the Red-house, or opposite	3	6
Red-house to Swan-stairs, Chelsea, or opposite	3	6
Swan-stairs, Chelsea, or opposite, to Battersea-bridge . . .	3	6

By this simple table it will be seen, that any of the fares between London and Battersea or Chelsea-bridge may be readily calculated. Supposing a person wishes to ascertain the charge from London-bridge to Westminster-bridge, he has only to add together the sums at the end of the first four lines, and he will perceive that it is 1*s.* for sculls, and 2*s.* for oars. Or from Westminster-bridge to Battersea-bridge, add together the sums of the last six lines, which will be 1*s.* 6*d.* for sculls, and 3*s.* for oars; and so on for any other distances.

If a boat be hired at stairs between any two of the above-mentioned places, the fare will be 3*d.* to either of them. Thus from Hungerford stairs to Waterloo-bridge, or to Westminster-bridge, the charge is 3*d.*

From Chelsea-bridge to, or towards, Windsor, the fare is 3*d.* per half mile for sculls, or 6*d.* for oars. Posts are placed on the bank of the river, in order to point out the distance from Battersea-bridge.

The stairs, or landing-places, at either end, or on either side, of tho bridges, are to be considered as part of the respective bridges.

EASTWARD OF LONDON BRIDGE.

	Sculls.	Oars.
London-bridge to Iron-gate, or opposite	3*d.*	6*d.*
Iron-gate to Union-stairs, or opposite	3	6
Union-stairs to King Edward-stairs, or opposite	3	6
King Edward-stairs to Shadwell-dock-stairs, or opposite . .	3	6
Shadwell-dock-stairs to Kidney-stairs, or opposise	3	6
Kidney-stairs to Limehouse-hole-stairs, or opposite . . .	3	6
Limehouse-hole-stairs to the Torrington-arms, Limehouse-reach, or opposite	3	6
The Torrington-arms to George's-stairs, Deptford, or opposite .	3	6
George's-stairs, Deptford, to L. Watergate, Deptford, or opposite	3	6
Lower Watergate, Deptford, to Crawley's-wharf, Greenwich, or opposite	3	6

From Crawley's-wharf, Greenwich, to Broadness-point, Gray's, or any other place to the eastward, at the rate of 6*d.* for every half-mile. Posts are placed on the bank of the river, to shew the distances. No sculler can be compelled to go below Crawley's-wharf, Greenwich.

* The stairs at New Palace-yard are to be considered the same as Westminster-bridge.

FERRIES.

Over the water directly, at any part between Windsor and Crawley's-wharf, Greenwich, (excepting the Sunday ferries,) for one person, 3*d.*; two persons, 1½*d.* each; for any number exceeding two, 1*d.* each.

Over the water, between Crawley's-wharf, Greenwich, and Broadness-point, for one person, 6*d.*; for a number of persons, 3*d.* each.

HIRING BY TIME.

Persons taking a boat between Windsor and Crawley's-wharf, Greenwich, to be rowed upon, about, or up and down the river, not going directly up or down from place to place, to pay for every half-hour, for scullers, 6*d.*; for oars, 1*s.*

GOING ON BOARD OF VESSELS.

To or from steam or other vessels for passengers, for one person, 4*d.*; for any number of persons, 3*d.* each, including 56 lbs. of luggage for each person.

To or from ships or vessels lying opposite the shore westward of Greenwich, for one person, 2*d.*; for any number of persons, 1*d.* each; and where the distance from the shore to the ship does not exceed the distance directly across the river, the fare across the river shall be deemed and taken to be the fare to or from ships in all such cases.

To or from ships or vessels eastward of Greenwich, at the rate of 6*d.* for every half-mile.

Watermen detained by persons stopping at ships, wharfs, or otherwise, to be paid for time or distance at the option of the watermen.

PASSAGE-BOATS.

From London-bridge westward to

	s.	*d.*
Chelsea	0	6
Wandsworth	0	7
Putney, Fulham, or Barn-elms	0	8
Hammersmith or Chiswick	0	9
Barnes or Mortlake	1	0
Brentford, Isleworth, or Richmond	1	3
Twickenham, Tide-end-town, or Richmond	1	6
Hampton-court, Hampton-town, Sunbury, or Walton-upon-Thames	1	9
Shepperton, Weybridge, Chertsey, or Laleham	2	0
Staines	2	6
Datchet or Windsor	3	0

Scullers' fare, six passengers.—Oars' fare, eight passengers.

From London-bridge eastward to

	s.	*d.*
Deptford or Greenwich	0	6
Blackwall	0	9
Woolwich	1	0
Gravesend	1	6

Scullers' fare, six passengers.—Oars' fare, eight passengers.

GENERAL INDEX.

INDEX

TO

The Plan of London.

CONTRACTIONS.

abb. *abbey*.—al. *alley*.—bdgs. *buildings*.—br. *bridge*.—ct. *court*.—h. *hill*.—l. *lane*.—pl. *place*.—r. *row*.—rd. *road*.—sq. *square*.—st. *street*.—ter. *terrace*.—yd. *yard*.

*** The letters and figures which follow the name of each street &c. refer to the letters on the top, and the figures on each side of the Plan, which is divided into squares; lines drawn from the given letter and figure would meet in the square where the street is to be found.

BR—CA

Broad-st. Lambeth, E 7
——— Ratcliffe, L 5
——— Royal Exchange, H 4
——— Wapping, K 5
Broadwall, Blackfriars-rd. F 5
Broadway, Blackfriars, F 4
——— Westminster, D 6
Brompton, A 6, A 7
———crescent, Brompton, A 7
———row, A 6
——— sq. A 7
Bronti-pl. G 8
Brook-st. Grosvenor-sq. B 5
——— Holborn, F 4
——— New-rd. C 3
——— Ratcliff-cross, L 5
——— St. George-fields, F 7
Brooksby-st. F 1
Brown's-l. Spitalfields, I 3
Brownlow-st. Drury-l. D 4
Brudenel-pl. Hoxton, G 2
Brunswick-sq. E 3
——— st. Blackfriars-rd. F 5
——— Hackney-rd. I 2
——— ter. Pentonville, E 1
Bruton-pl. C 5
——— st. Berkeley-sq. C 5
Bryanstone-sq. B 4
——— st. Portman-sq. B 4
Brydges-st. Covent-garden, E 5
Buckingham-row, C 6
——— st. Strand, D 5
Bucklersbury, G 4
Budge-row, Watling-st. G 5
Bullhead-dock, L 5
Bull and Mouth-st. G 4
Bulstrode-st. Manchester-sq. B 4
Bunhill-row, G 3
Burdett-st. Surrey-rd. F 6
——— Walworth, G 8
Burlington-house, C 5
——— pl. H 8
Burr-st. I 5
Burton-crescent, D 3
——— st. Tavistock-sq. D 3
——— B 7
Bury-st. Bloomsbury, D 4
——— Chelsea, A 7
——— St. James's, C 5
——— St. Mary Axe, H 4
Bush-l. Cannon-st. G 5
Butcherhall-l. G 4
Buxton-pl. E 7
Byng-st. D 3
Cable-st. St. George's in the East, I 5
Cadogan-pl. Sloane-st. B 7

CA—CA

Cadogan sq. Sloane-st. B 7
——— st. Sloane-st. A 7
Calthorpe-st. E 3
Camberwell-rd. G 8
——— new-rd. F 8
Cambridge-heath, Hackney-rd. K 2
——— pl. Hackney-rd. K 2
——— row, Hackney-rd. K 1
——— st. Hackney-rd. I 2
Camden-cottages, Kentish-to. C 1
——— row, C 1
——— st. Bethnal-green-rd. K 2
——— Camden-town, C 1
——— Islington, F 1
——— Lisson-grove, A 3
——— Walworth, G 8
——— terrace, C 1
——— town, C 1
Camomile-st. Bishopsgate-st. H 4
Canal, St. James's-park, D 6
——— rd. H 1, G 2
Cannon-row, Westminster, D 6
——— st. Ratcliff-highway, K 5
——— rd. I 4
——— Watling-st. G 5
Cannonbury-l. F 1
——— pl. G 1
Canterbury-pl. Walworth, G 8
——— Kennington-rd. F 8
——— row, E 7
——— st. F 6
——— terrace, Lambeth, E 7
Canton-pl. K 7
Capland-st. Regent's-park, A 3
Carburton-st. C 3
Cardigan-crescent, D 1
Cardington-st. Hampstead-rd. C 2
Carey-st. Lincoln's-inn-fields, E 4
Carlisle-l. Lambeth, E 6
——— pl. Carlisle-l. Lambeth, E 7
——— st. Regent's-park, A 3
——— Soho-sq. D 4
Carmarthen-sq D 3
——— st. D 3
Carnaby-st. C 4, C 5
Caroline-pl. Chelsea, A 7
——— st. Hackney-rd. I 2
Carter-l. St. Paul's-churchyd. F 4
——— st. Spitalfields, I 3
——— Walworth, G 8
——— Westminster, D 6
Cartwright-st. I 5
Carey-st. E 4
Castle-l. Borough, G 6
——— Pimlico, C 6
——— st. Borough, G 6

CH—CL

Chichester-pl. E 2
China-terrace, Lambeth, E 7
Chiswell-st. Finsbury-sq. G 3
Christian-st. Cable-st. I 5
Church-l. Borough, G 6
—— Whitechapel, I 4
—— r. Bethnal-green, I 3
—— Horsleydown, H 6
—— Sun-tavern-fields, K 5
—— st. Bethnal-green, H 3, I 3
—— Blackfriars-rd. F 5
—— Bloomsbury, E 4
—— Chelsea, A 8
—— Clapham-rd. E 8
—— Hackney, K 1
—— Islington, F 1
—— Lambeth church, E 7
—— Rotherhithe, K 6
—— Shoreditch, I 3
—— Soho, D 4
—— Spitalfields, I 4
—— Whitechapel, I 4
—— stairs, Rotherhithe, K 6
Churchyard-row, Newington, F 7
Cinnamon-st. Wapping, K 6
Circus, Blackfriars-rd. F 6
—— st. New-rd. A 3
City-gardens, City-rd. F 2
—— road, F 2, G 2, G 3
—— Saw-mills, G 2
Clandon-st. G 8
Clapham-rd. E 8
Clare-market, E 4
—— st. Clare-market, E 4
Claremont-pl. Islington, F 1
—— Kent-rd. H 8
—— sq. Pentonville, F 2
—— terrace, F 2
Clarence-sq. C 2
—— st. Regent's park, C 2
—— Rotherhithe, K 6
—— terrace, Regent's - park, B 3
Clarendon-sq. Somers-town, D 2
—— st. Somers-town, D 2
Clarges-st Piccadilly, C 5
Clark-st. K 4
Clay-st. B 7
Clayton-st. Kennington-green, E 8
—— cross, F 8
Clement's-inn, E 4
—— lane, Clare-market, E 4
—— Lombard-st. G 5
Clerkenwell-green, F 3
Cleveland-st. Fitzroy-sq. C 3
—— r. St. James's-palace, C 6

CL—CO

Clifford-st. New Bond-st. C 5
—— Walworth, H 8
Clifton-pl. K 1
—— st. H 3
Clink-st. Borough, G 5
Clipstone-st. Fitzroy-sq. C 3
Cloak-l. Queen-st. G 5
Cloth-fair, Smithfield, F 4
Cloudesley-sq. F 1
Cobham-row, F 3
Cobourg-road, H 8
Coburg-pl. E 8
—— row, C 7
—— st. F 6
Cochrane-terrace, A 2
Cock-hill, Ratcliff cross, L 5
—— lane, Snow-hill, F 4
Cockspur-st. D 5
Colchester-st. Whitechapel, I 4
Cold-bath-sq. Clerkenwell, F 3
Cold-harbour, Blackwall, L 7
—— st. I 2
Colebrook-r. Islington, F 1
Cole-harbour, G 5
Coleman-st. Old Jewry, G 4
Collate-st. F 6
College-h. Upper Thames-st. G 5
—— pl. Chelsea, A 7
—— Camden-town, D 1
—— st. Camden-town, C 1, D 1
—— Chelsea, A 7
—— Lambeth, E 6
—— Tooley-st. H 6
—— Westminster, D 7
Collier-st. Pentonville, E 2
Collingwood-pl. Chelsea, A 8
—— st. Bethnal-gr. K 3
—— Blackfriars - road, F 6
Commercial-docks, L 6
—— rd. K 4, L 4
—— Waterloo-br. E 5
—— Chelsea, B 8
—— row, H 8
Compton-pl. E 3
—— st. Goswell-st. F 3
—— Soho, D 4
—— Tavistock-sq. D 3
—— terrace, F 1
Conduit-st. New Bond-st. C 5
Connaught-pl. A 4
—— sq. A 4
Constitution-hill, Green-park, C 6
Conway-st. Fitzroy-sq. C 3
Cook's-ground, A 8
—— r. D 1

DO—EA

Dorset-st. Spitalfields, H 4
Doughty-st. E 3
Douglas-st. Vincent-sq. D 7
Dove-r. near Hackney, I 2
Dover-pl. Greenwich-rd. G 7
—— st. Kent-rd. H 8
—— Piccadilly, C 5
Dowgate-hill, G 5
Downham-rd. H 1
—— st. Kingsland, H 1
Downing-st. Westminster, D 6
Drapers' almshouses, I 2
Draycott-pl. Chelsea, A 7
Drummond-st. C 3, D 2
Drury-l. E 4
Duchess-st. Portland-pl. C 4
Duck-l. Westminster, D 7
Duckett's, sir G., canal, L 2
Duckett-st. Stepney, L 3
Ducking-pond-r. Whitechapel, K 4
Duke's-pl. Houndsditch, H 4
—— r. Pimlico, C 7
—— New-rd. D 3
—— st. Bloomsbury, D 4
—— Somers-town, D 2
—— Chelsea, A 8
—— Grosvenor-sq. B 4
—— Lincoln's-inn-fields, E 4
—— Lisson-grove, A 3
—— Manchester-sq. B 4
—— Portland-pl. C 4
—— Smithfield, F 4
—— Spitalfields, H 4
—— Stamford-st. F 5
—— St. James's, C 5
—— Turk-st. I 3
—— Waterloo-rd. F 6
—— Westminster, D 6
Duncan-pl. Hackney, K 1
—— terrace, City-rd. F 2
Dunstan-st. Kingsland-rd. K 1
Durham-grove, A 8
—— pl. Chelsea, A 8
—— Lambeth, F 7
Eagle-st. Red Lion-sq. E 4
—— Spitalfields, I 3
Earl-st. Blackfriars, F 5
—— Edgeware-rd. A 3
—— Finsbury, H 3
—— Seven-dials, D 4
—— Westminster, D 7
—— Hoxton, H 2
Earnes-st. Mile-end, L 3
East India Docks, L 7
—— l. Rotherhithe, I 6
—— Walworth, G 8

EA—EV

East-st. Finsbury, H 4
—— Kent-rd. H 8
—— Lambeth, E 7
—— Manchester-sq. B 4
—— Red Lion-sq. E 3
—— Walworth, G 8
—— West-sq. F 7
Eastcheap, G 5
Eastfield-st. L 4
East Smithfield, I 5
Easton-st. F 3
Eaton-st. Pimlico, C 7
—— pl. Pimlico, B 7
—— sq. Pimlico, B 7
Ebenezer-pl. St. George's-fields, F 7
Ebury chapel, B 7
—— pl. Chelsea-rd. B 7
—— sq. Pimlico, B 7
—— st. B 7, C 7
Eccleston-st. C 7
Eden-st. Tottenham-ct.-rd. D 3
Edgeware-rd. A 3
Edith-pl. Hackney-rd. I 2
Edward-st. Blackfriars-rd. F 5
—— Hampstead-rd. C 2
—— Portman-sq. B 4
—— Spitalfields, I 3
—— Stepney, L 4
—— City-rd. G 2
—— ter. E 1
Eggleston-st. B 7
Egmont-pl. Greenwich-rd. I 8
Elder-st. Spitalfields, H 3
Eldon-st. Finsbury, H 4
Elephant-l. K 6
—— stairs, Rotherhithe, K 6
—— and Castle, F 7
Elim-st. H 6
Eliza-st. Pimlico, B 7
Elliot's-r. St. George's-fields, F 7
Elizabeth-st. Belgrave-sq. B 7
—— Goodman's-fields, I 5
—— Sloane-st. A 6
—— ter. Islington, F 1
Elm-lodge, D 1
—— st. E 3
Ely-pl. Holborn, F 4
Ernest-st. C 2
Essex-st. Kingsland-rd. H 2
—— Strand, E 5
—— Whitechapel, I 4
Euston-gr. Euston-sq. D 3
—— pl. D 3
—— sq. New Road, D 3
—— st. Euston-sq. D 3
Everett-st. Brunswick-sq. D 3

HE—HO

Hertford-rd. H 1
—— st. Fitzroy-sq. C 3
—— May-fair, B 5
Hickman's-folly, Horsleydown, I 6
High-Holborn, E 4
—— row, Knightsbridge, A 6
—— st. Borough, G 5, G 6
—— Islington, F 2
—— Kennington, F 7
—— Lambeth, E 7
—— Mary-le-bone, B 4, B 3
—— Portland-town, A 2
—— St. Giles's, D 4
Higler's-l. Blackfriars-rd. F 6
Hill-st. Berkeley-sq. B 5
—— Finsbury, H 3
—— St. George's-fields, F 6
—— Walworth, G 8
Hind-st. Manchester-sq. B 4
Hog-l. Shoreditch, H 3
Holborn, E 4
—— hill, F 4
—— r. Lincoln's-inn-fields, E 4
Holland-st. Blackfriars-rd. F 5
Holles-st. Cavendish-sq. C 4
Holloway New-rd. E 1
—— st. I 4
Hollywell-l. H 3
—— r. Finsbury, H 3
—— st. Strand, E 5
Holmes-st. K 4
Homer-r. Lisson-green, A 4
Hope-town, I 3
—— st. I 3
—— Hackney-rd. K 2
Hornsey-l. H 7
Horse-st. Commercial-rd. L 4
Horseferry-rd. Millbank, D 7
—— stairs, D 7
Horse-guards, D 6
Horsleydown, H 6
—— l. Horsleydown, H 6
—— Old-stairs, H 6
—— New-stairs, I 6
—— sq. I 6
Horsemonger-l. Sessions'-house, and Gaol, G 6
Horseshoe-al.-stairs, G 5
Hosier-l. Smithfield, F 4
Houghton-st. Clare-market, E 4
Houndsditch, Bishopsgate-st. H 4
House of Correction, E 3
—— Commons, D 6
—— Lords, D 6
Howard's-pl. Hackney, K 2
Howick-pl. C 7

HO—JO

Howland-st. Fitzroy-sq. C 3
Hoxton, G 2, H 2
—— rd. H 2, H 3
—— sq. H 2, H 3
Hungerford-market or st. Strand, D 5
—— stairs, Strand, E 5
Hunter-st. Brunswick-sq. D 3
—— Kent-st. H 7
Huntingdon-st. Kingsland-rd. H 2
Huntley-st. Hampstead-rd. D 3
Hyde-park, A 5
—— corner, Piccadilly, B 6
—— ter. A 4
—— pl. A 4
—— pl. Rosemary B. H 1
—— Vincent-sq. D 7
—— st. Bloomsbury-sq. D 4
Jacob-st. Horsleydown, I 6
James-pl. Shadwell, L 5
—— st. Bedford-r. E 3
—— Bethnal-green, K 3
—— Buckingham-gate, C 6
—— Camden Town, C 1
—— Covent-garden, D 5
—— Goodman's-fields, I 4
—— Haymarket, D 5
—— Lambeth-marsh, E 6
—— Lisson-grove, A 3
—— Oxford-st. B 4
—— Spitalfields, I 3
—— Stepney, L 4
Jane-st. K 4
Jenkin's Botanical-garden, A 3
Jermyn-st. St. James's, C 5
Jetsom-st. Blackfriars-rd. F 6
Jewin-st. Aldersgate-st. G 4
Jewry-st. Leadenhall-st. H 5
Jews' burying-ground, L 3
—— walk, Bethnal-green, K 2
Imperial Gas-works, D 2, I 2
John's-r. City-rd. G 3
John-st. Adelphi, E 5
John's-st. Bethnal-gr. L 2 and 3
John-st. Berkeley-sq. C 5
—— Blackfriars-rd. F 5
—— Chelsea, A 7
—— Curtain-rd. H 3
—— Dog-r. K 3
—— Edgeware-rd. A 4
—— Fitzroy-sq. C 3
—— Gray's-inn-l. E 3
—— Horsleydown, H 6
—— Kent-rd. G 7
—— Hackney-rd. K 2
—— Islington, F 1

LA—LO

Lansdown-pl. I 1
Lant-st. Borough, G 6
Lark-r. K 2
Lawrence-l. Cheapside, G 4
———— Pountney-l. G 5
Laystall-st. E 3
Leadenhall-st. H 4
Leader-st. A 7
Leather-l. Holborn, F 3, F 4
Lebanon-pl. H 8
Leicester-sq. D 5
Leigh-st. Tavistock-sq. D 3
Leman-st. Goodman's-fields, I 4
Leonard-st. Shoreditch, H 3
Lewkner's-l. Drury-l. E 4
Lime or Lyme-st. H 5
Limehouse-dock, K 7
Lincoln's-inn, E 4
Lincoln's-inn-sq. E 4
Lion-st. Bloomsbury, E 4
——— Greenwich-rd. G 7
Liquor-pond-st. Gray's-inn-l. E 3
Lisle-st. Leicester-sq. D 5
Lisson-grove, A 3
——— st. Dog-r. K 3
———— Paddington, A 3, A 4
Litchfield-st. Soho, D 4
Little Ayliff-st. I 4
——— Britain, Aldersgate-st. G 4
——— Brook-st. Hanover-sq. C 4
——— Distaff-l. G 5
——— Earl-st. D 4
——— Eastcheap, Fish-st.-hill, H 5
——— Guildford-st. Borough, G 6
——— James-st. Bedford-r. E 3
——— Maddox-st. C 5
——— Mary-le-bone-st. B 4
——— Moorfields, G 4
——— Pulteney-st. Golden-sq. D 5
——— Queen-st. Lincoln's-inn, E 4
——— Russell-st. Bloomsbury, D 4
——— Suffolk-st. Borough, G 6
——— Surrey-st. F 6
——— Wild-st. E 4
——— Windmill-st. D 5
Liverpool-rd. F 1, F 2
———— st. H 4
Lock's-fields, G 7
Loddige's Nursery, K 1
Lodge-rd. A 2
Loman's-pond, F 6
Lombard-st. G 4
————— Borough, G 6
London-bridge, G 5
——— docks, I 5, K 5
——— fields, Hackney, K 1

LO—MA

London-hospital, K 4
——— l. Hackney, K 1
——— pl. Hackney, K 1
——— rd. St. George's-fields, F 7
——— st. Bethnal-green, K 3
————— Fenchurch-st. I 5
————— Fitzroy-sq. C 3
————— Horsleydown, I 6
————— Ratcliffe, L 5
————— Paddington, A 4
——— ter. Hackney, I 1
——— University, D 3
——— wall, Moorfields, C 4
Long-acre, D 5, E 4
—— al. Moorfields, H 4
—— l. Borough, G 6, H 6
——— West-Smithfield, F 4
Lord's Cricket-ground, A 2
Lothbury, G 4
Louisa-st. Mile-end-rd. L 3
Love-l. Bankside, F 5
——— Lambeth, E 7, E 6
——— Lower Thames-st. H 5
Lovell-st. Rotherhithe, K 6
Lowdell's-st. F 6
Lower Berkeley-st. B 4
——— Chapman-st. K 4
——— College-st. C 1
——— Frederick-st. A 4
——— Grosvenor-pl. Pimlico, C 6
——— Grove-st. I 5
——— rd. Islington, G 1
——— st. Islington, F 1, G 1
——— St. James's-pl. C 6
——— Sloane-st. Sloane-sq. B 7
——— Thames-st. H 5
Lucas-st. Commercial-rd. K 4
———— Rotherhithe, K 6
Ludgate-hill, Fleet-st. F 4
———— st. St. Paul's, F 4
Luke-st. Finsbury-sq. H 3
——— Houndsditch, H 4
Macclesfield-st. City-rd. G 2
—————— Soho, D 5
Maddox-st. Hanover-sq. C 4, C 5
Magdalen-hospital, F 6
Maiden-l. Covent-garden, E 5
————— Pancras, D 1, E 1
Maize, the, H 6
Mall, St. James's-park, D 6
Manchester-buildings, D 6
————— sq. B 4
————— st. Manchester-sq. B 4
Manley-pl. F 8
Manor-pl. Chelsea, A 8
———— Walworth, G 8

MO—NE

Motcomb-st. B 6
Mount-pl. Whitechapel, I 4
—— st. Grosvenor-sq. B 5
—— Shoreditch, I 3
—— Walworth, G 8
—— Westminster-rd. E 6
—— Whitechapel, I 4
Museum-st. D 4
Mutton-hill, F 3
—— l. Hackney, K 1
Myddleton-sq. F 2
—— terrace, F 2
Myrtle-st. H 2
Narrow-wall, Lambeth, E 6
Nassau-st. Middlesex-hospital, C 4
Neat-houses, Chelsea, C 8
—— row, C 8
—— st. Greenwich-rd. H 8
Neckinger-rd. Bermondsey, I 6, I 7
Nelson-pl. Lock's-fields, G 7
—— sq. Blackfriars-rd. F 6
—— st. Borough, G 6
—— Commercial-rd. K 4
—— Hackney-rd. I 2
—— terrace, F 2
Neptune-st. Rotherhithe, K 6
New Bond-st. C 4, C 5
—— Burlington-st. Piccadilly, C 5
Newcastle-st. E 4
New Cavendish-st. Hoxton, G 2
—— Portland-pl. C 4
—— church-rd. Camberwell, G 8
—— st. Edgeware-rd. A 3
—— Compton-st. St. Giles's, D 4
—— cut, Lambeth, F 6
—— Gloucester-st. Hoxton, H 2
—— inn-yard, Shoreditch, H 3
—— Norfolk-st. B 5
—— North-st. Finsbury, H 3
—— Palace-yard, D 6
—— Peter-st. Westminster, D 7
—— Pye-st. D 7
—— Quebec-st. B 4
—— river, F 2
—— river-head, F 2
—— road, B 3, C 3, D 2
—— Bermondsey, H 7
—— Chelsea, B 6
—— Blue-anchor-rd. H 7
—— Kentish-town, C 1
—— row, Kennington, F 8
—— Smithfield, Islington, G 1
—— sq. Lincoln's-inn, E 4
—— st. Baker-st. N. B 3
—— Bishopsgate-st. H 4
—— Brompton, A 6

NE—NO

New-st. Covent-garden, D 5
—— Horsleydown, H 6
—— Kennington, F 8
—— Kent-rd. G 7
—— New-cut, F 6
—— Rotherhithe, K 6
—— Southwark-bridge, G 6
—— Spring-gardens, D 5
—— Whitechapel, I 4
—— terrace, Pentonville, F 2
—— Tothill st. Westminster, D 6
Newington-causeway, F 7, G 7
—— butts, F 7
—— pl. Kennington-rd. F 8
Newgate-st. F 4
Newman-st. Oxford-st. D 4
Newnham-st. Edgeware-rd. A 4
New Swan, A 8
Newport-st. D 5
Newton-st. Holborn, E 4
Nicholas-l. Lombard-st. G 5
Nightingale-st. I 5
Nine-elms, Vauxhall, D 8
Noble-st. Foster-l. G 4
—— Goswell-st. G 3
Norfolk-st. Bethnal-green. I K 3
—— Commercial-rd. K 4
—— Globe-l. L 3
—— Somer's-town, D 2
—— Middlesex-hospital, C 4
—— Southwark, G 6
—— Strand, E 5
North-bank, Regent's-park, A 2
—— London-hospital, D 3
—— pl. Hampstead-rd. C 2
—— r. Grosvenor-sq. B 4
—— st. Bethnal-green, K 2
—— Brompton, A 6
—— Finsbury, H 3
—— Goodman's-fields, I 4
—— Hackney-rd. K 1
—— Lambeth, E 7
—— Lock's-fields, G 7
—— Mary-le-bone, B 4
—— Pentonville, E 2
—— Regent's-park, A 3
—— Stepney, L 4
—— Westminster, D 7
Northampton-sq. F 3
—— st. Bethnal-green, K 3
—— Islington-rd. F 3
—— Kent rd. H 8
—— Lock's-fields, G 7
—— terrace, G 1
North Audley-st. B 4, B 5

RO—SA

Robert-st. Bedford-r. E 3
—— Bethnal-green, I 2, 3
—— Blackfriars-rd. F 6
—— Chelsea, A 8
—— Hampstead-rd. C 2
—— Hoxton, H 2
Robinson's-r. Chelsea, A 8
Roch-st. D 7
Rochester-st. Tothill-fields, C 7
Rockingham-r. G 7
Rodney-buildings, G 7
—— r. Greenwich-rd. G 7
—— st. Pentonville, E 2
Rood-l. Fenchurch-st. H 5
Ropemaker-st. G 4
Rosamond's-r. F 3
—— st. F 3
Rose-l. Shadwell, L 5
—— Whitechapel, I 4
—— st. Shoreditch, I 3
—— Soho, D 4
—— pl. L 3
Rosemary-branch, G 1
——l. Tower-hill, I 5
Ross-alley, H 6
Rotherfield-st. Islington, G 1
Rotherhithe-st. K 6
——wall, I 6
Rotton-r. G 3
Roxburgh-pl. C 4
Rowland's-r. Mile-end, K 3
Royal Hospital, Chelsea, B 8
—— Military Asylum, B 8
—— r. Bridge-rd. Westminster, E 6
Rupert-st. Goodman's-fields, I 4
——Haymarket, D 5
Russell-pl. Fitzroy-sq. C 3
—— sq. D 3
—— st. Covent-garden, E 5
Russia-l. Hackney-turnpike, K 2
Rutland-pl. F 5
—— st. Hampstead-rd. C 2
—— Whitechapel, K 4
Sackville-st. Piccadilly, C 5
Sadler's Wells, F 2
Saffron-hill, Hatton-garden, F 3
Saint Alban's-pl. D 5
—— r. E 7
—— Andrew's-pl. Regent's-park, C 3
—— Hackney, K 1
——st. Seven-dials, D 4
—— Ann's-st. Westminster, D 7
—— Catherine's, I 5
—— docks, I 5

SA—SA

Saint Catherine's-hospital, C 2
—— Clement's-l. G 5
—— Dunstan's-hill, H 5
—— George's Burial-ground, A 4
——pl. Hyde-park-corner, B 6
—— Walworth, H 8
—— Chelsea, C 7
—— rd. F 7, G 7
—— r. Chelsea, C 8
—— Tyburn, A 4
—— Giles's Burying-ground, D 1
—— Helen's-pl. H 4
—— James's Burial-ground, C 2
—— palace, C 6
—— park, D 6
—— pl. St. James's-st. C 5
—— sq. Pall-mall, D 5
—— st. Piccadilly, C 5
—— John's-l. Smithfield, F 3
—— pl. F 6
—— sq. Clerkenwell, F 3
—— st. Smithfield, F 3
—— Spitalfields, I 3
—— Walworth, G 8
—— rd. F 2
—— wood-farm, A 1
—— rd. A 2
—— ter. A 2
—— Luke's-hospital, G 3
—— Mark's-rd. F 8
—— Martin's Burial-ground, C 1
—— l. Cannon-st. G 5
—— Charing-cross, D 5
—— le-grand, G 4
—— st. Borough-rd. F 6
—— Mary-axe, Leadenhall-st. H 4
——'s-l. H 5
—— Pancras' Old Church, D 1
—— Workhouse, D 1
—— Paul's, G 4
—— st. G 8
—— Peter-st. G 8
—— Saviour's Dock, I 6
—— Swithin's-l. Lombard-st. G 5
—— Thomas Apostle, Queen-st. G 5
Salcombe-pl. B 3
Sale-st. Edgeware-rd. A 4
Salisbury-crescent, G 7
—— pl. Lock's-fields, G 7
—— l. Rotherhithe-wall, I 6
—— pl. Rotherhithe-wall, I 6
—— st. Edgeware-rd. A 3
—— Lock's-fields, G 7
—— North-rd. G 1

VA—WE

Vauxhall-terrace, E 8
——— well, D 8
Vere-st. Bond-st. C 4
Veterinary college, D 1
Victory-pl. Lock's-fields, G 7
Vigo-l. Piccadilly, C 5
Villiers-st. Strand, D 5
Vimeira-pl. D 8
Vincent-sq. Tothill fields, D 7
——— st. Tothill-fields, D 7
Vine-st. Minories, H 5
——— Lambeth, E 6
——— Westminster, D 7
——— yard, Tooley-st. H 6
Vinegar st. Commercial rd. K 4, 5
Virginia-st. Hackney-rd. I 2
——— terrace, Great Dover st. G 7
Wakefield-st. Regent-sq. E 3
Walbrook, G 5
——— r. H 2
——— pl. Hoxton, G 2
Walburg-st. K 5
Walcot-pl. Lambeth, F 7
Walker-st. L 3
Wallis's-green, I 2
Walmer-garden, H 1
Walney-st. K 4
Walnut-tree-walk, Lambeth, E 7
Walworth, G 8
——— pl. G 8
——— common, G 8, H 8
Wandsworth-rd. D 8
Wapping, I 6, K 6
——— dock-stairs, K 6
——— New-stairs, K 6
——— Old-stairs, I 6
——— wall, K 5
Ward's-r. Bethnal-green, I 3
——— Pimlico, C 6
Wardour-st. Soho, D 4
Warren-st. Fitzroy-sq. C 3
Warwick-l. Newgate-st. F 4
——— st. Golden-sq. C 5
Water-l. Blackfriars, F 5
——— Fleet-st. F 4
Waterloo-bridge, E 5
——— rd. E 5, E 6, F 6
——— pl. D 5
——— I 1
——— st. I 1
——— Walworth, G 8
——— terrace, L 1
——— town, Bethnal grn. I 3
Watling-st. G 4
Webb-st. Bermondsey, H 6

WE—WH

Webb-st. Walworth, G 8
Webber-st. Blackfriars-rd. F 6
Welbeck-st. Cavendish-sq. B 4
Wellclose-sq Ratcliffe-highway, I 5
Well-st. Hackney, K 1
——— Wellclose-sq. I 5
Wells-st. Gray's-inn-l. E 3
Well's-st. Brick-l. Whitechapel, I 4
——— Oxford-st. C 4
Wellesley-st. Chelsea, A 8
Wellington-pl. D 8
——— Stepney, L 4
——— Hackney, I 2
——— rd. Portland-town, A 2
——— ter. A 2
——— st. Blackfriars-rd. F 6
——— Camden-town, C 1
——— Chelsea, A 8
——— Goswell-st. F 3
——— Strand, E 5
——— Waterloo-town, I 3
Wenlock-st. G 3
Wentworth-st. Spitalfields, H 4, I 4
Westbourne-st. B 7
Westham-reservoir, L 3
West India-docks, K 7
——— l. Rotherhithe, K 6
——— sq. St. George's-fields, F 7
——— Smithfield, F 4
——— st. Bethnal-green, L 2
——— K 3
——— Seven-dials, D 4
——— Borough, G 6
——— Finsbury, G 4
——— Smithfield, F 4
——— West-sq. F 7
Westminster-abbey, D 6
——— bridge, E 6
——— rd. E 6
——— rd. F 6
Westmorland-pl. City-rd. G 2
Weston-st. Bermondsey, H 6
——— Pentonville, E 2
——— Somers-town, D 2
Weymouth-st. Greenwich-rd. G 7
——— Portland-pl. B 3, C 3
——— Hoxton, G 2
——— ter. Hackney-rd. I 2
Wharton-st. E 2
Wheeler-pl. Hampstead-rd. B 1
——— st. Spitalfields, H 3
Whetstone-park, E 4
Whiston-st. F 3
Whitcombe st. Leicester-sq. D 5
White-st. Spitalfields, H 4
——— Borough, High-st. G 6

THE END.

LONDON:
PRINTED BY ROBSON, LEVEY, AND FRANKLYN,
46 St. Martin's Lane.

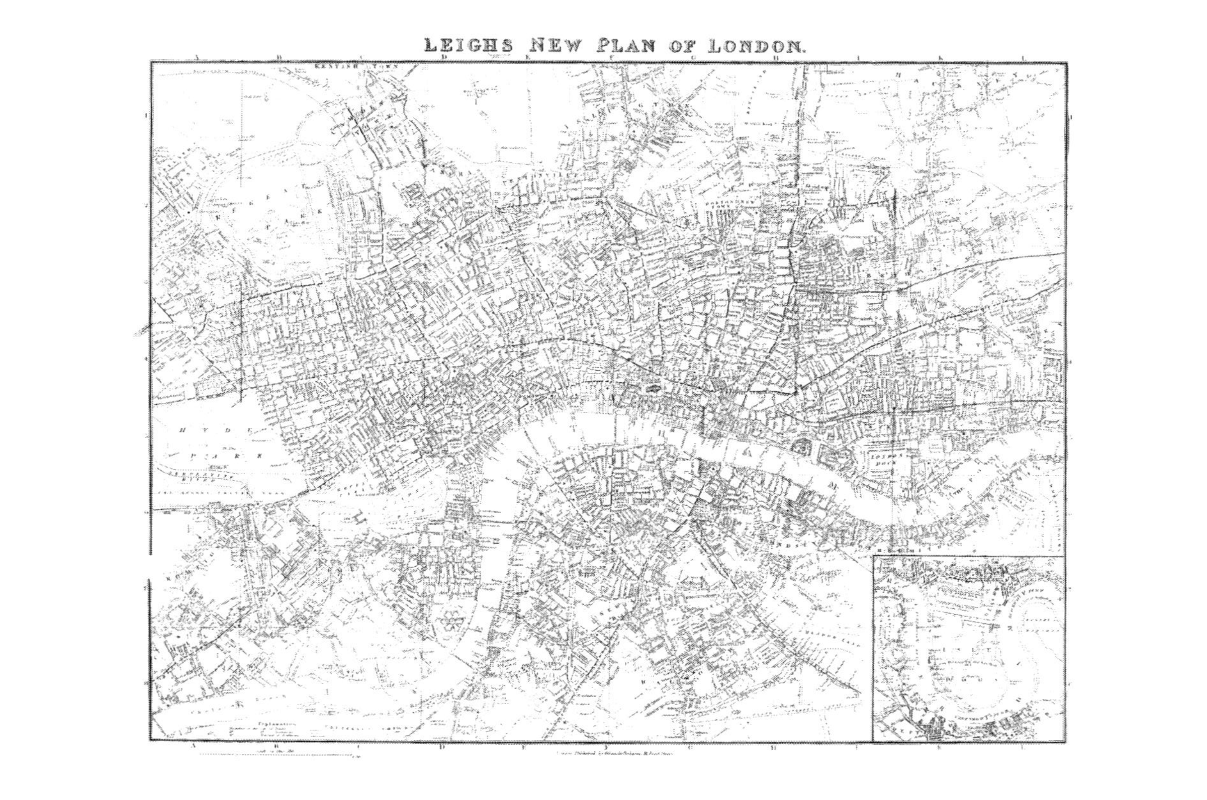
LEIGHS NEW PLAN OF LONDON.
KENTISH TOWN
HYDE PARK

Printed in Great Britain
by Amazon.co.uk, Ltd.,
Marston Gate.